COMPETITION LAW IN THE EU

COMPETITION LAW IN THE EU

PRINCIPLES, SUBSTANCE, ENFORCEMENT

JOHAN W. VAN DE GRONDEN

Professor of European Law, Department of International and European Law, Radboud University Nijmegen, and State Counsellor in Extraordinary Service at the Dutch Council of State, the Netherlands

CATALIN S. RUSU

Associate Professor of European Law, Department of International and European Law, Radboud University Nijmegen, the Netherlands

 Edward Elgar
PUBLISHING

Cheltenham, UK • Northampton, MA, USA

Published by
Edward Elgar Publishing Limited
The Lypiatts
15 Lansdown Road
Cheltenham
Glos GL50 2JA
UK

Edward Elgar Publishing, Inc.
William Pratt House
9 Dewey Court
Northampton
Massachusetts 01060
USA

A catalogue record for this book
is available from the British Library

Library of Congress Control Number: 2020950935

ISBN 978 1 78897 474 5 (cased)
ISBN 978 1 78897 476 9 (paperback)
ISBN 978 1 78897 475 2 (eBook)

Typeset by Servis Filmsetting Ltd, Stockport, Cheshire
Printed and bound by CPI Group (UK) Ltd, Croydon, CR0 4YY

CONTENTS IN BRIEF

FULL CONTENTS

PART II   ANTITRUST LAW

PART III ENFORCEMENT OF THE ANTITRUST RULES

PART V COMPETITION RULES ADDRESSED TO THE MEMBER STATES

ABBREVIATIONS

AAC	Average avoidable cost
ACM	Autoriteit Consument en Markt
AG	Advocate General
AIC	Average incremental cost
ATC	Average total cost
AVC	Average variable cost
Awb	Algemene wet bestuursrecht (General Administrative Law Act)
BKA	Bundeskartellamt (Federal Cartel Office)
CC	Competition Commission
CFI	Court of First Instance
CJEU	Court of Justice of the European Union
CMA	Competition and Markets Authority
EC	European Communities
ECHR	European Convention on Human Rights
ECN	European Competition Network
ECSC	European Coal and Steel Community
ECtHR	European Court of Human Rights
EEA	European Economic Area
EEC	European Economic Community
EU	European Union
FRAND	Fair, reasonable and non-discriminatory
GC	General Court
GWB	Gesetz gegen Wettbewerbsbeschränkungen (Act against Restraints of Competition)
HHI	Herfindahl-Hirschman Index
ICN	International Competition Network
IP	Intellectual property
LRAIC	Long-run average incremental cost
M&A	Mergers and acquisitions
Mw	Mededingingswet

NCA	National competition authority
NZa	Nederlandse Zorgautoriteit (Dutch Healthcare Authority)
OFT	Office of Fair Trading
PSO	Public service obligation
R&D	Research and development
SAM	State Aid Modernisation
S-C-P	Structure-Conduct-Performance
SEP	Standard essential patent
SGEI	Service of General Economic Interest
SGI	Service of General Interest
SIEC	Significant impediment to effective competition
SLC	Substantial lessening of competition
SME	Small and medium-sized enterprise
SSGI	Social Service of General Interest
SSNIP	Small but significant and non-transitory increase in price
TEC	Treaty Establishing the European Community
TEU	Treaty on the European Union
TFEU	Treaty on the Functioning of the European Union
WEM	Wet Economische Mededinging (Act on Economic Competition)

TABLE OF CASES, LEGISLATION AND OTHER SOURCES

COMMISSION DECISIONS

DOMESTIC CASE-LAW AND DECISIONAL PRACTICE

HARD-LAW

SOFT-LAW

PART I
PREREQUISITES OF COMPETITION LAW

1

The context of European competition law

1 INTRODUCTION

Strikingly, no clear definition can be given as to what competition entails. It is clear from the outset that some rivalry between companies is an important element of this concept. Furthermore, it is safe to state that this rivalry is one of the pillars on which free markets are based. Moreover, it may even be submitted that competition and the market could be regarded as synonyms for the same phenomenon, that is, the process of supplying goods and services by companies to customers in a (to a certain extent) free arena. However, unlike other concepts of law, there exists no clear definition of what competition is. As will be clear in the next chapters, in competition law many well-delineated definitions are given for a wide array of terms, such as 'agreement', 'concerted practice', 'trade between the Member States', 'dominance' and 'merger'. This is not to say that these definitions are not open for debate, but at least there is some common ground to base the arguments exchanged on. As for the concept of competition, it is difficult to find such common ground. It depends on the view one has on how the concept of competition is dealt with. The aim of this chapter is to set the scene for the rest of the book, by reflecting on this concept, discussing the institutional setup of European competition law, and explaining the approach of the book.

2 WHAT IS COMPETITION (LAW) ABOUT?

In order to grasp what the concept of competition entails, various schools of thought should be explored. As the cradle of competition law is in the United States, the first view to be discussed is developed in this jurisdiction. In 1890, the Sherman Act was adopted by the US Congress, in order to address the problems arising from various large trusts and the economic power resulting from these trusts.[1] Against this backdrop, it could be argued that at its initial inception, US antitrust law was concerned with protecting small businesses.[2] Later, this view on competition changed dramatically.

---

[1] Gerber 2010, p. 123.

[2] Hovenkamp 2008, p. 41.

2.1 Schools of thought

To start with, attention should be paid to the view based on the Structure-Conduct-Performance (S-C-P) paradigm, developed at Harvard University.[3] This paradigm implies that market performance is dependent on the conduct of sellers and buyers, which in its turn is determined by the structure of the relevant market.[4] In this view the role played by the structure of the market is emphasised. In other words, the US antitrust laws should be focused on the setup of the market, rather than on protecting competitors. In essence, the S-C-P paradigm entailed that a given market structure dictated certain types of conduct and performance, which meant that a hostile approach was adopted towards concentrated markets.[5] Some Harvard school authors even argued that mergers at relatively low market shares are illegal, and that practices of firms having economic power had to be condemned, even if these practices were to the benefit of consumers.[6]

In reaction to the Harvard school, a new theory was developed, known as the Chicago school. The point of departure of this theory is that firms behave in a rational manner and, therefore, seek to maximise their profits.[7] Furthermore, most markets were believed to be capable of correcting imperfections by themselves and were considered to be competitive, even if only a few companies were active in the market.[8] A very important feature of the Chicago school is the trust placed in the efficient functioning of the markets and, therefore, efficiency is at the heart of this school of thought. Interventions based on competition law should be limited to taking action against practices not leading to efficient outcomes on the market. The pursuit of efficiency should be the sole goal of competition law and, accordingly, the only concern is whether the practices under review lead to reduction of output or to higher prices.[9] In comparison with the Harvard school, Chicago scholars believe that antitrust authorities must refrain from intervening on the market, whenever possible. An important element of the Chicago school is its confidence that the entry of new firms in the market will solve almost all market problems, an approach which stands in sharp contrast with the Harvard school, which feared that, on highly concentrated markets, entry of newcomers was very problematic.[10]

Both the Harvard and Chicago schools have been very influential in US antitrust law. It should be noted that competition law is capable of accommodating new (economic) theories relatively easily, given the open manner of drafting of its norms. This is not only true for US antitrust law, but also for EU competition law. It must be pointed out that, in its turn, the Chicago school, which questioned various views held by Harvard scholars, was corrected by

---

[3] Van den Bergh, Camesasca and Giannaccari 2017, p. 34.

[4] Ibid.

[5] Hovenkamp 2008, p. 36.

[6] Jones, Sufrin and Dunne 2019, p. 14.

[7] Van den Bergh, Camesasca and Giannaccari 2017, p. 45.

[8] Ibid.

[9] Jones, Sufrin and Dunne 2019, p. 15.

[10] Hovenkamp 2008, p. 32

subsequently developed theories. For example, it was stressed that some markets are more prone to competition problems than others, given their structure and the economic activities concerned.[11] The uneven balancing of information, for instance, could cause competition problems.[12] An interesting theory was developed by behavioural economists. These scholars questioned whether, as a rule, companies and consumers are well informed and act in a rational way, doubts which made these scholars introduce the concept of 'bounded rationality': rationality is not perfect as collecting the necessary information may prove to be very difficult.[13] One of the points made by behavioural economists is that consumers do not always take decisions serving their own wealth-maximising interests, and competition authorities should pay due interest to this when developing policies and enforcement strategies.[14]

The US was the first jurisdiction to introduce a competition law system, which entails that this system has had and continues to have an important impact on the shaping of competition law around the world. Nevertheless, it should not be forgotten that some European countries also have gained vast experience with rules dealing with competition, even before the European Treaties were signed into force. Most notably, in Germany the Kartellverordnung (Cartel Regulation) was adopted in 1923, on the basis of which action could be taken in the event of harmful excesses of the cartel system ('schädlicher Auswüchse des Kartellwesen').[15] The oversight activities of the competent authority, which was the Minister of Economic Affairs, were based on 'Missbrauchsaufsicht' (control of cartel abuse): restrictive agreements were only prohibited upon action of this authority. Also, other European countries enacted competition laws before the Second World War: for example, in the 1930s, in the Netherlands, the Act on the Agreements Concluded by Firms 1935 was adopted, on the basis of which agreements concluded by firms could be declared both generally binding or non-binding, if this was required in the public interest.[16] So, in this system, which was based on control of cartel abuse, like the German rules, attention was paid not only to negative effects caused by restrictive agreements, but also to possible benefits achieved through these agreements; this was not surprising, against the backdrop of the deep economic recession of the 1930s, and the need to address problems of overcapacity. In France, where the first specific competition law regulation was adopted after the Second World War, the principle of free competition and the right to set up businesses was already established by a Decree in 1791 and dominated commerce in the 19th and early 20th centuries.[17] The status of these principles was reinforced by a provision of criminal law banning agreements on uniform pricing strategies concluded by firms supplying the same products.[18]

In sum, despite the huge impact of US antitrust law on the competition law systems in

---

[11] Ibid, p. 38.

[12] Ibid.

[13] Van den Bergh, Camesasca and Giannaccari 2017, p. 70.

[14] Jones, Sufrin and Dunne 2019, p. 24.

[15] Bechtold and Bosch 2018, p. 2.

[16] Mulder and Mok 1962, pp. 9–15.

[17] Vogel 2015, p. 16.

[18] Ibid.

Europe, it is an oversimplification to argue that these systems are only a copy of the US rules, as the European experiences have merits of their own.[19] In Europe, the Freiburg school has been very influential. This German school of thought is also known as Ordoliberalism. Already in the 1930s, a group of scholars worked on a doctrine that departed from the need to protect economic freedom from state and private accumulations of power, doctrine which, as is clear from the outset, was developed in the hostile environment of the Nazi regime.[20] According to the Freiburg school, competitive markets are based on economic freedom and legally protected individual rights.[21] The role of competition law is to protect competition as a system, within which individuals are free to make their own choices.[22] A legal framework should be in place in order to make '*vollständige Wettbewerb*' (complete competition) possible: the legislature must introduce competition provisions as rules of the game, and must then step back.[23] Of great importance is that the task of competition law enforcement is entrusted to an independent authority, being free from pressure of political stakeholders and pressure groups.[24] This task was assigned to the Bundeskartellamt (the Federal Cartel Office), the authority of which is undisputed in Europe. After the Second World War, Germany adopted its own competition laws, also instigated by the US, as occupying power of post-Nazi Germany. These competition laws have been very influential as far as EU competition law is concerned.[25] It is, therefore, not surprising that traces of the Freiburg school (Ordoliberalism) could be found in EU competition law. For example, the requirement of Article 101(3) TFEU that restrictive agreements are justified provided that, inter alia, competition is not totally eliminated, has its roots in this school of thought, which emphasised that the competition process, as prerequisite for economic freedom, must be preserved.

Also, other schools of thought emerged in Europe. Worth mentioning is the Austrian school, an important exponent of which was von Hayek. As firms only have imperfect knowledge of the preferences of consumers, it is important for them to find out what these preferences are by making use of the signals given by prices.[26] The price system provides enterprises with important information that enables them to adapt to changing circumstances. As no administrator or judge will have the same understanding of the competitive process as market operators have, von Hayek was opposed to interventions based on competition law.[27]

Notwithstanding this restrictive view of von Hayek, during the last decades, the importance of competition law has steadily increased in the EU and also in its Member States. This may be partly explained by pointing to the neo-liberal view on the role of governments and markets. Another notable development is the emergence of the 'more economic approach' in

---

[19] Gerber 2010, p. 159.

[20] Ibid, pp. 167–8.

[21] Van den Bergh, Camesasca and Giannaccari 2017, p. 30.

[22] Jones, Sufrin and Dunne 2019, pp. 27–8.

[23] Van den Bergh, Camesasca and Giannaccari 2017, p. 32.

[24] Ibid.

[25] Gerber 2010, p. 182.

[26] Van den Bergh, Camesasca and Giannaccari 2017, p. 54.

[27] Ibid, p. 55.

EU competition law, which means that, in accordance with the view of the Chicago school, the interpretation of the competition rules is geared towards the effects of the practices and the conduct under review.[28]

During the last years, the criticism as to whether markets and competition should be viewed as the default solution for problems at play in society has grown. This criticism has its bearing also on the discussion of how to define competition. In response to this criticism, the current Commissioner for competition, Margrethe Vestager, has put forward the concept of 'fair competition/fairness in competition law', which seems to entail that not only big enterprises but also other players, among which consumers, should get their fair deal of the positive results of the markets.[29] Consumers, as well as small and medium-sized enterprises (SMEs) are entitled to their fair shot of the deal. In this respect, Vestager has pointed out that businesses need a level playing field to reach their full potential.[30] This point of view has much in common with what Stucke and Ezrachi have put forward recently: competition should not simply be about stealing business from rivals, but about creating value.[31] They are in favour of introducing the concept of 'noble competition', which means that each market operator competes fiercely, but with respect for societal and moral standards, which means that the competitiveness of a firm helps other market operators to reach their full potential.[32]

From the foregoing it is clear that various and even opposing views as to what competition is about are developed over time. On one hand, the doctrines outlined have had some impact on the interpretation of the EU competition rules, including the theories developed in the United States. On the other hand, the Court of Justice of the European Union (CJEU) has not singled out one particular school of thought as a leading doctrine, in the sense that it has acknowledged a particular theory as the official doctrine to be adhered to in EU competition law. As was already stated in relation to US antitrust law, the drafting the EU competition rules is very flexible. The open norms are capable of accommodating new views and developments. Having said that, we would like to argue that, at the very least, competition law is about free markets and the competitive process that must be preserved. It is also undeniable that economic theory plays an important role, in order to understand how competition works in the markets. Therefore, in Chapter 3 attention will be paid to the economics of competition law.

2.2 Challenges ahead

The challenges which competition law has to address are concerned with various, serious problems of society. The emergence of digital markets has forced competition authorities, such as the Commission, to rethink what competition law is about. For example, Big Data

---

[28] Gerber 2010, pp. 192–8.

[29] E.g. Vestager 2019 (c), 2018 (a), 2018 (b), 2018 (c).

[30] Vestager 2020 (b).

[31] Stucke and Ezrachi 2020, ch 9.

[32] Ibid, ch 10.

plays an important role in many current commercial practices, as many companies adopt business models based on personal data as key input.[33] Big Data represents significant value enabling big tech companies to provide services to huge numbers of consumers.[34] The scale of data leads to enormous network effects: the more people make use of a digital service and, by doing so, provide data, the more the company concerned can learn and improve its service, the more attractive this service becomes to other users, and the more new consumers will make use of it.[35] This process may also lead to spillover effects, which enable the enterprise concerned to offer new products closely related to the first service.[36] This example shows that digital markets lead to new questions, as the services offered to users are not (fully) based on pricing, which commonly plays an important role in competition law, but on Big Data. It is not surprising that the Commission has adopted a wide range of policy proposals dealing with digital markets.[37] Recently, the Commission has adopted its Communication, Shaping Europe's Digital Future,[38] which, inter alia, concerns competition policy.

Another problem is related to global warming. The Green Deal proposed by the Commission[39] may also lead to updating the view on how the competitive process should be shaped. Moreover, the Corona crisis, which started in 2020, also poses new challenges in competition law. It is unprecedented how many businesses, state bodies, and citizens are depending on digital services and networks owned by large enterprises. These firms are in control of facilities the access to which is indispensable in order to work from home or to operate otherwise in accordance with the rules on social distancing. The Commission has also given guidance as to how to deal with business cooperation projects aimed at addressing shortages of essential services and products (resulting from the Corona crisis), in light of the Treaty provisions on competition.[40] Furthermore, many companies encounter great economic difficulties, as they have to close their business premises and shops, or have to limit their commercial activities considerably. The EU Member States' response to these economic problems was to give financial support of an unprecedented size, which the Commission had to approve on the basis of the EU state aid rules[41] (which are part of competition law in our view), after having adopted the 2020 Temporary Framework for State Aid Measures to Support the Economy in the Current COVID-19 Outbreak. Rethinking how to protect competition in a time when many companies have become heavily dependent on state aid is challenging, to put it mildly.

---

[33] Stucke and Grunes 2016, p. 37.

[34] Ibid, pp. 44–5.

[35] Ibid, p. 170.

[36] Ibid 2016, p. 186.

[37] On this matter, see e.g. Rusu, Looijestijn-Clearie and Veenbrink 2018, p. 15 *et seq.*

[38] (2020) COM/2020/67 final.

[39] Green Deal Communication 2019.

[40] Temporary Framework 2020, par. 6–16.

[41] For an overview of the measures approved, see <https://ec.europa.eu/competition/state_aid/what_is_new/covid_19.html> accessed 23 June 2020.

2.3 The role of the law in competition

All in all, it is clear that competition is a process that remains subject to lively and, from time to time, heated debate. In this regard it must be pointed out that a difference exists between competition and the law governing it, that is, competition law. The function of each area of law, including competition law, is, inter alia, to set out which conduct is prohibited and, accordingly, which conduct is deemed to be permitted. In close relation to this, the principle of legal certainty must be observed, which means that market operators, consumers, enforcement agencies, and other players know where they stand.[42]

It goes without saying that another important function of competition law is to ensure that the competition process is preserved. According to many schools of thought (although not all of them), competition rules are needed in order to oblige companies to not jeopardise this process. In other words, introducing competition in a sector or relying on the competitive process in a particular branch without having in place an adequate set of competition rules is very problematic, as it remains to be seen whether companies will be engaged in competitive behaviour in the first place. Consequently, the task of competition law is to prevent companies operating on the free market set up practices leading to hampering or even blocking this free market.[43]

Moreover, the applicability of EU competition law also entails that general principles of EU law are of importance. The authorities applying and enforcing the rules must observe legal guarantees and rights enshrined in the law. As will become apparent in the next chapters of this book, more in particular Chapter 8 dealing with public enforcement of the EU antitrust rules, competition law is not only a means for achieving various objectives, but it also grants rights to undertakings, consumers and other stakeholders. Hellingman and Mortelmans have pointed out that economic law, including competition law, constitutes a 'guarantee function' (the Dutch word used is 'waarborgfunctie'), meaning that the quality of the provisions of law (e.g. transparency), legal protection and the general principles of law are of great interest.[44] Against this backdrop, it is no wonder that open norms of competition law are specified in a wide array of communications and notices (issued by, for example, the Commission), that both EU and national courts are called upon to review decisions taken by competition authorities, and that enforcement actions are reviewed in the light of fundamental rights.[45] In other words, apart from pursuing competition objectives (EU and national) competition law ensures that rights of undertakings, individuals and other stakeholders, as well as certain legal guarantees, are protected. The reason for this is simply that competition law is part of an overarching legal system. In addition, it must be pointed out that in EU law the applicability of a set of EU rules, including competition law, triggers the applicability of

---

[42] Vedder and Appeldoorn 2019, p. 4.

[43] Hellingman and Mortelmans 1989, p. 304.

[44] Ibid, pp. 81–8.

[45] E.g. case C-94/00 *Roquette Frères*, ECLI:EU:C:2002:603. In Chapter 8, attention will be paid to the CJEU case-law on fundamental rights in enforcement cases.

general principles of law,[46] including fundamental rights.[47] Accordingly, the applicability of the EU competition rules adds a 'legal protection dimension' to markets, on which, next to rivalry, basic norms and values of an EU nature must be respected.

3 OBJECTIVES OF COMPETITION LAW

Many argue that one of the objectives of EU competition law is to achieve consumer welfare. At least the Commission has made many references to this goal in its publications.[48] The welfare of consumers must be maximised by stimulating efficient markets.[49] It must be pointed out that in this respect EU competition law is influenced by US antitrust law, where it is commonly held that the protection of consumer welfare is the ultimate purpose of antitrust law.[50] In some judgments, the CJEU has held that one of the aims is to protect the interests of consumers,[51] which is a little confusing. Protection of consumers seems to be concerned with addressing the uneven position of consumers being engaged in commercial transactions with traders, which is a classic goal of consumer law rather than competition law. Maximising consumer welfare cannot be equated with consumer protection.[52] In other judgments it is put forward that the EU competition rules aim at preventing competition from being distorted, to the detriment of not only the public interest and individual undertakings, but also consumers.[53] This seems to be more in line with consumer welfare, as undistorted competition promotes efficiency, which is believed to result in the enhancement of consumer welfare. Although the wording of the CJEU is somewhat ambiguous, it may be argued that it endorses the view that consumer welfare is an objective of EU competition law. Consequently, the Chicago school, which has changed the course of the antitrust rules in the US, has also had some bearing on the direction of travel of the TFEU provisions on competition. However, unlike in US antitrust law, consumer welfare is not the sole objective pursued in EU competition law.

Before the other (possible) goals will be discussed, it must be pointed out that the efficiencies boosting consumer welfare may take different forms: allocative efficiency, productive efficiency and dynamic efficiency.[54] Allocative efficiency means that goods and services are

---

[46] E.g. case C-206/13 *Siragusa*, ECLI:EU:C:2014:126. On this matter, see Jans, Prechal and Widdershoven 2015, pp. 139–40.

[47] Charter of Fundamental Rights of the EU, Article 51.

[48] E.g. Guidelines on Article 101(3) TFEU 2004, par. 13; Enforcement Priorities Guidelines 2009, par. 2–8; Guidelines on Vertical Restraints 2010, par. 7.

[49] Jones, Sufrin and Dunne 2019, p. 28.

[50] Hovenkamp 2008, p. 31.

[51] Joined cases C-501, C-513, C-515 and C-519/06 P *GlaxoSmithKline*, ECLI:EU:C:2009:610, par. 63; case C-8/08, *T-Mobile*, ECLI:EU:C:2009:343, par. 38.

[52] Cseres 2006, p. 121 *et seq.*

[53] Cases C-52/09 *TeliaSonera*, ECLI:EU:C:2011:83, par. 22; C-94/00 *Roquette Frères*, ECLI:EU:C:2002:603, par. 42.

[54] Whish and Bailey 2018, pp. 5–8; Sauter 2016, p. 64.

allocated between the consumers concerned in the best possible way on the basis of the prices these consumers want to pay.[55] Productive efficiency is achieved if goods and services are produced at the lowest cost possible.[56] Dynamic efficiency means that competition stimulates companies to develop new products, which may further technological research and development (R&D).[57] The efficiencies identified may not only lead to consumer welfare, but also to total welfare. The latter concept adds the producer surplus to the consumer surplus.[58] It should be pointed out that generally it is not believed that total welfare is an objective of EU competition law.

In contrast with US antitrust law, where consumer welfare is considered the ultimate objective to pursue, in EU competition law another objective, which is typical to the EU, is acknowledged, that is, the establishment of the Internal Market.[59] In the past, Article 3(3)(g) of the TEC used to provide that a system ensuring that competition in the Internal Market is not distorted was part of the policy of the European Communities, whereas Article 2 of this Treaty clearly set out that the establishment of a Common Market was a goal to be achieved. Now, the TEU, which, together with the TFEU, has replaced the TEC, stipulates in its Article 3(3) that the EU is based on an Internal Market, while the Protocol on the Internal Market states that a system of undistorted competition is part of this market.[60] In this respect, it is of interest to note that the Single Market imperative runs as a common thread through many CJEU judgments and Commission decisions. As will be seen in Chapter 5, which deals with the cartel prohibition, absolute territorial protection, which leads to the partitioning of national markets, is considered as a very serious violation of EU competition law.[61] The reason for this is that such practices run counter to the idea of establishing one Internal Market in the EU. In *GlaxoSmithKline*, the CJEU held that given the objectives of competition law these practices continue to give rise to serious competition issues and rejected the point of view that these practices were only harmful if final consumers were deprived of certain benefits.[62] The CJEU specifically pointed to 'the Treaty's objective of achieving the integration of national markets through the establishment of a Single Market . . .',[63] in support of its point of view. As a result, even if consumer welfare is not at stake, business practices being contrary to the Single Market imperative are condemned in EU competition law.[64] In this regard, it must be noted that, as in EU competition law, the Treaty provisions on free movement (laid down, for example, in Articles 34–36 and Articles 45–66

---

[55] See Whish and Bailey 2018, pp. 5, 7.

[56] Ibid, p. 6.

[57] Ibid, p. 7.

[58] Jones, Sufrin and Dunne 2019, p. 11.

[59] Sauter 2016, p. 73.

[60] Internal Market and Competition Protocol 2008.

[61] This view was advanced by the CJEU already in the 1960s, in joined cases 56 and 58/64 *Grundig/Consten*, ECLI:EU:C:1966:41.

[62] Joined cases C-501, C-513, C-515 and C-519/06 P *GlaxoSmithKline*, ECLI:EU:C:2009:610, par. 62.

[63] Ibid, par. 61.

[64] Cf. Van den Bergh, Camesasca and Giannaccari 2017, p. 110.

TFEU) pursue the establishment and proper functioning of the Internal Market. The most significant addressees of these provisions are the Member States, which are precluded from taking measures leading to non-justified restrictions of free movement. In fact, from the perspective of the Single Market imperative, competition law and free movement law are different sides of the same coin: EU competition law pursues the Internal Market objective by imposing obligations upon undertakings, whereas free movement law achieves this objective by directing instructions to Member States.

Apart from establishing the Internal Market and consumer welfare, a couple of other objectives may be distinguished in EU competition law. In this regard, the following state-ment made by the CJEU in *GlaxoSmithKline* should be considered: EU competition law 'aims to protect not only the interests of competitors or of consumers, but also the structure of the market and, in so doing, competition as such'.[65] As already put forward, protecting the interests of consumers may be understood as enhancing consumer welfare. In our view the 'structure of the market' and 'competition as such' should be considered as belonging to the same category. The competition process must be preserved. This process is deemed to have merits of its own. This highly reflects the views articulated by the Freiburg school (Ordoliberalism), which emphasised the importance of economic freedom and competition as a system. The well-functioning of competitive markets is regarded as an important value. Moreover, also in the S-C-P paradigm, developed by the Harvard school, the structure of the market plays an essential role.

Returning to the statement made by the CJEU in *GlaxoSmithKline*, we would like to point out that the aim of protecting the interests of competitors is somewhat puzzling. Although in its time of inception, US antitrust law was deemed to protect competitors, nowadays it is commonly accepted that a system of competition law does not aim to give a helping hand to companies having difficulties in matching competitive performances of other companies. Some firms, not operating efficiently on a competitive market, are outper-formed by other firms, which do a better job. It goes without saying that the competition rules are not destined to solve this problem, which is, at the end of the day, not a problem but a consequence of how markets should work. What did the CJEU mean by its reference to the protection of the interests of competitors? In our view, the crux of this statement is constituted by the word 'interest'. In general, a competitive market is in the interest of companies performing business on the market. It is in the interest of an average, circum-spect market operator that competition is not restricted, whereas protection of a company not being able to match what efficient firms deliver is definitely not in the interest of such a market operator. Accordingly, a competitive market enabling average circumspect market operators to deliver what they have in store is seen an objective of competition law by the CJEU. To our mind, this point of view has a lot in common with that which was advocated by the Freiburg school.

The ambiguous wording of what competition law is about does not only lead to debates, but also enables the competent (administrative and judicial) authorities to incorporate new developments in this area of law. To put it differently, its flexibility allows for responding

---

[65] Joined cases C-501, C-513, C-515 and C-519/06 P *GlaxoSmithKline*, ECLI:EU:C:2009:610, par. 63.

aptly to new challenges. On the basis of the current case-law it may, for example, be argued that societal welfare is part of the goals of EU competition law. This goal takes the public interest as the point of departure and stresses that the well-being of the EU as whole should be pursued.[66] In *Roquette Frères*[67] and *TeliaSonera*,[68] and in *CK Telecoms UK Investments*,[69] the CJEU and the General Court (GC), respectively, have pointed out that the function of EU competition law is 'to prevent competition from being distorted to the detriment of the public interest, individual undertakings and consumers, thereby ensuring the well-being of the European Union'. This wording seems to suggest that next to economic goals, objectives of social and environmental nature, as well as aims related to fundamental rights and significant values, may also play a role. As was outlined above, the Green Deal policy developed in order to address the very serious problems caused by climate change may lead to developments in competition law. The same is true for the Corona crisis and the emergence of digital markets. Adapting (to a certain extent) the competition law goals is possible given the flexible approach developed by the EU courts, which may result in paying due consideration to these major developments.

Accordingly, it cannot be excluded that new goals will be articulated in EU competition law. Above, some attention was paid to views on fair competition. Recently, views have been developed, stressing that not only big enterprises but also other players are entitled to obtain a share of the positive results of the markets and putting forward that businesses should be stimulated to reach their full potential. In our view, what matters is that markets and competition produce incentives prompting undertakings to engage in practices that are both *efficient* and *fair*. If this is accepted, competition law should permit business conduct being in line with these two values. This means that an aim of competition law is to ensure equal opportunities for companies, consumers and other stakeholders, in the sense that these entities are free to pursue their goals on the market as they see fit (subject to the legal rules in place), without having any disadvantages in comparison with others. It should be noted that in the case-law of the CJEU on free movement and the transparency principle, it is required that an exclusive right to provide services should be granted through a competitive procedure, since competition does justice to equal treatment.[70] In this case-law a clear connection is made between competition and equal opportunities. As already pointed out, in EU law the competition rules are closely related to free movement law, which is also apparent from the transparency case-law. It goes without saying that a lot of research, as well as much case-law and decisional practice, is needed in order to establish how objectives such as fairness and equal opportunities should be fleshed out.

In close relation to this, an important debate is to what extent public interest goals, such as environmental protection and healthcare objectives, should be accommodated in the

---

[66] Rusu 2010, pp. 102–3.

[67] Case C-94/00 *Roquette Frères*, ECLI:EU:C:2002:603, par. 42.

[68] Case C-52/09 *TeliaSonera*, ECLI:EU:C:2011:83, par. 22.

[69] Case T-399/16 *CK Telecoms UK Investments*, ECLI:EU:T:2020:217, par. 93.

[70] E.g. case C-203/08 *Betfair*, ECLI:EU:C:2010:307.

application of the competition rules.[71] As will be seen in the next chapters of this book, doctrines and approaches are developed in competition law in order to take public interest goals into account, such as the *Wouters* case[72] (discussed in Chapter 5) and Services of General Economic Interest (analysed in Chapters 11 and 12). A strict view is that competition law is not suitable for taking such objectives into account, while a more flexible view will emphasise that integrating these objectives in competition law does not affect the fundamental features of this area of law. To our mind, it is not necessary to settle the dispute as to whether non-competition goals should be included in the objectives pursued by competition law. What matters the most is whether certain competition rules may be moderated or even disapplied, if this is necessary in order to achieve a significant public interest goal.[73] In other words, does the setup of competition law allow for making a trade-off between competition and non-competition goals[74] and does it acknowledge that companies have some responsibilities with regard to certain significant public interest goals? Although the question on the role of public interest goals has given rise to important judgments and developments, it may be expected that the dust has not settled yet, with regard to this question. Moreover, in our view it is an educated guess that competition authorities and judicial bodies will accept that some public interest objectives must be taken into account in competition law. Given the gravity of the problems caused by, inter alia, global warming, the Corona crisis and the emergence of digital markets, it seems inevitable to abandon a very strict approach to the goals of competition law.

4 THE INSTITUTIONAL SETUP

The task to apply and to enforce the EU competition rules is assigned to the Commission. As will become apparent in the next chapters and more in particular in Chapter 8, the Commission has at its disposal far-reaching powers to fulfil this task. Within the Commission, a special unit, called DG Competition, deals with competition matters on a daily basis; this unit is managed by one of the Commissioners. It should be pointed out that this Commissioner does not adopt decisions on her own, as all decisions are taken by the entire Commission. The Commission is in its entirety responsible for the decisions taken and the policies developed, also in the field of competition law. This EU institution acts in accordance with the principle of collegiate responsibility.[75] As a result, commissioners responsible for policy areas other than competition could exert influence on the decision-making process in competition law. At least, the appearance of such influence, which may also be of a political nature, cannot be avoided. On the one hand, it is clearly set out in the Treaties that the Commission should act

---

[71] On this matter, see e.g. Lavrijssen 2015, p. 636 *et seq.*; Gerbrandy 2017, p. 539 *et seq.*; Gerbrandy 2015, p. 769 *et seq.*; Townley 2009, p. 11 *et seq.*

[72] Case C-309/99 *Wouters*, ECLI:EU:C:2002:98.

[73] Cf. Sauter 2016, p. 70.

[74] Cf. Townley 2009, p. 42.

[75] Article 250 TFEU.

independently from other institutions, as well as the EU Member States, and look after the interests of the Union.[76] On the other hand, the Commission, as one of the key EU players, operates in a political arena and, accordingly, the Commissioner for competition affairs is not in a position not to take the interests of her fellow commissioners into account.

It goes without saying that the rule of law must be respected in EU law, as stipulated in Article 2 TEU. For that reason, the decisions taken by the Commission, also in the field of competition law, are subject to judicial review of the EU courts. Article 47 of the Charter of Fundamental Rights of the EU lays down the right to an effective remedy before a tribunal, a provision which largely echoes Article 6(1) of the European Convention on Human Rights (ECHR). It flows from Article 263 TFEU that Commission decisions may be annulled by the EU courts and that an action may be brought by any natural and legal person, if the Commission decision is addressed to such a person, or when the decision is of direct and individual concern to that person. Moreover, as a result of what is stipulated in Article 261 TFEU, these courts have unlimited jurisdiction with regard to fines and penalties imposed by the Commission in competition law cases.[77] In first instance, the GC handles cases brought against the Commission, while in higher appeal the CJEU is the competent judicial body. It should be noted that the higher appeal to the CJEU may only concern points of law and should not question the establishment of the facts by the GC.[78]

The EU competition law rules are not applied and enforced only by the Commission, but also by national competition authorities (NCAs) and domestic courts. This competence is derived from the concept of direct effect: every administrative authority and each judicial body is obliged to give full effect to the provisions of EU law having direct effect,[79] including the competition rules.[80] Accordingly, the power to apply the directly applicable competition rules also amounts to an obligation to do so. The position of the national authorities has been reinforced by the entering into force of Regulation 1/2003, on 1 May 2004. It is apparent from Article 1 of this Regulation that not only the prohibitions contained in Articles 101(1) and 102 TFEU should be applied by the national authorities, but also that these authorities have the authority to review anti-competitive practices under the exception enshrined in Article 101(3) TFEU. This process of fostering the implementation of EU competition law at the national level is referred to as the decentralised application of EU competition law,[81] which means that a great deal of the EU competition law responsibilities are shifted from the EU level (Commission) to the national level (domestic administrative and judicial authorities). Commonly, in a non-competition law context, decentralisation is associated with the process of delegating powers to regional and/or local authorities. In EU antitrust law, however, this term is connected with the transfer of tasks from the EU level to the national level.

In the EU Member States NCAs apply and enforce domestic competition rules. Article 35

---

[76] Article 17(1) TEU; Articles 245–250 TFEU.

[77] Jones, Sufrin and Dunne 2019, p. 983.

[78] Article 256(1) TFEU.

[79] E.g. cases 103/88 *Fratelli Costanzo*, ECLI:EU:C:1989:256; 106/77 *Simmenthal*, ECLI:EU:C:1978:49.

[80] E.g. case C-198/01, *CIF*, ECLI:EU:C:2003:430.

[81] Modernisation White Paper 1999, par. 41–73.

of Regulation 1/2003 requires that every Member State designates an authority responsible for the application of the Treaty provisions on competition. It is apparent from this provision that the task of implementing the national competition rules must be combined by the NCAs with the application and enforcement of EU competition law. In other words, NCAs have a dual task, as they are responsible for the implementation of both sets of competition rules. Of importance also is that, on the basis of Article 35(1) of Regulation 1/2003, the Member States ensure that NCAs are able to apply the EU competition rules effectively. It may be assumed that this can be realised by, inter alia, granting an independent position to NCAs.[82] The majority of the NCAs operate in an independent fashion, as they are not subject to supervision by another body.[83] As will be outlined in section 4.3.1 of Chapter 8, the ECN+ Directive 2019 requires that the position of NCAs is independent, which means that every Member State must guarantee that this requirement is complied with, once the implementation term of the Directive expires. Above, it was put forward that according to the Freiburg school, a competition authority should be independent in order to protect the competition process. What the ECN+ Directive 2019 provides is, for that reason, in line with this school of thought. Strikingly, given the setup framed in the European Treaties, the design of the Commission does not entirely mirror the independence requirements imposed on NCAs. Due to the principle of collegiate responsibility, which is set out in primary EU law and has, therefore, a constitutional dimension, it is not possible to let the Commissioner for competition affairs take the decision independently from the other commissioners. Then again, it must be borne in mind that, as was outlined above, the Treaties ensure the independent status of the Commission as a body vis-à-vis other institutions and EU Member States.

It goes without saying that everyone being confronted with a decision taken by an NCA must have recourse to a court proceeding. In the jurisdictions of the EU Member States the domestic courts review the decisions adopted by NCAs. It must be pointed out that, in so far as these decisions concern the application of EU competition law, the Charter of Fundamental Rights of the EU applies,[84] including Article 47 of this Charter, which lays down the right to an effective remedy and a fair trial. If a domestic court, while reviewing an NCA decision, entertains any doubts regarding the interpretation of EU (competition) law, it may pose preliminary questions to the CJEU.[85] In some Member States the responsibility of applying the EU competition rules is shared by an administrative authority and a judicial authority (which means that the task of the latter is not limited to granting judicial protection but also encompasses matters such as imposing sanctions).[86] Article 30(1) of the ECN+ Directive 2019 requires that these Member States enable their NCAs to bring cases directly or indirectly before these national judicial authorities.[87]

---

[82] Cf. case C-439/08 *VEBIC*, ECLI:EU:C:2010:739.

[83] ECN Staff Working Document 2014, p. 6.

[84] This flows from Article 51 of the Charter of Fundamental Rights of the EU.

[85] Article 267 TFEU.

[86] In these countries, the NCA carries out investigations and brings the case before a national court, which decides on the merits of the case and on the imposition of fines. See ECN Staff Working Document 2014, p. 5.

[87] This provision codifies the CJEU ruling in case C-439/08 *VEBIC*, ECLI:EU:C:2010:739.

The Commission and the NCAs work together in the European Competition Network (ECN). Article 11 of Regulation 1/2003 requires that they apply the EU competition rules in close cooperation. In the ECN+ Directive 2019 many references are made to the ECN. Given the increasing role of the NCAs, the proper functioning of this network greatly contributes to the successful enforcement of EU competition law.[88] In this regard, it must be noted that even at the global level such a network is established, called the International Competition Network (ICN).[89]

It is apparent from the foregoing that both at the EU and at the national level a comprehensive (multi-layered) governance system is set up for enforcing the European (and also national) competition rules. In Chapter 8 the enforcement of these rules will be analysed both from an EU and a national perspective.

Actions taken by the Commission and the NCAs amount to the public enforcement of EU competition law. It should be pointed out that competition law may also be subject to private law actions, which concerns the private enforcement of the competition rules. Remarkably, Article 101(2) TFEU contains a provision of private law, as it states (in short) that certain restrictive agreements are void. On top of that, the Union legislature has adopted Private Damages Directive 2014 dealing with damages actions related to competition law infringements. It is in the hands of private law courts of the Member States to decide on damage claims, nullity and other matters of private law. In Chapter 9 the private enforcement of the competition rules will be discussed.

The decentralisation process of EU competition law has resulted in European and national law being closely intertwined in this policy field. It must be recalled that, according to settled case-law of the CJEU, EU law takes precedence over national law.[90] The supremacy of EU law is one of the core principles to observe, when it comes to the interplay between European and national rules. However, in competition law, the direction of travel of this principle has given rise to intriguing developments. In *Walt Wilhelm*,[91] the CJEU accepted that European and national competition law may be applied in parallel, even if this leads to the imposition of sanctions by both the Commission and an NCA.[92] The reason for this finding is that the systems of European and national competition law pursue different objectives, that is, preserving competition on the Internal Market and addressing competition problems on the national market. Regulation 1/2003 has slightly moderated the doctrine developed in *Walt Wilhelm*, by providing that in the event the trade between the Member States is influenced the NCAs and domestic courts are obliged to apply the Treaty provisions on competition, whereas it is at their discretion to apply the domestic competition rules in parallel.[93]

---

[88] An interesting development was the ECN Joint Statement 2020, which sets out that legitimate cooperation projects between companies ensuring the supply of essential services and products will not give rise to serious issues under competition law.

[89] See <https://www.internationalcompetitionnetwork.org/about/> accessed 23 June 2020.

[90] Cases 26/62 *Van Gend en Loos*, ECLI:EU:C:1963:1; 6/64 *Costa v E.N.E.L.*, ECLI:EU:C:1964:66.

[91] Case 14/68 *Walt Wilhelm*, ECLI:EU:C:1969:4.

[92] This point of view is confirmed by the CJEU in case C-17/10 *Toshiba*, ECLI:EU:C:2012:72.

[93] Regulation 1/2003, Article 3(1).

Consequently, finding an effect on the trade between the Member States triggers the duty to base a national decision or ruling dealing with competition law on Article 101 TFEU and/or Article 102 TFEU, while freedom exists as to whether such a decision or ruling should also be based on national competition rules. Moreover, national rules governing restrictive agreements and similar practices may not be stricter than Article 101 TFEU.[94] What is permitted under this Treaty provision may not be banned under domestic law. However, Member States are not precluded from adopting or applying national laws prohibiting unilateral conduct of undertakings, which is not in violation of the EU competition rules.[95] Stricter national requirements for unilateral conduct (which is assessed under Article 102 TFEU) are allowed by Regulation 1/2003.

Brexit may pose some challenging issues regarding the enforcement of the competition rules at the national level. Once Brexit is fully effective, the United Kingdom competition authority, which is the Competition and Markets Authority (CMA), no longer has the authority to apply the TFEU provisions on competition. However, as will be outlined in section 2.3.2 of Chapter 5 and section 4.4 of Chapter 10, enterprises of third countries (which is now the status of the UK) may be confronted with EU competition law, when their practices have an impact on the EU Internal Market.[96] This means that, in many instances, British companies continue to be obliged to comply with the EU competition rules.[97] The UK is so close to the EU Member States and its economy is so interwoven with the economies of these states that effects on the EU Internal Market occur with regard to a great deal of business deals and operations. Cooperation between the Commission, the CMA and the NCAs of the EU Member States is very important for that reason. When writing this book, it was not yet clear whether and, if so, which deals were concluded between the UK and the EU regarding Brexit.

5 THE APPROACH OF THIS BOOK

In the next chapters the relevant provisions, principles and doctrines of EU competition law will be analysed. This unique body of law applies throughout the EU and has contributed considerably to the economic success of the EU. It also sets an example for competition law systems for other countries.[98] In the light of this, a thorough and systematic analysis of EU competition law is warranted.

In the previous section, however, the role of NCAs and domestic courts has also been highlighted. This has shown that the national dimension of competition law has grown significantly over time. A proper understanding of the implementation and enforcement of the

---

[94] Ibid, Article 3(2).

[95] Ibid.

[96] E.g. joined cases 89, 104, 114, 116, 117 and 125 to 129/85 *Wood Pulp*, ECLI:EU:C:1988:447, par. 16; case C-413/14 *Intel*, ECLI:EU:C:2017:632, par. 40–65.

[97] Brexit Notice 2019, p. 2.

[98] Gerber 2010, pp. 202–4.

EU competition rules requires that national competition law is addressed too. In this respect, it must be noted that the national substantive competition laws of the EU Member States have converged, as these systems are modelled after the EU experience: in the past, Germany was the only country of the six founders of the European Treaties having competition laws in place, whereas now all Member States have such laws in place.[99] Due to the ECN+ Directive 2019, convergence on the procedural and sanctioning matters will be furthered. Nevertheless, as will be outlined in the next chapters of this book, some remarkable differences between the European and national systems continue to exist and, therefore, it is of great importance to discuss the national experience with competition law. It should be noted that the ECN+ Directive 2019 does not oblige the Member States to align their substantive competition rules with the EU norms, while it contains minimum harmonisation for the procedural matters (leaving, accordingly, some room for manoeuvre to the Member States).

All in all, attention must be paid to various aspects of the national competition laws of the EU Member States. Given the wide variety and the multitude of the national rules, rulings and decisional practice, it is not possible to analyse all the national competition law systems with the same depth as EU competition law. Therefore, this book will focus on examples and representative developments at the national level, in order to show how EU competition law plays out in the legal framework of the Member States. The aim is not to give a comprehensive overview of the national law systems; the endeavour is rather to reveal some key features of the complex and delicate interplay between European and national competition law.

As was pointed out above, the first piece of legislation dealing with competition was adopted in the US. For that reason, this book will highlight some discussions conducted in this jurisdiction. The purpose of this is to learn lessons in order to enhance the understanding of the issues at play in EU competition law. It is, therefore, not necessary to engage in a consistent and systematic discussion of US antitrust law in this book. Only if needed, some aspects of this competition law system will be brought up.

This book discusses the law as it stands on 30 June 2020.

6 CONCLUSIONS

Not only competition, but also competition law has given rise to lively and heated debates. Although it remains strongly debatable what competition law is about, the various schools of thought and the case-law of the CJEU have given some important clues. Consumer welfare and the establishment of the Internal Market are significant objectives to be achieved in competition law, while other objectives may also play a role. It may be expected that EU com-petition law will be shaped by the significant challenges that society faces nowadays, more in particular by the emergence of digital markets, the global warming phenomenon, and the Corona crisis of 2020. EU competition law is applied and enforced both at the European and at the national level. As a result, not only the Commission, but also the NCAs and domestic

---

[99] OECD 2005, p. 13.

courts play a significant role in this respect. A proper understanding of the issues at play in EU competition law requires that due consideration is paid to its national dimension: the interplay between the Commission and the national competent authorities, as well as between European and national law must be explored.

2

Key concepts and categorisations

1 INTRODUCTION

In the previous chapter, the context of EU competition law was discussed. The objectives pursued and the setup of the rules were outlined. In this chapter, the most important concepts being used throughout competition law will be analysed. For example, what is meant by an undertaking for the purposes of competition law and how the market must be defined are themes running as a red thread throughout EU competition law. Furthermore, attention is paid to the institutional design of these rules. In other words, the categorisations EU competition law is based on will be explored. A significant component of the institutional design is by the organisation of enforcement. A separate section is dedicated to this matter.

2 BASIC CONCEPTS

2.1 The concept of undertaking

As was already mentioned in the previous chapter, Articles 101 and 102 TFEU and the Merger Control Regulation 2004 are directed at undertakings. Moreover, the EU rules on state and competition, such as state aid law, apply in so far as public authorities deal with undertakings. This raises the question, 'What is meant by the concept of undertaking for the purposes of competition law?'

In its case-law dealing with this question, the CJEU has developed a functional approach. This means that the legal form of a particular organisation is not of importance in establishing the applicability of the competition rules. The CJEU ruled that every entity engaged in economic activities is an undertaking within the meaning of EU competition law.[1] The offering of goods or services on the market is regarded as an economic activity.[2] It is clear from the outset that the concept of undertaking is interpreted in an expansive way by the CJEU. Nevertheless, it is apparent from its case-law that there are also a few limits to this concept.

---

[1] Case C-41/90 *Höfner*, ECLI:EU:C:1991:161.

[2] E.g. case C-35/96 *Commission v Italy*, ECLI:EU:C:1998:303.

To start with, it is settled case-law that the exercise of official authority does not amount to an economic activity.[3] Thus, the surveillance activities carried out by a limited corporation in the harbour of Genoa in order to verify compliance with the public laws on the environment did not qualify as economic activities.[4] The reason for this was that these activities were typical for the public domain.

Another limit is concerned with social security, such as pension schemes, health insurance and insurance against occupational diseases and accidents. It depends on the design of the social security system concerned whether the bodies managing this system are engaged in economic activities and, accordingly, qualify as undertakings. The case-law of the CJEU comes down to exploring whether the social security scheme concerned is predominantly based on solidarity and subject to substantial state control.[5] Consequently, the Dutch pension schemes, according to which the affiliates were entitled to benefits based on the financial results of the investments made by the pension schemes on the market, fell within the scope of competition law.[6] In contrast, German sickness funds were not deemed to be engaged in economic activities, as the benefits concerned were fixed in national law, profit making was not permitted and these funds were obliged to take part in a risk equalisation scheme.[7] According to such a scheme, the funds insuring the least costly risks contribute to the financing of the funds insuring more onerous risks. Conversely, a French health insurance company operating a solidarity-based scheme was found to be engaged in economic activities for the reason that it was not subject to substantial state control. Then again, in *Dôvera zdravotná poist'ovňa and Union zdravotná poist'ovňa*, the CJEU held that Slovak health insurance companies, although engaged in some competition, were not undertakings, since the benefits insured persons are entitled to and the amount of the contributions due are fixed in national law. The CJEU found that that the health insurance scheme under review pursued a social objective and applied the principle of solidarity under state supervision.[8] A striking statement made by the CJEU with respect to the Slovak healthcare scheme was that the introduction of

> a competitive element which is intended to encourage operators to operate in accordance with principles of sound management, that is to say, in the most effective and least costly manner possible, in the interests of the proper functioning of the social security system, is not such as to change the nature of that scheme.[9]

---

[3] E.g. cases C-364/92 *Eurocontrol*, ECLI:EU:C:1994:7; C-687/17 *Aanbestedingskalender*, ECLI:EU:2019:932.

[4] Case C-343/95 *Diego Calì*, ECLI:EU:C:1997:160.

[5] E.g. joined cases C-159 and C-160/91 *Poucet et Pistre*, ECLI:EU:C:1993:63; joined cases C-264, C-306, C-354 and C-355/01 *AOK Bundesverband*, ECLI:EU:C:2004:150; case C-437/09 *AG2R*, ECLI:EU:C:2011:112.

[6] Case C-67/96 *Albany*, ECLI:EU:C:1999:430.

[7] Joined cases C-264, C-306, C-354 and C-355/01 *AOK Bundesverband*, ECLI:EU:C:2004:150.

[8] Joined cases C-262 and C-271/18 P *Dôvera zdravotná poist'ovňa and Union zdravotná poist'ovňa*, ECLI:EU:C:2020:450, par. 51.

[9] Ibid, par. 43.

In our view, it is apparent from this line of reasoning that consumer welfare and efficiency are not the only objectives in competition law under the approach developed by the CJEU. In the previous chapter, it was outlined that the Chicago school has advocated to base competition law only on consumer welfare considerations. Clearly, the CJEU does not agree with that vision and is even of the opinion that cost savings realised by efficiency gains, in themselves, do not satisfy the finding that competition law applies. As a result, *Dôvera zdravotná poist'ovňa and Union zdravotná poist'ovňa* confirms the conclusion that EU competition law is not only concerned with consumer welfare but also with other objectives, such as, possibly, societal welfare. As far as the latter objective is concerned, it could be argued that doing justice to the social functions of a national healthcare scheme contributes to the achievement of social policy goals. All in all, from these examples, it is clear that in social security cases the CJEU scrutinises the various relevant aspects of a scheme in its assessment.[10] To a certain extent, interpreting the concept of undertaking in social security settings boils down to making all pieces of the puzzle fit together.

A third limit is, in our view, connected with, inter alia, education. In *CEPPB*,[11] the CJEU found that a school that predominately is financed by the state in order to fulfil its social, cultural and educational obligations towards its population is not engaged in an economic activity.[12] It should be noted that other activities, such as nature conservation and cultural activities, also amount to important values in society and are, largely, dependent on government funding. This raises the question whether such activities should be immune from competition law, if the sole reason that entities perform them is that these entities receive funding from the state. If the answer to this question is affirmative, it could be considered that the following test must be carried out to find the non-applicability of the EU competition law rules: (1) the supply of the goods or services concerned is mainly dependent on public funding; (2) the aim of this funding is the pursuit of a public interest goal; and (3) the activities under review are closely related to this goal. It should be awaited to see to what extent the CJEU will elaborate on its judgment in *CEPPB*.[13]

It should be noted that an undertaking may be engaged in both economic and non-economic activities. This means that the activities of such an entity must be severed in two parts: one part being governed by competition law and one part falling outside the scope of this area of law.[14] Special attention must be paid to buying activities in relation to the supply of goods or services by an undertaking. It is apparent from case-law that the subsequent use of the goods or services purchased is determinant for the qualification of the buying

---

[10] Case C-437/09 *AG2R*, ECLI:EU:C:2011:112.

[11] Case C-74/16 *CEPPB*, ECLI:EU:C:2017:496. Cf case C-393/17 *Kirschstein*, ECLI:EU:C:2019:563.

[12] The CJEU took this approach from its case-law on free movement, the concept service and education. In cases 263/86 *Humbel*, ECLI:EU:C:1988:451 and C-109/92 *Wirth*, ECLI:EU:C:1993:916, the CJEU held that educational activities financed by public means do not constitute services for the purposes of the Treaty provisions on free movement, as the state, while financing the educational system, does not seek gainful activity but aims to fulfil 'its duties towards its own population in the social, cultural and educational fields'.

[13] Van de Gronden 2018, pp. 214–16.

[14] E.g. cases T-128/98 *Aéroport de Paris*, ECLI:EU:T:2000:290; C-82/01 P *Aéroport de Paris*, ECLI:EU:C:2002:617.

activities.[15] If a state body purchases goods with a view to exercise official authority (e.g. police authorities order cars for surveillance purposes), this activity is not governed by EU competition law. In contrast, if the goods purchased will be used for carrying out economic activities (such as offering private security services), competition law does apply.

Another important issue regarding the concept of undertaking is related to the structure of firms. As this concept is based on a functional approach, an undertaking may be comprised of various legal and even natural persons. Such groups are referred to as 'single economic units'.[16] A conglomerate consisting of a parent company and subsidiaries is an important example of such a single economic unit, provided that this company is in full control of its subsidiaries.[17] The consequence of this is that agreements concluded between various entities within this conglomerate do not fall within the ambit of Article 101 TFEU.[18] This is a positive aspect of the doctrine of single economic unit for the legal entities concerned. The downside of this doctrine for them is, however, that the parent companies can be held liable for the anti-competitive practices of their subsidiaries both in cases concerning the imposition of fines[19] and when it comes to civil law damages.[20]

2.2 Market definition

Applying the competition law rules will only be successful if there is a profound understanding of the markets concerned. One could only argue that certain practices of firms may be harmful for competition, if the special characteristics of a given market are identified. An important step that must be taken in this respect is the definition of the relevant market. The aim of this technique is to establish the competition constraints of particular goods or services on a given market. The European Commission has published a Notice setting out how to define the relevant market in EU competition law.[21] From this Notice it is apparent that the market must be defined both on the basis of product/service and of location considerations: the relevant product market, as well as the relevant geographic market.

When it comes to the relevant product market, the criterion of substitution must be applied. It should be examined whether a particular product could be replaced by another product. This assessment can be carried out from the perspective of both the demand and the supply side. Demand substitution entails that a product may be replaced by another product from the perspective of the consumer. Supply substitution entails an examination of whether suppliers are able to switch production. Could firms easily start supplying other products for the reason, for example, that the costs for switching are relatively low?

A test to be carried out in order to establish whether products can be substituted is

---

[15] Cases C-319/99 *FENIN*, ECLI:EU:T:2003:50; C-205/03 *FENIN*, ECLI:EU:C:2006:453.

[16] Jones, Sufrin and Dunne 2019, p. 151.

[17] E.g. case 15/74 *Centrafarm*, ECLI:EU:C:1974:114.

[18] Case C-73/95 *Viho*, ECLI:EU:C:1996:405.

[19] E.g. case C-97/08 P *Akzo Nobel*, ECLI:EU:C:2009:536.

[20] Case C-724/17 *Skanska*, ECLI:EU:C:2019:204.

[21] Notice on Relevant Market 1997.

examining the features and intended use of the products concerned. A classic, but also somewhat odd, example of this technique is the definition of the product market by the CJEU in *United Brands*.[22] Here, it was found that bananas could not be replaced by other fruit, as bananas could be smashed and were, for that reason, very suitable food for babies and elderly people. In this case substitution was determined on the basis of the special features of the products concerned. The outcome of this case shows, however, that such an approach may be arbitrary.[23] Another way of defining the relevant market is applying the so-called SSNIP test: 'Small but Significant Non-transitory Increase in Price'. If a relatively small change of price (ranging between 5 and 10 per cent) for a product determines the consumer to switch to another product, these two products belong to the same market.[24] If not, these products are part of two separate markets. A problem with this test is that on non-competitive markets, the price level is already high. If on such markets the consumers are confronted with an increase in price of approximately 5 to 10 per cent, they will indicate that they are prepared to switch to other products. This does not mean, however, that these other products are part of the same market as the product under review as, in fact, on a well-functioning market the prices would have been considerably lower and a potential increase in price would then not have been an incentive for consumers to switch. This problem is also known as the 'cellophane fallacy', named after the first case in US antitrust law, where this effect was found.[25] Moreover, on digital markets, the SSNIP test may give rise to problems, as price is not always a decisive factor for consumers making use of IT services, such as search engines and platforms.[26] This means that applying this test to services offered on digital markets requires that not only price-related factors, but also matters regarding data and the quality of these services must be taken into account.

As for the geographic market, the test to be carried out is to establish the area where the competition conditions are sufficiently homogenous, which implies that this area can be distinguished from other areas. Important factors in this regard are the costs of transport of a product in relation to its value, the national laws in place and the preferences of consumers. Changes in prices in different areas and the consequent reaction by customers may indicate how the geographic market must be defined.[27] Furthermore, the preferences of consumers may vary from region to region.[28] Moreover, information on trade flows may be very helpful for establishing the relevant geographic market.[29]

All in all, defining the relevant market could be challenging. Nevertheless, it is an important technique, since it enables the competition authorities and other parties to fine-tune the (broadly drafted) competition rules in accordance with the features of the case concerned. It

---

[22] Case 27/76 *United Brands*, ECLI:EU:C:1978:22.

[23] Van den Bergh, Camesasca and Giannaccari 2017, p. 135.

[24] Ibid, p. 142.

[25] Case *United States v E.I. du Pont de Nemours & Co. (Cellophane)*, (1956) 351 US 377.

[26] Van den Bergh, Camesasca and Giannaccari 2017, pp. 150–51.

[27] Notice on Relevant Market 1997, par. 45.

[28] Ibid, par. 46.

[29] Ibid, par. 50.

should be noted that in June 2020 the Commission started a public consultation in order to evaluate the current Notice on Relevant Market 1997.[30] It may be expected that this action may eventually lead to the adoption of a new Notice or to an amendment of the current Notice.

2.3 Trade between the Member States

Articles 101 and 102 TFEU apply in so far as the trade between the Member States is influenced. It is settled case-law that not only actual effects but also potential competition effects are capable of influencing this trade.[31] The same is true for the rules dealing with state and competition, such as the Treaty provisions on state aid. With regard to state aid, the CJEU has contended that it will suffice that the intervention concerned is *liable* to affect the trade between the Member States.[32]

If particular practices change the pattern of trade between two or more Member States, it goes without saying that the TFEU provisions on competition are relevant. Accordingly, an agreement concluded between undertakings operating in two or more Member States may be caught by these Treaty provisions. However, it must also be noted that an agreement concluded between undertakings operating only within one Member State could be capable of influencing intra-Union trade. Such an agreement could prevent enterprises from other Member States from penetrating the national market concerned and, by doing so, reinforcing the compartmentalisation of markets on a national basis.[33]

In various judgments, the CJEU has held that the trade between the Member States is affected if it is possible to foresee with a sufficient degree of probability on the basis of a set of objective factors that the practice concerned may have an influence, direct or indirect, actual or potential, on the pattern of this trade.[34] With regard to Articles 101 and 102 TFEU the Commission has elaborated on the case-law concerning the trade between the Member States by issuing Guidelines,[35] in which it sets out that the application of the effect on trade criterion is based on three elements: (1) 'trade between the Member States', (2) 'may affect', and (3) 'appreciability'.[36]

The element of 'trade between the Member States' encompasses all kinds of cross-border effects, including those resulting from practices inside one Member State that prevent firms

---

[30] See <https://ec.europa.eu/info/law/better-regulation/have-your-say/initiatives/12325-Evaluation-of-the-Commission-Notice-on-market-definition-in-EU-competition-law> accessed 12 June 2020.

[31] E.g. joined cases 56 and 58/64 *Grundig/Consten*, ECLI:EU:C:1966:41.

[32] Joined cases C-197 and C-203/11 *Libert*, ECLI:EU:C:2013:288, par. 74.

[33] Case 8/72 *Vereeniging van Cementhandelaren*, ECLI:EU:C:1972:84.

[34] E.g. case 56/65 *Société Technique Minière*, ECLI:EU:C:1966:38, pat. 7; joined cases 240, 241, 242, 261, 262, 268 and 269/92 *Stichting Sigarettenindustrie*, ECLI:EU:C:1985:488, par. 48; joined cases T-24, T-25, T-26 and T-28/93 *Compagnie Maritime Belge Transports*, ECLI:EU:T:1996:139, par. 201; case T-286/09 *Intel*, ECLI:EU:T:2014:547, par. 317.

[35] Guidelines on Effect on Trade 2004.

[36] Ibid, par. 18.

based in other Member States from penetrating the national market concerned. As for the element of 'may affect', the Commission puts forward that the condition of intra-Union trade is connected with the pattern of trade. This means that both actual and potential effects are caught by this condition. With regard to the element of 'appreciability', the Commission points out that according to the case-law of the CJEU, insignificant effects do not fall with the ambit of the Treaty provisions on competition.[37] In other words, an appreciable effect on the trade between the Member States is required in order for Articles 101 or 102 TFEU to apply. In its Guidelines, the Commission discusses various factors, such as the nature of the agreement and practice, the nature of the products concerned and the market position of the companies involved,[38] which are of interest for answering the question whether an appreciable effect can be identified.

On top of that, the Commission also formulates quantitative rules for establishing such an effect with regard to agreements. It is stressed that these rules are not capable of covering all categories of agreements and practices having an appreciable effect on intra-Union trade. Therefore, the outcome of the test introduced in the Guidelines may be rebutted.[39] In the Commission's view, no appreciable effect on the trade between the Member States occurs, if the following cumulative conditions are satisfied:

- The aggregate market share of the parties on any relevant market within the EU does not exceed 5 per cent; and
- In the case of horizontal agreements, the aggregate annual EU turnover of the undertakings concerned, in the products covered by the agreement, does not exceed EUR 40 million; in the case of vertical agreements, the aggregate annual EU turnover of the supplier of the products covered by the agreement does not exceed EUR 40 million.

It should be noted that, in Chapter 5, a Notice of the Commission dealing with the notion of appreciable effect on competition[40] will also be discussed. This *De Minimis* Notice, however, concerns the question whether *competition*, rather than *the trade between the Member States*, is appreciably restricted. These two concepts must be sharply delineated, as they constitute separate conditions for Article 101(1) TFEU to apply. Furthermore, the quantitative rules on appreciable effect on the trade between the Member States apply, in principle, to all kinds of agreements, whereas the Notice on appreciable effects on competition is only concerned with practices that have the effect to restrict competition (and not restrictions by object).[41] Moreover, the Commission rules on appreciable effect on competition have a long-standing tradition in EU competition law, while this is not the case for the rules on appreciable effect on the trade between the Member States. In our view, the quantification of appreciability of

---

[37] E.g. case 5/69 *Völk/Vervaecke*, ECLI:EU:C:1969:35, par. 5–7 and 84–7; joined cases 100 to 103/80 *Musique Diffusion Française*, ECLI:EU:C:1983:158; case C-306/96 *Javico*, ECLI:EU:C:1998:173, par. 16–17.

[38] Guidelines on Effect on Trade 2004, par. 45–9.

[39] Ibid, par. 50.

[40] *De Minimis* Notice 2014.

[41] In Chapter 5, section 2.2.1, the EU approach to restrictions by object and by effect will be discussed.

the effect on the trade between the Member States, introduced by the Guidelines on Effect on Trade 2004, should be regarded as a rule of thumb that particularly aims at assisting SMEs, when it comes to the review of their contracts under Article 101 TFEU.[42]

2.4 Extraterritorial application of the EU competition rules

Closely related to the issue of the trade between the Member States is the question whether EU competition law may be applied to undertakings based outside the EU. For example, in cases such as *Intel*,[43] *Microsoft*[44] and *Google*,[45] the Commission has imposed huge fines on undertakings established in the US. It is settled case-law that the Treaty provisions on competition apply to practices having effects in the EU Internal Market, even if these practices are set up in third countries.

In *Wood Pulp*, the CJEU held that in establishing the applicability of the Treaty provisions on competition, the decisive factor is the place where a particular agreement is implemented.[46] As the pricing agreement under review was (partly) implemented in the EU Internal Market, EU competition law applied to this conduct, which was in line with the territoriality principle 'universally recognized in public international law'.[47] In *Intel*,[48] Article 102 TFEU was found to be applicable since the effects of the practices of Intel (based in the US) in the EU Internal Market were substantial, immediate and foreseeable.[49] The tests used in these cases are referred to as the 'implementation' and the 'qualified effects' doctrines, respectively.[50] It is thus argued in legal doctrine that two bases can be identified for the extraterritorial application of the TFEU provisions on competition: the place of implementation and the place of the qualified effects (i.e. the immediate, substantial and foreseeable effects).[51]

In our view, the EU approach to the extraterritorial dimension of EU competition law is of great importance for digital markets. The services and products offered on these markets can be supplied globally by enterprises based in one country. As the effects of a practice are decisive for the applicability of EU competition law, such enterprises will not be immune from the scrutiny of the Commission and of the domestic authorities of the EU Member States, for the sole reason that they are established outside the EU. In other words, the expansive construction of the extraterritorial dimension of EU competition law enables these authorities to take action against anti-competitive conduct on digital markets. Furthermore,

---

[42] Guidelines on Effect on Trade 2004, par. 50.

[43] Case COMP/37.990 *Intel*, (2009) OJ C 227/13.

[44] Case COMP/C-3/37.792 *Microsoft*, (2007) OJ L 32/23.

[45] Case AT.40099 *Google Android*, (2018) 4761 final.

[46] Joined cases 89, 104, 114, 116, 117 and 125 to 129/85 *Wood Pulp*, ECLI:EU:C:1988:447, par. 16.

[47] Ibid, par. 17–18.

[48] Cases T-286/09 *Intel*, ECLI: EU:T:2014:547, par. 231–52; C-413/14 *Intel*, ECLI:EU:C:2017:632, par. 40–65.

[49] Jones, Sufrin and Dunne 2019, pp. 1208–9.

[50] Ibid, pp. 1199–209.

[51] Ibid.

the EU approach to extraterritorial effects is also very relevant for the relationship between EU competition law and Brexit. This matter will be discussed in section 2.3.2 of Chapter 5.

3 CATEGORISATIONS

EU law is composed of primary law and secondary law. The provisions of the TFEU, for example, are part of primary law, whereas EU regulations and directives qualify as secondary law. EU competition law contains both primary and secondary law. On top of that, judgments of the EU courts and all kinds of soft-law documents are of great importance for this area of law. This vast body of law should be distinguished in two categories: substantive and procedural rules.

3.1 The substantive rules on competition

The core provisions are of a binding nature and contain the substantive norms. The ban on restrictive agreements (Article 101 TFEU) and abuse of dominance (Article 102 TFEU) are laid down in the Treaty and the same is true for rules preventing the state from distorting competition (Article 106 TFEU, Articles 107–109 TFEU and Article 4(3) TEU in conjunction with Article 101 TFEU or Article 102 TFEU). It goes without saying that these rules are of a binding nature. It should be noted that derogations from the ban on restrictive agreements, the so-called Block Exemptions, are laid down in EU regulations.

The EU rules dealing with concentrations, such as mergers and acquisitions are also binding, but are enshrined in an EU regulation.[52] As will become apparent in Chapter 10, in this Regulation the (substantive) provisions governing competition on the market and those of a procedural nature are closely intertwined. The reason for this is that, unlike the other regimes, merger control is based on *ex ante* control, as transactions (meeting specific turnover thresholds) must be notified to, and be approved by, the Commission before they may be implemented. Accordingly, the application of the EU merger control rules is highly dependent on compliance with a provision of procedural nature. The oversight of the compliance with provisions such as Articles 101 and 102 TFEU usually takes place after competition problems have occurred on the market. In other words, these provisions are based on *ex post* control.

Apart from merger control, it should be noted that throughout EU competition law a clear distinction exists between substantive and procedural rules. The substantive rules come down to prohibiting agreements and similar practices restricting competition (Article 101 TFEU), abuses by dominant undertakings (Article 102 TFEU), mergers distorting competition (Merger Control Regulation), state aid distorting competition (Article 107 TFEU), anti-competitive measures taken by the state with regard to specific undertakings (Article 106(1) TFEU), and state measures jeopardising the useful effect of the Treaty provisions on competition (Article 4(3) TEU in conjunction with Article 101 TFEU or Article 102 TFEU).

---

[52] Merger Control Regulation 2004.

Policies developed by undertakings and the competent bodies of the EU Member States must be reviewed under these rules.

The substantive rules on competition must be divided into two groups. Articles 101 and 102 TFEU, which together are often referred to as antitrust law, and the Merger Control Regulation are directed at undertakings. So, the addressees of these norms are companies whose behaviour on the market is reviewed. The EU state aid rules and the other rules dealing with the state and competition are directed at the EU Member States, that is, all competent bodies of these states. It should be noted, however, that a key aspect of these rules is that, apart from the involvement of a state body, the measures taken by this body are somehow related to undertakings. For example, state aid given to entities not qualifying as an undertaking for the purposes of EU competition law is not caught by Article 107 TFEU (which precludes Member States from granting aid that distorts competition and influences the trade between the Member States).

Given the broad drafting of the EU substantive rules, considerable room for interpretation exists. As a result, the judgments of the EU courts have played a major role in shaping these rules. Although since the entering into force of the Treaty of Rome (establishing the European Economic Community) in 1957, the wording of the provisions on competition is virtually unamended, the interpretation of these provisions has been subject to major developments. One of the reasons for this is that the EU courts have determined the direction of travel of this area of law by handing down landmark judgments. Thus, the evolution of EU competition law is partly shaped by EU case-law.

Another factor that has been decisive for the change of course in EU competition law is the role the Commission has played. Not only were significant decisions taken by this EU institution (by which, for instance, fines were imposed on enterprises), but also important guidelines, notices and communications were issued. From a formal point of view, it must be pointed out that these documents are soft-law and, accordingly, not binding. Then again, it must be stressed that the Commission documents dealing with competition law have acquired much authority and are considered with great care by both the EU judiciary and the domestic authorities. As a result, a communication or notice of the Commission may pave the way for new developments. For example, the economic approach to vertical restraints was, among others, boosted by the Commission issuing the Guidelines on Vertical Restraints 2000. The substantive rules on competition are interpreted and, to a certain extent, as testified by the example of these Guidelines, also modified in soft-law documents. Therefore, it could be argued that these substantive rules are not only shaped by primary and secondary law (as interpreted by the EU judiciary), but also by soft-law.

3.2 The procedural competition rules

Over time, a great body of procedural rules facilitating the application and enforcement of the substantive provisions on competition has been developed. In the past, Regulation 17/62 contained the majority of the procedural rules. Since the entering into force of Regulation 1/2003 this has been changed. Not only has Regulation 17 been replaced by Regulation 1/2003, but also other pieces of EU legislation have seen the light of day. In 2014, the Private

Damages Directive 2014 was adopted, and in 2019 the Directive boosting the enforcement of EU competition law by NCAs[53] was published. Apart from these developments, a regulation elaborating on some procedural issues has also been adopted.[54] The Commission has also issued notices and communications dealing with procedural issues.[55] Also, in EU state aid law regulations on procedural matters have been adopted, and guidelines dealing with such matters have been issued. For example, Regulation 2015/1589 sets out which steps the Commission must take when enforcing the Treaty provisions on state aid. Furthermore, the Commission published the Unlawful Aid Notice 2019 in order to explain how the recovery of unlawful and incompatible aid must be conducted.

From this overview it is apparent that the following categorisations can be made. The first categorisation takes the nature of the legal source as the point of departure. The procedural rules are laid down partly in hard-law and partly in soft-law, which is also the case with the substantive provisions on competition. As was already stated, soft-law is not binding but has a great authority in EU competition law. As for the binding rules, it must be noted that they mainly concern secondary law. There is one significant exception: the provision that agreements and decisions of associations of undertakings restricting competition are void is laid down in Article 101(2) TFEU. Accordingly, one of the procedural rules dealing with the application of the cartel prohibition in private law has the status of primary law. The second categorisation focuses on the level of application and enforcement of EU competition law. Part of the procedural rules governs the actions taken by the Commission at the EU level. Another part of procedural law is concerned with the decentralised application of EU competition law, in the national legal order of the Member States. In this respect, the Private Damages Directive 2014 and the ECN+ Directive 2019 stand out. Again, attention must be paid to Article 101(2) TFEU. In fact, this provision of primary law deals with the application of the cartel prohibition in the national legal orders. This does not mean that the relationship between EU competition law and national law is only governed by hard-law. The Commission has also issued guidelines assisting the application of the EU competition rules by, for example, national courts.[56] It goes without saying that soft-law adopted by the Commission is not binding for the national judiciary. However, as already stated, the guidelines, notices and communications of the Commission enjoy much authority.

4 THE ROLE OF ENFORCEMENT IN EU COMPETITION LAW

A very important achievement of EU competition law is the structure and network developed for its enforcement. This section aims to explain the main principles of the enforcement of EU competition law. Chapters 7–9 deal with this subject in detail.

---

[53] ECN+ Directive 2019.

[54] Conduct of Proceedings Regulation 2004.

[55] E.g. Notice on Handling of Complaints 2004.

[56] E.g. Guidelines on Passed-on Overcharges 2019; Notice on Enforcement by National Courts 2009.

During the period in which Regulation 17/62 was in force, the enforcement of the EU competition rules was mainly in the hands of the Commission, with a marginal role for the domestic courts, which could review practices of undertakings in the light of Articles 101(1) and 102 TFEU on the basis of the direct effect doctrine. Now, the Commission and the NCAs oversee compliance with EU competition law. A wide range of competences are at their disposal to this end. Furthermore, national courts have the power to award damages if claimants suffer harm from infringements of competition law.

The EU competition law rules are enforced both at the EU and the national level. Regulation 1/2003 lays down powers for the Commission to carry out investigations and to impose sanctions. The Commission directly derives the necessary powers from this Regulation. From the drafting of Article 1 of Regulation 1/2003 it is clear that Articles 101(1) and (3) and 102 TFEU have direct effect. Under Regulation 17/62, the national authorities already had the power to apply the prohibitions contained in Articles 101(1) and 102 TFEU, but the Commission had the exclusive authority to assess whether restrictive agreements were justifiable under Article 101(3) TFEU. Consequently, by giving direct effect, next to the antitrust bans, also to the exception of Article 101(3) TFEU, Regulation 1/2003 has considerably stimulated the decentralised enforcement of EU competition law. It should be noted that, in this area of EU law, national enforcement is referred to as decentralised enforcement (as opposed to the central enforcement at the EU level).[57] As a result, in EU competition law, as it now stands, enforcement actions are undertaken both at the European and national level.

Pursuant to Article 5 of Regulation 1/2003, NCAs must also have the power to enforce EU competition law. It is up to the Member States to designate the competent authorities and to confer powers to these authorities. Accordingly, the enforcement powers of the NCAs are primarily a matter of national law. However, it must be pointed out that these powers have been harmonised by the ECN+ Directive 2019. This means that national laws conferring enforcement powers to NCAs must be compatible with the requirements laid down in this Directive. The NCAs derive their powers from national legislation, but these powers are characterised by an EU dimension. An important consequence of this is that the CJEU has the final say in matters concerning the interpretation of the NCAs' powers outlined in the ECN+ Directive 2019. Moreover, national courts may pose preliminary questions to the CJEU with regard to these matters on the basis of Article 267 TFEU. As a result, many powers of the NCAs could be subject to a process of increasing Europeanisation in the future.

Moving on, it is clear from the outset that decisions imposing fines or penalties are subject to judicial review. In EU (competition) law, pursuant to Article 263 TFEU, the decisions taken by the Commission may be appealed against before the GC and, in higher appeal, in front of the CJEU. Although the Commission enjoys some discretion in exercising its powers, the EU judiciary will carry out a full review of such sanctioning decisions. This is evident from both Article 6 ECHR and Article 47 of the Charter of Fundamental Rights of the EU, provisions which contain the right to an effective remedy and to a fair trial. Both the European Court of Human Rights (ECtHR) and the CJEU have held that in cases concerning the enforcement of competition law, the decision by which sanctions are imposed must

---

[57] Modernisation White Paper 1999, par. 46–7.

be subject to a full judicial review.[58] This entails that the court must examine whether the evidence used is accurate, reliable and consistent, and also whether that evidence contains all relevant information in order to assess a complex situation.[59] Moreover, the courts must examine whether the evidence concerned is capable of substantiating the conclusions drawn from it.[60]

Article 6 ECHR also applies to the sanctions imposed by NCAs. Furthermore, Article 51(1) of the Charter of Fundamental Rights of the EU provides that national authorities implementing EU law are bound by the fundamental rights enshrined in this Charter. Accordingly, the decisions of NCAs enforcing the EU competition rules must be subject to full judicial review, as this is required by Article 47 of the Charter. The decisions adopted by the NCAs are subject to the review of the national judiciary in the national jurisdiction of the Member State concerned. If issues of EU law arise in national cases, preliminary questions may be asked to the CJEU, on the basis of Article 267 TFEU.

Apart from public enforcement, which is in the hands of the Commission and the NCAs, private enforcement is also of importance in competition law. Generally, private enforcement consists of two components: the nullity of agreements and decisions of associations of undertakings in violation of Article 101 TFEU, as well as damage claims. As already pointed out, Article 101(2) TFEU contains the civil law sanction of nullity. In cases, such as *Courage and Crehan*,[61] the CJEU held that any person who has suffered harm resulting from an infringement of EU competition law must have the right to claim damages from the undertaking having committed this infringement. This right is codified and harmonised by the Private Damages Directive 2014. Only national civil courts have the authority to declare that a contractual provision is void and to grant damages to claimants. Accordingly, private enforcement takes place only at the national level. In this regard, it must be stressed that neither the Commission nor an NCA have the power to award damages. Civil courts derive their judicial powers from national legislation. However, with the handing down of the *Courage and Crehan* judgment, the CJEU has set conditions with which the national rules on non-contractual liability must comply. The Private Damages Directive 2014 has even harmonised these conditions to a great extent. As a result, the national right to claim damages has a considerable EU dimension.

When it comes to the EU rules on state and competition, special attention must be paid to state aid law. The CJEU has derived from Article 108(3) TFEU that state aid that is not notified and approved by the Commission must be recovered. This TFEU provision is referred to as the standstill provision. Not only the Commission has the task to take action against unlawful aid, but also national judicial authorities are obliged to order the recovery of unlawful aid, as Article 108(3) TFEU has direct effect, according to the settled case-law of the

---

[58] Cases 43509/08 *Menarini*, ECtHR, 27 September 2011; C-386/10 *Chalkor*, ECLI:EU:C:2011:815; C-389/10 *KME Germany*, ECLI:EU:C:2011:816.

[59] Cases C-389/10 *KME Germany*, ECLI:EU:C:2011:816, par. 121; C-386/10 *Chalkor*, ECLI:EU:C:2011:815, par. 54.

[60] Ibid.

[61] Case C-453/99 *Courage and Crehan*, ECLI:EU:C:2001:465.

CJEU.[62] From the foregoing it is apparent that the EU state aid rules can be enforced both at the EU and the national level. Chapter 12, which discusses the EU state aid rules, will further elaborate on the enforcement of these rules.

5 CONCLUSIONS

The efficient application and enforcement of the competition rules is an important value in EU law. This is apparent, for example, from the broad concept of undertaking, the expansive interpretation of the concept of trade between the Member States, and the extraterritorial dimension of EU competition law. The functional approaches developed ensure that the competition rules are applied in many circumstances and that circumvention of these rules is made very difficult. It may be argued that the *effect utile* of EU law is the principle underpinning the interpretation of these concepts. Moreover, the EU has built up an impressive set of rules and networks dealing with the enforcement of competition law. The result of this is that EU competition law has a very important impact on the national legal orders of the Member States. Last but not least, it should be noted that, in enforcement cases, the rule of law must be observed. An important development in this regard is the case-law requiring that the sanctions imposed by the Commission and the NCA must be subject to full judicial review.

---

[62] E.g. case C-284/12 *Lufthansa*, ECLI:EU:C:2013:755, par. 29.

3

The economics of competition law

1 INTRODUCTION

Economics and competition law are inextricably linked. Ever since competition law came into existence, the economic theory of competition has exercised its influence upon it. Economics plays a prominent role in the formulation of substantive competition rules and their enforcement. This impact is clearly visible in the relevant legislation and the enforcement practice of many jurisdictions, including the EU,[1] and it essentially relates to the so-called 'effects-based approach' to competition law:[2] focusing on the outcomes of a particular practice in the market and its effects on consumers and competitors, rather than on the formalistic features of the behaviour. More specifically, economics can be employed in relation to competition law via macro-economic arguments, namely explaining and remedying market failure, on one hand, and via micro-economic arguments relied upon on a case-by-case basis, to justify intervention, or to defend a company's position, on the other hand.[3] But why is this so? Why is economics influential in competition law? What is the exact role that economics plays in relation to competition law? In other words, why can it be rightfully argued that economics is best placed to explain the design and functioning of the competition law rules? It is important to correctly understand this relation from the outset, since this endeavour brings clarity with respect to: the fundamental rationale of competition law, the drivers and effects of the behaviour of market players, the motivation of enforcement authorities to intervene in the workings of the market, and to that end, the value of economic evidence in competition law analysis. Beyond this, the chapter at hand sheds light on certain important economic theories and concepts which are used throughout this book, and which stand as the basis of understanding the intricacies of substantive competition rules and their enforcement mechanisms.

---

[1] Van den Bergh, Camesasca and Giannaccari 2017, pp. 1, 13.

[2] On the development and implications of the effects-based approach to competition law, see Bourgeois and Waelbroeck 2012.

[3] Marco Colino 2011, p. 7.

2 GENERAL SETUP AND BASIC CONCEPTS

Economics has contributed significantly to competition law by developing practical tests and criteria, which make the application of the law more workable and sound, and statistical and econometric techniques, which may serve as extremely valuable evidence in competition cases.[4] In theory, these tools are generally used to explain what has happened or what will happen in a market, by contrasting various (and somewhat extreme) scenarios: a market with perfect competition as opposed to a market which is fully monopolised. The former scenario entails a market with many buyers and suppliers, homogeneous goods with insignificant differences of quality and price, perfect information and no costs for customers to switch between suppliers, no entry or exit barriers, and so on. In the latter scenario, a single seller caters for the entire demand in the market, due to, for example, the existence of high barriers to entry.[5] The monopolist thus faces neither actual, nor potential competition.[6]

Regardless in which scenario we place the discussion, competition economics is premised on analysing the firms' behaviour and incentives,[7] and the elements which curb the buyers' willingness to engage in transactions of goods or services with the suppliers. In this context it becomes evident that concepts such as supply and demand, cost and price, profit maximisation, economies of scale and scope, and the like, play a key role. Yet, such concepts, and their value for explaining the functioning of the market mechanisms, are to be interpreted having in mind the perfect competition versus full monopoly scenarios mentioned above. Given that competition takes places in market contexts, it is important to understand that markets are social arrangements in which the demand and supply for products and services interact. Therefore, Figure 3.1 depicts the relationship between such concepts in the two extreme scenarios mentioned above: perfectly competitive and fully monopolised markets.

2.1 Demand and supply

In Figure 3.1 the horizontal axis represents the quantity of goods or services which are sold in a market, while the vertical axis represents the price at which they are sold. The starting point is the assumption that the higher the price is, the lower the amount of goods or services will be purchased, and vice versa, the lower the price, the higher the amount of goods or services which form the subject of transactions in the market.[8] In other words, the price and quantity variables are linked in this exercise by a demand curve, which is sloping from top-left to bottom-right; to be clear, by demand curve we essentially mean an indication of the volume of sales a supplier will make for the various prices it may set, provided that other factors (such

---

[4] Niels, Jenkins and Kavanagh 2016, p. 4.

[5] Bishop and Walker 2010; Jones, Sufrin and Dunne 2019, ch 1, section 3; Geradin, Layne-Farrar and Petit 2012, ch 2; Dunne 2015, pp. 14–18.

[6] Van den Bergh, Camesasca and Giannaccari 2017, p. 23.

[7] Gore, Lewis, Lofaro and Dethmers 2013, p. 14.

[8] Dunne 2015, p. 7.

as prices of competing products or services, their characteristics, and so on) do not change.[9] In other words, the demand curve also shows how the customers' demand for a product or service varies depending on its price.[10] This setup is not to be taken in absolute terms though, since consumers are different, as they place different value on different features of such transactions. This is so, given that consumers have diverse preferences, and overall different degrees of willingness to pay a particular price for a product or service. In any case, the maximum amount a consumer is willing to pay, for any of the reasons mentioned above, is called the consumer's reservation price. Furthermore, some goods or services are more prone than others to be price sensitive, that is, to experience a more or less abrupt change in the consumers' willingness to pay when the price marginally increases.[11] This setting relates to the so-called price elasticity of demand, namely the sensitivity of quantity purchased by consumers in relation to price increases: consumers' demand is said to be elastic if an increase in price results in a significant fall in demand, and inelastic price increases render insignificant demand shifts.[12] Still, the demand curve should not be set in stone based on a static scenario as described above. This is so, given that the suppliers' pricing decision is influenced by a multitude of factors, including for instance the need for accommodating various categories of consumers, with differing reservation prices, or the interaction with the demand for other competing products. In relation to the latter consideration, the concepts of cross-price elasticity of demand and substitutability are relevant, since these concepts measure the shift of demand for one product, in relation to variations of prices for another product. The interaction between the demand curves for these products (or services) is the essence of how they can be substituted for each other and lies at the heart of market definition in competition law cases,[13] as pointed out in Chapters 2 and 6.

The flipside of the demand curve discussion relates to the concept of supply. The rationale is therefore (somewhat) similar. The supply curve is depicted in Figure 3.1 from bottom-left to top-right, signalling that the relationship between supply and price is that the higher the price the greater the level of supply.[14] Similar to demand curves, supply curves can also be described as elastic or inelastic depending on the fluctuations they exhibit in relation to the price – quantity ratio. Furthermore, other considerations may be inserted in the discussion, relating to differences in the costs various suppliers incur, or to limitations relating to the capacity to cater for the whole demand in the market. These are considerations relating to the concept of supply substitutability, which is again relevant in defining the relevant markets in competition cases. Above all, what supply curves relate to greatly is the concept of cost. At the end of the day, the supply of a given product or service is determined by the cost of production, and of course, as portrayed above, by the existence of demand in the market. In

---

[9] Gore, Lewis, Lofaro and Dethmers 2013, p. 14.

[10] Lindsay and Berridge 2017, p. 3.

[11] Niels, Jenkins and Kavanagh 2016, pp. 7–8.

[12] Jones, Sufrin and Dunne 2019, p. 5.

[13] Niels, Jenkins and Kavanagh 2016, p. 9.

[14] Marco Colino 2011, p. 13.

general terms, a rational market player will produce and sell a product if the price charged can cover the costs incurred. But what are costs composed of?

2.2 Costs

Various categorisations of costs may be put forward, depending on diverse criteria. Fixed costs are those costs that do not change when the output of products or services on the market increases or decreases. Of course, fixed costs differ depending on the company's activities, or the timeframe over which output decisions are considered, but examples of typically fixed costs include rent and managerial staff costs.[15] Variable costs, on the other hand, fluctuate depending on increases or decreases of the level of production, as is normally the case for input costs or costs related to raw materials.[16] In practice, depending on the economic sector in which a case may unfold, the ratio of fixed and variable costs may differ extensively. For example, in the telecommunications sector fixed costs tend to be high (since building the network infrastructure is very cost-intensive), whereas variable costs may be low (since making a phone call or sending a text message is rather cheap). Furthermore, in practice it may often be difficult to distinguish between these two types of prices, since they may vary depending on a number of other considerations, including, for example, whether the company produces multiple types of products, for which (some of) the fixed costs may be shared. A different type of costs that is highly relevant for competition economics is marginal costs, that is, the costs of an additional unit of production, or in other words, the change in total costs that arises when one extra unit is produced. As Figure 3.1 depicts, there is a strong connection between the supply curve and marginal costs, since as long as the price which can be obtained is higher than the marginal costs, it makes sense for the producer to produce that extra item. Generally, marginal costs drop, as production increases. In other words, costs drop when more of the same is produced. This is due to the operation of the so-called economies of scale: while the input (variable) costs may increase with increasing production, other (primarily fixed) costs remain unchanged; this results in a drop in the average production costs (namely the total costs divided by the quantity of items produced), and thus efficiency in production, as output of the given product is increased.[17] Connected to the economies of scale concept, achieving economies of scope relates to situations where it is cheaper to produce two different products together rather than separately, thus expanding the range of products a market player produces. Economies of scope occur primarily when fixed costs are shared, for example when a producer moves from being a single-product company to a multi-product company, saving costs by using the same production plant and the same team of employees.[18]

While the costs categories and related concepts explained above are useful for market players when they devise their pricing policies on the market, in competition cases several

[15] Gore, Lewis, Lofaro and Dethmers 2013, p. 20.

[16] Graham 2010, p. 20.

[17] Graham 2010, p. 20; Marco Colino 2011, p. 14.

[18] On the ins and outs of the economies of scale and scope concepts, see Whish and Bailey 2018, pp. 10–11.

cost benchmarks are employed when assessing whether the price-related conduct of under-takings infringes the competition law rules. Without aiming to exhaustively discuss all cost benchmarks which may be used in diverse practical scenarios,[19] in the following lines we will explain some of the most relevant cost standards used by competition authorities and courts. While the total production costs include all the fixed and variable costs, the concept of average total cost (ATC) covers the total production costs spent on the production of one unit. In other words, here we are talking about dividing the total production costs by the number of units produced. Similarly, the concept of average variable cost (AVC) covers the variable costs spent for the production of one unit, that is, dividing the variable costs by the number of units produced. Further, the concept of avoidable costs includes those costs (variable and fixed – for the reference period) which are not incurred if a particular action is not undertaken or a product is not produced. This concept obviously does not include sunk costs, since such costs relate to non-recoverable amounts already spent. Average avoidable costs (AAC) relate to the average of the costs that could have been avoided if a discrete amount of extra output is not produced. In most cases, AAC and AVC are similar, as it is often only variable costs that can be avoided. Moving on, long-run average incremental cost (LRAIC) is the average of all the (variable and fixed) costs that a company incurs to produce a particular product. LRAIC and ATC are good proxies for each other, and are the same in the case of single-product undertakings. If multi-product undertakings have economies of scope, LRAIC would be below ATC for each individual product, as true common costs are not taken into account in LRAIC. LRAIC is usually above AAC because, in contrast to AAC (which only includes fixed costs if incurred during the period under examination), LRAIC includes product-specific fixed costs made before this reference period. Applying this cost benchmark is also particularly useful in the sectors of the economy where fixed costs are high (due to the required investments, for example) and variable costs are low.[20]

2.3 Profit maximisation, consumer and producer surplus

In close connection to the costs discussion above is the matter of profit maximisation and surplus created when participating in market transactions. Economic theory assumes that market players act rationally on the market, with a view to maximise profits.[21] By profit we mean the difference between the revenues obtained and the costs incurred when trading a product or service on the market. Yet, this assumption may not always be accurate, since the approaches that firms may embark on in this respect vary depending on the perfect compe-tition versus the monopoly scenario, and also on the production costs and the consumers' sensitivity to price shifts. Either way, when it comes to profit maximisation and while taking these variables into account, firms perform an analysis, or better yet a trade-off, when setting the prices that they will charge on the market. This trade-off essentially revolves around the

---

[19] For more info on cost benchmarks, see Jones, Sufrin and Dunne 2019, pp. 394-5, Lianos, Korah and Siciliani 2019, p. 1001.

[20] Enforcement Priorities Guidelines 2009, par. 26.

[21] Dunne 2015, p. 7.

decision to set high prices, yielding high margins on few sales and the decision to set low prices, which render lower margins on a greater sales volume. Of course, this rationale is predicated on the prerequisite that firms will supply products or services on the market when the projected revenue exceeds the costs incurred. Yet, in this respect, the firms' profit maximisation decisions will factor in the marginal cost and marginal revenue (i.e. the additional revenue created by selling one extra unit), in relation to the volume of goods or services placed on the market: where marginal revenue exceeds marginal cost, the volume will be increased, and vice versa, where marginal cost exceeds marginal revenue, the volume will be reduced.[22] Naturally, a firm's incentive and ability to alter the output on the market (i.e. the volume of products or services) will very much depend on the features of the scenario in which it is present, namely a monopolised or a (perfectly) competitive market.

The price-setting exercise discussed above impacts the surplus that is generated by trading goods on the market. The concept of producer surplus measures the producer's gains from trading on the market, by looking at the difference between the sums that would have induced producers to supply the product or service and the sums they actually receive;[23] in other words, the difference between the selling price and the marginal cost of production.[24] Thus, the producer surplus is connected to the marginal cost incurred by the producer, to the supply and demand curves and their elasticity, and to the price-setting decisions adopted by the producer. In Figure 3.1, the producer surplus is embedded in the area demarcated by the supply curve (or marginal cost), the point where the demand curve intersects with the supply curve, and the line where the market price sits. While acknowledging that the features of a market (monopoly or perfect competition) influence the positioning of the supply and demand curves, and consequently this impacts on the firm's output and pricing decisions, one may observe that the producer surplus may increase or decrease, as the case may be. Furthermore, the producer surplus may experience shifts in the context where the producer is able to price discriminate, by charging different prices for the same product or service, depending on each customer's reservation price. Of course, such a setting is more prone to occur when the supplier enjoys some degree of market power and cannot prevent the resale of the goods between the customers that have different reservation prices.

The consumer surplus concept, on the other hand, relates to the difference between the consumers' reservation price and the market price.[25] It is self-evident that this concept pertains greatly to the demand curve, and for that matter, similarly to the producer surplus concept just discussed, to the price-setting decisions of the supplier. In Figure 3.1, the consumer surplus is depicted by the area that sits below the demand curve and above the line where the market price is set. If the concept of consumer surplus is understood to represent the consumers' gains from trade, it has to be acknowledged that these gains differ, depending on each consumer's evaluation of the value attached to a good or service, as expressed through his or her willingness to pay a particular price: who is willing to pay more, while

---

[22] Gore, Lewis, Lofaro and Dethmers 2013, pp. 23–4.

[23] Lindsay and Berridge 2017, p. 7.

[24] Van den Bergh, Camesasca and Giannaccari 2017, p. 23.

[25] Jones, Sufrin and Dunne 2019, p. 5.

having to pay less, would arguably 'gain more', and vice versa. This willingness to pay relates thus also to the price discrimination possibilities discussed above. At the end of the day, the producer would want to capitalise on the differences in the customers' willingness to pay and thus capture as much consumer surplus as possible, without losing the sales to those who are willing to pay less. All in all, the consumer surplus discussion is important in competition economics, and consequently competition law, since it forms part of the broader concept of consumer welfare. This is because, as we have already pointed out in Chapter 1, fostering consumer welfare is one of the key objectives pursued by (modern) competition law systems.

2.4 Efficiency and costs of monopoly

What is important to understand at this stage is that somewhere on the spectrum described above suppliers and consumers meet when goods and services are traded on a market. The point where demand and supply meet is highly dependent on the cost structures market players manage, on the price-setting decisions, on the extent and (cross-)elasticity of demand, and thus also on the (more) external factors which, at the end of the day, characterise the two extreme scenarios: perfect competition and full monopoly. It is important to understand the merits of this discussion since the scope and need for competition law intervention in the market depends also on the features of the market at hand in a given practical setting.

As already pointed out in Chapter 1, competition law may be conceived to aim for (among other goals) fostering economic efficiency, which in turn is believed to lead to benefits for society and its diverse constituents, and thus generally speaking, maximising welfare.[26] But how is the concept of efficiency to be conceived in this context? How is efficiency to be achieved (if at all) in the perfect competition and fully monopolised market scenarios? Simply put, the yardstick for measuring the efficiency of the market outcome is the sum of consumer and producer surplus. This joint surplus makes it possible to compare the social welfare consequences of the competitive equilibrium and a market in disequilibrium.[27]

In a perfect competition setting efficiency is maximised or secured by the market itself, to the point where it is argued that (external) intervention via competition rules application is redundant.[28] The features of markets characterised by perfect competition make it so that sellers are most often 'price takers', not 'makers', since the availability of diverse choice allows consumers to 'shop around'. This is so, also having in mind the pressure stemming from competitive constraints imposed by existing and potential competitors. Therefore, sellers in such markets will most likely not be able to price above marginal cost. In other words, marginal cost equals marginal revenue.[29] The only profit such firms would make would be

---

[26] Niels, Jenkins and Kavanagh 2016, p. 15 *et seq.*

[27] Van den Bergh, Camesasca and Giannaccari 2017, p. 23.

[28] Dunne 2015, p. 9.

[29] Graham 2010, p. 20; Jones, Sufrin and Dunne 2019, pp. 7–9; Van den Bergh, Camesasca and Giannaccari 2017, p. 23.

that which covers the initial capital investments, thus keeping the firms alive in the market. So what types of efficiency are achieved in this scenario?[30]

First, perfect competition is said to lead to allocative efficiency, namely allocating resources so as the net benefit of their use is maximised. Allocative efficiency depicts a setting in which producers produce the goods that are desired by consumers (as shown by their willingness to pay) and continue to do so until the market price equals marginal cost. No more, no less. Allocative efficiency is achieved when the prices could not be further reduced and the volume of sales could not be further increased, without producers incurring losses. This essentially entails an equilibrium, which cannot be further perfected. Second, perfect competition is said to lead to productive efficiency, by pressuring firms to make optimal use of the available resources and produce at the lowest cost possible. When this is not the case, and a firm's prices are set above marginal cost, consumers will switch to a competitor's product, given the perfect information and lack of switching costs presupposed in perfectly competitive markets. Competitive pressure is thus key in inducing producers to efficiently manage the production process, to the point where production factors can no longer be reorganised, so costs are further minimised and output is further increased. Third, the concept of dynamic efficiency is also important, yet unlike the previous types of efficiency discussed, which depict static situations, dynamic efficiency is concerned with how well markets deliver innovation and technological progress.[31] Dynamic efficiency relates to improvements to products or services and to the production process, which are identifiable in the longer run. The question here though is in which scenario is dynamic efficiency fostered: perfect competition or monopoly? Who is more prone to innovate: the market players needing an edge in order to stay competitive in the market, or the monopolist with 'deep pockets' who has the resources to invest in R&D and further innovate?[32]

This brings us to the next point of discussion, namely what are the drawbacks and costs of monopolies? And for that matter, why is competition law intervention needed in such a scenario? From the outset, it must be understood that in monopolised markets the monopolist is a 'price maker', as opposed to perfectly competitive markets where firms are 'price takers'. As is evident in Figure 3.1, the monopolist can influence the equilibrium price and quantity by its production decisions;[33] it can allow itself to reduce the output and increase the selling price above marginal cost. This essentially entails a redistribution of surplus from the consumer to the producer. For the sake of completeness, even in markets which are not monopolised, but are prone to cartelisation, such surplus redistribution may occur if competitors collude in order to mirror monopoly-like outcomes of reducing output and increasing prices. What does this mean for the different types of efficiency discussed above, under the perfect competition model?

Since the consumers' demand and desires are not fully satisfied, the price is increased

---

[30] For more info on types of efficiency, see Whish and Bailey 2018, pp. 5–7; Lindsay and Berridge 2017, pp. 8–9; Dunne 2015, p. 8.

[31] Jones, Sufrin and Dunne 2019, p. 8.

[32] For more on this matter, see Mooij and Rusu 2016; Whish and Bailey 2018, pp. 6–7.

[33] Van den Bergh, Camesasca and Giannaccari 2017, p. 23.

and the output reduced, allocative efficiency is lacking. This is so, because a more optimal allocation of resources could be possible under the monopoly model, as opposed to the perfect competition scenario, where such reallocation is not possible. Further, a monopolist is not pressured to lower its costs by competitors, to the same extent as actors in perfectly competitive markets. This may result in productive inefficiency, but it may also be connected to other types of inefficiency.[34] Due to lack of competitive pressure, and consequently the inexistence of production examples and best practices stemming from competitors, the monopolist will prefer a 'quiet life', with no incentives to produce efficiently. This leads to the so-called risk of internal slack and 'X-inefficiency', relating to a lack of managerial efficiency (i.e. high salaries, lack of reorganisation, excessive managing, and the like), and which may be furthered by wasteful behaviour in an effort to defend a monopoly position. This also brings us to the point of the resources spent while seeking to achieve monopoly power (lobbying, excessive advertising, and so on), given the attractiveness of the possibility to charge monopoly prices. This rent-seeking behaviour may also lead to inefficiency, in circumstances where welfare gains do not result from such actions. But there is more to the cost of monopolies. In the context of the surplus redistribution discussion, while in perfectly competitive markets consumers pay the competitive price (i.e. marginal cost), in monopolised markets some consumers choose to pay the increased monopolistic price (and thus surplus is diverted from consumers to producers), while other consumers will choose not to spend the available resources. This essentially relates to the so-called deadweight loss, or the overall loss to the economy and to societal welfare. This concept represents the welfare which is lost, since it is not enjoyed by either the consumer of the monopolist producer, or in other words the loss of consumer surplus which is not transformed into producer surplus. All in all, it is with a view to these inefficiency concerns that arguments may be phrased that monopolies may cause market failure,[35] and therefore competition law intervention is needed.

3 IN-BETWEEN SCENARIOS AND ONGOING DEVELOPMENTS

The discussion so far is predicated on the functioning of market mechanisms in the context of two extremes: perfect competition and full monopoly. Yet, the fact of the matter is that in real life monopolies are rare. They exist primarily when they are created via state regulation or in situations of natural monopoly. Also, perfectly competitive markets are rather rare.[36] While these scenarios are useful in explaining the market dynamics in general terms and constitute good benchmarks to measure the competitiveness of real markets, the reality is that most of such markets lie somewhere in between these two extremes: firms have different degrees of market power, products are heterogeneous, the degree of transparency in the market and

---

[34] For more on this matter, see Van den Bergh, Camesasca and Giannaccari 2017, p. 25; Whish and Bailey 2018, pp. 7–8; Lindsay and Berridge 2017, pp. 12–17; Niels, Jenkins and Kavanagh 2016, pp. 11–15.

[35] Dunne 2015, p. 9.

[36] Whish and Bailey 2018, p. 9.

the availability of information varies, and so on.[37] One particularly problematic setting in this 'in-between' area relates to oligopolistic markets. Furthermore, the discussion so far tackled, although not always evidently and explicitly, scenarios normally embedded in the traditional economy. Yet lately, we are faced with interesting and challenging developments brought about by the digitalisation phenomenon. Many sectors of the economy are impacted by this phenomenon, resulting in a pressing need for the law to address the problems and the enforcement gaps that the digital dimension of markets brings to the forefront.

Peculiar scenarios such as oligopolies and digital markets thus require a somewhat fine-tuned understanding of the economic theories and concepts discussed so far. This exercise is valuable since it is apparent that such markets pose specific problems to competition enforcement authorities. Therefore, the next paragraphs will dedicate attention to oligopolies and digital markets, in turn.

3.1 Oligopolies

Oligopolies are prone to be formed in markets that generally exhibit the following features: a small number of players that enjoy a certain degree of market power; market transparency, which results in players being aware of the identity of their competitors and their price, output, and quality decisions; entry barriers, which make the threat of potential competitors less immediate, thus allowing the oligopolists to reinforce their behaviour. In such markets, all players may influence to some extent, but may not fully determine, the market price and output. The decisions of an oligopolist influence not only its business, but that of its competitors too, and therefore such decisions must also factor in the decisions of the other market players. This results in a somewhat strange mutual awareness and interdependence between players. This strategic interaction[38] may induce players to quickly realise that their profit maximisation strategies may be repositioned, that there is something to gain from adopting a policy of not competing, and thus collusion may creep in, at times explicitly and at times tacitly. This results in the same price being charged on the market, similar to the perfect competition model, yet in oligopolistic settings this price may be set higher than marginal cost, sometimes even close to monopoly levels, due to the mutual dependence and/or collusion which may settle on the market. This outcome is not always very easy to identify in practice, and that is why, at times, oligopolies may appear as fiercely competitive environments. The difficulties which competition authorities encounter in tackling such market scenarios are caused not only by the players' interdependent approach to market tactics, but are also exacerbated by the fact that oligopolies pertain to structural market problems, or better yet limitations that such markets exhibit, as indicated at the beginning of this paragraph. This is why competition authorities often struggle with using antitrust tools (which essentially entail prohibitions, implying that the undertakings might have done something wrong – which may not always be true in oligopolistic markets)[39] or merger control tools (which may not

---

[37] Jones, Sufrin and Dunne 2019, p. 11.

[38] Decker 2009, p. 13; Lindsay and Berridge 2017, p. 18.

[39] Graham 2010, p. 374; Decker 2009, p. 17 *et seq.*

always be useful, for example if no concentration transactions are present), to address the oligopoly problem.[40]

There are many models which explain the mechanisms that underpin oligopolies. We will not dwell extensively upon such discussion,[41] but for the purpose of exemplification, we will briefly refer to the following: the Cournot model provides that each producer will take its own output decision, aiming to maximise profits while predicting the output of competitors. Therefore, in such a setting the demand curves pertaining to each individual producer are less important than the response that each oligopolist devises in reaction to the output decisions taken by others. Thus, as the output produced by one company increases, the profit-maximising output of the second falls, reflecting the fact that it is generally profitable to restrict industry output below the competitive level.[42] The Bertrand model, on the other hand, focuses on the producers' pricing decisions, while attempting to predict the competitors' actions. In such a setting, the producers' inclination will be to set prices at a lower level, in an attempt to win the market. Competing on prices thus renders higher output quantities on the market, which gets us closer to a competitive market situation, rather than a monopoly.[43] Lastly, a different way of understanding the outcomes of the internal mechanisms in an oligopoly is by way of analogy to a simplified and adapted version of the so-called 'prisoner's dilemma' theory,[44] which essentially observes the dynamic of the oligopolists' pricing decision-making process, when they have no information about each other's actions, in relation to the potential outcomes measured in profit. In this context, game theory shows what the profit consequences are of choosing to price high or low, and what opportunities are created by the ability to compete less fiercely, depending on what other variables are inserted in the scenario: having to make a 'once and for all' pricing choice or not, being able to observe the competitor's market moves, and so on. For the sake of completeness, we must also point out that the prisoner's dilemma idea is also instrumental when competition authorities design their leniency policies, tools which are extremely important for their efforts of fighting cartels, by stimulating undertakings to confess their involvement in such practices. Briefly, the leniency policy essentially offers companies involved in cartels, which self-report and hand over evidence, either total immunity from fines or a reduction of fines which the competition authority would have otherwise imposed on them. This policy benefits the competition authorities, allowing them not only to pierce the cloak of secrecy in which cartels operate, but also to obtain insider evidence of the cartel infringement. Lastly, for now, the concept of leniency deters cartel formation and destabilises the operation of existing cartels.[45] We will detail this rationale further in Chapter 8, when we will deal with the topic of public enforcement of the antitrust rules.

---

[40] On addressing oligopoly problems relating to collective dominance and collusion, see Filippelli 2013.

[41] For more on this matter, see e.g. Scherer and Ross 1990; Shapiro 1989; Martin 2001.

[42] Lindsay and Berridge 2017, p. 18.

[43] Rusu 2010, pp. 190–91.

[44] On how this theory is applied to competition law, see Graham 2010, p. 371 *et seq.*

[45] On the EU Commission' leniency policy, see <http://ec.europa.eu/competition/cartels/leniency/leniency.html> accessed 13 June 2020.

3.2 Digital markets

As pointed out above, the digitalisation phenomenon has brought about interesting developments which challenge our understanding of how markets function. The emergence of the digital economy entails a reshaped interaction between the players active on digital markets, whereby new and faster paths for consumers to reach the suppliers of the products and services they desire have been created. Furthermore, digitalisation has facilitated the development of novel technologies, consequently of new types of products and services, and of new types of businesses and markets, where existing market players are forced to adapt their business models.[46] These new challenges pose the natural question of how does competition law account for these market developments, both when it comes to its substantive provisions and the enforcement exercise? This is particularly important since the law as we know it, conceived and designed chiefly with a view to the traditional, analogue economy, pre-dates the emergence of digital markets. Consequently, exploring the need for potential adjustments of the law to accurately tackle the digitalisation challenges is an exercise which sits high on the legislative, regulatory, enforcement and, why not, academic agendas.[47] But how do the features of digital markets and the dynamics which take place therein relate to the economic theories and concepts discussed above? In other words, are there circumstances which set digital markets apart and which require a different interpretation of the economic principles discussed above?

Indeed, digital markets are unique in a number of ways,[48] and therefore this calls for a careful understanding of competition economics in this environment. Digitalisation allows businesses to cut costs and achieve cost efficiencies, yet success in digital markets requires more than that. Such markets are characterised by fast-pace, costly and resource-demanding innovation, if one hopes to stay one step ahead of competitors. Therefore, digital markets are dynamic, or better yet cyclical, since market power is transient due to vulnerability to displacement by the next cycle of innovation. Competition between the players active in such markets exhibits tendencies towards 'winner takes all' competition *for* the market.[49] If there are low entry barriers, newcomers can challenge the incumbent market power more easily than in traditional economy settings,[50] because a large segment of end users may be reached quickly through various routes of delivering digital content. This is why digital markets are frequently contestable. Further, such markets are often built on multi-sided platforms, the creation of which require large investments (i.e. fixed costs), and which essentially entail an intermediary operating a digital infrastructure used to match buyers and sellers of certain

---

[46] Mundt 2017.

[47] E.g. the Digital Single Market Strategy 2015; the Roaming Regulation 2015; the General Data Protection Regulation 2016; the Portability of Online Content Regulation 2017; the E-Commerce Sector Inquiry 2017. See also Veenbrink, Looijestijn-Clearie and Rusu 2018; Kadar 2015; Solano Diaz 2017; Hoppner 2015; Graef 2015.

[48] Commission, DG for Internal Policies 2015, p. 7; Robertson 2017.

[49] Rusu, Looijestijn-Clearie and Veenbrink 2018, p. 2; OECD 2012, pp. 5–6.

[50] Commission, DG for Internal Policies 2015, p. 7.

goods or services.[51] The success of the platform rests with the intermediary's ability to attract many buyers and sellers, and therefore the respective markets are characterised by direct and indirect network effects.[52] This may lead to high market concentration, since the more the platform grows, the more difficult it becomes for competitors to challenge the position of the (dominant) platform. Furthermore, such a platform may assume the role of a so-called 'gatekeeper', preventing market entry for new players. On a connected note, such scenarios also reframe the relationship between producers and consumers. The consumers often face high and diverse switching costs,[53] or in other words they are more likely than not to be 'locked-in' to the producer's product or service, since switching to another supplier is difficult. This essentially entails a reframed dynamic of the demand and supply curves discussed above in the context of the traditional economy. The same assertion is valid when one thinks of pricing strategies too. For example, tools available in the digital environment (e.g. using algorithms, cookies) allow market players to interact differently with their competitors, by automatically adjusting prices, for instance, when competitors do so, and with their consumers, by being better able to target the consumer's reservation price, and through engaging in personalised pricing tactics. While the former scenario can lead to coordination between competitors, the latter scenario can result in price increases and price discrimination, even if the supplier does not hold a specific degree of market power. A different example relating to pricing strategies relates to situations when services are provided in the digital marketplace for free, an approach that is often used on multi-sided platforms. In such settings, the suppliers will obtain their revenue from selling advertising space.[54] Thus, it is not the consumer of the service that pays for it, or at least this is the misleading appearance; the reality is that consumers will often, and at times unknowingly, 'pay by disclosing their personal data' for the 'purchased' services.[55] While data becomes the 'currency' in digital markets, it is actually also a crucial asset for the platform and for businesses active on the platform, particularly when it cannot be easily replicated by competitors, but also when it comes to behavioural advertising, or for the purpose of reselling it to third parties. However, and lastly for now, when real money comes into the picture, consumers in digital markets are highly price sensitive and will quickly search for substitutes when price becomes a factor in their decision-making. Thus, the products or services that consumers view as interchangeable change rapidly, which makes the assessment of demand substitutability a more dynamic and demanding process, than in the case of the traditional economy. The same is valid for supply-side substitutability, as its assessment in digital markets is arguably more speculative than in traditional industries, due to the fast pace of innovation.[56]

---

[51] Kadar 2015; Solano Diaz 2017; Hoppner 2017.

[52] On network effects and multi-sided markets, see Whish and Bailey 2018, pp. 11–13.

[53] Weber 2017.

[54] Monopolkommission 2015, p. 5.

[55] Rusu, Looijestijn-Clearie and Veenbrink 2018, pp. 3–4.

[56] Pleatsikas and Teece 2001.

4 CONCLUSIONS AND OVERALL REMARKS ON THE USE OF ECONOMICS IN COMPETITION LAW ANALYSIS

Having explored the basic economic theories and concepts which are relevant for competition law, it is now time to draw the lines together and reflect on the importance of the role that economics plays in competition law (assessment). In plain terms, competition law translates into legal terms the application of economic principles. More specifically, economics has provided competition law with a better understanding of the effects of business practices, with practical concepts and criteria, and with quantitative tools that generate empirical evidence to support theories and arguments.[57] It is therefore understandable why, especially nowadays, economics is so influential in competition law enforcement, that the large majority of cases involve economic analysis of a certain depth. This is because while economic theory provides the framework within which a competition case is assessed, competition authorities need to reach consistent and evidence-based decisions, which are supported by observations regarding the operation of the market.[58] It is thus not surprising that competition authorities currently employ many economists and have furthermore created Chief Competition Economist positions;[59] these are essentially advisory positions, the purpose of which is to provide an economic viewpoint to decision-makers and ongoing guidance to the authorities' investigative staff in the enforcement process. In addition, a substantial economic consulting sector has developed, providing law firms and businesses with economic expertise in relation to competition law matters.[60] Yet, in this multi-actor relationship, lawyers, economists, competition authorities and judges need to acknowledge the tasks they each fulfil, and the limitations that their roles come with. For example, when defending a company's position, the lawyers and economists on its side must work alongside each other as complements and not substitutes, to deliver an integrated legal submission, that reflects both the business reality and sound economic reasoning, and that may be complemented by a separate, more technical economic submission containing supporting empirical evidence.[61]

While employing economics in competition cases, a wide range of techniques are used and a multitude of types of economic evidence are collected and submitted to and by the respective actors. These range from statistical evidence to market share information, diversion ratios, win/loss analyses and critical loss analyses, and to more sophisticated econometric instruments such as regressions, and bid and merger simulation models.[62] Naturally, the use of these tools varies extensively depending on the type of case at hand: cartels, dominance

---

[57] Niels, Jenkins and Kavanagh 2016, p. 470.

[58] Gore, Lewis, Lofaro and Dethmers 2013, p. 27.

[59] E.g., at EU level, the Chief Competition Economist is part of the Commission's Competition Directorate General (DG COMP). For further details, see <http://ec.europa.eu/dgs/competition/economist/role_en.html> accessed 13 June 2020.

[60] Decker 2009, pp. 1–2.

[61] See Niels, Jenkins and Kavanagh 2016, p. 460.

[62] Rusu 2010, p. 164 *et seq.*; Gore, Lewis, Lofaro and Dethmers 2013, pp. 27–30.

abuse, mergers. The same stands for the weight attached to the evidence and the manner in which the evidence is presented in the submissions made by the parties. In this respect, competition authorities have issued guidelines and best practices[63] for the submission of economic evidence in competition cases, which essentially call for transparency, clarity, completeness, robustness, and suchlike of the submission, and give valuable guidance as to the interpretation of the results.

All these elements are important because, while competition authorities (as pointed out above) employ economists that are able to decipher complex economic submissions, when a case involving economic evidence comes before a judge, things may become trickier. Of course, judges are accustomed to reviewing and evaluating reports drawn up by all kinds of scientists. In this context, while acknowledging that judges are apt to deal with economic reasoning, they normally do not have thorough economics training and thus courts may appear less equipped than competition authorities to interpret technical economic evidence. Nevertheless, judges do have various approaches they may embark on in this respect: performing reliability checks of the conclusions submitted; contrasting these conclusions with the counter-party's arguments; appointing independent experts, and so on. Different jurisdictions have chosen different paths to deal with such uncertainties, by designing, for example, more or less strict regimes under which independent experts can work with the courts, or by putting forward a duty to cooperate with the courts.[64]

In any case, and to conclude for now, the trend seems to be that economics will continue to strengthen its contribution to competition law and its enforcement.[65] This is evidenced not only by the 'more economic' or 'effects-based' approach to competition enforcement adopted by competition authorities throughout the world, but also by the steady expansion of the role that economics plays in legal fields closely connected to competition law: think of, for example, regulated and newly liberalised sectors, areas dominated by natural monopolies, even healthcare and international trade law and, why not, the digital economy.

---

[63] E.g. Staff Working Document 2010.

[64] On such alternatives, see Niels, Jenkins and Kavanagh 2016, p. 464 *et seq.*

[65] Niels, Jenkins and Kavanagh 2016, p. 470 *et seq.*

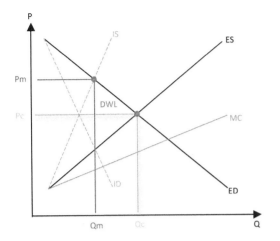

Figure 3.1 Interaction between demand and supply in monopolised and perfectly competitive markets

PART II
ANTITRUST LAW

4

Introduction to antitrust law: the scope of EU and national antitrust provisions

1 INTRODUCTION

This part of the book deals with the substantive rules addressed to undertakings, which form part of so-called antitrust law, namely the prohibition to engage in cartels and other anti-competitive agreements and the prohibition to abuse a dominant position. In this chapter, we will provide a brief overview of the pillars of antitrust law, which will be then discussed in depth in Chapters 5 and 6. This chapter sheds light on the specificity of the construction of antitrust law at both the EU and the Member States level.

The concept of antitrust law originates in the US, where in 1890 the Sherman Act was passed, in order to deal with major changes to the American economy, triggered by the growth of large and highly influential corporations, also referred to as 'trusts'. Sections 1 and 2 of the Sherman Act contain the core provisions of antitrust law. They refer to the prohibition to engage in contracts, combinations in the form of trust or otherwise, or conspiracies, in restraint of trade or commerce and the prohibition to (attempt to) monopolise, or combine or conspire with any other person or persons, to monopolise any part of the trade or commerce. Put simply, antitrust law consists of rules dealing with coordination between economic operators and behaviour of players possessing market power, which both (may) restrict trade in various forms. The Sherman Act antitrust provisions are at the heart of modern competition law systems and are still in force today, despite being supplemented by other pieces of legislation adopted as time passed. These provisions were broadly formulated and contain concepts which were not defined in the law per se. The vast body of case-law developed by the US Courts continuously shaped the antitrust provisions,[1] rendering them essential to the functioning of the US economy. Furthermore, these provisions are underpinned by economic principles which are very much valid regardless of borders and jurisdictions.[2] It is thus no surprise that US antitrust law constituted the inspiration for adopting similar rules in the large majority of the world's jurisdictions.

In the EU, a dual layer of antitrust rules has been adopted, at EU level, and in the domestic jurisdictions of the Member States. However, as already previewed in Chapter 1, it has to be

---

[1] E.g. cases *Standard Oil Co of New Jersey*, (1911) 221 US 1; *Grinnel Corp*, (1966) 384 US 563.

[2] Graham 2010, pp. 5–6; Marco Colino 2019, p. 7; Jones, Sufrin and Dunne 2019, pp. 35–6.

acknowledged from the outset that the EU antitrust rules are not identical copies of the US provisions. While similar in content and manner of drafting, they also differ in certain major respects, having to do with goals and policy orientations, substantive perception of market power, enforcement priorities and roadmaps, institutional design of enforcement agencies, sanctions, and so forth.[3]

2 EU ANTITRUST LAW

The EU antitrust provisions are now embedded in Part III, Title VII, Chapter 1 of the TFEU. It is worth mentioning that antitrust provisions have been part of the European Treaties since the early stages of European integration: Articles 65 and 66 of the 1951 ECSC Treaty and Articles 85 and 86 of the 1957 EEC Treaty. The current Articles 101 and 102 TFEU (numbering valid after the 2009 Treaty of Lisbon) have remained largely unchanged (when compared with Articles 85 and 86 EEC) since the Constitutive Treaties, despite the expiry of the European Community and of the European Coal and Steel Community.[4]

Article 101 TFEU is structured in three paragraphs containing a prohibition to engage in anti-competitive coordination between undertakings (paragraph 1), the civil law consequences of such coordination (paragraph 2) and the legal exception to the prohibition contained in paragraph 1 (paragraph 3). As will be detailed in Chapter 5, the prohibition contained in Article 101(1) TFEU is built on the fulfilment of certain cumulative conditions: coordination between undertakings in the form of agreements, concerted practices, or decisions of associations of undertakings, which have the object or effect to restrict, distort or prevent competition in the Internal Market, provided that the trade between the Member States may be affected. Article 101(1) TFEU also contains a list of examples of conduct that may be prohibited. Remarkably, no distinction is made as to whether such conduct occurs between actual or potential competitors, or between undertakings which are vertically related.[5] Article 101(2) TFEU provides that agreements and decisions of associations of undertakings which infringe paragraph 1 of the Article are void. This means that such provisions of contracts or decisions are unenforceable. Article 101(3) TFEU declares paragraph 1 inapplicable to coordination which yields certain benefits, provided that four cumulative conditions are met: improving production or distribution of goods, or promoting technical or economic progress, while allowing the consumers a fair share of the benefits, while not imposing non-indispensable restrictions on the parties that coordinate their behaviour and while not eliminating competition from the market.

Article 102 TFEU is primarily geared towards catching unilateral behaviour of undertakings that enjoy a certain degree of market power. It thus prohibits abuses of a dominant position established in the Internal Market or a substantial part of it, provided that the trade between the Member States may be affected by such conduct. In a similar fashion to Article

---

[3] On such differences, see Jones, Sufrin and Dunne 2019, pp. 38–40.

[4] Lianos, Korah and Siciliani 2019, p. 1.

[5] Ibid, p. 3.

101 TFEU, Article 102 provides a list of examples of what kind of conduct may constitute abusive behaviour. This Treaty provision tackles the behaviour of one or more undertakings, only if it/they hold a dominant position. Similar behaviour of non-dominant undertakings is not caught by this provision. A first glance at the content of Article 102 TFEU reveals that it does not contain a provision outlining the civil law consequences of abusive practices. This makes sense, having in mind that abuses are mostly not materialised through contracts, or conceived as decisions or otherwise enforceable legal means. Furthermore, Article 102 TFEU does not contain a legal exception as Article 101(3) TFEU does. However, the CJEU in its case-law,[6] and the Commission in its Enforcement Priorities Guidelines 2009, acknowledge that dominant undertakings may justify their abusive practices, by demonstrating either that the conduct is objectively necessary, or that its effects may be counterbalanced, outweighed even, by advantages in terms of efficiency.

The structure of Articles 101 and 102 TFEU seems straightforward and somewhat minimalistic. Key concepts of these substantive provisions are not defined in the text of the TFEU. The EU judiciary and legislator have nevertheless, throughout time, developed the content, scope and rationale of EU antitrust law. The extensive body of the EU courts' case-law sheds light on the constitutive elements of the concept of concerted practice,[7] the object/effect dichotomy,[8] the notion of dominance,[9] the concept of abuse,[10] just to give a few examples. As already shown in Chapter 1, the CJEU has also not shied away from bringing clarifications to the question of what the goals of competition law should be.[11] It went even further, by interpreting the provisions of Articles 101 and 102 TFEU teleologically, allowing for new theories of harm to be developed and broadening the scope of application of the said provisions, to catch conduct which is not literally described in the Treaty text.[12] The CJEU has also created and developed the right to claim damages resulting from infringements of EU antitrust law.[13] The role of the EU courts in developing the antitrust rules was supplemented by the EU institutions, with the Commission in the driving seat, which adopted legislative and soft-law instruments that nuance the provisions of Articles 101 and 102 TFEU.[14] As we will detail in Chapters 5–9, such instruments provide valuable guidance to the market players as to how

---

[6] E.g. case C-209/10 *Post Danmark I*, ECLI:EU:C:2012:172, par. 40 *et seq.*

[7] E.g. cases 48/69 *ICI*, ECLI:EU:C:1972:70; C-8/08 *T-Mobile*, ECLI:EU:C:2009:343.

[8] E.g. cases C-32/11 *Allianz Hungaria*, ECLI:EU:C:2013:160; C-67/13 *Cartes Bancaires*, ECLI:EU:C:2014:2204; C-373/14 *Toshiba*, ECLI:EU:C:2016:26.

[9] E.g. case 27/76 *United Brands*, ECLI:EU:C:1978:22.

[10] E.g. case 85/76 *Hoffmann-La Roche*, ECLI:EU:C:1979:36.

[11] E.g. joined cases 56 and 58/64 *Grundig/Consten*, ECLI:EU:C:1966:41; joined cases C-501, C-513, C-515 and C-519/06 P *GlaxoSmithKline*, ECLI:EU:C:2009:610.

[12] E.g. case C-52/09 *TeliaSonera Sverige*, ECLI:EU:C:2011:83.

[13] E.g. case C-453/99 *Courage and Crehan*, ECLI:EU:C:2001:465; joined cases C-295 to C-298/04 *Manfredi*, ECLI:EU:C:2006:461.

[14] See <https://ec.europa.eu/competition/antitrust/legislation/legislation.html> accessed 28 May 2020, for a complete list of such instruments adopted at EU level.

antitrust concepts are to be interpreted;[15] they also define policy priorities and give body to the enforcement activities performed by the European Commission.[16]

3 DOMESTIC ANTITRUST LAWS OF THE EU MEMBER STATES: ALIGNMENT WITH THE EU MODEL

Nowadays a dual layer of (EU and domestic) antitrust rules exists in Europe. However, this has not always been so: when the Treaty of Rome was adopted, Germany was the only Member State with competition law enforced by an administrative authority, while the other five original Member States had in force only provisions related to unfair or disloyal competition, or to regulated prices in large sectors of their economies.[17] Nowadays, all EU Member States have adopted laws on cartels and abuse of dominance. Interestingly, the EU antitrust rules have often been regarded by the Member States as a model when adopting or reframing their domestic laws. Several reasons underlie this choice: a renewed trust in the Single Market integration in the late 1980s and early 1990s, the alignment to a level-playing regulatory field meant to attract foreign investments, and so on.[18] Adopting the 'EU model' may range from a literal 'textual harmonisation' with the EU antitrust provisions, to making different terminological choices, to straightforwardly referring to EU antitrust law and the case-law of the EU courts in domestic law.[19] In the Member States that acceded to the EU in 2004 and later, EU competition law had an even more profound influence on the construction of domestic laws,[20] because having in place such national rules, which are in tune with EU competition law, was subject to complex pre-accession negotiations between the Commission and the national governments.

This process of alignment of national antitrust regimes to the EU model is also referred to as 'spontaneous/soft harmonisation', which ensured a remarkable degree of substantive convergence between the domestic and EU legal regimes. However, as Vedder rightfully argues, this process differs from classic harmonisation techniques adopted at EU level via Articles 114 and 115 TFEU. First, the antitrust alignment originates primarily within the Member States, who pro-actively show their willingness to adopt the EU route. Second, such legal alignment allows for differing domestic approaches to the incorporation of the EU model. Rather than resulting in identical (minimum) rules throughout Europe, spontaneous harmonisation has resulted in the adoption of a more or less uniform culture of competition and an acceptance of the need to have rules that will effectively protect competition.[21] Consequently, the degree of convergence is definitely not absolute, since, as we will detail in Chapters 5 and

---

[15] E.g. Notice on Relevant Market 1997; Guidelines on Effect on Trade 2004.

[16] E.g. Enforcement Priorities Guidelines 2009; Leniency Notice 2006; Notice on Fines 2006.

[17] Lianos, Korah and Siciliani 2019, pp. 1–2.

[18] For a thorough discussion in this respect, see Dabbah 2010, p. 187 *et seq.*

[19] Vedder 2004, p. 8; Dabbah 2010, p. 189.

[20] Dabbah 2010, pp. 176–7.

[21] Vedder 2004, p. 9.

6, certain Member States maintained a domestic flavour to the manner in which the antitrust prohibitions are adopted in domestic legislation.

The alignment of domestic substantive antitrust rules to the EU model constitutes only one of the facets which characterises the relationship between the EU and the domestic antitrust regimes. Achieving a fully coherent competition culture throughout the EU, however, also requires convergence of institutional and procedural/enforcement features. These aspects will be discussed in Chapters 7–9. The integration of the competition law regimes in the EU was not achieved overnight, but in several stages, which entailed thorough coordination between EU and national competition law regimes. Regulation 1/2003, the creation of the ECN, the Private Damages Directive 2014 and the ECN+ Directive 2019 are important landmarks in this respect, shaping the constantly evolving EU–domestic competition laws dynamic. This evolution is thus bound to move beyond the mere formal jurisdictional criteria,[22] which in the early years established more or less rigid boundaries between EU and domestic law application, as will be discussed just below.

4 EU AND DOMESTIC ANTITRUST LAW: REALMS OF APPLICATION

When do the respective domestic or EU rules apply to a given case? Despite the substantive similarity between EU and national antitrust rules, in Chapter 2 we showed that Articles 101 and 102 TFEU only apply if conduct may appreciably affect intra-Union trade, whereas domestic antitrust laws apply when such an effect is missing. The effect on the intra-EU trade concept is an autonomous EU law criterion, which must be assessed separately in each case,[23] in order to distil which law applies to a given practical situation. It essentially acts as a jurisdictional operational tool which limits the reach of the EU antitrust rules: if the effect is confined to one Member State, the EU has no jurisdiction.[24] This criterion has been broadly interpreted in the case-law of the EU courts, allowing the Commission to liberally assume jurisdiction in many cases. This was particularly useful at the time when the Member States had no, or weak, domestic competition laws in place.[25] Nowadays, this is rarely the case, which does not necessarily mean that the effect on the intra-Union trade concept is emptied of relevance.

The jurisdictional setup as discussed just above does not mean that the national antitrust rules may not be applied in parallel with the Treaty provisions on competition. Such rules may be applied concurrently by the Commission and the NCAs to the same set of facts. As shown in Chapter 1, in the *Walt Wilhelm* case,[26] the CJEU validated the approach according

---

[22] Dabbah 2010, p. 189.

[23] Guidelines on Effect on Trade 2004, par. 12. See also Lianos, Korah and Siciliani 2019, p. 65.

[24] Case 22/78 *Hugin*, ECLI:EU:C:1979:138. See also Jones, Sufrin and Dunne 2019, p. 197; Lianos, Korah and Siciliani 2019, p. 62.

[25] Whish and Bailey 2018, p. 151.

[26] Case 14/68 *Walt Wilhelm*, ECLI:EU:C:1969:4.

to which one and the same agreement may, in principle, be the object of two sets of parallel proceedings, one before the EU authorities under Article 101 TFEU, the other before the national authorities under national law,[27] since these authorities assess the conduct from different standpoints: the obstacles for trade between the Member States, and other national considerations, respectively. This approach reflects the special system of sharing jurisdiction between the EU and the Member States.[28] Yet, in light of the principles of supremacy of EU law[29] and sincere cooperation,[30] the parallel application of the national systems may not prejudice the uniform application throughout the Internal Market of the EU antitrust rules, meaning that NCAs cannot authorise practices prohibited by EU antitrust law. The *Walt Wilhelm* judgment did not clarify whether a practice could be declared anti-competitive under national law, if it was authorised under EU antitrust law.[31] In subsequent case-law,[32] the CJEU stated that potential conflicts should be avoided when national authorities give decisions on agreements or practices which may subsequently be the subject of a decision by the Commission. Furthermore, domestic courts were able to apply Articles 101(1) and 102 TFEU, due to the direct effect of their provisions,[33] while the application of Article 101(3) TFEU was fully reserved by Article 9 of Regulation 17/62 for the Commission. Thus, during the early years of European integration, the relationship between EU and domestic competition laws was a particularly vague one.[34] The entry into force of Regulation 1/2003 brought some clarity in this respect.

As already signalled in Chapters 1 and 2, and as Chapters 7 and 8 will further reveal, this Regulation has gone considerably deeper in regulating the relationship between EU and domestic antitrust law, and importantly, the role of national authorities in applying the TFEU antitrust provisions. This exemplifies the ongoing trend of a more cooperative and integrated framework for the EU competition law regime.[35] The decentralisation exercise that Regulation 1/2003 put forward is important in this respect, since it obliged domestic authorities to apply the EU antitrust provisions when the trade between the Member States is affected.[36] In the context of enforcement decentralisation, the effect on intra-Union trade remains of central importance.[37] Whish and Bailey[38] accurately identify scenarios which emphasise the importance of the practical application of this criterion, by pointing, for

---

[27] This approach is equally applicable to Article 102 TFEU cases.

[28] Case 14/68 *Walt Wilhelm*, ECLI:EU:C:1969:4, par. 3, 4, 9, 11.

[29] Case 6/64 *Costa v E.N.E.L.*, ECLI:EU:C:1964:66.

[30] Article 4(3) TEU. See also Marco Colino 2019, pp. 59–60; Dabbah 2010, p. 177.

[31] Jones, Sufrin and Dunne 2019, pp. 1010–11.

[32] E.g. cases C-234/89 *Delimitis*, ECLI:EU:C:1991:91; C-344/98 *Masterfoods*, ECLI:EU:C:2000:689.

[33] Case C-127/73 *BRT v SABAM*, ECLI:EU:C:1974:25, par. 15, 16.

[34] Dabbah 2010, p. 177.

[35] Ibid, p. 180 *et seq.*

[36] Rusu and Looijestijn-Clearie 2017 (a), p. 5 *et seq.*; Sauter 2016, p. 30. On how the idea of decentralisation caught shape, see Dabbah 2010, pp. 179–87.

[37] Whish and Bailey 2018, p. 151; Parret 2011, p. 45 *et seq.*

[38] Whish and Bailey 2018, p. 151; Marco Colino 2019, p. 63 *et seq.*

example, to the following. Where there is an effect on trade between the Member States, national courts and NCAs cannot apply stricter national competition law to agreements, although they can apply stricter national law to unilateral conduct.[39] This means that if an agreement is authorised by Article 101 TFEU, either because it does not restrict competition within the meaning of Article 101(1) TFEU, it fulfils the criteria of Article 101(3) TFEU or satisfies the conditions of a Block Exemption, it cannot be prohibited by national law. Regarding unilateral conduct, NCAs are, however, free to apply national competition laws which are stricter than Article 102 TFEU to unilateral conduct. They may thus prohibit or impose sanctions on unilateral conduct engaged in by undertakings which does not constitute an abuse of a dominant position under Article 102 TFEU.[40] Further, NCAs that apply Articles 101 and 102 TFEU have an obligation to inform the Commission of that fact before the adoption of the decision.[41] Clearly, an NCA could avoid this obligation by reaching the conclusion that there is no effect on trade between the Member States. Also, when the Commission is informed that an NCA intends to adopt a decision on the basis of EU competition law, it has the power to initiate its own proceedings and thereby to terminate the proceedings of the NCA.[42] When the Commission has finished its investigation, the NCAs' power to apply EU and domestic antitrust law revives, subject to their obligation not to adopt decisions that run counter to the Commission's decision.

Lastly for now, Recital 9 and Article 3(3) of Regulation 1/2003 clarify that domestic authorities may apply national provisions that predominantly pursue an objective different from that pursued by Articles 101 and 102 TFEU and may implement legislation which protects other legitimate interests than that pursued by these TFEU articles, if it is compatible with general principles and other provisions of EU law. National sectoral regulators are thus not obliged to apply the EU antitrust provisions.[43]

5 CONCLUSIONS

Summing up, the antitrust rules in Europe have their seeds in US antitrust law. Yet, in the EU, the adoption of antitrust rules has been modelled according to the EU's legal architecture. EU antitrust law was conceived to cater to the EU's needs, particularly related, but not limited to, the Internal Market integration endeavour. At Member State level, antitrust policies have been developed with the observance of the EU model, yet also considering domestic specificities. The construction of antitrust law in the EU and its Member States is thus unique in itself and may be best described by pointing to EU antitrust law as a centre of gravity, to which national regimes are primarily connected.[44]

---

[39] Regulation 1/2003, Article 3(2).

[40] Jones, Sufrin and Dunne 2019, pp. 1011–12.

[41] Regulation 1/2003, Article 11(4).

[42] Ibid, Article 11(6).

[43] Jones, Sufrin and Dunne 2019, p. 1012.

[44] Dabbah 2010, p. 190.

5

The cartel prohibition and the ban on anti-competitive agreements

1 INTRODUCTION

In the previous chapter it was outlined that Article 101 TFEU constitutes one of the pillars of EU competition law. It was also pointed out that this provision applies in so far as the trade between the Member States is impacted. Nevertheless, in cases where this trade is not affected, competition law may still be relevant, as the EU Member States have adopted legislation modelled after Article 101 (and Article 102 TFEU).[1]

In this chapter the cartel prohibition and the prohibition to engage in other anti-competitive agreements contained in Article 101 TFEU will be explored. In many official documents the term cartel is connected with a serious infringement of this Treaty provision, such as price fixing.[2] It is clear from the outset that other contractual arrangements may also be caught by Article 101 TFEU and, therefore, the legislation and the case-law discussed below are not only concerned with cartels. However, for reasons of convenience, a reference made to cartels also encompasses other restrictive agreements, unless stated otherwise. At first, the ban on cartels will be discussed in this chapter. The evolution of the case-law, including the role of economic theory, will be at the heart of this analysis. Then, attention will be paid to the exceptions to this prohibition. Also, with regard to this subject matter the case-law of the EU courts and the economic approach play a role. Subsequently, national examples of the cartel prohibitions will be highlighted. It will be made clear that a coherent layer of EU and national rules for cartels is in place.

In this regard it must be noted that Article 101(2) TFEU contains a civil law sanction in the event that an agreement or a decision of an association of undertakings is incompatible with the cartel prohibition and cannot be justified by exceptions. Such an agreement or decision is void pursuant to this provision. This entails that the undertakings concerned are not bound by the agreement or decision at stake. They are not obliged to live up to what is stipulated in this agreement or decision. On the contrary, it is even not permitted for them to do so, as the practices concerned are considered to be harmful for the competition process. It is apparent from the case-law of the CJEU that the automatic nullity applies to

---

[1] E.g. in case C-32/11 *Allianz Hungaria*, ECLI:EU:C:2013:160, par. 20, the CJEU put forward that the Hungarian rules on cartels and restrictive practices faithfully reproduce Article 101 TFEU.

[2] E.g. Private Damages Directive 2014, Article 2(14); Leniency Notice 2006, par. 1.

the individual clauses of an agreement or decision, rather than the entire legal act.[3] In *Société Technique Minière*,[4] the CJEU held that in that case the contract as a whole was not void, unless its provisions were not severable from the clauses affected by the cartel prohibition. Accordingly, as a rule a distinction must be made between the contractual provisions restricting competition and the contractual provision not restricting competition. It is up to national (private) law to determine to what extent the clauses of an agreement or contract are severable.[5] Furthermore, parties having suffered damages from infringements of Article 101 TFEU may start a proceeding against the wrongdoers before a private law court. In Chapter 9, the private enforcement of the antitrust rules (including Article 101 TFEU) will be discussed.

2 ARTICLE 101(1) TFEU: THE BAN ON CARTELS

Pursuant to Article 101(1) TFEU, agreements between undertakings, concerted practices between undertakings and decisions of associations of undertakings that restrict competition and may affect the trade between the Member States are not permitted (save for some exceptions). To our mind, this provision consists of the following elements: (1) a form of cooperation between undertakings; (2) the restriction of competition; and (3) an effect on the trade between the Member States. These elements are the cumulative conditions that must be satisfied for Article 101(1) TFEU to be applicable.

2.1 Agreements, concerted practices and decisions of associations of undertakings

From the drafting of Article 101(1) TFEU, it is apparent that unilateral behaviour is not caught by this provision. The cartel prohibition involves a form of cooperation between undertakings. It should be noted that cooperation based on a lasting change of control of the governance structure of the companies concerned is likely to amount to a concentration, which is governed by the EU Merger Control Regulation 2004. In that case, the undertakings cooperating will become part of one business unit and, as a result, Article 101 TFEU is not applicable.[6] Cooperation forms not impacting on the governance structure of the enterprises concerned are subject to Article 101(1) TFEU. Three cooperation forms have to be distinguished: (1) an agreement, (2) a concerted practice, and (3) a decision of an association of undertakings.

---

[3] Jones, Sufrin and Dunne 2019, p. 204.

[4] Case 56/65 *Société Technique Minière*, ECLI:EU:C:1966:38.

[5] Jones, Sufrin and Dunne 2019, p. 204.

[6] An exception to this is that particular joint ventures must be assessed in the light of Article 101 TFEU, although these transactions are subject to the notification obligation under the Merger Control Regulation 2004. This matter is discussed in Chapter 10.

2.1.1 Agreements

As in private law, an agreement is deemed to be present if there is a concurrence of wills.[7] The form of this is not important, as long as it constitutes the faithful expression of the parties' intention.[8] In other words, the will of the parties is decisive. Even non-binding agreements (e.g. gentleman's agreements) may fall within the ambit of Article 101(1) TFEU, that is, when the parties have the intention to abide by what is agreed upon.[9]

In this regard, it must be pointed out that even companies or persons facilitating the smooth operation of a cartel between other undertakings, regarding markets these companies or persons do not operate on, could be found to be part of that cartel.[10] Thus, in *Treuhand*,[11] a consultancy firm based in Zurich, which offered business management and administration services, was held liable for the cartel under review, as this firm organised a number of meetings, during which the prices for tin and heat stabilisers were aligned. Although the consultancy firm did not operate on the markets for these stabilisers but rather offered management services to the companies manufacturing the products concerned, this firm was assumed to be part of the cartel too, as it facilitated the smooth operation of this anti-competitive practice.

Collective labour agreements are a special type of agreement. It is clear from the outset that reviewing such agreements under the competition law rules would have massive consequences for social policy. As the employees' pay is at the heart of collective bargaining, the fair chance exists that this bargaining will be found incompatible with Article 101(1) TFEU. This would put the social policy of the Member States under pressure, as it is common in Europe that collective labour agreements play a significant role in pursuing employment and social objectives. For that reason, the CJEU has developed a specific approach in order to strike a balance between competition and social policy goals.

In its so-called *Brentjens* case-law,[12] the CJEU held that collective labour agreements are immune from Article 101(1) TFEU, if the following conditions are fulfilled. First, the agreement at issue is the outcome of collective negotiations between organisations representing employers and workers. Second, the aim of this agreement is to improve the employment and working conditions. The fulfilment of these conditions entails that the collective agreement concerned does not fall within the scope of Article 101 TFEU.

The approach developed in the *Brentjens* case-law highly mirrors the US antitrust experience with collective bargaining.[13] This does not come as a surprise, as the Advocate General

---

[7] E.g. joined cases C-2 and C-3/01 P *Bayer*, ECLI:EU:C:2004:2.

[8] Ibid, par. 97.

[9] Case 41/69 *ACF Chemiefarma*, ECLI:EU:C:1970:71, par. 110–12.

[10] Jones, Sufrin and Dunne 2019, p. 195.

[11] Case C-194/14 *AC Treuhand*, ECLI:EU:C:2015:717.

[12] Joined cases C-115, C-116 and C-117/97 *Brentjens*, ECLI:EU:C:1999:434; cases C-67/96 *Albany*, ECLI:EU:C:1999:430; C-219/97 *Drijvende Bokken*, ECLI:EU:C:1999:437; C-222/98 *Van der Woude*, ECLI:EU:C:2000:475.

[13] Fox and Gerard 2017, p. 112, refer, inter alia, to Section 6 of the US Clayton Act, which contains an antitrust exemption to agreements among workers. US courts have expanded this exemption to collective bargaining agreements between workers and employers.

in *Brentjens* referred to this experience in his ground-breaking and illuminating Opinion on this matter.[14] In our view, the *Brentjens* case-law comes down to making a distinction between the labour market and the market for goods (commodities) and services. As long as the sole aim of a collective labour agreement is to regulate the labour market, Article 101 TFEU does not apply. In contrast, clauses of collective labour agreements affecting the functioning of goods and services markets are not immune from this Treaty provision and are, accordingly, capable of raising serious competition issues. Thus, in *Pavlov*[15] the CJEU held that the collective bargaining under review fell within the scope of Article 101(1) TFEU, as the organisations concerned did not represent employees, but self-employed persons (i.e. medical specialists). These entities qualify as undertakings for the purposes of competition law and, therefore, the outcome of the negotiations had an impact on the market for health services. In *FNV Kunsten*,[16] the CJEU made it clear that it must be examined with great care whether the persons provide services and assume the risks attached to these services or whether they are 'false' self-employed persons, meaning that they perform services under the direction of another person. If a supervisory relationship exists between a person providing services and somebody else, this person qualifies as a worker and, accordingly, the collective bargaining does benefit from immunity from Article 101(1) TFEU.

To date, the case-law dealing with competition and collective labour agreements only concerns Article 101 TFEU. The CJEU has not handed down judgments regarding collective bargaining and Article 102 TFEU. Given the rationale of the *Brentjens* approach, which takes the distinction between the labour market and the goods and services markets as point of departure, it seems a logical step to extend this approach to dominance cases too. Applying Article 102 TFEU may also hinder the proper functioning of the labour market and such hindrances should, therefore, not be accepted. On the other hand, it may be assumed that Article 102 TFEU applies in the event that the conclusion of a collective labour agreement leads to abusive practices on goods and services markets. All in all, further case-law on this matter must be awaited.

2.1.2 Concerted practices

Collusion between undertakings may occur, despite the fact that no agreements are concluded. In that case, commercial policies are aligned through the actual operations of the companies involved. It goes without saying that the impact of such operations on competition could be considerable. For that reason, concerted practices fall within the ambit of Article 101(1) TFEU. According to settled case-law of the CJEU, a concerted practice constitutes a form of coordination between undertakings that knowingly substitutes practical cooperation between them for the risks of competition.[17] Two elements must be distinguished: parallel behaviour and coordination. On the market, prices and other commercial matters of various

---

[14] Par. 96–107 of the Opinion of Advocate General Jacobs in case C-67/96 *Albany*, joined cases C-115, C-116 and C-117/97 *Brentjens* and case C-219/97 *Drijvende Bokken*, ECLI:EU:C:1999:28.

[15] Joined cases C-180 and C-184/98 *Pavlov*, ECLI:EU:C:2000:428.

[16] Case C-413/13 *FNV Kunsten*, ECLI:EU:C:2014:2411.

[17] E.g. case 48/69 *ICI*, ECLI:EU:C:1972:70, par. 64.

undertaking could be similar or evolve in a similar direction. For example, prices increase in the same time span. This is parallel behaviour and it cannot be excluded that this is the result of undertakings cooperating. However, the mere occurrence of parallel behaviour in itself does not prove the existence of concerted practices.[18] These practices must be caused by coordination. In other words, a causal link between parallel behaviour and the concerted practices at issue must be demonstrated. Consequently, three steps must be taken in order to apply Article 101(1) TFEU to situations involving concerted practices: (1) coordination between undertakings must be proven, (2) (subsequent) parallel behaviour has to be identified on the market, and (3) a causal link between this behaviour and the coordination must be demonstrated.

It goes without saying that establishing that undertakings were engaged in concerted practices could give rise to evidentiary problems. In many cases, it will not be difficult to show parallel behaviour on the market. However, coordination usually takes place behind closed doors and, therefore, it will be problematic to prove that the undertakings involved have aligned their commercial policies. On top of that, these undertakings may question whether this alignment forms the basis of the parallel behaviour that occurred on the market. For instance, companies that frequently meet could argue that the increase of prices is not the result of these meetings but of autonomous developments (such as economic downturn or the oligopolistic nature of the market).[19]

As for the last issue, it should be noted that the CJEU has offered a helping hand in its case-law. If undertakings take part in a concerted action and remain active on the market, a causal link between this action and the market conduct of these undertakings is presumed to be present.[20] The parties concerned may rebut this presumption by giving proof to the contrary. It is clear that the burden of proof is reversed when it comes to the causal connection between parallel behaviour and coordination. For example, undertakings that have met in order to discuss the 'appropriate level of pricing' and subsequently have increased the prices for their products are presumed to be engaged in concerted actions. The burden of proof that this is not true rests with them. Such undertakings could try to give other explanations for the increase of prices, by for instance pointing to the rising costs of particular raw materials. But it is clear that in these circumstances it will be very hard for them to come up with an alternative explanation that convincingly lines out why prices went up.[21] The presumption is even more difficult to rebut if the undertakings concerned have had meetings for a long period of time.[22] In any event, mere assertions that alternative explanations could be given will never be regarded as convincing explanations.[23]

In the *E-TURAS* preliminary ruling,[24] the presumption of a causal link was applied to

---

[18] E.g. joined cases 89, 104, 114, 116, 117 and 125 to 129/85 *Ahlström*, ECLI:EU:C:1993:120, par. 71, 72.

[19] Cf. ibid, par. 126.

[20] Case C-8/08 *T-Mobile*, ECLI:EU:C:2009:343, par. 44–53.

[21] E.g. Loozen 2010, p. 150.

[22] Bailey 2010, p. 366

[23] Ibid.

[24] Case C-74/14 *E-TURAS*, ECLI:EU:C:2016:42.

digital markets. At issue was an information system used by travel agencies for selling travel packages on their websites. The administrator of this system sent an e-mail to the personal mailbox of the agencies, stating that the discounts to be given were reduced to 3 per cent maximum. Subsequently, the administrator implemented a few technical modifications that precluded the travel agencies from granting discounts higher than 3 per cent. The question arose whether the dispatch of the e-mail amounted to participation in concerted actions. The CJEU held that the agencies were presumed to have taken part in concerted practices if they were aware of the message sent by the administrator. This could be rebutted by, for example, showing that the economic operator concerned had publicly distanced itself from these practices, had reported these practices to the administrative authorities or had applied higher discounts outside the digital platform. In our view, the most sensitive matter concerns the question whether the travel agencies were aware of the e-mail on the reduction of the discount.[25] Unlike the issue of the presumption of the causal link, the CJEU framed this question as a matter of national procedural law. This implies that, on one hand, the national court had to decide on the basis of national rules whether the operators were aware of the e-mail and that, on the other hand, the national court was obliged to take into account the principles of equivalence and effectiveness.[26] On top of that, the Charter of Fundamental Rights of the EU, including Article 48(1), which is about the presumption of innocence, had to be observed. This principle does not preclude the domestic court from considering that the dispatch of the e-mail justifies the presumption that the travel agencies were aware of the content of this mail. However, the presumption of innocence requires that the agencies have the opportunity to rebut this presumption.

It is apparent from the foregoing that the exchange of data through electronic means could lead to concerted practices under Article 101(1) TFEU. Admittedly, the CJEU has developed a detailed and sophisticated approach in *E-TURAS*, leaving considerable freedom to national law, which also raises the question how the CJEU would deal with the issue of the dispatch of the e-mail in direct appeal cases against Commission decisions. In such cases the role of national law is different from cases where Article 101(1) TFEU is applied by domestic (judicial) authorities. Then again, in *E-TURAS* the CJEU did not shy away from adapting the concept of concerted practices to ICT operations on digital markets. The electronic/automatic transfer of data, which is common on such markets and is even facilitated by algorithms, could amount to concerted practices and, for that reason, give rise to serious concerns under EU competition law. Any contact between competitors should be carefully reviewed, as it is capable of reducing or eliminating the risk of competition.[27] The main point is that the CJEU did not exclude that the enterprises taking part in a digital system of exchange of data were aware or ought to be aware of the content of these data. If these data stimulate anti-competitive conduct, this is a very sensitive matter. However, the issue that remains to be resolved is how to establish the awareness of the content of the data transferred. In *E-TURAS*, solving this issue was mainly left to the domestic court. In our view,

---

[25] Rusu 2016, p. 397.

[26] These principles are discussed in Chapter 7, section 4.3.

[27] Pereira 2018, p. 226.

given the importance of the emerging digital markets, it is inevitable that the CJEU will shed more light on this in future case-law.

2.1.3 Decisions of associations of undertakings

Associations of undertakings play an important role in economic life. They represent the undertakings associated with them and look after their interests. In other words, these associations provide for excellent mechanisms for companies to cooperate. For that reason, their decisions must be reviewed under Article 101(1) TFEU. On many occasions, cooperation between undertakings is very fruitful for the market and delivers great benefits, as associations of undertakings can carry out administrative tasks and provide other services of facilities management. But the policies adopted in the framework of an association of undertakings could also be very harmful for competition, for example, when such policies lead to the alignment of pricing. Consequently, the decisions taken by these associations must be compatible with the 'cartel prohibition'.

For purposes of qualification, it is not important whether a particular organisation is governed by national private or public law. What matters is that an organisation represents the interest of the undertakings associated and manages certain economic activities with a view to these interests.[28] It is not required that the association itself is engaged in economic activities but rather its members must qualify as undertakings within the meaning of EU competition law.[29] It is apparent from settled case-law that the CJEU assigns great value to the commonality of interests between the association and its members.[30] If these interests coincide, a change of the governance structure of the association according to which the majority of the board does not represent the members anymore cannot call into question the applicability of Article 101(1) TFEU. Although the commonality of interests is not the exclusive criterion, it is a significant analytical element in applying Article 101(1) TFEU to associations of undertakings.[31]

Many decisions taken by associations of undertakings are binding. It goes without saying that these decisions fall within the scope of EU competition law and must be in line with the cartel prohibition. It is not permitted that such decisions distort competition. It should be noted, however, that non-binding decisions could also fall within the scope of Article 101(1) TFEU. This is the case, if such decisions constitute the faithful reflection of the association concerned to coordinate the conduct of its members on the market.[32] If, for example, these members closely follow the recommendations issued by the association, their conduct is aligned and may, therefore, lead to distortions of competition.

---

[28] Case C-309/99 *Wouters*, ECLI:EU:C:2002:98, par. 56–71.

[29] Ibid, par. 64.

[30] Case C-382/12 *Mastercard*, ECLI:EU:C:2014:2201, par. 62–77.

[31] Van Cleynenbreugel 2015, p. 288.

[32] Case 45/85 *Verband der Sachversicherer*, ECLI:EU:C:1987:34, par. 32.

2.2 Restriction of competition

The second condition of Article 101(1) TFEU is related to the prevention, distortion or restriction of competition. An agreement, concerted practice or a decision of an association of undertaking is only forbidden in so far as it restricts competition. Freedom of contract is of great value in EU law and, therefore, it is permitted for undertakings to cooperate in order to achieve the commercial objectives they have set. Interventions based on Article 101(1) TFEU are only appropriate if the proper functioning of the market is at stake. In this section, the central question is how to determine whether an agreement, concerted practice or decision of an association of undertakings restricts competition. In this regard, it should be noted that for reasons of convenience only reference will be made to agreements. These references also encompass concerted practices and decisions of an association of undertakings.

2.2.1 Restriction by object and by effect

Article 101(1) TFEU stipulates that agreements having the object or the effect to restrict competition are not permitted. From the wording of this Treaty provision, it is apparent that a distinction must be made between restrictions 'by object' and restrictions 'by effect'. The CJEU's case-law departs from a sharp divide between these two categories of restrictions. The CJEU has consistently held that once the anti-competitive object of an agreement is established, the concrete effects of this agreement do not need to be analysed.[33] In contrast, establishing an anti-competitive effect entails that the concrete effects caused by the agreement at issue on competition must be examined with great care.[34]

To a certain extent, this EU case-law has some resemblance with the US experience with the cartel prohibition, laid down in Section 1 of the Sherman Act. Pursuant to this provision every contract, combination in the form of trust or otherwise, or conspiracy leading to restraining trade or commerce among the several states, is banned. Some forms of collusion are regarded as so harmful that they fall within the per se illegality category and are, accordingly, prohibited irrespective of the effects caused by these forms of collusion, whereas other practices are subject to a review under the Rule of Reason, which means that pro- and anti-competitive effects are balanced.[35] These practices are illegal to the extent that the negative effects outweigh the positive effects. So, both the US and EU rules on restrictive agreements are based on a distinction between two kinds of practices: those that are deemed to lead to serious competition issues and those that merit an in-depth analysis for establishing such issues. It should, however, be stressed that the EU approach does not entirely coincide with the US approach, as under the latter regime pro-competitive effects are accommodated in the review under Section 1 of the Sherman Act, while under the former regime, these effects are taken into account under the legal exception of Article 101(3) TFEU.[36] Moreover,

---

[33] E.g. joined cases 56 and 58/64 *Grundig/Consten*, ECLI:EU:C:1966:41 (at p. 342); cases C-49/92 P *Anic*, ECLI:EU:C: 1999:356, par. 99; C-209/07 *BIDS*, ECLI:EU:C:2008:643, par. 15–17; C-8/08 *T-Mobile*, ECLI:EU:C:2009:343, par. 29.

[34] Ibid.

[35] Nagy 2013, p. 7; Van den Bergh, Camesasca and Giannaccari 2017, pp. 1–2.

[36] Nagy 2013, p. 7.

in EU competition law, restrictions by object could also be justifiable, at least theoretically, whereas such justification is not acceptable in the concept of per se illegality of US antitrust law.

All in all, in EU competition law it is of great importance to examine whether an agreement leads to a restriction by object or by effect. In this respect, the agreement concerned must be considered in its economic and legal context and close regard must be paid to the objectives that it is intended to attain.[37] The Commission has given some guidance by listing the most well-known types of 'by object' restrictions, such as price fixing, market sharing, bid rigging and sales restrictions, in the *De Minimis* Staff Working Document 2014.

In various judgments, the CJEU has explained how to make a distinction between the two types of restrictions. It is clear from the outset that the Commission, NCAs as well as any individual claimant having suffered damage are inclined to argue that the object of a certain agreements is restrictive. The burden of proof is in such circumstances considerably lower than in the event that a contractual clause may have a restrictive effect. On the other hand, an expansive interpretation of the concept of restriction by object could trigger the applicability of the cartel prohibition to practices that are in fact harmless. This could even lead to banning potentially welfare-enhancing agreements.[38] Consequently, the CJEU had to proceed with great care in specifying the constituting elements of a restriction by object.

Already in *BIDS*,[39] the CJEU made it clear that the point of departure is that certain forms of collusion between undertakings can be regarded, by their very nature, as being injurious to the proper functioning of competition.[40] Textbook examples of such practices are horizontal and vertical price fixing, market sharing, output restrictions and bid rigging. Such forms of collusion are also known as hardcore restrictions. It goes without saying that hardcore restrictions are very controversial in EU competition law. Furthermore, in *GlaxoSmithKline* the CJEU held that nothing in Article 101(1) TFEU or in the case-law indicates that only contractual provisions that deprive end users from certain advantages may have an anti-competitive object, as EU competition law does not only pursue objectives such as consumer welfare, but also goals related to the protection of the market structure and competition as such.[41] Restrictions that go to the detriment of other groups than final consumers can also have the object of restricting competition. Then, in *Cartes Bancaires*,[42] it held that certain types of coordination between undertakings reveal a sufficient degree of harm to competition that it may be found that there is no need to examine their effects. Apparently, such practices may be considered very harmful by their nature. The negative effects caused by the restriction

---

[37] E.g. joined cases 96 to 102, 104, 105, 108 and 110/82 *IAZ*, ECLI:EU:C:1983:310, par. 25; case C-8/08 *T-Mobile*, ECLI:EU:C:2009:343, par. 27.

[38] Niels, Jenkins and Kavanagh 2016, p. 239.

[39] Case C-209/07 *BIDS*, ECLI:EU:C:2008:643.

[40] Ibid, par. 17.

[41] Joined cases C-501, C-513, C-515 and C-519/06 P *GlaxoSmithKline*, ECLI:EU:C:2009:610, par. 62.

[42] Case C-67/13 *Cartes Bancaires*, ECLI:EU:C:2014:2204, par. 49–52. See also case C-469/15 P *FSL*, EU:C:2017:308, par. 103.

justify the avoidance of a full analysis of these effects.[43] In *Budapest Bank,* the CJEU added to this that sufficiently reliable and robust experience must show that the restriction under review is harmful to competition.[44]

It is apparent from this approach that the central test for establishing the object of the restriction is whether the practice reveals a sufficient degree of harm to competition.[45] Thus, in *Cartes Bancaires,* the CJEU pointed out that the credit card system under review would only function properly if the acquisition and issuing activities of the banks participating in this system are in balance.[46] For that reason, the requirement that banks not engaged actively in acquiring new customers and banks entering the system must pay a fee to banks that have put much effort in such acquisition did not have the object to restrict competition. The rationale of this requirement was to solve a 'free rider' problem, caused by banks that left the acquisition largely to other banks.[47]

In *Toshiba*[48] and *Hoffmann-La Roche,*[49] it was outlined which factors needed to be analysed in order to identify a sufficient degree of harm to competition. The following factors were named in this respect: (1) the content of the provision, (2) the objectives pursued, and (3) the economic and legal context. What is meant by the economic and legal context is specified with a reference to the nature of the goods or services rendered, the real conditions of the functioning, and the structure of the market or markets in question. It is apparent from the factors specified in the case-law that one should not jump to conclusions when confronted with the issue of restriction by object or effect. All the relevant factors must be scrutinised. It is a bit puzzling that the examination of the economic and legal context entails, inter alia, an analysis of the real conditions of the functioning and the structure of the market. The line between analysing these conditions and analysing the effects on the market, which is inherent in an assessment related to restrictions by effect, is very thin.

In some cases, it may be inevitable to go, to a certain extent, into the effects of a certain practice in order to learn more about the real conditions of the functioning and the structure of the market. This statement can be illustrated by pointing to the *Hoffmann-La-Roche* case. This case concerned the marketing of a medicine that was developed for cancer treatment but that turned out to be also effective with regard to eye diseases. The result of this was that this medicine was supplied on the market in competition with other medicines for eye treatment. In order to address these competition restraints two pharmaceutical companies concluded an agreement, according to which information was disseminated questioning the effectiveness of the cancer medicine concerned for eye treatment. Both the public authorities competent for overseeing the quality of pharmaceutical products and the public had to be warned about this use of the medicine. The CJEU was called upon to decide whether the agreement on

---

[43] Brankin 2016, p. 380.

[44] Case C-228/18 *Budapest Bank*, ELCI:EU:2020:265, par. 76.

[45] Heng Alvin Sng 2016, p. 182.

[46] Cf. case C-228/18 *Budapest Bank*, ECLI:EU:C:2020:265, par. 66.

[47] In this regard, it was not excluded that this requirement could lead a restriction by effect.

[48] Case C-373/14 *Toshiba*, ECLI:EU:C:2016:26.

[49] Case C-179/16 *Hoffmann-La Roche*, ECLI:EU:C:2018:25.

disseminating information on the medicine concerned had the object of restricting competition. It pointed out that the information was misleading and encouraged doctors to refrain from prescribing this medicine for treatment of eye diseases. It was also put forward that specific European and national laws are in place for guaranteeing the proper use of medicines and preventing health problems. Eventually, the CJEU found that the agreement on the dissemination of information on the use the medicine at issue had the object of restricting competition.

Also, in the case *Generics and GlaxoSmithKline*[50] it appeared that a quick scan of the effects was inevitable in order to establish whether a contractual arrangement constitutes a restriction by object. At issue was an agreement whereby a manufacturer of generic medicines committed itself to not challenging the validity of a patent of an originator medicine. As a result, the generic manufacturer refrained from producing the medicine concerned and, accordingly, did not enter the market for that medicine. In return, it received some compensation for this commitment from the manufacturer of the medicine protected by the patent at stake (the originator medicine). Such deals are known as 'pay-for-delay' agreements (a pharmaceutical company pays a competitor for delaying its plans to produce particular medicines) and may have an anti-competitive purpose.[51] In *Generics and GlaxoSmithKline* the sole intent of the manufacturer of the originator medicine could have been to convince the manufacturer of the generic medicine not to enter the market and, by doing so, to distort competition. Then again, the deal clinched could also have been based on a genuine assessment of the intellectual property (IP) right issues at play and may have reflected a justified settlement of the dispute between the companies concerned. Consequently, it depends on the circumstances of the case concerned whether issues under competition law arise. The transfer of value is, in itself, not sufficient to conclude that the agreement restricts competition by object. It should be established whether it is clear from the analysis of the settlement agreement under review that the transfer of value provided by it cannot have any explanation other than the commercial interest of both the manufacturer of the originator medicine and the manufacturer of generic medicines not to engage in competition on the merits.[52]

The *Hoffmann-La Roche* and *Generics and GlaxoSmithKline* judgments show that qualifying a practice as a restriction by object requires a good understanding of the working of the markets under review. The CJEU analysed with great care how the contractual arrangements at issue functioned. To a certain extent the appreciation of the (potential) effects of such arrangements is required in order to find that these arrangements reveal a sufficient degree of harm to competition.

In the same vein, the CJEU addressed the impact of agreements concluded between Hungarian insurance companies and car repair shops in *Allianz Hungaria*,[53] in the context of a preliminary ruling proceeding. According to these agreements, the shops would not only fix damaged cars of the insured persons, but also offer car insurance to their customers. If the

---

[50] Case C-307/18 *Generics and GlaxoSmithKline*, ECLI:EU:C:2020:52.

[51] E.g. case T-472/13 *Lundbeck*, ECLI:EU:T:2016:449.

[52] Case C-307/18 *Generics and GlaxoSmithKline*, ECLI:EU:C:2020:52, par. 87.

[53] Case C-32/11 *Allianz Hungaria*, ECLI:EU:C:2013:160.

car repair shops had been successful in selling insurance policies, they would receive higher remuneration than usual for their repair services. The CJEU contended that special regard had to be given to domestic legislation that provided that insurance agents were obliged to act independently from insurance companies. The referring national judge had to examine whether against the backdrop of this legislation the proper functioning of the insurance market would be disrupted by the agreements under review (which were based on conditionality between the parties concerned). Moreover, the referring court had to verify whether it was likely that the competition on the market would be weakened or eliminated by the conclusion of the agreements under review. In that context special attention had to be given to the role of alternative distribution channels and their importance in relation to the market power of the parties to the agreements. Again, determining the restrictive object of a contractual clause requires some appreciation of the likelihood of the effects caused by this clause.

In sum, the next steps must be taken for determining a restriction by object. It should be examined whether the agreement concerned amounts to a sufficient degree of harm to competition. The factors that are relevant in this respect are the following:

1. The content of the provisions;
2. The objectives pursued;
3. The economic and legal context:
    a. The nature of the goods or services rendered; and
    b. The real conditions of the functioning and structure of the market(s) concerned.

If an agreement does not have the object of restricting competition, it cannot be excluded that it may have an effect of doing so. It could be argued that the negative impact on competition is a side effect of the contract under review, although the intent of the parties concerned was not related to competition matters. In order to establish an effect on competition, a counterfactual analysis must be carried out: how would the market(s) have evolved in the absence of the contract under review?[54] It should be examined whether the agreement is liable to have an adverse impact on the parameters of competition, such as the price, the quantity and the quality of the goods or the services.[55] However, it is not required that these effects must be harmful for end users.[56] As already pointed out, consumer welfare is not the only objective to be attained by EU competition law.

Strikingly, as with the restriction by object, the effects of an agreement on competition must be assessed in the economic and legal context in which it occurs and where it might combine with others to have a cumulative effect on competition.[57] Consequently, the economic and legal context is a common thread running through the assessment carried out under Article 101(1) TFEU. Not only actual, but also potential effects must be taken into

[54] Niels, Jenkins and Kavanagh 2016, p. 237; Whish and Bailey 2018, p. 134.

[55] Whish and Bailey 2018, p. 132.

[56] Ibid.

[57] Cases C-345/14 SIA 'Maxima Latvija', ECLI:EU:C:2015:784, par. 26; C-234/89 Delimitis, ECLI:EU:C:1991:91, par. 14.

account.[58] The purpose of the counterfactual analysis is to establish the realistic possibilities with regard to the conduct of the undertakings concerned in the absence of the restrictive agreement(s) under review.[59]

In many cases, the relevant markets will be defined in order to find an adverse effect on competition. In SIA 'Maxima Latvija' the CJEU was asked whether commercial lease agreements concluded by a large supermarket chain for the rental of premises in shopping centres was compatible with Article 101(1) TFEU. Pursuant to one of the clauses inserted in these contracts, the supermarket concerned was the 'anchor tenant' and had, accordingly, the right to agree with the selection of other businesses, to which a premise was let. These clauses enabled the supermarket to exercise control over other companies wishing to enter the market. The agreements under review were not deemed to restrict competition by object, as the supermarket was not in competition with the owners of the shopping centres with which it had concluded these agreements. Then, the CJEU made clear that, in order to find an anti-competitive effect, the conditions of the relevant market had to be assessed. This entails, of course, that at first a definition of the relevant market should be made. Furthermore, it was of importance to have regard to the number and the size of the operators present on this market, as well as the degree of concentration of that market, customer fidelity to existing brands and consumer habits. Only after a thorough analysis of the economic and legal context of the agreements under review it is possible to find that access to the relevant market is made difficult and that foreclosure effects occur.[60] In other words, analysing the effects of an agreement is definitely not an easy matter but, on the contrary, requires extensive and sound research. In EU competition law the importance of the economic approach has increased during the last 20 years.[61] As a result, proving that (actual or potential) effects may be caused by an agreement is a demanding (and hopefully rewarding) operation.

In sum, it could be argued that, although suggested both in the wording of Article 101(1) TFEU and in the case-law, no sharp divide exists between restrictions by object and by effect. In our view, this is apparent from the emphasis put by the CJEU on the economic and legal context of the agreement under review.[62] Contractual clauses should not be considered in isolation, but rather be reviewed in close relation to the circumstances under which they are concluded and implemented. A sound understanding of the market conditions, the relevant (EU and national) laws and other factors is indispensable for reaching a well-founded decision. For example, price recommendations issued by an association of undertakings may have a different impact on a highly concentrated market, on which homogenous products are offered, than on a market on which a great number of players operate, as well as sophisticated and divergent services are supplied. At least, making an appreciation of the possible effects that could occur is inevitable. Applying the cartel prohibition to contractual clauses without understanding the market(s), to which these clauses relate, could lead to problematic

---

[58] Case C-345/14 SIA 'Maxima Latvija', ECLI:EU:C:2015:784, par. 30.

[59] Case C-307/18 Generics and GlaxoSmithKline, ECLI:EU:C:2020:52, par 120.

[60] Case C-345/14 SIA 'Maxima Latvija', ECLI:EU:C:2015:784, par. 29.

[61] Niels, Jenkins and Kavanagh 2016, p. 4.

[62] Cf. Murray 2015, pp. 48–9.

outcomes: welfare-enhancing agreements may be forbidden or harmful agreements may be permitted.

To our mind, the object-effect dichotomy is in fact a 'gliding scale', which means that the burden of proof is higher for restrictions by effect than for restrictions by object. In the event that an agreement having the object of restricting competition – in other words, a practice that reveals a sufficient degree of harm to competition – is reviewed, the negative effects are likely to occur and, accordingly, are not (very) difficult to prove. In the event that an agreement may have adverse effects on competition, experience has taught us that the occurrence of negative effects is not self-evident, which warrants an in-depth and comprehensive analysis of those effects.

2.2.2 Appreciability

It is settled case-law that anti-competitive agreements are caught by Article 101(1) TFEU, in so far as they lead to appreciable restrictions. Appreciability is a constituent element for finding an infringement of the cartel prohibition.[63] Minor distortions of competition are immune from Article 101(1) TFEU, as their impact on the market is negligible. This raises the question how this requirement relates to the object-effect dichotomy. To what extent is it possible to assess the level of the effects caused by a restriction by object? After all, according to the settled case-law of the CJEU, there is no need to analyse the concrete effects of a restriction by object.

Strikingly, the CJEU addressed this question for the first time in *Expedia*,[64] a judgment that was handed down in 2012. Here, the CJEU emphasised the distinction between restrictions by object and effect. It recalled that no concrete effects had to be analysed in the event of an anti-competitive object. For that reason, the CJEU ruled that such agreements (i.e. object restrictions) are deemed to constitute an appreciable restriction on competition.[65] Once the anti-competitive object is established, the appreciability of the clause under review is given.

Consequently, appreciability is only an issue for agreements that may have an adverse effect on competition. The Commission has adopted the Notice on Agreements of Minor Importance,[66] in order to give guidance with respect to this issue. In this Notice, which is also known as the *De Minimis* Notice, a distinction is made between vertical agreements and horizontal agreements. Vertical agreements are treated more favourably than horizontal agreements. This does not come as a surprise, as parties to a vertical agreement are, as a rule, not in competition with each other, whereas parties to a horizontal agreement usually compete with each other.

According to the *De Minimis* Notice 2014, an agreement is deemed not to restrict competition appreciably if the aggregate market share of the parties concerned does not exceed 10 per cent in the event that this agreement is concluded between undertakings, which are

---

[63] E.g. cases 5/69 *Völk/Vervaecke*, ECLI:EU:C:1969:35; C-286/13 P *Dole Food Company*, ECLI:EU:C:2015:184, par. 116; C-345/14 *SIA 'Maxima Latvija'*, ECLI:EU:C:2015:784, par. 17.

[64] Case C-226/11 *Expedia*, ECLI:EU:C:2012:795.

[65] Ibid, par. 37.

[66] *De Minimis* Notice 2014.

actual or potential competitors.[67] Such agreements are normally of horizontal nature. In the event that an agreement is concluded by undertakings, which are not actual or potential competitors, the threshold of the market share is set at 15 per cent, held by each party.[68] Such agreements are normally of vertical nature.[69] Accordingly, the *De Minimis* Notice 2014 leaves more room for concluding vertical agreements than horizontal agreements for the following two reasons. The threshold for vertical restraints is higher than for horizontal restraints (15 per cent respectively 10 per cent) and, what is more important, the starting point for vertical agreements is the market share of each individual undertaking, whereas the market shares of all parties concerned must be taken together with regard to horizontal agreements. If, for example, the parties to a vertical agreement each have a market share of approximately 10 per cent, the threshold of the Notice is not exceeded, whereas this Notice does not apply if, for instance, the parties to a horizontal agreement each hold a market share of 7 per cent.

From the foregoing, it is apparent that the relevant market must be defined in order to apply the *De Minimis* Notice 2014. This is, in our view, not surprising, as in general this market has also to be defined in order to find concrete effects of the restrictive practices concerned. It must be borne in mind that appreciability is only an issue for agreements having the effect of restricting competition. For the same reason, it is specifically put forward that the *De Minimis* Notice 2014 does not apply to agreements having the object of restricting competition.[70] The appreciability of these agreements is, as already discussed, given according to the *Expedia* ruling of the CJEU.

It should be noted that the sole reason of exceeding the thresholds set out in the *De Minimis* Notice 2014 does not automatically entail that the practice under review is anti-competitive. It is required that this practice must be examined closely in order to find negative effects.

2.2.3 Rule of Reason in Article 101(1) TFEU?

In US antitrust law the concept of the Rule of Reason plays an important role. According to this concept, as stated above, it must be examined whether the pro-competitive effects of an agreement outweigh its anti-competitive effects.[71] If so, the agreement is regarded to be compatible with the Sherman Act. If not, this agreement is considered to be unlawful.[72] The question was raised as to whether a Rule of Reason approach is in place also in EU competition law. In its judgment in the *Métropole Television* case,[73] the GC answered this question in the negative. It should be pointed out that in US antitrust law the most serious anti-competitive practices, such as horizontal price fixing, are condemned on the basis of the

---

[67] Ibid, par. 8(a).

[68] Ibid, par. 8(b).

[69] Cumulative effects may occur for parallel networks of agreements having similar effects. In those circumstances the threshold of the market share is reduced to 5 per cent. See *De Minimis* Notice 2014, par. 10.

[70] *De Minimis* Notice 2014, par. 2.

[71] Case *Standard Oil Co of New Jersey*, (1911) 221 US 1.

[72] E.g. Hovenkamp 2008, pp. 105–8; Wesseling 2000, pp. 101–5.

[73] Case T-112/99 *Métropole Television*, ECLI:EU:T:2001:215.

so-called per se rule.[74] This means that they are not permitted irrespective of their possible beneficial effects. Other practices are assessed under the Rule of Reason. The setup of the EU rules on anti-competitive agreements is different, as all types of restrictive practices, including the restrictions by object, are assessed under Article 101(1) TFEU and, what is more important, are also reviewed under the exception laid down in Article 101(3) TFEU. Accordingly, the (possible) anti-competitive effects of an agreement must be considered under Article 101(1) TFEU, whereas the (possible) beneficial effects, including the pro-competitive effects, must be taken into account under Article 101(3) TFEU. Consequently, in *Métropole Television* the GC held that the positive effects of an agreement on competition must be accommodated in an assessment based on Article 101(3) TFEU. This point of view has been confirmed by the CJEU in *Generics and GlaxoSmithKline*.[75]

In *Wouters*,[76] however, the CJEU contended that some restrictions of competition are inherent in the pursuit of objectives connected with professional ethics. At issue was a ban for lawyers on setting up a partnership with accountants, issued by the Dutch Bar Association (which qualified as an association of undertakings under EU competition law). Although, this ban gave rise to some restraints of competition, the CJEU ruled that it was not in violation of the cartel prohibition enshrined in Article 101(1) TFEU, as its aim was to avoid conflicts of interests. A lawyer is supposed to act in the interest of her/his client, whereas an accountant has to undertake an objective examination of the accounts of a firm.[77] The approach adopted by the CJEU led to the finding that the cartel prohibition was not infringed upon. The following conditions had to be satisfied in this respect: the objectives to be achieved must be connected with professional ethics, the restrictive effects have to be inherent in the pursuit of these objectives, and must not go beyond what is necessary to achieve those objectives.[78]

In subsequent case-law, the CJEU applied the doctrine developed in *Wouters* to anti-doping rules of a sports association,[79] to rules on permanent education adopted by an association for accountants,[80] to rules adopted by a professional body for geologists[81] and to provisions dealing with the amount of minimum costs determined by a body representing transport companies.[82] Given these developments and also against the background of the *ONP* case,[83] in which the GC reviewed practices of pharmacists in the light of the *Wouters* doctrine, it could be argued that this doctrine is now well-established in EU competition law.

Strikingly, some of the cases did not concern professional ethics but the pursuit of other objectives, such as combatting doping in sports and road safety. It is apparent from these

---

[74] E.g. Nagy 2013, pp. 93–101.

[75] Case C-307/18 *Generics and GlaxoSmithKline*, ECLI:EU:C:2020:52, par. 104.

[76] Case C-309/99 *Wouters*, ECLI:EU:C:2002:98.

[77] Ibid, par. 100–107.

[78] Ibid, par. 97, 109.

[79] Case C-519/04 P *Meca-Medina*, ECLI:EU:C:2006:492.

[80] Case C-1/12 *OTOC*, ECLI:EU:C:2013:127.

[81] Case C-136/12 *Consiglio nazionale dei geologi*, ECLI:EU:C:2013:489.

[82] Joined cases C-184 to 187, C-194, C-1953 and C-208/13 *API*, ECLI:EU:C:2014:2147.

[83] Case T-90/11 *ONP*, ECLI:EU:T:2014:1049.

cases that the *Wouters* approach is also relevant for matters falling outside the scope of liberal professions. It cannot be excluded that the CJEU is developing a doctrine geared towards justifying restrictive practices for public interest reasons under Article 101(1) TFEU. This doctrine could constitute an *EU-style Rule of Reason*, which is, in contrast with the *US-style Rule of Reason*, concerned with balancing competition and public interest goals. If the public interest goals outweigh the aims connected to undistorted competition, the cartel prohibition laid down in Article 101(1) TFEU is not violated.[84]

The conditions to be fulfilled are that the interest at issue is of a public (and non-economic) nature and that the competition restrictions do not go beyond what is necessary to fulfil that interest. It remains to be seen whether the requirement that the practice is inherent must also be satisfied, as this requirement is – on first sight – closely connected with the professional ethics of liberal professions. Without the restrictions being inherent to the provision of professional services, conflicts of interests may occur. This market failure does not necessarily play a role in other markets. All in all, more case-law is needed in order to clarify in which types of cases the EU-style Rule of Reason can be applied. In particular, more light should be shed on the question which public interests may be accommodated in this Rule of Reason.

In this regard it should also be pointed out that the Corona crisis of 2020 and the position adopted by the Commission following this crisis are of great relevance. Due to shortage of essential products and services, more in particular medicines, medical equipment and medical devices, many undertakings were compelled to cooperate. In the Temporary Framework dealing with this challenge,[85] the Commission set out under which circumstances cooperation projects aimed at addressing the shortage of essential products and services were permitted under Article 101 TFEU. This action was supported by a Joint Statement by the ECN.[86] In the Commission's view, projects amounting to, for example, joint transport for input materials or to identification of essential medicines for which there are risks of shortages are not likely to give rise to antitrust concerns, provided that these projects are subject to safeguards, such as no flow of individualised company information to competitors.[87] Moreover, the measures to be taken may even lead to exchange of commercially sensitive information. Under normal circumstances, this is forbidden under the EU antitrust rules. However, in the wake of the Corona crisis the Commission has put forward that such an exchange of information is permitted, provided that: (1) it is designed and objectively necessary to address the shortages of the essential products and services; (2) it is temporary in nature; and (3) it does not go beyond what is necessary.[88] As the Commission notes that in these circumstances no problems with EU competition law occur or that at least no enforcement action will be taken,[89] the question is left open whether given the public interests at stake the restrictive practices concerned are

---

[84] Townley 2009, p. 65.

[85] Temporary Framework 2020.

[86] ECN Joint Statement 2020.

[87] Temporary Framework 2020, par. 12–13.

[88] Ibid, par. 15.

[89] Ibid.

justifiable, for instance, on the basis of an EU-style Rule of Reason type of reasoning. In any event, the response of the Commission to the Corona crisis has revealed that competition law should allow for balancing the competition goals and the public interest objective of ensuring access for all to particular essential products and services. From the foregoing, it is clear that discussions on *Wouters* and the EU-style Rule of Reason will continue to occur.

2.3 Impact on the trade between the Member States

The third condition for the application of Article 101(1) TFEU is that the trade between the Member States is influenced. The rationale of this requirement is that the said Treaty provision only applies to practices that matter from an EU perspective. If the effects of a contract are limited to the domestic market of a Member State, it would not make sense to subject this contract to EU competition law. In these circumstances, it is up to the Member States to determine whether such a contract must be condemned under national competition law.

2.3.1 General observations

It is settled case-law of the CJEU that the condition of the effect on the trade between the Member States is not only met in the event of an actual effect on this trade, but is also satisfied if a potential effect is identified.[90] If the pattern of trade between the Member States could be changed, the applicability of Article 101(1) TFEU is triggered. Many practices of undertakings are capable of being caught by the condition of intra-Union trade. It goes without saying that this is the case, if an agreement is concluded between firms operating in various Member States and supplying products or services in these states. It should be pointed out that the trade between the Member States could also be influenced if a particular practice, such as an agreement, only covers the territory of one country. If such a practice leads to an obstacle for companies based in other Member States for entering the national market concerned, a potential effect can be identified. In that event, it is difficult for foreign companies to penetrate that national market.[91] Especially in the case of hardcore restrictions, such as price fixing and market sharing, the problem is that compartmentalisation of markets on a national basis could be reinforced, which runs counter to the Single Market imperative.[92] A vertical agreement between a supplier and its customer in one Member State could trigger the applicability of EU competition law if this agreement is part of a network of similar contracts concluded by the supplier (or customer) with other undertakings. This may give rise to a cumulative effect, which justifies the applicability of Article 101(1) TFEU.[93] If, for example, a beer brewer concludes an agreement with pubs for supplying beer under the same conditions, the cumulative effects resulting from this commercial policy may lead to, at least, a potential effect on the trade between the Member States, even if all the parties concerned operate in one jurisdiction.

---

[90] E.g. joined cases 56 and 58/64 *Grundig/Consten*, ECLI:EU:C:1966:41.

[91] Case 8/72 *Vereeniging van Cementhandelaren*, ECLI:EU:C:1972:84.

[92] Ibid, par. 29.

[93] Cases 23/67 *Brasserie De Haecht*, ECLI:EU:C:1967:54; C-234/89 *Delimitis*, ECLI:EU:C:1991:91.

2.3.2 Extraterritorial scope

Furthermore, as was pointed out in Chapter 2, it is apparent from the case-law of the CJEU that even undertakings based in third countries could conclude agreements impacting the trade between the Member States. In *Wood Pulp*, for example, the CJEU held that, in establishing the applicability of Article 101(1) TFEU, the decisive factor is the place where the agreement under review is implemented.[94] Consequently, if the effects caused by an agreement, concerted practice or decision of association of undertakings occur in the EU, Article 101(1) TFEU applies. Even if the parties to a contract are situated in countries outside the EU, this provision constitutes, nevertheless, the legal framework for review, if this contract is operative in the territory of the EU Internal Market.[95] Also, in *Intel*, the CJEU found that the practices of this enterprise based in the US were caught by EU competition law, as their impact on the EU Internal Market was substantial, immediate and foreseeable.[96] In Chapter 2, the extraterritorial scope of EU competition law was discussed.

The extraterritorial dimension of Article 101 TFEU is an important feature of EU competition law, especially with regard to Brexit. It may be assumed that many enterprises established in the UK will continue to be engaged in business in the EU Internal Market. These UK companies will be subject to Article 101(1) TFEU and, accordingly, their commercial policies must be compatible with this Treaty provision. For that reason, the Commission will continue to exercise its jurisdiction on agreements that are concluded by UK companies and which affect competition in the EU Internal Market.[97] In this regard, it must be noted that the UK competition authority, the CMA, will no longer have the authority to apply the Treaty provisions on competition after Brexit. However, pursuant to Section 60A of the UK Competition Act 1998, it is bound by the obligation to ensure that no inconsistency with the pre-Brexit EU competition rules occur, when interpreting UK competition law; in particular circumstances, however, derogations from this obligation are permitted.[98]

2.3.3 The Guidelines on the Effect on Trade

With regard to the condition of the effect on the trade between the Member States, the Commission has issued specific Guidelines.[99] The aim of these Guidelines is to codify the case-law of the CJEU on this matter. The Commission has identified three elements that must be addressed: the concept of 'trade between the Member States', the notion of 'may affect' and the concept of 'appreciability'.[100] When it comes to the first element, the Commission stresses that all cross-border activity, such as the exchange of goods and services across borders as well as cross-border establishment, is covered.[101] The element of 'may affect' requires that it

---

[94] Joined cases 89, 104, 114, 116, 117 and 125 to 129/85 *Wood Pulp*, ECLI:EU:C:1988:447, par. 16.

[95] Case 22/71 *Béguelin*, ECLI:EU:C:1971:113, par. 11.

[96] Case C-413/14 *Intel*, ECLI:EU:C:2017:632, par. 40–65.

[97] Brexit Notice 2019.

[98] Brexit Guidance 2018.

[99] Guidelines on Effect on Trade 2004.

[100] Ibid, par. 18.

[101] Ibid, par. 19.

is possible to foresee with a sufficient degree of probability on the basis of objective factors that the agreement or practice concerned has some influence on the pattern of trade between the Member States.[102] As a potential effect already triggers the applicability of Article 101(1) TFEU, it will suffice to examine whether this agreement or practice is capable of influencing the trade pattern.[103] The third element is related to appreciability. It is settled case-law that an appreciable effect is required for establishing an effect on the trade between the Member States.[104] Accordingly, this requirement plays a role both in finding an adverse effect on competition and an impact on the intra-Union trade. It was already put forward that the Commission has adopted the *De Minimis* Notice 2014 for determining an appreciable competition effect. In the same vein, the Commission has laid down rules for establishing an appreciable effect on the trade between the Member States. The approach adopted comes down to a quantification of such an effect. It is specifically pointed out that the aim is to indicate when trade is normally not capable of being appreciably affected.[105] In other words, quantitative criteria indicate when an appreciable effect on the trade between the Member States is likely to be absent. It is not possible to draft quantitative rules that capture all agreements and practices having an appreciable effect.[106] Consequently, agreements and practices not falling within the scope of the quantitative rules of the Guidelines are not deemed to have such an effect. A separate analysis of the effects caused must be carried out before arriving at this conclusion.[107]

The quantitative criteria for not finding an appreciable effect developed by the Commission are as follows: (1) the aggregate market share of the parties in any relevant market within the EU, affected by the agreement, does not exceed 5 per cent; and (2) in the case of horizontal agreements, the aggregate annual Union turnover of the undertakings concerned does not exceed 40 million EUR, while in the case of vertical agreements the threshold is 40 million EUR of the annual turnover of the supplier.[108] It should be noted that these criteria apply both to hardcore restrictions and other restrictive practices. This stands in sharp contrast with the *De Minimis* Notice 2014 for competition restrictions, which does not cover restrictions by object. In our view, this difference is not surprising, as the main function of the condition of the effect on intra-Union trade is establishing whether an agreement or practice falls with the scope of Article 101(1) TFEU. In fact, the main question is whether the impact of the conduct under review matters from an EU perspective. In essence, this is a neutral assessment, the outcome of which does not reveal whether this conduct is acceptable or not. As a result, extending the scope of the rules for appreciable effect on the trade between the Member States to hardcore restrictions is not problematic.

---

[102] Ibid, par. 23.

[103] Ibid.

[104] E.g. cases 5/69 *Völk/Vervaecke*, ECLI:EU:C:1969:35; C-306/96 *Javico*, ECLI:EU:C:1998:173.

[105] Guidelines on Effect on Trade 2004, par. 50.

[106] Ibid.

[107] Ibid, par. 51.

[108] Ibid, par. 52, which also contains more refined criteria for specific agreements and practices.

3 THE EXCEPTIONS TO THE CARTEL PROHIBITION

Restrictive agreements and practices could be justified on the basis of exceptions available in competition law. Three exceptions should be distinguished. The first group is laid down in Block Exemptions. These exemptions contain a carve-out for certain categories of agreements and practices restricting competition. In advance, it is set out that these agreements, even if they are restrictive, are permitted under Article 101 TFEU. The second exception is laid down in Article 101(3) TFEU, which is designed as a legal exception since the entry into force of Regulation 1/2003. In the past (before this piece of EU legislation came into force), the Commission had the sole power to exempt an agreement on the basis of the criteria of Article 101(3) TFEU. However, since 1 May 2004 this Treaty provision can be applied not only by the Commission, but also by the domestic authorities. As a result, this provision has direct effect and undertakings alleged of having violated the cartel prohibition may rely on it. The third exception can be found in Article 106(2) TFEU and concerns Services of General Economic Interest. As this matter is closely related to the theme of state and competition, Article 106(2) TFEU will be discussed in Chapter 11. In what follows, attention will be paid to the Block Exemptions and Article 101(3) TFEU.

3.1 The Block Exemptions

An important function of Block Exemptions is to facilitate the decentralised application of Article 101 TFEU. If an agreement satisfies the conditions of a Block Exemption, it is clear from the outset that it is justified. Moreover, it is even not necessary to assess whether this agreement is in violation of the cartel prohibition, as in any case it will be permitted. An important advantage of Block Exemptions is, furthermore, that they provide legal certainty to the undertakings. In EU competition law the Block Exemptions are laid in regulations. These pieces of EU legislation are directly applicable pursuant to Article 288 TFEU and can, accordingly, be relied upon by undertakings. The regulations containing the Block Exemptions are adopted by the European Commission, which is enabled to do so by the Council in, for example, Regulation 19/65 and Regulation 2821/71.

A Block Exemption specifies which categories of agreements are exempted from the prohibition laid down in Article 101(1) TFEU. It goes without saying that the special features that the agreement concerned must have are lined out. Furthermore, as a rule, the Block Exemptions also contain market share thresholds, in excess of which the exemption does not apply. Moreover, specific clauses are banned in Block Exemptions. Such clauses are referred to as 'black list' and 'grey list' clauses. If such a clause is inserted in an agreement, the exemption does not apply. In the event a clause is black-listed, the entire agreement does not benefit from the exemption, which means that all provisions of this agreement must be reviewed in the light of Article 101 TFEU. In the event that a clause is grey-listed, only this clause (if severable from the agreement itself) falls outside the scope of the Block Exemption, which means that other provisions may still benefit from the exemption. The clause not being exempted must be reviewed under Article 101 TFEU. In the past, Block Exemptions also contained 'white list' clauses, stipulating which types of clauses had to be included in an agreement in order to be exempted.[109] The criticism was that this method led to a 'straight jacket' for companies and did not leave sufficient room for manoeuvre. Consequently, the current Block Exemptions do not contain any white list clauses. The Commission, when enacting Block Exemptions, confines itself to stipulating what must not be inserted in a contract and does not set out how a contract must be drafted.

It cannot be excluded that particular agreements that are exempted have serious and adverse effects on competition. In that case, it is not appropriate that these agreements benefit from the Block Exemption. Article 29(1) of Regulation 1/2003 specifically provides that in these circumstances the Commission has the power to withdraw the benefit of the Block Exemption concerned. If it finds that the agreement under review has effects incompatible with Article 101(3) TFEU, the Commission may adopt an official decision stating that the Block Exemption does not apply to this agreement anymore. According to Article 29(2) of Regulation 1/2003 the national competition authority of an EU Member State has the same powers in respect of the territory of its jurisdiction.

The Commission has adopted various Block Exemptions.[110] In legal practice the exemption dealing with vertical restraints and those concerning two specific types of horizontal contracts, that is, specialisation agreements and R&D agreements, are of great interest. These exemptions will be discussed below.

3.1.1 Block Exemption for vertical restraints

The Commission has based its policy for vertical agreements, which is set out in the Guidelines on Vertical Restraints 2010, on an economic approach. The point of departure is that vertical agreements lead to economic efficiencies and are beneficial for the economy. For example, such agreements are capable of addressing 'free rider' problems. An official dealer of a product may be assigned a territory for selling the products of a specific supplier in order to give this dealer the possibility to invest in promotional activities without being confronted by other companies selling the same contract products and free riding on its promotion.[111]

3.1.1.1 Market power

At the heart of the Commission's approach is the distinction between *inter-brand* competition and *intra-brand* competition.[112] Inter-brand competition relates to competition between suppliers of various brands, whereas intra-brand competition concerns competition within one brand (an example of which is the competition occurring when retailers resell products of the same brand to end users). As long as inter-brand competition is at an adequate level, restraints of intra-brand competition are not deemed to be harmful. Many vertical agreements could have some restrictive effects on intra-brand competition, but as long as there is sufficient inter-brand competition this is not a problem. In that case, consumers and other

---

[109] Jones, Sufrin and Dunne 2019, p. 785.

[110] The Block Exemptions that are currently in force may be found at <http://ec.europa.eu/competition/antitrust/legislation/legislation.html> accessed 23 June 2020.

[111] Guidelines on Vertical Restraints 2010, par. 63.

[112] Ibid, par. 6 *et seq.*

buyers have the possibility to switch to other brands. If, for instance, a supplier of perfumes introduces restrictions regarding its products, the consumer can decide to purchase another brand of perfume, provided that other brands are available on the market. In contrast, if inter-brand competition is not at an adequate level, intra-brand competition does matter. In those circumstances, agreements restraining intra-brand competition can be harmful, as consumers and other buyers cannot switch to alternative products. In other words, in the event that the supplier has some market power, the vertical agreements this company concludes may give rise to competition concerns.

In fact, the Block Exemption for vertical restraints adopted by the Commission comes down to exempting vertical agreements, as long as the parties concerned do not have market power.[113] Market power is framed as a particular percentage of the market share held by these parties. Pursuant to Article 2(1) of Regulation 330/2010,[114] vertical agreements may benefit from the exemption if neither of the parties have a market share on the relevant market in excess of 30 per cent. Accordingly, the threshold for the applicability of the Block Exemption is 30 per cent of the relevant market. It should be noted that this is true for both the supplier and the buyer. The Regulation for vertical restraints preceding the one that is now in force was only concerned with the market share of the supplier and did, therefore, not address buying power.[115] This approach has been changed by the entering into force of Regulation 330/2010. This seems reasonable, since it goes without saying that, for example, some super-markets are able to exercise market power over their suppliers, when buying products such as bread and milk.

All in all, the first condition for the applicability of the exemption contained in Regulation 330/2010 is that neither the supplier nor the buyer have a market share on the relevant market exceeding 30 per cent. The second and third conditions relate to the clauses inserted in the vertical agreement concerned. Some clauses may be black-listed, whereas other clauses may be grey-listed.

3.1.1.2 Black-listed clauses

The second condition concerns the clauses on the black list. Article 4 of Regulation 330/2010 provides that such clauses contain hardcore restrictions and may, for that reason, not be included in an agreement. Pursuant to Article 4(a) of this Regulation, fixed and minimum resale prices are not permitted. It is not allowed to restrict the buyer's ability to determine its resale price. Nevertheless, it is specifically set out that the parties are allowed to agree upon maximum or recommended resale prices. It should be noted that contract provisions containing maximum or recommended prices ought not to be enforced in such a way that in fact they come down to a fixed or minimum price. For example, a supplier must refrain from taking action if a retailer resells the contract products below the recommended price. It goes

---

[113] When writing this book, the Commission was in the midst of a process of evaluating this Block Exemption. See Consultation Strategy for the Evaluation of the Vertical Block Exemption Regulation, available at <http://ec.europa.eu/competition/consultations/2018_vber/consultation_strategy.pdf> accessed 23 June 2020.

[114] Vertical Block Exemption Regulation 2010.

[115] Vertical Block Exemption Regulation 1999, Article 3(1).

without saying that forcing resellers to observe recommended prices comes down to applying fixed or minimum prices.

In this respect, it must be noted that according to some economic theories, vertical price restrictions, such as resale price maintenance, could lead to efficiencies, such as preventing 'free rider' problems for products the marketing of which is based on pre-sale services (vertical price fixing ensures that these services can be financed from the gains resulting from prices on a higher level).[116] In other words, it is believed that resale price maintenance may not go to the detriment of inter-brand competition and could even stimulate it. In the US, these theories have inspired the Supreme Court to hand down the *Leegin* judgment,[117] according to which resale price maintenance is not automatically banned but subject to the (US-style) Rule of Reason.[118] This means that the positive and negative effects must be balanced in order to find out whether the resale price maintenance system under review is harmful for competition.[119] In EU competition law the stance towards vertical price fixing (being minimum vertical prices and fixed vertical prices) remains hostile and therefore these practices are still on the black list. In the view of the Commission, such practices may, inter alia, facilitate collusion between suppliers and also between distributors (the buyers reselling the products concerned), by enhancing price transparency on the market, and may soften competition between manufacturers and also between retailers.[120] In our view, it may be expected that these divided views on both sides of the Atlantic will continue to give rise to debates.

The aim of Article 4(b) of Regulation 330/2010 is to prevent the parties to a vertical agreement from restricting parallel trade. Therefore, according to this provision, the territory into which, or of the customers to whom, the buyer may sell the contract products may not be restricted. In other words, absolute territorial protection is not allowed. This is compatible with the long-established idea of the Single Market imperative in EU competition law. In one of its oldest judgments, *Grundig/Consten*,[121] the CJEU held that parallel trade greatly contributes to the establishment of the Single European Market and, accordingly, practices partitioning this market run counter to the Treaty provisions on competition. However, the approach adopted in Regulation 330/2010 is sophisticated, since it accommodates 'free rider' concerns. The benefit of allocating, for example, a particular territory to an official dealer is that action will be taken and investments will be made for launching a new product in that territory. In that event, other traders are prevented from making use of these efforts, entering the markets and reselling the contract goods without incurring costs in connection with the introduction of a new product. From an economic point of view, it makes sense that some protection is offered by the supplier to a buyer being prepared to market its products and taking risks inherent to this marketing. For that reason, the ban on *active* sales is not

---

[116] Van den Bergh, Camesasca and Giannaccari 2017, pp. 294–5, 247–60.

[117] Case *Leegin v PSKS*, (2007) 551 US 877.

[118] Elhauge and Geradin 2011, pp. 743–67; Van den Bergh, Camesasca and Giannaccari 2017, pp. 273–4.

[119] Nagy 2013, pp. 155–7.

[120] Guidelines on Vertical Restraints 2010, par. 224.

[121] Joined cases 56 and 58/64 *Grundig/Consten*, ECLI:EU:C:1966:41.

black-listed in Article 4(b)(i) of Regulation 330/2010. This means that a supplier is entitled to preclude a buyer from actively entering a territory, or approaching a customer group, reserved to another buyer. According to a ban on active sales, a buyer may not take the initiative to operate in the territories reserved to other resellers or to contact the consumer groups reserved to other buyers. However, a ban on *passive* sales is black-listed, which means that a buyer must not be precluded from reselling the contract products to a customer from a reserved territory or group who decides on his own initiative to approach the buyer concerned. In that event, the initiative is not taken by the buyer/reseller, but by the customer. A considerable disadvantage of a ban on passive sales is that it leads to partitioning of markets. It is not surprising that such bans are black-listed.

Next to bans on active sales other practices are also permitted according to Article 4(b) (ii), (iii) and (iv). The restriction of sales to end users by a wholesaler does not lead to the non-applicability of the Block Exemption. Another practice that is not on the black list is related to selective distribution. One of the core features of such a system is that the contract products are only resold to end users by traders satisfying special conditions. Against this backdrop it is not surprising that the black list does not cover the restriction of sales by the members of a selective distribution system to unauthorised distributors within the territory reserved by the supplier concerned. Furthermore, it is permitted for a supplier to prohibit a buyer from reselling components to customers who will incorporate these components in a product that will compete with a product of the supplier.

Article 4(c) of Regulation 330/2010 also deals with selective distribution systems. A retailer that is a member of such a system must have the possibility to sell the contract goods to all end users. Therefore, a restriction of active or passive sales to end users imposed on a retailer taking part in a system of selective distribution is black-listed. The aim of this is to guarantee the freedom of retailers to resell the contract products to the end users of their preference. It should be noted that the prohibition on operating out of an unauthorised place of establishment is not black-listed. To our view, this makes sense, as the main feature of selective distribution is that contract products are resold by traders satisfying specific conditions. These conditions include the establishment from which the products concerned are sold.

Nevertheless, in the Guidelines on Vertical Restraints 2010 it is set out that restrictions on the use of the internet for reselling products are not permitted.[122] Accordingly, provisions in vertical agreements precluding resellers making use of the internet are regarded as hardcore restrictions that are also black-listed.[123] In *Pierre Fabre*,[124] the CJEU also held that a ban on the use of the internet for distributing products is not permitted. At issue was a clause inserted in contracts concluded with pharmacists. According to this clause, pharmacists were precluded from reselling cosmetic products on the internet. The CJEU held that this practice was not compatible with Article 101(1) TFEU and did not fall within the ambit of the Block Exemption. The reason for this was that its object was to restrict passive sales to end users

---

[122] Guidelines on Vertical Restraints 2010, par. 56.

[123] Ibid.

[124] Case C-439/09 *Pierre Fabre*, ECLI:EU:C:2011:649.

wishing to purchase the contract goods online. In this respect, it should be pointed out that according to settled case-law of the CJEU,[125] selective distribution systems based on qualitative criteria are permitted, whereas the quantitative criteria are regarded as problematic.[126] It could be argued that an absolute ban on the use of internet amounts, in fact, to a quantitative criterion.

It must be noted that the EU rules for vertical restraints do not require that no provisions regulating the use of the internet may be inserted in vertical agreements. It is important that provisions containing specific obligations for selling on the internet are justified by the specific features of the contract products. As a result, criteria dealing with methods of online reselling may be acceptable, if, for example, the aim of these criteria is to preserve the luxurious image of the contract products.[127] Thus, in *Coty*,[128] the CJEU held that a clause precluding authorised dealers from using third-party platforms for online selling was not incompatible with EU competition law, provided that it did not go beyond what is necessary. Third-party platforms, such as Amazon and eBay, are operated by enterprises not being part of the selective distribution system concerned. Traders could make use of such platforms, which facilitates their online selling activities. However, it is clear from the outset that enterprises operating such platforms have not concluded an agreement with the supplier of the contract goods and are, therefore, not bound by the conditions of the selective distribution system concerned. Consequently, the CJEU decided that the restriction on the use of third-party platforms did not restrict competition if it was proportionate and was also not black-listed in the Block Exemption for vertical restraints. In this respect, it was of importance that the official dealers were entitled to resell the contract products on their own web shops, which entailed that the use of the internet for selling products was not made entirely impossible. The significant difference between *Coty* and *Pierre Fabre* is that in the former case no absolute ban on the use of the internet was in place, while in the latter case all online sales activities were not permitted.

Article 4(d) of Regulation 330/2010 again concerns selective distribution. Restrictions of cross-supplies between distributors within such a system (including those operating at different levels of trade) are black-listed. Such a clause may lead to partitioning the markets, which would have adverse effects on competition. It must be prevented that the traders of a selective distribution system are forced to purchase the contract goods exclusively from a given source.[129]

The last black-listed clause is set out in Article 4(e) of Regulation 330/2010. This practice is related to the sale of components by manufacturers to a buyer that incorporates those parts into its own products. The supplier may not be restricted to sell the components as spare parts to end users, as well as to independent repairers or other service providers. However,

---

[125] This case-law line started with the handing down of the judgment in case 26/76 *Metro I*, ECLI:EU:C:1977:167.

[126] Jones, Sufrin and Dunne 2019, pp. 777–8.

[127] Guidelines on Vertical Restraints 2010, par. 56.

[128] Case C-230/16 *Coty*, ECLI:EU:C:2017:941.

[129] See Guidelines on Vertical Restraints 2010, par. 58.

the original equipment manufacturer is allowed to require its own repair and service network to buy spare parts from it.[130]

Inserting a black-listed clause in an agreement has far-going consequences. The entire agreement does not benefit from the Block Exemption. In other words, not only the clause concerned but also the other provisions of this agreement are not exempted. The sanction on agreeing on black-listed clauses is serious. It must be noted that not satisfying the conditions of the Block Exemption does not suffice in itself to reach the conclusion that the cartel prohibition is violated. At first, the agreement must be reviewed under Article 101 TFEU, which entails both an assessment based under Article 101(1) TFEU (the ban on restrictive agreements) and Article 101(3) TFEU (the legal exception to be discussed below). However, it must be borne in mind that the clauses on the black list are regarded as hardcore restrictions. For that reason, the Commission has stated in the Guidelines on Vertical Restraints 2010 that these practices are presumed to restrict competition and that it may be expected that they are not justifiable under Article 101(3) TFEU.[131]

3.1.1.3 Grey-listed clauses

Pursuant to Article 5 of Regulation 330/2010 a couple of restrictions are grey-listed. The most important practice in this regard is the non-compete clause. According to such a clause a buyer is, for example, prohibited from manufacturing, purchasing, selling or reselling products or services that compete with the contract goods or services of the supplier. As already pointed out, vertical restraints may be able to address 'free rider' problems. It is clear from the outset that non-compete clauses are inserted in agreements in order to tackle these problems. A buyer may benefit from the reputation, expertise and knowledge of a supplier from which it purchases the contract products. After having terminated its commercial relationship with the supplier, the buyer could make (mis)use of the benefits of this relationship while selling competing products. Non-compete clauses address this problem and protect suppliers from these practices. However, the disadvantages will outweigh the advantages of a non-compete clause if the duration of this clause is too long, which is the case when entering the market will become very difficult. In Regulation 330/2010 the line is drawn at five years. Non-compete clauses in excess of five years are grey-listed pursuant to Article 5(1)(a) of Regulation 330/2010. Consequently, in order to benefit from the Block Exemption, the parties to a vertical agreement must not insert non-compete clauses the duration of which is longer than five years. It is allowed to agree that after termination of the contract the buyer will not sell competing products for a period of five years or shorter.

The other clauses of the grey list are set out in Article 5(1)(b) and (c). The restriction under (b) concerns the obligation causing the buyer, after the termination of the contract, not to manufacture, purchase, sell or resell goods and services and the restriction under (c) imposes on the members of a selective distribution system the obligation not to sell the brands of *particular* competing suppliers. As regards the last restriction, it is permitted that a selective

---

[130] Ibid, par. 59.

[131] Ibid, par. 47.

distribution system is combined with a non-compete obligation.[132] This obligation should, however, oblige the dealers not to resell competing brands in general. The point is that the ban to resell competing products must not target specific brands. The objective of this is that it must be avoided that various suppliers use the same selective distribution system in order to prevent one specific competitor or certain specific competitors from using outlets of this distribution system.[133]

The consequences of inserting grey-listed clauses in a contract is less serious than including black-listed clauses. The clause itself does not benefit from the exemption but it is not excluded that other provisions of the contract do. If the parties possess market shares below 30 per cent, these provisions are exempted. The restrictions mentioned in Article 5 of the Block Exemption must be assessed under Article 101 TFEU. As these restrictions do not amount to hardcore restrictions, the presumption of incompatibility with Article 101 TFEU does not apply. It depends on the market circumstances, the drafting of the contract, the details of the clause under review and its duration whether this Treaty provision is infringed.

3.1.1.4 Future developments

The Block Exemption on vertical restraints expires on 31 May 2022.[134] For that reason, the Commission has launched a review process in order to extend the validity of the current Regulation, or to adopt a new set of rules.[135] It is not surprising that the emergence of digital markets is one of the developments that must be paid due consideration to in this respect. Price transparency has increased due to the digitalisation of the markets and has enabled, strikingly, at the same time, consumers to find affordable products and companies to monitor prices and to coordinate them.[136] Furthermore, increased price competition may lead to benefits for consumers but also to disadvantages, if it affects quality and innovation.[137] A report, commissioned by the European Commission, has revealed that the Block Exemption on vertical restraints remains relevant, but that this piece of EU legislation does not sufficiently address the latest developments, such as online platforms.[138] It is clear that companies and customers increasingly make use of platforms, but that some 'brick and mortar' retailers responded to these developments with recourse to vertical restraints.[139] This is not surprising against the backdrop of the increasing competitive pressure on undertakings, which have been confronted with buyers being able to shop around both on the EU and the global markets.[140] In general, due to the developments in e-commerce the current EU rules for vertical

---

[132] Ibid, par. 69.

[133] Ibid.

[134] Vertical Block Exemption Regulation 2010, Article 10.

[135] See <https://ec.europa.eu/info/law/better-regulation/have-your-say/initiatives/1936-Evaluation-of-the-Vertical-Block-Exemption-Regulation> accessed 15 June 2020.

[136] E-Commerce Sector Inquiry 2017, par. 11, 13.

[137] Ibid, par. 12.

[138] Support Studies for the Evaluation of the VBER 2019, p. 143.

[139] E-Commerce Staff Working Document 2017, par. 23.

[140] Support Studies for the Evaluation of the VBER 2019, p. 144.

restraints have to be revisited and the lack of clear definitions and guidelines specifically dealing with online sales must be addressed.[141] It should be made clear which practices occurring on digital markets are permitted, and which are banned in EU competition law.

A noteworthy development in this respect are the co-called hub-and-spoke arrangements. Such arrangements can be characterised as any number of vertical exchanges or agreements between firms at one level of the supply chain (referred to as the spokes) and common trading partners on another level of the chain (the hub), leading to anti-competitive practices.[142] Such practices may, for instance, amount to price alignments. E-commerce platforms may facilitate hub-and-spoke arrangements by making use of price algorithms and pricing monitoring software.[143] Hub-and-spoke cartels could affect competition seriously and, for that reason, EU competition law must take action against these cartels. This example clarifies which challenges EU competition law has to meet.

All in all, it may be assumed that the review process of the EU rules for vertical restraints will lead to some important changes. However, it is not likely that the general Block Exemption will be abolished, as this exemption contributes greatly to legal certainty and, accordingly, reduces the costs of distribution trade practices considerably.[144] As a result, also in the future a Block Exemption dealing with vertical restraints will play an important role in European competition law.

3.1.2 Horizontal cooperation agreements

In EU competition law no general Block Exemption for horizontal agreements is in place. This is not a surprise, as such agreements are normally concluded between competitors operating on the same level of the market. Horizontal agreements are more prone to give rise to serious competition concerns than vertical agreements. Nevertheless, some horizontal agreements could also lead to efficiencies and, for that reason, Block Exemptions for specific forms of such agreements are adopted by the Commission. Below, the exemptions for specialisation agreements[145] and for R&D agreements[146] will be discussed. It should be noted that the Commission has adopted Guidelines that set out its policy regarding horizontal agreements.[147]

3.1.2.1 Block Exemption for specialisation agreements

In the view of the Commission, agreements on specialisation in the production or in the preparation of services are likely to contribute to the improvement of production or distribution, if the parties concerned have complementary skills, assets or activities.[148] The aim of

---

[141] Ibid.

[142] OECD 2019, p. 5.

[143] Ibid.

[144] Support Studies for the Evaluation of the VBER 2019, p. 147.

[145] Specialisation Agreements Block Exemption Regulation 2010.

[146] R&D Agreements Block Exemption Regulation 2010.

[147] Guidelines on Horizontal Agreements 2011.

[148] Specialisation Agreements Block Exemption Regulation 2010, Recital 6.

a specialisation agreement is that a particular undertaking or undertakings concentrate on supplying a specific product or service that will be purchased by other companies. Expertise and skills are bundled in one or a limited group of undertakings.

According to the Block Exemption three forms of specialisation agreements should be distinguished. In the event of a *unilateral specialisation agreement*, two parties operating on the same market agree that one of them ceases production of certain products in order to purchase these products from the other company, who has committed itself to producing and supplying the products concerned.[149] A *reciprocal specialisation agreement* is based on a mutual pattern of cooperation. Two or more parties active on the same market agree to cease production of certain, but different, products and to buy these products from the other party, who has, of course, promised to produce and supply the products concerned.[150] In other words, one party will stop production of a particular good and will be concerned with manufacturing another good, while the other party will purchase this good but also will produce and supply the product the first party had ceased production of. *Joint production agreement* means that the parties concerned produce certain products together.[151]

Pursuant to Article 3 of the Block Exemption, a specialisation agreement is exempted from the cartel prohibition of Article 101(1) TFEU, if the combined market share of the parties does not exceed 20 per cent on any relevant market. From this wording it is clear that the aggregate market shares of all undertakings party to the agreement must be taken into account. As in the Block Exemption for vertical agreements, market power is an important issue and the level of market shares is regarded as an appropriate yardstick in this regard.

Another important parallel between the Block Exemptions for vertical restraints and specialisation agreements is that particular practices are black-listed. Pursuant to Article 4 of Regulation 1218/2010, no safe harbours exist for price fixing, the limitation of output or sales and the allocation of markets or customers. The sanction for including such clauses in an agreement is that the entire agreement will not benefit from the Block Exemption.

With regard to the limitation of output or sales, it must be borne in mind that the parties concerned must make arrangements as to how many units of certain products have to be produced. A firm specialising in the production of a certain good should know how many units of this good will be purchased by the other party to the specialisation agreement. Accordingly, contract provisions dealing with the amount of products in the context of unilateral or reciprocal specialisation agreements or contract provisions dealing with the setting of the capacity and production volume in the context of joint contribution are not black-listed.[152] Moreover, the setting of sales targets in the context of joint distribution is also not on the black list.[153] In our view, it can be questioned whether sales targets, which in fact specify the ambitions of firms in terms of the amount of products to be sold on the market,

---

[149] Ibid, Article 1(1)(b).

[150] Ibid, Article 1(1)(c).

[151] Ibid, Article 1(1)(d).

[152] Ibid, Article 4(b)(i).

[153] Ibid, Article 4(b)(ii).

leads to a distortion of competition. Do contract provisions setting out these targets fall within the scope of Article 101(1) TFEU?

The Block Exemption for specialisation agreements does not contain a grey list. As a result, this exemption applies, if an agreement is geared towards specialisation of production, the market shares of the parties concerned are not in excess of 20 per cent and no black-listed clauses are included in this agreement.

3.1.2.2 Block Exemption for research and development agreements

It goes without saying that an agreement concluded in order to implement a R&D project could lead to efficiencies. For that reason, the Commission has adopted a Block Exemption for R&D agreements. The following conditions must be satisfied for this exemption to be applicable. First, the agreement at issue must be concerned with R&D. Second the implementation of the agreement is geared towards dissemination of the results of the project. Third, the market shares of the parties concerned must not exceed a particular threshold. Fourth, no clauses that are on the black and grey lists may be included.

As for the first condition, Article 1(1)(c) of Regulation 1217/2010 gives a rather broad definition of what is meant by R&D. These activities entail the acquisition of know-how relating to products, technologies or processes, as well as the carrying out of theoretical analysis, systematic study or experimentation. In our view a great range of projects could fall within the scope of this definition.

The second condition, which takes the dissemination of results as the point of departure, is specific to R&D agreements. Access to the results obtained is a very significant requirement for the Commission. Every party must have full access to the results, as soon as they become available, for the purpose of further R&D and also for exploitation. However, academic institutions, such as universities, being part of the project concerned may confine the use of the results to purposes of further research.

The third condition is concerned with the market shares of the parties to the agreement. According to Article 4 of Regulation 1217/2010 a distinction must be made between agreements concluded by non-competing undertakings and agreements concluded by competing undertakings. In the first case, the exemption will apply for the entire duration of the project and the first seven years of the joint exploitation. After these seven years have elapsed, the exemption will continue to apply in so far as the combined market share of the firms concerned does not exceed the threshold of 25 per cent on the relevant product and technology markets. It is clear that the Block Exemption gives great room for manoeuvre for non-competing firms. In the second case, the combined market shares of the parties to the contract must not exceed 25 per cent of the relevant market for the duration of the R&D project. Moreover, joint exploitation of the results is permitted for seven years, again under the condition that the threshold of 25 per cent of the aggregate market shares of the parties concerned is not exceeded.

3.1.2.3 Future developments

Both the Specialisation Agreements Block Exemption Regulation 2010 and the R&D Agreements Block Exemption Regulation 2010 expire on 31 December 2022. The Commission launched a public consultation in order to find out whether the Block Exemptions, as well as the Guidelines on Horizontal Agreements 2011 should be revised.[154] It is apparent from the report[155] drafted by the Commission following this consultation that the EU rules for horizontal agreements have added value, as they have contributed to uniform application across the EU.[156] However, it was also put forward that major developments require that these rules are updated; references were made to climate change, digitalisation and globalisation.[157] Strikingly, it was argued in the public consultation that due to recent market developments and business realities, the EU rules for horizontal agreements do not provide sufficient legal certainty.[158] Against this backdrop it may be expected that, as with the EU policy for vertical restraints, the Block Exemptions and the Guidelines on Horizontal Agreements will continue to play a role in the future, but that updating these measures seems to be a sensible course of action.

3.2 Article 101(3) TFEU: the legal exception

Pursuant to Article 101(3) TFEU individual agreements distorting competition may be justifiable. On a case-by-case basis, it must be assessed whether the conditions outlined in this Treaty provision are satisfied. At the heart of the legal exception of Article 101(3) TFEU is the acknowledgement that efficiencies should be permitted, even in cases in which competition is distorted. Article 101(3) TFEU specifically provides that the improvement of production, distribution or innovation may lead to the conclusion that a restrictive practice is allowed. In its Guidelines on Article 101(3) TFEU, the Commission contends that this provision is relevant for restrictive agreements that 'generate objective benefits so as to outweigh the negative effects of the restriction of competition'.[159] The resemblance with US antitrust law is particularly evident. As already stated, in this jurisdiction the weighing of pro- and anti-competitive effects is important to find a violation of the Sherman Act (if the practice under review is subject to the Rule of Reason). A similar assessment must be carried out in a review under Article 101 TFEU. Nevertheless, it must be recalled that in EU competition law appreciation of the positive effects is accommodated in Article 101(3) TFEU. This difference in the setup of balancing of pro- and anti-competitive effects eventually boils down to a matter of the burden of proof. According to Article 2 of Regulation 1/2003, the burden of proving that Article 101(1) TFEU is violated rests with the authority or the party alleging an infringement, while the company claiming the benefits of Article 101(3) TFEU has the burden to prove that the conditions of this provision are fulfilled.[160]

---

[154] See <https://ec.europa.eu/info/law/better-regulation/have-your-say/initiatives/11886-Evaluation-of-EU-competition-rules-on-horizontal-agreements/public-consultation> accessed 16 June 2020.

[155] Factual Summary 2020.

[156] Ibid, pp. 20–21.

[157] Ibid, pp. 16–17.

[158] Ibid, pp. 6–7.

[159] Guidelines on Article 101(3) TFEU 2004, par. 33.

[160] Van Ginneken 2002, p. 82.

For Article 101(3) TFEU to be applicable, four cumulative conditions must be fulfilled:[161]

1. The agreement under review contributes to the improvement of production, distribution or innovation (referred to as technical and economic progress in Article 101(3) TFEU);
2. A fair share of the benefits is for the consumers;
3. The agreement is indispensable; and
4. Competition is not totally eliminated.

It is clear from the outset that these conditions leave room for interpretation and even for discretion. This is not surprising given the historical background of Article 101(3) TFEU. In the past, the Commission had the sole power to apply this provision. Undertakings claiming that their agreement led to efficiencies had to apply for prior authorisation from the Commission in order to rely on Article 101(3) TFEU. On 1 May 2004, however, Regulation 1/2003 entered into force, which brought about a significant change. According to Article 1 of this Regulation, Article 101(3) TFEU has direct effect. Before this change, the direct applicability of the Treaty provisions on competition was limited to Articles 101(1) and 102 TFEU. In its 1999 White Paper on the modernisation of competition law the Commission explained the rationale for turning Article 101(3) TFEU into a directly applicable provision. The Commission had to refocus its activities on combatting the most serious of violations of competition law.[162] A considerable part of its workload needed to be shifted to the national level. In this regard, it must be noted that before the entering into force of Regulation 1/2003, the Commission was forced to spend a lot of time on interpreting and applying Article 101(3) TFEU, activities which prevented it from taking action against hardcore restrictions. An administrative practice, coming down to sending an informal letter, called a 'comfort letter', which explained that the Commission saw no reason for taking action, was developed.[163] This practice was, however, not capable of relieving the Commission's workload sufficiently, due to the limited legal certainty generated by a 'comfort letter'.[164] Since the entry into force of Regulation 1/2003, Article 101(3) TFEU is directly applicable. This entails that undertakings are compelled to assess for themselves whether their arrangements satisfy the conditions set out by this Treaty provision. Although many competition law issues are clarified in the case-law of the Union courts, as well as in the decisional practice and soft-law documents of the Commission, undertakings may be faced with complicated questions and, accordingly, with a lack of legal certainty. Especially, in exceptional circumstances, this may be very problematic. It is, therefore, not surprising that in the wake of the Corona crisis of 2020 the Commission

---

[161] E.g. joined cases 56 and 58/64 *Grundig/Consten*, ECLI:EU:C:1966:41; case T-9/93 *Schöller Lebensmittel*, ECLI:EU:T:1995:99.

[162] Modernisation White Paper 1999, par. 42.

[163] Wesseling 2000, p. 84.

[164] Ibid.

announced that it was prepared to give ad hoc 'comfort letters' in order to give guidance to companies engaged in necessary cooperation projects.[165]

NCAs and domestic courts must interpret and apply Article 101(3) TFEU as from 1 May 2004. The discretionary wording of this provision may give rise to various interpretations. In order to prevent this, the Commission has issued Guidelines on Article 101(3) TFEU.[166] As already pointed out, according to these Guidelines, efficiencies play an important role. Two types of efficiencies are distinguished in the Guidelines, but it is stressed that these types are only examples and are not intended to be exhaustive.[167] The first type concerns cost efficiencies, which may result from the development of new technologies and methods as well as from economies of scale.[168] The second type stems from qualitative efficiencies, which may constitute the improvement of the quality of production or the improvement of the services rendered.[169] It is difficult to give clear examples of this type of efficiencies. It is clear from the outset that opinions may differ considerably as to whether a particular commercial practice has contributed to the enhancement of quality. As one of the other conditions for the applicability of Article 101(3) TFEU is related to the position of the consumer, it should be argued that at least the quality is improved from the perspective of the consumer.

As for the role of non-competition goals (such as environmental protection and health-care), the Guidelines contain an ambiguous statement in paragraph 42, which states that objectives pursued by other Treaty provisions can be taken into account to the extent that they can be subsumed under the four conditions of Article 101(3) TFEU. In our view, this means that public interest goals cannot serve as a separate head of justification. Whether such goals could play a role depends largely on the interpretation of the words 'improvement of production, distribution or innovation'. It goes without saying that this could give rise to (fierce) legal debates. The ambiguous statement on the role of non-competition goals in the Guidelines is somewhat at odds with the *CECED* Decision[170] of the Commission from 24 January 1999.[171] In this Decision the Commission accepted that a restrictive agreement that limited the manufacturing of washing machines to energy friendly products was justifiable under Article 101(3) TFEU, as environmental benefits were achieved by this practice. In our view, the need to realise environmental objectives served as a separate head of justification in *CECED*. It remains to be seen how the relationship between Article 101(3) TFEU and non-economic goals (such as environmental protection) will evolve. This development is of particular interest for cases in which restrictive agreements concluded in order to address climate change problems must be assessed.[172] Given the challenges the EU and the rest of the

---

[165] See Temporary Framework 2020, par. 5, 7, 18.

[166] See Guidelines on Article 101(3) TFEU 2004.

[167] Ibid, par. 63.

[168] Ibid, par. 64–8.

[169] Ibid, par. 69–72.

[170] See case IV.F.1/36.718 *CECED*, (2000) OJ L 187/47.

[171] Vedder 2003, pp. 433–4.

[172] Cf. Townley 2009, pp. 141–76.

world are facing, specific guidance on this relationship given by the Commission would be welcome.[173]

4 NATIONAL EXAMPLES OF THE CARTEL PROHIBITION

As outlined in Chapters 1 and 2, the national competition rules may be applied in parallel with the Treaty provisions on competition, as long as the requirements laid down in Regulation 1/2003 are met and the useful effect of the Treaty provisions is not jeopardised. As a rule, the EU Member States have in place competition laws laying down provisions on cartels. These provisions are modelled after the EU experience with Article 101 TFEU.

4.1 Germany

Germany has a long-standing tradition, when it comes to competition law. Its legislation dealing with competition is even older than the equivalent EU rules (EEC and ECSC) on competition. In the 1920s, Germany adopted Europe's first laws in order to protect competition and to control abuse.[174] In 1958 the Gesetz gegen Wettbewerbsbeschränkungen (GWB – Act against Restraints of Competition) entered into force, which sets out the competition rules for the German Federal Republic. In the past, German competition law used to have separate provisions dealing with horizontal and vertical agreements. In general terms, it prohibited horizontal agreements having the object or effect of restricting competition,[175] while there was only a ban on resale price maintenance in place for vertical agreements.[176] However, over time, the German legislator has decided to align its rules on restrictive agreements with Article 101 TFEU.[177]

Accordingly, pursuant to Section 1 of the current version of the GWB, agreements between undertakings, decisions by associations of undertakings and concerted practices which have as their object or effect the prevention, restriction or distortion of competition are prohibited. This drafting highly mirrors what is provided in Article 101(1) TFEU. As a result, the core cartel provision of German competition law does not make a distinction between horizontal and vertical agreements anymore.[178] Although EU law does not impose on the Member States

---

[173] Vedder 2003, p. 434.

[174] OECD – Germany 2005, pp. 10–11.

[175] OECD – Germany 2004, p. 13.

[176] See the old version of Section 14 GWB.

[177] The Siebtes Gesetz zur Änderung des Gesetzes gegen Wettbewerbbeschränkungen has amended the GWB in order to align this piece of national legislation with EU competition law. This alignment also plays a role in the Achtes Gesetz zur Änderung des Gesetzes gegen Wettbewerbbeschränkungen and Neuntes Gesetz zur Änderung des Gesetzes gegen Wettbewerbbeschränkungen.

[178] It goes without saying that in the policy measures and case-law dealing with Section 1 GWB this distinction may still matter, as it also does in EU competition law.

the obligation to shape their rules on cartels in accordance with Article 101(1) TFEU, the German legislator has decided to follow the European example.

Important concepts and approaches developed in EU competition law are therefore also of relevance for German competition law. As a result, practices such as horizontal price fixing are regarded as serious infringements of the competition rules. For example, firm action was taken by the German competition authority against five producers of ophthalmic lenses, as these enterprises had fixed prices and by doing so distorted competition for years.[179] Similarly, agreements on allocating customers or territories are regarded as illegal practices.[180] In German competition law, the distinction between restrictions by object and by effect is emphasised, as in the EU case-law. In line with CJEU judgments, such as *Cartes Bancaires*, it is put forward that particular collusion practices, such as price fixing, are deemed to be so harmful for competition that the concrete effects do not need to be analysed.[181] The cartel prohibition of Section 1 GWB is violated in so far as the restrictions identified are appreciable. In line with EU competition law, restrictions by object are deemed to have an appreciable effect.[182] As a result, appreciability is only an issue for restrictions by effect.

As in EU competition law, the German (judicial) authorities have been called upon to shed light on the application of the cartel prohibition to digital markets. In *ASICS*,[183] the Federal Court of Justice (Bundesgerichtshof) had to decide whether a general ban on the use of price engines on the internet laid down in a selective distribution agreement (between, in this case, a supplier and a retailer) was in violation of the EU and German rules on cartels. It held that such a ban amounted to a hardcore restriction, as it restricts passive sales to end-consumers.[184] Consequently, the cartel prohibition was infringed and the Block Exemption on vertical restraints did not apply. The reason for this finding was that the possibilities available on the internet were considerably restricted by the clause at stake, which clause was also not based on qualitative criteria.[185] More in particular, it was pointed out that in the event of the supply of a broad range of products on the internet, price comparison engines will be very beneficial for consumers in order to make a good selection.[186] In the view of the Federal Court, its ruling was not at odds with the *Coty* judgment,[187] in which the CJEU held that a clause prohibiting retailers from using third-party platforms did not amount to a hardcore restriction. An absolute ban on the use of price comparison engines restricts passive sales, whereas this is not the case for a clause prohibiting the selling of the contract goods on

---

[179] Esken, Von Graevenitz, Slobodenjuk, Kammer, Jorias, Lemmens and Gronemeyer 2014, pp. 287–8.

[180] Ibid, p. 288.

[181] See Bechtold and Bosch 2018, p. 48.

[182] Ibid, p. 51.

[183] Case *ASICS*, Bundesgerichtshof 12 December 2017, ECLI:DE:BGH:2017:121217BKVZ41.17.0.

[184] Klauß and Dos Santos Goncalves 2018, pp. N65, N66.

[185] Case *ASICS*, Bundesgerichtshof 12 December 2017, ECLI:DE:BGH:2017:121217BKVZ41.17.0, par. 17.

[186] Ibid, par. 25.

[187] Case C-230/16 *Coty*, ECLI:EU:C:2017:941.

third-party platforms.[188] In our view, it remains to be seen whether the CJEU endorses this view: on one hand, a clause preventing retailers from using price comparison engines does not preclude these traders from selling the contract products on the internet, but on the other hand, restrictions to making price reviews could have negative effects on price competition. It cannot be excluded that at a certain point in time preliminary questions will be asked on these matters to the CJEU.

All in all, as in EU competition law, Section 1 GWB is infringed upon, if a form of cooperation between undertakings (an agreement, a decision of an association of undertakings or a concerted practice) exists and competition is distorted. A significant difference between German and EU competition law lies in the role of the condition of the effect on the trade between the Member States. It is not a surprise that this condition is absent in German competition law, while it is decisive for the applicability of Article 101(1) TFEU. In the former system, the objective is to protect the competition structure on the domestic market, whereas in the latter system the establishment of the EU Internal Market is a key value. Firms being engaged in anti-competitive practices in Germany may escape from the application of the EU competition rules if no effect on intra-Union trade can be established, but these practices may nevertheless give rise to serious issues of competition law under the domestic system.

The alignment with EU competition law has also resulted in the GWB containing a legal exception. According to Section 2(1) GWB, restrictive agreements, decisions of associations of undertakings and concerted practices are permitted, if: (1) they contribute to the improvement of the production or distribution of goods or to promoting technical and economic progress; (2) they allow consumers a fair share of the benefits created; (3) the restrictions concerned are indispensable for the objectives pursued; and (4) competition in respect of a substantial part of the products in question is not eliminated. These conditions have a great resemblance with Article 101(3) TFEU. Consequently, as in EU competition law, parties to a restrictive agreement could argue that this agreement is permitted in the light of the efficiencies to be achieved.

Above, the Block Exemptions carving out specific practices from Article 101(1) TFEU were discussed. Section 2(2) GWB specifically provides that these Block Exemptions are also capable of carving out agreements, decisions of associations of undertakings and concerted practices from the scope of the German cartel prohibition. Accordingly, the EU Block Exemptions are turned into domestic ones for the purposes of German competition law. On top of these exemptions, carve-outs that are typical for German competition law are in place. For example, Section 3 GWB lays down an exemption for cartels of SMEs. If these practices are geared towards the rationalisation of economic activities through inter-firm cooperation, in order to improve the competitive position of these enterprises without having any substantial impact on competition, they are deemed to fulfil the conditions set out by Section 2(1) GWB. In fact, Section 3 GWB gives further effect to the conditions of Article 101(3) TFEU, by adapting them to the specific needs of SMEs. In any event, it must be avoided that on the

---

[188] Case *ASICS*, Bundesgerichtshof 12 December 2017, ECLI:DE:BGH:2017:121217BKVZ41.17.0, par. 28–30. See also Klauß and Dos Santos Goncalves 2018, p. N66.

basis of Section 3 GWB, agreements are permitted that are in violation of Article 101 TFEU. As a result, this German exception for SMEs is only of relevance for practices not influencing the trade between the Member States.[189] Another interesting example is Section 30 GWB, which exempts certain vertical price agreements concluded by publishers from the cartel prohibition of Section 1 GWB. As long as these agreements do not influence intra-Union trade, no issues under EU competition law arise. However, if such effects are identified, the question must be addressed whether the vertical prices agreed upon by publishers could benefit from Article 101(3) TFEU. There is a precedent showing that at least the Commission is willing to accept that a system for vertical price fixing set up by publishers is justifiable under Article 101(3) TFEU in order to guarantee the offer of a wide range of media products to the public.[190] As the general approach to vertical price fixing is hostile in EU competition law, it cannot be excluded that in the future the regime of Section 30 GWB will clash with EU judgments based on Article 101 TFEU.

4.2 The UK

An important point in time for UK competition law is 1998, when the Competition Act 1998 was passed. Another important reform resulted in the passing of the Enterprise Act 2002. The substantive rules of the Competition Act 1998 mainly echo Articles 101 and 102 TFEU. The Chapter 1 Prohibition of this Act deals with cartels, whereas the Chapter 2 Prohibition is concerned with dominance.

The Chapter 1 Prohibition is modelled after Article 101(1) TFEU. Section 2(1) of the Competition Act 1998 stipulates that agreements, decisions by associations of undertakings or concerted practices which may affect trade within the UK, as well as have as their object or effect the prevention, restriction or distortion of competition within the UK are prohibited unless they are exempted in accordance with the relevant provisions of the Act. As is the case in German competition law, the conditions, which are common in EU law, are incorporated in the Chapter 1 Prohibition: some form of cooperation (being either an agreement, or a decision of an association of undertakings or a concerted practice) and distortion of competition must be proven. Section 2(2) lists a few examples of practices that are considered to be anti-competitive, such as price fixing and market sharing.

A landmark case,[191] where serious competition issues arose under the Chapter 1 Prohibition, is the *Replica Football Kit* case.[192] This case concerned the retail in, inter alia, football jerseys of famous clubs, such as Manchester United, and of the English national team. Umbro was the supplier of these kits, while JJB and Sports Soccer were two major players on the retail market, reselling the Umbro products. The UK competition authority

---

[189] Bechtold and Bosch 2018, p. 99.

[190] See the Belgian *AMP* case (cases IV/C-2/31.609 and 37.306, (1999)), discussed in the XXIX Competition Report of the Commission, p. 161. On this, see Bechtold and Bosch 2018, p. 290. Cf De Vries 2006, pp. 214–19.

[191] Rodger 2013, pp. 321, 322.

[192] Decision CA98/06/2003, 1 August 2003, *Replica Football Kit*, available at <https://www.gov.uk/cma-cases/replica-football-kit-price-fixing> accessed 9 January 2020.

found that Umbro enforced in practice compliance with its recommended resale prices, which in fact were turned into fixed or minimum prices.[193] Furthermore, JJB was exerting pressure on Umbro to reduce the amount of discounting by other retailers.[194] As a result, it was believed that the practices under review amounted to restrictive vertical and horizontal agreements: conspiracy was found between the supplier and the retailers, as well as between the retailers.[195] As for the horizontal dimension of *Replica Football Kit* case, the pricing information was deemed to be passed on by JJB indirectly to other retailers, such as Sports Soccer, making use of the supplier as an intermediator. The practices were considered to restrict competition by object. The competent courts upheld the decision taken by the UK competition authority as to whether the Chapter I Prohibition was violated.[196] A very important finding was that, in the given circumstances, it was acceptable to conclude that JJB, as a retailer, provided confidential price information to Umbro (supplier), knowing that the latter, in its turn, would pass on this information to another important retailer, that is, Sports Soccer, in order to persuade this retailer to raise its prices.[197] Sports Soccer did so, foreseeing that other retailers would do the same given the role Umbro played on the market.[198] In other words, the facts and circumstances of the case justified the finding that a trilateral concerted practice had occurred on the market: direct conspiracy between the supplier and the retailer, as well as indirect conspiracy between the retailers.[199]

Another important case concerned the deals made by Hasbro, Argos and Littlewoods.[200] Hasbro was a large manufacturer of toys and games. It received complaints from two retailers, Argos and Littlewoods, that the margins on its products were too low. In response to this, Hasbro organised separate meetings with Argos and Littlewoods in order to find out for which products a system of resale and price maintenance needed to be implemented. Hasbro discussed the price levels needed with the retailers individually. Subsequently, the manufacturer informed each retailer that the other had agreed with introducing a system of resale and price maintenance for a particular range of products. As a result, the manufacturer acted as a hub in order to facilitate anti-competitive practices (price alignment) of the retailers

---

[193] Case *Replica Football Kit*, Decision CA98/06/2003, 1 August 2003, par. 125.

[194] Ibid, par. 445.

[195] Ibid, par. 495.

[196] Cases 1021/1/1/03 and 1022/1/1/03, Competition Appeal Tribunal, *JJB Sports and Allsports*, (2004) CAT 17; 2005/1071, 1074 and 1623, Court of Appeal, *Argos Limited and JJB Sports*, (2006) EWCA Civ 1318.

[197] Rodger 2013, p. 326.

[198] Ibid.

[199] Ibid, p. 326, 327. Cf case 2005/1071, 1074 and 1623, Court of Appeal, *Argos Limited and JJB Sports*, (2006) EWCA Civ 1318, par. 141.

[200] Case *Agreements between Hasbro, Argos and Littlewoods*, Decision No. CA98/8/2003 of the OFT, 21 November 2003, available at <https://webarchive.nationalarchives.gov.uk/20140402170242/http://www.oft.gov.uk/OFTwork/competition-act-and-cartels/ca98/decisions/argos2> accessed 15 June 2020; cases 1014 and 1015/1/1/03, Competition Appeal Tribunal, *Argos and Littlewoods*, (2004) CAT 24; 2005/1071, 1074 and 1623, Court of Appeal, *Argos Limited and JJB Sports*, (2006) EWCA Civ 1318.

concerned.[201] This amounted to a hub-and-spoke cartel and, accordingly, a breach of the competition rules was found.

Section 2(1) of the Competition Act 1998 specifically provides that the trade within the UK should be influenced. As the Competition Act 1998 is concerned with preventing competition problems from occurring on the domestic market, an effect on the trade between the Member States does not need to be established. Domestic cartels not having any impact on the trade between the Member States are still under surveillance of a competition authority, which is the body responsible for the enforcement of the UK competition rules, the CMA. This is also an important conclusion with regard to issues arising from Brexit. After the UK has left the EU, UK businesses remain bound by a set of national rules inspired by the TFEU provisions on competition.[202] On top of that, it is settled case-law of the CJEU, which is based on the 'qualified effects' doctrine, that EU competition law applies to companies, regardless of whether they are based within or outside the EU, being engaged in practices having an effect on the EU market. In this regard, it must be pointed out that also after Brexit, many UK firms will be obliged to observe Articles 101 and 102 TFEU, in so far as they are engaged in cross-border activity on the European continent.[203] Strikingly, the voluntary incorporation of the European competition rules into the UK competition laws and the close business ties with EU Member States mean that British firms will not be immune from the Treaty provisions on competition.

In the event the UK leaves the EU without a deal, Article 60A of the Competition Act 1998 will enter into force.[204] According to this provision the British competition rules must be applied in accordance with EU competition law, as it stood before the exit day. It should be noted that some exceptions apply to this rule, allowing for some flexibility. When writing this book, the outcome of the negotiations between the EU and UK was not yet known.

Section 3 excludes various practices from the Chapter 1 Prohibition. These carve-outs do not appear in EU competition law. For example, agreements are excluded if they are subject to competition scrutiny under other legislation, such as the laws on financial markets.[205] Other carve-outs concern, inter alia, Services of General Economic Interest and public policy.[206]

As in EU competition law, the Competition Act 1998 contains a legal exception, which is laid down in Section 9(1) of this Act. According to this provision, an agreement is exempted from the Chapter 1 Prohibition if it contributes to the improvement of production or distribution, or to promoting technical or economic progress, while allowing consumers a fair share of the benefits concerned, while the restrictions imposed are not indispensable and competition is not eliminated. It is clear from the outset that this drafting is inspired by Article 101(3) TFEU. Pursuant to Section 9(2) of the Competition Act 1998, the undertaking

---

[201] OECD 2019, p. 6.

[202] Brexit Notice 2019.

[203] Joined cases 89, 104, 114, 116, 117 and 125 to 129/85 *Wood Pulp*, ECLI:EU:C:1988:447; case C-413/14 *Intel*, ECLI:EU:C:2017:632.

[204] See <http://www.legislation.gov.uk/uksi/2019/93/regulation/23/made> accessed 4 June 2020.

[205] Whish and Bailey 2018, pp. 366, 367.

[206] Ibid, pp. 368–70.

claiming the benefit of the previous subsection is obliged to submit evidence for this. This rule on the burden of proof is similar to Article 2 of Regulation 1/2003, according to which it is also up to the undertaking making the claim of the beneficial effects of an agreement to demonstrate the alleged effects.

In UK competition law, it was debated whether the conditions of both Article 101(3) TFEU and Section 9(2) of the Competition Act 1998 leave room for taking into account non-economic benefits.[207] In the *Lucite and BASF* case,[208] the UK competition authority put forward that an agreement that led to the improvement of safety and the local environment constituted benefits within the meaning of Article 101(3) TFEU and Section 9(2) of the Competition Act 1998. Reference was made to the *CECED* Commission Decision.[209] Although this decision supports the interpretation adopted by the UK competition authority, it should be recalled that in its Guidelines on Article 101(3) TFEU 2004, the Commission refocused its approach towards an efficiencies-based test. As already stated above, guidance is needed as to whether non-competition goals may be accommodated in a review under Article 101(3) TFEU and the national provisions based on this Article.

In UK competition law, Block Exemptions are also in place. Section 10 of the Competition Act 1998 provides that the EU Block Exemptions also apply in UK competition law. Also, in order to ascertain that beneficial agreements that do not fall under an EU Block Exemption for the sole reason of the absence of an effect on intra-Union trade, it is specifically set out that these agreements, which satisfy all conditions set out in an EU Block Exemption, without having an interstate dimension, nevertheless are exempted from the Chapter 1 Prohibition. For the purposes of UK competition law, the EU Block Exemptions are referred to as parallel exemptions.[210]

The Competition Act 1998 also allows for the adoption of national Block Exemptions. Section 6 of this Act has conferred on the Secretary of State the power to create such exemptions. At this moment a Section 6 Block Exemption is in place for particular ticketing schemes in public transport.[211]

4.3 The Netherlands

In 1998, the Competition Act (Mededingingswet – Mw) entered into force in the Netherlands. With the enactment of this piece of legislation, an end was put to the era of the Dutch Act on Economic Competition (Wet Economische Mededinging – WEM), under which cartels were permitted, unless they were specifically banned by the competent authorities.[212] At

---

[207] Ibid, p. 373.

[208] Decision of the Director General of Fair Trading in case CP/1288-02, *Lucite and BASF*.

[209] Case IV.F.1/36.718 *CECED*, (2000) OJ L 187/47.

[210] Competition Act 1998, Section 10(3).

[211] Whish and Bailey 2018, p. 375.

[212] E.g. WEM, Articles 10, 19. One of the characteristics of the WEM system was that the competition conditions and possibilities varied from sector to sector. See Mulder and Mok 1962, pp. 72–3.

that time the Netherlands was known as the cartel paradise of Europe.[213] The general view and business climate changed dramatically when the WEM was replaced by the Mw. In the latter piece of national legislation, anti-competitive practices were prohibited, save for some exceptions. When it comes to cartels, the core provision is Article 6 Mw, which is modelled after Article 101(1) TFEU. It is, therefore, not a surprise that according to the first paragraph of this provision of national law agreements, decisions of associations of undertakings and concerted practices that have the object or effect of distorting competition are prohibited. It goes without saying that a condition related to the effect on intra-Union trade is not required. Article 6(1) Mw does refer to the Dutch market or a part of this market.

The distinction between restriction by object and by effect, the importance of which was emphasised in the judgments of the EU courts, has given rise to a heated debate in Dutch case-law. As already stated, in *Expedia* the CJEU held that in the event an agreement has the object to restrict competition the appreciable effect is given. Before this judgment was handed down in Luxembourg, the Dutch courts competent to review the decisions taken by the Dutch competition authority were of the view that, although the concrete effects of practices containing a restriction by object do not need to be analysed, the appreciability of the effect on competition of such practices had to be examined.[214] After the *Expedia* judgment was handed down, the national administrative law courts (entrusted with the task to review the NCA decisions) changed their approach by contending that agreements having the object of distorting competition are deemed to give rise to an appreciable effect.[215] On the other hand, after *Expedia*, the Dutch Supreme Court continued to assess the appreciable effect of a restriction by object.[216] In subsequent case-law, however, the Supreme Court seemed to have changed its view, as it put forward that once a restriction by object of a particular agreement is established, a separate assessment of an appreciable effect is not required anymore.[217] All in all, from these developments it is apparent that the doctrine of restriction by object and effect is surrounded by some unclarity in Dutch competition law.

Above, it was put forward that in EU competition law the Commission has developed an approach based on market shares in order to determine whether a restriction by effect is appreciable. This is laid down in the *De Minimis* Notice 2004, which is soft-law. In the Mw, Article 7, which contains binding rules, deals with the matter of appreciable effect of agreements. This Article has introduced two thresholds, laid down in Article 7(1) and (2), respectively, for restrictive agreements. If the conditions of one of these thresholds are satisfied, the cartel prohibition enshrined in Article 6 Mw does not apply. According to Article 7(1) Mw, an anti-competitive agreement is immune from the cartel prohibition, if no more than eight undertakings are involved and the combined turnover of these undertakings does not exceed 5.5 million EUR, in the event the agreement concerns the supply of goods, or this

---

[213] De Jong 1990, p. 244 *et seq.*

[214] E.g. case *Secon*, ECLI:NL:CBB:2005:AU8309, College van Beroep voor het Bedrijfsleven 7 December 2005.

[215] E.g. case *Flour*, ECLI:NL:CBB:2016:184, College van Beroep voor het Bedrijfsleven, 14 July 2016. See also Outhuijse 2019, pp. 117–18.

[216] Case *Petrol Station on Texel*, ECLI:NL:HR:2013:CA3745, HR, 25 October 2013.

[217] Case *Association of Veterinarians*, ECLI:NL:2017:1354, HR, 14 July 2017.

turnover is not excess of 1.1 million EUR, in the event of other agreements.[218] According to Article 7(2) Mw, the cartel prohibition does not apply if the combined market share of the parties concerned does not exceed 10 per cent on any of the relevant markets impacted by the agreement at issue and the trade between the Member States is not influenced.

The last threshold is very generous and was introduced in order to give SMEs the opportunity to exercise countervailing power vis-à-vis large enterprises.[219] The carve-out of Article 7(2) Mw does not apply, if the agreement concerned has an impact on the trade between the Member States, in order to avoid that EU competition law is infringed. It should be noted that the thresholds of Article 7 apply equally to restrictions by object and effect. The scope of the EU-based *de minimis* rules is limited to restrictions by effect. By requiring that no effect on intra-Union trade occurs Article 7(2) Mw prevents that restrictions by object that do fall within the ambit of Article 101(1) TFEU are permitted under Dutch competition law. All in all, in Dutch competition law, the appreciable effect doctrine as developed in the case-law of the CJEU (such as *Expedia*) and in the Commission *De Minimis* Notice 2004 is combined with Article 7 Mw. This may result in a complicated review based on various factors and considerations.

As in EU competition law and other systems of national competition law, the Mw provides for exceptions: the legal exception and Block Exemptions. Article 6(3) is modelled after Article 101(3) TFEU and therefore provides that a particular restrictive agreement is justified if: it contributes to the improvement of the production or distribution, or to technical or economic improvement, a fair share of the benefits is allowed for the consumers, the restrictions are indispensable to achieve the objectives pursued and competition is not eliminated. The EU Block Exemptions are turned into Block Exemptions for the purposes of Dutch competition law, as Article 12 Mw provides that these exemptions carve restrictive agreements out from the scope of Article 6(1) Mw. Moreover, according to Article 13 Mw this also applies to agreements that satisfy all conditions of an EU Block Exemption, but do not fall within its scope for the sole reason of absence of an effect on intra-Union trade. Also, in Dutch competition law, 'home-made' exemptions are in place. On the basis of Article 15 Mw national Block Exemptions can be adopted through Royal Decrees. Of interest is also Article 16 Mw, which exempts collective labour agreements, pension agreements concluded by employers' associations and trade unions, as well as agreements or decisions by organisations of professionals, from the scope of Article 6(1) Mw. This provision has a lot in common with the approach developed by the CJEU in cases such as *Brentjens*, in which a safe harbour has been created for collective labour agreements. An important difference is, though, that in the CJEU's view these agreements (provided that they are the result of bargaining between trade unions and employers and concern labour conditions) do not fall within the scope of the cartel prohibition at all, whereas in Article 16 Mw the need of collective bargaining is framed as an exception. What is more important, and may give rise to problems, is that even agreements and decisions by organisations of professionals may be exempted by Article 16 Mw. As these agreements and decisions are not the result of collective bargaining between

---

[218] The majority of these 'other agreements' pertain to the provision of services.

[219] Parliamentary Documents 2007–08.

trade unions and employers, the *Brentjens* approach does not apply.[220] In other words, the agreements and decisions concerned could give rise to competition issues under Article 101(1) TFEU, whereas they are permitted under Dutch competition law.

4.4 Other Member States

The examples given above are representative of the design of the national competition rules of some of the Member States of the EU: a general ban on cartels and other restrictive agreements, with a few exceptions. A brief discussion of provisions of some other national systems of competition law shows that the rules on cartels of other Member States have a similar setup.

For instance, it must be pointed out that in France a ban on cartels is in place. According to Article L420-1 of the Commercial Code, agreements and arrangements between companies, having the object or effect of restricting competition, are not allowed. Firm action has been taken against enterprises engaged in anti-competitive practices such as horizontal price fixing and market sharing.[221] In practice, such practices are not regarded to be justifiable under Article L420-4 of the Commercial Code, according to which anti-competitive practices are permitted, if they contribute to economic progress, allow a fair share of the benefits to the consumer, do not eliminate competition and are indispensable.[222]

In the same vein, Article 5(1) of the Romanian Competition Law 21/1996 bans agreements that restrict competition. Article 5(2) is identical to Article 101(3) TFEU and, accordingly, exempts anti-competitive practices that contribute to the achievement of efficiencies.[223] Article 5(3) of the Competition Law provides that the EU Block Exemptions are also capable of carving out practices falling within the scope of the Romanian cartel prohibition of Article 5(1). Furthermore, Article 8 of the Competition Law incorporates the provisions of the Commission *De Minimis* Notice 2004 in this piece of national legislation.[224] Consequently, horizontal agreements are deemed not to have an appreciable effect, if the combined market share of the parties involved is not in excess of 10 per cent, whereas this threshold is 15 per cent of every individual party to a vertical agreement. It goes without saying that hardcore restrictions do not benefit from the *de minimis* rule of Article 8.

In Belgium, all agreements between undertakings, all decisions by associations of undertakings and all concerted practices having the object or the effect of restricting competition are banned according to Article IV.1(1) of the Code de Droit Économique. It is clear from the outset that this provision is modelled after Article 101(1) TFEU. Also, Article IV.1(3) of this piece of national legislation echoes EU competition law, in this case Article 101(3) TFEU. In other words, anti-competitive practices are justifiable, if they contribute to the improvement of production or distribution or to innovation, enable users to benefit from

---

[220] Joined cases C-180 and C-184/98 *Pavlov*, ECLI:EU:C:2000:428.

[221] Philippe, Trabucchi and Guyon 2014, p. 270.

[222] Ibid, p. 269.

[223] OECD – Romania 2014, p. 16.

[224] Ibid.

a fair share of the resulting efficiencies, they are indispensable and they do not eliminate competition. In Belgian competition law, Block Exemptions are also in place. To start with, Article IV.4(4), first and second sections, provides that the Belgian ban on cartels does not apply if the conditions of the EU Block Exemptions are satisfied, irrespective of whether the trade between the Member States is influenced or not. Furthermore, on the basis of Article IV.5 of the Code de Droit Économique, a Royal Decree may be adopted in order to introduce national Block Exemptions.[225]

In Greece, the rules on cartels are also designed in tune with Article 101 TFEU. Thus, Article 1 of the Greek Competition Act 2011 highly mirrors what is laid down in the first section of this Treaty provision. This national provision applies if the conditions common to many systems of competition law are satisfied: a form of cooperation between undertakings (agreements, decisions by associations of undertakings or concerted practices) the object or effect of which is distorting competition.[226] Also, Article 1(3) is in accordance with Article 101(3) TFEU, which exempts restrictive practices that deliver pro-competitive benefits.[227] Furthermore, pursuant to Article 1(4) of the Competition Act, the EU Block Exemptions also apply in Greek competition law. Interestingly, the Greek competition authority has had particular interest in the policies of trade associations and took action against minimum price regulations of the Technical Chamber of Greece, of the associations of estate agents, and professional associations of foreign language schools.[228]

5 CONCLUSIONS

Article 101 TFEU contains the rules for restrictive agreements in the EU. Given its broad wording it is not a surprise that the interpretation and application of this provision have evolved over time. Two important developments are worth mentioning in this respect.

First, the importance of the economic approach has increased. This has resulted in significant changes in European competition law. Most notably, the EU rules for vertical restraints are now based on economic theory, which emphasises that a distinction must be made between inter-brand and intra-brand competition. As a result, a generous Block Exemption for vertical restraints is in place. This does not mean, however, that the criticism inspired by economic theory has come to an end. In this regard, it must be noted that the hostile stance of EU competition law to resale price maintenance was met with fierce opposition by some scholars. Moreover, this stance does not sit well with developments that have taken place across the Atlantic, in US antitrust law. Furthermore, the struggle the CJEU has experienced with the object/effect dichotomy has led to a lot of confusion and, accordingly, refinement of its case-law on this matter is still needed. Additionally, the emergence of digital markets has given rise to challenges. In the near future, the EU rules for vertical restraints and horizontal

---

[225] Code de Droit Économique, Article IV.4 §4, third section.

[226] OECD – Greece 2018, p. 27.

[227] Ibid.

[228] Pelecanos, Gerakinis and Themelis 2014, p. 306.

cooperation agreements must be revised and an important issue is how to accommodate the role played by e-commerce and digital platforms in these rules.

Second, the entering into force of Regulation 1/2003 has given a considerable boost to the decentralised enforcement of Article 101 TFEU, by the NCAs. Parallel with this a process of spontaneous harmonisation unfolded in the EU Member States, leading to the adoption of national competition laws containing provisions on restrictive agreements based on Article 101 TFEU. As a result, cartels are, in principle, banned, even if the trade between the Member States is not influenced. This coherent set of EU and national competition rules signals that anti-competitive practices, such as price fixing and market sharing, is not permitted throughout Europe, be it on the EU level, the national level, regional or local level. Strikingly, no harmonisation measures needed to be adopted by the Union legislator in order to achieve this result. The experience with the national rules on cartels shows that new interesting case-law is created, which is an enrichment for the supranational EU system. Derogation from what is decided and ruled on at the EU level cannot be excluded, but this does not call into question the finding that the experience at the national level of the Member States has resulted in an extended set of national judgments and decisions on cartels that firms doing business in Europe can benefit from. Moreover, these national judgments and decisions are capable of contributing significantly to the further development of EU competition law.

6

The prohibition to abuse a dominant position

1 INTRODUCTION

In Chapter 4 we pointed out that EU antitrust law is built on two pillars, namely the cartel prohibition, in Article 101 TFEU, and the prohibition to abuse a dominant position embedded in Article 102 TFEU. From an economic point of view, Articles 101 and 102 TFEU are meant to form a coherent system which, having regard to the constitutive elements of the prohibitions embedded in these two articles, is meant to address behaviour of undertakings resulting in economic inefficiency, to the detriment of consumers. While the former article tackles *coordination* between undertakings that has the object or effect the restriction of competition, the latter provision tackles *unilateral behaviour* of undertakings holding a certain degree of (economic) power in one or more markets. In other words, Article 102 TFEU constrains the behaviour of undertakings which are not sufficiently restrained by other competitors.[1]

Article 102 TFEU is said to have drawn inspiration from the (West-)German GWB (Section 19) and the US Sherman Antitrust Law (Section 2). These laws were, however, adopted due to considerations peculiar to those jurisdictions, namely in order to safeguard free trade, diffuse power and address the risk of resurgence of the Nazi regime, in Germany, and as a response to excessive concentration of private power in the hands of big businesses, in the US. In the EU, beyond the economic (in)efficiency argument pointed out above, Article 102 TFEU was historically seen as a vehicle to regulate behaviour of firms with economic power, rather than addressing distrust of big business. In this respect, Article 102 TFEU, much like Article 101 TFEU, was conceived to cater to multiple and diverse interests: consumer welfare, the integration of the Internal Market, level playing field and access to the market for all players, and so on. Since the late 1990s/early 2000s, the focus in Article 102 TFEU analysis shifted from a formalistic method, to a more effects-based approach, culminating with the adoption of the Enforcement Priorities Guidelines in 2009.[2] Still, Article 102 TFEU has not suffered textual changes since it came into being as Article 86 of the EEC Treaty (renumbered as Article 82 of the TEC). It is thus no surprise that discussions surrounding digitalisation, big tech and

---

[1] Jones, Sufrin and Dunne 2019, p. 278.

[2] Fox and Gerard 2017, pp. 159–61.

dominance are nowadays quite prominent in connection to the need to re-modernise the application of Article 102 TFEU.[3]

This chapter discusses the second component of antitrust law: Article 102 TFEU. It will first focus on the constitutive elements of this Treaty article, some of which were already previewed in Chapters 2 and 4. Next the possible defences and justifications that undertakings could make use of, will be explored. Last but not least, domestic experience of the abuse of dominance doctrine will be elucidated with reference to several national jurisdictions.

2 ARTICLE 102 TFEU: CONSTITUTIVE ELEMENTS

Article 102 TFEU provides that any *abuse* by one or more *undertakings* of a *dominant position within the Internal Market or in a substantial part of it* shall be prohibited as incompatible with the Internal Market in so far as it may *affect the trade between the Member States*. The italicised words point to the cumulative conditions for establishing an infringement of Article 102 TFEU.

Thus, a finding of dominance *only*, without an abuse being established, is not problematic under Article 102 TFEU, as clarified as early as the CJEU's *Michelin I* ruling.[4] Achieving market dominance through innovativeness and entrepreneurship should not be stifled. To the contrary, competition law and policy should encourage such courses of action. This also means that one and the same type of conduct is not caught by the prohibition when engaged in by a non-dominant firm, while it would be prohibited when performed by a dominant undertaking. This finding sheds light on the fact that dominant and non-dominant undertakings are in crucially different positions.[5] Two further findings stem from this: first, correctly identifying the existence of dominance, which in turn relies on a proper definition of the relevant market, is key when it comes to not arriving at flawed analysis results under Article 102 TFEU. Second, once dominance is established, the undertaking concerned has a 'special responsibility' not to allow its conduct to impair genuine undistorted competition on the market. The scope of this responsibility must be considered in light of the specific circumstances of each case.[6]

As pointed out, inspiration was drawn from US antitrust law for the drafting of Article 102 TFEU. Section 2 of the US Sherman Act sets out that no person is permitted to monopolise or attempt to monopolise, or combine or conspire with any other person or persons to

---

[3] See intervention of Commissioner Vestager at the 2020 American Bar Association roundtable discussions, available at <https://ourcuriousamalgam.com/event-schedule/livestream-enforcers-roundtable/?_cldee=Yy5ydXN1QGplci55ydS5ubA%3d%3d&recipientid=contact-60beb1d3b778e511abd8005056a02f56-58cf6c131a2e4742afac7f995febef6b&esid=c9b87485-a78f-ea11-8129-0050569432d7> accessed 8 May 2020. See also e.g. Wiggers, Struijlaart and Dibbits 2019.

[4] Case C-322/81 *Michelin I*, ECLI:EU:C:1983:313.

[5] Jones, Sufrin and Dunne 2019, p. 280.

[6] Enforcement Priorities Guidelines 2009, par. 1, 9, and essentially almost every judgment of the EU courts dealing with Article 102 TFEU.

monopolise any part of the trade or commerce.[7] Monopolisation comes down to: (1) the possession of monopoly power, and (2) anti-competitive or exclusionary conduct.[8] Although the setup of Section 2 of the Sherman Act is not entirely the same as Article 102 TFEU, also under this former provision, the mere possession of economic power is not problematic. It should be pointed out that attempted monopolisation too is prohibited under US antitrust law. In that event, the intent of the anti-competitive or predatory conduct was to monopolise, while a dangerous probability of achieving monopoly power exists.[9] Conspiracy to monopolise may occur if an agreement is reached among firms having the specific intent to monopolise and an overt act to that effect is present.[10] These offences also require that apart from economic power, practices of an anti-competitive nature are proven. Consequently, like Article 102 TFEU, the US approach to monopolisation is concerned with taking action against the conduct leading to the misuse of this power, rather than punishing the mere possession thereof.

2.1 One or more undertakings

In EU competition law, the special responsibility not to abuse the dominant position rests on the shoulders of one or more undertakings, as the case may be. In Chapter 2 we showed that EU law adopts a functional and broad definition of the concept of undertaking: every entity engaged in economic activities is an undertaking within the meaning of EU competition law, regardless of legal status or financing methods. In a nutshell, the concept of undertaking relies on the single economic unit doctrine: such a unit may comprise diverse structures including various legal and natural persons. It is important to keep in mind that the agreements concluded within such a unit between its various members are not caught by the prohibition of Article 101 TFEU.

Article 102 TFEU is also framed in terms of a prohibition addressed to *undertakings*. Yet, certain peculiarities pertaining to this concept in the context of Article 102 TFEU may be identified. First, Lorenz[11] argues that an important distinction between the application of the concept of undertaking in Articles 101 and 102 TFEU, respectively, is that the single economic unit doctrine does not apply in the context of the latter. With a reference to the *GT-Link* case,[12] he argues that dominant undertakings may not favour their own subsidiaries to the detriment of third-party competitors, since this may result in the application of dissimilar conditions to equivalent transactions. As we will see in section 2.4.5.5 below, the concept of margin squeeze abuse could be a good exemplification of this discussion.

Second, Chapter 11 focuses on the relationship between Articles 102 and 106 TFEU, regarding public undertakings and undertakings having exclusive or special rights. In

---

[7] Section 2 of the Sherman Antitrust Act, 15 U.S.C.

[8] Elhauge and Geradin 2011, p. 265.

[9] Ibid, p. 266.

[10] Ibid.

[11] Lorenz 2013, pp. 190–91.

[12] Case C-242/95 *GT-Link*, ECLI:EU:C:1997:376.

essence, the fact that an undertaking has a monopoly conferred by the state does not make it escape per se the application of Article 102 TFEU. Member States may thus not confer undertakings immunity from this TFEU prohibition, unless the conditions of Article 106(2) TFEU are met, that is, we are dealing with the behaviour of an undertaking charged with the execution of a Service of General Economic Interest (SGEI).[13] If an undertaking is forced to behave abusively by the state, while having no room for manoeuvre, it cannot be held to have violated Article 102 TFEU. However, the state measure concerned may be in violation of Article 106 TFEU in combination with Article 102 TFEU.

Third, the reference in Article 102 TFEU to *one* or *more* undertakings holding a dominant position relates to the concepts of 'single' and 'collective' dominance, respectively. To establish collective dominance, certain specific market circumstances (i.e. so-called oligopolistic features) need to be present. The undertakings in question have a responsibility not to abuse that position. In *CMB*,[14] the CJEU clarified that a dominant position may be held by two or more economic entities legally independent of each other, provided that from an economic point of view they present themselves or act together on a particular market as a collective entity, particularly when it comes to their relationship with their competitors, their trading partners and consumers. To ascertain this setting, the existence of an agreement or of other *legal* links between the undertakings concerned is not indispensable. Instead, it is necessary to examine the *economic* links or factors which give rise to a connection between the undertakings concerned and which enable them to act together independently of their competitors, their customers and consumers. This would thus depend on an economic assessment and, in particular, on an assessment of the structure of the market in question. In *Irish Sugar*,[15] the GC confirmed the Commission's finding that the undertakings held to be collectively dominant must not necessarily be active in the same market; a vertical commercial relationship, such as between a producer and distributor, can also fit that concept. In *Piau*,[16] with reference to the *Airtours* (merger control) case,[17] the Court spelled out the three cumulative conditions that need to be met for a finding of collective dominance: each member of the dominant oligopoly must be able to know and monitor the behaviour of the other members, their tacit coordination must be sustainable over time, and the foreseeable reaction of current and future competitors and consumers must not jeopardise the results expected from the common policy. In Chapter 10 we will discuss these conditions in more detail. Given that cases involving abuses of collective dominant position do not occur often, this chapter focuses primarily on the concept of single dominance.

---

[13] Whish and Bailey 2018, p. 185.

[14] Joined cases C-395 and 396/96 P *CMB*, ECLI:EU:C:2000:132, par. 36–48.

[15] Case T-228/97 *Irish Sugar*, ECLI:EU:T:1999:246, par. 63.

[16] Case T-193/02 *Piau*, ECLI:EU:T:2005:22, par. 111.

[17] Case T-342/99 *Airtours*, ECLI:EU:T:2002:146.

2.2 Dominant position

For the Article 102 TFEU prohibition to apply, the undertaking(s) in question must hold a dominant position. The concept of dominance is not defined in the TFEU itself. This task was taken on by the CJEU in early judgments, such as *United Brands* and *Hoffmann-La Roche*,[18] when the Court defined the concept of dominant position as relating to *a position of economic strength enjoyed by an undertaking, which enables it to prevent effective competition being maintained on the relevant market by affording it the power to behave to an appreciable extent independently of its competitors, its customers and ultimately of the consumers*. This definition is essentially repeated in all subsequent Article 102 TFEU cases handled by the EU courts. The notion of dominance entails that the undertaking at hand holds a degree of *market power*, although not necessarily a monopoly, which enables it, if not to determine, at least to have an appreciable influence on the conditions under which competition will develop, and in any case to *act largely in disregard* of it so long as such conduct does not operate to its detriment.[19] The Commission's interpretation of dominance and market power is very much in tune to the EU courts' approach: paragraph 10 of the Enforcement Priorities Guidelines 2009, while dwelling on why dominant undertakings may behave *independently*, provides that the notion of *independence* is related to the degree of *competitive constraint* exerted on the undertaking in question. Dominance entails that these competitive constraints are not sufficiently effective and hence that the undertaking in question enjoys substantial market power over a period of time. This means that the undertaking's decisions are largely insensitive to the actions and reactions of competitors, customers and, ultimately, consumers. Paragraph 12 spells out where exactly the constraints in discussion may stem from: existing supplies from, and the position on the market of, *actual competitors* (the market position of the undertaking in question and its competitors), credible threat of future expansion by actual competitors or entry by *potential competitors* (expansion and entry), bargaining strength of the undertaking's *customers* (countervailing buyer power). Not all these aspects are always determinative in every case though, as far as establishing whether an undertaking is or is not dominant in a given market.

Identifying the presence and the degree of market power allows the filtering of the potential sources of competition problems.[20] This is important, since every firm may be said to have a certain degree of market power, at one point in time. And yet, should Article 102 TFEU apply in all such situations? There are several theories explaining the different dimensions of market power:[21]

- The power to increase prices: while in a competitive market prices are set in light of the consumers' demand, a firm with market power may increase (and maintain)

---

[18] Cases 27/76 *United Brands*, ECLI:EU:C:1978:22, par. 65; 85/76 *Hoffmann-La Roche*, ECLI:EU:C:1979:36, par. 38.

[19] Case 85/76 *Hoffmann-La Roche*, ECLI:EU:C:1979:36, par. 39.

[20] Monti 2007, p. 124.

[21] Lianos, Korah and Siciliani 2019, p. 821 *et seq.*; Lorenz 2013, pp. 194–5; Monti 2007, pp. 124–7.

prices profitably above the competitive level.[22] Increasing prices may also be used as shorthand for the various ways in which the parameters of competition, such as output, innovation, quality, can be influenced to the advantage of the dominant undertaking and to the detriment of consumers.[23] Generally speaking, the greater and the more durable the market power, the greater the number and degree of competition risks that may occur in a market;

- Greater commercial power: this indicates that a firm enjoys significant advantages when compared to other market players, advantages (e.g. 'deep pockets', better positioning on the market, stronger negotiation powers, and the like) which may be used to harm the interests of other parties;
- Exclusionary power: this relates to the ability of a firm to devise strategies that can harm rivals,[24] for example by raising their input costs, a scenario which may eventually put this firm in the future in a position to increase prices and reduce output. Thus, harming competitors may be regarded as an intermediary step to harming consumers; and
- Market power as a jurisdictional concept: this relates to labelling an undertaking as having market power, when specific jurisdictional thresholds (e.g. based on market shares) are met.

The Commission's understanding of market power and dominance borrows from all these four dimensions. In paragraph 11 of the Enforcement Priorities Guidelines 2009, it is shown that an undertaking which is capable of profitably increasing prices above the competitive level (or reducing innovation, quality, output, and suchlike) for a significant period of time does not face sufficiently effective competitive constraints and can thus generally be regarded as dominant. All in all, the Commission essentially equates *dominance* with the concept of *substantial market power*. It does so not only in the context of Article 102 TFEU, but also with reference to Article 101 TFEU and the Merger Control Regulation 2004.[25]

To assert whether an undertaking is dominant, two analytical steps need to be run through: first, the relevant market must be defined, since an undertaking may not be dominant 'in abstract'. Indeed, in *Continental Can*,[26] the CJEU also explained that the definition of the market is of paramount importance in competition cases, since the possibilities of competition can only be judged in relation to those characteristics of the products/services which make them substitutable or interchangeable. The Enforcement Priorities Guidelines 2009,[27] too, speak of a dominant position on one or more relevant markets, and to the fact that dominance actually relates to preventing effective competition from being maintained on a relevant market. Second, once the relevant market is defined, the factors which are indicative of substantial market power are investigated to conclude whether dominance exists or not.

---

[22] See Chapter 3, Figure 3.1.

[23] Enforcement Priorities Guidelines 2009, par. 11.

[24] Krattenmaker, Lande and Salop 1987.

[25] Lianos, Korah and Siciliani, pp. 824–6.

[26] Case 6/72 *Continental Can*, ECLI:EU:C:1973:22, par. 32.

[27] Par. 4, 10.

Indeed, paragraphs 10 and 12 of the Enforcement Priorities Guidelines 2009 state that the assessment of dominance will take into account the competitive structure of the market and in particular a combination of factors (including the power of actual and potential competition and countervailing buyer power), which, taken separately, are not necessarily determinative.[28]

When the market is defined narrowly (both as far as the product/service and geography are concerned), as competition authorities may often be swayed to do, dominance may be more prone to be established, for obvious reasons (e.g. less competitive constraints present, higher market share, and so on). It is then expected that the allegedly dominant undertaking will attempt to show that competitive pressure may be exerted from players not falling within the market defined as such. When such pressure is strong, the undertaking may argue that it is futile to focus only on its behaviour.[29] In other words, in order to escape the Article 102 TFEU prohibition, the undertaking in question may argue that the market should be defined in a broader manner, thus rendering it non-dominant.

2.2.1 Relevant market

In Chapter 2 we discussed the main points pertaining to the market definition requirement in EU competition law. In a nutshell, the definition of the relevant market is not an end in itself, but better yet a tool which serves to establish the framework within which competition policy is applied. By defining the market, the Commission aims to identify those actual competitors of the undertakings involved that are capable of constraining those undertakings' behaviour and of preventing them from behaving independently of effective competitive pressure. This makes it possible inter alia to calculate market shares that would convey meaningful information regarding market power, for the purposes of assessing dominance when applying Article 102 TFEU. It is thus no surprise that the definition of the relevant product and geographic market often has a decisive influence on the assessment of a competition case.[30]

A fresh, new market definition must be performed in each particular case, in order to identify the conditions of competition relevant to that case. The Commission cannot bluntly adopt previous findings of dominance in the same economic sector, although it may take into account, as evidence, preceding patterns of defining the market in that sector of the economy, when nothing indicates that the conditions of competition have changed in the meantime.[31]

The Notice on Relevant Market 1997 contains valuable information on how the definition of the market is performed in practice, as a combination of the product/service and geographic dimensions.[32] The Notice is currently under revision, in order to ensure that the

---

[28] Cases 27/76 *United Brands*, ECLI:EU:C:1978:22, par. 66; 85/76 *Hoffmann-La Roche*, ECLI:EU:C:1979:36, par. 39.

[29] Lianos, Korah and Siciliani 2019, p. 251.

[30] Notice on Relevant Market 1997, par. 2, 4.

[31] E.g. case T-699/14 *Topps Europe*, ECLI:EU:T:2017:2, par. 93.

[32] Notice on Relevant Market 1997, par. 9.

market definition exercise accurately captures the changes triggered by the globalisation and digitalisation developments in the recent past.[33]

2.2.1.1 Product/service market

Paragraph 7 of the Notice on Relevant Market 1997 provides that the relevant product market comprises all those products and/or services which are regarded as interchangeable or substitutable by the consumer, by reason of the products' characteristics, their prices and their intended use. Paragraphs 13 to 24 indicate the basic principles of market definition. Identifying the competitive constraints in the market essentially relies on three sources, discussed just below: demand substitutability, supply substitutability and potential competition.[34] The concept of substitutability/interchangeability is key to correctly identifying the relevant product/service market.

- Demand substitutability:[35] this entails a determination of the range of products which are viewed as substitutes by the consumer. From an economic point of view, demand substitution constitutes the most immediate and effective disciplinary force on the suppliers of a given product, since a market player cannot significantly control prices, if its customers are in a position to switch easily to available substitute products. In Chapter 2 we have already indicated that the so-called SSNIP test, which is essentially a speculative experiment, postulating a hypothetical small, lasting change in relative prices and evaluating the likely reactions of customers to that increase, is probably the most prominent tool to measure demand substitution. Its functionality is described neatly in paragraphs 17 and 18 of the Notice. The test is based on a repetitive exercise of hypothetical price increases, until the point where they become profitable. In other words, where there are no alternative candidate products/services that consumers could switch to, the boundaries of the market would be reached. The SSNIP test is, however, not free of limits and difficulties of application, particularly when it comes to Article 102 TFEU cases: in Chapter 2 we have already discussed the so-called 'cellophane fallacy' problem. In section 2.2.1.4 below, we will further explore the limitations of the SSNIP test in relation to digital markets. Lastly for now, for the sake of clarity, the SSNIP test is only one of the tools used by the Commission in the market definition process, be it probably one of the most important ones. This means that should the Commission find this test unhelpful in a given case, or when data necessary for its application is not available, it is not obliged to use it.[36]

---

[33] See <https://ec.europa.eu/info/law/better-regulation/have-your-say/initiatives/12325-Evaluation-of-the-Commission-Notice-on-market-definition-in-EU-competition-law> accessed 4 June 2020.

[34] Potential competition and barriers to entry are normally evaluated when establishing the existence of a dominant position. See section 2.2.2 of this chapter.

[35] Notice on Relevant Market 1997, par. 13, 15–19.

[36] Case T-699/14 *Topps Europe*, ECLI:EU:T:2017:2, par. 82.

- Supply substitutability:[37] competitive constraints arising from supply substitutability are generally less immediate, and therefore such analysis is used much less than demand substitutability analysis. However, supply substitutability may be relevant when its effects would be equivalent to those of demand substitutability, in terms of immediacy and effectiveness: that is, when suppliers are able to switch production to the relevant products and market them in the short term without incurring significant additional costs or risks, thus disciplining the competitive behaviour of the companies involved. Useful examples of such scenarios are provided in paragraphs 21 and 22 of the Notice.

The Commission will start its analysis by broadly establishing the possible relevant markets. It may then identify several alternative working scenarios, based on which further analysis is carried out. Such analysis will differ from case to case, and will call for diverse ranges of evidence to be submitted, depending very much on the characteristics and specificity of the industry and products or services that are being examined. No specific evidence will always be determinative in every case. Nevertheless, paragraphs 38 to 43 of the Notice on Relevant Market 1997 show that the following categories of evidence may be relevant in asserting demand substitutability: evidence of substitution in the recent past; econometric and statistical estimates of (cross-price) elasticities; views of customers and competitors; market studies and consumer surveys; existence of regulatory obstacles, and so on.

Particularly when it comes to products which have identifiable features, their *physical characteristics* and *intended use* allow the Commission, as a first step, to limit the field of investigation of possible substitutes. Paragraph 36 of the Notice on Relevant Market 1997 nevertheless shows that such tools are insufficient to show whether two products are demand substitutes. Functional interchangeability or similarity in characteristics may not, in themselves, provide sufficient criteria, because the responsiveness of customers to relative price changes may be determined by other considerations (e.g. markets for original equipment and spare parts, respectively, may feature different competitive constraints and may thus constitute separate relevant markets). And yet, in *United Brands*, the CJEU relied heavily on the product's characteristics and intended use when identifying the banana market to be separate from the market from fresh fruit. The Court stated that 'the banana has certain characteristics, appearance, taste, softness, seedlessness, easy handling, a constant level of production, which enable it to satisfy the constant needs of an important section of the population consisting of the very young, the old and the sick'.[38]

All in all, to our minds, the product market definition entails complex analyses, in which the overall picture of the interaction between goods or services must, at the end of the day, match economic and business realities. This is why, reliance on SSNIP only, or on physical characteristics or intended use only, may lead to erroneous definitions of the market. In our view, once such tools are applied to a practical setting, 'taking a step back' and considering whether the market boundaries as identified make sense in the economic and business reality of the case (and economic sector) may be a good idea. This is so, particularly in complex

---

[37] Notice on Relevant Market 1997, par. 14, 20–23.

[38] Case 27/76 *United Brands*, ECLI:EU:1978:22, par. 31.

market scenarios, such as aftermarkets/spare parts markets/secondary markets (referring to complementary products which are normally purchased after a primary product to which they relate has been purchased),[39] markets entailing chains of substitution (namely, cases in which products at the extreme of the geographic/product are not substitutable)[40] or multi-sided and digital markets.[41]

2.2.1.2 Geographic market

Paragraph 8 of the Notice on Relevant Market 1997 defines the relevant geographic market as the area in which the undertakings concerned are involved in the supply and demand of products or services, in which the conditions of competition are sufficiently homogeneous and which can be distinguished from neighbouring areas because the conditions of competition are appreciably different in those areas. In *United Brands*,[42] the CJEU made it clear that it is in relation to the geographic market, defined as such, that an evaluation of the effect of the market power of the undertaking in question should take place. A number of factors are relevant in this exercise, and their correct assessment may render markets to being defined as local, regional, national, European, or global.[43] The perception of such factors must not always render the conditions of competition in different geographic areas perfectly homogeneous, for such areas to be brought within one and the same relevant geographic market. It is sufficient if the conditions of competition are similar or sufficiently homogeneous and, accordingly, only areas in which the objective conditions of competition are heterogeneous may not be considered to constitute a uniform market.[44] Defining the geographic market is meant to identify the various alternative sources of supply that may be chosen by the consumers.

The Commission will first draw a working hypothesis of the relevant geographic market definition: this is a preliminary view of the scope of the geographic market, on the basis of broad indications as to the distribution of market shares between the parties and their competitors, as well as a preliminary analysis of pricing and price differences at national and EU level. The Commission then fine-tunes this initial view, by checking the working hypothesis against demand characteristics, supply factors and trade flows, in order to essentially identify whether companies located in a given area may be isolated from the competitive pressure of companies located outside that area.[45] This analysis essentially boils down to performing a SSNIP test, similar to the one described above and mentioned in Chapter 2. The difference is, however, that, in the case of the geographic market definition, the question is whether, faced

---

[39] Notice on Relevant Market 1997, par. 56. See cases 22/78 *Hugin*, ECLI:EU:C:1979:138; T-427/08 *CEAHR*, ECLI:EU:T:2010:517.

[40] Notice on Relevant Market 1997, par. 57.

[41] See section 2.2.1.4 of this chapter.

[42] Case 27/76 *United Brands*, ECLI:EU:1978:22, par. 11.

[43] Notice on Relevant Market 1997, par. 51.

[44] Case T-229/94 *Deutsche Bahn*, ECLI:EU:T:1997:155, par. 92.

[45] Notice on Relevant Market 1997, par. 28–31.

with an increase in price, consumers located in a particular area would switch their purchases to suppliers established elsewhere, in the short term and at negligible cost.[46]

Paragraphs 44 *et seq.* of the Notice on Relevant Market 1997 shed light on the factors which the Commission may take into account as evidence for the purpose of defining the relevant geographic market: past evidence of diversion of orders to other areas; consumers' national preferences, or preferences for national brands and language; views of customers and competitors; geographic patterns of purchasing; statistic evidence on trade flows and patterns of shipments; (regulatory) barriers isolating the national market (e.g. quotas and tariffs); transport costs (especially for bulky, low-value products); significant switching costs in procuring supplies, and so on.

A good example of the use of such factors is the *Michelin I* case.[47] In this case, the market for supply of tyres for heavy duty vehicles to dealers was confined to the territory of the Netherlands because: Michelin NV (Dutch subsidiary of Michelin) concentrated its activities in the Netherlands, the main competitors' activities were also performed in the same territory, again via subsidiaries, dealers in the Netherlands were only shopping within the boundaries of this Member State, the pricing behaviour of Michelin NV was only addressed to the dealers in this territory, and so on.

Lastly, it is important to understand that the perception of (geographic) markets changes over time. This is due to various reasons which, as Commissioner Vestager acknowledges,[48] the review of the Notice on Relevant Market 1997 is bound to take into account. For example, digitalisation and the integration of the Internal Market[49] allow consumers to find supplies beyond just the local providers. Indeed, markets develop continuously, yet one should not be easily swept away into thinking that (almost) every market is nowadays EU-wide or world-wide. Certain markets (e.g. production of cement), despite the worldwide presence of market players, are nevertheless bound to remain (geographically) local, due to high transport costs.

2.2.1.3 Temporal market

In certain cases, it may be necessary to define the relevant temporal market too, although when temporal aspects may be relevant to a particular case, such considerations are subsumed in the product/service market definition.[50] Temporal aspects are normally relevant when the competition conditions vary during a calendar year, as is the case, for example, with the production and supply of seasonal products, or with transport services. In such scenarios, an undertaking may face competitive constraints during certain periods of the year, and enjoy market power during other periods. Cases in which a definition of the temporal market is necessary are nevertheless rare.[51]

---

[46] Ibid, par. 29; Whish and Bailey 2018, p. 39.

[47] Case C-322/81 *Michelin I*, ECLI:EU:C:1983:313.

[48] Vestager 2019 (b).

[49] Notice on Relevant Market 1997, par. 32.

[50] E.g. joined cases T-374, T-375, T-384 and T-388/94 *European Night Services*, ECLI:EU:T:1998:198.

[51] In case 27/76 *United Brands*, ECLI:EU:1978:22, for example, evidence was put forward regarding the existence

2.2.1.4 Market definition in the digital economy

While the sections above approach the definition of the market primarily from the perspective of the analogue/offline traditional economy, it is by now commonly accepted that the advent of the digital economy has led to the emergence of new types of markets, that is, digital markets. We have already signalled in Chapter 3 that the digitalisation phenomenon has brought about new types of products and services, new technologies and business models, and also new channels through which end-consumers may be reached. Such features signal that the market definition in the digital economy is a 'different kind of beast'.

The challenges of defining the relevant market in cases embedded in the digital economy relate primarily to the product market definition. Traditional tools used in this respect, both with regard to demand-side and supply-side substitutability, seem to be somewhat ill-suited when it comes to digital markets. For example, when prices are a factor in the consumers' decision-making regarding purchasing of digital goods and services, consumers are highly price sensitive and will quickly search for substitutes. Often though, prices do not play a role in digital markets, since services are offered for free. In such scenarios, the application of the SSNIP test is rendered useless. Mandrescu[52] actually argues that the SSNIP test of demand elasticity will require an overhaul in order to maintain its relevance in the case of zero-pricing strategies commonly used by online platforms. The author suggests that, in such cases, the only feasible option for assessing demand elasticity for the purpose of performing the hypothetical monopolist test entails converting the price-centred analysis into a quality-oriented one, namely based on a *small but significant non-transitory decrease in quality*. The *Google Shopping* decision[53] seems to be a good example in this respect, where Google allegedly engaged in self-preferencing conduct, resulting in leveraging market power from the search engine market to the neighbouring comparison shopping market. Also, in *Google Android*,[54] the Commission, having to deal with the fact that the Android operating system was offered for free, questioned what would happen if Google reduced the quality of Android: would consumers switch to other providers? Other authors,[55] however, argue that quality might be a subjective concept and it is unclear how a change in the quality could be quantified. Either way, although focusing on quality rather than price might make economic sense, the practical implementation of such an approach is difficult.

It seems that where price does not play a role the competition process is placed on other considerations, such as innovation and the role of data. In so-called innovation markets, emphasis is placed on investments in R&D and the market players' ability to be the first to introduce a new or improved product or process, which will give this undertaking an edge in its relationship with other market players. It is argued that in such markets, reliance on

---

of seasonal markets for bananas and fresh fruit, yet the Commission and the CJEU did not take such evidence into account.

[52] Mandrescu 2018 (a).

[53] Case AT.39740 *Google Search (Shopping)*, (2017) 4444 final.

[54] Case AT.40099 *Google Android*, (2018) 4761 final.

[55] Schwalbe 2019.

market shares should be treated with great care,[56] because due to the fast pace of innovation, the supply-side substitutability dynamics may differ greatly from markets in the traditional economy. Data, on the other hand, becomes a crucial asset in digital markets, particularly when it cannot be easily replicated by competitors, and especially when digital products or services are offered 'for free'. Customers actually often allow access to their data, in exchange for the products or services 'purchased', data which may be later monetised in subsequent transactions, relating to, for example, personalised advertisements. This is particularly so when exchanges in the digital economy take place on so-called multi-sided platforms. Thus, on multi-sided markets data is important on the user side. The collection of data is also important, since it can determine the economic position vis-à-vis competitors, and it should be therefore regarded as a competitive parameter.[57] The focus on data does not, however, mean that the price parameter is completely 'out of the picture'. On multi-sided markets, on the advertisement side, price considerations are still important, since companies seeking to sell goods and services have to pay the platform to this end.

This takes us to the next complication relating to market definition in the digital economy. Applying the traditional market definition tools in multi-sided platform settings may yield unreliable market definitions, for example when the SSNIP test is applied only to one side of this market/platform. Further, if the SSNIP test was applied to both sides of the market, should all prices be increased or just the price on one side of the market, and if so, which one? Should the sum of the two prices be increased and in which proportion? Should the two prices be increased simultaneously or sequentially? In any case, how can one account for the fact that the hypothetical price increase may affect both sides of the platform?[58] To this end, Mandrescu[59] actually argues that in order to adequately reflect the business reality of online platforms in the digital economy and the degree of competitive pressure they may experience in practice, the key initial step in the approach to market definition is to identify the number of relevant markets in a given case. This should be determined based on the typology of the interactions facilitated by the online platform and the degree of substitutability of such online platform with other non-platform undertakings from the perspective of its customer groups. In this respect, the author argues that the main challenges when it comes to market definition in cases involving online platforms relate not to the availability of tools, but rather to their correct application and translation of the existing concepts to platforms.

Speaking of practical challenges, as opposed to traditional markets where the homogeneity of the goods traded may be identified with a more or less accurate degree of precision (e.g. fruits, soft drinks, guitars, and so forth), digital platforms may evolve into becoming their own 'ecosystems'. Such entities offer a range of products and services which are often complementary to each other, which may lock the consumers in, by making it difficult to switch to competing suppliers.[60] Competition does not occur thus on individual products or

---

[56] Bishop and Walker 2010.

[57] Kerber 2016.

[58] Schwalbe 2019.

[59] Mandrescu 2018 (b).

[60] Vestager 2019 (b).

services per se, but on bundles of such offerings. The difficulties of defining markets in such settings are by now well acknowledged. The Commission's 2019 Report on Competition Policy for the Digital Era[61] states that digital market boundaries are not as clear as in the 'old economy', and therefore less emphasis should be placed on the analysis of market definition in the digital sector, and more emphasis should be devoted to theories of harm and the identification of anti-competitive strategies. In this sense, it is sensible that the Commission's recent attention seems to be turning to developing new competition tools for digital markets, and particularly in relation to potential *ex ante* regulation of digital platforms that play a so-called gatekeeper role and with regard to preventing that markets that exhibit certain characteristics (e.g. network and scale effects, lack of multi-homing and lock-in effects) face the risk of 'tipping'.[62]

In any case, it will be interesting to see how the review of the Notice on Relevant Market 1997 will account for the digitalisation challenges, as far as market definition is concerned. One thing, however, should be crystal clear: market definition requires transparency and consistency, in order to confer legal certainty to the market players. This is so, particularly when thinking of the consequences of labelling an undertaking dominant or non-dominant, based on a narrow or broad market definition.

2.2.2 Establishing dominance

Once the relevant market is defined, it is time to establish whether a dominant position is held by one or more undertakings on that market. In general, a dominant position derives from a combination of several factors which, taken separately, are not necessarily determinative.[63] Paragraph 12 of the Commission's Enforcement Priorities Guidelines 2009 indicates that the assessment of dominance will take into account the competitive structure of the market, meaning a focus on the market shares of the undertaking at hand and of its competitors, on barriers to entry and the constraints that potential competitors may exert, and on the countervailing force of buyers. This enumeration is not exhaustive; depending on the features of each case, other market aspects or features of the undertakings concerned may be taken into account.

2.2.2.1 Market shares and positioning on the market

Paragraph 13 of the Enforcement Priorities Guidelines 2009 states clearly that market shares provide a useful *first indication* of the market structure and of the relative importance of the various undertakings active on the market.[64] This approach is in line with the CJEU's

---

[61] Crémer, de Montjoye and Schweitzer 2019.

[62] Press Release IP/20/977.

[63] Enforcement Priorities Guidelines 2009, par. 10.

[64] On the calculation of market shares, see Notice on Relevant Market 1997, par. 53–55. Essentially, the volume and/or value of sales of the relevant products in the relevant area are important in this exercise. However, when sales figures are not at stake, other factors may be taken into account: e.g. in case AT.39740 *Google Search (Shopping)*, (2017) 4444 final, the Commission evaluated the volume of user traffic in general search services.

well-established case-law.[65] Yet, concluding that an undertaking is dominant *solely* based on market share information, particularly in complex market scenarios, may not be the smartest thing to do.[66] Market shares must be interpreted in light of the relevant market conditions, and in particular in light of the volatility and dynamics of the market. They must be perceived in the broader context: for example, high market shares may not be indicative of dominance if the market has no barriers to entry, as players not yet active in the market may easily constrain the incumbent's behaviour by threatening swift and aggressive market entry. Nevertheless, regardless of how tentative the Commission's and EU courts' language is when it comes to market shares, the fact of the matter is that, in practice, market shares are key in assessing the existence of dominance. The same is true for the practice in US antitrust law.[67] Although the precise dividing line is unclear, the Supreme Court has indicated that market shares above 66 per cent point to the existence of monopoly power (the US equivalent of dominance).[68]

The practical perception of market shares resembles a gliding scale: low market shares are generally a good proxy for the absence of substantial market power, while the higher the market share and the longer the period of time over which it is held, the more likely it is that it constitutes an important preliminary indication of the existence of a dominant position.[69] In practice, certain thresholds of market power are being used, although these are not necessarily bright-line measures which establish *legal* presumptions. In other words, no safe harbour is established per se in Article 102 TFEU. For example, while the Commission does not exclude the possibility of dominance being established at market share levels below 40 per cent, it acknowledges at paragraph 14 of its Enforcement Priorities Guidelines 2009 that dominance in such scenarios is *not likely*. At such low levels, there may be cases which deserve attention, specifically when competitors are not in a position to constrain effectively the conduct of a dominant undertaking, because, for example, they face serious capacity limitations. In the case-law of the EU courts, the lowest market share resulting in dominance was registered in the *British Airways* case,[70] at 39.7 per cent. Market shares over 50 per cent, on the other hand, are considered according to the CJEU (e.g. *Hoffmann-La Roche*, *AKZO*[71] and *AstraZeneca*[72]) as very large, which are in themselves, and save in exceptional circumstances, evidence of the existence of a dominant position. It is often argued that such levels of market share provide a (rebuttable) presumption, or better yet, a permissible inference of dominance.[73] This does not mean that when market shares exceed quite high levels (e.g.

---

[65] E.g. cases 85/76 *Hoffmann-La Roche*, ECLI:EU:C:1979:36, par. 39–41; T-30/89 *Hilti*, ECLI:EU:T:1991:70, par. 90–92.

[66] Enforcement Priorities Guidelines 2009, par. 15.

[67] Elhauge and Geradin 2011, p. 284.

[68] Ibid, pp. 284–5.

[69] Enforcement Priorities Guidelines 2009, par. 14–15.

[70] Case T-219/99 *British Airways*, ECLI:EU:T:2003:343.

[71] Case C-62/86 *AKZO Chemie v Commission*, ECLI:EU:C:1991:286, par. 60.

[72] Case C-457/10 P *AstraZeneca*, ECLI:EU:C:2012:770, par. 176.

[73] Jones, Sufrin and Dunne 2019, p. 334, with reference to Faull and Nikpay 2014.

over 70 per cent), other factors are not taken into account, to see whether such exceptional circumstances exist. The flipside of this statement is equally valid: the lower the market share of the undertaking in question, the higher will be the importance of other factors (e.g. structure of the market and the positioning of undertakings, entry barriers, countervailing buyer power), in order to establish dominance. This is particularly so, when dealing with so-called 'grey area' cases, of market share levels between 40 and 50 per cent, when such other factors may be used to establish the existence of a dominant position, where market shares alone are not enough to reach the rebuttable presumption, or permissible inference mentioned above. Yet, such factors may also be used to rebut this presumption when the market shares are over 50 per cent. For example, an undertaking holds more than half of the market shares and argues that it should not be labelled dominant due to the presence of strong competitors, the lack of barriers to entry, and suchlike.

Thus, market shares must not be viewed only as absolute values, but also in their relative context, as the Court signalled in *Gøttrup Klim*:[74] the market shares of the undertaking allegedly dominant have to be viewed in relation to the strength and number of its competitors. In *Hoffmann-La Roche*,[75] the Court highlighted the importance of the relationship between the market shares of the undertaking concerned and of its competitors, especially those of the next largest. For example, an undertaking with 45 per cent market share enjoys a different degree of market power if it has one competitor holding 35 per cent and several other competitors each with around 10 per cent of the market, than when it has 25 competitors all with market shares around 1 per cent and 2 per cent.

Lastly, timing is also important. Market shares must be held for a period of time for them to trustworthily indicate dominance. The more dynamic the market, the longer this period should be. In practice, we are talking about years, rather than months or weeks, in this respect. For market power to trigger the Commission's attention, it should not be transitory.

2.2.2.2 Expansion and entry

The Commission argues in paragraphs 16 and 17 of its Enforcement Priorities Guidelines 2009 that competition is a dynamic process and an assessment of the competitive constraints on an undertaking cannot be based solely on the existing market situation. The potential impact of expansion by actual competitors or market entry by potential competitors, including the threat of such expansion or entry, is also relevant, since it may deter price increases by the allegedly dominant undertaking. However, for such outcomes to actually occur in practice, certain basic requirements must be met: first, expansion or entry must be *likely*, in that it must be sufficiently profitable, taking into account barriers to expansion or entry, the likely reactions of the allegedly dominant undertaking and other competitors, and the risks and costs of failure; second, it must be *timely*, in that it must be sufficiently swift to deter or defeat the exercise of substantial market power; third, it must be *sufficient*, in that it must have a certain magnitude, going beyond small-scale entry into a niche segment of the market.

---

[74] Case C-250/92 *Gøttrup Klim*, ECLI:EU:C:1994:413, par. 48.

[75] Case 85/76 *Hoffmann-La Roche*, ECLI:EU:C:1979:36, par. 48.

For these three conditions to be met, much will depend on the concept of so-called 'barriers to expansion/entry'. The concept of barriers to entry can be defined in multiple ways, and may exhibit diverse features, which all, nevertheless boil down to costs which must be borne by a company which seeks to enter a market or an industry, but are not borne by the firms already established in the industry.[76] Barriers to entry thus relate to specific features of a given market, which give incumbent firms advantages over potential competitors. The recipe is quite straightforward: high barriers to entry may insulate a particular market, giving the incumbent undertaking the possibility to raise prices and reduce output, even if its market share is not too high; low or no barriers to entry may result in likelier and timelier market entry by potential competitors, especially if high prices in that market signal to these players that that market may be quite profitable.

The Enforcement Priorities Guidelines 2009, much like the Horizontal Merger Guidelines 2004, discussed in Chapter 10, categorise barriers to entry as legal, technical or strategic advantages. Legal advantages relate to regulatory (tariff-related or not) barriers, which essentially limit the number of market participants. In Article 102 TFEU cases, it seems that technical and strategic advantages (i.e. factors which are more 'internal' to the undertaking in question) seem to bear more weight. For example, in *United Brands*, the CJEU discussed the structure and characteristics of the company.[77] It noticed that the undertaking was highly vertically integrated, covering multiple levels of the production–distribution chain. As also mentioned in *Michelin I*,[78] such integration, or owning an established distribution and sales network, or having long-term supply contracts with customers may have important consequences which make market entry less attractive: the incumbent company may be able to deliver the product to the end-consumer in a smoother manner, or as the case may be, it may protect itself more effectively against competition. Moving on, economies of scale, allowing the spread of an investment over larger quantities of products,[79] as well as technological advances enjoyed by the undertaking, may constitute deterrent signals to outsiders. Next, a company that is constantly involved in research, or has efficient internal organisational structures and the ability to mount large-scale advertisement campaigns, can compete more successfully with its competitors. Also, owning strong brand names, or essential facilities, or preferential access to natural resources or inputs that are unavailable to entrants, may render a company an 'unavoidable trading partner'. Further, the so-called portfolio power of an undertaking, its overall size and strength and its investment capabilities, could also deter entry. Lastly for now, and specifically (but not exclusively) with reference to digital markets, network effects, the ability to lock-in consumers,[80] or to increase the customer's costs of switching to an alternative supplier, are also circumstances which may make market entry less attractive, and consequently good indicators for establishing dominant positions.

---

[76] Stigler 1968, p. 67.

[77] Case 27/76 *United Brands*, ECLI:EU:1978:22, par. 69 *et seq.*

[78] Case C-322/81 *Michelin I*, ECLI:EU:C:1983:313, par. 58.

[79] Lorenz 2013, p. 201.

[80] E.g. case AT.40153 *Amazon (E-book MFNs)*, (2017) 2876 final.

2.2.2.3 Buyer power

The Commission dedicates one single paragraph (18) in its Enforcement Priorities Guidelines 2009 to the matter of countervailing buyer power as a relevant factor in establishing a dominant position. Essentially, the Commission argues that, even when an undertaking has a high market share, it may not be able to act to an appreciable extent independently of customers, when such customers are able to exercise constraints on its behaviour due to their bargaining strength. This power, however, must be of magnitude to amount to effective constraint:[81] for example, buyers may have a certain size or commercial significance to the seller, they may switch quickly to competing suppliers, they may promote new entry, vertically integrate, or credibly threaten to do so. Such buyers should not be 'selfish' though. Negotiating favourable terms for themselves only is not enough to label the seller non-dominant. They should instead react to any price increase in the market, for their countervailing power to actually constrain price increases upstream. All in all, put bluntly, a powerful seller will only be as dominant as the buyers downstream are able to allow it to be.

2.2.2.4 Dominance in the digital economy

Dominance and market power seem to be exhibiting new dimensions when it comes to digital markets, for many reasons. For example, as discussed in Chapter 3, digital markets exhibit tendencies towards 'winner takes all' competition *for* the market, rather than competition *in* the market. Also, in such markets, establishing the existence of dominance requires a more encompassing view of multiple parameters. A few examples in this respect are briefly provided in the lines below.

Market shares are less reliable in digital markets, since in such markets the innovation coming from competitors, be them fringe competitors, may displace market power in the short run. Also, market share analysis, as known in the context of traditional markets, is static, whereas the dynamics of new types of (digital) markets seem to require a more in-depth look, going beyond market shares. This stance was evident as early as the *France Télécom* case,[82] in which the GC did not dismiss the claimant's contention that, in emerging markets, market shares are not always the most reliable indicator, and that the market should be looked at from a dynamic perspective by assessing potential as well as actual competition. This is, however, not to be interpreted that market share analysis no longer plays a role in digital markets. In recent Commission decisions (e.g. *Google Shopping* and *Amazon*[83]) high market shares kept over a period of time are still a factor discussed while assessing dominance.

Measuring market power in cases involving multi-sided platforms is further complicated when pricing is not a factor to be taken into account, and when instead, what counts more are incentives to increase scale, network effects and externalities, and the use of data. For example, if data that is not available to market entrants provides a strong competitive advantage, its possession may lead to market dominance. Further, this dominance can extend to

---

[81] E.g. case T-228/97 *Irish Sugar*, ECLI:EU:T:1999:246.

[82] Case T-340/03 *France Télécom*, ECLI:EU:T:2007:22; C-202/07 P *France Télécom*, ECLI:EU:C:2009:214. See also Jones, Sufrin and Dunne 2019, p. 340.

[83] Case AT.40153 *Amazon (E-book MFNs)*, (2017) 2876 final.

adjacent markets where the same data conveys strong competitive advantages in providing complementary services.[84] Also, direct and indirect network effects may often amount to barriers to entry when talking about multi-sided markets, thus requiring a different outlook on the constraints imposed by potential competition. In this context, taking the discussion further, cross-platform network effects can magnify the competitive constraints that exist, while also raising entry barriers to potential rivals and restricting the emergence of new competitive constraints.[85]

Market power in digital markets may be exacerbated by vertical integration, where businesses expand into upstream and downstream markets, becoming competitors of, for example, the traders or app developers that use their platforms (e.g. Apple and Amazon). Companies that expand in such manner may have better ability to collect data, which in turn improves their competitiveness, to the point where they may become gatekeepers of online stores and application markets, in which they are both owners and users.[86] It is thus not surprising that the attention of competition authorities is triggered when dominant undertakings assume such a role in the relevant online ecosystem.[87] Yet, complications arise when the boundaries and features of the term gatekeeper are not yet properly defined. Is this gatekeeper undertaking supposed to be dominant? Or does this term entail something more than dominance?[88] While this seems to be the case, it is self-evident that the consequences of introducing new thresholds in the enforcement of Article 102 TFEU will not come free of challenges.

Lastly for now, such challenges may also be connected to the notion of 'modern bigness' and the concerns surrounding the power of 'Big Tech'. Gerbrandy[89] argues that technological developments and the accumulation of economic and digital power have consequences for the application of the law, when large tech firms impact markets. Yet, the definition of bigness is not limited to the law only; it relates to different facets of power (i.e. economic, corporate, power of governance, market power, digital power, and more). In this respect, when it comes to 'modern bigness' attention should be paid to how the behaviour of such large tech firms impacts not only market, but also non-market values. This takes us back to the discussion provided in Chapter 1, regarding non-economic interest analysis in competition law.

Summing up, asserting dominance in the digital economy seems to often require adopting a different stance. Competition issues created by market power in such realms are by now a reality. This is why competition authorities and legislators are leaning more and more towards appropriately conceptualising market power and dominance in the digital economy. A perfect example in this respect is the new Section 18(3a) of the German GWB, which provides that, in particular in the case of multi-sided markets and networks, in assessing

---

[84] Crémer, de Montjoye and Schweitzer 2019, p. 49.

[85] OECD 2018, pp. 16–21.

[86] UNCTAD 2019, p. 7.

[87] See e.g. in the Netherlands, the ACM Memorandum 2019; in Germany, see Market Power of Platforms and Networks 2016. See also Press Release IP/20/977.

[88] Mandrescu 2019.

[89] Gerbrandy 2018.

the market position of an undertaking account shall also be taken of factors such as those discussed just above. In section 4.1 below, this provision of German competition law will be highlighted.

2.3 Internal Market or substantial part of it

For Article 102 TFEU to apply, it needs to be ensured that the dominant position is held in the EU Internal Market or a substantial part of it. This criterion acts as a jurisdictional threshold, calling for EU or domestic intervention, respectively. For example, cases in which the dominant position is localised in one (area of a) Member State have probably less, or no EU interest, to necessarily trigger the application of this TFEU article. Given the enlargement of the EU in the recent decades, and given the deeper integration of the Internal Market, the delineation of geographic markets becomes broader.[90] This is why bright-line, percentage-based delineations of what is a substantial part of the Internal Market were not endorsed by the EU courts. For the sake of clarity, this requirement is not the same as the definition of the relevant geographic market, which belongs to the substantive assessment of whether an undertaking has a dominant position.[91] Speaking of the geographic dimension, this aspect is not decisive in establishing whether dominance is held in a substantial part of the Internal Market. As indicated in *Suiker Unie*,[92] substantiality is instead judged in light of the pattern and volume of production and consumption of goods/services, and the habits and economic opportunities of vendors and purchasers. This is why a Member State, or a part of it, is likely to be considered a substantial part of the Internal Market, especially where legal monopolies are established, and in so-called 'single facility' cases (e.g. harbours, airports, and the like).[93]

2.4 Abuse

In section 2 above we pointed out that, once dominance is established, the undertaking concerned has a special responsibility not to allow its conduct to impair genuine undistorted competition on the market. This essentially means that Article 102 TFEU imposes a prohibition on dominant undertakings to abuse the power they have on the market. It is important to understand that this responsibility pertains only to dominant undertakings, meaning that the same type of behaviour is not caught by the Article 102 TFEU prohibition when engaged in by a non-dominant firm.

The concept of abuse is not defined in the TFEU. Article 102 TFEU nevertheless contains a non-exhaustive list of practices that may amount to abusive behaviour. As we will see in the subsections below, the Commission, the EU courts and also the NCAs have dealt

---

[90] Jones, Sufrin and Dunne 2019, p. 288.

[91] Whish and Bailey 2018, p. 196.

[92] Joined cases 40 to 48, 50, 54 to 56, 111, 113 and 114/73 *Suiker Unie*, ECLI:EU:C:1975:174.

[93] E.g. cases C-18/93 *Corsica Ferries*, ECLI:EU:C:1994:195; C-179/90 *Merci Convenzionali Porto di Genova*, ECLI: EU:C:1991:464. See also Guidelines on Effect on Trade 2004, par. 98.

under Article 102 TFEU with diverse types of practices, not mentioned specifically in this provision. The exemplificative list in Article 102 TFEU resembles closely the enumeration contained in Article 101 TFEU. This similarity makes sense, at least from an economic point of view, since behaviour caught under both TFEU articles may result in price increases and reduction of output, in the presence of a degree of market power. (One of) the difference(s) between the two provisions is that while Article 101 TFEU tackles the coordination between undertakings, Article 102 TFEU applies to the unilateral behaviour of undertakings holding a dominant position.[94]

Labelling the behaviour of a dominant undertaking as abusive is not an easy task. The enforcement authorities must decide whether that behaviour deviates from 'normal' or 'fair' or 'undistorted' competition, or from 'competition on the merits', none of which expressions is free from difficulty.[95] The CJEU has, however, provided valuable indications of what the notion of abuse entails, in its case-law. The Enforcement Priorities Guidelines 2009 also provides clarity and predictability as regards the general framework of analysis which the Commission employs, thus helping undertakings assess if certain behaviour is likely to result in intervention by the Commission under Article 102 TFEU.[96]

Giving a fully encompassing definition of the concept of abuse is a difficult task, especially having in mind that the scope of the special responsibility not to engage in abusive conduct must be considered in the light of the specific circumstances of each case.[97] The CJEU has nevertheless consistently provided in its early[98] and more recent case-law[99] that concept of *abuse is an objective concept relating to the conduct of a dominant undertaking which, on a market where the degree of competition is already weakened precisely because of the presence of the undertaking concerned, through recourse to methods different from those governing normal competition in products or services on the basis of the transactions of commercial operators, has the effect of hindering the maintenance of the degree of competition still existing in the market or the growth of that competition.*

Certain clarifications about this definition are in order at this point. First, the notion of abuse is an objective concept. This means that, as highlighted in *Continental Can*,[100] abusive conduct may be caught under Article 102 TFEU irrespective of any fault or subjective intention of the dominant undertaking. However, if the dominant undertaking's behaviour has an anti-competitive intent, this *may* be used as one of the factors taken into account to establish the existence of an abuse. Also, with regard to certain types of abuses (e.g. predation, vexatious litigation), the dominant undertaking's intent plays a more intense role. In any case, the

---

[94] See also Regulation 1/2003, Article 3.

[95] Whish and Bailey 2018, p. 197.

[96] Enforcement Priorities Guidelines 2009, par. 2.

[97] Ibid, par. 9, referring to cases such as C-322/81 *Michelin I*, ECLI:EU:C:1983:313, par. 57; T-83/91 *Tetra Pak II*, ECLI:EU:T:1994:246, par. 114; T-228/97 *Irish Sugar*, ECLI:EU:T:1999:246, par. 112.

[98] E.g. case 85/76 *Hoffmann-La Roche*, ECLI:EU:C:1979:36, par. 91.

[99] E.g. case C-52/09 *TeliaSonera*, ECLI:EU:C:2011:83, par. 27.

[100] Case 6/72 *Continental Can*, ECLI:EU:C:1973:22, par 29.

flipside of the statements above, namely that the dominant undertaking intends to 'compete on the merits', cannot prove the absence of an abuse.[101]

Second, it is extremely rare to encounter so-called 'one-product undertakings'. Indeed, companies are often active on different, often connected markets. It is thus not inconceivable that an undertaking dominates one particular market, while behaving in an abusive manner on another market, for example, to leverage the market power from the dominated to the non-dominated market. In *Tetra Pak II*,[102] the CJEU clarified that an abuse may occur in a market different from the one dominated, while in *AstraZeneca*,[103] the GC argued that an abuse of a dominant position does not necessarily have to consist in the use of the economic power conferred by a dominant position. Consequently, what matters is that the undertaking at hand enjoys a degree of power which 'supports' its abusive behaviour, without necessarily using that power.

Third, at times, when referring to the notion of abuse, the CJEU alters slightly the language used in the *Hoffmann-La Roche* definition, by adding interesting (and to a certain extent surprising) remarks.[104] In *Post Danmark I*,[105] the CJEU added a specific requirement of consumer detriment to the notion of abuse. In *Intel*,[106] the focus was also placed on consumer welfare, when the CJEU spoke of competitors that are less attractive to consumers from the point of view of price, choice, quality or innovation. Granted, in *Post Danmark I*, the Court argued that Article 102 TFEU applies *in particular* to conduct detrimental to consumers. This signals that detriment to consumer is not a constitutive element of the notion of abuse, but rather an example of who could be 'on the receiving end' of abusive practices of dominant undertakings. In this respect, this discussion seems reminiscent of the points made by the GC and CJEU in the *GlaxoSmithKline* case,[107] discussed in Chapter 1.

2.4.1 Categorisations

Abuses may be categorised as *price* and *non-price* related. The former category includes, for example, excessive high pricing, predatory pricing, price discrimination, and the latter, for instance, refusal to supply or vexatious litigation. Another categorisation distinguishes between abuses which threaten the integration of the Internal Market, by partitioning it into separate smaller markets, price discrimination abuses, and reprisal abuses, which relate to punishing other market players.

The most prominent categorisation relates to so-called *exploitative* and *exclusionary* abuses. Exploitative conduct relates to drawing advantages from the opportunities provided by the dominant company's strength, in order to exploit the undertaking's trading partners, be they customers or consumers downstream, or suppliers upstream. Paragraph 7 of the

---

[101] Case C-549/10 P *Tomra*, ECLI:EU:C:2012:221, par. 19–22.

[102] Case C-333/94 P *Tetra Pak II*, ECLI:EU:C:1996:436.

[103] Case T-321/05 *AstraZeneca*, ECLI:EU:T:2010:266, par. 354.

[104] Jones, Sufrin and Dunne 2019, p. 367.

[105] Case C-209/10 *Post Danmark I*, ECLI:EU:C:2012:172, par. 24.

[106] Case C-413/14 *Intel*, ECLI:EU:C:2017:632, par. 134.

[107] Joined cases C-501, C-513, C-515 and C-519/06 P *GlaxoSmithKline*, ECLI:EU:C:2009:610, par. 63.

Enforcement Priorities Guidelines 2009 provides that conduct which is directly exploita-tive of consumers, for example, charging excessively high prices or certain behaviour that undermines the efforts to achieve an integrated Internal Market, is liable to infringe Article 102 TFEU. The Commission may intervene in relation to such conduct; however, such inter-vention is not per se within its top priorities. Exclusionary abuses, on the other hand, relate to conduct likely to limit the remaining competitive constraints on the dominant company, forcing the exit or limiting entry or expansion by competitors, and thus obviously impacting on the actual structure of the market. As indicated by the actual title of the Commission's Enforcement Priorities Guidelines 2009 (i.e. *Guidance on the Commission's enforcement priorities in applying Article 82 of the EC Treaty – now Article 102 TFEU – to abusive exclusionary conduct by dominant undertakings*), the focus of the Commission's enforce-ment activities in the context of Article 102 TFEU is on exclusionary abuses. Paragraphs 5 and 6 of the Guidelines state clearly that the Commission will focus on those types of conduct that are most harmful to consumers. In this respect, it will direct its enforcement to ensuring that markets function properly and that consumers benefit from the efficiency and productivity which result from effective competition between undertakings. The emphasis pertains to safeguarding the competitive process in the Internal Market and ensuring that dominant undertakings do not exclude their competitors by other means than competing on the merits. The Commission is thus mindful that what really matters is protecting an effective competitive process and not simply protecting competitors. This may very well mean that competitors who deliver less to consumers in terms of price, choice, quality and innovation will leave the market. All in all, the rationale for focusing on exclusionary abuses seems straightforward: ensuring that markets function well entails that efficient market players compete with each other, thus preventing exploitative behaviour to take place, to the ultimate benefit of consumers.

Regardless of these categorisations, abuses are not mutually exclusive. The same conduct may be both exploitative and exclusionary, or both exclusionary and discriminatory, at the same time.[108] Also, certain types of abuses may consist of several different kinds of abusive behaviour: for example, margin squeeze practices may comprise elements of predation, price discrimination and excessive pricing.

2.4.2 Object/effect analysis in Article 102 TFEU?

While drawing a parallel between Articles 101 and 102 TFEU, an interesting question is whether, similar to the object/effect dichotomy in Article 101 TFEU, there are abuses 'by object' and abuses 'by effect' in Article 102 TFEU?

In *Michelin II*,[109] the GC (Court of First Instance (CFI), at that time) stated that, for the purposes of applying Article 102 TFEU, establishing the anti-competitive object and the anti-competitive effect are one and the same thing. If it is shown that the object pursued by the conduct of an undertaking in a dominant position is to limit competition, that conduct will also be liable to have such an effect. The academic community has nuanced this assertion.

---

[108] Jones, Sufrin and Dunne 2019, p. 362.

[109] Case T-203/01 *Michelin II*, ECLI:EU:T:2003:250, par. 241.

Whish and Bailey[110] argue that nowadays there is no per se illegality in Article 102 TFEU analysis. It is true that in *Hoffmann-La Roche* the Court established that the loyalty rebates at issue in that case amounted to a per se abuse of dominance. However, in *Intel*,[111] the Court argued that this line of reasoning must be clarified, when the undertaking concerned submits that its conduct was not capable of restricting competition and, in particular, of producing the alleged foreclosure effects. In other words, a practice would be considered abusive only when it can be shown to be capable of having anti-competitive effects. This, let us call it 'effects analysis', seems to require differing degrees of intensity in different cases/types of abuses/practical scenarios, though. For example, in *TeliaSonera*[112] the Court stated that in order to establish whether such a practice is abusive, that practice *must* have an anti-competitive effect on the market, but the effect does not necessarily have to be concrete, and it is sufficient to demonstrate that there is an anti-competitive effect which may potentially exclude competitors who are at least as efficient as the dominant undertaking. In other cases, such as *Post Danmark II*[113] and *MEO*,[114] where 'all circumstances of the case' had been evaluated before establishing the existence of an abuse, the analysis of potential exclusionary effects seems to be merely one of the tools in the competition authorities' arsenal.

Ibáñez Colomo,[115] on the other hand, puts forward a somewhat different view, while nevertheless acknowledging the *Intel* line of reasoning mentioned above. He argues that the legal tests applicable to undertakings' behaviour on a market may be placed on a spectrum in Article 102 TFEU, much like under Article 101 TFEU, ranging from prima facie lawful behaviour (such as quantity rebates, or pricing above average total cost) to prima facie unlawful (such as exclusive dealing, or pricing below average variable cost); for the latter category, the practice is presumed to have no other purpose than the restriction of competition and it is presumed to be capable of having restrictive effects. In such cases there should be no need to perform an effects analysis. Indeed, paragraph 22 of the Commission's Enforcement Priorities Guidelines 2009 seems to point in the same direction: a detailed assessment is not always necessary, and anti-competitive effects may be inferred when the conduct can only raise obstacles to competition and when it creates no efficiencies.

In between these prima facie lawful and prima facie unlawful types of behaviour, Ibáñez Colomo identifies different degrees of intensity that the analysis of effects of a practice would have to embody: a standard 'effects analysis', as would be the case for margin squeeze and standardised rebates abuses, or an 'enhanced effects analysis', as is the case for refusal to deal abuses. The difference between these types of analyses is, arguably, the remedy that would have to be applied: in the former scenarios we deal with reactive remedies (i.e. the undertaking would be required not to do something), while in the latter scenario the remedy would be proactive (i.e. certain positive obligations would be imposed on the undertaking).

---

[110] Whish and Bailey 2018, p. 204 *et seq.*

[111] Case C-413/14 *Intel*, ECLI:EU:C:2017:632, par. 138.

[112] Case C-52/09 *TeliaSonera*, ECLI:EU:C:2011:83, par 64.

[113] Case C-23/14 *Post Danmark II*, ECLI:EU:C:2015:651, par. 29.

[114] Case C-525/16 *MEO*, ECLI:EU:C:2018:270, par. 31.

[115] Ibáñez Colomo 2018 (a) and 2020.

Thus, the object/effect dichotomy, although not present literally in the text of Article 102 TFEU, seems to have left some traces in the interpretation of this provision. The bottom line is that applying Article 102 TFEU entails that the markets concerned are analysed and, accordingly, a good understanding of how these markets work is gained.

2.4.3 Competition on the merits

We have mentioned several times by now the concept of 'competition on the merits', or 'competing by means of normal competition'. The CJEU and the Commission seem to attach specific weight to these notions, in the context of establishing whether a particular practice is abusive or not. In paragraph 1 of the Enforcement Priorities Guidelines 2009, the Commission states that dominant undertakings are entitled to *compete on the merits*, while in paragraph 6 it is shown that such undertakings may not exclude their competitors by other means than *competing on the merits of the products or services they provide*. In *Hoffmann-La Roche*,[116] the Court referred to methods different from those which condition *normal competition*. In *Post Danmark I*,[117] the Court stated that not every exclusionary effect is necessarily detrimental to competition and that *competition on the merits* may, by definition, lead to departure from the market or marginalisation of competitors that are less efficient and so less attractive to consumers from the point of view of, among other things, price, choice, quality or innovation. The Court also stated that not all competition by means of price may be regarded as legitimate, and it placed this statement in the context of exclusionary behaviour which results in strengthening of a dominant position by using methods other than those that are part of *competition on the merits*.

The concept of competition on the merits points to effective competition between undertakings, which is prone to deliver benefits to consumers, that results from the efficiency and productivity of market players. Practices that meet these requirements, even if they result in vivid competition between undertakings, are not prohibited by Article 102 TFEU. Practices such as vexatious litigation, or misleading the authorities,[118] on the other hand, have nothing to do with competing on the merits of the products or services with regard to which undertakings assumedly compete. Thus, in our opinion, the concept of competition on the merits may arguably be used by the Commission and the EU courts to delineate legal from illegal behaviour under Article 102 TFEU.

Delineating what constitutes and what does not constitute competition on the merits is not always easy, since there are no objective criteria that may be used to this end. In *Microsoft*,[119] for example, the GC referred to the 'intrinsic merits' of the product on which competition is based. In other cases, different economic tools are used in order to identify the boundaries of competition on the merits. The Enforcement Priorities Guidelines 2009[120] prefers the 'equally efficient competitor' and the 'sacrifice' tests. The former entails that conduct should

---

[116] Case 85/76 *Hoffmann-La Roche*, ECLI:EU:C:1979:36, par. 91.

[117] Case C-209/10 *Post Danmark I*, ECLI:EU:C:2012:172, par. 22, 25.

[118] See section 2.4.5.8 of this chapter.

[119] Case T-201/04 *Microsoft*, ECLI:EU:T:2007:289.

[120] Par. 23–25 and 64–66, respectively.

be unlawful only if it is capable of excluding a hypothetical competitor, which is as efficient as the dominant undertaking, for example, having the same costs as the dominant player, because only some kind of anti-competitive conduct can exclude equally efficient rivals. This test is also echoed in *Post Danmark I*.[121] The latter, that is, the 'sacrifice' test, is used by the Commission in cases of predatory pricing, for example. The test is meant to check if the dominant undertaking is sacrificing profits in circumstances where it would only be rational to do so if the undertaking was thereby able to exclude competitors.[122]

2.4.4 Exclusionary conduct and anti-competitive foreclosure

In *Post Danmark I*, the CJEU stated that not every exclusionary effect is necessarily detrimental to competition. To determine whether this is the case, the Court devised a two-prong test:[123] (1) (pricing) practices must have an exclusionary effect on competitors as efficient as the dominant company itself, and (2) this company's dominant position is strengthened by using methods other than those that are part of competition on the merits. But, in *Intel*[124] the Court accepted that the exclusionary effect may be counteracted by evidence put forward by the dominant undertaking, which may show that its conduct was not capable of restricting competition and, in particular, of producing the alleged foreclosure effects. Also, in *Post Danmark II*,[125] while applying the 'as efficient competitor' test, the Court showed that there is no legal obligation that stems from Article 102 TFEU or the Court's case-law, to *always* use this test: it should not be per se excluded from the analysis, but there are also practical scenarios in which applying the 'as efficient competitor' test is of no relevance, inasmuch as the structure of the market makes the emergence of an as efficient competitor practically impossible. In such scenarios, entailing markets with high barriers to entry, the presence of a less efficient competitor might actually contribute to intensifying the competitive pressure on that market and, therefore, to exerting a constraint on the conduct of the dominant undertaking.[126] Thus, the 'as efficient competitor' test is merely *one tool among others* for assessing whether conduct is abusive. Still, when the Commission uses this test, and the dominant undertaking criticises the Commission's method, in order to show that the conduct could not result in foreclosure effects, the GC must take into consideration the undertaking's arguments seeking to expose alleged errors committed by the Commission in the 'as efficient competitor' test.[127]

The Commission's conceptualisation of exclusionary abuses approaches the matter from a different angle, synthesised in the first sentence of paragraph 19 of the Enforcement Priorities Guidelines 2009:

---

[121] Case C-209/10 *Post Danmark I*, ECLI:EU:C:2012:172, par. 25.

[122] Whish and Bailey 2018, p. 204; Jones, Sufrin and Dunne 2019, pp. 373–5.

[123] Case C-209/10 *Post Danmark I*, ECLI:EU:C:2012:172, par. 25.

[124] Case C-413/14 *Intel*, ECLI:EU:C:2017:632, par. 138.

[125] Case C-23/14 *Post Danmark II*, ECLI:EU:C:2015:651, par. 57 *et seq.*

[126] The Commission also acknowledges that in certain circumstances less efficient competitors may exercise constraints which should be taken into account. See Enforcement Priorities Guidelines 2009, par. 24.

[127] Case C-413/14 *Intel*, ECLI:EU:C:2017:632, par. 142 *et seq.*

the aim of the Commission's enforcement activity in relation to exclusionary conduct is to ensure that dominant undertakings do not impair effective competition by fore-closing their competitors in an anti-competitive way, thus having an adverse impact on consumer welfare, whether in the form of higher price levels than would have otherwise prevailed or in some other form such as limiting quality or reducing consumer choice.

Two observations stem from this statement: first, exclusionary abuses may be very well per-ceived as precursors for exploitative abuses, the latter being the ultimate embodiment of one's market power: the ability to raise prices, reduce output and consumer choice. By preventing the former type of conduct, the Commission essentially fosters consumer welfare.[128] Second, this focus on consumers is a perfect exemplification of the consumer welfare objective the Commission strives to attain, as discussed in Chapter 1. At the same time, both points taken together signal the important move in EU competition analysis in the 2000s, towards a more effects-based, economic approach to assessing market behaviour of undertakings.[129]

As a side note in this last respect, the Commission's 2009 Guidelines signal an important turn in how Article 102 TFEU is to be conceived. Jones, Sufrin and Dunne[130] show, with reference to *Post Danmark I* and *II* and *Intel*, that the implications of the Guidelines extend beyond the Commission itself: the case-law increasingly recognises the merits of the 'more economic approach', as evidenced by the courts' reception of concepts, tests and methods such as 'as efficient competitor', efficiency defence, average incremental costs, and suchlike. This stance is even more special, if one has in mind that the EU courts often state that they are not bound by the viewpoints taken by the Commission in its soft-law documents.[131]

Returning to the Commission's conceptualisation of exclusionary abuses, the cornerstone of intervention in Article 102 TFEU cases is the concept *of anti-competitive foreclosure*, defined as a situation where effective access of actual or potential competitors to supplies or markets is hampered or eliminated as a result of the conduct of the dominant undertak-ing whereby the dominant undertaking is likely to be in a position to profitably increase prices above the competitive level, or influence other parameters of competition such as output, innovation, quality, to the detriment of consumers. The concept of anti-competitive foreclosure is thus built on two limbs: first, foreclosure, which, second, must be anti-com-petitive. Reference must be made here to excluding competitors who are equally efficient and via means other than competition on the merits. The second limb relates to identifying consumer (i.e. direct and indirect users, including intermediate producers, distributors and end-consumers) harm, which may be done either via qualitative or quantitative means. From an enforcement perspective, one may perceive the reference to consumer detriment,

---

[128] Enforcement Priorities Guidelines 2009, par. 5.

[129] See also <https://ec.europa.eu/competition/antitrust/art82/index.html> accessed 14 June 2020, where the Commission actually states that the Guidelines comprehensively show how the Commission uses an economic and effects-based approach to establish its enforcement priorities under Article 102 TFEU in relation to exclusionary conduct.

[130] Jones, Sufrin and Dunne 2019, p. 296 *et seq.*

[131] E.g. case C-226/11 *Expedia*, ECLI:EU:C:2012:795.

in light of the Commission's right to set its own priorities: when the Commission would not identify consumer harm, it may relinquish action under Article 102 TFEU. Should there be consumers or competitors unhappy with such an outcome, they may also submit complaints to the NCAs which may also be competent to handle the case, or file a lawsuit before the domestic private law courts.[132]

Assessing whether the first limb of the test is fulfilled in practice requires an analysis of general factors, conduct-specific factors and other factors which the Commission may consider relevant in a given case. This analysis is fed into a counterfactual scenario, which entails comparing the actual or likely future situation in the relevant market (with the dominant undertaking's conduct in place) with the absence of the conduct in question or with another realistic alternative scenario, having regard to established business practices.[133] The general factors that may be relevant for an analysis of anti-competitive foreclosure are spelled out in paragraph 20 of the Guidelines. These may include: the position of the dominant undertaking; the conditions on the relevant market (for example barriers to entry, network effects); the position of the dominant undertaking's competitors, customers or input suppliers; the extent of the allegedly abusive conduct; direct or possible evidence of actual foreclosure.

Lastly for now, when the allegedly exclusionary conduct is price-related, the Commission will use specific tools and cost benchmarks, meant to help it assess whether an equally efficient competitor is likely to be foreclosed.[134] The cost benchmarks the Commission normally uses may at times differ from the ones used by the EU courts in their case-law. Yet, they are not necessarily incompatible or contradictory to each other. Instead, certain cost benchmarks are better suited than others, for different market scenarios, or different industries.[135]

The bottom line is that, if the data clearly suggest that an equally efficient competitor can compete effectively with the pricing conduct of the dominant undertaking, the Commission will, in principle, infer that the dominant undertaking's pricing conduct is not likely to have an adverse impact on effective competition, and thus on consumers, and will therefore be unlikely to intervene. If, on the contrary, the data suggest that the price charged by the dominant undertaking has the potential to foreclose equally efficient competitors, then the Commission will integrate this finding in the general assessment of anti-competitive foreclosure, taking into account other relevant quantitative and/or qualitative evidence.[136]

2.4.5 Examples of abusive conduct

In the following subsections we will discuss several examples of conduct which may be considered abusive and thus prohibited under Article 102 TFEU. It goes without saying that the discussion below does not encapsulate an exhaustive account of every type of behaviour which may qualify as such. We have shown above that Article 102 TFEU contains a non-exhaustive list of practices that may amount to abusive behaviour. The Commission's

---

[132] Rusu 2015 (c) and 2018.

[133] Enforcement Priorities Guidelines 2009, par. 21.

[134] Ibid, par. 23–27. See also description of cost benchmarks provided in Chapter 3.

[135] Case C-209/10 *Post Danmark I*, ECLI:EU:C:2012:172, par. 31 *et seq.*

[136] Enforcement Priorities Guidelines 2009, par. 27.

Enforcement Priorities Guidelines 2009 tackle only a limited number of examples of such behaviour too. Since Article 102 TFEU practice is constantly developing, we can only predict that many other types of conduct which may be deemed abusive will emerge in practice. The subsection below dealing with abusive conduct in the digital economy, for example, is the perfect testimony to this end.

2.4.5.1 Excessive (high) pricing

The ability to charge high prices is arguably what drives businesses to want to increase their market power. In Chapter 3 we showed that, from an economic perspective, the higher the degree of market power of an undertaking, the more it may be inclined to reduce output and increase prices. The mirage of 'monopoly pricing' relates to increased profitability on behalf of the undertaking at hand. But high profitability may also pertain to a reward for risk-taking, or for the innovativeness, or superior efficiency of the respective firm.[137] At the same time, high profits may signal a competition problem. In this respect, what is the benchmark for intervention under Article 102 TFEU? When is the level of pricing sufficiently high to trigger competition law intervention? How to calculate what is high profitability and what is excessive pricing, since, these notions evidently entail a subjective element in their meaning? Lastly, say that a particular practice is deemed abusive particularly because the price was set at a too high level: what would be the remedy available in this respect? Would the remedy not entail, one way or the other, some sort of price regulation on the market, with all the consequences that such an assertion would bring about, especially for the idea of 'free market'? Such questions are good indicators why the inclination of competition authorities throughout the world to tackle excessive pricing differs extensively. For example, in the US, in *Verizon/Trinko*,[138] it was signalled that the ability to charge high prices is an important element in the free market system. Therefore, enforcement of exploitative practices is virtually inexistent. In the EU, the Commission's focus on exclusionary, rather than exploitative, conduct indicates that the excessive high pricing might be quite unlikely in absence of a high degree of market power. In other words, healthy and vivid competition on the merits might itself prevent high pricing from occurring. This does not mean that the Commission is not preoccupied by such behaviour: the scarcity of sanctioning decisions should not mislead us though, since most enforcement action taken by the Commission in respect of such practices is handled via commitment decisions.[139]

The CJEU attempted to define, in *United Brands*,[140] what should be the test for deciding whether prices are excessively high thus warranting intervention under Article 102(a) TFEU. In this case the dominant undertaking was selling its bananas in some areas with prices 100 per cent higher than those charged in other areas, 20 to 40 per cent higher than the prices of unbranded bananas, and 7 per cent higher than the prices of other brands of bananas.

---

[137] Graham 2010, p. 130 *et seq.*; Katsoulacos and Jenny 2018.

[138] Case *Verizon/Trinko*, (2004) 540 US 398.

[139] E.g. Press Release IP/18/3921. In Chapter 8, section 3.3 we will discuss in more detail the concept of commitments. See Regulation 1/2003, Article 9.

[140] Case 27/76 *United Brands*, ECLI:EU:1978:22, par. 250 *et seq.*

The CJEU, while annulling the Commission decision finding an infringement of the said TFEU provision, stated that charging a price which is excessive because it has no reasonable relation to the economic value of the product supplied constitutes an abuse. The question is then how does one decide what this excess amounts to? The Court provided that a possible method would amount to an objective determination, by comparison between the selling price of the product in question and its cost of production, thus disclosing the amount of the profit margin. As complex as this exercise may be, once the profit margin is established as being excessive, a decision must be taken whether the price is either unfair in itself or when compared to competing products. The Court does not explain in clear terms what 'unfair in itself' means, and what is more, it acknowledges that other techniques may be available to make such an evaluation. Comparisons with competing products is also not free of challenges, since judging substitutability is not always an exact science. This 'open' two-prong test was refined in later case-law. In *Bodson*,[141] the Court adopted a method called 'yardstick competition',[142] by suggesting that when it comes to funeral services, comparisons may be drawn between the prices charged by the undertaking that had exclusivity in a certain area, with the prices charged in other areas where markets were open to competition. In several cases dealing with royalty rates,[143] the CJEU accepted that comparisons could be made with prices charged in other Member States. In *AKKA/LAA*,[144] dealing with whether the fees collected by a copyright management organisation in Latvia were unfair or not, the CJEU explained that it is appropriate to compare its rates with those applicable in neighbouring Member States, as well as with those applicable in other Member States. However, given the significant differences in price levels between Member States for identical services, which are closely linked with the differences in citizens' purchasing power, the comparison must be adjusted in accordance with the so-called 'Purchasing Power Parity' index. The reference Member States must nevertheless be selected in accordance with objective, appropriate and verifiable criteria and the comparisons must be made on a consistent basis. The difference between the rates compared must be regarded as appreciable, and thus pointing to an abuse of dominance, if that difference is significant and persistent.

2.4.5.2 Price discrimination

In section 2.4.1 above we showed that price discrimination may constitute a category of abusive practices in itself. This is so, given that discrimination may be a component of particular types of abuses, such as rebates or margin squeeze. Viewed from a different angle, price discrimination may constitute an abusive practice in itself, caught by Article 102(c) TFEU. To make things even more interesting, such a practice may exhibit both exploitative and exclusionary features: the former relates to extracting the highest reservation price from each particular buyer thus trying to capture as much as possible from the consumer surplus.[145] The

---

[141] Case 30/87 *Bodson*, ECLI:EU:C:1988:225.

[142] Lorenz 2013, p. 223.

[143] E.g. joined cases 110, 241 and 242/88 *Lucazeau*, ECLI:EU:C:1989:326.

[144] Case C-177/16 *AKKA/LAA*, ECLI:EU:C:2017:689.

[145] Geradin and Petit 2005, p 5.

latter may result in foreclosure of competitors or of other trading partners. Viewed from this angle, academic writing[146] makes a distinction between primary-line injury (i.e. producing detriments to the competitors of the dominant undertaking) and secondary-line injury (i.e. harming customers of this undertaking, which compete with each other – e.g. purchasers from different Member States). In line with the Commission's focus on exclusionary conduct, primary-line injury scenarios seem to be higher on the enforcement priority list, due to the impact on competition that such discrimination may create. Some authors[147] also identify different degrees of price discrimination: first degree (i.e. charging each customer the exact highest amount it is willing to pay); second degree (i.e. setting of a price/unit sold which can vary depending on the volume of units sold); and third degree (i.e. charging different prices to different customers depending on their characteristics, or on how elastic their demand is). From a competition law perspective though, this classification is not telling, since one cannot argue that a particular price discrimination degree is, or is not, likely to be caught by the antitrust rules.

For price discrimination as a market tactic to work, several circumstances need to be present:[148] (1) the undertaking engaging in such behaviour must have a degree of market power allowing it to charge different prices which sit above competitive levels; (2) the undertaking should be able to filter the customers that are willing to pay, and identify the reservation price of each customer; (3) the undertaking should be able to prevent the customer to resell the products between themselves. Absent any of these circumstances price discrimination may not yield the expected results.

The CJEU clarified the application of Article 102(c) TFEU, which precludes dominant undertakings from applying dissimilar conditions to equivalent transactions with other trading parties, thereby placing them at a competitive disadvantage, in the *MEO* preliminary ruling.[149] This case dealt with different tariffs charged to different customers by a cooperative organisation managing the rights relating to copyright of artists and performers in Portugal, this being the sole entity responsible for the collective management of related rights in this Member State. The Court, with reference to the *British Airways* ruling,[150] observes first that market conduct may create distortions upstream or downstream, without it being necessary that the abusive conduct affects the competitive position of the dominant undertaking itself on the same market in which it operates, compared with its own potential competitors. Then, the Court states that Article 102(c) TFEU catches such behaviour if two cumulative conditions are met: first, the behaviour of the dominant undertaking is discriminatory, and second, it tends to hinder the competitive position of some of the business partners of that undertaking in relation to the others. For the latter point, the mere presence of an immediate disadvantage affecting operators who were charged more, compared with the tariffs applied to their competitors for an equivalent service, does not, however, mean that competition is

---

[146] E.g. Jones, Sufrin and Dunne 2019, p. 550; Geradin and Petit 2005, p. 9.

[147] E.g. Graham 2010, p. 157; Geradin and Petit 2005, p. 5.

[148] Geradin and Petit 2005, p. 5.

[149] Case C-525/16 *MEO*, ECLI:EU:C:2018:270, particularly par. 23 *et seq.*

[150] Case C-95/04 P *British Airways*, ECLI:EU:C:2007:166.

distorted or is capable of being distorted. The situation of the customers who paid more must be affected (e.g. in terms of costs, profits or any other relevant interest), for a practice to be capable to create a competitive disadvantage. To establish that a competitive disadvantage, required by Article 102(c) TFEU, is (capable to be) produced by the price discrimination, the Court argues that all relevant circumstances of the case must be examined: for example, the undertaking's dominant position, the negotiating power as regards the tariffs, the conditions and arrangements for charging those tariffs, their duration and amount, and the possible existence of a strategy aiming to exclude from the downstream market one of its trade partners which is at least as efficient as its competitors. The Court thus applies a clear effects-focused approach, in line with modern competition law analysis.

2.4.5.3 Predatory pricing

This type of conduct entails pricing below production cost, with the goal of driving competitors out of the market. Predation is thus an exclusionary abuse, which assumes that the dominant undertaking has sufficient resources to incur losses for a particular period of time, resources that its rivals do not have. Once these competitors, unable to cope with the low pricing of the dominant player, are excluded from the market, the assumption would be that the dominant player, having its dominance consolidated and strengthened, would raise prices to a level higher than the pre-predation period, in order to recoup its losses and to reap monopoly benefits.

Successful predation is nevertheless premised on a market that is sheltered by barriers to entry, otherwise the monopoly prices post-predation would signal to potential competitors the profit-making potential of the market, and thus, this market entry would constrain the dominant undertaking to reduce prices. Yet, predation may be perceived in itself as creating barriers to entry, as when the incumbent is a known predator, market entry of potential competitors may be deterred. Alternatively, predation may also give inaccurate pricing signals to newcomers, specifically during the predation period: low prices may signal low profitability to such potential competitors, who would thus find the market less attractive to access altogether. Furthermore, in practice, it may be that the undertaking engaged in predation is dominant in another (potentially adjacent) market, and the predation is performed on the non-dominated market; the losses in the latter market are subsidised through the monopoly gains in the former market, and at the end of the process market power may be leveraged from the dominated to the non-dominated market.[151] This is why evaluating predation must be performed in a more dynamic manner, and with due care.

This assertion is even more important if one observes the counterintuitive nature of the arguments surrounding predation: at the end of the day, low prices are something that consumers would gladly embrace. Yet, if these low prices would turn into supra-competitive prices in the longer run, the stance will differ. Viewed from a different standpoint, low prices in a market may also be interpreted as signalling that that market is competitive. Furthermore, there may be plenty of reasons why prices are low, and even below cost, such as

---

[151] E.g. case C-333/94 P *Tetra Pak II*, ECLI:EU:C:1996:436.

promotional pricing, end of the line clearances, using spare capacity in a period of economic downturn, and so forth.[152] Thus, distinguishing licit from illicit behaviour is a tough task.

Different tests have been developed to draw this line, most having their origin in the so-called Areeda-Turner cost-based method of identifying predatory pricing.[153] This test used the concept of AVC (explained in Chapter 3) as a benchmark: a price at or above reasonably anticipated AVC is presumed lawful, whereas a price below reasonably anticipated AVC should be presumed unlawful. This method is predicated on a short-run interval. Posner,[154] on the other hand, argued that long-run marginal cost proxies are better suited to judge predation, since the predator pricing at short-run marginal cost could eliminate efficient competitors who lack the ability or willingness to sustain short-term losses. This test would also require proof that the market is prone to effective predation and that the predator intended to exclude the prey from the market.

The EU test for predatory pricing was developed in the *AKZO* case.[155] AKZO's product (i.e. benzoyl peroxide) was used as a catalyst in plastic production and as a bleaching agent in flour. ECS produced benzoyl peroxide, and while being active mainly in the flour market, intended to expand in the plastics sector. AKZO retaliated by lowering prices in the flour sector, primarily for ECS's main customers. The Commission fined AKZO for predatory pricing abuse of dominance, while focusing primarily on the intent of this undertaking. On appeal, the CJEU distinguished between two scenarios, while devising the test for predatory pricing under Article 102 TFEU:[156] prices below AVC (i.e. those costs which vary depending on the quantities produced) by means of which a dominant undertaking seeks to eliminate a competitor must be regarded as abusive. A dominant undertaking has no interest in applying such prices except that of eliminating competitors so as to enable it subsequently to raise its prices by taking advantage of its monopolistic position, since each sale generates a loss, namely the total amount of the fixed costs (i.e. those costs which remain constant regardless of the quantities produced) and, at least, part of the variable costs relating to the unit produced. Moreover, prices below ATC (i.e. fixed costs plus variable costs, divided by number of units produced) but above AVC must be regarded as abusive if they are determined as part of a plan for eliminating a competitor. Such prices can drive from the market undertakings which are perhaps as efficient as the dominant undertaking but which, because of their smaller financial resources, are incapable of withstanding the competition waged against them. All in all, the *AKZO* test noticeably builds on the Areeda-Turner method mentioned above.

In *AKZO*, the Court did not literally weigh-in on the matter of whether there needs to be proof that the dominant undertaking will recoup its losses post-predation. However, it may be argued that the ability to recoup losses is self-evident, since we are talking about a dominant undertaking, which assumedly has 'deep pockets'. It is remarkable how recoupment

---

[152] Graham 2010, p. 140.

[153] Areeda and Turner 1975.

[154] Posner 1976.

[155] Case C-62/86 *AKZO Chemie v Commission*, ECLI:EU:C:1991:286.

[156] See par. 71–72 of the CJEU's judgment.

is perceived in US antitrust law, where courts do not recognise predatory pricing as a form of monopolisation unless the plaintiff demonstrates that the alleged predator had a dangerous probability of recouping its investment in below-cost prices.[157] The CJEU in *Tetra Pak II*[158] and *France Télécom*[159] took a significantly different approach, by arguing that the Commission must not bring proof of recoupment to establish the existence of an abuse of dominance. Recoupment is thus not a necessary precondition for the predation test. What matters in such scenarios is whether the pricing policy may result in foreclosure of competition. However, the above is not to say that the possibility of recoupment is totally irrelevant. In *France Télécom*,[160] the CJEU acknowledged that the Commission may find recoupment of losses to be a relevant factor in assessing whether or not the practice concerned is abusive, in that it may, for example where prices lower than AVC are applied, assist in excluding economic justifications other than the elimination of a competitor, or, where prices below ATC but above AVC are applied, assist in establishing that a plan to eliminate a competitor exists.

In more recent judgments the CJEU showed flexibility regarding the cost standards put forward in *AKZO*. For the sake of clarity, the test based on AVC and ATC is still valid today, yet in some sectors of the economy, it may be better suited to judge predation based on other cost benchmarks, which reflect economic reality more appropriately. In *Post Danmark I*,[161] the CJEU acknowledged the use of the 'average incremental cost' (AIC) standard, which points to those costs destined to disappear in the short or medium term (three to five years), if the undertaking at hand were to give up a specific business activity. In the same case, the concept of average total costs was referred to as average incremental costs to which were added a portion, determined by estimation, of the undertaking's common costs connected to activities other than those covered by the universal service obligation which it had.[162] Importantly, the CJEU clarified in *Post Danmark I* that prices below ATC but above AIC may be abusive, but there is no presumption that they are. Instead, it must be demonstrated that such pricing tactics produce an actual or likely exclusionary effect, to the detriment of competition and thereby of consumers' interests.[163]

This approach is in tune with the Commission's take on predation in the Enforcement Priorities Guidelines 2009.[164] The Commission employs the benchmarks of sacrifice and anti-competitive foreclosure in devising its intervention priorities: it will generally intervene where a dominant undertaking deliberately incurs losses or foregoes profits in the short term so as to foreclose or be likely to foreclose one or more of its actual or potential competitors with a view to strengthening or maintaining its market power, thereby causing consumer harm. In assessing whether such sacrifice occurs, the Commission will essentially check

---

[157] Jones, Sufrin and Dunne 2019, p. 407; Graham 2010, p. 143.

[158] Case C-333/94 P *Tetra Pak II*, ECLI:EU:C:1996:436.

[159] Case C-202/07 P *France Télécom*, ECLI:EU:C:2009:214.

[160] Par. 111 *et seq.*

[161] Case C-209/10 *Post Danmark I*, ECLI:EU:C:2012:172, par. 31 *et seq.*

[162] Ibid, par. 4.

[163] Ibid, par. 44. See also Lianos, Korah and Siciliani 2019, pp. 1011–12.

[164] Enforcement Priorities Guidelines 2009, par. 63–74.

whether the undertaking incurs losses that could have been avoided, by taking the AAC (explained in Chapter 3, which in most circumstances can be a good proxy for AVC) as a starting benchmark: if a dominant undertaking charges a price below AAC for all or part of its output, it is not recovering the costs that could have been avoided by not producing that output. In order to show a predatory strategy, the Commission may also investigate whether the allegedly predatory conduct led in the short term to net revenues lower than could have been expected from a reasonable alternative conduct, that is to say, whether the dominant undertaking incurred a loss that it could have avoided. In applying the anti-competitive fore-closure part of the test, the Commission will use the LRAIC (explained in Chapter 3, which in most circumstances can be a good proxy for ATC) benchmark, since normally only pricing below this level is capable of foreclosing as efficient competitors from the market. Market exclusion is, however, not a per se requirement for predation, in the Commission's eyes, since such pricing tactics may also be used to discipline competitors, not only to eliminate them from the market. Lastly, consumer welfare is likely to be harmed by predation when the dominant player may expect its market power to increase post-predation, thus benefiting from the sacrifice. Also, consumer harm may occur if conduct would be likely to prevent or delay a decline in prices that would otherwise have occurred.[165]

Recently, the Commission fined Qualcomm for abusing its dominance in the market for 3G baseband chipsets.[166] This type of abuse thus lends itself to diverse sectors of the economy, covering also the behaviour of tech firms in the digital economy. Qualcomm's market share was almost three times as large as its closest competitor (Icera) in a relevant market that exhibited high barriers to entry. Based on price-cost tests and qualitative evidence regarding Qualcomm's rationale behind its conduct, the Commission found that this undertaking sold its products, to two strategically important customers, below cost, for a period of two years. The intention was specifically to foreclose Icera (who was emerging as a growing threat for Qualcomm's chipset business) from one of the specific segments of the market. The targeted nature of the pricing policy ensured minimal impact on Qualcomm's revenues and a negative impact on Icera's business, which eventually was acquired by another company at the end of the two-year period, and its baseband chipset business was wound down in a matter of a few more years.

2.4.5.4 Refusal to supply

This type of conduct may also be labelled as an exclusionary abuse, yet intervention in such behaviour requires a certain degree of caution, as also recognised by the Commission in its Enforcement Priorities Guidelines 2009.[167] This is because, generally speaking, any under-taking, whether dominant or not, should have the right to choose its trading partners and to dispose freely of its property. And in the alternative, should an infringement of Article 102 TFEU be identified, the remedy would be an obligation placed on that undertaking to supply

---

[165] Ibid, par. 69–71.

[166] Case AT.39711 *Qualcomm*, (2019) available at <https://ec.europa.eu/competition/elojade/isef/case_details.cfm?proc_code=1_39711> accessed 17 June 2020.

[167] Enforcement Priorities Guidelines 2009, par. 75.

its products, or grant access to its assets. Even if this would be done for fair remuneration, such an obligation may undermine undertakings' incentives to invest and innovate and may make room for 'free riding'.

The Commission focuses on scenarios in which the dominant undertaking competes on the downstream market with the buyer whom it refuses to supply,[168] while nevertheless acknowledging that other types of conduct do fit in its understanding of what the concept of refusal to supply covers: refusal to supply products to existing or new customers, refusal to license IP rights, including when the licence is necessary to provide interface information, or refusal to grant access to an essential facility or a network. The Commission will intervene if three conditions are met:[169]

1. The refusal relates to a product or service (for which there is demand from at least potential purchasers, in a market that can be identified) which is objectively necessary to be able to compete effectively on a downstream market. This does not mean that, without the refused input, no competitor could ever enter or survive on the downstream market (essentially meaning that these criteria apply to both disruption of existing supply and *de novo* refusal to supply). This also means that the concept of indispensability is important in this respect: an input is indispensable where there is no actual or potential substitute on which competitors in the downstream market could rely so as to counter the negative consequences of the refusal. The main question to be asked here is whether competitors could effectively duplicate the input produced by the dominant undertaking in the foreseeable future.

2. The refusal is likely to lead to the elimination of effective competition on the downstream market.

3. The refusal is likely to lead to consumer harm, that is, for consumers, the likely negative consequences of the refusal to supply in the relevant market outweigh over time the negative consequences of imposing an obligation to supply (e.g. when the foreclosed competitors are prevented from bringing innovative goods or services to market).

Should the market at hand be regulated (in accordance with EU law), to the extent that an undertaking is obliged to supply, the Commission will be unlikely to identify competition concerns, since it will normally start from the assumption that that regulation has already balanced the incentives to innovate and invest, on one hand, with the obligation to supply, on the other hand.

The case-law of the EU courts, old or more recent, covers scenarios going beyond the Commission's enforcement focus. In *Commercial Solvents*,[170] the CJEU assessed the behaviour of an undertaking which was dominant in the market for raw material and therefore able to control the supply to manufacturers of derivatives, which decided to start manufacturing such derivatives, in competition with its former customers. The Court held that such an

---

[168] Ibid, par. 76–78.

[169] Ibid, par. 81 *et seq.*

[170] Joined cases 6 and 7/73 *Commercial Solvents*, ECLI:EU:C:1974:18, par. 25.

undertaking which, with the object of reserving raw material for manufacturing its own derivatives, refuses to supply a customer, which is itself a manufacturer of these derivatives, and therefore risks eliminating all competition on the part of this customer, is abusing its dominant position within the meaning of Article 102 TFEU.

An interesting stream of refusal to supply case-law relates to the so-called 'essential facilities doctrine'. An essential facility may be an infrastructure without access to which competitors cannot provide services to their users. This occurs where competitors downstream require access to something owned or controlled by a vertically integrated dominant undertaking, in order to provide products or services to customers. This is sometimes referred to as a 'bottleneck monopoly'.[171] In EU jurisprudence, the essential facilities doctrine was first acknowledged in connection with cases concerning access to port facilities.[172] The leading case-law in this area of law remains the 1998 *Bronner* preliminary ruling.[173] In this case, Oscar Bronner intended to publish a newspaper competing with the more prominent daily newspaper published by Mediaprint, in Austria. Bronner sought access to Mediaprint's home-delivery system, arguing there was no alternative means of delivery, and it would be too costly to create such a system given the small size of his business. The Court argued that, for an abuse to be established, not only should the refusal of the home-delivery service be likely to eliminate all competition in the daily newspaper market, but such refusal should also be incapable of being objectively justified, and that service should in itself be indispensable to carrying on that person's business, inasmuch as there is no actual or potential substitute in existence for that home-delivery scheme. The Court pointed out that other methods of distributing daily newspapers existed. For access to be granted, it had to be shown that it was impossible or even unreasonably difficult to create an alternative distribution system, and thus access to the existing system was indispensable. Arguments to the effect that it was not economically viable by reason of the small circulation of the newspaper to build such a system do not suffice.

In *IMS Health*[174] and *Magill*,[175] the Court had to assess whether a refusal to grant a licence for an IP right constituted an abuse caught by Article 102 TFEU. Such rights essentially shelter the holder from competition on the market in which it is active, but may also create competition issues on markets downstream, where the protected product is a necessary input. In *IMS Health*, dominance was identified on the market for data on sale of pharmaceuticals, data which were purchased by pharmaceutical companies in order to monitor their sales force.[176] While recalling the relationship between IP law and competition law, the Court,[177] with reference to the *Magill* ruling, first stated that refusal to grant a licence, even if it is the act of an undertaking holding a dominant position, cannot in itself constitute

[171] Jones, Sufrin and Dunne 2019, p. 487; Lorenz 2013, pp 236–7.

[172] Case IV/34.174 *Sealink/B&I Holyhead: Interim Measures*, (1992) available at <https://ec.europa.eu/competition/antitrust/cases/dec_docs/34174/34174_2_2.pdf> accessed 4 May 2020.

[173] Case C-7/97 *Bronner*, ECLI:EU:C:1998:569, par. 41 *et seq*. See also Graham 2010, p. 174.

[174] Case C-418/01 *IMS Health*, ECLI:EU:C:2004:257.

[175] Joined cases C-241 and C-242/91 P *RTE and ITP*, ECLI:EU:C:1995:98.

[176] Lorenz 2013, p. 235.

[177] Case C-418/01 *IMS Health*, ECLI:EU:C:2004:257, par. 34 *et seq*.

abuse of a dominant position. However, the Court continued, in exceptional circumstances such refusal may be caught by Article 102 TFEU. These circumstances boiled down to: the undertaking which requested the licence intends to offer, on the market for the supply of the data in question, new products or services not offered by the owner of the IP right and for which there is a potential consumer demand; the refusal is not justified by objective considerations; the refusal is such as to reserve to the owner of the IP right the market for the supply of data on sales of pharmaceutical products in the Member State concerned, by eliminating all competition on that market. Similarly, in *Magill*, the Court found such exceptional circumstances in the fact that the refusal in question concerned a product (information on the weekly schedules of television channels) the supply of which was indispensable for carrying on the business in question (the publishing of a general television guide), in that, without that information, the person wishing to produce such a guide would find it impossible to publish it and offer it for sale, the fact that such refusal prevented the appearance of a new product for which there was a potential consumer demand, the fact that the refusal was not justified by objective considerations, and that it was likely to exclude all competition in the secondary market of television guides.

Refusal to supply may also be conceived in cases dealing with interoperability in the IT sector (i.e. ensuring that software developers create products that can work with each other's systems). In *Microsoft*,[178] the company Sun complained that Microsoft refused to disclose to those who provided server operating systems sufficient interface information to enable them to create workgroup server operating systems that would operate satisfactorily with Microsoft's Windows desktop and server operating systems. The Commission held that Microsoft held a dominant position on both the client PC operating systems market and the workgroup server operating systems market, and that it had committed an abuse by refusing to supply the interface information. The GC upheld the Commission decision, largely based on the *Magill* exceptional circumstances reasoning.[179]

Refusal to supply lends itself well to be applied to conduct in various sectors of the economy, and in connection to other areas of the law (e.g. IP law), which makes its application equally challenging and interesting. In this respect, we fully agree with Jones, Sufrin and Dunne[180] when they argue that the next frontier for refusal to supply case-law under Article 102 TFEU is the possibility of treating access to valuable consumer data as a type of essential facility, thus generating an antitrust duty to supply. The 'ins and outs' of this matter are far from being settled though. The interplay of data-related issues in the context of the 'essential facilities doctrine' with, for example, matters relating to the application of the General Data Protection Regulation 2016, re-conceptualising the requirement of indispensability of data for the purpose of antitrust cases, and balancing the incentives to invest with market contestability, are simple examples in this respect. The Commission's 2019 Report on Competition

---

[178] Case T-201/04 *Microsoft*, ECLI:EU:T:2007:289.

[179] Jones, Sufrin and Dunne 2019, pp. 510–11, 516–17.

[180] Ibid, p. 519.

Policy for the Digital Era[181] rightfully dedicates due attention to such matters. In our opinion, for this area of the law to properly develop, further case-law is bound to arise.

2.4.5.5 Margin squeeze

This is a complex type of exclusionary abuse, which, as we have already pointed out, may encapsulate other types of abuses, such as excessive pricing, price discrimination and predatory pricing. It is interesting to note that the Commission treats margin squeeze as an alternative of refusal to supply, in its Enforcement Priorities Guidelines 2009:[182] instead of refusing to supply, a dominant undertaking may charge a price for the product on the upstream market which, compared to the price it charges on the downstream market, does not allow even an equally efficient competitor to trade profitably in the downstream market on a lasting basis. When evaluating this latter setting, the Commission will use the LRAIC of the downstream division of the integrated dominant undertaking.

These excerpts from the Enforcement Priorities Guidelines 2009 highlight that margin squeeze entails leaving competitors with no margin at the retail level, thus foreclosing their access to, or expelling them from, the market. Lorenz[183] observes that such scenarios are prone to occur in the freshly liberalised telecommunication markets sector, where the previous monopolist still owns part of the infrastructure, and also competes downstream with newcomers on the retail market.[184] Margin squeeze cases are very specific, in that they require a special set of circumstances for the abusive strategy to be successful:

- There must be two levels of the market, vertically connected to each other (e.g. production–retail, or wholesale–retail);
- There must be dominance in the upstream market, but not necessarily in the downstream market (since the whole point of foreclosing competitors downstream would be to leverage the market power from the upstream to the downstream level of the market);
- The dominant player should be vertically integrated (e.g. it should be active in both the production/wholesale and the retail markets); and
- There should be barriers to entry both upstream and downstream (since otherwise, foreclosure downstream could be counteracted by new retailers entering the market, while excessive prices or refusal to deal by the dominant undertaking in the upstream market could be counteracted by potential competitors entering the upstream level of the market).

When such circumstances are met, a dominant supplier could discriminate between the prices charged to its division downstream (these could be low or even predatory prices) and those charged to the retail competitors of its downstream division (these could be excessive

---

[181] Crémer, de Montjoye and Schweitzer 2019.

[182] Enforcement Priorities Guidelines 2009, par. 80.

[183] Lorenz 2013, pp. 237–8.

[184] E.g. cases C-280/08 P *Deutsche Telekom*, ECLI:EU:C:2010:603; T-336/07 *Telefónica*, ECLI:EU:T:2012:172.

high prices, or in any case higher than the ones charged to the dominant undertaking's downstream division). When an equally efficient downstream competitor could not cope with such a policy (since it would probably have to sell its product at a loss, to keep up with its competitor favoured by the dominant undertaking upstream), and would be forced to leave the downstream market, an abuse caught by Article 102 TFEU could be established.

In the *TeliaSonera* preliminary ruling,[185] the CJEU strikingly identified margin squeeze as a self-standing type of abuse, rather than merely an alternative to refusal to supply. The Court also provided a number of valuable answers, regarding questions about how this type of abuse works in practice: for example, the wholesale and retail prices charged by the dominant player must not be abusive (predatory or excessively high) in themselves (paragraph 34); the practice must have at least a potential effect affecting equally efficient competitors, which does not necessarily have to be actual or concrete (paragraph 64); an abuse may be established even if the input is not indispensable to the retail activities (paragraph 69 *et seq.*); it is irrelevant for finding an abuse if the practice drives out of the market an existing retailer or a new client of the dominant undertaking (paragraphs 94–95); and last but not least, the extent of the maturity of the markets (i.e. whether they are markets that grow rapidly and involve new technology, requiring high levels of investment) is also irrelevant for a finding of a breach of Article 102 TFEU (paragraphs 110–111).

2.4.5.6 Rebates and exclusive purchasing

The Commission deals with such conduct in its Enforcement Priorities Guidelines 2009,[186] by referring to the concept of exclusive dealing. This encapsulates exclusive purchasing obligations, requiring a customer to purchase exclusively or to a large extent only from the dominant undertaking, and conditional rebates, that is, those rebates granted to customers in order to reward them for a particular form of purchasing behaviour. In reality, this kind of behaviour may embody various forms, depending on the detailed features of the scheme adopted by the dominant player: *quantity rebates* (discounts linked to the quantity of products purchased), *loyalty/exclusivity rebates* (rewards for purchasing exclusively, or largely from one supplier), *loyalty-inducing rebates* (rebates having a similar effect to the previous type), *target rebates* (awarded if a specific target of orders is met), *retroactive rebates* (awarded for all orders only once the order target is met), *incremental rebates* (awarded only for purchases above a specific threshold of orders), and more.[187] The reasoning for setting up rebate schemes is to attract more demand from consumers. While everyone loves a discount, some types of rebates may lead to foreclosure of the dominant undertaking's competitors, by hindering them from selling to customers.[188]

The Commission's approach to exclusive purchasing starts from the observation that in order to convince customers to accept exclusive purchasing, the dominant undertaking may have to compensate them, in whole or in part, for the loss in competition resulting from the

---

[185] Case C-52/09 *TeliaSonera*, ECLI:EU:C:2011:83.

[186] Par. 32–46.

[187] On the various types of rebate schemes, see Jones, Sufrin and Dunne 2019, pp. 449–50.

[188] Enforcement Priorities Guidelines 2009, par. 32.

exclusivity. Such a setting will result in anti-competitive foreclosure in particular where, without the obligations, an important competitive constraint would be exercised by competitors who either are not yet present in the market at the time the obligations are concluded, or who are not in a position to compete for the full supply of the customers. If competitors can compete on equal terms with the dominant undertaking for each individual customer's entire demand, exclusive purchasing obligations are generally unlikely to hamper effective competition, unless the switching of supplier by customers is rendered difficult due to the duration of the exclusive purchasing obligation. In general, the longer the duration of the obligation, the greater the likely foreclosure effect.[189] The Commission's approach to conditional rebates is similar in many respects to its view on exclusive purchasing obligations: for example, the likelihood of anti-competitive foreclosure is higher where competitors are not able to compete on equal terms for the entire demand of each individual customer.[190] Yet, conditional rebates, be they retroactive or incremental, may lead to anti-competitive foreclosure in the Commission's view, even if they do not entail a sacrifice for the dominant undertaking. So, prices do not necessarily have to exhibit predatory features, for a rebate scheme that has exclusionary effects and which, for this reason, is already capable of restricting competition, a stance which was also validated by the CJEU in its *Tomra* judgment.[191] Nevertheless, the Commission explains in a detailed manner the relationship between the price charged and the LRAIC and AAC cost benchmarks: as long as the effective price remains consistently above the LRAIC of the dominant undertaking, this would normally allow an equally efficient competitor to compete profitably notwithstanding the rebate, and thus the rebate is normally not capable of anti-competitive foreclosure. Where the effective price is below AAC, the rebate scheme is capable of foreclosing even equally efficient competitors. Where the effective price is between AAC and LRAIC, the Commission will investigate whether other factors point to the conclusion that entry or expansion even by equally efficient competitors is likely to be affected (e.g. do competitors have realistic and effective counterstrategies at their disposal?).[192]

The case-law of the EU courts regarding rebates spreads the various shapes in which this kind of conduct may materialise on a different spectrum. We have already shown in section 2.4.2 above, that in the opinion of certain authors, this spectrum ranges from prima facie lawful behaviour to prima facie unlawful behaviour, and in between these extremes, different kinds of 'effects analyses' are required. The relevant judgments of the EU courts also show that, over time, different kinds of rebates-related conduct may shift towards different ends of this spectrum.

With reference to previous case-law,[193] the GC explained in its 2014 *Intel* judgment,[194] that a distinction should be drawn between three categories of rebates: first, *quantity rebates*

---

[189] Ibid, par. 33–36.

[190] Ibid, par. 39.

[191] Case C-549/10 P *Tomra*, ECLI:EU:C:2012:221, par. 78. See also Lorenz 2013, p. 232.

[192] Enforcement Priorities Guidelines 2009, par. 43–44.

[193] Cases 85/76 *Hoffmann-La Roche*, ECLI:EU:C:1979:36; C-322/81 *Michelin I*, ECLI:EU:C:1983:313; C-95/04 P *British Airways*, ECLI:EU:C:2007:166; C-549/10 P *Tomra*, ECLI:EU:C:2012:221.

[194] Case T-286/09 *Intel*, ECLI:EU:T:2014:547, par. 74–78.

linked solely to the volume of purchases made from a dominant undertaking are generally considered not to have foreclosure effects, as they are deemed to reflect gains in efficiency and economies of scale made by that undertaking. Such behaviour is thus not prohibited by Article 102 TFEU. Second, there are *exclusivity/fidelity rebates*, through which the dominant undertaking ties purchasers – even if it does so at their request – by an obligation or promise on their part to obtain all or most of their requirements exclusively from that undertaking, whether the obligation is stipulated without further qualification or whether it is undertaken in consideration of the grant of a rebate; scenarios in which, even without tying the purchasers by a formal obligation, the dominant undertaking would apply a system of loyalty rebates/discounts conditional on the customer's obtaining all or most of its requirements – whether the quantity of its purchases be large or small – from the undertaking in a dominant position, also fall in this category. Such rebates are designed to remove or restrict the purchaser's freedom to choose his sources of supply and to deny other producers access to the market, and are therefore prohibited under Article 102 TFEU. Third, there are *other rebate systems* where the mechanism for granting the rebate may also have a *fidelity-building effect*, such as systems depending on the attainment of individual sales objectives which do not constitute exclusivity rebates. In examining whether the application of such a rebate constitutes an abuse of dominant position, it is necessary to consider *all the circumstances of the given case*.

In its 2015 preliminary ruling in *Post Danmark II*,[195] the CJEU elaborated on this third category of rebates, while dealing with a complex scheme, which entailed standardised and conditional rebates, given on a yearly basis, in a retroactive manner. Determining whether such a rebate scheme is capable of having exclusionary effects contrary to Article 102 TFEU, requires the examination of *all the circumstances of the case*, in particular, the criteria and rules governing the grant of the rebates, the rebate's duration, amount and market coverage, the extent of the dominant position of the undertaking concerned, whether it is an unavoidable trading partner, or whether it devised an exclusionary strategy, the market conditions including the presence of barriers to entry. Thus, while in *Hoffmann-La Roche* and *Michelin I*, loyalty rebates (i.e. the second category above) were 'assumed' to be capable of having exclusionary effects, in *Post Danmark II*, for non-loyalty rebates (i.e. the third category) a multitude of factors must be investigated to identify the likelihood of an anti-competitive exclusionary effect (for which no assumption is made).

Lastly, in its 2017 appeal judgment in *Intel*,[196] the CJEU embraced even more evidently the effects-oriented approach, when it comes to rebate practices. With regard to the second category mentioned above (i.e. exclusivity/loyalty rebates), which, if we recall *Hoffmann-La Roche, Michelin I, British Airways* and even the GC's judgment in *Intel*, seem to constitute prima facie unlawful behaviour under Article 102 TFEU, the CJEU stated that this case-law must be further clarified. When the dominant undertaking submits, during the administrative procedure, on the basis of supporting evidence, that its conduct was not capable of restricting competition and, in particular, of producing foreclosure effects, the Commission must engage in an in-depth analysis of all the features of the case, as suggested in *Post*

---

[195] Case C-23/14 *Post Danmark II*, ECLI:EU:C:2015:651, par. 29 *et seq.*

[196] Case C-413/14 *Intel*, ECLI:EU:C:2017:632, par. 137 *et seq.*

Danmark II, in order to identify the rebate system's capacity to foreclose. The GC must examine this analysis against all of the dominant undertaking's arguments which call into question the validity of the Commission's findings concerning the foreclosure capability of the rebate concerned.

All in all, the EU law on rebates as it currently stands, at least from the CJEU's perspective, may be summarised as follows: quantity rebates are permitted under Article 102 TFEU; for loyalty rebates to be prohibited under Article 102 TFEU, all relevant circumstances of the case must be evaluated in order to identify that exclusionary effects may result from the rebate, when the dominant undertaking claims on the basis of substantial arguments that its conduct is not capable to restrict competition in such manner; lastly, for (complex) rebates which are neither quantity nor loyalty rebates, all circumstances of the case must be evaluated in order to check whether it is capable of having exclusionary effects contrary to Article 102 TFEU.

2.4.5.7 Tying and bundling

This type of practice may fall under Article 102(d) TFEU: making the conclusion of contracts subject to acceptance by the other parties of supplementary obligations which, by their nature or according to commercial usage, have no connection with the subject of such contracts. This type of conduct involves different products/services, more often than not belonging to different markets. It may also entail both exploitative and exclusionary features. The Enforcement Priorities Guidelines 2009[197] indicate that tying and bundling may be used by an undertaking which is dominant in one market, namely the market for the tying product, to foreclose competition in the non-dominated market for the tied product. In this way, the dominant undertaking may leverage its power from one market to the other. Further, tying practices often involve no choice for the buyer to obtain the product it desires, without buying a different product, which but for the tying practice, the buyer would have not purchased. In such scenarios, tying may be perceived as an exploitative practice, too.

Tying refers to situations where customers that purchase one product (the tying product) are required also to purchase another product (the tied product). This may be done on a technical or contractual basis. Bundling refers to the way products are offered and priced. Therefore, tying and bundling may embody different variants: pure bundling (i.e. products are only sold jointly in fixed proportions, meaning that buyers cannot obtain the two products separately); mixed bundling or multi-product rebates (i.e. the products are also made available separately, but the sum of the prices when sold separately is higher than the bundled price).[198]

The Commission uses a two part test in evaluating whether the practice of a dominant undertaking in the market for the tying product infringes Article 102(d) TFEU: first, based on customer demand information, the tying and the tied products must be distinct (i.e. in absence of the tying practice, customers would purchase the tying product without also buying the tied product from the same supplier, thereby allowing stand-alone production for

---

[197] Par. 47–62.

[198] Enforcement Priorities Guidelines 2009, par. 48.

both the tying and the tied product); second, the practice must lead to anti-competitive fore-closure normally in the tied product market, but also possibly in the tying product market, or in both markets at the same time.[199] Technical tying, which is costly to reverse, signals that the tying strategy is a lasting one, thus increasing the risk of such foreclosure. When it comes to bundling, the greater the number of products in a bundle, and the greater the number of such products that an undertaking is dominant for, the higher the risks of foreclosure, particularly when competitors cannot replicate the bundle.

In the case-law of the EU courts, a regular occurrence are cases dealing with tying specific devices with the consumables sold on an aftermarket: in *Hilti*,[200] the dominant undertaking attempted to argue that nail guns and nails are not distinct products, but instead a 'powder actuated fastening system', while in *Tetra Pak II*,[201] the manufacturer of packaging machines attempted to oblige customers to buy the packaging material exclusively from the same sup-plier. Such cases often hinge on the definition of the relevant markets and on the possibility to objectively justify the practice. In *Hilti*, the Court did not accept arguments regarding health and safety of consumers put forward to justify the infringement of Article 102 TFEU, while in *Tetra Pak II*, the Court clarified that once the tied products/services are established to be distinct, the dominant undertaking can no longer rely on the 'nature and commercial usage' provision in Article 102(d) TFEU, because the 'commercial usage' may merely have been established by the dominant undertaking itself.[202] In *Microsoft*,[203] the GC reached the rightful conclusion that the Windows operating system (tying product) and Windows Media Player (tied product) were indeed two distinct products. Microsoft was held to be dominant in the market for operating systems, while the market for the tied product (i.e. the media players market) was populated with other, potentially more efficient competitors. The Commission argued that the bundling of Windows Media Player with Windows protected Microsoft's position in the market for media players, deterred innovation and allowed this company to leverage its market power in adjacent markets.[204] In paragraph 862 of the appeal judgment, the GC validated the four factors the Commission used for establishing unlawful tying, by stating that the constituent elements of abusive tying identified by the Commission coincide effectively with the conditions laid down in Article 102(d) TFEU. These factors are: first, the tying and tied products are two separate products; second, the undertaking concerned is dominant in the market for the tying product; third, the undertaking concerned does not give customers a choice to obtain the tying product without the tied product; and fourth, the practice in question forecloses competition. Although the language used in this enumeration differs slightly from the wording of the Enforcement Priorities Guidelines 2009, the essence of the Commission's approach to tying and bundling is certainly unitary.

A different *Microsoft* case entailed the alleged tying of the Internet Explorer web browser

---

[199] Ibid, par. 51–52.

[200] Case T-30/89 *Hilti*, ECLI:EU:T:1991:70.

[201] Cases T-83/91 *Tetra Pak II*, ECLI:EU:T:1994:246; C-333/94 P *Tetra Pak II*, ECLI:EU:C:1996:436.

[202] Jones, Sufrin and Dunne 2019, p. 464.

[203] Case T-201/04 *Microsoft*, ECLI:EU:T:2007:289.

[204] Graham 2010, p. 166.

to the Microsoft operating system. Microsoft was labelled dominant in the market for the latter product. The Commission accepted commitments from Microsoft in 2009,[205] which essentially entailed giving users the choice to install different browsers. However, Microsoft did not comply with this assumed obligation for a period of more than a year. This is why, in 2013, the Commission imposed a heavy fine on Microsoft, based on Article 23(2)(c) of Regulation 1/2003.[206] The *Microsoft* cases in particular show that the tying and bundling theory of harm lends itself appropriately to conduct connected to digital markets. Furthermore, these cases show the Commission's propensity to deal with such cases way before the upsurge of digital markets in various sectors of the economy, throughout the world. As we will see in section 2.4.5.9 below, tying practices in digital markets are today more relevant than ever, as evidenced by the *Google Android* decision.[207]

2.4.5.8 Vexatious litigation and other abuses connected to the enforcement of legal rights

In a series of cases, the EU courts dealt with behaviour of dominant undertakings which started court proceedings in order to enforce certain rights. Such course of action may also infringe Article 102 TFEU and in this context it is often referred to as vexatious litigation. The key legal issue in this respect is asserting when such litigation against a competitor may be deemed normal litigation and when it is abusive and thus prohibited by Article 102 TFEU.[208] While Article 47 of the EU Charter of Fundamental Rights guarantees the right to access a tribunal, dominant undertakings may abuse their position if, as confirmed by the GC in *ITT Promedia*,[209] two cumulative conditions are met: the action initiated by the dominant undertaking cannot reasonably be considered as an attempt to establish the rights of the undertaking concerned and can therefore only serve to harass the opposite party, and the action is conceived in the framework of a plan the goal of which is to eliminate competition. The question here is not whether the rights claimed by the dominant player exist, but whether this undertaking may reasonably consider that they do. Thus, litigation can be an abuse, but only where it is, in effect, vexatious.[210] This is obviously a matter of interpretation.

Not only vexatious court proceedings may qualify as abusive practices under Article 102 TFEU, but also the use of regulatory procedures, which may harm competitors. In *AstraZeneca*,[211] the Commission fined this dominant undertaking which was found to have made deliberately misleading representations to the patent offices of certain Member States, with the goal of maintaining supplementary protection certificates for a particular drug (Losec), granting an extension of the protection under the patent, to which the dominant player was not entitled or to which it was entitled for a shorter duration. This tactic was designed to keep manufacturers of generic products away from the market. Furthermore,

---

[205] Case COMP/39.530 *Microsoft (Tying)*, (2009) C/2009/10033.

[206] Case AT.39530 *Microsoft (Tying)*, (2013) C/2013/1210 final.

[207] Case AT.40099 *Google Android*, (2018) 4761 final.

[208] Lorenz 2013, p. 238.

[209] Case T-111/96 *ITT Promedia*, ECLI:EU:T:1998:183, par. 55.

[210] Jones, Sufrin and Dunne 2019, p. 535.

[211] Case C-457/10 P *AstraZeneca*, ECLI:EU:C:2012:770.

AstraZeneca submitted requests for deregistration of the marketing authorisations for Losec capsules in certain countries, in order to delay or make more difficult the marketing of generic products, and to prevent parallel imports of Losec. In rejecting AstraZeneca's appeal, the CJEU held that such behaviour amounts to a breach of competition on the merits and thus an abuse of a dominant position under Article 102 TFEU.[212]

Speaking of patents, the EU courts, while seeking a balance between free competition and the exercise of exclusive rights linked to an IP right, held that a proprietor's right to bring an action for patent infringement is guaranteed, even if the proprietor holds a dominant position. Such a court action cannot in itself constitute an abuse of a dominant position, unless certain circumstances are met.[213] The patent may become a so-called standard essential patent (SEP), in that it is indispensable to all competitors who envisage manufacturing products that comply with the standard. This may be the case when the proprietor irrevocably commits in front of a standardisation entity to grant licences to third parties on fair, reasonable and non-discriminatory terms (so-called FRAND terms). In *Huawei*,[214] this company brought actions before the German competent court against users of its SEP that had not paid it royalties, seeking *first*, an injunction prohibiting the patent infringement and the recall of products, and *second*, the rendering of accounts and an award of damages. In its preliminary ruling, with regard to the *former request* of Huawei, the CJEU argued that the SEP proprietor who committed to licensing on FRAND terms does not abuse its dominant position by bringing such an action as long as two cumulative conditions are met: (1) prior to bringing the action, the proprietor has alerted the alleged infringer of the infringement and presented to that alleged infringer, after it has expressed its willingness to conclude a licensing agreement on FRAND terms, a specific, written offer for a licence on such terms; (2) the alleged infringer continues to use the patent and has not diligently responded to that offer, in conditions of good faith, and thus without any delaying tactics. Regarding the *latter request* of Huawei, the Court stated that Article 102 TFEU does not prevent such a dominant undertaking from bringing an action with the goal of rendering of accounts or an award for damages, since such actions do not have a direct impact on standard-compliant products manufactured by competitors appearing or remaining on the market.[215]

2.4.5.9 Abusive conduct on digital markets

Cases such as *Microsoft* and *Intel*, discussed above, show that the EU authorities are not foreign to handling cases connected to the digital world under Article 102 TFEU. The Commission has shown appetite for such cases in the recent past too, showing that it has no reservations in applying this antitrust provision to behaviour of large tech corporations.

For example, the Commission has recently adopted an interim measures decision ordering Broadcom to cease the application of certain contractual agreements it has with its

---

[212] Press Release 158/12.

[213] E.g. case C-418/01 *IMS Health*, ECLI:EU:C:2004:257.

[214] Case C-170/13 *Huawei*, ECLI:EU:C:2015:477.

[215] Press Release 88/15.

customer, in order to prevent serious and irreparable harm to competition.[216] According to the Commission, Broadcom was, at least on first sight, dominant in the markets for system-on-a-chip for TV set-top boxes, fibre modems and xDSL modems. Broadcom applied different measures in its contracts with its customers, such as exclusive or quasi-exclusive purchasing obligations, rebates and other non-price related advantages, in order to either strengthen its dominant position in these markets, or to leverage its market power in other markets in which it is present.[217] Despite disagreeing with the Commission's findings, Broadcom has proposed commitments under Article 9 of Regulation 1/2003,[218] meant to address the Commission's concerns, by promising to suspend existing agreements and not to enter into new agreements of the sort identified as problematic by the Commission. When writing this book, the Commission was evaluating these proposed commitments through market tests.[219]

In a different case,[220] the Commission accepted commitments put forward by Amazon, after it took the preliminary view that this undertaking may have abused its dominant position on the markets for retail distribution of English and German language e-books. The allegedly abusive conduct consisted of Amazon imposing in its e-books distribution agreements so-called 'most-favoured-nation' clauses, to Amazon's requiring publishers to offer Amazon similar (or better) terms and conditions as those offered to its competitors, and/or to inform Amazon about more favourable or alternative terms given to competitors. The clauses covered not only price but many aspects that a competitor can use to differentiate itself from Amazon, such as an alternative business (distribution) model, an innovative e-book or a promotion. In the Commission's view, Amazon could thus always offer the same prices and conditions as its competitors. Such behaviour had the capacity to strengthen Amazon's dominant position and foreclose other e-book platforms, by reducing publishers' and competitors' ability and incentives to develop new and innovative e-books and alternative distribution services, thus leading to less choice, less innovation and higher prices in the market. Amazon's commitments to no longer use the parity clauses were deemed appropriate by the Commission and are binding on Amazon for a period of five years starting with 2017.[221]

Far more prominent, in the context of applying Article 102 TFEU to conduct on digital markets, are the three infringement decisions addressed to Google, based on which the Commission fined this tech giant a total of over 8 billion EUR. Appeals have been lodged by

---

[216] Case AT.40608 *Broadcom*, (2019) available at <https://ec.europa.eu/competition/elojade/isef/case_details.cfm?proc_code=1_40608> accessed 16 June 2020.

[217] Press Release IP/19/6109.

[218] See <https://ec.europa.eu/competition/antitrust/cases/dec_docs/40608/40608_2511_10.pdf> accessed 16 June 2020.

[219] See Commission, Communication published pursuant to Article 27(4) of Council Regulation 1/2003 in case AT.40608 – *Broadcom*, 2020/C 142/03, (2020) OJ C 142/04.

[220] Case AT.40153 *Amazon (E-book MFNs)*, (2017) 2876 final.

[221] Press Release IP/17/1223.

Google, and are pending in front of the GC, when writing this book.[222] In *Google Shopping*,[223] the Commission held that Google was dominant as a search engine. Its search engine was also an important source of traffic for comparison shopping services, which rely to a large extent on traffic to be competitive: more traffic leads to more clicks and thus generates revenue. According to the Commission, since 2018, Google changed its strategy concerning comparison shopping services, by relying on Google's dominance in general internet search, instead of competition on the merits in comparison shopping markets. Google has engaged in so-called self-preferencing behaviour, or in other words it has systematically given prominent placement to its own comparison shopping service and it has algorithmically demoted rival comparison shopping services in its search results, consequently rendering Google's comparison shopping service much more visible to consumers in Google's search results, while rival comparison shopping services are much less visible. Google has thus used its dominance in the search engine market to decrease internet traffic to competing price comparison services and increase traffic from its search page to its own price comparison page.[224] In *Google Android*,[225] the Commission argued that Google was dominant in the markets for general internet search services, licensable smart mobile operating systems and app stores for the Android mobile operating system. It sanctioned this undertaking since it believed that Google imposed illegal restrictions on Android device manufacturers and mobile network operators meant to reinforce its dominant position in general internet search. Specifically, the Commission found that Google required manufacturers to pre-install the Google Search and Chrome apps, as a condition for licensing Google's Play Store, it has made payments to certain large manufacturers and mobile network operators on condition that they exclusively pre-installed the Google Search app on their devices, and it has prevented manufacturers wishing to pre-install Google apps from selling mobile devices running on alternative versions of Android (i.e. 'Android forks'), that were not approved by Google. While the first two practices relate to (at least somewhat) familiar conduct of tying and rebate granting, the third type of conduct connected to 'Android forks' entails a more *sui generis* abuse, namely illegal obstruction of development and distribution of competing Android operating systems, which seems to resemble a non-compete obligation found in franchising arrangements, or obligations seeking to protect business goodwill.[226] Lastly, in *Google AdSense*,[227] the Commission found that Google abused its dominance by imposing restrictive clauses in contracts with third-party websites, which prevented Google's rivals from placing their search adverts on these websites. Google has done so through AdSense/ Ads, which is a Google application allowing third parties to add a search function to their website. When a user uses this search function, the website delivers both search results and

---

[222] See cases T-612/17 *Google and Alphabet v Commission*; T-604/18 *Google and Alphabet v Commission*.

[223] Case AT.39740 *Google Search (Shopping)*, (2017) 4444 final.

[224] Press Release IP/17/1784.

[225] Case AT.40099 *Google Android*, (2018) 4761 final.

[226] Jones, Sufrin and Dunne 2019, p. 549; Ibáñez Colomo 2018 (b); Press Release IP/18/4581.

[227] Case AT.40411 *Google AdSense*, (2016) available at <https://ec.europa.eu/competition/elojade/isef/case_details. cfm?proc_code=1_40411> accessed 16 June 2020.

search adverts, which appear alongside the search result. Google was held to be dominant in in the markets for online search advertising intermediation and general search. In its contracts with the most important publishers Google inserted certain clauses relating to online search advertising intermediation services. These entailed, among others, exclusivity obligations (i.e. publishers were prohibited from placing any search adverts from competitors on their search results pages), 'premium placement' clauses (i.e. preventing Google's competitors from placing their search adverts in the most visible parts of the websites' search results pages), and 'approval' clauses (i.e. requiring publishers to seek Google's approval before making changes to the way in which any rival adverts were displayed). The Commission thus found that Google's strategy evolved from exclusive supply obligations being imposed, to a more relaxed exclusivity strategy, aimed at reserving for its own search adverts the most valuable positions and at controlling competing adverts' performance. Nevertheless, the Commission argued that this conduct does not amount to competition on the merits, since it prevented rivals from competing, thus harming competition and stifling innovation. By 2016, shortly after the Commission issued its Statement of Objections, Google had already changed its policies in this respect.[228]

In our opinion, such developments show that the Commission is indeed not shying away from applying the antitrust rules to conduct of tech giants on digital markets. Wiggers, Struijlaart and Dibbits[229] actually argue that the Commission has slowly but surely taken on a leading role as far as enforcement in the digital sector is concerned, as it initiated more enforcement proceedings than the UK, French, Dutch and Belgian competition authorities taken together. The cases discussed above also show, in our opinion, that the Commission displays remarkable agility in its enforcement activity: first, it made use of a broad array of enforcement techniques, ranging from interim measures, to full-blown infringement decisions, and from commitments to imposing record-level fines for unilateral conduct of dominant players. Second, the Commission showed aptitude in applying well-established theories of harm (e.g. tying, exclusive dealing) to the digital realm, while addressing conduct not amounting to competition on the merits: leveraging market power, restricting rivals' access to the market, or obstructing the development of novel products. It has done so in line with its enforcement priorities relating to exclusionary behaviour and its effects-oriented analysis. Third, the Commission shows interest in applying Article 102 TFEU to diverse sectors of the digital economy, ranging from online advertising to distribution via platforms, and from operating systems to tech-related hardware components. Lastly, it is often said that competition law is not a medicine for all problems in the market. This statement stands also for digital markets.[230] That is why the Commission has proposed legislative means which could be used to address the behaviour of such undertakings.[231]

---

[228] Wiggers, Struijlaart and Dibbits 2019, pp. 15–16; Press Release IP/19/1770.

[229] Wiggers, Struijlaart and Dibbits 2019, p. 119 *et seq.*

[230] E.g. Shapiro 2018.

[231] E.g. Regulation 2019/1150; Commission, 'Proposal for a Regulation: A New Tool to Combat Emerging Risks to Fair Competition', available at <https://ec.europa.eu/info/law/better-regulation/have-your-say/initiatives/12416-New-competition-tool> accessed 16 June 2020.

In our opinion, the floodgates are only now beginning to open as far as antitrust-related case-law in the EU digital economy is concerned. When writing this book, several complaints/investigations/cases were in the midst of unfolding, once again emphasising that potentially abusive conduct on digital markets occupies an important role on the EU antitrust agenda. In July 2019, the Commission opened investigations into Amazon's use of sensitive data from independent retailers that use the Amazon platform.[232] Essentially, Amazon plays a dual role in this scenario: retailer and marketplace where independent sellers can sell their products to consumers. In the latter capacity, Amazon collects data from such sellers, which it may use in its former capacity, as retailer competing with these sellers. The Commission is currently investigating if and how such conduct may affect competition and infringe the EU antitrust provisions. In March 2019, music streaming service Spotify submitted a complaint to the European Commission, against Apple, alleging that the latter company is using its App Store to favour its own streaming music service, Apple Music, a direct competitor of Spotify. According to Spotify, Apple charges content creators, such as itself, a 30 per cent fee when Apple's payment system is used for subscriptions concluded in the App Store. In an answer given to parliamentary questions on 15 November 2019,[233] Commissioner Vestager pointed out that as of July 2020, Regulation 2019/1150 obliges all online platforms, including Apple's App Store, to include a description of any differentiated treatment on their platforms of their own services in comparison to those of third parties (i.e. main economic, commercial or legal considerations for such differentiated treatment). On 16 June 2020, the Commission opened a formal investigation into Apple's behaviour, in particular the mandatory use of Apple's own proprietary in-app purchase system and the restrictions on the ability of developers to inform iPhone and iPad users of alternative cheaper purchasing possibilities outside of apps. One of the striking features in the press release announcing the start of this investigation is that Commissioner Vestager identifies Apple as a gatekeeper when it comes to the distribution of apps and content to users of Apple's devices.[234] This shows that the proposals to design new competition tools to tackle the behaviour of companies providing the market environment while also acting as player on that market, which we mentioned in section 2.2.2.4 above, seem closer to becoming reality.[235] On the same day, a second investigation into Apple's conduct was launched, this time in connection with the Apple Pay system. The Commission's concerns relate to Apple's terms, conditions and other measures for integrating Apple Pay in merchant apps and websites on iPhones and iPads, Apple's limitation of access to the Near Field Communication functionality on iPhones for payments in stores (Apple Pay being the only mobile payment solution that may access this technology embedded on iOS mobile devices for payments in stores), and alleged refusals of

---

[232] Case AT.40462 *Amazon*, (2019) available at <https://ec.europa.eu/competition/elojade/isef/case_details.cfm?proc_code=1_40462> accessed 16 June 2020.

[233] See <https://www.europarl.europa.eu/doceo/document/E-9-2019-002996-ASW_EN.html> accessed 16 June 2020.

[234] Cases AT.40437 *Apple – App Store Practices – music streaming*; AT.40652 *Apple – App Store Practices – e-books/audiobooks*; AT.40716 – *Apple – App Store Practices – In-app Purchases*. See Press Release IP/20/1073.

[235] Press Release IP/20/977.

access to Apple Pay for specific products of rivals on iOS and iPadOS devices. Commissioner Vestager stated that investigating such conduct is particularly relevant, especially in times of the Corona crisis, where social-distancing measures and increased online payments seems to have accelerated the growth of mobile payment solutions.[236]

2.4.6 'De minimis' threshold in Article 102 TFEU?

A striking observation is that, as opposed to Article 101 TFEU analysis, the EU courts do not seem to have fixed an appreciability threshold to Article 102 TFEU infringements. Neither is the Commission's *De Minimis* Notice 2014 applicable to scenarios falling under this TFEU provision. The EU courts have emphasised this stance on various occasions, with different degrees of assertiveness. In *Intel*,[237] the GC pointed out that the CJEU has *rejected* the application of an 'appreciable effect' criterion or a *de minimis* threshold for the purposes of applying Article 102 TFEU. In *Post Danmark II*[238] and *MEO*,[239] the CJEU argued that fixing an appreciability threshold for the purposes of determining whether there is an abuse of a dominant position is *not justified*. In other words, there is no need to look into the seriousness of the competition restriction to find an infringement of Article 102 TFEU.

The CJEU's rationale in all these cases can be traced back to the *Hoffmann-La Roche* ruling,[240] where the Court stated that where an undertaking occupies a dominant position on a market, the structure of competition on that market is already weakened precisely for this reason. Any further weakening of the structure of competition may constitute an abuse of dominance. This is why in *Post Danmark II* the CJEU stated that an anti-competitive practice engaged in by a dominant undertaking is, by its very nature, liable to give rise to restrictions of competition which are not insignificant. AG Kokott argued in the same case[241] that the use of a *de minimis* threshold in Article 102 TFEU seems to be unnecessary for two reasons: first, the exclusionary effects are to be determined on the basis of a specific examination of 'all the relevant circumstances of the individual case' and their presence must be more likely than their absence. Second, the prohibition embedded in Article 102 TFEU is in any event directed only at conduct capable of affecting the trade between the Member States. Viewed from a different standpoint, the applicability of the *de minimis* doctrine, as we are familiar with it in the context of Article 101 TFEU, is tied to the degree of market power of the undertakings concerned. It is self-evident that undertakings in a dominant position must hold a considerably higher degree of market power than the market shares thresholds embedded in the *De Minimis* Notice 2014 to be labelled as dominant altogether. Thus, the idea of dominance cannot be reconciled with the Commission's *De Minimis* Notice 2014, at least in its current shape.

---

[236] Case AT.40452 *Apple – Mobile Payments – Apple Pay*. See Press Release IP/20/1075.

[237] Case T-286/09 *Intel*, ECLI:EU:T:2014:547, par. 116.

[238] Case C-23/14 *Post Danmark II*, ECLI:EU:C:2015:651, par. 73

[239] Case C-525/16 *MEO*, ECLI:EU:C:2018:270, par. 29.

[240] Case 85/76 *Hoffmann-La Roche*, ECLI:EU:C:1979:36, par. 123.

[241] Case C-23/14 *Post Danmark II*, Opinion of Advocate General Kokott, ECLI:EU:C:2015:343, par. 93.

However, some authors[242] argue that the lack of a *de minimis* threshold in Article 102 TFEU does not mean that any impact on the market structure is sufficient to establish an abuse of a dominant position. Indeed, the Court in *Post Danmark II* clarified that even though appreciability must not be established, the restriction of competition must be *probable*, while in *Intel*,[243] it accepted that the dominant undertaking may submit evidence showing that its practices were not *capable* of restricting competition, and in particular, of producing foreclosure effects. Other authors[244] argue strongly in favour of introducing a *de minimis* threshold in Article 102 TFEU, because the law should not concern itself with trivial or insignificant effects on competition. Lastly, other authors,[245] in line with the arguments of AG Kokott mentioned above, suggest that the *de minimis* analysis has already been introduced in Article 102 TFEU through the back door, especially when talking about those cases where the Court requires an examination of 'all circumstances of the case'.

2.5 Effect on the trade between the Member States

The last condition which needs to be met in order to establish an infringement of Article 102 TFEU is that the conduct yields actual or potential effects on the trade between the EU Member States. In Chapters 2 and 5, the features of this concept were discussed. Much of what was discussed there is equally valid for the interpretation of this concept under Article 102 TFEU. In essence, the effect on trade between the Member States serves as a jurisdictional division criterion, when it comes to the application of domestic and EU competition law, respectively.

The EU courts' case-law is neatly codified in the Commission's Guidelines on Effect on Trade 2004, which as far as Article 102 TFEU is concerned, covers four main scenarios, in which the Commission refers to and, where necessary, distinguishes between exploitative and exclusionary abuses. First, paragraphs 73–76 discuss abuses covering several Member States. Such scenarios are by their very nature capable of affecting trade between the Member States. Second, when the abusive practice covers a single Member State a more detailed inquiry is necessary. Exclusionary abuses will normally make it more difficult for competitors from other Member States to penetrate the market, they may dissuade such competitors from attempting to compete aggressively, or they may eliminate competitors from the same Member State which export to or import from other Member States.[246] Exploitative abuses normally do not affect trade between the Member States when the customers of the dominant undertaking are local, unless such customers are engaged in export activities, or if discriminatory pricing is imposed by the dominant undertaking to dissuade imports.[247] Third, if the dominant position covers only a part of a Member State and the abuse makes

---

[242] Ibáñez Colomo 2016, p. 651 *et seq.*

[243] Case C-413/14 *Intel*, ECLI:EU:C:2017:632, par. 138.

[244] Whish and Bailey 2018, p. 207.

[245] E.g. Sidiropoulos 2015.

[246] Guidelines on Effect on Trade 2004, par. 77, 93–94.

[247] Ibid, par. 95.

it more difficult for competitors from other Member States to gain access to the market where the undertaking is dominant, trade between the Member States must normally be considered capable of being appreciably affected.[248] Fourth, abusive practices are capable of affecting trade between the Member States even if one or more of the parties are located outside the EU, as we have already pointed out in Chapter 2, with reference to the *Microsoft*, *Google* and *Intel* cases.[249] The practice must nevertheless fit the requirements of the 'qualified effects' or 'implementation' doctrines, thoroughly discussed in the latter case just mentioned. Paragraph 100 *et seq.* of the Guidelines on Effect on Trade 2004 explain how, for example, when the practice relates to imports into one of the EU Member States, the conditions of competition in that Member State may be affected, which in turn can have an impact on exports and imports of competing products to and from other Member States. When the object of the practice is to directly impact on competition inside the EU, it is normally by its very nature capable of affecting trade between the Member States. Should this not be the case, a more detailed inquiry of the effects of the practice on customers and other operators in the EU is needed, in order to identify exactly how the patterns of trade may be affected.

3 DEFENCES AND JUSTIFICATIONS

The fact that one or more undertakings are found to have infringed Article 102 TFEU does not mean that possibilities to defend or save abusive practices are not available in practice. Put differently, behaviour which would otherwise seem, at first sight, abusive may be justified by the undertaking in question. Below we will discuss such opportunities to escape the prohibition of Article 102 TFEU. It is important to mention that such a possibility is also provided by Article 106(2) TFEU, which states that undertakings entrusted with the operation of SGEIs or having the character of a revenue-producing monopoly are subject to the TFEU competition rules, in so far as the application of such rules does not obstruct the performance of the particular tasks assigned to them. We will discuss this matter further in Chapter 11.

Article 102 TFEU does not contain a legal exception in its text similar to Article 101(3) TFEU. Indeed, it may be hard to conceptualise a 'way out' for practices which essentially reduce output and increase prices. This is so especially when observing that the notion of dominance itself entails the ability to behave independently of, inter alia, consumers, and thus assumedly a lack of incentives to pass on efficiencies and cost savings to consumers. Yet, it would be strange if the significance of efficiencies, for example, would be recognised under Article 101 TFEU, but not under Article 102.[250]

This is why the CJEU and the Commission developed a number of so-called 'defences' and 'justifications' which allow otherwise abusive behaviour to escape the Article 102 TFEU

---

[248] Ibid, par. 97.

[249] See cases COMP/C-3/37.792 *Microsoft*, (2007) OJ L 32/23; AT.40099 *Google Android*, (2018) 4761 final; T-286/09 *Intel*, ECLI:EU:T:2014:547; C-413/14 *Intel*, ECLI:EU:C:2017:632.

[250] Whish and Bailey 2018, p. 217.

prohibition.[251] The burden of proof in this respect rests on the dominant undertaking's shoulders.[252]

Defences and justifications may embody different shapes. Some authors[253] argue that defences entail scenarios in which an infringement exists, and the arguments of the dominant undertaking save it from the consequences of the infringement; justifications refer to scenarios in which the arguments of the dominant undertaking prevent the existence of an infringement altogether. The CJEU in *AstraZeneca*[254] also suggested a delineation between the *defence of the legitimate interests* and *objective justification*. In *Syfait*,[255] AG Jacobs took issue with the two-prong analysis in Article 102 TFEU, according to which, first, an infringement needs to be established and, second, an objective justification needs to be investigated. The AG argued that it would be more accurate to say that certain types of conduct on the part of a dominant undertaking do not fall within the category of abuse at all.

The Enforcement Priorities Guidelines 2009 simply refer to *objective necessity* and *efficiencies*, as justification grounds. The Commission seems to regard efficiencies and objective necessity as inherent in Article 102 TFEU; it examines claims put forward by a dominant undertaking that its conduct is justified, in the context of the overall assessment of the conduct, by inspecting whether the conduct in question is indispensable and proportionate to the goal allegedly pursued by the dominant undertaking.[256] The CJEU, in *Post Danmark I*,[257] on the other hand, suggests that the justification discussion comes *after* carrying out the assessment of the dominant undertaking's conduct, and thus after making a finding of anti-competitive effects that are liable to be caught by the prohibition under Article 102 TFEU. Either way, while referring to the *objective necessity* and *efficiencies* as justification grounds, the CJEU, in *Post Danmark I*,[258] states that these two avenues *in particular* are available to undertakings aiming to justify their behaviour. This formulation suggests that other possibilities exist for dominant undertakings to escape an Article 102 TFEU infringement.

Indeed, in *United Brands*,[259] the CJEU accepted that the fact that an undertaking is in a dominant position cannot disentitle it from protecting its own commercial interests if they are attacked. Therefore, such an undertaking must be conceded the right to take such reasonable steps as it deems appropriate to protect its said interests. However, such behaviour cannot be approved if its actual purpose is to strengthen this dominant position and abuse it. Even if the possibility of a counterattack is acceptable, that attack must still be *proportionate* to the threat, taking into account the economic strength of the undertakings confronting

---

[251] Enforcement Priorities Guidelines 2009, Section III D; cases C-209/10 *Post Danmark I*, ECLI:EU:C:2012:172, par. 40–41; C-52/09 *TeliaSonera*, ECLI:EU:C:2011:83, par. 76.

[252] Enforcement Priorities Guidelines 2009, par. 31; case C-209/10 *Post Danmark I*, ECLI:EU:C:2012:172, par. 40.

[253] E.g. O'Donoghue and Padila 2013.

[254] Case C-457/10 P *AstraZeneca*, ECLI:EU:C:2012:770, par. 134.

[255] Case C-53/03 *Syfait*, Opinion of Advocate General Jacobs, ECLI:EU:C:2004:673, par. 72.

[256] Enforcement Priorities Guidelines 2009, par. 28.

[257] Case C-209/10 *Post Danmark I*, ECLI:EU:C:2012:172, par. 40.

[258] Case C-209/10 *Post Danmark I*, ECLI:EU:C:2012:172, par. 41.

[259] Case 27/76 *United Brands*, ECLI:EU:1978:22, par. 189–90.

each other. In other words, 'meeting competition' is acceptable in the eyes of the Court, while 'beating competition' is not. In *Sot. Lélos kai Sia*[260] the Court reiterated this stance. In practice, the meeting competition defence is most often encountered in cases relating to price-related conduct. The subtleties of the conduct are important, though: while in *AKZO*[261] it acknowledged that a dominant undertaking accused of practising predatory pricing may meet the competition by making defensive price adjustments to the level of its competitor, in order to keep the customers which were originally its own, in *France Télécom*,[262] the Court stated that the 'meeting competition' approach cannot save predatory pricing from constituting an abuse, since there is no absolute right for a dominant undertaking to align its prices with those of its competitors, where that conduct constitutes an abuse of its dominant position.[263] In other words, similar conduct conceived as defensive or offensive strategies may lead to different outcomes.

In the following two sections we will focus on the two justifications which the Commission discusses in its Enforcement Priorities Guidelines 2009, and which are also referred to by the CJEU in its recent case-law: *objective necessity* and *efficiencies*.

3.1 Objective necessity

The CJEU mentioned objective necessity as a potential justification alternative in *Post Danmark I*, yet without further discussing the content of this ground. In *Centre belge d'études de marché Télémarketing v CLT*,[264] the Court held that an abuse is committed where, without any objective necessity, a dominant undertaking reserves to itself or to an undertaking belonging to the same group an ancillary activity which might be carried out by another undertaking as part of its activities on a neighbouring but separate market, with the possibility of eliminating all competition from such undertaking. The Court was a bit more forthcoming in this case, by explaining that the justification for the refusal to supply in this case related to the technical or commercial requirements relating to the nature of television, which was the service at issue in the case. In *Hilti*[265] and *Tetra Pak II*,[266] the Court dealt with the question whether tying practices which were claimed to be necessary to protect legitimate public interest objectives, such as health and safety of consumers, could escape the Article 102 TFEU prohibition. The Court argued that the attainment of such objectives rests within the tasks of public authorities, which must enforce health and safety standards, and not in the hands of undertakings which may through their behaviour eliminate competitors

---

[260] Joined cases C-468 to C-478/06 *Sot. Lélos kai Sia*, ECLI:EU:C:2008:504, par. 50.

[261] Case C-62/86 *AKZO Chemie v Commission*, ECLI:EU:C:1991:286, par. 156.

[262] Case C-202/07 P *France Télécom*, ECLI:EU:C:2009:214, par. 47.

[263] Jones, Sufrin and Dunne 2019, p. 389.

[264] Case C-311/84 *Centre belge d'études de marché Télémarketing v CLT*, ECLI:EU:C:1985:394, par. 26–27.

[265] Case T-30/89 *Hilti*, ECLI:EU:T:1991:70, par. 102–119.

[266] Cases T-83/91 *Tetra Pak II*, ECLI:EU:T:1994:246, par. 136–140; C-333/94 P *Tetra Pak II*, ECLI:EU:C:1996:436, par. 37.

from the market. Nevertheless, in *AstraZeneca*,[267] the Court accepted that pharmacovigilance obligations may constitute an objective justification.

Paragraphs 28 and 29 of the Enforcement Priorities Guidelines 2009 require first that the conduct in question is indispensable and proportionate to the goal allegedly pursued by the dominant undertaking; and second, that the necessity and proportionality are determined on the basis of factors external to the dominant undertaking, such as was the case in *Hilti* and *Tetra Pak II*, health or safety reasons. However, nothing in the text of the Guidelines points to an obligation of balancing between the conduct's negative and positive effects on competition, as long as the necessity and proportionality requirements are met.[268] The Commission insists that it is not the task of a dominant undertaking to take steps on its own initiative to exclude products which it regards, rightly or wrongly, as dangerous or inferior to its own product. In other words, successfully establishing a case of objective necessity in practice, especially in cases of exclusionary abuses, is difficult.[269]

3.2 Efficiencies

The second possibility to escape the Article 102 TFEU prohibition which was explicitly mentioned by the Court in *Post Danmark I* relates to counterbalancing or outweighing the exclusionary effects produced by the dominant undertaking's conduct, by advantages in terms of efficiency that also benefit consumers.[270] In judgments prior to *Post Danmark I*, the Court signalled the existence of an efficiency defence/justification in Article 102 TFEU. For example, in *British Airways*[271] and *TeliaSonera*[272] the Court made clear that the assessment of efficiencies (i.e. economic justifications) must be made on the basis of all circumstances of the case. If the exclusionary effects bear no relation to advantages for the market and consumers, or if they go beyond what is necessary in order to attain those advantages, the conduct must be regarded as an abuse. The concept of efficiency relates thus to a trade-off between the negative effects on competition, on one hand, and the gains in terms of efficiency, on the other hand.[273]

In *Post Danmark I*,[274] the CJEU spelled out the cumulative requirements that a dominant undertaking must meet, in order to successfully establish the efficiency defence. It must show that:

---

[267] Case C-457/10 P *AstraZeneca*, ECLI:EU:C:2012:770, par. 135.

[268] Jones, Sufrin and Dunne 2019, p. 3385, with reference to Faull and Nikpay 2014.

[269] E.g. cases COMP/39.525 *Telekomunikacja Polska*, (2011) available at <https://ec.europa.eu/competition/antitrust/cases/dec_docs/39525/39525_1916_7.pdf > accessed 25 May 2020; T-486/11 *Orange Polska*, ECLI:EU:T: 2015:1002.

[270] Case C-209/10 *Post Danmark I*, ECLI:EU:C:2012:172, par. 41.

[271] Case C-95/04 P *British Airways*, ECLI:EU:C:2007:166, p. 86.

[272] Case C-52/09 *TeliaSonera*, ECLI:EU:C:2011:83, par. 76.

[273] See also the Enforcement Priorities Guidelines 2009, par. 31.

[274] Case C-209/10 *Post Danmark I*, ECLI:EU:C:2012:172, par. 42.

- The efficiency gains likely to result from the conduct counteract any likely negative effects on competition and consumer welfare in the affected markets;
- Those gains have been, or are likely to be, brought about as a result of that conduct;
- That such conduct is necessary for the achievement of those gains in efficiency; and
- The conduct does not eliminate effective competition by removing all or most existing sources of actual or potential competition.

The Enforcement Priorities Guidelines 2009[275] provide more details: efficiencies may include technical qualitative improvements of goods, or production or distribution cost savings; the indispensability of the conduct for realising the efficiencies relates to the unavailability of less anti-competitive alternatives to this end, and suchlike. The elimination of effective competition expectedly receives slightly more attention (given that the Guidelines deal in essence with exclusionary behaviour): the Commission emphasises the importance of rivalry as a driver for economic efficiency, of incentivising companies to innovate and pass on efficiency gains, and of protecting the competitive process when actual or potential competitors cannot constrain the dominant undertaking. Furthermore, when it comes to approaching each specific form of abusive conduct the Commission discusses in the Guidelines, efficiencies are dedicated specific attention. The Commission provides handy explanations as to how cost savings and other transaction-related advantages may be achieved, how economies of scale may be realised, how incentives to continue investments and innovation may be fostered, and so forth, in cases dealing with predation, refusal to supply, exclusive dealing or tying practices.[276]

All in all, despite the useful guidance provided by the Commission in its Guidelines, the dominant undertaking must meet rather stringent conditions for establishing the efficiency defence, with a sufficient degree of credibility, by producing verifiable evidence to this end. This is a high standard to clear, since vague, general and theoretical arguments put forward by the dominant undertaking will not suffice.[277]

Lastly for now, one may notice the striking resemblance between efficiency defence conditions in Article 102 TFEU cases, and the conditions in Article 101(3) TFEU, and the Horizontal Merger Guidelines 2004 efficiency defence conditions in concentration control cases. All these relate to efficiencies which counteract certain negative competition effects. Yet, Article 101(3) TFEU requires a fair share of the practice's resulting benefits to accrue to the consumers, while paragraphs 79 et seq. of the Horizontal Merger Guidelines 2004 require the presence of benefits to consumers, when talking about mergers that may bring about efficiencies. Sauter[278] notes that it is remarkable that in relation to Article 102 TFEU the presence of consumer benefits is not part of the cumulative conditions embedded in the Enforcement Priorities Guidelines 2009. However true this may be, to our minds, the consumer is still at the centre of mounting an Article 102 TFEU efficiency

---

[275] Enforcement Priorities Guidelines 2009, par. 30.

[276] Ibid, par. 46, 62, 74, 89–90.

[277] See e.g. case T-201/04 *Microsoft*, ECLI:EU:T:2007:289, par. 698.

[278] Sauter 2016, p. 204.

defence: paragraphs 30 and 31 of the Guidelines talk about guaranteeing that no net harm to *consumers* is likely to arise, about outweighing negative effects on *consumer welfare*, and about the likelihood of *consumer* harm in the context of the 'efficiencies versus anti-competitive effects' balancing exercise; also, the Court itself, in *Post Danmark I*, *British Airways* and *TeliaSonera*, specifically refers to advantages in terms of efficiency that *also benefit consumers*.

4 EXAMPLES FROM NATIONAL JURISDICTIONS

As stated in Chapter 4, the national antitrust rules may be applied in parallel with the TFEU antitrust provisions, provided that the conditions set out in Regulation 1/2003 are satisfied and the useful effect of the TFEU provisions is respected. As with the cartel prohibition, the EU Member States have adopted competition laws that, inter alia, preclude undertakings from abusing dominant positions. These bans are modelled after the EU experience with Article 102 TFEU.

4.1 The example of Germany

As already put forward in Chapter 5, Germany has a long-standing tradition in competition law. For that reason, it also has much experience with dominance. This subject is dealt with by Sections 18–20 of the GWB. It should be noted that, unlike EU competition law, the concept of market dominance is regulated in a separate provision. This concept is described in Section 18, whereas Sections 19 and 20 are geared towards abusive behaviour.

4.1.1 Dominant position

Pursuant to Section 18(1) GWB an undertaking may be dominant both in its capacity of supplier and purchaser. In German competition law establishing dominance requires that two steps are taken: the relevant market must be defined and, subsequently, the competition conditions have to be determined.[279] The first paragraph of Section 18 GWB sheds some light on the factors which are important for establishing dominance. It is specified that dominance exists if the firm concerned has no competitors, or it is not exposed to any substantial competition, or it has a paramount market position in relation to its competitors. In Section 18(3) GWB various factors that are of importance for the assessment of the market position are listed, such as market share, financial strength, barriers to market entry by other undertakings as well as actual or potential competition from other undertakings. In EU competition law market shares constitute the point of departure for assessing dominance, while the other factors are of additional value. In German competition law the same approach is adopted, as the market shares are considered to be the most important criterion for establishing dominance.[280]

---

[279] Bechtold and Bosch 2018, p. 108.

[280] Ibid, p. 120.

In order to give guidance as to how to examine positions on digital markets, Section 18(3a) GWB provides that in the event of multi-sided markets and networks, attention must be paid to, inter alia, direct and indirect network effects, the undertaking's access to data relevant for competition and the innovation-driven competitive pressure. In its decisional practice, the Bundeskartellamt (BKA – Federal Cartel Office) distinguishes between '*Matchingplatformen*' (matching platforms) and '*Aufmerksamkeitsplattformen*' (attention platforms).[281] The purpose of the '*Matchingplatform*' is to act as an intermediate channel for direct interactions between various users of the platform (e.g. traders and consumers).[282] An '*Aufmerksamkeitsplattform*' enables a group of users to get access to another group of users.[283]

In Section 18 GWB presumptions of existence of dominance based on thresholds related to particular percentages of market shares are laid down. For example, a single firm is considered to be dominant if it has a market share of at least 40 per cent. This presumption may be rebutted by the undertaking concerned, by showing that it is exposed to substantial competition and does not hold a paramount market position.[284]

4.1.2 Abuse of dominance

Section 19(1) GWB provides that the abuse of dominance is prohibited. It is clear from the outset that this provision highly echoes Article 102 TFEU, save for the condition that the trade between the Member States is influenced. This GWB provision contains a general clause, which applies to practices harmful to competition and does not require a moral appreciation of the practices concerned.[285] As in EU competition law, Section 19(1) GWB covers both exclusionary conduct ('*Behinderungsmissbrauch*') and exploitative conduct ('*Ausbeutungsmissbrauch*').[286] The general prohibition of the first paragraph of Section 19 GWB is elaborated on in the second paragraph of this provision, which lists a few examples of abusive practices. As a result, this general prohibition is specified by a series of examples and, accordingly, subjected to explanation in greater detail.[287] A concrete example of abuse is, according to the first indent of Section 19(2) GWB, the unfair impediment of another undertaking, or the different treatment of another undertaking, in so far as this difference is not objectively justified. The second indent specifies that demanding payments or other business terms which differ from those in the event of effective competition also amounts to abusive behaviour. The benchmark is, as is apparent from the drafting of this provision, the situation of the hypothetical competition, referred to as '*Als-Ob-Wettbewerb*' (as if competition).[288] The difference between the terms imposed and the terms that would

---

[281] Fuchs 2020, marginals 74 and 74a.

[282] Ibid.

[283] Ibid.

[284] Bechtold and Bosch 2018, p. 134.

[285] Ibid, p. 141.

[286] Fuchs 2020, marginal 4.

[287] Ibid, marginal 8.

[288] See Bechtold and Bosch 2018, p. 162.

have been imposed under effective competition must be substantial.[289] The third indent of Section 19(2) GWB makes it clear that also charging less favourable prices or imposing less favourable business terms than applied by the dominant undertaking to similar purchasers operating in comparable markets constitutes abusive conduct. The differences between these business practices may, however, be permitted on the basis of an objective justification. The fourth indent of Section 19(2) GWB deals with the refusal to give access, and is based on the doctrine of essential facilities. If a dominant firm does not grant access to its own networks or other infrastructure facilities charging adequate fees, it is engaged in abusive behaviour, provided that this access is necessary for the other undertaking to operate as a competitor of this dominant firm. The exception to this ban is that joint use of the network cannot reasonably be expected for operational or other reasons. It is clear that the rules set out in the fourth indent have a lot in common with the essential facilities doctrine developed in EU competition law.[290] The fifth and last indent of Section 19(2) GWB precludes dominant firms from making requests to other undertakings in order to obtain advantages without any objective justification.

Given its long-standing tradition in competition law, it goes without saying that the BKA has a lot of experience with applying Section 19 GWB. Of special interest are its various enforcement actions on digital markets.[291] Without any doubt, a case in point is the *Facebook* saga.[292] The BKA found that Facebook was dominant on the German market for social networks. The users of Facebook are requested to give their consent for the use of their data. If this consent is not given, they cannot make use of the Facebook platform. The BKA was not opposed to the processing of the data for Facebook's own website. The point was that Facebook was also allowed to collect a virtually unlimited set of data from other sources. These data were allocated to the Facebook accounts and processed for various purposes. Some of these sources concerned platforms owned by Facebook, such as Instagram or WhatsApp, but other sources were third-party websites (not owned by Facebook), that is, those that applied Facebook features, such as the 'Like button'. In the view of the BKA this amounted to exploitative behaviour towards the consumers making use of Facebook.[293] Interestingly, also a breach of the EU privacy rules, more in particular of the General Data Protection Regulation 2016, was found. The BKA adopted a multidisciplinary approach, as it cooperated closely with the leading data protection authorities. It could even be argued that the BKA heavily relied on data protection rules in order to find a violation of the competition rules.[294] Consequently, privacy issues play a role in the interpretation of the competition rules. In an interim ruling, however, the Düsseldorf OLG (Higher Regional Court) suspended the Facebook decision of the BKA, partly because the consumers' loss of control resulting

---

[289] Ibid.

[290] Ibid, p. 168.

[291] Israel, MacLennan and Jeram 2019, pp. 21–3; Wiggers, Struijlaart and Dibbits 2019, pp. 63–72.

[292] See <https://www.bundeskartellamt.de/SharedDocs/Entscheidung/EN/Fallberichte/Missbrauchsaufsicht/2019/B6-22-16.html?nn=3591568> accessed 23 June 2020.

[293] Wiggers, Struijlaart and Dibbits 2019, p. 70.

[294] Fountoukakos, Nuys, Penz and Rowland 2019, p. 56.

from the data collection is not seen as exploitative abuse, while data are also easy to be duplicated.[295] From this reasoning it is clear that the Düsseldorf OLG based its rejection on fundamental arguments, as the availability and processing of data belong to the key features of the digital markets.[296] The Düsseldorf OLG ruling is based on the findings that the data collection by Facebook did not amount to abusive behaviour and that consumers consented to the use of data on a voluntary basis.[297] In higher appeal, the BKA was more successful. On 23 June 2020, the Bundesgerichtshof (the German Federal Court of Justice) overturned the ruling of the Düsseldorf OLG and confirmed, on a preliminary basis, that the BKA was right in finding that Facebook's practices were abusive.[298] Nevertheless, it should be pointed out that the Bundesgerichtshof did not base its line of reasoning on the same point of departure, as the BKA did. As stated above, the view of the latter was focused on privacy issues. In contrast, the Bundesgerichtshof argued that it is not relevant whether the practices of Facebook were not in tune with the EU privacy rules. The cornerstone of the reasoning of this Court was that the private users of Facebook had virtually no freedom of choice. The users cannot switch to other platforms offering services that match those supplied by Facebook. As such competing services are not offered due to network effects, no real alternatives exist for the private users. For that reason, the intensive processing of the personal data amounted to an abuse, in the preliminary view of the Bundesgerichtshof. It should be noted that the main court proceedings geared towards reaching a final decision are still due. Further case-law, which is likely to shed more light on the fundamental issues at play in the digital economy, must be accordingly awaited.

4.1.3 Relative market and superior market power

Relative market and superior market power are dealt with in Section 20 GWB. According to this provision firms may not be engaged in particular practices vis-à-vis undertakings that are depending on them, such as SMEs. For example, it may be virtually impossible for SMEs, supplying or buying goods from undertakings holding a strong position on the market, to switch to other business partners. This extension of the dominance rules in the GWB goes beyond what is stipulated in Article 102 TFEU, but it may be expected that it is permitted on the basis of the last sentence of Article 3(2) of Regulation 1/2003.[299] As explained in Chapter 2, this provision states that Member States are not precluded from adopting laws prohibiting unilateral conduct of undertakings. Of interest is also Section 21 GWB, which precludes undertakings and associations of undertakings from boycotting other undertakings and associations of undertakings, or from being engaged in illicit behaviour. It may be argued

---

[295] Beschluss vom (ruling of) 26 August 2019, case *Facebook*, VI-Kart 1/19 (V), OLG Düsseldorf.

[296] See 'German Cartel Office to Take Facebook Case to High Court', available on the following website: <https://www.reuters.com/article/us-facebook-germany/german-cartel-office-to-take-facebook-case-to-high-court-idUSKCN1VG1AJ> accessed 17 June 2020.

[297] Botta and Widermann 2019, p. 470.

[298] See the Press Release available at <https://www.bundesgerichtshof.de/SharedDocs/Pressemitteilungen/DE/2020/2020080.html> accessed 30 June 2020. When writing this book, the judgment itself was not yet made available.

[299] Markert 2020, marginal 1.

that this provision extends the ban on boycotting laid down in private law and in fair-trading rules to German competition law. As with Section 20 GWB, this is not contrary to EU law in light of Article 3(2) of Regulation 1/2003.

4.1.4 Future developments

The German Ministry of Economic Affairs has proposed to add new provisions to the GWB dealing with dominance on digital markets, by issuing a draft bill, called the GWB-Digitalisierungsgesetz (GWB Digitalisation Act).[300] According to this draft, a new Section 19a should be added to the GWB. The first paragraph of this provision states that the BKA will have the power to find that an undertaking operating on multi-sided markets and making use of networks has paramount market power. This finding should, inter alia, be based on its position on various markets, its vertical integration and its activities on markets related to this integration, as well as on its access to data relevant for competition. In the event paramount market power is established, according to Section 19a(2), the BKA will have the power to prohibit, for instance, that in the bargaining process for getting access to procurement and sales markets, the offers of competitors are treated differently from their own offers, that the dominant firm impedes competitors to extend their market positions, that the dominant firm creates barriers to entry to markets by making use of the data it has obtained, and that the dominant firm complicates the interoperability of products or services or the interoperability of data in order to distort competition. The aim of the proposed provisions is to strengthen the enforcement of the rules on dominance on the digital markets.[301] Of significance is that the concept of '*Intermediationsmacht*' (intermediation power), which is defined as the role of 'agents' acting as intermediates (by offering platform services), has grown in importance.[302] For that reason, according to Section 18(3b), as proposed in the GWB-Digitalisierungsgesetz, when it comes to the assessment of market power, due consideration must be paid to the significance of the intermediate services necessary for ensuring access to procurement and sales markets. Interestingly, also the protective scope of Section 20 GWB, dealing with relative and superior power, will be extended from SMEs to large enterprises, as the latter may also be dependent on digital platforms.[303] It is clear from the foregoing that the German legislature endeavours to make the dominance provisions of the GWB fit for the challenges of the digital markets.

4.2 The example of France

The rules of French competition law are laid down in the Code de Commerce (Commercial Code). The rules are enforced by the Autorité de la concurrence (Competition authority, hereinafter Autorité). In French competition law, three sets of rules dealing with dominance

---

[300] This draft bill is available at <https://www.bmwi.de/Redaktion/DE/Downloads/G/gwb-digitalisierungsgesetz-referentenentwurf.pdf?__blob=publicationFile&v=10> accessed 23 June 2020.

[301] GWB-Digitalisierungsgesetz, p. 59.

[302] Ibid, p. 71.

[303] Ibid, p. 59.

are set out in the Code: Article L420-2, first paragraph, containing a ban on the abuse of a dominant position, Article L420-2, second paragraph, prohibiting the abuse of economic dependence and Article L420-5, dealing with abusively low pricing.

4.2.1 Abuse of a dominant position

The first set of rules governing the abuse of dominance have a lot in common with Article 102 TFEU. It is apparent from the drafting of Article L420-2(1) of the Code that the dominant position may concern both individual and collective dominance.[304] The Code does not contain a definition of the concept of dominance. As in EU competition law, however, the level of market shares in possession of a firm on the relevant market is a decisive factor in establishing a dominant position.[305] As a result, market shares around 50 per cent or higher are a strong indication that an undertaking is dominant.[306] In French competition law the definition used for dominance has a lot in common with the definition developed in the CJEU judgments in *United Brands* and *Hoffmann-La Roche* (already mentioned in section 2.2. of this chapter).[307] Apart from the significant role of market shares, other factors must also be paid attention to, such as the market structure and the corporate structure.[308]

The mere fact that an undertaking holds a dominant position is not prohibited under French competition law. As for abusive behaviour, a distinction is made between exclusionary behaviour and exploitative behaviour.[309] Exploitative behaviour flows from elements inherent in the actions of the undertaking concerned, whereas exclusionary behaviour is geared towards the effects caused by the practices under review, that is, the extent to which competitors are forced out of the market or are disciplined.[310] The anti-competitive effects caused by the abuse must be appreciable, a requirement which entails that either actual or potential effects are established.[311] Consequently, it suffices that a particular conduct is likely to render restrictive effects for finding a violation of Article L420-2(1) of the Code. The practices under review are subject to a broad assessment of the relevant circumstances, whereby particular conduct is not regarded as per se illegal but attention is paid to the question of the objective necessity of this conduct.[312] Gradually, an effect-based approach has been developed regarding the concept of abuse in French competition law.[313] It should be noted that, in contrast with Article 102 TFEU, abusive behaviour may be justifiable on the basis of the same exceptions which apply to the ban on restrictive agreements (enshrined in

---

[304] Vogel 2015, p. 271.

[305] Ibid, p. 284.

[306] See Prunet 2020, Section 4.1.1.2.

[307] Ibid.

[308] See Vogel 2015, pp. 285–8.

[309] Ibid, p. 291.

[310] Ibid.

[311] Ibid, p. 301.

[312] Ibid, pp. 302–3.

[313] Ibid, p. 303.

Article L420-1 of the Code). Most notable is Article L420-4(I)(2), which contains conditions very similar to Article 101(3) TFEU.[314]

Article L420-2(1) of the Code lists a few examples of abusive practices, such as the refusal to sell, linked sales and discriminatory sale conditions. An interesting example is a case where the French Football Federation refused to sell licences for broadcasting matches to a certain television channel.[315] Rebates based on discriminatory conditions may also be in violation of this Code provision.[316] It should be noted that the list in Article L420-2(1) of the Code is not exhaustive and that other practices may be caught by this provision too.

An interesting case in which the Autorité applied Article L420-2(1) of the Code is *Janssen-Cilag*.[317] This pharmaceutical company marketed the medicine Durogesic in France and intervened in the decision process of the health authority competent for issuing a market authorisation for the generic version of this medicine. Janssen-Cilag tried to convince this authority not to grant this authorisation and questioned the quality of the generic medicine under review. On top of that, it started a campaign in order to discredit this medicine. As these actions caused the delay of the introduction of the generic medicine to the French market, the Autorité found an infringement of the ban on the abuse of dominance.[318] The Cour d'Appel de Paris (Paris Court of Appeal), which is competent to review the Autorité's decisions in first instance, upheld the decision, as far as the substance is concerned, but has reduced the fine imposed from 25 million EUR to 21 million EUR.[319] The Cour d'Appel argued that putting forward illegal arguments before a competent health authority may restrict competition, while launching a campaign which disseminates unreliable information on a generic medicine may also be anti-competitive.[320] The reduction of the fine was based on the finding that the impact of Janssen-Cilag's intervention on the delay of issuing the market authorisation for the generic medicine was not as serious as assumed by the Autorité.[321] The judgment of Cour d'Appel was appealed against at the Cour de cassation (Court of Cassation), which is the competent court in higher appeal in cases brought against the Autorité;[322] at the moment of writing this book, the outcome of this higher appeal was

---

[314] See Chapter 5.

[315] Prunet 2020, Section 4.1.2.1, referring to the ruling of the Paris Court of Appeals, 10 February 1992, *La Cinq* and to Cour de Cassation no. 92-12.124 of 1 March 1994.

[316] Prunet 2020, Section 4.1.2.2, referring to the Decision of the Competition Council no. 93-D-56 of 7 December 1993, *Société Bandai*.

[317] See the Autorité's Decision no. 17-D-25 of 20 December 2017, case *Janssen-Cilag*.

[318] Reille 2018, p. N64.

[319] Judgment of the Cour d'Appel de Paris of 11 July 2019, case *Janssen-Cilag*, (2019) 8/01945 – No Portalis 35L7-V-B7C-B44MU.

[320] Newsletter of July/August 2019 of the firm Cleary Gottlieb, pp. 7–8, available at <https://www.clearygottlieb.com/-/media/files/french-competition-reports/frenchcompetitionnewsletterjulyaugust2019-pdf.pdf> accessed 19 June 2020.

[321] Ibid, p. 8.

[322] See <https://www.autoritedelaconcurrence.fr/en/decision/decision-17-d-25-regarding-practices-implemented-sector-transdermal-patches-fentanyl> accessed 19 June 2020.

not known. It should be outlined that in EU competition law the dissemination of incorrect information on generic medicines may also lead to a violation of the competition rules. However, in section 2.2.1 of Chapter 5 the discussion of the *Hoffmann-La Roche* judgment[323] revealed that in the CJEU's view such dissemination amounted to an infringement of Article 101 TFEU (pertaining to cartels) in the circumstances at play in that case. It has to be noted that in *Hoffmann-La Roche* an agreement on the dissemination of the incorrect information was concluded, whereas in *Janssen-Cilag* this dissemination was the result of unilateral conduct of a dominant pharmaceutical company. The French experience with the competition rules on dominance shows that, in the latter circumstances, enforcement action may be based on these rules.

As in EU and German competition law, the Autorité pays much attention to the competition problems occurring on the digital markets. More in particular, Google Ads, Google's advertisement service, which was also subject to scrutiny by the Commission,[324] has given rise to various actions and decisions taken by the French Competition Authority.[325] These developments resulted at the end of 2019 in the adoption of a decision,[326] by which a fine of 150 million EUR was imposed. The competition problems identified were related to the multi-sided platforms of Google: its search engine shows users the results of a search by displaying various products and services. These products and services are listed on the basis of not only relevance, but also advertisements sponsored by companies. The results generated may, eventually, lead to transactions between the users and the companies. The rules adopted by Google with regard to Ads turned out to be very opaque and subject to many changes. Moreover, the advertisers were not informed about these changes, whereas, on top of that, the rules were applied in discriminatory fashion, in the view of the Autorité. Consequently, some advertisers were confronted with refusals to place advertisements, with the blocking of their sites, and with the suspension of their accounts. As a result, as highlighted in the press release of the Autorité, this 'volatility of the rules has the effect of keeping certain advertisers in a situation of legal and economic insecurity, the latter being exposed to Google's position changes, and therefore to the suspension of their site or even their account, which they couldn't anticipate'.[327] The policies developed by Google for Ads have discouraged innovative products and services, and were anti-competitive in the view of the Autorité. For that reason, an infringement of both Article L420-2(1) of the Code and Article 102 TFEU was found.[328] Given the huge financial interests at stake, it is not surprising that legal action was brought against the decision of the Autorité in the *Google Ads* case. When writing this book,

---

[323] Case C-179/16 *Hoffmann-La Roche*, ECLI:EU:C:2018:25.

[324] Section 2.4.5.9 of this chapter.

[325] On this matter, see Wiggers, Struijlaart and Dibbits 2019, pp. 56–8.

[326] Decision no. 19-D-26 of 19 December 2019 of the Autorité de la concurrence, case *Google Ads* (2019).

[327] Press Release: 'The Autorité de la concurrence Hands Down a € 150M Fine for Abuse of a Dominant Position', available at <https://www.autoritedelaconcurrence.fr/en/press-release/autorite-de-la-concurrence-hands-down-eu150m-fine-abuse-dominant-position> accessed 19 June 2020.

[328] Regulation 1/2003, Article 3(1).

the outcome of this legal proceeding was not known.[329] In any event, it is clear that Google's practices have not only given rise to enforcement action undertaken by the Commission at the EU level, but also to competition law scrutiny at the national level. It may be expected that both the European and national cases brought against Google will result in case-law that will clarify fundamental issues at play on digital markets.

4.2.2 Abuse of economic dependence

The second set of rules dealing with dominance is laid down in Article L420-2(2) of the Code. According to this provision, the abuse of economic dependence is prohibited. An undertaking or group of undertakings is precluded from making misuse of the state of economic dependence in which a client or supplier finds itself. The aim of this ban was, inter alia, to control hyper-/supermarket pools.[330] More in general, the aim was to protect distributors, who were confronted with 'aggressive' practices of mass retailers and in particular of purchasing groups of retailers.[331] In order to qualify a position as a state of economic dependence, the Autorité must have regard to the reputation of the supplier's brand, the significance of the supplier's market share, the significant part of the supplier in the retailer's market share, and the difficulty for the retailer to find alternative suppliers of equivalent products.[332] The problem with Article L420-2(2) of the Code is that a distributor claiming to be a victim of a violation of this provision must prove that there is no equivalent solution for selling its products. In practice, it turned out that in many cases the Autorité was of the opinion that the distributor had recourse to other retail channels.[333] The legislature decided, therefore, to take out the 'equivalent solution' requirement.[334] However, the competition authority maintained the position that this requirement had to be complied with in legal practice, also after this change of law.[335] All in all, the application of Article L420-2(2) of the Code does not seem to be very successful, since, inter alia, distributors depending on mass retailers fear reprisal, while the violation of this provision is hard to prove.[336]

4.2.3 Abusively low pricing

The third set of rules is concerned with abusively low pricing. Article L420-5 of the Code prohibits prices that are excessively low compared to the relevant costs, if the offers or practices

---

[329] See <https://www.autoritedelaconcurrence.fr/fr/decision/relative-des-pratiques-mises-en-oeuvre-dans-le-secteur-de-la-publicite-en-ligne-liee-aux> accessed 19 June 2020.

[330] Prunet 2020, Section 4.2.

[331] Vogel 2015, p. 305.

[332] Prunet 2020, Section 4.2, referring to the Decisions of the Autorité in the following cases: no. 09-D-02 of 20 January 2009, *Syndicat National des Dépositaires de Presse*; no. 11-D-09 of 10 June 2011, *Sociétés EDF and RTF*; no. 11-D-20 of 16 December 2011, *Practices implemented by Carrefour in the food retail sector*; and no. 12-D-11 of 6 April 2012, *Société Roland Vlaemynck Tisseur*.

[333] Prunet 2020, Section 4.2.

[334] Vogel 2015, p. 306

[335] Prunet 2020, Section 4.2.

[336] Vogel 2015, p. 306.

have the purpose, or may have the effect of eliminating, a firm or one of its products from the market or of barring market access. It should be noted that this provision does not require that the undertaking charging these prices has a dominant position. In fact, Article L420-5 of the Code does not deal with dominance but only with a particular abusive practice, which is known as predatory pricing in, for example, EU competition law. Of course, in the latter area of law, predatory pricing is banned, in so far as the company concerned is dominant. The Autorité has put forward that the term abusively low pricing must be interpreted along the same lines as the EU case-law on predatory pricing,[337] which is discussed in section 2.4.5.3 of this chapter. For Article L420-5 of the Code to be applicable, the pricing policy must have an anti-competitive object or effect.[338]

4.2.4 Future developments

At the end of this section, it must be pointed out that the Autorité has responded to the challenges posed by the emergence of the digital markets,[339] already at an early stage.[340] For example, in 2012 it published a Report on E-commerce.[341] Furthermore, it published a Report on Data and Competition Law,[342] as well as a Report on Algorithms and Competition,[343] together with the German BKA. In 2020, the Autorité published its position paper on the competition reforms needed for digital markets.[344] The Autorité proposed to make the competition rules fit for the issues at play on the digital markets. In particular, the Autorité paid attention to the role of platforms. It recommended to introduce a few changes, such as: the broadening of the concept of dominance so that it includes platforms (playing the role of gatekeepers), the redefining of the doctrine of essential facilities in order to accommodate the significance of some databases, and drafting a (non-exhaustive) list of practices giving rise to competition concerns, such as the misuse of data as barriers to enter markets.[345]

An important aspect of the position adopted by the Autorité is related to the definition of

---

[337] Ibid, p. 315.

[338] Ibid, p. 316.

[339] Cf the Common Understanding of G7 Competition Authorities on 'Competition and the Digital Economy' adopted on 5 June 2019, available at <https://www.autoritedelaconcurrence.fr/sites/default/files/2019-11/g7_common_understanding.pdf> accessed 19 June 2020.

[340] Wiggers, Struijlaart and Dibbits 2019, p. 51.

[341] Available at <https://www.autoritedelaconcurrence.fr/fr/avis/relatif-au-fonctionnement-concurrentiel-du-commerce-electronique> accessed 19 June 2020.

[342] Available at <https://www.autoritedelaconcurrence.fr/sites/default/files/2019-05/rapport-concurrence-donnees-vf-mai2016.pdf> and <https://www.bundeskartellamt.de/EN/AboutUs/Publications/Reports/reports_node.html> accessed 19 June 2020.

[343] See <https://www.autoritedelaconcurrence.fr/sites/default/files/2019-11/2019-11-04_algorithms_and_competition.pdf> and <https://www.bundeskartellamt.de/SharedDocs/Publikation/EN/Berichte/Algorithms_and_Competition_Working-Paper.pdf?__blob=publicationFile&v=5> accessed 19 June 2020.

[344] L'Autorité de la concurrence 2020.

[345] See <https://www.osborneclarke.com/insights/french-competition-authority-proposes-competition-reforms-digital-platforms/> accessed 19 June 2020.

the so-called structuring platforms (*'plateformes numériques structurantes'*). This definition should revolve around the question whether the platform in question has an intermediary function.[346] Subsequently, the strategic character of the conduct of platforms (e.g. the gate-keeper role) for the markets dominated by these platforms, but also for other markets, must be established.[347] Then, it must be examined how important the platforms are for other market operators in order to obtain access to certain markets, which other competing platforms may be identified, as well as which are the users of the platform services and the traders being dependent on these services for their commercial activities.[348] On the basis of these factors structuring platforms may be defined as enterprises which offer online intermediary services in order to facilitate commercial transactions and have structural market power towards their competitor, their users and traders being dependent on their intermediary services.[349] The list containing the possible anti-competitive practices (mentioned above) should be used in order to enforce the competition rules on the platforms satisfying the criteria of this definition.

4.3 The example of the Netherlands

The Mw is a faithful copy of the TFEU provisions on competition, in so far as the substantive rules are concerned. Article 24(1) Mw deals with abusive behaviour. According to this provision, undertakings are precluded from making misuse of a dominant position. Unlike EU, German and French competition law, no examples of abusive practices are given in this provision of Dutch law. The Mw does, however, give a definition of the concept of dominance. Article 1 Mw sets out how some key concepts of competition law must be defined, among which is dominance. Article 1(i) specifies that a dominant position is a position of one or more undertakings, which enables them to prevent effective competition being maintained on the Dutch market or on a part thereof, by giving them the power to behave to an appreciable extent independently of their competitors, their suppliers, their customers or end users. It is clear from the outset that this definition is taken from the CJEU's case-law, such as *United Brands*[350] and *Hoffmann-La Roche*.[351] In other words, the Dutch legislature dwelt upon the settled case-law of the CJEU, when describing dominance. It should be noted that, for obvious reasons, Article 24(1) Mw does not refer to the EU Internal Market and the intra-Union trade, but rather to the Dutch market. Strikingly, what is meant by abuse is not defined. Although this term is also defined in the case-law of the CJEU,[352] the Dutch legislature has not opted for transposing this definition into the Mw. However, as the substantive

---

[346] See L'Autorité de la concurrence 2020, p. 7.

[347] Ibid.

[348] Ibid, p. 8.

[349] Ibid.

[350] Case 27/76 *United Brands*, ECLI:EU:C:1978:22, par. 65.

[351] Case 85/76 *Hoffmann-La Roche*, ECLI:EU:C:1979:36, par. 38.

[352] See section 2.4 of this chapter.

rules of Dutch competition law are aligned with the equivalent EU rules, the term abuse must be interpreted in accordance with the settled case-law of the CJEU.[353]

Two remarkable differences from the EU rules on dominance stand out in the Dutch provisions on dominance. The first divergence is contained in Article 24(2) Mw. This provision specifically states that the implementation of a concentration is not deemed to be an abuse of a dominant position. This provision is closely related to the *Continental Can* judgment of the CJEU,[354] in which the Court found that a merger could amount to abusive behaviour for the purposes of Article 102 TFEU. At the time of the handing down of this CJEU judgment, no specific rules for merger control were in place in EU competition law and, for that reason, mergers could be reviewed on the basis of the Treaty provision dealing with dominance.[355] Currently, not only EU competition law, but also the Dutch Mw contains a merger control regime. In order to avoid concurrence between the rules on dominance and those governing concentrations, Article 24(2) Mw excludes concentrations from the scope of the ban on the abuse of dominance.[356]

Another difference from EU competition law is the approach of Article 25 Mw to SGEIs. As will be explained in section 3.2 of Chapter 11, the need to provide SGEIs may justify anti-competitive practices that are caught by Articles 101 and 102 TFEU. This exception is laid down in Article 106(2) TFEU and is directly applicable. The Dutch legislature, seeking convergence with the substantive EU competition rules, specified for the rules on cartels and dominance that the provision of SGEI is an exception, provided that the proportionality principle is met. For that reason, Article 11 Mw exempts agreements necessary to supply these services from the cartel prohibition of Article 6 Mw, whereas originally, in the draft Mw, Article 25 Mw was supposed to contain the same exemption for abusive behaviour. However, the Dutch parliament feared that an exemption for abusive behaviour of undertakings being entrusted with SGEI missions would come down to giving a carte blanche for these undertakings and, accordingly, to making the control of these enterprises virtually impossible.[357] The point was that an exemption is directly applicable and does not require prior permission from a public authority. As a result, the draft provision dealing with SGEI in dominance cases was amended, and now Article 25 Mw provides that undertakings entrusted with a SGEI must ask for prior authorisation from the Dutch Competition Authority (ACM – Autoriteit Consument en Markt/Authority for Consumers and Markets) in order to justify their abusive behaviour. This stands in sharp contrast with Article 11 Mw, as well as with Article 106(2) TFEU, which can be relied upon without applying for prior authorisation. In section 5.1 of Chapter 11, more attention will be paid to the role of SGEI in Dutch competition law. In our view, the discrepancy between Article 106(2) TFEU and Article 25 Mw is not in violation of EU law, as the last sentence of Article 3(2) of Regulation 1/2003 specifically provides that

---

[353] Van de Gronden 2017, p. 170.

[354] Case 6/72 *Continental Can*, ECLI:EU:C:1973:22.

[355] See also Chapter 10, section 2.3.

[356] On this matter, see Mok 2004, p. 352.

[357] Mok 2004, pp. 353–4.

Member States are not precluded from having in place stricter national rules dealing with unilateral conduct.

In cases concerning dominance, both the ACM and the national courts reviewing the decisions of this NCA have endeavoured to closely follow the case-law developed at the EU level.[358] The *Sandd* case is a good example of the approach adopted in this respect. In this case Sandd, a firm operating on postal markets, argued that the pricing policy of its competitor, PostNL, amounted to predation. PostNL is the incumbent in the Dutch postal services sector and had the task to ensure the continuous delivery of mailings not exceeding 2 kg and parcels not exceeding 10 kg in the Netherlands. Sandd, mainly active on the markets for delivering business mail and parcels, claimed that the tariffs for business mail of PostNL were of a predatory nature, as the latter made use of its network for small mailings to deliver this mail too. The additional costs of delivering business mail was for that reason very low. The ACM, however, assessed the costs of PostNL and found that the tariffs charged by this company for business mail were not predatory, as the level of these tariffs were above the LRAIC.[359] According to this approach, as was outlined in Chapter 3, the costs incurred with providing an extra economic unit constitute the benchmark for the assessment carried out. In appeal, the Rechtbank Rotterdam (District Court of Rotterdam) found that applying the LRAIC benchmark has as a result that intervening on the basis of the competition rules is deemed appropriate only in so far as the competitors as efficient as the dominant firm are not able to match the pricing policy of this dominant firm. The Rechtbank Rotterdam referred to both the *Post Danmark I* judgment of the CJEU and the Commission's Enforcement Priorities Guidelines 2009 (both were discussed in section 2.4.5.3 of this chapter),[360] and held that the approach adopted by the ACM was in line with Article 24(1) Mw and, accordingly, this authority was correct in finding that the prices of PostNL were not predatory.[361] In the view of Rechtbank Rotterdam, it had to be avoided that a competitor less efficient than PostNL would force the dominant firm to raise its prices to the detriment of the end users.[362]

The ACM has paid great attention to digital markets and more in particular to platforms. In 2016, the ACM published the report 'Grote Platforms, Grote Problemen' (Big Platforms, Big Problems).[363] At the heart of this report was the dominant position resulting from the collection of data by big platforms.[364] As a follow-up, the ACM issued its report 'Market Study into Mobile App Stores'.[365] One of the competition issues identified in this report is that Apple and Google (responsible for the most important operating systems on mobile phones) control the app stores, which function as an 'app-ecosystem' for installing applications of

---

[358] Pijnacker Hordijk 2016, p. 257.

[359] Case 6207 *Sandd*, (2012) Decision of the ACM of 21 May 2012.

[360] Van de Gronden, 2017, p. 174

[361] Case *Sandd*, (2013) ECLI:NL:RBROT:2013:7337, Rechtbank Rotterdam, 26 September 2013.

[362] De Rijke 2019, p. 320.

[363] ACM Report 2016.

[364] Wiggers, Struijlaart and Dibbits 2019, p. 83.

[365] See <https://www.acm.nl/sites/default/files/documents/market-study-into-mobile-app-stores.pdf> accessed 22 June 2020.

third parties.[366] It is of utmost importance for a third-party developer of apps to have access to these stores. Providers of paid apps must pay a commission of 30 per cent and, in the event of a subscription, 15 per cent in the second year, to Apple and Google.[367] Competition problems might arise when Apple and Google favour their own apps over competing apps, when comparable apps are treated in a discriminatory fashion, and when Apple and Google are not transparent in their communication (e.g. with regard to their general terms and conditions) towards third-party developers of apps.[368] Interestingly, shortly after the publication of 'Market Study into Mobile App Stores' the ACM announced that it had started an investigation in order to examine whether Apple had abused its dominant position in its App Store.[369] One of the issues explored is whether Apple had favoured its own apps over the apps developed by competing developers. Priority is given to Apple's App Store, as the ACM had received the most concrete complaints with regard to this platform.[370] Moreover, the investigation is focused on Dutch news media apps, as various signals received by the ACM concerned these apps.[371] When writing this book it was not yet known whether the ACM would adopt an official decision in this case. In section 2.4.5.9 it was outlined that the Commission has also started investigations against Apple. As a result, Apple now faces enforcement actions based on competition law both at the EU and at the national level.

Lastly for now, it should be noted that in relation to its actions on the digital markets the ACM has advocated that *ex ante* regulation of platforms needed to be developed.[372] In fact, in 2019 such a proposal was made by the ACM itself;[373] this development will be discussed in more detail in section 4.4.2.3 of Chapter 8, dealing with public enforcement of the EU antitrust rules, as this proposal is concerned with the introduction of new enforcement powers.

5 CONCLUSIONS

After having discussed Article 102 TFEU and the practice developed around this provision, it is not striking at all to find that the conclusions which we may draw are on par with the conclusions we drew in relation to Article 101 TFEU, at the end of Chapter 5. While the wording of Article 102 TFEU has remained unchanged since its creation, its scope of application, and the interpretation of the concepts embedded in its text, have been consistently broadened, through the case-law of the EU courts and the Commission's decisional practice. It is thus no surprise that practices of dominant undertakings, which are not literally mentioned in Article

---

[366] ACM Market Study into Mobile App Stores 2019, p. 5.

[367] Ibid.

[368] Ibid, p. 7.

[369] See <https://www.acm.nl/nl/publicaties/acm-start-onderzoek-misbruik-machtspositie-apple-app-store> accessed 22 June 2020; Wiggers, Struijlaart and Dibbits 2019, p. 84.

[370] Ibid.

[371] Ibid.

[372] Wiggers, Struijlaart and Dibbits 2019, p. 85; Market Study into Mobile App Stores 2019, p. 108.

[373] ACM Memorandum 2019.

102 TFEU, have, over time, been found to infringe this Treaty provision. Furthermore, the Commission and the EU courts seem to have embraced more and more evidently the economic, effects-based approach in relation to Article 102 TFEU, as well. This has resulted in case outcomes which are better connected to economic realities of the markets, especially when it comes to exclusionary conduct of dominant undertakings. And last but not least, in the recent past, the Commission seems to have developed a solid appetite for addressing the challenges which the digitalisation phenomenon brings about, by making use of Article 102 TFEU. It is interesting to note that theories of harm, which are well established in Article 102 TFEU practice, and which have been validated over time in the case-law of the EU courts, are being revived and applied to conduct taking place in complex digital market settings (e.g. tying, refusal to supply, essential facilities, discrimination, and suchlike). This shows once more that the concepts embedded in Article 102 TFEU are apt to broad and diverse interpretations. Nevertheless, digital markets may require more than that. This is where new concepts and methods, such as a potential *ex ante* control of the behaviour of the so-called gatekeeper platforms, seem to be making their way in Article 102 TFEU analysis. The future certainly holds interesting developments in this respect for Article 102 TFEU.

As far as the domestic experience with market power is concerned, the spontaneous harmonisation of national bans on abuse of dominance with the EU approach has resulted in a broad and coherent set of rules, addressing such practices throughout the EU Internal Market. Yet, (some of) the Member States have not hesitated to put or to keep in place their own 'take' on abuse of dominance. This is acceptable, especially since Article 3(2) of Regulation 1/2003 is more permissive in this respect, when it comes to addressing unilateral conduct, than it is as far as collusive practices are concerned. In the recent past, the national authorities' approach to abusive conduct is probably most visible when it comes to digital markets. Important cases, addressing the conduct of giant digital players, have unfolded not only at EU level, but also in the domestic jurisdictions. This shows that competition authorities in the EU are apt to take on the digitalisation challenge. Furthermore, domestic authorities have shown innovativeness also at the policymaking level, when it comes to the digital economy and digital markets. National competition laws are in the process of being amended and new enforcement tools are being developed, to ensure the competitiveness of the digital sector, also in the domestic ambits. Similar to our conclusion in the paragraph just above, we expect interesting developments on this front too, in the near future.

PART III
ENFORCEMENT OF THE ANTITRUST RULES

7
Preliminary enforcement considerations

1 INTRODUCTION AND THE CONNECTION BETWEEN SUBSTANTIVE AND PROCEDURAL RULES

For the objectives of EU antitrust law to be achieved, effective enforcement of Articles 101 and 102 TFEU must take place. Otherwise, the meaning of the law will not be developed and elucidated, breaches of the rules will not be halted, punished or deterred, and victims of violations will not be compensated.[1] This is why, in the design of the EU antitrust system, it may be rightfully argued that the real-world success of the antitrust prohibitions depends on their practical enforcement.[2] In other words, the enforcement of Articles 101 and 102 TFEU and the procedural law developed to support this enforcement have been frequently referred to as the 'nuts and bolts' of the law, since these procedures regulate the way the substantive law is applied and enforced.[3] Therefore, procedures may be viewed as tools used to shape and implement effective enforcement, thereby giving competition law practical meaning. They impose structure on the parties involved, and can be linked to the concepts of effectiveness and legitimacy of the law. The procedural rules prescribe the steps that must be taken to ensure that the enforcement of the substantive rules leads to legally valid results.[4]

In this chapter we will deal with the main themes regarding the enforcement of Articles 101 and 102 TFEU in the EU: distinguishing various enforcement methods, identifying the entities involved in the enforcement process, discussing the goals of the enforcement exercise, delineating the legal ambits in which the enforcement takes place, and so on. Then, Chapter 8 will deal with public enforcement mechanisms, while Chapter 9 will zoom in on the private enforcement phenomenon.

---

[1] Jones, Sufrin and Dunne 2019, p. 1020, referring to Wils 2009 and Dunne 2014 (b).

[2] Rusu and Looijestijn-Clearie 2017 (a), p. 2.

[3] Marco Colino 2011, p. 73

[4] Sauter 2016, pp. 117–18; Parret 2011, pp. 162–3.

2 TYPES OF ENFORCEMENT AND THEIR INTER-RELATIONSHIP

The enforcement of the EU antitrust prohibitions can be categorised based on the broad areas of law in which the diverse enforcement mechanisms are embedded: private law and public law enforcement, respectively. While the former refers to the use of Articles 101 and 102 TFEU in litigation between private parties in domestic courts, the latter refers to proceedings conducted by competition authorities (Commission or NCAs), even if they are triggered by complaints lodged by private parties to such authorities.[5] In public enforcement, a further sub-categorisation relates to the use of administrative or criminal law concepts and frameworks. For example, the EU public enforcement system based on Regulation 1/2003 relates to administrative enforcement, since Article 23(5) of this Regulation provides that fining decisions issued by the Commission shall not be of a criminal law nature. Nevertheless, this does not preclude domestic criminal enforcement in the EU Member States, since according to Article 5 of Regulation 1/2003, domestic authorities may impose the sanctions provided in their domestic laws.[6] Private enforcement too comprises mechanisms belonging to various areas of the law, such as civil law, tort law (e.g. actions for damages, collective redress and class actions, injunctions), and even alternative dispute resolution[7] (e.g. arbitration and mediation), which may be used for enforcing Articles 101 and 102 TFEU.

Public and private enforcement involve different actors, various types of tools and procedures, and quite diverse consequences for the parties involved. Public enforcement, on one hand, is premised on public law institutions (i.e. enforcement agencies) applying the antitrust prohibitions, as part of public policies of the EU or of the Member States. Consequently, such entities find themselves in a vertical relationship with the undertakings under investigation. It is thus no surprise that, as discussed in Chapter 8, enforcement agencies are often endowed with wide-ranging enforcement powers, allowing them to uncover, stop and potentially sanction anti-competitive practices. Further, in some jurisdictions, it is the courts (and not the enforcement agencies) that are tasked with the power to rule whether the antitrust prohibitions have been infringed, and to impose sanctions of an administrative or even criminal law nature. Private enforcement, on the other hand, is premised on a horizontal relationship between the antitrust infringer(s) and the victims of their anti-competitive behaviour, be they consumers, customers or competitors. Such enforcement mechanisms unfold in front of private law domestic courts, in adversarial procedures, in which the issues debated relate not only to the existence of an infringement, and if so bringing the infringement to a stop, but also to identifying the harm created to one or more of the parties involved, and affording the compensation due in this respect.

Public and private enforcement are thus built on different frameworks, they seem to serve different tasks, they employ different tools and, as detailed below, they may be conceived

---

[5] Wils 2017, pp. 3–4.

[6] Bucan 2013, p. 19.

[7] Private Damages Directive 2014, Articles 18, 19.

as catering for different goals and interests.[8] This stance stems, for example, from Article 105 TFEU, which tasks the Commission with the prerogative to define and implement the orientation of the EU competition policy, while ensuring the application of the principles laid down in Articles 101 and 102 TFEU,[9] and from classic private enforcement case-law, such as *Courage and Crehan*[10] and *Manfredi*.[11] If public and private enforcement are indeed separate, a safe conclusion would be that, if public enforcement is effective, fewer (or more ambitiously, no) infringements would occur, and consequently, the need for private enforcement would be limited.[12] As illusory as this may sound, for both economic and psychological reasons,[13] this statement nevertheless suggests the existence of a close connection between the two enforcement ambits.

More recently, it has been highlighted that public and private enforcement together form a complete system of enforcement, albeit with two limbs, that should be regarded as a whole.[14] Such an assertion may also be justified by pointing to the aims the enforcement system, taken as a whole, strives to achieve. Also, it is important to view these dimensions of antitrust enforcement through the same lens, since as discussed in Chapters 8 and 9, a correct balance between public and private enforcement mechanisms should be struck, for effective antitrust enforcement to exist: for now, it will suffice to exemplify this by pointing to the protection granted to leniency applicants when it comes to disclosure of evidence and establishing liability to pay damages in private enforcement,[15] the binding effect of Commission decisions, according to Article 16 of Regulation 1/2003, which the domestic courts (including civil courts ruling on damages claims) may not ignore, recognising the strength of NCAs' decisions in private damages actions,[16] the NCAs' ability to take into account any compensation paid as a result of a consensual settlement in private enforcement, when calculating the public law fines,[17] using the NCAs' expertise in private enforcement when determining the quantum of damages,[18] and so on.

Thus, public and private enforcement must be viewed in conjunction, also because they work together to achieve the objectives of the enforcement exercise.[19] They are indeed complementary: where one of the two enforcement limbs exhibits gaps (e.g. limited resources in

---

[8] White Paper 2008, p. 3. See also Wils 2009, pp. 12–15; Bucan 2013, p. 20.

[9] Rusu 2015 (c), p. 166.

[10] Case C-453/99 *Courage and Crehan*, ECLI:EU:C:2001:465.

[11] Joined cases C-295 to C-298/04 *Manfredi*, ECLI:EU:C:2006:461.

[12] Jones, Sufrin and Dunne 2019, p. 1024.

[13] See analysis of Wils 2009, p. 11.

[14] Case C-724/17 *Skanska*, Opinion of Advocate General Wahl, ECLI:EU:C:2019:100, par. 76. See also Jones, Sufrin and Dunne 2019, pp. 1023–4, and the cited literature.

[15] Private Damages Directive 2014, Articles 6, 11.

[16] Ibid, Article 9.

[17] ECN+ Directive 2019, Article 14(3), Recital 47.

[18] Private Damages Directive 2014, Article 17(3).

[19] Waller 2006, p. 368.

public enforcement may prevent addressing all infringements),[20] these can be offset by the strengths of the other limb. Public and private enforcement pertain to different facets of the same phenomenon, both being necessary for the effectiveness of the whole of competition law enforcement.[21]

3 OBJECTIVES OF THE EU ANTITRUST ENFORCEMENT MECHANISMS

The enforcement of the antitrust rules is driven by multiple goals: clarifying and developing the content of the prohibitions, preventing violations of these prohibitions, in particular through deterrence and punishment, dealing with the consequences when violations have nevertheless happened, in particular by providing compensation to achieve corrective justice, and ensuring procedural fairness of the overall application of the antitrust prohibitions.[22] Some authors[23] choose to categorise the aims of enforcement as injunctive, restorative and punitive. Regardless of the categorisation preferred, the different enforcement goals may be achieved either primarily by one of the enforcement limbs, or by both (public or private). In other words, law enforcement may pursue different, although substantively inter-connected, objectives.[24]

3.1 Clarifying the substantive prohibitions

Bringing clarifications to the manner in which the abstractly formulated Articles 101 and 102 TFEU should be applied (and further developed) may be achieved through formal means (i.e. decisions of enforcement agencies, court judgments) and informal means (e.g. soft-law guidelines). These means allow for the potential reinterpretation of the prohibitions throughout time, if societal or economic circumstances call for such an approach: think, for example, of adapting competition law to the challenges of digitalisation. Wils[25] aptly shows that public enforcement is superior in performing the task of clarifying the substantive prohibitions, since competition authorities are better endowed with powers to gather relevant information and are better able to link competition enforcement with other areas of the law. Furthermore, public enforcement is about public interest, meaning that enforcers seek interpretations of the law with a view to the general merit, and not with a view to individual interests, as is the case in private enforcement.[26] However, with this caveat in mind, as showed in Chapter 9, also private actions may provide the springboard for the law to be developed,[27] primar-

---

[20] Whish and Bailey 2018, p. 306.

[21] Komninos 2006, p. 10.

[22] Wils 2009, p. 5 *et seq.*, Graham 2010, pp. 237–9.

[23] E.g. Harding and Joshua 2003.

[24] Bucan 2013, p. 21; Monti 2007, pp. 425–6.

[25] Wils 2009, pp. 5–6.

[26] Harding and Joshua 2003, p. 239.

[27] Jones, Sufrin and Dunne 2019, p. 1023.

ily in so-called 'stand-alone' actions, in which the merits of what constitutes an antitrust infringement are normally thoroughly discussed.

3.2 Deterrence

One may (rightfully) argue that the real harm caused by antitrust infringements is the so-called deadweight loss resulting from such infringements, namely the loss of economic efficiency experienced by society as a whole.[28] If this is so, deterring anti-competitiveness is an important goal to pursue, in order to prevent antitrust violations.[29] Undertakings will only engage in anti-competitiveness if this would be a profitable avenue to pursue. Deterrence occurs when such undertakings find that the likelihood of being detected and sanctioned imposes greater costs on them, than their activity is profitable.[30] In order to prevent anti-competitive practices the authorities may first provide guidance to the market players.[31] Still, the most effective way to deter anti-competitiveness is probably by altering the parameters of the calculation that undertakings contemplating to engage in anti-competitive behaviour perform, as briefly described above. In other words, (future) deterrence may be achieved by threatening the imposition of public law sanctions, of varying degrees of intensity, in case the antitrust prohibitions are violated: for example, criminal law sanctions, such as imprisonment of directors of cartelist companies, have a high deterrence effect.[32] Administrative fines can also achieve deterrence, if they credibly disrupt the balance between the gains to be obtained from anti-competitive behaviour and the costs of setting up a cartel, or engaging in abusive practices. Yet, identifying the optimal level of fines (keeping in mind the gravity and duration of the infringement, and factoring in leniency reductions) is important to ensure that they are effective and dissuasive, not only for the infringers, but also for other undertakings (i.e. the so-called general deterrence).[33] All in all, such public law sanctions are apt to ensure deterrence given that public law mechanisms are characterised by wider investigation, discovery and coercion powers, and benefit from a more adequate structure in imposing sanctions.[34]

Private enforcement mechanisms, on the other hand, are driven by private interests that relate to personal gains (i.e. victims obtaining reparation), and which are not connected to the cost/benefit calculation that the alleged infringers engage in when contemplating a particular behaviour.[35] Nevertheless, private enforcement adds an extra layer to the deterrent effect of public law action: first, the threat of paying damages in civil proceedings may alter this

---

[28] See section 2.4 of Chapter 3. See also Graham 2010, p. 237 and case C-724/17 *Skanska*, Opinion of Advocate General Wahl, ECLI:EU:C:2019:100, par. 50.

[29] Bucan 2013, p. 21.

[30] Graham 2010, p. 238.

[31] E.g. the Enforcement Priorities Guidelines 2009; Guidelines on Article 101(3) TFEU 2004.

[32] Wils 2005; Whelan 2014.

[33] Notice on Fines 2006, p. 4.

[34] On why public enforcement is superior to private enforcement when it comes to deterrence, see Wils 2017, pp. 17–21.

[35] Bucan 2013, p. 23; Wils 2003.

calculation;[36] second, the vigilance of consumers and competitors, if they have effective private law remedies at their disposal, increases the likelihood of a greater illegal restrictions detection rate; third, the large number of potential claimants adds to the effectiveness of the deterrent effect;[37] lastly, where allowed (e.g. the US) punitive or exemplary damages may yield effective deterrence. In the EU the Private Damages Directive 2014 prohibits the award of such damages, since they contradict the idea of not affording overcompensation to anyone concerned by an antitrust infringement.[38] All in all, private damages actions may increase the costs that infringers have when they violate the antitrust prohibitions. The CJEU's case-law recognised that the existence of a right to claim damages strengthens the working of the EU antitrust rules and discourages conduct liable to distort competition. Actions for damages can thus make a significant contribution to the maintenance of effective competition in the EU.[39] Advocate General Wahl went even further in *Skanska*, by arguing that public and private enforcement are complementary and constitute composite parts of a whole. Actions for damages form an integral part of the enforcement of EU competition law, a system that (taken as a whole) aims primarily at deterring undertakings from engaging in anti-competitive behaviour. In his view, actually, the compensatory function of an action for damages remains subordinate to that of its deterrent function.[40] Having in mind the above, deterrence can therefore be served by both limbs of the enforcement system, although through various means.

3.3 Compensation

Public enforcement mechanisms do not compensate the victims of antitrust infringements. The financial sanctions imposed on infringers go in the public purse. Public enforcement mechanisms nevertheless take away from antitrust infringements the benefits accrued through their behaviour. Furthermore, when anti-competitive harm caused by antitrust violations is still unfolding, it may be possible to limit or mitigate this harm.[41] Public enforcement would achieve this when competition authorities are able to adopt so-called interim measures.[42] A similar result may be achieved through private enforcement injunction actions. Public and private enforcement may thus achieve corrective justice; yet, when speaking of corrective justice, it is the concept of compensation that is often viewed as more prominent, since it essentially entails giving each person what she or he deserves.[43] Compensation, by its very

---

[36] Veenbrink and Rusu 2014, p. 113.

[37] Case C-724/17 *Skanska*, Opinion of Advocate General Wahl, ECLI:EU:C:2019:100, par. 48.

[38] Private Damages Directive 2014, Article 3(3). See also discussions in sections 5.1 and 5.7 of Chapter 9.

[39] Case C-453/99 *Courage and Crehan*, ECLI:EU:C:2001:465, par. 27; joined cases C-295 to C-298/04 *Manfredi*, ECLI:EU:C:2006:461, par. 91; case C-199/11 *Otis*, ECLI:EU:C:2012:684, par. 42; case C-557/12 *Kone*, ECLI:EU:C:2014:1317, par. 23.

[40] Case C-724/17 *Skanska*, Opinion of Advocate General Wahl, ECLI:EU:C:2019:100, par. 50 and 80.

[41] Wils 2009, p. 11.

[42] Regulation 1/2003, Article 7; ECN+ Directive 2019, Article 11.

[43] Bucan 2013, p. 22.

nature may be best achieved through private enforcement though, primarily through actions for damages initiated by those harmed by the antitrust violations.

In this context of corrective justice, contrary to Advocate General Wahl's arguments discussed above, the *main aim* of private damages actions is not preventing antitrust violations, but to correct the consequences of the infringement, namely the harm suffered by the victims.[44] This would be achieved by placing the person who has suffered harm in the position in which that person would have been had the antitrust infringement not been committed: that is, the victim is entitled to receive *full* compensation (actual loss, loss of profit, plus the payment of interest) for the harm suffered.[45] However, the Court has often clarified that such compensation should nevertheless not result in the unjust enrichment of the claimant.[46] All in all, achieving corrective justice through compensation is better achieved through private enforcement rather than public enforcement mechanisms.

3.4 Procedural fairness

Lastly, the enforcement of the (EU) antitrust rules is also about ensuring procedural fairness throughout the process of applying the antitrust provisions. Put simply, enforcement systems and procedures should work in a fair manner, ensuring effective judicial protection of the parties involved in the proceedings, respect for due process, adequate transparency of the procedure, and so on. As far as public enforcement is concerned, the issue of 'checks and balances' with regard to how enforcement agencies perform their tasks is important particularly when competition authorities bundle prosecutorial and administrative adjudication functions. In such a setting, the only control over the manner in which such tasks are discharged is by appeal to the courts.[47] Such a system could conflict with the right to a fair trial, embedded in Article 6 of the European Convention of Human Rights and Article 47 of the Charter of Fundamental Rights of the EU. Nevertheless, case-law of both the ECtHR[48] and of the CJEU[49] has clarified that such frameworks are compatible with the law as it stands. Going further, effective judicial protection, which in the EU constitutes a general principle of EU law,[50] covers a wide range of aspects, to which due regard must be ensured: for example, the rights of the defence, the principle of equality of arms, the right of access to a tribunal, and the right to be defended, and represented.[51] What is more, the protection against self-incrimination and the respect for the right to privacy, as well as observing the

---

[44] Bucan 2013, p. 22; Wils 2009, p. 12; Graham 2010, p. 238.

[45] Joined cases C-295 to C-298/04 *Manfredi*, ECLI:EU:C:2006:461, p. 95 *et seq.*; Private Damages Directive 2014, Article 3.

[46] E.g. case C-453/99 *Courage and Crehan*, ECLI:EU:C:2001:465, par. 30; joined cases C-295 to C-298/04 *Manfredi*, ECLI:EU:C:2006:461, par. 94.

[47] Sauter 2016, p. 118; Graham 2010, p. 239.

[48] Case 43509/08 *Menarini*, ECtHR, 27 September 2011.

[49] Cases C-386/10 *Chalkor*, ECLI:EU:C:2011:815; C-389/10 *KME Germany*, ECLI:EU:C:2011:816.

[50] Case C-199/11 *Otis*, ECLI:EU:C:2012:684, par. 46.

[51] Ibid, par. 48.

ne bis in idem principle, are matters enshrined in both the European Convention of Human Rights and in the Charter of Fundamental Rights of the EU, and have formed the subject of the ECtHR's and CJEU's case-law. Such matters also form the corollary of the principle of effective judicial protection and are embedded in the broad idea of a right to a fair trial.[52] Chapter 8 will discuss such matters further.

Private enforcement mechanisms too must afford procedural fairness, yet this discussion is less nuanced, since, as detailed in Chapter 9, the rights of antitrust victims in relation to private enforcement mechanisms are given expression in the domestic legal ambits. EU law provides the safe-net of protection in this respect, by obliging Member States to ensure effective legal protection in the fields covered by Union law: each Member State is required to provide effective remedies and, consequently, appropriate procedural rules ensuring the effective exercise of the right of antitrust victims to claim damages.[53] Such guarantees are embedded in the Private Damages Directive 2014, they are supported by the application of the principles of equivalence and effectiveness, and also through the work of the CJEU, which throughout time, shaped the development of the law in this respect.

Concluding, the design of antitrust enforcement systems and procedural frameworks must ensure that the application of the antitrust prohibitions unfolds in a fair environment. While various components of the enforcement frameworks have been tried and tested over time in the EU, an important corollary of the application of the substantive rules, both in public and private enforcement proceedings, relates to appropriately observing the rights of all parties involved. It is only so that effectiveness and legitimacy of the EU antitrust substantive rules may be fostered.[54]

4 EU/NATIONAL DELINEATION

As far as public enforcement is concerned, it is important to delineate the entities in charge of the enforcement system. When talking about enforcement at EU level, it is the Commission who takes the leading enforcement role. The procedural rules which guide the Commission's actions are embedded in EU law. Articles 101 and 102 TFEU are currently also enforced by the NCAs and, given the direct effect of these provisions,[55] by the domestic courts. The enforcement exercise and the procedural rules in this respect are embedded in a mixture of EU law and domestic law. To be more precise, first, the EU enforcement regulations and directives (i.e. Regulation 17/62, Regulation 1/2003 and the ECN+ Directive 2019) provide(d) certain important dimensions of the procedural ambits in which these national entities perform public enforcement activities. Second, the detailed procedural rules for the enforcement of the EU antitrust prohibitions by the NCAs and the domestic courts are provided in national public law (i.e. administrative and/or criminal law) norms. Naturally,

---

[52] Jones, Sufrin and Dunne 2019, p. 882 *et seq.*

[53] Private Damages Directive 2014, Recital 4.

[54] Sauter 2016, p. 117.

[55] Case C-127/73 *BRT v SABAM*, ECLI:EU:C:1974:25, par. 15–16.

the NCAs and national courts use their domestic procedural frameworks in order to enforce the national competition laws in the Member States.

With regard to private enforcement of the EU antitrust prohibitions, for a long period of time, there was no specific enforcement framework provided for at EU level. This is due to the specific nature of private enforcement, where the adversarial process unfolds between two private parties (i.e. infringer(s) and victims), which do not have direct access to the EU courts for the purpose of repairing the harm caused by such infringements of EU law. Furthermore, the EU courts do not have jurisdiction based on EU law to afford compensation to the victims of cartels and abuses of dominance. Such legal conflicts unfold in front of the domestic private law courts, which use their national procedural rules for the effectuation of the private enforcement exercise. Actually, the early case-law of the CJEU, namely the *Courage and Crehan*[56] and *Manfredi*[57] rulings, made it clear that, in the absence of EU rules governing the matter, it is for the domestic legal system of each Member State to designate the courts and tribunals having jurisdiction and to lay down the detailed procedural rules governing actions for safeguarding rights which individuals derive directly from EU law. While the private enforcement of the EU antitrust prohibitions, and for that matter of the domestic antitrust prohibitions, is eminently performed based on domestic procedural grounds, the Private Damages Directive 2014 harmonised some of these domestic procedural rules. Therefore, in private enforcement too, we are facing a mixture of EU and national law rules.

4.1 EU and national public enforcement: decentralisation and the multi-level enforcement system

In Chapters 1 and 2 we pointed out that the current Articles 101 and 102 TFEU have been in force since 1958, and were initially enforced based on Regulation 17/62, which granted the Commission the central role in the enforcement of European antitrust law. This centralised enforcement system was far from ideal,[58] and it was overhauled by Regulation 1/2003, which fundamentally changed the organisation of antitrust enforcement in the EU. This Regulation expanded the competition enforcement culture in the Member States by mandating the NCAs and the domestic courts to apply the TFEU antitrust rules in their entirety, alongside their national antitrust material rules.[59] This amounted to a decentralisation of the enforcement exercise and the creation of a multi-level enforcement system, which essentially entails a horizontal and vertical interplay between different actors (Commission, NCAs and national courts), across different levels (European and national).[60]

The decentralisation of the EU antitrust enforcement yielded several important consequences: first, the centralised individual exemption regime of Article 101(3) TFEU was abolished. Consequently, second, the NCAs have become important enforcement pillars in the

---

[56] Case C-453/99 *Courage and Crehan*, ECLI:EU:C:2001:465, par. 29.

[57] Joined cases C-295 to C-298/04 *Manfredi*, ECLI:EU:C:2006:461, par. 62.

[58] Brammer 2008, p. 8; Montag 1998, p. 826; Ehlermann 1996, pp. 88–95.

[59] Regulation 1/2003, Article 3(1). See also Dzino, Van de Gronden and Rusu 2019.

[60] Manganelli, Nicita and Rossi 2010.

EU. This seems reasonable, given their closer knowledge of the functioning of the domestic markets.[61] Therefore, third, the decentralisation process allowed more prioritisation room for the Commission and more efficient use of the enforcement resources, by multiple enforcers throughout the EU. Lastly, Regulation 1/2003 cemented the alignment of national substantive rules on cartels and abuse of dominance to the European model, a process which already began in the late 1990s.[62] This phenomenon seems sensible, given the NCAs' obligation to apply domestic and EU antitrust law in parallel. In turn, this led to Articles 101 and 102 TFEU becoming the law of the land in the Member States.[63]

In this multi-layered enforcement system, it is important that Articles 101 and 102 TFEU are applied uniformly and consistently, thus ensuring a level enforcement playing field, despite the involvement of different actors.[64] Because the Commission and the NCAs enforce the same substantive rules, endowing these authorities with the appropriate enforcement tools, and also cooperation and information exchange mechanisms between themselves, is key in this respect. Chapter 8 will explore in greater detail the Commission's wide-ranging investigative, decision-making and sanctioning powers granted by Regulation 1/2003, the basic mechanisms for the institutional and enforcement cooperation between the Commission and the NCAs, including the role of the ECN, and more. Regulation 1/2003 was far-reaching, as far as the Commission's enforcement framework and its cooperation with the NCAs are concerned. Yet, it was far less forthcoming with regard to the NCAs' abilities to enforce the EU antitrust prohibitions: Article 5 recognised the NCAs' decision-making abilities, yet when it comes to their fact-finding powers, the Regulation was completely silent. Such powers, and also the types of sanctions that can be imposed, were left in the hands of the domestic laws.

4.2 National institutional and procedural autonomy in EU public and private enforcement

Thus, when it comes to domestic enforcement of the EU antitrust prohibitions, those enforcement matters not touched upon by EU law mechanisms (i.e. absence of harmonisation measures) remain a matter of the national law of the Member States.[65] In other words, it is the Member States that remain responsible for designing the institutional and procedural frameworks with which domestic antitrust enforcers work. This setup allows the national authorities to be consistent within their own jurisdictions whether they are applying the EU rules or their own domestic competition laws.[66] This national institutional and procedural autonomy stems clearly from the CJEU's early case-law[67] and it relates closely to the Member

---

[61] Rusu 2018, p. 30.

[62] Monti 2018, p. 103.

[63] Antitrust Communication 2014, par. 23.

[64] Dzino and Rusu 2019.

[65] Sauter 2016, p. 118.

[66] Ibid, p. 119, with reference to Maher 2009.

[67] Cases 33/76 *Rewe*, ECLI:EU:C:1976:188, par. 5; 45/76 *Comet*, ECLI:EU:C:1976:191, par. 15.

States' duty of sincere cooperation and their obligation to provide remedies sufficient to ensure effective legal protection in the fields covered by EU law.[68]

Regarding public enforcement, the Member States' institutional autonomy stems directly from the provisions of Regulation 1/2003. Article 35 and Recital 35 provide that the Member States should designate and empower authorities (administrative or judicial) to apply the EU antitrust prohibitions as public enforcers. The only requirement imposed by Regulation 1/2003 on the Member States is that, while designating their domestic enforcers, the provisions of the Regulation are effectively complied with,[69] meaning that the enforcement process is not jeopardised. An example of how this may occur in practice stems from the *VEBIC* ruling,[70] where the CJEU made it clear that Article 35 of Regulation 1/2003 precludes national rules which do not allow an NCA to participate, as a defendant or respondent, in judicial proceedings brought against a decision that the authority itself has taken. National institutional autonomy works in a similar fashion in private enforcement: the CJEU in *Courage and Crehan* and *Manfredi* recognised the Member States' right to designate the courts and tribunals having jurisdiction with regard to actions for damages, in absence of EU harmonisation measures.

The setup is similar when it comes to the Member States' procedural autonomy: they are free to determine how to design and implement the procedural framework in which EU law is enforced in their national legal systems.[71] This means that the domestic enforcement activities of the EU antitrust prohibitions unfold based on national procedural rules, in the absence of harmonisation measures (e.g. the NCAs' public enforcement *investigation* powers). This freedom resulted in a great variation in the public enforcement systems of Member States, an issue recognised by Regulation 1/2003 itself,[72] and by the ECN.[73] This rendered an uneven enforcement playing field in the Internal Market, in which different stakeholders were facing differing degrees of enforcement depth (e.g. some NCAs lacked powers to inspect non-business premises, others could not access data stored on servers from other countries, while the level of fining differed greatly from country to country).[74] Nevertheless, throughout time, the NCAs cooperated in the context of the ECN in order to achieve effective and consistent application of the EU antitrust rules.[75] The work of the ECN pushed towards some voluntary harmonisation of certain aspects of national procedural regimes, such as domestic leniency policies, which were steadily aligned to the (soft-law) ECN Model Leniency Programme.[76]

---

[68] Articles 4(3) and 19 TEU.

[69] Regulation 1/2003, Article 35(1).

[70] Case C-439/08 *VEBIC*, ECLI:EU:C:2010:739, par. 64.

[71] Parret 2011, p. 161.

[72] Regulation 1/2003, Recital 35.

[73] Network Notice 2004, par. 1, 2.

[74] Impact Assessment accompanying the initial Proposal of the ECN+ Directive 2019, p. 16. See also Sinclair 2017, pp. 627–8.

[75] Notice on Handling of Complaints 2004, par. 20.

[76] See <http://ec.europa.eu/competition/ecn/mlp_revised_2012_en.pdf> accessed 6 May 2020.

The Member States' procedural autonomy is equally visible in private enforcement. The CJEU has played an important role in pushing the law in this field, by creating the EU right to claim damages for antitrust infringements in *Courage and Crehan*, and by modelling important elements of the Member States' procedural frameworks in subsequent case-law such as *Manfredi* and *Kone*.[77] Nevertheless, where there is no EU law on the matter, it falls on the Member States to lay down the detailed procedural rules governing actions for damages through which victims of antitrust infringements may satisfy their right to full compensation. This setup too created an uneven enforcement playing field, which allowed for forum shopping, with only a handful of jurisdictions in the EU experiencing (optimistically put, somewhat meaningful) private enforcement. Private enforcement of the EU antitrust provisions was thus scattered and underdeveloped.[78]

All in all, the institutional and procedural autonomy of the Member States when it comes to the enforcement of the EU antitrust prohibitions shaped a fragmented enforcement exercise in the EU, creating the risk of not only missing out on the benefits of effective enforcement, but also of rolling back the achievements attained so far.[79] In order to overcome such setbacks, two avenues have been embarked on, both curtailing the reach of the institutional and procedural autonomy of the Member States. First, the so-called Europeanisation of EU antitrust enforcement through the harmonisation of the enforcement and procedural rules brought about in both private and public enforcement by the Private Damages Directive 2014 and the ECN+ Directive 2019, respectively. Chapters 8 and 9 will dwell further on these instruments. Second, for those enforcement matters not touched upon by such EU harmonisation measures, the principles of effectiveness and equivalence are valuable mechanisms for the enforcement exercise at the domestic level. These principles ensure a (light) control of the domestic institutional and procedural frameworks, by preventing Member States from frustrating the effectiveness of the EU antitrust prohibitions.

4.3 EU law safe-net: the principles of equivalence and effectiveness

The Member States' institutional and procedural autonomy is not unlimited. In areas characterised by the absence of EU law rules, the Member States have not retained their entire sovereignty. With regard to the domestic enforcement of EU law, there is a risk that the rights that private parties derive from EU law could be protected at a lower standard than the rights based on national law, and that the effective and uniform application of EU law could be undermined.[80] To address this risk, the CJEU formulated in the *Rewe* and *Comet* cases[81] the principles of effectiveness and equivalence, which are meant to ensure that domestic rules used for the enforcement of EU law should not be less favourable than those rules used

---

[77] Case C-557/12 *Kone*, ECLI:EU:C:2014:1317.

[78] Rusu 2017 (a), pp. 796, 802.

[79] Rusu and Looijestijn-Clearie 2017 (a), p. 7; Rusu 2018, p. 41.

[80] Bucan 2013, pp. 46–7.

[81] Cases 33/76 *Rewe*, ECLI:EU:C:1976:188, par. 5; 45/76 *Comet*, ECLI:EU:C:1976:191, par. 13.

for similar actions based on domestic law, nor render practically impossible or excessively difficult to pursue EU law-based actions.

The CJEU has developed an extensive body of case-law in which it examined whether national rules are prone to frustrate the effectiveness of EU law provisions, and in which it provided for a base level of homogeneity and convergence in the field of legal remedies.[82] This 'judicial harmonisation' leaves scope for the Member States to exercise their procedural autonomy above the minimum level of protection required by EU law through the principles of equivalence and effectiveness. Nevertheless, if any obstacles arise from national law in the enforcement of the EU law rules, these principles oblige setting aside those domestic norms. Thus, the principles of equivalence and effectiveness created a balance between the Member States' autonomy, on one hand, and the effectiveness of EU law and the need to protect rights derived from EU law, on the other hand.[83]

In the field of EU antitrust enforcement in the domestic legal orders, the principles of equivalence and effectiveness have played an important role in both private and public enforcement, especially before the entry into force of the 2014 and 2019 Directives.[84] Chapters 8 and 9 will shed more light in this respect.

5 CONCLUSIONS

The enforcement system is meant to ensure that the substantive antitrust prohibitions can be effectively applied. The procedural frameworks developed in this respect serve thus as a means to an end for enforcing the substantive law accurately, therefore contributing to the overall legitimacy of antitrust law.[85] The public and private enforcement systems of the EU antitrust prohibitions have been developed through numerous legislative, soft-law and judicial means, with a view to catering for various objectives, such as deterrence and compensation. To this end, and also for ensuring the effectiveness of Articles 101 and 102 TFEU, the enforcement system was based on a mixture of EU and national action. The coherency of such an approach required a functional balance in this respect. The enforcement groundwork was carried out at first by the European Commission (in the context of public enforcement). Subsequently, the role of domestic enforcement (both public and private) has steadily increased. Nevertheless, a process of so-called Europeanisation of antitrust enforcement has persistently shaped the manner in which the EU antitrust prohibitions are worked out in practice. The following two chapters will discuss the public and private law mechanisms which animate the practical application of Articles 101 and 102 TFEU.

---

[82] E.g. joined cases C-6 and C-9/90 *Francovich and Bonifaci*, ECLI:EU:C:1991:428; case C-261/95 *Palmisani*, ECLI:EU:C:1997:351; case C-199/82 *San Giorgio*, ECLI:EU:C:1983:318. See also Parret 2011, p. 165 *et seq.*

[83] Parret 2011, p. 166; Bucan 2013, pp. 49–50.

[84] E.g. joined cases C-295 to C-298/04 *Manfredi*, ECLI:EU:C:2006:461; cases C-681/11 *Schenker*, ECLI:EU:C:2013:404, par. 36; C-439/08 *VEBIC*, ECLI:EU:C:2010:739, par. 61–64.

[85] Parret 2011, p. 162.

8

Public enforcement of the EU antitrust rules

1 INTRODUCTION

The Commission has far-reaching powers for enforcing the antitrust rules. Regulation 1/2003 governs these powers. From this Regulation it is clear that the enforcement of antitrust law is a shared responsibility between the Commission and the NCAs. Regulation 1/2003 does not only set out the powers of the Commission to initiate investigations and to impose sanctions, but also lays down rules for the national level. In fact, the first provision thereof contains a hidden but very important point of departure: only agreements restricting competition and not satisfying the conditions of Article 101(3) TFEU are prohibited, whereas restrictive agreements satisfying these conditions are permitted. Before 1 May 2004, when Regulation 1/2003 entered into force, the Commission enjoyed the sole power to decide whether an agreement was in line with Article 101(3) TFEU, which meant that undertakings were obliged to notify such an agreement in advance.[1] Article 1 of Regulation 1/2003 reveals that national authorities play a significant role in enforcing the Treaty provisions on competition, as they are entitled to subject business practices to a full review on the basis of all the relevant aspects of Article 101(3) TFEU; it goes without saying that the same is true for Article 102 TFEU.

In this chapter, the enforcement powers of the Commission will be discussed. Of relevance are the powers used by the Commission to start investigations in order to collect evidence, or to form a good impression of the competition structure of a given market. Moreover, the Commission's powers to adopt decisions resulting from the investigations conducted, such as imposing sanctions, will be explored. Given the importance of the decentralised enforcement of the competition rules, attention will also be paid to enforcement at the national level. For that reason, the ECN+ Directive 2019, harmonising to some extent the public enforcement at the national level, will be analysed. Furthermore, two national enforcement systems will be highlighted in order to give an idea of the national setup of the competition law enforcement system.

---

[1] Until 1 May 2004, Regulation 17/62 was in force. Pursuant to Article 4(1) of this Regulation, prior notification to the Commission was required in order to benefit from the exception laid down in (then) Article 85(3) EEC Treaty (now Article 101(3) TFEU).

2 INVESTIGATIONS BY THE COMMISSION

Regulation 1/2003 confers specific powers to the Commission with a view to start investigations. Some of those powers are of a general nature and enable the Commission to obtain information on the functioning of a particular market. Other competences are geared towards collecting evidence, which could eventually lead to the imposition of sanctions.

2.1 Investigations into sectors of the economy and into types of agreements

It is clear from the outset that the Commission has limited capacity and should set priorities. A very useful power for setting these priorities is contained in Article 17 of Regulation 1/2003. If competition is flawed in a particular sector, the Commission is entitled to examine this sector. In the words of this provision, such examination may be initiated, if the rigidity of prices or other circumstances suggest that competition is restricted or distorted. The sector or sectors concerned may be subjected to an inquiry by the Commission.

The Commission has the power to request undertakings or associations of undertakings to supply information necessary for the enforcement of the TFEU antitrust rules. This request could amount to providing all the agreements, decisions and concerted practices by the enterprises concerned. The Commission is even entitled to carry out inspections when exercising its powers under Article 17. The competences of making requests for information or conducting inspections are governed in separate provisions of Regulation 1/2003, that is, Articles 18 and 20, respectively. It does, therefore, not come as a surprise that Article 17(2) declares as equally applicable what is set out in these (and some other) provisions.

The inquiries of the Commission normally result in the publication of reports on the sectors that have been examined.[2] These reports serve as a stepping stone for taking specific enforcement actions.

2.2 Request for information

It is clear from the outset that the success of the enforcement actions undertaken by the Commission is largely dependent on collecting case-specific evidence. The Commission could simply ask for information from undertakings in order to collect this evidence. This matter is governed by Article 18 of Regulation 1/2003, which states that the Commission may, by simple request or by decision, require undertakings and associations of undertakings to provide all the necessary information. The same competence is laid down in Article 11 of the Merger Control Regulation 2004. This will be dealt with in section 3.2.4.2 of Chapter 10. The discussion below will only be concerned with Article 18 of Regulation 1/2003.

The competence conferred to the Commission is very broad. The Commission is not

---

[2] These reports are available at <http://ec.europa.eu/competition/antitrust/sector_inquiries.html> accessed 25 May 2020.

required to show that the requests for information are necessary.[3] However, despite the widely formulated provision, it is not permitted for the Commission to engage in a so-called 'fishing expedition', that is, asking an excessive amount of questions of different natures.[4] When making requests, the Commission must comply with the principle of proportionality and these requests must be reasonable: there must be a correlation between the requested information and the alleged infringement.[5]

Article 18 of Regulation 1/2003 refers to *simple requests* and requests made by way of *decisions*. It is of great importance to make a distinction between these two settings. No sanctions are in place for non-compliance with simple requests made by the Commission. An undertaking not sending information to the Commission will not be fined. In contrast, if an undertaking does not respond to a request for information made through a decision, the Commission is entitled to impose a fine, according to Article 23(1)(b) of Regulation 1/2003. Another possibility is imposing a periodic penalty payment on the company refusing to provide information. Requests by decision are more effective than simple requests. It is apparent from the case-law of the CJEU that Article 18 does not envisage a fixed order for requesting information. In other words, the Commission is not required to make a simple request at first and, subsequently, in the event of the refusal of the undertaking concerned to provide the necessary information, to proceed to the stage of making a request by decision. The first request for information of the Commission may be made by decision. The drafting of Article 18(1) of Regulation 1/2003 leaves room for manoeuvre for the Commission.

It should be noted that providing incorrect, incomplete or misleading information is not permitted in the event of both simple requests and requests by decisions. The Commission will then have the power to adopt sanctions.[6] It does not come as a surprise that supplying information leading to confusion is illegal and may give rise to sanctions. Consequently, in the case of simple requests for information it is a better strategy for an undertaking not to respond to this request, than providing incorrect information.

Requests made by decisions are subject to judicial review by the Union courts (on appeal before the GC and on higher appeal before the CJEU). The point of departure for reviewing these appeals is that a company being confronted with a request for information must cooperate. The obligation to provide the necessary information rests on the owners of the undertakings, on their representatives, as well as on the persons authorised to represent the undertakings and associations of undertakings concerned.

It should be pointed out that there is a very important exception to the obligation to cooperate actively. The CJEU has acknowledged the right that no one must be obliged to incriminate oneself. This principle is not expressly embodied in Article 18. In the view of the CJEU the right to remain silent is part of the general principles of EU law.[7] The Commission must, therefore, refrain from compelling a company to provide it with answers, which might

---

[3] E.g. case 374/87 *Orkem*, ECLI:EU:C:1989:387, par. 15.

[4] Case C-94/00 *Roquette Frères*, ECLI:EU:C:2002:603, par. 54. See also Jones, Sufrin and Dunne 2019, p. 902.

[5] E.g. case C-94/00 *Roquette Frères*, ECLI:EU:C:2002:603, par. 42, 76–77.

[6] Regulation 1/2003, Articles 23(1)(a) and (4), 24(1).

[7] Case 374/87 *Orkem*, ECLI:EU:C:1989:387, par. 28–34.

involve an admission of the existence of an infringement. Accordingly, persons representing an undertaking may not be forced to give answers establishing the involvement of this undertaking in an infringement of the competition rules. It should be noted that according to the ECtHR, the right to remain silent does not extend to materials (such as documents) that exist independently from the will of the suspect.[8] As a result, the CJEU held in *SGL Carbon*[9] that the Commission is entitled to request documents in the possession of an undertaking and that these documents must be produced by this undertaking, even if the materials concerned contain proof establishing the infringement committed by the undertaking under investigation.[10] In sum, documents must always be handed over to the Commission but (oral or written) answers must only be given to the extent that they do not lead to an admission of guilt.[11] In concrete cases, it is difficult to make a distinction between compelling an undertaking to incriminate itself and obliging it to just produce materials, such as a document that exists independently from the undertaking's will. In any event, the freedom from self-incrimination is infringed if there is some form of coercion on the part of the Commission and an actual interference with this freedom.[12]

2.3 Power to take statements

According to Article 19 of Regulation 1/2003, the Commission may interview any natural or legal person who consents to be interviewed. By exercising this power, the Commission has the opportunity to collect information connected with an ongoing investigation. The effectiveness of Article 19 of Regulation 1/2003 could be questioned, as no sanctions in relation to this power are in place. This entails that nobody is obliged to cooperate with the interviews of the Commission. The success of the interview is fully dependent on the goodwill of the (legal) persons concerned, as they have to give their consent. What is even worse, is that providing incorrect, incomplete or misleading information does not result in any sanctions under Regulation 1/2003. Undertakings having a peculiar take on the facts and giving confusing information to the Commission will not be punished for this behaviour. The added value of the Article 19 powers is not clear from the outset. Nevertheless, the Commission has regularly used these powers, although this institution is aware of the disincentive of providing correct information resulting from the absence of sanctions.[13]

2.4 The inspection of business premises

A very important instrument for collecting evidence, which is at the Commission's disposal, is laid down in Article 20 of Regulation 1/2003. This provision confers the competence to

---

[8] Case *Saunders v UK*, Application No. 19187/91, 17 December 1996, ECLI:CE:ECHR:1993:1207DEC001918791.

[9] Case C-301/04 *SGL Carbon*, ECLI:EU:C:2006:432.

[10] Ibid, par. 44.

[11] Veenbrink 2020, p. 147.

[12] Ibid, pp. 147–55.

[13] Staff Working Document 2009, par. 84.

this institution to inspect any premises, land and means of transport of undertakings and associations of undertakings. In this regard, it should be pointed out that the Merger Control Regulation 2004 also provides that the Commission is entitled to carry out inspections. The drafting of these provisions, which will be dealt with in section 3.2.4.2 of Chapter 10, highly mirrors what is written in Article 20 of Regulation 1/2003. For that reason, only the latter provision will be analysed below.

2.4.1 The powers of the Commission

The inspection powers are set out in Article 20(2) of Regulation 1/2003. The officials of the Commission are empowered:

a) to enter any premises, land and means of transport of undertakings and associations of undertakings;
b) to examine the books and other records related to the business, irrespective of the medium on which they are stored;
c) to take copies from such books or records;
d) to seal any business premises and books or records; and
e) to ask any representative or member of staff of the entity under investigation for explanations on facts or documents related to the investigation carried out and to record the answers.

It is apparent from this provision that the inspection powers of the Commission are great tools for collecting evidence. Its officials may search books and records in order to find information supporting the claim that competition law is infringed. Furthermore, they may seal premises for the period, and to the extent this is necessary. By doing so, the Commission officials prevent that evidence being removed in the event that an investigation is spread over various days.

2.4.2 Legal privilege

However, these powers are subject to important limitations and safeguards. To start with, the correspondence between the representatives of the undertaking under investigation and lawyers is protected by legal privilege. In *AM&S*,[14] the CJEU held that the confidentiality of this correspondence must be respected by the Commission, when carrying out investigations. This principle is known as the concept of legal privilege. Similar to the right to remain silent, legal privilege is not expressly embodied in Regulation 1/2003. However, it is regarded to be part of the principles of Union law. The written communication between the lawyer and the company is protected against disclosure if the following two conditions are fulfilled: (1) such communications are made for the purposes and in the interest of the clients' rights of defence, and (2) they originate from independent lawyers, that is, lawyers who are not bound to the client by a relationship of employment.[15] In subsequent case-law, the importance of

---

[14] Case 155/79 *AM&S*, ECLI:EU:C:1982:157.

[15] Ibid, par. 21.

the independent position of lawyers is underlined by the CJEU. The written communications from in-house lawyers do not benefit from the protection of legal privilege.[16] As a result, such communications must be disclosed to the Commission.

The Commission officials and the representatives of the undertaking under investigation could have differing opinions as to whether a particular document is protected by legal privilege. This dispute cannot be solved by giving access to the Commission officials concerned, because then the content of the document is known to these officials. In such an event, a copy of the document concerned is put in a sealed envelope.[17] The Hearing Officer, who holds an independent position in the enforcement process at the level of the Commission, could open the envelope and verify the document therein, if the parties concerned give their consent to this solution.[18] If the matter remains unsolved, the Commission can take a decision ordering the disclosure of the document at stake, a decision which may be appealed against by the undertaking concerned before the GC on the basis of Article 263 TFEU, while, if necessary, interim measures may be requested under Articles 278 and 279 TFEU.[19]

2.4.3 Inspections on the basis of a written authorisation or a decision

Article 20 of Regulation 1/2003 specifies some conditions for the inspection of business premises. From this provision it is clear that an inspection can be conducted on the basis of a written authorisation or a decision. Either way, the subject matter and purpose of the inspection must be specified[20] in order to prevent the Commission engaging in a 'fishing expedition'.[21]

Article 20(3) of Regulation 1/2003, which applies to inspections based on written authorisations, does not say that the undertakings concerned are obliged to submit to these inspections. In contrast, if the inspection is ordered by a Commission decision, the undertaking is obliged to submit to this inspection pursuant to Article 20(4) of Regulation 1/2003. It is not surprising that both the written authorisation and the decision must specify the subject matter and purpose of the inspection. The company under investigation is entitled to this information for reasons connected with the right of defence. It should also be made known which sanctions are provided for non-compliance.

Article 23 of Regulation 1/2003 states with regard to both types of inspections (by written authorisation and by decision) that giving incorrect or misleading answers, providing books and other records in incomplete form, and breaking seals can result in imposing fines. In addition to this, this provision specifies that the refusal to submit to an inspection ordered by decision can lead to the imposition of a fine. Such a refusal could also give rise to a periodic penalty payment provided for in Article 24 of Regulation 1/2003.

It is possible for the Commission to involve the NCA of the Member State, where the

---

[16] Case C-550/07 *Akzo Nobel*, ECLI:EU:C:2010:512.

[17] Best Practices 2011, par. 54.

[18] Decision Regarding the Hearing Officer 2011, Article 4(2)(a).

[19] Jones, Sufrin and Dunne 2019, p. 919.

[20] Regulation 1/2003, Article 20(3) and (4).

[21] Vedder and Appeldoorn, 2019, p. 251.

premises under investigation are located, in the inspection. Article 20(5) of Regulation 1/2003 states that officials of such an authority can assist the Commission at the request of the authority concerned or of the Commission. It is important to note that, according to this provision, the national officials enjoy the same powers as the Commission officials when inspecting the premises concerned. In fact, Regulation 1/2003 confers powers directly to national officials. As soon as these persons are entrusted with the task to carry out an inspection together with the Commission, they are entitled to exercise the powers given to them by this Regulation. It is clear from the outset that given the supremacy of EU law over national law, these powers cannot be affected or amended by the domestic legislator. Therefore, it may be assumed that in a considerable number of Member States, inspection powers of national officials differ depending on whether they conduct an inspection together with the Commission or on a stand-alone basis. In the last case, it is up to national procedural law, rather than Regulation 1/2003, to determine the powers of the national officials.

The involvement of national officials could be of great use for the Commission. If the undertaking (the premises of which are under investigation) opposes an inspection ordered by decision, the national officials must help the Commission, which could even entail that the police or an equivalent enforcement authority would intervene.[22] The exercise of police enforcement powers will give the Commission access to the premises it wishes to enter.

All in all, the Commission has more powers during inspections ordered by decision than during inspections carried out on the basis of authorisations. Importantly, as already stated, the Commission is not obliged to start first an inspection on the basis of an authorisation and, only in the event of a refusal to cooperate on the part of the undertaking concerned, to move to the stage of an inspection by decision. It is permitted for the Commission to immediately order an inspection by decision,[23] which enables this institution to get access to business premises without any delay. The point is that in the event of an inspection based on a written authorisation, an undertaking could refuse the Commission to enter in order to gain time to destroy evidence. Immediate action by the Commission on the basis of an inspection ordered by decision prevents that evidence will disappear.

2.4.4 Fundamental rights and inspections

When exercising its inspection powers, the Commission must respect fundamental rights. In cases concerning inspections, undertakings rely on the right to respect for private life, as enshrined in Article 8 ECHR and Article 7 of the Charter of Fundamental Rights of the EU. In *Hoechst*,[24] the CJEU contended that this fundamental right did not extend to legal persons. Nevertheless, it held that any intervention by a public authority in the sphere of both natural or legal persons must have a legal basis and be justified on the grounds laid down by law in order to protect against arbitrary or disproportionate intervention.[25] Developments in the case-law of the ECtHR made the CJEU reconsider its view on the scope of the right to respect

---

[22] Regulation 1/2003, Article 20(6).

[23] Case 136/79 *National Panasonic*, ECLI:EU:C:1980:169.

[24] Case 46/87 *Hoechst*, ECLI:EU:C:1989:337.

[25] Ibid, par. 19.

for private life. In *Colas Est*, the ECtHR pointed out that legal persons are protected by Article 8 ECHR and, accordingly, may invoke the right to respect for family life. In response to this, the CJEU performed a U-turn as regards the scope of this fundamental right and held in *Roquette Frères*[26] that, given the case-law of the ECtHR, more in particular in *Colas Est*,[27] the protection of the respect for private life may be extended in certain circumstances to cover business premises.[28]

It goes without saying that the safeguards set out by the CJEU in *Hoechst* continued to be adhered to. Despite its view in this case, that undertakings could not rely on the right to respect for private life, the CJEU had acknowledged that the Commission inspections of business premises are subject to certain limitations. No wonder that in *Roquette Frères*, where the CJEU adopted a more favourable approach to the scope of this fundamental right, the safeguards were elaborated on. It should be noted that the EU rules dealing with the procedural aspects of inspections do not envisage any prior involvement of the EU courts in the conduct of the inspection by the Commission. As a result, it is left to the national courts to review, prior to an inspection of the business premises, a request of the Commission that NCA officials assist its officials. It should be recalled that this assistance may entail the involvement of the police, if the undertaking under investigation opposes the inspection concerned. This judicial task amounts to a delicate matter, as a domestic authority assesses whether a Union institution has respected the limitations that are in place. In *Roquette Frères*, the aim of the CJEU was to strike a balance between the need for judicial protection and the hierarchical order between national and EU law. It held that the invasion of privacy necessitates that a national body carries out a judicial review. It should examine whether the coercive measures sought by the Commission are not arbitrary. So, at the heart of the assessment to be performed by a national court is the compliance with the principle of proportionality. However, the *necessity* of the inspection ordered by the Commission may not be reviewed by a national court. The CJEU held that a national court is not entitled to demand that it be provided with the information and evidence in the file of the Commission.[29] The reason for this is that, in the CJEU's view, the Member States, including apparently their judiciary, must ensure that the Commission action is effective.[30]

The judgment in *Roquette Frères* is codified in Article 20(8) of Regulation 1/2003, which, in the same vein, provides which information should be given by the Commission to the national court. Furthermore, this provision also stresses that the national judicial authority is neither entitled to question the necessity for the inspection, nor to demand that it is provided with information in the Commission's file. That means that these aspects can only be reviewed by the Union courts afterwards, that is, when the Commission has adopted a decision, by which a fine is imposed on the undertaking concerned, and this decision is appealed against.

---

[26] Case C-94/00 *Roquette Frères*, ECLI:EU:C:2002:603.

[27] Case 37971/97 *Colas Est*, ECtHR, 16 April 2002.

[28] Case C-94/00 *Roquette Frères*, ECLI:EU:C:2002:603, par. 29.

[29] Ibid, par. 62.

[30] Ibid, par. 63.

It should be pointed out that neither the CJEU in *Roquette Frères*, nor Article 20 of Regulation 1/2003 require that the inspections of business premises involving the assistance of NCA officials have to be subjected to prior judicial authorisation by domestic courts. It is left to national law whether such review must be carried out.[31] Consequently, if national law requires such prior authorisation, the Commission must apply for it before conducting an inspection. Conversely, if national law is silent on this matter or provides that no prior authorisation must be asked, the Commission can conduct its inspection without involving any national judicial body.

The question arose as to whether the limited involvement of national judicial bodies in the inspections of business premises was compatible with Article 8 of the ECHR. According to the EU rules on these inspections, judicial authorisation must only be sought if national law so requires, whereas the national review carried out is limited to verifying whether the coercive measures asked for are arbitrary. This question is addressed in case-law subsequent to *Roquette Frères*.

In *Pekárny*,[32] the ECtHR was of the opinion that the inspection of the business premises by the Czech competition authority was incompatible with Article 8 ECHR, given the absence of prior judicial authorisation and the flawed *ex post* judicial review. In *Deutsche Bahn*,[33] the EU GC derived from the case-law of the ECtHR that absence of prior judicial authorisation may be counterbalanced by a comprehensive *ex post* inspection review.[34] It then moved on by arguing and specifying in great detail that the EU rules for inspections contain sufficient safeguards in order to counterbalance the limited prior judicial authorisation. This point of view was confirmed by the CJEU in its ruling in *Deutsche Bahn*.[35] The CJEU stressed that the *ex post* review carried out by the Union courts entails that these courts perform an in-depth assessment of the law and of the facts on the basis of the evidence adduced by the defendant.[36] Eventually, the CJEU concluded that the absence of prior judicial authorisation does not disregard the right to respect for private life, as this absence is compensated by a wide range of safeguards, the compliance with which is subject to substantial *ex post* review.[37] In other words, the drawbacks resulting from an absent or limited *ex ante* judicial review system must be offset by the effective safeguards of the *ex post* judicial review system.[38]

From the foregoing, it is apparent that the CJEU has struggled with the relationship between the rules on the inspection of businesses and the fundamental right laid down in Article 8 ECHR and Article 7 Charter of Fundamental Rights of the EU. It should be pointed out that some issues still need some consideration. For example, the time gap between an inspection and the final decision by which a fine is imposed could be huge. To what extent

---

[31] Regulation 1/2003, Article 20(7).

[32] Case 97/11 *Delta Pekárny v Czech Republic*, ECtHR, 2 October 2014.

[33] Joined cases T-289, T-290 and T-521/11 *Deutsche Bahn*, ECLI:EU:T:2013:404.

[34] Ibid, par. 66.

[35] Case C-583/13 *Deutsche Bahn*, ECLI:EU:C:2015:404.

[36] Ibid, par. 34.

[37] Andersson 2018, p. 75.

[38] Ibid, p. 101.

could this lead to the conclusion that *ex post* review falls short in compensating the limited prior judicial authorisation? Moreover, it cannot be excluded that, in specific cases, the Commission will exercise its inspection powers in contravention of what is provided in EU law or in the ECHR. This could also amount to legal problems in relation to the absence of prior judicial authorisation. Further case-law on these issues must be awaited.

2.5 The inspection of other premises, such as private homes

An important power for collecting evidence is laid down in Article 21 of Regulation 1/2003. The heading of this provision is euphemistic as it refers to 'other premises' (than business premises) that can be inspected. Mention is made of land and means of transport but also of the homes of directors, managers and other members of staff of the undertaking or the association of undertakings under investigation. It is clear from the outset that the main aim of Article 21 is to enable the Commission to search private homes. Telling in this context is Recital 26 of Regulation 1/2003, which states that, in some cases, business records are kept in homes of, inter alia, directors and, accordingly, the Commission officials should be empowered to enter these premises. In this section, the Article 21 inspection will be referred to as the power to search private homes.

Inspections of private homes are very intrusive for the persons living in these residences and, therefore, these inspections are subject to important safeguards. It should be noted that the power of searching homes of suspects belongs, as a rule, to the domain of criminal law. As the TFEU does not provide for criminal enforcement of the competition rules and, moreover, criminal law is regarded as being part of the national competences, the power to search homes is laid down in administrative law, which is, of course, in this context Regulation 1/2003. All in all, Article 21 of Regulation 1/2003 concerns a sensitive matter and it is, therefore, surprising that to date no case-law on this provision is available. No wonder that the Commission has used its powers under this provision with caution by searching private homes only in very few cases.[39]

The power provided in Article 21 of Regulation 1/2003 can only be exercised in so far as a reasonable suspicion exists that books or other records related to the business are being kept in a home of a director or other member of staff. On top of that, the evidence to be collected must be relevant to prove a serious infringement of Articles 101 or 102 TFEU. The conditions for starting an Article 21 inspection are stricter than those governing Article 20 inspections. When it comes to the former, the Commission must carry out a two-prong test: demonstrating the existence of reasonable suspicion that books or other records are kept in such premises, and making it plausible that an infringement of a serious nature is committed. It should be pointed out that the reasonable suspicion has to be related to the location of the evidence and does not necessarily entail that the person living in the premises concerned is alleged of having violated or having contributed to the violation of Articles 101 or 102 TFEU. Inspections of private homes can only be ordered by Commission decisions. Given the considerable impact of such an inspection, it is sensible that an order by simple written

---

[39] Ibid, p. 223.

authorisation is not possible. The decision of the Commission is subject to *ex post* judicial review by the EU courts. The decision must specify the subject matter and purpose of the investigation. It must also outline the reasons that have led to the conclusion that a reasonable suspicion exists. Before a decision to search private homes is ordered, the Commission is obliged to consult the competition authority of the Member State, where the inspection must take place.

It is apparent from the foregoing that substantial safeguarding mechanisms must be in place. The most important mechanism is laid down in Article 21(3) of Regulation 1/2003. Pursuant to this provision, prior authorisation from the judicial authority of the Member State concerned is required. Unlike the inspection of business premises, it is not left to the national legislator to determine whether an inspection of private homes is subject to prior judicial review by a national court. In all circumstances, the involvement of a national court is compulsory. In our view, this prerequisite is of great importance in order to preclude that the fundamental right to respect for private life, as enshrined in Article 8 ECHR and Article 7 of the Charter of Fundamental Rights of the EU, is violated.

The point is, however, that Article 21(3) of Regulation 1/2003 limits the judicial review to be carried out by the national court involved. In this regard, there is a striking resemblance with the inspections of business premises. The national court, being asked for prior permission by the Commission, does not have the power to assess every aspect of the inspection of a private home. Also, in Article 21(3) a distinction is made between the possible arbitrary and excessive character of the coercive measure and the necessity for the inspection requested. Similar to cases concerning the inspection of business premises, the national courts are not allowed to assess the necessity of the inspection of private homes. This review is in the hands of the GC and the CJEU. In our view it is not clear whether an intensive and comprehensive review conducted *ex post* by the EU courts would be able to compensate for the limited *ex ante* review carried out by the national courts. The cases *Pekárny* and *Deutsche Bahn* (discussed above) did not concern the inspection of private homes. Moreover, it is not excluded that the ECtHR and CJEU could have different views on this matter. Further case-law and developments dealing with the inspection of private homes must be awaited.

3 DECISIONS AND SANCTIONS ADOPTED BY THE COMMISSION

Once the Commission has gathered sufficient evidence, it can take action against the undertakings under investigation. Regulation 1/2003 envisages a wide range of decisions that can be taken, based on the results stemming from the investigation. The most important one is the power to impose fines. Below, these decisions will be discussed.

3.1 Finding and termination of infringement

If an infringement of Article 101 TFEU or Article 102 TFEU is detected by the Commission, it could make use of its power laid down in Article 7 of Regulation 1/2003. It could decide that one of the Treaty provisions on competition is violated and order the undertakings or associations of undertakings concerned to bring such violation to an end. In many cases, such a decision is combined with the imposition of a fine. It is important to note that pursuant to Article 27(1) of Regulation 1/2003 the undertakings or associations of undertakings concerned have the right to be heard and the decision must be based on objections on which the parties concerned have been able to comment. In practice the Commission sends the parties concerned the so-called statement of objections. In section 3.5.1 of this chapter, this statement will be elaborated on, as at the heart of this section is the imposition of fines.

3.1.1 Procedural issues

Article 7 of Regulation 1/2003 stipulates that the Commission, when finding an infringement and ordering the termination thereof, can act both on a complaint and on its own initiative. The second paragraph of this provision states that natural or legal persons who can show a legitimate interest are entitled to lodge complaints.[40] In other words, a complaint can play an important role when it comes to triggering Commission action against violations of the competition rules. This is so, also having in mind the limited resources the Commission possesses for uncovering anti-competitive practices.

According to Article 27(1) of Regulation 1/2003 the undertakings and associations of undertakings subject to investigations of the Commission have the right to be heard. Article 10(1) of the Conduct of Proceedings Regulation 2004 specifies that a statement of objections must be sent by the Commission to them. Section 3.5.1 will further outline what such a statement entails.

Article 7 of Regulation 1/2003 specifically provides that the Commission is entitled to impose behavioural or structural remedies, which are proportionate and necessary. It is clear from the wording of Article 7 that structural remedies are means of last resort, as these remedies may only be imposed if the behavioural remedies are not capable of addressing the competition problems at play, or are not sufficiently proportionate. Unfortunately, this provision and the recitals of Regulation 1/2003 do not explain what is meant by structural remedies. An indication of what a structural remedy may entail, though, can be found in Recital 12 of Regulation 1/2003.[41] There it is stated that, if strict requirements of proportionality and necessity are satisfied, the structure of an undertaking, as it existed before the infringement was committed, can be changed. In our view, this suggests that an enterprise can be obliged to divest one or more units of its business. To date, however, the Commission has not made use of its power to impose structural remedies but has confined itself to imposing behavioural remedies. The reason for this is that the Commission has preferred to confront undertakings with the need of taking structural remedies in the framework of the commitment decisions,[42] which will be discussed below.

---

[40] Remarkably, the Member States also have the right to do this.

[41] Faul and Nikpay 2014, p. 125.

[42] Staff Working Document 2014, par. 188. Nevertheless, in a recent speech (Vestager 2020 (c)), Commissioner Vestager suggested that, especially in relation to problems occurring in digital markets, intervention should not necessarily entail fines, but could also be conceived as obligations (such as duty to share data), or, as a last resort,

3.1.2 Priority decisions

It goes without saying that the Commission cannot act upon every complaint lodged. The capacity of this Union institution is limited and, therefore, there is a need for setting priorities. This is accepted in the case-law of the EU courts, as the Commission is entrusted with the task of applying the EU antitrust rules and of implementing the competition policy of the EU, which entails that it has discretion as to how to deal with complaints.[43]

Nevertheless, the Commission decision not to take up a complaint is subjected to some constraints. In *Automec I*,[44] the GC held that the procedure for complaints is composed of three stages. During the first stage, the Commission collects information and gives the complainant the opportunity to clarify his views. In the second stage, the Commission communicates its intent not to act upon the complaint and the reasons for this. The complainant is given the opportunity to react to what the Commission has put forward. In the third stage, the Commission considers the reaction of the complainant and takes a decision, in which the complaint is rejected. This decision, which is adopted at the end of the third stage, is subject to judicial review, whereas the other statements made by the Commission in the first and second stage are not.

As already stated, the Commission is entitled to set priorities. In *Automec II*,[45] the GC pointed out that, unlike civil courts, the task of which is to safeguard the individual rights of private persons, an administrative authority must act in the public interest.[46] This could entail that no action is taken, because such an action would not serve the Union interest appropriately. However, the Commission must state reasons for not taking up the case at issue. This means that the Commission must take account of the circumstances of the case concerned, and more particularly, of the legal and factual particularities set out in the complaint.[47] In this respect, the Commission must balance the significance of the alleged infringement in relation to the functioning of the Internal Market, the probability of establishing an infringement, and the scope of the investigation required.[48]

In *UFEX*,[49] the CJEU has also shed light on the right of the Commission to set priorities. Like the GC, the CJEU stressed that the Commission must state reasons if it declines to continue with the examinations resulting from a complaint.[50] These reasons must be sufficiently precise and detailed to enable the Union courts to review the Commission's use of its discretion to define priorities.[51] Furthermore, in principle, it is not permitted for the

---

breaking up companies, to protect competition. This stance seems to signal that structural remedies in EU antitrust law 'are still alive, although not really kicking'.

[43] E.g. case T-355/13 *easyJet*, ECLI:EU:T:2015:36, par. 17.

[44] Case T-64/89 *Automec I*, ECLI:EU:T:1990:42.

[45] Case T-24/90 *Automec II*, ECLI:EU:T:1992:97.

[46] Ibid, par. 85.

[47] Ibid, par. 86.

[48] Ibid.

[49] Case C-119/97 *Ufex*, ECLI:EU:C:1999:116.

[50] Ibid, par. 90.

[51] Ibid, par. 91.

Commission to exclude from its purview situations that come under the task entrusted to it by the Treaties.[52]

From the foregoing it is apparent that initially the right to lodge complaints has been developed in the case-law of the Union courts. Later the Commission issued the Conduct of Proceedings Regulation 2004,[53] codifying the case-law and elaborating on it.[54]

A special reason for not acting upon a complaint is contained in Article 13(2) of Regulation 1/2003. The Commission is entitled to reject a complaint against an alleged anti-competitive practice if this practice has already been dealt with by a national competition authority. In *Si.mobil*,[55] the GC held that the Commission has the power to apply this provision, if the following two conditions are satisfied: an NCA is dealing with the same case, and this case relates to the same agreement, decision of an association of undertakings, or concerted practice.[56]

As regards the condition of 'dealing with', the NCA must have carried out some review. However, the Commission needs only to verify whether the NCA concerned was engaged in an investigation, without assessing whether the decision of this NCA is well-founded.[57] In *easyJet*,[58] the GC held that national decisions based on priority grounds can also be considered as matters already dealt with at the national level. In *Agria Polska*,[59] it was not considered of relevance that the NCA has based its decision on the ground that the limitation period had expired; the reason for the expiration of this period was that the companies concerned took action too late.[60] The requirement of the 'same case' entails that the complaint received by the Commission relates to the same alleged infringements, on the same markets, within the same timeframe.[61]

Strikingly, the judgments in the cases being dealt with by the NCAs seem to exempt the Commission from the obligation to perform a weighting exercise regarding the Union interest at stake in a given case. While in *Automec II* the Commission is obliged to explain why the Union interest does not necessitate taking action, the Commission may confine itself to pointing to the review and investigations of an NCA, if the latter is already dealing with the practice concerned.[62]

---

[52] Ibid, par. 92.

[53] Conduct of Proceedings Regulation 2004.

[54] See, in this respect, also Notice on Handling of Complaints 2004.

[55] Case T-201/11 *Si.mobil*, ECLI:EU:T:2014:1096.

[56] Ibid, par. 33–34.

[57] Rusu 2015 (c), p. 169

[58] Case T-355/13 *easyJet*, ECLI:EU:T:2015:36.

[59] Case C-373/17 *Agria Polska*, ECLI:EU:C:2018:756.

[60] Ibid, par. 82.

[61] Rusu 2015 (c), p. 168.

[62] Ibid, p. 169.

3.2 Interim measures

Investigations take up a lot of time in competition law cases and many years could have passed before the Commission takes its final decision. This can give rise to lengthy proceedings before the Union courts. The outcome of these investigations and proceedings could come too late in order to address the competition problems that were at play when the case was initiated. Article 8 of Regulation 1/2003 aims at solving this issue by empowering the Commission to take interim measures. Already in the 1980 *Camera Care* judgment,[63] the CJEU had acknowledged that the power to adopt such measures was at the disposal of the Commission, although Regulation 17/62, which was then in force, did not contain any provision on interim decisions.

Article 8 of Regulation 1/2003 sets out two conditions. In the first place, there must be a prima facie finding of an infringement. In the second place, a risk of serious and irreparable damage to competition exists. It goes without saying that interim measures are of temporary character. No wonder that Article 8(2) of Regulation 1/2003 provides that a decision adopting such a measure applies for a specific period of time. It may be renewed in so far as this is necessary and appropriate.

The test of serious and irreparable damage is very strict and, therefore, it is not surprising that the Commission has hardly made use of the power to adopt interim measures.[64] A solution for dealing with this strict test is to negotiate an interim settlement with the firms concerned.[65] All in all, it is disappointing that the tool, the rationale of which is to take swift action in order to protect the competition process, turns out not to be very effective. Given the duration of proceedings in competition law, which can go beyond six years in many cases, this is very worrying, as an interim measure is capable of addressing adverse effects of anti-competitive practices in the short run. More in particular, the limited effectiveness of the interim measure tool gives rise to serious problems on digital markets, since these markets are subject to rapid changes and developments.[66] The Dutch competition authority has launched a proposal to address these problems. Below, in section 4.4.2.3, this proposal will be discussed.

3.3 Commitments

Both for the Commission and for the undertakings under investigation, enforcement proceedings in EU competition law could be very burdensome and may lead to complicated legal and economic issues of, for example, fact finding and assessment of the effects of certain practices on the market structure. Article 9 of Regulation 1/2003 has introduced an instrument meant to avoid these complex problems. This provision deals with the commitments that enterprises being subject of investigations of the Commission can make. If the

---

[63] Case 792/79 *Camera Care*, ECLI:EU:C:1980:18.

[64] Whish and Bailey 2018, p. 263.

[65] Ibid.

[66] Van de Gronden 2019, p. 344.

Commission wishes to adopt a decision targeting specific anti-competitive practices and the enterprises engaged in these practices offer commitments addressing the problems identified, the Commission is entitled to adopt a decision, by which these commitments are made binding. The undertakings having offered the commitments at issue are then bound by this decision. The use of commitment decisions may lead to an efficient and relatively inexpensive solution of the competition problems at play, as the Commission and the undertakings concerned are actively engaged in negotiations aimed at terminating the anti-competitive behaviour.[67]

From the drafting of Article 9 it is apparent that the following conditions must be fulfilled for adopting a commitment decision: (1) the Commission had the intent to adopt a decision requiring that an infringement must be brought to an end, and (2) the undertakings under investigation have made commitments in order to address the concerns expressed by the Commission.

It is at the discretion of the Commission to make use of the power laid down in Article 9. If the Commission adopts a commitment decision, it is not entitled anymore to take action against the companies concerned. According to the last sentence of Article 9(1) of Regulation 1/2003, as long as the commitment decision is in force, there are no longer grounds for action by the Commission.

It should be stressed that a commitment decision does not say anything about the compatibility of the business practices at stake with the competition rules. It does not contain a final judgement as to whether the companies concerned have infringed Article 101 TFEU or Article 102 TFEU.[68] For that reason, the NCAs and courts are not bound by a Commission commitment decision. It is still permitted for them to take action against the undertakings that have offered commitments, as was apparent from the *Gasorba* case.[69] The general rule is, of course, that NCAs do not take any decisions in contravention of the decisions adopted by the Commission.[70] However, in a commitment decision the Commission has carried out 'a mere "preliminary assessment" of the competition situation . . .' without 'establishing whether there has been or still is an infringement . . .', and, for that reason, a national or judicial body is still entitled to conclude that the practice that is subject to this commitment decision infringes the Treaty provisions on competition.[71] Accordingly, the Commission could have come to the conclusion that its concerns are addressed by specific commitments, whereas the national authorities consider that imposing penalties is the right course of action. Moreover, it should be pointed out that in *Gasorba*, the CJEU also held that the preliminary assessment, carried out by the Commission and having led to the competition concerns of this institution, should be taken into account by the national authorities as an indication, if not prima facie evidence, of the anti-competitive nature of the practices at

---

[67] Ottow 2015, p. 180.

[68] Regulation 1/2003, Recital 13.

[69] Case C-547/16 *Gasorba*, ECLI:EU:C:2017:891.

[70] Cases C-234/89 *Delimitis*, ECLI:EU:C:1991:91; C-344/98 *Masterfoods*, ECLI:EU:C:2000:689.

[71] Case C-547/16 *Gasorba*, ECLI:EU:C:2017:891, par. 26.

hand; this obligation was derived from the principle of Union loyalty/sincere cooperation.[72] As a result, commitment decisions give rise to a circumstantial probative value.[73] In sum, a commitment decision of the Commission does not shield the undertakings concerned from enforcement actions taken by national authorities and may even provide fuel for such action.

Like the Commission, the undertakings are also bound by the commitment decision. They are obliged to comply with the commitments they have offered and are embodied in the decision taken by the Commission on the basis of Article 9. Article 9(2)(b) of Regulation 1/2003 empowers the Commission to reopen the proceedings, where the commitments are not respected. Pursuant to Article 23(2)(c) of Regulation 1/2003 the Commission may even impose a fine of up to 10 per cent of their turnover on the undertakings not living up to the commitments. Reopening the proceedings is also possible in the event that there has been a material change in the relevant facts or that incomplete, incorrect or misleading information is provided by the parties.

The commitment decision is a very effective tool for the Commission to enforce the competition rules.[74] It can ensure compliance with these rules without starting proceedings leading to the imposition of a fine. As already stated, such proceedings are very lengthy and complex. Once the fine is imposed and all proceedings before the GC and the CJEU have been completed, the competition problems at stake could no longer be of relevance, as many markets evolve rapidly. The great advantage of commitment decisions is that immediate action is possible.

Since the *Alrosa* judgment,[75] the effectiveness of this instrument has even been increased. In this case, the CJEU decided that the undertakings involved are obliged to live up to the commitments made, even if these commitments go further than would have been required of the respective undertakings under Articles 101 or 102 TFEU. In its view, it is not relevant whether the commitments prevent practices infringing those Treaty provisions. What does matter, is that the proportionality principle is observed by the Commission when designing the commitment decision. This comes down to examining whether the commitments offered are capable of addressing the concerns of the Commission and whether the undertakings concerned have not offered less onerous commitments that also address the problems at stake in an adequate way.[76] In this regard, the interests of the third parties must also be taken into account. All in all, heavier obligations could fall on undertakings under a commitment decision than under a decision establishing an infringement of Article 101 TFEU or Article 102 TFEU.

The Commission has frequently made use of its power to adopt commitment decisions.[77] As already pointed out, the Commission has accepted structural remedies under Article 9 of Regulation 1/2003, whereas it did not impose any obligations of structural nature under

---

[72] Ibid, par. 29.

[73] Fratea 2018, p. 504.

[74] Staff Working Document 2014, par. 189.

[75] Case C-441/07 *Alrosa*, ECLI:EU:C:2010:377.

[76] Ibid, par. 41.

[77] Staff Working Document 2014, par. 183–190.

Article 7 of the Regulation, although this provision specifically makes mention of such obligations. An example of structural remedies contained in a commitment decision concerns the *ENI* case.[78] Here, the Commission was of the opinion that ENI, which operates on the energy markets mainly in Italy, abused its dominant position by not granting access to its network. ENI offered to divest its shares in three international pipelines to Italy. As this offer was capable of addressing the competition problems resulting from the vertical integration of ENI in both the transport and supply of gas, the Commission accepted the commitments made. As a result, the decision adopted on the basis of Article 9 of Regulation 1/2003 imposes on ENI structural remedies leading to the divestiture of parts of its enterprise.

Despite its flexible character, the commitment decision is subject to some limitations. As already submitted, it should be compliant with the principle of proportionality. Moreover, Recital 13 of Regulation 1/2003 specifically states that the commitment decision is not appropriate in cases where the Commission intends to impose a fine.

3.4 Finding of inapplicability

In section 3.2 of Chapter 5 and section 4.1 of Chapter 7, it was put forward that one of reasons for adopting Regulation 1/2003 was to free-up capacity of the Commission for intensifying its enforcement actions. The sole competence of the Commission to exempt agreements from the cartel prohibition on the basis of Article 101(3) TFEU was, therefore, abolished. Since the entry into force of this Regulation, next to the Commission, the NCAs and the domestic courts were also entitled to review business practices in the light of Article 101(3) TFEU. Against this backdrop, it is clear that Article 10 of Regulation 1/2003 is somewhat peculiar, as it empowers the Commission to adopt a decision finding the inapplicability of Article 101 TFEU or Article 102 TFEU. The fair chance exists that exercising this competence could lead to reintroducing partly the exemption procedure that made many undertakings to apply for permission from the Commission on the basis of Article 101(3) TFEU through the back door: undertakings may be tempted to ask the Commission to approve their agreements on the basis of Article 10 of Regulation 1/2003 and, if the Commission were to show considerable willingness to do so, many undertakings would be triggered to apply for such Commission approval. Admittedly, Article 10 does not take away the powers of the national authorities to apply Article 101 TFEU. But, unlike the Commission's exemption power that was in place on the basis of Regulation 17/62 and was solely related to Article 101(3) TFEU, Article 10 of Regulation 1/2003 also extends to Article 102 TFEU. It is clear from the outset that the Commission should be reluctant in exercising its powers under Article 10 of Regulation 1/2003.

No wonder that this provision stipulates that the Commission may take action if the Union interest so requires. Furthermore, a decision finding inapplicability will only be taken by the Commission on its own initiative and not at the request of undertakings or other parties. According to Recital 14 of Regulation 1/2003 it is appropriate to take these decisions only in exceptional circumstances in order to give clarifications on specific issues of the

---

[78] Case COMP/39.315 *ENI*, (2010) Commission Decision of 29 September 2010.

competition rules and to ensure the consistent application of these rules throughout the Union. For example, new light could be shed on types of agreements or practices that have not been settled in the case-law or the decisional practices of the Commission.

It is an understatement to put forward that the Commission has strictly observed the point of departure that Article 10 is reserved for exceptional cases. To date, no decisions have been adopted on the basis of this provision.[79] The reason for this is that, in the view of the Commission, the uniform and consistent application of the EU competition rules is ensured through cooperation within the ECN.[80] In other words, by cooperating closely with the NCAs of the EU Member States, the Commission has been able to realise the objectives that are at the heart of Article 10. Consequently, it was not needed to adopt a decision on the basis of this provision.

In this regard it must be pointed out that the CJEU held in *Tele2 Polska*,[81] that the NCAs are not entitled to apply Article 10 of Regulation 1/2003 and, accordingly, they do not have the power to adopt a decision finding that Article 101 TFEU or Article 102 TFEU is not violated. The reason for this is that Article 5 of Regulation 1/2003 specifies the decisions an NCA may take in relation to EU competition law. The decision finding the inapplicability of the EU antitrust rules is not mentioned in this provision. Apparently, in the CJEU's view the list of decisions outlined in Article 5 of Regulation 1/2003 is exhaustive.

The Commission can also shed light on new questions of competition law by issuing guidance letters.[82] However, the Commission is only prepared to address novel questions. Furthermore, giving such guidance should be in line with the enforcement priorities set.

3.5 Fines

Infringements of the competition rules could result in the imposition of sanctions. The Commission has the power to impose both fines and periodic penalties. In this section the fines will be discussed and in the next section periodic penalties will be dealt with. The majority of the enforcement cases of the Commission are concerned with fines rather than periodic penalties. For that reason, more attention will be paid to the former category of sanctions rather than the latter.

The Commission decisions by which fines are imposed have given rise to a great dearth of case-law. Most judgments deal with fines resulting from infringements of the substantive competition rules, that is, Articles 101 and 102 TFEU. As is apparent from the previous sections, fines can also be imposed due to violations of procedural obligations, such as breaking a seal or providing misleading information. Given the importance of the violations of the substantive competition rules the emphasis of the discussion below will be on the fines resulting from such violations.

---

[79] Staff Working Document 2014, par. 191.

[80] Ibid, par. 193.

[81] Case C-375/09 *Tele2 Polska*, ECLI:EU:C:2011:270.

[82] Informal Guidance Notice 2004.

3.5.1 Statement of objections

One of the most significant principles in enforcement cases is the right to be heard. This right was already acknowledged at an early stage in EU competition law.[83] Nowadays, Article 27(1) of Regulation 1/2003 provides that before a sanction is imposed the Commission must give the undertakings and associations of undertakings under investigation the opportunity of being heard. Furthermore, this provision states that the Commission decisions must be based on objections the parties concerned have been able to comment on. Consequently, the objections that have given rise to imposing a fine must be known to the parties in advance.[84] Pursuant to Article 10(1) of the Conduct of Proceedings Regulation 2004, the Commission is obliged to inform the parties concerned in writing of these objections.

It is the Commission's consistent practice to send the parties a statement of objections in order to comply with this requirement. In this statement, the established facts and alleged violations of the competition rules are outlined. The undertakings that have received a statement of objections have the right to develop their arguments in an oral hearing.[85]

An important point of criticism is that the investigatory and sanctioning tasks are in the hands of one body, that is, the Commission. The question arises whether sufficient checks and balances are built in, at the stage leading to the imposition of fines. In order to meet this criticism, the Commission has introduced the function of the Hearing Officer,[86] who is independent from the other units of the Commission. An oral hearing will be conducted by this official in full independence.[87] Another task of the Hearing Officer is to decide on the access to documents.[88]

3.5.2 General observations on the fines in EU competition law

The key provision on fines in EU competition law is Article 23 of Regulation 1/2003. The first paragraph of this provision deals with fines for the infringement of procedural rules, such as providing incorrect and misleading information, whereas the second paragraph is concerned with infringements of the substantive rules. Violations of Articles 101 and 102 TFEU, as well as contraventions of interim decisions and non-compliance with commitment decisions belong to the last category. Fines for infringements of the procedural rules must not be in excess of 1 per cent of the turnover of the preceding business year, whereas the maximum fine for violations of the substantive rules is set at 10 per cent of this turnover, of the undertaking(s) under investigation. Given the impact that violations of Articles 101 and 102 TFEU and of the conditions laid down in commitment decisions and interim measures could have on the competition process, it is sensible that the maximum level of the fines for this type of offence is higher than the level being in place for procedural infringements. Articles 25 and 26 of Regulation 1/2003 deal with limitation periods regarding the imposition and implementation

---

[83] Case 17/74 *Transocean Marine Paint*, ECLI:EU:C:1974:106.

[84] Conduct of Proceedings Regulation 2004, Article 11(2).

[85] Ibid, Article 12.

[86] Decision Regarding the Hearing Officer 2011.

[87] Conduct of Proceedings Regulation 2004, Article 14(1).

[88] Decision Regarding the Hearing Officer 2011, Article 7.

of the sanctions of the Commission. The power to impose sanctions following infringements of a procedural nature expires after three years, whereas the duration of the limitation period for other sanctions (related to, for example, infringements of Articles 101 or 102 TFEU) is five years. The term starts to run on the day that the violation has been committed or in the event of continued or repeated offences on the day the violation has been terminated.

Regulation 1/2003 does not contain many requirements for setting fines. Both in the first and second paragraphs of Article 23 of Regulation 1/2003 reference is made to intent and negligence. In other words, some level of culpability must be identified before the Commission is entitled to impose fines. This is in line with legal doctrine and also the case-law of the ECtHR. Then again, it is virtually impossible to infringe competition law without any awareness of the illegal status of the practice concerned. In our view, the defence of an undertaking that it had no clue that concluding cartels was illegal cuts no ice. In the same vein, it is inconceivable that a company supplies the Commission with misleading information in a non-deliberate way. In *Miller International Schallplatten*,[89] the CJEU held that it is not necessary to prove that the company concerned was aware it violated Article 101 TFEU; what matters is that this company must have understood that its conduct affected competition.[90]

In other words, in cases concerning the enforcement of EU competition law rules culpability does not, as a rule, give rise to serious issues. Illustrative in this respect is that, in principle, a mother company is liable for its subsidiaries if it holds 100 per cent or a percentage close to 100 per cent of the shares of these subsidiaries.[91] In such circumstances the mother company is supposed to exercise decisive influence over the subsidiary concerned. This presumption can be rebutted, which is, however, difficult in practice. After all, the mother company has to provide evidence it was not able to give instructions. Generally, it is hard to prove that particular action has not taken place. The reason for holding a mother company liable for infringements of its subsidiaries lies in the concept of undertaking. This concept encompasses an economic unit that could be composed of several legal (or even natural) persons, which means that this economic unit is responsible for the violations committed and that these violations must be imputed to a legal person.[92] It is not surprising that in enforcement cases the Commission prefers to hold the mother company liable, as this company would usually have a greater amount of financial resources at its disposal than its subsidiaries.

Article 23(3) of Regulation 1/2003 provides that in fixing the amount of the fine the Commission must have regard both to the gravity and the duration of the infringement. On top of that, in the case-law of the CJEU more clarity is given. For example, as regards the duration of the violation, the CJEU has accepted that various acts could amount to one infringement, which is known as a single and continuous infringement. The test to be carried out is whether the different actions are part of an 'overall plan', given their identical object to restrict competition.[93] If these conditions are satisfied, the violation extends over a wider

---

[89] Case 19/77 *Miller International Schallplatten*, ECLI:EU:C:1978:19.

[90] Cases 246/86 *Belasco*, ECLI:EU:C:1988:233; 279/87 *Tipp-Ex*, ECLI:EU:C:1990:57.

[91] E.g. case C-97/08 P *Akzo Nobel*, ECLI:EU:C:2009:536.

[92] Ibid, par. 55–57.

[93] E.g. joined cases 243 and 294/13 *Fresh Del Monte*, ECLI:EU:C:2015:416, par. 156; joined cases C-239, C-489 and

period than would have been the case if the various actions had to be considered separately. It also means that the limitation period starts to run on the day that the continuous infringement has ceased to be implemented. This is on the day of the last act of this infringement and, accordingly, practices from a long time ago may still be punishable if the last act of the single and continuous infringement has taken place before the applicable limitation period has expired. Furthermore, the existence of the single and continuous infringement entails that every undertaking having participated in the implementation of the overall plan may be fined.

All in all, the guidance given by Article 23 of Regulation 1/2003 is abstract and leaves a great margin of appreciation to the Commission. It should be noted that general principles of law, such as the proportionality principle,[94] also apply to the Commission's competence to impose fines. The fine imposed must not be disproportionate to the objective pursued, which is compliance with the competition rules, and has to be proportionate to the infringement as a whole.[95] Another important principle is the *ne bis in idem* (double jeopardy) principle. This means that a (legal) person may not be prosecuted, tried and punished twice for the same offence or act.[96] This principle, however, has not prevented the CJEU from accepting that a firm can be fined by both the Commission and an NCA for the same anti-competitive practice[97] or from ruling that the Commission is entitled to impose fines on companies already being punished by competition authorities of third countries for the same wrongful conduct.[98] The reason for this is that the legal interest protected by the EU competition rules is not the same as the legal interest at play in national systems of competition law.[99]

It is clear from the outset that the general principles of EU law do not dictate the exact amount of the fine due. In terms of judicial protection, the Commission's wide margin of appreciation may cause problems. Then again, enterprises would have been tempted to calculate whether it is profitable to continue the infringement, if the provisions of Regulation 1/2003 specified in great detail the level of the fine to be imposed. Some middle ground needs to be found, when it comes to calculating the fines by the Commission. By issuing Guidelines on setting the level of fines, the Commission has given some clarity without writing in stone what the exact amount of the fine must be. It is clear from the outset that these Guidelines have limited the discretion of the Commission. All in all, it is of great importance to have a comprehensive understanding of these Guidelines.

C-498/11 *Siemens*, ECLI:EU:C:2013:866, par. 247–248.

[94] Jans, Prechal and Widdershoven 2015, pp. 305–6.

[95] E.g. case T-267/12 *Deutsche Bahn*, ECLI:EU:T:2016:110, par. 176.

[96] Veenbrink 2020, p. 33.

[97] Cases 14/68 *Walt Wilhelm*, ECLI:EU:C:1969:4; C-17/10 *Toshiba*, ECLI:EU:C:2012:72.

[98] Case C-397/03 *Archer Daniels Midland*, ECLI:EU:C:2006:328, par. 46 *et seq.*

[99] Veenbrink 2020, pp. 178–9; Petr 2020, pp. 84–8.

3.5.3 Guidelines on the fines imposed by the Commission

The first set of Guidelines on fines imposed in competition law were published in 1998.[100] These rules were replaced by the Notice on Fines 2006.

According to this Notice, the point of departure is that the basic amount of the fine will be based on the value of the undertaking's sales of goods or services to which the infringement at issue relates.[101] The basic amount of the fine is a portion of this value and depends on the gravity of the infringement; the maximum portion is 30 per cent.[102] Horizontal price fixing, market sharing and output limitation agreements are considered as very serious violations and will give rise to fines, the portion of which is at the end of the scale (i.e. close to 30 per cent). The amount determined on the basis of the relevant value will be multiplied by the number of years of participation in the infringement. In case of horizontal price fixing, market sharing and output limitation agreements the amount of the fine will be raised by a sum between 15 and 25 per cent of the value of the sales that relate to the infringement concerned.[103] This increase of the amount of fine is called an 'entrance fee' by the Commission[104] and its aim is to deter companies from entering into such anti-competitive behaviour. The 'entrance fee' could also be imposed in cases involving other types of infringements.

The basic amount of the fine is, subsequently, adjusted on the basis of aggravating and mitigating circumstances. Aggravating circumstances will be a reason to increase the fine to be imposed. The Notice on Fines 2006 lists the following circumstances: continuation of an infringement or repetition of a similar offence, refusal to cooperate with the Commission, and being the leader in, or having instigated an infringement, as well as having exercised coercion.[105] Mitigating circumstances could make the Commission lower the amount of the fines. The following circumstances are named in the 2006 Guidelines: the provision of evidence that the undertaking concerned terminated the infringement as soon as the Commission intervened (this circumstance will not be taken into account in secret agreements or practices), the provision of evidence demonstrating that the infringement is committed as a result of negligence, the provision of evidence leading to the finding that the involvement of the company concerned was limited, active cooperation with the Commission, as well as the authorisation or encouragement of anti-competitive conduct by public authorities or legislation.[106]

Apart from the aggravating and mitigating circumstances, the Commission will pay due consideration to the need to ensure the deterrence of the fines. To that end, the Commission may increase the fine in order to skim off the gains made as a result of the infringement at issue.[107]

---

[100] Notice on Fines 1998.

[101] Notice on Fines 2006, par. 13.

[102] Ibid, par. 19–21.

[103] Ibid, par. 25.

[104] Press Release IP/06/857.

[105] Notice on Fines 2006, par. 28.

[106] Ibid, par. 29.

[107] Ibid, par. 30–31.

Before the final amount of the fine is determined the Commission has to verify whether the legal maximum, enshrined in Article 23 of Regulation 1/2003, is observed.[108] Consequently, it is not permitted to impose a fine in excess of 10 per cent of the turnover of the undertaking concerned. Moreover, the level of the fine must be proportionate, which is verified by the EU courts, by examining whether all relevant factors are taken into account.[109] Veenbrink has pointed out that, in EU case-law,[110] the capping ceiling of 10 per cent of the turnover is seen as a general safeguard against excessive (disproportionate) fines.[111] This, however, does not, as this author rightly argues, exclude responsibility of the Commission for assessing in individual cases whether the fine envisaged may be excessive.[112]

In our view, it is of great importance, from the perspective of judicial protection, that the Commission has explained how it will make use of its discretionary powers to set fines in competition law cases. As is apparent from Article 31 of Regulation 1/2003, the EU courts have unlimited jurisdiction to review decisions, whereby the Commission has imposed a fine. Article 6 ECHR, as well as Article 47 of the Charter of Fundamental Rights of the EU, provisions which lay down the right to an effective remedy and to a fair trial, apply to these fines. The consequence of this is that the fines imposed by the Commission must be subject to full review by the Union courts. The Notice on Fines 2006 sets out which factors are of interest for calculating fines. Step by step, it is explained what the Commission is supposed to do. On the basis of the factors mentioned in these Guidelines, the EU courts are able to conduct a full review and to critically assess the fine imposed.

It should be noted that in *Menarini*[113] the ECtHR pointed out that, in cases concerning competition law fines, the courts must not limit their review to simply verifying the lawfulness of the fining decision. It is important that these courts are able to verify whether the competent competition authority has made use of its power in a proper way.[114] It has to be examined whether the decision imposing the fine is substantiated and proportionate and, on top of that, the technical findings must be checked.[115] The courts must thus have full jurisdiction.[116]

In *Chalkor*[117] and *KME*,[118] the CJEU has followed the approach of the ECtHR, strikingly without referring to the judgment in *Menarini*. It acknowledged that the Commission has a margin of discretion in complex economic matters, but it also pointed out that the Union courts must examine whether the evidence is accurate and consistent as well as whether the

---

[108] Ibid, par. 32–33.

[109] Veenbrink 2020, p. 215.

[110] Case T-62/02 *Union Pigments*, ECLI:EU:T:2005:430, par. 158.

[111] Veenbrink 2020, pp. 215–16.

[112] Ibid, p. 216. In this context the author refers to case T-410/09 *Almamet*, ECLI:EU:T:2012:676, par. 228.

[113] Case 43509/08 *Menarini*, ECtHR, 27 September 2011.

[114] Ibid, par. 63.

[115] Ibid, par. 64.

[116] Ibid, par. 65.

[117] Case C-386/10 *Chalkor*, ECLI:EU:C:2011:815.

[118] Case C-389/10 *KME Germany*, ECLI:EU:C:2011:816.

evidence contains all information needed in order to substantiate the conclusions drawn.[119] The CJEU also stated that the EU courts must carry out an in-depth review of the law and of the facts and, as a consequence, cannot use the Commission's margin of discretion as a basis for dispensing with the conduct of such a review.[120] The EU courts have unlimited jurisdiction and, therefore, they are empowered to substitute their own appraisal for the Commission's, which may lead to the cancellation, reduction or increase of the fine imposed.[121] However, the failure to review the entire decision of the Commission on own motion by the EU courts is not incompatible with the principle of effective judicial protection.[122] What is required, is that these courts respond to the pleas put forward by the parties.[123]

3.5.4 Leniency

It is very difficult for the Commission to detect cartels, as these practices are, as a rule, secret. In order to improve its enforcement activities, the Commission has introduced a leniency programme. In essence, this programme gives immunity from fines, if an undertaking party to a cartel provides the Commission with information that enables this institution to detect the cartel at issue. In EU competition law, most cartels have been detected through the Commission's leniency programme.[124] Between 2005 and 2010 the Commission imposed fines in 35 different cases, and in 33 of these cases the leniency programme played an important role.[125] It goes without saying that this programme contributes largely to the effective enforcement of EU competition law. As pointed out in section 3.1 of Chapter 3, the leniency policy is based on game theory, according to which undertakings are stimulated to be the first to report a cartel, because, if they fail to do so, other parties to this cartel may have already informed the Commission.[126] The success of a leniency policy depends, apart from the benefits an undertaking may receive (immunity from fines), on the transparent drafting of the programme concerned: it must be predictable under which circumstances an undertaking is entitled to immunity from fines.[127]

In this regard, it must be pointed out that private enforcement of the competition rules may interfere with the leniency policy. An undertaking having received immunity from fines could nevertheless be confronted with damage claims in private law proceedings. It cannot be excluded that successful damage claims have a negative bearing on the willingness of members of a cartel to step forward in order to apply for leniency. It is clear that the relationship between leniency and private enforcement is of a delicate nature. In Chapter 9, particularly in section 5.6 of that chapter, this relationship will be explored.

---

[119] Cases C-386/10 *Chalkor*, ECLI:EU:C:2011:815, par. 54; C-389/10 *KME Germany*, ECLI:EU:C:2011:816, par. 121.

[120] Cases C-386/10 *Chalkor*, ECLI:EU:C:2011:815, par. 62; C-389/10 *KME Germany*, ECLI:EU:C:2011:816, par. 129.

[121] Cases C-386/10 *Chalkor*, ECLI:EU:C:2011:815, par. 63; C-389/10 *KME Germany*, ECLI:EU:C:2011:816, par. 130.

[122] Case C-386/10 *Chalkor*, ECLI:EU:C:2011:815, par. 66.

[123] Ibid.

[124] Report on Competition Policy 2017, p. 3.

[125] Braat 2018, p. 46.

[126] Ibid, p. 21.

[127] Ibid, p. 25.

For the first time, the Commission published its policy on leniency in 1996.[128] This approach was replaced by the Notice introduced in 2002.[129] When writing this book the Leniency Notice 2006 was still in place. It should be noted that, over time, the Commission has added mechanisms to improve the efficiency of its leniency policy. In 2017, it introduced the anonymous whistle-blower tool.[130] The main aim of this tool is to enable individuals to provide information to the Commission, while maintaining anonymity. Also, the eLeniency tool, enabling companies to apply for leniency online, was launched.[131] This tool can also be used for cartel settlements procedures; this type of dispute resolution will be discussed in section 3.5.5.

3.5.4.1 Conditions for leniency
The Leniency Notice 2006 applies only to infringements of Article 101 TFEU. It is hard to imagine that an enterprise has incentives to report abusive behaviour within the meaning of Article 102 TFEU, as in many cases solely one undertaking is dominant and, accordingly, responsible for the illegal practices. Under the current leniency rules, undertakings can be entitled to two types of benefits.

The first type of benefit amounts to full immunity from fines. In this case the Commission will not impose any fine on the undertaking applying for leniency. The following conditions must be satisfied in order to receive full immunity. In the first place, the undertaking concerned is the first one to submit information and evidence related to a particular cartel.[132] In the second place, the information and evidence submitted enable the Commission either to carry out a targeted inspection or to find an infringement of Article 101 TFEU.[133] Immunity will not be given if at the time of submission the Commission already had sufficient information and evidence.[134] Furthermore, the undertaking wishing to receive immunity must submit a corporate statement specifying important details such as a description of the alleged cartel, as well as other evidence related to that cartel. Moreover, the undertaking applying for immunity must cooperate fully with the Commission and immediately terminate its involvement in the cartel.[135] A company that coerced other companies to join the cartel, or to remain in it, is not eligible for immunity: it is not acceptable to force other companies to engage in anti-competitive behaviour and, subsequently, to ask not to be fined for breaching Article 101 TFEU.

The second type of benefits concerns a reduction of the fine. If an undertaking is not

---

[128] Leniency Notice 1996.

[129] Leniency Notice 2002.

[130] Press Release IP/17/591. See also <https://ec.europa.eu/competition/cartels/whistleblower/index.html> accessed 26 May 2020.

[131] Press Release IP/19/1594. See also <https://ec.europa.eu/competition/cartels/leniency/eleniency.html> accessed 26 May 2020.

[132] Leniency Notice 2006, par. 8.

[133] Ibid.

[134] Ibid, par. 9–10.

[135] Ibid, par. 12.

the first one to report a cartel, it will not obtain full immunity but it may be eligible for a reduction of the fine to be imposed.[136] Also the undertaking coercing other companies to be engaged in a cartel could be granted a reduction of a fine.[137] Reduction of a fine will be granted if a company provides the Commission with evidence of added value, which means that it strengthens the ability of the Commission to prove the alleged cartel.[138] The first undertaking providing evidence of added value, which is in fact the second undertaking applying for leniency, will get a reduction of 30–50 per cent, the second one (which is the third applicant in line) will get a reduction of 20–30 per cent, and subsequent undertakings will get a reduction of up to 20 per cent.[139]

In the case-law of the EU courts, it is accepted that the Commission has developed a leniency policy.[140] The application of the leniency rules is subject to full review by the Union courts for obvious reasons: granting leniency is an integral part of the decision process regarding the fines.[141] Furthermore, information contained in the documents submitted by a leniency applicant may be included in a decision dealing with the infringement concerned by the Commission. In *Degussa*,[142] the CJEU held that the documents submitted by the applicant are protected from disclosure but that information derived from these documents could be used in such a decision.

3.5.4.2 Marker system

From the foregoing, it is apparent that timing is of great importance for undertakings considering stepping forward to inform the Commission about the existence of a cartel. In order to facilitate undertakings stepping forward, the Commission has introduced a marker system. An undertaking can contact DG Competition of the Commission and opt for either receiving a marker or making a formal application for leniency.[143] The marker secures the applicant's place in the queue. When a marker is granted, the Commission services will determine the period for perfecting this marker. The applicant must give the necessary information within this period. The advantage of the marker system is that an undertaking can show its willingness to step forward, without being obliged to submit a complete and detailed application at a very early stage.

3.5.5 Settlements

In leniency procedures, the immunity or the reduction of fines is considered at the initial stage of the investigations. Companies may also be given the possibility of such a reduction closer to the end of the proceedings leading to the imposition of a fine. When the

---

[136] Ibid, par. 23.

[137] Ibid, par. 13, last sentence.

[138] Ibid, par. 24–25.

[139] Ibid, par. 26.

[140] E.g. joined cases T-236, T-244 to 246, T-251 and T-252/01 *Tokai*, ECLI:EU:T:2004:118.

[141] Case C-557/12 *Kone*, ECLI:EU:C:2014:1317.

[142] Case C-162/15 P *Evonik Degussa*, ECLI:EU:C:2017:205.

[143] Leniency Notice 2006, par. 14.

Commission is in the midst of adopting a decision by which a fine will be imposed, it could try to reach a settlement with the undertakings concerned. This possibility is introduced by an amendment[144] of the Conduct of Proceedings Regulation 2004. If the undertakings concerned decide to settle with the Commission, they acknowledge that they are liable for the infringement concerned.[145] In exchange, the Commission will reduce the amount of the fine by 10 per cent.[146] It should be noted that it is permitted that undertakings benefit both from the reduction of fines in leniency procedures and from reduction of fines offered in settlement procedures.[147] The Commission has introduced the settlement procedure in order to free Commission resources to pursue other cases.[148] The settlements will lead to simplification of the administrative proceedings and are capable of reducing litigation before the Union courts.[149]

Of great importance is the *Timab* ruling, in which the CJEU held that the settlement procedure is not in violation of the rights of the defence of the undertakings under investigation.[150] The reason for this is that the cooperation with the Commission takes place on a voluntary basis. In *Timab*, the parties concerned were engaged in a settlement procedure and the Commission had communicated to them the amount of the fine it intended to impose. The undertakings concerned eventually terminated the negotiations. The Commission then decided to impose a fine that was substantially higher than initially communicated. The CJEU did not find a breach of EU law by the Commission, as this institution was entitled to consider new information when adopting the final decision setting the fine. Moreover, the parties concerned were aware of the allegations made by the Commission with regard to their conduct.

The *Timab* judgment has paved the way for an extensive application of the settlement procedures. Furthermore, it may be assumed that undertakings that are engaged in settlement procedures will think twice before they terminate the negotiations. In this regard it must be noted that in *Icap*[151] the GC has stressed that it must be prevented that the settlements made contravene the principle of the presumption of innocence. In hybrid settlement procedures, the compliance with this principle may be at stake. In such procedures, some of the undertakings take part in the settlement made with the Commission, while other undertakings refuse to do so. In these circumstances, the Commission must take the necessary steps in order to guarantee that the undertakings not being part of the deal still enjoy the presumption of innocence, which mostly will come down to adopting the decisions regarding the

---

[144] Regulation 622/2008.

[145] Settlement Notice 2008, par. 20.

[146] Ibid, par. 32.

[147] Ibid, par. 33.

[148] Press Release IP/08/1056.

[149] Ibid.

[150] Case C-411/15 *Timab*, ECLI:EU:C:2017:11. A similar approach was adopted by the General Court in case T-456/10 *Timab*, ECLI:EU:T:2015:296.

[151] Case T-180/15 *Icap*, ECLI:EU:T:2017:795.

participating and the non-participating undertakings on the same date.[152] The *Icap* judgment has restricted the Commission's room for manoeuvre in settlement proceedings, and may have some adverse effects on the efficiency of these proceedings.[153] Nevertheless, the settlement procedure is well-established in EU competition law and a considerable number of cases are dealt with under this procedure.[154]

3.6 Periodic penalties

According to Article 24 of Regulation 1/2003, the Commission has the power to impose periodic penalties upon undertakings and associations of undertakings. These penalties must not exceed 5 per cent of the average daily turnover in the preceding business year. The aim of a periodic penalty is to compel an undertaking or an association of undertakings to put an end to the infringement of the competition rules. The periodic penalty may be combined with an interim measure that is imposed on the basis of Article 8 of Regulation 1/2003. The same is true for a commitment decision within the meaning of Article 9 of Regulation 1/2003. To date, only limited case-law is available on periodic penalties. It should be noted that, according to Article 31 of Regulation 1/2003, the EU courts have unlimited jurisdiction to review Commission decisions whereby periodic penalties are fixed.

4 ENFORCEMENT AT THE NATIONAL LEVEL

Regulation 1/2003 is based on a system of decentralised enforcement, which, in the context of competition law, means that, next to the European Commission, NCAs play an important role. Accordingly, the term decentralisation refers to the relationship between the EU and national level, rather than to the relationship between the national and regional/local level. Below, the rules and policies governing the relationship between the Commission and the NCAs will be discussed. After that, the relationship between the domestic courts and the Commission will be explored. Then, attention will be paid to the ECN+ Directive 2019, which imposes on the Member States obligations concerning the public enforcement of the EU competition law rules at the national level. Subsequently, two national competition law enforcement systems will be touched upon.

4.1 The relationship between the Commission and the NCAs

The rationale of the cooperation mechanisms between the Commission and the NCAs is to ensure the uniform application of the competition rules. The point of departure is Article 16(2) of Regulation 1/2003, which stipulates that NCAs are precluded from taking decisions running counter to a decision of the Commission concerning the same anti-competitive

---

[152] Ibid, par. 268.

[153] Jones, Sufrin and Dunne 2019, p. 950.

[154] Whish and Bailey 2018, p. 273.

practices. Articles 11–14 of Regulation 1/2003 contain specific provisions governing the cooperation between the Commission and the NCAs. The common thread running through these provisions is reflected in Article 11(1) of the Regulation, which states that the Commission and the NCAs must apply the EU competition rules in close cooperation. This provision has led to the adoption of the Network Notice 2004,[155] laying down rules governing matters, such as case allocation, between the Commission and the NCAs.

The Commission has put forward that an important matter regarding cooperation between the Commission and the NCAs concerns the exchange of information.[156] This information concerns cases being handled by these authorities. For that reason, this exchange may also give rise to some controversy, as the information being forwarded could be of a confidential nature. Article 12(1) of Regulation 2003/1 states that for the purpose of enforcing Articles 101 and 102 TFEU, the Commission and the NCAs have the power to provide one another with and use in evidence any matter of fact or of law, including confidential information. The use of the information exchanged must be limited to the purpose of applying the competition rules of the Treaty and in respect of the subject matter for which it was collected by the transferring authority pursuant to Article 12(2) of Regulation 1/2003. However, it is specifically provided by Article 12(2) of Regulation 1/2003 that the evidence gathered may be used for the application of a provision of national competition law, where this national provision is applied in the same case and in parallel to EU antitrust law, provided that it does not lead to a different outcome. This approach derogates from the case-law developed under the predecessor of Regulation 1/2003, that is, Regulation 17/62. According to the judgment in *Spanish Banks*,[157] delivered at a time when Regulation 17/62 was in force, a national authority was precluded from using information obtained from another authority for the purpose of enforcing national competition law. The outcome of this judgment has been altered by the adoption of Regulation 1/2003. The current mechanism for exchange of information is more flexible than the previous one.

4.2 The relationship between the Commission and the domestic courts

The Commission has issued the Notice on Cooperation with National Courts 2004. This is a delicate matter, as the (national) judiciary is independent and its task is to review, inter alia, decisions taken by the administrative authorities. Then again, the Commission is responsible for the uniform and effective enforcement of the EU competition rules, which means that it also has to pay attention to cases being handled by national courts. All in all, a balance must be struck between the independent position of the national judiciary, on one hand, and the need to enforce the competition rules in a uniform and effective way, on the other hand.

---

[155] Cf also Regulation 1/2003, Recital 15, which underlines the importance of establishing such a network.

[156] Network Notice 2004, par. 26.

[157] Case C-67/91 *Spanish Banks*, ECLI:EU:C:1992:330.

4.2.1 Parallel application of the EU competition rules by the Commission and the domestic courts

In the Notice on Cooperation with National Courts 2004, attention is paid to parallel or consecutive application of the EU competition rules by the Commission and the domestic courts. To start with, it addresses the situation where a national court has handed down a judgment before the Commission has taken action. The point of departure is that the Commission is not bound by rulings of national courts. This entails that national courts must avoid taking decisions in a case that is still being handled by the Commission.[158] Accordingly, for reasons of legal certainty, a national court may decide to stay a procedure concerning a case that is also pending before the Commission. In the Notice, it is put forward that, in such an event, the Commission will endeavour to give priority to this case.[159] An important exception is given with regard to the starting point that national proceedings should be suspended. If a national court cannot reasonably doubt the outcome of the decision contemplated by the Commission or if the Commission already has decided on a similar case, the court may decide on the case pending before it. It goes without saying that this ruling of the court must be in accordance with the contemplated or earlier decision of the Commission.[160]

Where the Commission has already dealt with a case by taking a decision, the position of the domestic courts seems to be crystal clear, on first sight. They must refrain from handing down judgments running counter to this Commission decision. If a domestic court entertains serious doubts as to whether the Commission decision is compatible with EU law, it may ask preliminary questions to the CJEU.[161]

Nevertheless, it is apparent from the famous *Masterfoods* case[162] that a Commission decision preceding a national court ruling is capable of giving rise to complicated questions. In this case, the Commission decision was appealed against and the President of the GC had suspended this decision until judgment on the substance was given. The question arose whether an Irish court called upon to deal with the same contract that was at issue in the Commission decision was still under the obligation to give full effect to this decision. The CJEU ruled in *Masterfoods* that an interim measure suspending a Commission decision is only of a provisional nature and that the principle of Union loyalty/sincere cooperation enshrined in Article 4(3) TEU obliges national courts to fully respect such a Commission decision. As a result, it has to stay the national proceedings and, if necessary, to take interim measures to safeguard the rights of the parties concerned. Another solution pointed out by the CJEU did not come as a surprise: after having suspended the national proceedings the national court could ask the CJEU preliminary questions on the compatibility of the Commission decision (suspended by the President of the GC) with EU law. In other words, in such circumstances the preliminary ruling procedure could serve as a shortcut to an efficient settlement of a dispute that has led to parallel proceedings at the EU and the national level.

---

[158] Case C-234/89 *Delimitis*, ECLI:EU:C:1991:91.

[159] Notice on Cooperation with National Courts 2004, par. 12.

[160] Ibid.

[161] E.g. case 314/85 *Foto-Frost*, ECLI:EU:C:1987:452.

[162] Case C-344/98 *Masterfoods*, ECLI:EU:C:2000:689.

The approach developed by the CJEU in, inter alia, *Masterfoods* is codified in Article 16(1) of Regulation 1/2003. This provision clearly sets out that national courts must respect Commission decisions that are already adopted and those that will be taken. With regard to the latter type of decisions, it is put forward, in line with *Masterfoods*, that the national court may assess whether the national proceedings have to be stayed. According to the last line of Article 16(1) of Regulation 1/2003, referring to the CJEU is also an option, which is also in line with the *Masterfoods* ruling.

4.2.2 Cooperation between the Commission and the domestic courts

Article 15 of Regulation 1/2003 contains mechanisms facilitating cooperation between the Commission and the domestic courts. This concept is known as *amicus curiae* (friend of the court). The Commission acts as adviser to national courts handling cases of EU competition law.

4.2.2.1 Requests from national courts

Article 15(1) of Regulation 1/2003 elaborates on the general principle of Union loyalty/sincere cooperation laid down in Article 4(3) TEU. Pursuant to this provision of the Regulation, a national court is entitled to request the Commission to transmit information concerning a case involving Article 101 TFEU or Article 102 TFEU, or to ask its opinion on questions regarding the application of these Treaty provisions. Accordingly, two types of questions may be asked by a domestic court. The first type concerns information that is in the possession of the Commission and may be of relevance for the case pending before a national court. The second type of questions relates to the view the Commission has on particular matters of competition law. In the past, the CJEU had already derived similar obligations for the Commission from the principle of Union loyalty/sincere cooperation.[163] As for the Commission's obligation to provide information to national courts, it must be noted that some safeguards have to be observed. For example, confidential information and business secrets must be protected.[164] If this guarantee cannot be given, the information requested will be refused to be transmitted to the national court concerned.[165] Furthermore, other interests, such as the need to protect the interest of the Union or the independent functioning of the Commission, may be a reason for not giving information to the Commission too.[166]

4.2.2.2 Information given by the Commission on its initiative

Article 15(3) of Regulation 1/2003 deals with actions that are taken by the Commission but are not requested by domestic courts. The Commission has the right to submit its views on

---

[163] Case C-2/88 *Zwartveld*, ECLI:EU:C:1990:440. Cf also Notice on Cooperation with National Courts 2004, par. 15.

[164] Notice on Cooperation with National Courts 2004, par. 23; case C-2/88 *Zwartveld*, ECLI:EU:C:1990:440, par. 10–11.

[165] Notice on Cooperation with National Courts 2004, par. 25; case C-2/88 *Zwartveld*, ECLI:EU:C:1990:440, par. 10–11.

[166] Notice on Cooperation with National Courts 2004, par. 26; case C-2/88 *Zwartveld*, ECLI:EU:C:1990:440, par. 10–11.

cases pending before these courts on its own initiative. This has to be done in writing. Article 15(3) stipulates that the Commission is entitled to submit written observations to a national court on issues relating to Articles 101 and 102 TFEU, if the coherent application of these Treaty provisions so requires. On top of that, the NCA of the Member State concerned has the same power, without being obliged to show that its observations are required by the coherent application of EU competition law.

As a result, from a theoretical point of view, NCAs enjoy a wider margin for intervening in national proceedings than the Commission does. Then again, in practice it is hard for national courts to challenge the need of the Commission to put forward its views. It should be noted that in *Inspecteur van de Belastingdienst/X BV*,[167] the CJEU held that the Commission had the right to intervene in a tax law case where a national court had to decide as to whether a competition law fine imposed by the Commission could be deduced from the taxable profits. The concern of the Commission was that deductibility of such fines was capable of jeopardising the effective enforcement of EU competition law. The CJEU shared this concern by putting forward that the effectiveness of a fine could significantly be reduced if the wrongdoer were allowed to deduct the amount of this fine from its taxable profits, since such possibility would lead to offsetting the burden of this fine.[168] Strikingly, this consideration of the CJEU did not only confirm the power of the Commission to intervene in national tax law proceedings but also revealed the view of the CJEU on the fundamental question at issue: it is not permitted to deduct the EU competition law fines from the taxable profits (and, of course, from other taxable income and assets).

Moreover, Article 15(3) of Regulation 1/2003 does not even exclude that oral observations are put forward, both by the Commission and the NCA of the Member State concerned. However, these authorities need prior permission for this from the national court handling the case at issue. Consequently, it is up to a domestic court whether an official of the Commission or of an NCA has the right to speak at a hearing held with regard to a case involving EU competition law.

The right of the Commission and of the NCAs to intervene in national court proceedings on their own initiative is, to a certain extent, controversial. The aim of these interventions, which are – admittedly – not binding, is to influence the interpretation and application of the EU competition rules by judicial bodies at the national level. For that reason, it is of great importance that both the Commission and the NCAs proceed with great care when exercising their powers under Article 15(3) of Regulation 1/2003.[169] At the end of the day, the independent position of the national judiciary must be respected.

---

[167] Case C-429/07 *Inspecteur van de Belastingdienst/X BV*, ECLI:EU:C:2009:359.

[168] Ibid, par. 39.

[169] See <https://ec.europa.eu/competition/court/antitrust_amicus_curiae.html> accessed 24 April 2020, where the Commission observations made in national proceedings are reported. To date (April 2020), 18 interventions are reported by the Commission on this site.

4.3 EU requirements for enforcement at the national level

Strikingly, although competition law belongs to the core area of EU policies, enforcement of the competition rules by NCAs was hardly harmonised. Accordingly, it was left to the Member States to enact legislation dealing with this matter. As already stated in Chapter 1, all Member States have opted for a system of competition law that highly mirrors EU competition law. As a result, at the domestic level, both the national and the EU competition rules were enforced by the NCAs through national procedural rules. The point is, however, that, unlike the substantive rules, the national procedural rules could considerably differ from Member State to Member State. On top of that, some NCAs had comprehensive kits of enforcement tools at their disposal, while other NCAs only had few powers to take action.[170]

In order to create a level playing field for enforcement throughout all the Member States of the EU, the Union legislature has adopted the ECN+ Directive 2019. In fact, the aim of this Directive is to ensure that, except for the competence of adopting negative decisions (a power which is reserved by Article 10 of Regulation 1/2003 solely for the Commission), the NCAs have all the enforcement powers that the Commission also has and, by doing so, to create a common competition enforcement area.[171] The fundamental change of decentralisation brought upon by Regulation 1/2003 is further enhanced by the adoption of the ECN+ Directive 2019.[172] Various matters related to enforcement of the EU competition rules are now subject to harmonisation. It should be noted that the public enforcement by the NCAs has not been harmonised in an exhaustive fashion, as considerable room for adopting specific rules, for example dealing with criminal liability for violation of the competition rules, is left to the Member States.

4.3.1 Institutional design

It is widely accepted that the competition authorities should have an independent position in order to enforce the competition rules effectively, as the legitimacy and credibility of their actions is closely related to their ability to operate in an impartial fashion.[173] No wonder that Article 4 of the ECN+ Directive 2019 requires that the position of the NCAs is independent. It should be pointed out that Regulation 1/2003 also lays down a provision on the institutional design of NCAs, as Article 35 of this Regulation provides that a Member State must designate an NCA in such a way that the competition rules are effectively complied with. In *VEBIC*,[174] the CJEU held that national rules precluding an NCA from participating as a defendant in proceedings brought against its decision is incompatible with this Article. The added value of Article 4 of the Directive is that a couple of specific provisions elaborate on the requirement of the independent position of NCAs. For example, it is set out that an NCA must be able to perform its duties and to exercise its powers in relation to Articles 101 and 102 TFEU

---

[170] On this matter, see e.g. Sinclair 2017, pp. 627–8.

[171] Rizzuto 2019, p. 582.

[172] Ibid, p. 583.

[173] Sinclair 2017, pp. 626–7.

[174] Case C-439/08 *VEBIC*, ECLI:EU:C:2010:739.

independently from political and other types of influence.[175] This is further clarified by stipulating that an NCA should not receive any instructions from the government or any other public or private entity.[176] As for the influence exercised by public authorities, it is specifically outlined that general policy rules may be issued, as long as these rules are not concerned with sector inquiries and specific enforcement proceedings. It is believed that governments and other public bodies must not intervene in individual cases for reasons of equal treatment, whereas it is deemed acceptable that competition authorities are held accountable for their general activities to their governments and parliaments.[177]

It is apparent from the foregoing that Article 4 of the ECN+ Directive 2019 is mainly concerned with the operational independence of the NCAs, as it is geared towards their ability to act independently when taking enforcement actions.[178] Apart from this aspect, organisational and financial independence also play an important role, when it comes to the institutional design of competition authorities. Organisational independence means that an NCA needs sufficient and competent staff members, whereas financial independence is related to resources necessary to perform the tasks assigned to an NCA.[179]

Article 5 of the Directive deals with the organisational and financial independence of the NCAs. In general terms, the requirement of ensuring that an NCA has a sufficient number of qualified staff and sufficient resources is framed in the first paragraph of Article 5. This requirement is linked to the need for the effective performance of the duties assigned and the exercise of the powers related to Articles 101 and 102 TFEU. Importantly, Article 5(3) of the Directive provides that an NCA is granted independence in the spending of the allocated budget. In other words, important financial decisions regarding the application and enforcement of EU competition law must be taken by the NCAs, rather than the government or other institution at the national level. It should be borne in mind that the budget can function as an indirect instrument of political control by the government over competition authorities.[180] Article 5(4) is geared towards the accountability of the NCAs. According to this provision, NCAs are obliged to submit periodic reports on their activities to a governmental or parliamentary body.

4.3.2 Investigation powers

The ECN+ Directive 2019 aims at ensuring that every NCA has a minimum set of powers for carrying out investigations. Article 6 of the Directive provides that an NCA must have the authority to inspect business premises. The power set out in this provision largely mirrors the competences the Commission has under Regulation 1/2003. So, it does not come as a surprise that Article 7 states that inspecting other premises, including private homes, also has to be part of the toolkit of the NCAs. Such inspections may only be carried out

---

[175] ECN+ Directive 2019, Article 4(2)(a).

[176] Ibid, Article 4(2)(b).

[177] Wils 2019, p. 162.

[178] Dzino and Rusu 2019, p. 140.

[179] Ibid.

[180] Schinkel, Tóth and Tuinstra 2020, p. 253.

if prior authorisation is obtained from a national judicial body. Unlike the corresponding provisions of Regulation 1/2003, Articles 6 and 7 of the ECN+ Directive 2019 do not make a distinction between judicial review based on the necessity and proportionality of the inspections. This difference does not come as a surprise for the following reason. In the event the Commission carries out an inspection, the domestic and Union courts share the review powers, which entails that the former judicial body focuses on proportionality in the stage preceding the inspection under review, while the latter judicial body has sole power to assess the necessity of the inspections afterwards. In the event that NCAs inspect business and other premises, the national court is the sole judicial authority for reviewing the legality of the actions of the NCA concerned. This means that the national court involved has the duty to assess all aspects (including proportionality and necessity) of an inspection, an assessment which can be made prior to the inspection concerned. The role of the CJEU is limited to address the preliminary questions that might be asked by the national court handling the case under review. As a result, the setup of the judicial protection system against inspections carried out by NCAs does more justice to the rights of the parties involved than the design of the corresponding system against Commission decisions. The judicial protection system in relation to Commission decisions is based on an artificial distinction between necessity and proportionality review: as was pointed out in section 2.4.4 of this chapter, the domestic courts' power to review Commission inspections is limited to a proportionality test, while a necessity test should be carried out by Union courts. In our view, however, this problem cannot be solved, as long as no clear choice is made as to whether the judicial review of Commission inspections should be assigned to the Union or to the national judiciary.

Article 8 of the Directive deals with requests for information. It goes without saying that an NCA should be able to pose questions concerning commercial practices that could be incompatible with Articles 101 and 102 TFEU. For that reason, Article 8 of the ECN+ Directive 2019 stipulates that NCAs must have the power to require undertakings, associations of undertakings, and other natural or legal persons to provide all necessary information for the application of Articles 101 and 102 TFEU within a specified and reasonable time frame. Taking statements is an important inspection power for NCAs.

Article 9 of the ECN+ Directive 2019 introduces the power of conducting interviews. NCAs must have the power to summon representatives of undertakings, associations of undertakings, as well as natural and legal persons to appear for an interview. Strikingly, the provision is silent on the matter of cooperation. Should the representative concerned cooperate, or may this person choose not to answer the questions posed? It should be pointed out that failing to appear at an interview may lead to the imposition of a fine.[181] All in all, it remains to be seen whether this power will be effective; in any event, the Member States have the freedom to further regulate this power.[182]

---

[181] ECN+ Directive 2019, Article 13(2)(e).

[182] Dzino and Rusu 2019, pp. 145–6.

4.3.3 Decision-making and sanctioning powers

Article 5 of Regulation 1/2003 lists a few of powers of the NCAs for taking enforcement actions against infringements of EU antitrust law. Articles 10–16 of the ECN+ Directive 2019 elaborate on these powers and also add powers to the list, which are not mentioned in Article 5 of the Regulation.

Article 10 of the Directive states that NCAs must have the power to find an infringement of Articles 101 and 102 TFEU and to require the undertakings concerned to terminate this infringement. This power largely mirrors Article 7 of Regulation 1/2003, which confers similar powers upon the Commission. However, it must be noted that the NCAs do not have the authority to take a negative decision, that is, finding the inapplicability of the EU competition rules. This stands in sharp contrast with Article 10 of Regulation 1/2003, a provision which states that the Commission is entitled to take a decision in the public interest, finding the non-applicability of Articles 101 and 102 TFEU.

Article 11 of the ECN+ Directive 2019 provides that NCAs must be granted the competence to adopt interim measures. At least where there is urgency due to the risk of serious and irreparable harm to competition and a prima facie infringement can be established, an NCA has to be able to take action. In other words, if these two conditions are fulfilled the power to adopt interim measures must kick in. Article 11 is framed as minimum harmonisation, which means that NCAs could also be granted the competence to adopt interim measures under more flexible conditions. It should be pointed out, however, that the measures taken must be in line with the principles of necessity and proportionality. Moreover, it must be ensured that the legality of these measures can be challenged before a national court.

Above, it was outlined that the commitment decisions of the Commission have proven to be a very successful tool for enforcing the competition rules. It does not come as a surprise, therefore, that Article 12 of the ECN+ Directive 2019 provides that the power to adopt commitment decisions also must be granted to NCAs. By doing so, the Directive gives a considerable boost to the informal enforcement of EU competition law.

Article 13 of the ECN+ Directive 2019 deals with the fines that NCAs impose on infringements of the EU competition rules. It goes without saying that this is a very important matter for the enforcement of these rules. It is required that the fines imposed are effective, proportionate and dissuasive. These requirements largely echo what the CJEU has repeatedly held in cases concerning the enforcement of EU law.[183] It is left to the Member States whether the fine is imposed by the NCA in administrative law proceedings, or by a national court at the request of an NCA. Furthermore, the Directive requires that the system of parental liability for the conduct of subsidiaries, as developed by the CJEU under Articles 101 and 102 TFEU and Regulation 1/2003, is incorporated in the national rules on the imposition of fines in competition law cases.[184] So, if the conditions discussed in section 3.5.2 of this chapter are met, an NCA has the power to fine a legal person/mother company, a subsidiary of which was engaged in anti-competitive behaviour.

---

[183] E.g. case 68/88 *Commission v Greece*, ECLI:EU:C:1989:339; joined cases C-387, C-391 and C-403/02 *Berlusconi*, ECLI:EU:C:2005:270; case C-565/12 *LCL Le Crédit Lyonnais SA*, ECLI:EU:C:2014:190.

[184] ECN+ Directive 2019, Article 13(5).

It is specifically pointed out that the Directive leaves untouched the national system of criminal law dealing with infringements of the competition rules.[185] The disclaimer is that these systems do not affect the effective and uniform enforcement of Articles 101 and 102 TFEU, requirements which already flow from the case-law of the CJEU and the principle of Union loyalty/sincere cooperation enshrined in Article 4(3) EU Treaty.

The Directive contains specific requirements for the level of the fine. Article 14(1) starts off with putting forward that the NCA fines must be based on the gravity and the duration of the infringements. The reference to these factors is very common and is also present in Article 23(3) of Regulation 1/2003, which governs the Commission's competence to impose fines. Article 14(2) is more innovative, as it requires that in an enforcement proceeding the national competition laws empower the NCAs to consider compensations paid as a result of a consensual settlement. A company having caused damages by infringing upon the competition rules could reach an out-of-court settlement with the victims of these infringements, which is an example of enforcement by private law. It goes without saying that one of the main elements of such a settlement is the amount of compensation that will be paid. In order to stimulate this effective way of (alternative) dispute settlement, the Union legislature gives the NCAs the possibility to accommodate the outcome of consensual settlement in the level of the fine to be imposed. Article 14(2) of the ECN+ Directive 2019 links the public enforcement by the NCAs to the private enforcement, which is harmonised in the Private Damages Directive 2014. In this regard, it must be noted that Article 18 of the Private Damages Directive 2014 contains a provision very similar to Article 14(2) of the ECN+ Directive 2019. Chapter 9 will deal with private enforcement of the antitrust rules.

Article 15(1) of the ECN+ Directive 2019 introduces a remarkable mechanism for ensuring that the fines imposed are not set at too low a level. National competition laws lay down conditions for calculating the maximum amount of the fine. This maximum amount may vary from Member State to Member State. It is clear from the outset that the maxima set at a relatively low level may have a negative bearing on the dissuasive character of the fining policy of the NCA concerned. For that reason, the Directive has laid down conditions for calculating the maximum amount of the fine. As these conditions are framed as minimum harmonisation (leaving room for manoeuvre to the Member States), Article 15(1) contains a minimum requirement for the maximum amount of the fine: a minimum maximum fine provision! Also, of great interest is the turnover that must be considered for calculating the fine. Admittedly, it is very common to calculate the amount of a fine on the basis of the turnover realised, but Article 15(1) of the Directive requires that the benchmark must be the worldwide turnover. As a result, it is not permitted to take the European or national turnover as the point of departure. The maximum amount of the competition law fine may not be lower than 10 per cent of the worldwide turnover in the business year preceding the fining decision.

Article 16 of the ECN+ Directive 2019 deals with the periodic penalty payments. Apart from fining companies, an NCA must also be empowered to impose such penalties. The penalties imposed must be effective, proportionate and dissuasive, requirements which are,

---

[185] Ibid, Article 13(4).

as already stated, very common in EU enforcement law. Moreover, the periodic payments have to be determined in proportion to the average daily total worldwide turnover of the undertakings concerned, in order to compel them to live up to the competition rules.

4.3.4 Leniency

Before the ECN+ Directive 2019 entered into force, no EU rules harmonising national leniency policies were in place. However, it should be pointed out that the ECN had adopted the Model Leniency Programme[186] and by doing so fostered some convergence in this area. Nevertheless, it should be noted that compliance with this programme by the NCAs takes place on a voluntary basis, as the leniency rules are laid down in a soft-law document. As a result, national leniency policies may vary from Member State to Member State. It goes without saying that disparities occurring in the various national and EU leniency rules will deter parties to a cartel from stepping forward and reporting this cartel. As was already put forward in section 3.5.4 of this chapter, the predictability of these rules is a key factor for the success of the leniency policy. National divergent rules are capable, therefore, of jeopardising the functioning of this policy.

For that reason, it should be welcomed that Articles 17–23 of the ECN+ Directive 2019 harmonise various aspects of leniency. Member States are forced to have in place leniency programmes, granting immunity from fines or reductions of fines if specific conditions are met. As was outlined in section 3.5.4 of this chapter, the Commission has also adopted a leniency programme for its enforcement actions. This programme is laid down in soft-law: the Leniency Notice 2006. Strikingly, as the ECN+ Directive 2019 requires that NCAs must have the power to apply leniency programmes, the Member States are obliged to lay down these programmes in binding legislation. It should be borne in mind that according to settled case-law, directive provisions must be implemented by national measures with unquestionable binding force.[187] Accordingly, the national leniency programmes must be laid down in binding provisions of national law, whereas the equivalent EU programme has the status of soft-law. The result of the harmonisation process is that at the national level soft-law documents dealing with leniency will be turned into hard-law rules.

The conditions set out in the Directive largely echo the conditions of the Leniency Notice 2006. Immunity is granted to the first applicant, provided that, inter alia, evidence is submitted enabling the NCA concerned to carry out a targeted inspection or to find an infringement of the cartel prohibition (laid down in Article 101 TFEU or the corresponding provision of national competition law). Reduction of fines must be given to the subsequent applicants, provided that, inter alia, the evidence submitted has significant added value for the purpose of proving an infringement.

An important aspect is the marker system, which allows applicants to get a place in the queue and, meanwhile, to collect the evidence needed. As put forward in section 3.5.4.2 of this chapter, such a system greatly facilitates the smooth operation of the process of granting

---

[186] Available at <https://ec.europa.eu/competition/ecn/mlp_revised_2012_en.pdf> accessed 26 May 2020.

[187] Cases C-361/88 *Commission v Germany*, ECLI:EU:C:1991:224, par. 21; C-59/89 *Commission v Germany*, ECLI:EU:C:1991:225, par. 24.

leniency. Article 21 of the ECN+ Directive 2019 obliges Member States to have in place a marker system. Unfortunately, the Directive does not provide a one-stop-shop mechanism for leniency applicants. Under such a system, the application made would be valid in all relevant competition law jurisdictions, that is, in EU competition law and in the national competition laws of the Member States involved. The absence of a one-stop-shop mechanism is a missed opportunity in our view.[188] In order to address the problem of multiple leniency applications, Article 22 of the ECN+ Directive 2019 provides that NCAs must accept summary applications made by companies in cases handled by the Commission, subject to the condition that these applications cover more than three Member States as affected territories. This reduces the administrative burden of the applicant, as the file of the full application has to be put together only once, that is, at the EU level. Article 22, however, does not relieve a whistle-blower from the burden to send multiple applications to various authorities. Hopefully, in the future a one-stop-shop mechanism will be introduced, because this would improve the predictability of the leniency policy considerably and, accordingly, its success.

4.3.5 Cooperation

At the end of the ECN+ Directive 2019 a couple of provisions are found, dealing with cooperation between the NCAs. These provisions supplement the mechanism of Article 22(1) of Regulation 1/2003, according to which an NCA may carry out inspections on behalf of an NCA of another Member State. Article 24(1) of the ECN+ Directive 2019 sets out that officials of the requesting authority may assist the officials of the requested authority, when carrying out the inspections requested. In other words, the system of mutual assistance is enriched. Article 26 of the ECN+ Directive 2019 also provides for a transnational system of the enforcement of fines and penalty payments. If the firm concerned does not have sufficient assets in the Member State where the infringement is detected, or does not have an establishment in this country, the NCA of that Member State may request the NCA of another Member State to enforce the fining or penalty decision. The concrete requirements of the cooperation mechanisms are elaborated on in Article 27 of the Directive.

4.4 National laws on enforcement

The foregoing has shown that NCAs play a significant role in enforcing the competition rules. They are responsible for taking actions against both infringements of EU and national competition law. In this section, attention will be paid to two national systems of competition law. An overview of the German and Dutch enforcement systems will be given. It should be noted that competition law is interwoven with national administrative and – in some Member States – is partly connected with criminal law. Nevertheless, an in-depth-analysis of these national enforcement systems will not be given: the aim of this section is not to explore various national systems of administrative (and criminal) law but rather to give an impression how the (European) competition rules are enforced at the national level.

---

[188] Braat 2018, pp. 233–4; Rizzuto 2019, p. 583.

4.4.1 Enforcement of competition law in Germany

The GWB contains provisions dealing with both the substantive rules and enforcement matters. Germany is a federal state and, as a result, competition authorities operate both at the central level and the regional level ('*Länder*'). The principal decision-maker is the central authority in German competition law, that is, the BKA, and, for that reason, only the competences of this body will be discussed. It follows from Section 48 GWB that the BKA, the *obersten Landesbehörden* (highest regional authorities), as well as the Federal Ministry for Economic Affairs have the authority to apply and to enforce the German competition rules. Pursuant to Section 50 GWB, the BKA, together with the *obersten Landesbehörden*, is designated as the NCA responsible for applying and enforcing the EU competition law rules in Germany. In matters concerning cooperation with the Commission and other NCAs, the BKA is, in general, regarded as the authority to take action.

In the previous section, the ECN+ Directive 2019 was discussed. This piece of EU legislation has to be transposed into the national legal orders of the Member States. For that reason, the German Ministry of Economic Affairs has issued a draft bill in order to give effect to this obligation in Germany. It should be noted that this draft also deals with the challenges of the digital markets and, for that reason, it is called the GWB-Digitalisierungsgesetz (GWB Digitalisation Act).[189] When writing this book, the draft was not yet passed in the German Parliament. Below, the current powers of the BKA will be discussed, but a few references to this draft will be made as well.

4.4.1.1 The institutional design of the BKA

It is outlined in Section 51 GWB that the BKA is a '*selbständige Bundesoberbehörde*' (independent federal authority). This implies that this body is competent with regard to a particular policy field, that is, competition, and that the government is not permitted to take away the powers of the BKA related to this field.[190] For example, the Minister of Economic Affairs is precluded from taking over a specific case being handled by the BKA.

An important characteristic of the BKA is that decisions are adopted by so-called '*Beschlussabteilungen*' (Decisions Divisions).[191] That means that the decisions of the BKA are made in a panel, which is composed of one person or three persons (including chairman).[192] The panels operate on the basis of the principle of '*(Kollegial)spruchkörper*' (collegiate bodies).[193] It should be noted that even the President of the BKA does not have the authority to give instructions to the '*Beschlussabteilungen*'.[194] As a result, these panels have a significant influence on the way the competition rules are enforced in Germany. Within the BKA, cases

---

[189] This draft bill is available at <https://www.bmwi.de/Redaktion/DE/Downloads/G/gwb-digitalisierungsgesetz-ref erentenentwurf.pdf?__blob=publicationFile&v=10> accessed 24 June 2020.

[190] Stockmann 2020, Commentary on Section 51, marginal 4.

[191] GWB, Section 51(2).

[192] Ibid, Section 51(3).

[193] Stockmann 2020, Commentary on Section 51, marginal 20.

[194] Ibid, marginal 27.

are handled in a quasi-judicial fashion which arguably contributes to a great extent to the transparent and efficient enforcement of competition law in Germany.[195]

Above, it was put forward that the BKA and the regional authorities apply and enforce the EU competition rules together. The GWB-Digitalisierungsgesetz proposes to introduce a new provision that unambiguously states that the BKA is the authority responsible for the application of these rules in Germany, within the meaning of Article 35 of Regulation 1/2003. Furthermore, this draft bill lays down a couple of provisions governing the role of the BKA in the ECN with regard to matters such as cooperation with competition authorities of other Member States in cross-border cases.

4.4.1.2 Investigations

The German laws grant the BKA the necessary powers for carrying out investigations. These competences are mostly laid down in the Gesetz über Ordnungswidrigkeiten, which in its turn contains many references to the Strafprozeßordnung (German Code of Criminal Procedure). For example, according to Sections 105–107 of this Code, private and business premises may be searched; in this regard it is specifically provided that the order to perform these searches must be given by a court (save for some exceptional circumstances). Some investigatory powers are laid down in the GWB. Pursuant to Section 57 GWB, the BKA may conduct any investigations and collect any evidence required. For example, undertakings and associations of undertakings may be requested to provide information.[196] Also it is permitted that the BKA inspects and examines business documents on the premises of the undertakings concerned,[197] after prior authorisation of a judicial authority has been obtained.[198] The owners and representatives of the undertakings or associations of undertakings are obliged to cooperate when the BKA carries out investigations.[199] Some safeguards are in place, when it comes to the disclosure of documents and other information. For example, the correspondence between lawyers and businesses is protected by legal privilege, as is the case in EU law.[200] Furthermore, persons of undertakings under investigation have the right to refuse to give testimony, if such a testimony leads to self-incrimination.[201] According to Section 58, the BKA also has the competence to seize objects which may be of importance as evidence in a specific case.

The GWB-Digitalisierungsgesetz aims to transpose the ECN+ Directive 2019 into German law, by laying down various investigation powers set out in this Directive. For example, it is specifically stated in Section 59b GWB (as proposed by this draft bill) that the BKA has the power to search business premises, private homes, land and goods, where it is reasonable to suspect that documents related to a competition law investigation are kept there. As already

---

[195] OECD – Germany 2004, p. 22.

[196] GWB, Section 59(1)(1) and (2).

[197] Ibid, Section 59(1)(3).

[198] Ibid, Section 59(4).

[199] Ibid, Section 59(2).

[200] Bechtold and Bosch 2018, p. 615.

[201] Schnelle and Soyez 2020, Section 2.

stated, individuals must cooperate but are not obliged to testify, if this leads to self-incrim-ination. It should be pointed out that, according to the GWB-Digitalisierungsgesetz, the BKA will have the power to grant an individual representative of an undertaking under investigation a guarantee that no enforcement action will be taken against him.[202] The result of this will be that this person must give the information requested, even if it may reveal his/her involvement in the wrongdoing. This proposal has given rise to a heated debate in German competition law.[203]

4.4.1.3 Decisional powers

The BKA has the power to take action against infringements of both the German and EU competition law rules. For example, Section 32 GWB provides that the BKA is competent to order undertakings and associations of undertakings to put an end to practices contrary to these rules. The measures that may be taken in this respect could be geared towards both the behaviour of the firms concerned and to structural interventions. This highly mirrors what is set out in Article 10 of the ECN+ Directive 2019, according to which NCAs must have the power to adopt not only behavioural remedies but also structural remedies. Similar competences are granted to the Commission in Article 7 of Regulation 1/2003. Pursuant to Section 32(2) GWB, behavioural remedies should be preferred over structural remedies. It is only permitted to impose the latter measures, if these remedies are more effective than the behavioural ones or less intrusive on the companies concerned.[204] Interestingly, the decision requiring the termination of the infringement may also order the reimbursement of the ben-efits generated by this infringement.[205] The order may only concern pecuniary advantages, which means that other advantages cannot be skimmed off.[206]

Furthermore, according to Section 32a GWB, the BKA is entitled to adopt interim meas-ures in the event that a risk of serious and irreparable damage occurs. As already discussed above, Article 11 of the ECN+ Directive 2019 requires that NCAs have this competence. Also, the Commission may take interim measures on the basis of Article 8 of Regulation 1/2003. An important difference with Article 11 of the Directive and Article 8 of the Regulation is that German law does not require a prima facie violation and, accordingly, gives more room for manoeuvre.[207] It should be noted that, as already stated, Article 11 of the Directive is based on minimum harmonisation (the words 'at least' are used), which implies in our view that a wider power to intervene may be granted to an NCA. According to Section 32a(2) GWB, the interim orders must be limited in time. Although the time limit could be extended, the duration may not exceed one year in total.

Of interest is that it is proposed by the draft GWB-Digitalisierungsgesetz that the con-ditions for adopting an interim measure will be lowered. According to Section 32a GWB,

---

[202] Podszun and Brauckmann 2019, p. 437.

[203] Ibid.

[204] Bechtold and Bosch 2018, pp. 315–16.

[205] GWB, Section 32(2a).

[206] Bechtold and Bosch 2018, p. 316.

[207] Ibid, p. 320.

as envisaged by this draft, the BKA may intervene on the market on the basis of an interim measure, at the moment that it is very likely that the competition rules are infringed[208] and the protection of competition or the imminent threat of harm for another undertaking requires immediate action. It is put forward that the condition of irreparable damage is too stringent,[209] and prevents the BKA from taking action in urgent cases, more in particular those concerning digital markets, where innovations will follow each other in quick succession.[210] However, the undertaking being confronted with an intention of the BKA to adopt an interim measure will have the right to prove that this measure would lead to very hard consequences, not justified by public interest. If this claim can successfully be substantiated, the BKA will not be entitled to adopt an interim measure.

Pursuant to Section 32b GWB, the BKA has the power to accept commitments made by undertakings. These commitments must be able to meet the concerns communicated by the BKA to these undertakings. The promises made by the firms are made binding by a decision taken by the BKA. In return the BKA is precluded from taking enforcement against them. Nevertheless, it is specifically stated that such action may be carried out, if the undertakings involved do not meet the commitments made, the parties have given incomplete, incorrect or misleading information, or the factual circumstances have significantly changed. A decision based on Section 32 GWB has two constituent components: the BKA promises not to make use of its enforcement powers, and the companies are bound by the commitments specified in this decision.[211] If they fail to meet these commitments, the BKA is entitled to impose a fine. As in EU competition law, a commitment decision of the BKA does not set out that competition law is not violated and has, moreover, no binding effect in civil damages proceedings.[212] During the last years the BKA has made use of this power in various cases, although the number of cases being handled under Section 32b GWB (ranging currently between two and four per year) is decreasing.[213]

The GWB also provides a mechanism in the event that taking enforcement action does not seem appropriate. According to Section 32c GWB, which concerns enforcement of both the EU and the German competition law rules, the BKA may decide that no grounds for action exist on the basis of the findings in its possession. The decision to be adopted will state that the BKA will not exercise its enforcement powers, as long as no new findings are available. On the one hand, Section 32c GWB does not mirror the EU experience with setting priorities, as at the heart of the BKA's assessment is the appreciation of whether the conditions for the

---

[208] On p. 87 of the explanatory memorandum of the German Ministry of Economic Affairs on the GWB-Digitalisierungsgesetz, this condition is also referred to as 'more likely than not'. This memorandum is available at <https://www.bmwi.de/Redaktion/DE/Downloads/G/gwb-digitalisierungsgesetz-referentenentwurf.pdf?__blob=publicationFile&v=10> accessed 24 June 2020.

[209] Explanatory memorandum of the German Ministry of Economic Affairs on the GWB-Digitalisierungsgesetz, pp. 85, 91.

[210] Ibid, p. 84.

[211] Bach 2020, Commentary on Section 32b, marginal 20.

[212] Ibid, marginal 3.

[213] Ibid.

cartel prohibition and the ban on abuse of dominance are satisfied. This comes down to an assessment based on the merits of the case and is not concerned with a policy geared towards prioritising certain competition issues. On the other hand, the power granted by Section 32c GWB is not similar to the Commission decision based on Article 10 of Regulation 1/2003, which empowers this EU institution to find the non-applicability of Article 101 TFEU or Article 102 TFEU. The former decision (taken under German law) serves the interests of the undertakings concerned as it gives some legal certainty (no enforcement actions will be taken), while the latter decision (adopted under EU law) serves the general interest, as particular issues of competition law are clarified.[214] In contrast to Article 10 of Regulation 1/2003, the BKA only binds itself when exercising its powers under Section 32c GWB, which entails that it will not take any enforcement action in the absence of new findings.[215] Consequently, other authorities and, more in particular, national judicial bodies are not bound by a decision based on Section 32c of the GWB. Then again, it must be borne in mind that such a decision will influence these authorities, given the expertise and the authority of the BKA and will, accordingly, have some bearing on all parties concerned.[216]

In any event, as is outlined in section 3.4 of this chapter, it is settled case-law of the CJEU[217] that NCAs may not adopt a decision finding the non-applicability of Articles 101 and 102 TFEU and, accordingly, a decision based on Section 32c GWB may not officially state that these Treaty provisions are not infringed. In our view, in the light of this EU case-law it is of great importance that the BKA is only capable of binding itself, rather than other authorities, when taking the decision that no grounds for actions are found.

In this regard it must be noted that in the draft GWB-Digitalisierungsgesetz it is proposed to add a new paragraph to Section 32c GWB, according to which undertakings and associations of undertakings may ask the BKA to give its view on a particular form of cooperation and to decide that there are no grounds for action, provided that these undertakings and associations have a substantial, legal and economic interest with regard to this form of cooperation. It is put forward that this new mechanism should be used in order to give firms more legal certainty when developing new (ICT) products on the digital markets.[218] It is believed that on these markets the enterprises concerned have special interests that justify that guidance is given rapidly by the BKA; moreover the new mechanisms only apply to horizontal agreements due to the limited resources of the BKA.[219] Within six months, the BKA must decide on the application made by the parties concerned under Section 32c GWB, as proposed by the draft GWB-Digitalisierungsgesetz. In this regard, it must be pointed out that the BKA has shown a lot of interest in the digital markets and has intervened when

---

[214] Ibid, marginals 2 and 3.

[215] Bechtold and Bosch 2018, p. 329.

[216] Ibid.

[217] Case C-375/09 *Tele2 Polska*, ECLI:EU:C:2011:270.

[218] Explanatory memorandum of the German Ministry of Economic Affairs on the GWB-Digitalisierungsgesetz, p. 91.

[219] Ibid.

needed in its view, although without imposing sanctions on the firms concerned.[220] Against this backdrop, it does not come as a surprise that a competence is proposed which is aimed at giving clarifications on complicated issues at play, inter alia, on digital markets.

Also of interest to note is the competence of the BKA, laid down in Section 32e GWB, to carry out sector investigations. If the rigidity of prices or other circumstances suggest that domestic competition is distorted, the BKA has the power to conduct an investigation into a specific sector or into a particular type of agreement. The Commission is conferred similar powers by Article 17 of Regulation 1/2003. Noteworthy is also the BKA's competence based on Section 34 GWB to order disgorgement of the economic benefits gained by undertakings having violated the competition rules intentionally or negligently. This power cannot be exercised, if the economic benefit is disgorged by the payment of damages, the imposition of a fine, by an order of forfeiture or by reimbursement. It should be noted that the practical significance of this power is limited, as to date it is (virtually) not exercised.[221]

4.4.1.4 Sanctions in German competition law

It must be noted that in Germany, the competition law rules are enforced by administrative law save for one exception: bid rigging is a criminal offence according to Section 298 of the Strafgesetzbuch (Criminal Code).[222] The maximum sanction that may be imposed for this offence is five years of imprisonment. Given the limited role of criminal law enforcement (initiated by public prosecutors), this section will only focus on the sanctions of administrative law that may be imposed by the BKA.

Fines

It does not come as a surprise that the BKA has the power to impose fines on undertakings and associations of undertakings having violated both the German and the EU competition law rules. The competence is partly governed by Section 81 GWB and partly by the so-called Gesetz über Ordnungswidrigkeiten (Administrative Offences Act).[223] Undertakings, associations of undertakings, as well as individuals may be fined pursuant to this provision of German competition law. According to the 'Opportunitätsprinzip' (opportunity principle), it is up to the BKA to decide whether a fine will be imposed or not.[224] This decision (to fine a company or to refrain from doing so) cannot be challenged in court.[225] This stands in sharp contrast with the decision of the Commission not to follow up on a complaint lodged by a party, a decision which may be contested before the EU courts.[226]

---

[220] Wiggers, Struijlaart and Dibbits 2019, p. 74.

[221] Bach 2020, Commentary on Section 34, marginal 4.

[222] Schnelle and Soyez 2020, Section 1.

[223] Ordnungswidrigkeit relates to administrative offences and is a special area of German administrative law. As this book is not concerned with discussing various national systems of administrative law, this area of German law will not be elaborated on.

[224] Bechtold and Bosch 2018, p. 688.

[225] Ibid.

[226] On this matter, see section 3.1 of this chapter.

In Section 81(1) and (2) GWB it is spelled out under which circumstances fines may be imposed. References are made to both rules of German and EU law. These rules concern not only substantive matters (practices contrary to the cartel prohibition and the ban on the abuse of a dominant position) but also issues of a procedural nature (e.g. not giving the information requested or providing incorrect information).

The maximum level of the fines due is dealt with in Section 81(4) GWB. Undertakings and associations of undertakings having violated the substantive competition rules of EU and German law could be confronted with a fine of maximum 10 per cent of the worldwide turnover. In the *Grauzement* cartel case,[227] the Bundesgerichtshof (Supreme court) interpreted this provision not as a cap (like the equivalent maximum level in Regulation 1/2003) but as a turnover-based upper limit, being part of a framework in the light of which the fines imposed must be reviewed by the German judiciary.[228] In German enforcement law, it is required that the lower and upper limits for fines are fixed in legislative acts in order to serve as benchmarks for the level of the individual sanctions.[229] This entails for competition law that, together with the lower limit of 5 EUR,[230] the upper limit of 10 per cent functions as an orientation framework for the actual individual BKA decisions, by which the fines are imposed.[231] In the view of the Bundesgerichtshof, the constitutional principle of legal certainty ('*Rechtssicherheit*') requires that the maximum of 10 per cent is interpreted as a turnover-based upper limit.[232] From this judgment it is apparent that the requirement of German constitutional law that the conditions for imposing fines must be clearly articulated in legislative acts does not sit well with the approach of the EU rules on maximum fines.[233] The limit of 10 per cent of Section 81(4) GWB was modelled after EU competition law by the German legislature and it took the Bundesgerichtshof's 'interpretative acrobatics' to find this limit compatible with the German constitutional tradition.[234]

According to the sixth sentence of Section 81(4) GWB, when deciding on the level of the fine the BKA must pay due consideration to the gravity and duration of the infringement under review.[235] Furthermore, the economic situation of the company concerned has to be taken into account.[236] The fine imposed must also be in line with the principle of proportionality.[237] A system of judicial protection is in place against decisions taken by the BKA.[238] Consequently, fines may be annulled or lowered by the competent court. It is even apparent

---

[227] Case *Grauzement*, KRB, (2013) 20/12, BGH, Decision of 26 February 2013.

[228] Ibid, par. 63.

[229] Ibid, par. 56.

[230] This flows from Ordnungswidrigkeitengesetzes (Administrative Offences Act), Section 17(1).

[231] BGH *Grauzement* cartel case, par. 64, 65.

[232] Ibid, par 66.

[233] Cf. e.g. Pustlauk 2013, pp. 293–4.

[234] Ibid, p. 295.

[235] Ordnungswidrigkeitengesetzes, Section 17(3).

[236] GWB, Section 81(4a).

[237] Ordnungswidrigkeitengesetzes, Section 17(3).

[238] GWB, Section 63.

from the *Flüssiggas* cartel judgment that in German competition law the competent courts may raise fines when reviewing BKA decisions ('*reformatio in peius*').[239] It does not come as a surprise that this has discouraged firms from bringing cases to court and, moreover, had made them withdraw pending cases.[240]

It must be noted that the draft GWB-Digitalisierungsgesetz will introduce some specific provisions dealing with the level of fining. The point of departure is again, as is apparent from the proposed Section 81c(2) GWB, that the maximum level of the fine for undertakings and associations of undertakings is 10 per cent of the total worldwide turnover. Pursuant to Section 81d GWB (as proposed by this draft bill), the duration and the gravity of the infringement are regarded as factors to be taken into account, as is also the case under the current rules. Furthermore, attention has to be paid to the nature and size of the infringement, the impact of the infringement on the goods and services affected, the dimension of the turnover related to the infringement, the level of organisation of the parties involved and their contribution to the wrongdoing, the involvement of the undertaking in violation in previous infringements, and the post-violation behaviour of the undertaking. Of further significance is the economic strength of the undertaking concerned. In comparison with the current GWB provisions on fines, the proposed changes are more extensive, as they articulate the various factors to be taken into account with great care. It is apparent from the explanatory memorandum that these changes are also a response to the *Grauzement* judgment of the Bundesgerichtshof, where the importance of the principle of legal certainty was stressed.[241]

The BKA has issued Guidelines for the setting of fines in competition law cases.[242] In these Guidelines it is set out that the turnover achieved from the infringement is an appropriate starting point for determining the fine.[243] The BKA assumes that the gain and harm potential of an infringement is 10 per cent of the company's turnover achieved from this infringement.[244] A multiplication factor is applied in order to account for the size of the company concerned; a factor of 2–3 is applied for firms the total turnover of which is less than 100 million EUR, a factor of 3–4 for firms the total turnover of which is in the range of 100 million EUR to 1 billion EUR, a factor of 4–5 for firms the total turnover of which is in the range of 1 billion EUR to 10 billion EUR, a factor of 5–6 for firms the total turnover of which is in the range of 10 billion EUR to 100 billion EUR, and a factor of more than 6 for firms the total turnover of which is in excess of 100 billion EUR.[245] Furthermore aggravating and mitigating factors will be taken into account; that means, for example, that the role that the

---

[239] Case *Flüssiggas*, (2013) VI-4 Kart 2-6/10 OWi, Oberlandesgericht Düsseldorf, 14 April 2013.

[240] Outhuijse 2019, p. 73.

[241] Explanatory memorandum of the German Ministry of Economic Affairs on the GWB-Digitalisierungsgesetz, p. 138.

[242] Leitlinien für die Bussgeldzumessung in Kartellordnungswidrigkeitenverfahren of 25 June 2013, available at <https://www.bundeskartellamt.de/SharedDocs/Publikation/DE/Leitlinien/Bekanntmachung%20-%20Bu%C3%9Fgeldleitlinien-Juni%202013.pdf?__blob=publicationFile&v=5> accessed 24 June 2020.

[243] BKA Guidelines 2013, par. 5.

[244] Ibid, par. 10.

[245] Ibid, par. 13.

firm under investigation played in the cartel will be paid attention to.[246] The BKA specifically puts forward that, apart from imposing a fine, it is entitled to skim off the economic benefits obtained by the anti-competitive practices pursuant to Section 34 GWB.

Leniency

On 7 March 2006, the BKA also issued a Notice on leniency: Bonusregelung über den Erlass und die Reduktion von Geldbußen in Kartellsachen (Leniency programme on the immunity and reduction of fines in cartel cases).[247] According to this Notice, an undertaking is entitled to immunity from a fine, if it is the first participant in a cartel, providing information or evidence on this cartel, which enables the BKA to obtain a search warrant.[248] On top of that, it is set out that a successful application requires that the undertaking was not the only ringleader of the cartel and did not coerce other firms to join the cartel. Furthermore, this undertaking is obliged to cooperate fully on a continuous basis with the BKA.[249] If the BKA already is in the position of obtaining a search warrant, an undertaking can still apply for immunity, if it is able to provide information or evidence to the BKA as first participant, enabling this authority to prove the offence.[250] The other conditions to be met are that the applicant was not the only ringleader, is committed to full and continuous cooperation, and no immunity based on another application which led to a search warrant is already granted.[251] It is apparent from the last condition that an immunity application enabling the BKA to obtain a search warrant has priority over an immunity application enabling the BKA to prove a violation. Like in EU law, the BKA leniency programme also provides for a mechanism leading to a reduction of the fine to be imposed. This mechanism applies to all undertakings that have not stepped forward first, as participants in a cartel. They are entitled to such a reduction (up to 50 per cent), if the information and evidence given significantly contributes to proving the offence and cooperation is warranted on a full and continuous basis.[252] The amount of the reduction granted depends on the added value of the information and evidence given, as well as the sequence of the applications (place in the queue).[253]

The timing of an application plays a decisive role, because only the undertaking stepping forward first as participant in a certain cartel will be granted full immunity. For that reason, the BKA leniency programme has introduced a marker system, as the Commission also did for EU competition law. A cartel participant may contact an official of the BKA division responsible for the leniency applications. If only the core details of a cartel are provided, a

---

[246] Ibid, par. 16.

[247] Available at <https://www.bundeskartellamt.de/SharedDocs/Publikation/DE/Bekanntmachungen/Bekanntmach ung%20-%20Bonusregelung.html?nn=4136556> accessed 24 June 2020.

[248] See BKA Leniency Programme 2006, par. 3.

[249] Ibid.

[250] Ibid, par. 4.

[251] Ibid.

[252] Ibid, par. 5.

[253] Ibid.

marker, which will be decisive for the timing of the application concerned, will be given.[254] Within 8 weeks maximum, a full application must be filed, unless it turns out that the European Commission is the best placed authority for taking action against the cartel concerned.[255] In that case, the BKA can exempt the undertaking concerned from filing a full leniency application.

The GWB-Digitalisierungsgesetz implements the provisions of the ECN+ Directive 2019 dealing with leniency by adding a new paragraph to the GWB. As in the current leniency programme of the BKA, the core of the proposed rules is that no fine will be imposed, if a party to a cartel provides evidence that enables the BKA to carry out an inspection or proves an offence.[256] If an undertaking is not the first party to a cartel that provides evidence, reduction of the fine will, nevertheless, be given, provided that this evidence has significant added value.[257] Also a marker system is introduced by the GWB-Digitalisierungsgesetz.[258] Although the proposed provisions largely mirror what is laid down in the current BKA leniency programme, as of the moment that the GWB-Digitalisierungsgesetz will have entered into force, the rules dealing with leniency will no longer be contained in soft-law, but rather will be enshrined in provisions of binding law. Consequently, in the future, the leniency rules cannot as easily be changed as is the case under the law as it stands now (when writing this book).

Settlements

As under the EU rules on enforcement, a set of provisions is in place dealing with the settlements and the imposition of fines by the BKA in German competition law (although these provisions are laid down in a Notice). When in an administrative proceeding the BKA considers imposing a fine, it could engage in a settlement with the parties concerned. According to the Notice – Das Settlement-Verfahren des Bundeskartellamtes in Bußgeldsachen (The settlement proceeding of the BKA in fining cases),[259] an undertaking willing to settle the dispute on the competition law fine must make a statement in which it acknowledges the grounds of the charges and accepts the level of the fine envisaged by the BKA. In return, the BKA will take the settlement statement into account as a mitigating factor that will lead to a reduction of the fine due. If the case at issue concerns horizontal cartels, the reduction will amount to 10 per cent maximum of the fine due. Interestingly, this slightly differs from the EU experience with settlements. The reduction given by the Commission in settlements is fixed at 10 per cent, irrespective of the nature of the anti-competitive practices at issue. In German competition law, more fine-tuning is possible when it comes to the fine reductions in settlement proceedings. A parallel with the EU experience is, however, that both under German and EU competition law, an undertaking may be granted a reduction on the basis

---

[254] Ibid, par. 11.

[255] Ibid, par. 12–14.

[256] Section 81k GWB, as proposed by the GWB-Digitalisierungsgesetz.

[257] Section 81l GWB, as proposed by the GWB-Digitalisierungsgesetz.

[258] Section 81m GWB, as proposed by the GWB-Digitalisierungsgesetz.

[259] This Notice of February 2016 is available at <https://www.bundeskartellamt.de/SharedDocs/Publikation/DE/ Merkbl%C3%A4tter/Merkblatt-Settlement.pdf?__blob=publicationFile&v=3> accessed 24 June 2020.

of both the leniency programme and the settlement proceeding. Above, it was put forward that in enforcement cases, the German judiciary has raised a fine imposed by the BKA. It is believed that this case-law may explain the high percentage of the settlements reached during the last years, since these settlements are reached without any judicial involvement.[260]

Periodic penalties

Next to the competence to fine undertakings, the BKA has the authority to impose periodic penalties in the event that the competition rules are violated. Primarily, this authority is governed by the Verwaltungs-Vollstreckungsgesetz (Administrative Enforcement Act), more in particular Section 11 of this piece of legislation.[261] Pursuant to Section 86a(2) GWB, the minimum level of the periodic penalty is 1000 EUR and the maximum level is 10 million EUR. The GWB-Digitalisierungsgesetz proposes to replace the current second paragraph of Section 86a with a provision that sets the maximum of the periodic penalty at 5 per cent of the average daily turnover of the undertaking.[262]

4.4.2 Enforcement of competition law in the Netherlands

The Mw lays down a few provisions dealing with the enforcement of competition law rules in the Netherlands. Most of the rules on this subject, however, are contained in the Algemene wet bestuursrecht (Awb – General Administrative Law Act) and the Instellingswet ACM (Instellingswet – Establishment Act of the Authority for Consumers and Markets). The ACM is responsible for enforcing competition law rules in the Netherlands. According to Article 88 Mw, the ACM is designated as the authority for the application of EU competition law in the Netherlands, for the purposes of Regulation 1/2003.

The ECN+ Directive 2019, which was discussed in section 4.3 of this chapter, lays down provisions on the public enforcement in the Member States and must be implemented in the Netherlands. As in Germany, a proposal has been issued to that effect: Wijziging van de Mededingingswet en de Instellingswet ACM in verband met de implementatie van Richtlijn 2019/1 (Amendment of the Competition Act and Establishment Act of the Authority for Consumers and Markets in relation to the implementation of Directive 2019/1).[263] When writing this book, this draft bill was not yet adopted by the Dutch legislature and, for that reason, the rules in place at that moment are discussed below, although some attention is paid to the proposed changes as well.

4.4.2.1 The institutional design of the ACM

The ACM is a '*zelfstandig bestuursorgaan*' (independent administrative authority). It does not have legal personality and it is part of the Dutch Ministry of Economic Affairs.[264] As a

---

[260] Outhuijse 2019, p. 73.

[261] Bechtold and Bosch 2018, p. 741.

[262] ECN+ Directive 2019, Article 16 requires that the Member States grant to their competition authorities the competence to impose periodic penalties based on a particular proportion of the average daily turnover.

[263] Kamerstukken (Dutch parliamentary documents) II 2019–2020, 35 467, nr. 2.

[264] On this matter, see Dzino 2020, p. 37 *et seq.*

result, the final decision regarding its budget is taken by the Minister of Economic Affairs, although the draft budget is made by the board of the ACM. In light of Article 5 of the ECN+ Directive 2019, which deals with the financial independence of NCAs, the question has been raised whether the ACM should have the power to adopt its own budget.[265] The point is that the ACM also does not have legal personality and nevertheless must take action against enterprises managed by the Ministry of Economic Affairs,[266] of which the ACM is officially part.[267]

The position of a *'zelfstandig bestuursorgaan'*, such as the ACM, is governed by the Kaderwet zelfstandige bestuursorganen (Public Bodies Framework Act). As a result, the Minister of Economic Affairs has the authority to give instructions of general nature to the ACM, which are called *'beleidsregels'* (guidelines) in Dutch administrative law.[268] These instructions may concern policy matters related to particular competition issues. For example, instructions are issued, setting out how the ACM has to determine the level of the fines. Other instructions adopted by the Minister deal with the leniency policy of the ACM. However, it is not permitted for the Minister to direct case-specific instructions at the ACM, as this competition authority should handle individual cases in an independent fashion. Article 9(1) Instellingswet specifically provides that the Minister must refrain from giving instructions concerning individual cases. The second paragraph of this provision adds that the officials of the ACM are not allowed to request or to accept instructions concerning individual cases. In other words, under Dutch competition law a sharp divide exists between instructions of a general nature and instructions with regard to individual cases. The ban directed at the Minister not to give case-specific instructions is one of the core elements of the independent position of the ACM.

The board of the ACM is charged with the task to adopt decisions and to implement the relevant policies. This board is composed of three persons, including the chairperson.[269] The staff of the ACM drafts the decisions and performs other tasks, such as carrying out investigations. In order to guarantee the objective nature of enforcement actions, the following safeguard is laid down in Dutch competition law: prior to the imposition of a fine, a report (comparable to the statement of objections sent by the Commission to the undertakings under investigation) will be drafted. Pursuant to Article 12q Instellingswet a staff member involved in the drafting of this report may not work on the decision imposing the fine on the firms concerned. It could be argued that a Chinese wall exists between the staff members engaged in the investigations and the staff members preparing the fining decision. However, it should be noted that both the report and the fining decision are adopted on behalf of the same body, which is the board of the ACM. In other words, the Chinese wall is only in place in the preparatory phase and is absent at the moment a binding decision is adopted.

---

[265] Dzino, Van de Gronden and Rusu 2019, pp. 539–40; Dzino 2020, pp. 53–6.

[266] These enterprises mostly concern businesses in the utilities sector, such as energy.

[267] Case C-530/16 *Commission v Poland*, ECLI:EU:C:2018:430.

[268] Kaderwet zelfstandige bestuursorganen, Article 21.

[269] Instellingswet, Article 3(1).

4.4.2.2 Investigations

The Mw, the Instellingswet and the Awb confer the necessary powers on the ACM to carry out investigations. The powers are divided over these acts and it requires a close reading of the relevant provisions in order to find out which powers the ACM has. The Awb contains provisions applicable in all domains of Dutch administrative law, the Instellingswet is concerned with the powers the ACM has in order to carry out all the tasks assigned to it (among which are the application and enforcement of the competition rules) and the Mw only deals with matters of competition law.

According to Article 12a Instellingswet the officials appointed by a decision of the ACM are entrusted with the enforcement of, inter alia, the competition law rules. As a result, they are entitled to exercise investigatory powers. Some of these powers are set out in the Awb, more in particular in Articles 5:15–5:19. These powers include the inspection of business premises (Article 5:15), the requests for information (Article 5:16) and the inspection of business information and documents (Article 5:17).

When inspecting business premises, the ACM officials may look around in order to collect certain items of evidence (referred to as '*zoekend rondkijken*' in Dutch administrative law) but must refrain from searching the premises (referred to as '*doorzoeken*').[270] It goes without saying that in practice it could be hard to distinguish between activities leading to 'looking around' and activities amounting to 'searching'. ACM officials may enter business premises without the consent of the undertaking. No prior permission from a judicial authority is required.

The power to request information may be exercised by sending a letter to the undertakings under investigation and other market players. Such requests could also be made by an official that is engaged in an inspection of business premises.

The power to require inspection of business information and documents concerns both paper files and electronic data. As a result, the ACM has developed an approach, enabling it to make a forensic image of a hard disk or another data medium. The ACM Guidance on digital inspection[271] specifies how this approach will be applied and also addresses the rights of the firms involved.

The Instellingswet also confers investigation powers on the ACM. Of importance is Article 12b of this Act, which states that officials of the ACM are authorised to seal off business premises and objects. This power may be exercised in so far as is reasonably necessary for investigation purposes.

Another important competence is the inspection of private homes. Pursuant to Article 12c Instellingswet, ACM officials are authorised to enter a private home without the resident's permission, provided that this is necessary for investigation purposes. Prior judicial permission is required for exercising the powers under Article 12c. As with the power to enter business premises, the ACM officials are entitled to look around for finding items of evidence

---

[270] E.g. case *Mejia Amaya A.*, (1985) NJ 1985, 822, Hoge Raad, 28 May 1985.

[271] ACM Werkwijze digitaal onderzoek 2014 (ACM approach to digital inspection 2014) available at <https://www.acm.nl/nl/publicaties/publicatie/12594/ACM-Werkwijze-digitaal-onderzoek-2014> accessed 24 June 2020.

('*zoekend rondkijken*'), but are not permitted to search ('*doorzoeken*') the private home under investigation.

It should be recalled that the Instellingswet governs all (investigation) tasks assigned to the ACM, which, apart from competition law, concern consumer matters and regulatory oversight in the area of energy and telecommunications. Strikingly, solely for the purposes of investigations in competition law cases, the Mw adds a special power for inspecting private homes to the power laid down in Article 12c Instellingswet. Article 50 Mw states that, subject to prior authorisation from a judicial body,[272] the ACM officials are authorised to search ('*doorzoeken*'), if this is necessary for investigation purposes. From this provision, it is apparent that, if needed in competition law cases, the inspection powers of the ACM are extended and also encompass searching, which under administrative law is a huge step.[273] It should be pointed out that in the event of inspection of business premises, the powers of the ACM cannot be extended and, accordingly, do not encompass searching. This is a remarkable difference, as entering a private home is more intrusive for the persons residing there, than entering business premises.

It is apparent from the foregoing that the Dutch rules on inspecting premises are complicated. In fact, these rules are even more complicated if the ACM is involved in a Commission inspection of premises located in the Netherlands. According to Article 89b Mw, the ACM is obliged to assist Commission officials in inspections, if this is required on the basis of Regulation 1/2003. The ACM officials have the same powers as the Commission officials have in the event business premises located in the Netherlands are inspected under the regime of Regulation 1/2003.[274] This entails that ACM officials are authorised to search the business premises under investigation in that event, which stands in sharp contrast with the inspections of business premises carried out autonomously by the ACM (in the absence of Commission officials). It must be pointed out that prior permission of a judicial authority is required if the inspection planned by the Commission and the ACM will lead to a search.

The ACM is also obliged to assist the Commission in inspections of private homes under Article 21 of Regulation 1/2003. Irrespective of the fact whether this would lead to searching activities, prior permission from a judicial authority is required by Article 89d Mw in that case, which is, by the way, also set out by Article 21 of the Regulation.

According to Article 5:20(1) Awb, everyone is obliged to cooperate with a public official, as long as this cooperation is reasonable. Cooperation may be refused by any person bound by a duty of secrecy by virtue of his/her office or profession.[275] Of great importance is Article 5:10a Awb, which provides that no one is obliged to incriminate themselves by giving a statement with regard to an alleged offence. Another significant safeguard is derived from EU law: it is apparent from both Article 129 Instellingswet and Article 5:20(2) Awb that the correspondence between the lawyer and the undertaking concerned is protected by legal

---

[272] Mw, Article 51.

[273] It is believed that the power of searching belongs to the domain of criminal law, rather than administrative law. See Mok 2004, p. 505.

[274] This flows directly from Regulation 1/2003, Article 20(5). See also section 2.4 of this chapter.

[275] Awb, Article 5:20(2).

privilege. Consequently, the EU approach to the communication exchanged between lawyer and the undertakings under investigation, developed by the CJEU for EU competition law in *AM&S*,[276] is incorporated by the Dutch legislature in provisions of binding law.

4.4.2.3 Decisional powers

The powers of the ACM to apply competition law rules are divided over two pieces of legislation: the Instellingswet and the Mw. The reason for this is that some of the powers are not exercised only in competition law cases, but are also relevant for other tasks assigned to the ACM. These powers are contained in the Instellingswet, while the competition law-specific powers are laid down in the Mw.

If a provision of law is violated and the ACM is entrusted with the task to enforce compliance with that provision, this authority is entitled to impose a binding instruction on the offender according to Article 12j Instellingswet. This power comes very close to the power of the Commission from Article 7 of Regulation 1/2003, on the basis of which a violation can be found and termination thereof may be ordered. It also highly mirrors what is provided by Article 10 of the ECN+ Directive 2019, according to which each NCA must have the power to find and terminate an infringement of Articles 101 and 102 TFEU.

In the past, the ACM had the power to adopt interim measures. Pursuant to then Article 83 Mw, the ACM could impose a provisional order subject to periodic penalty payments, if on first sight it was probable that the competition rules were violated as well as immediate action was required in view of the interests of the undertakings affected or of the interest of preserving effective competition. This sanction was legally structured as a special form of a periodic penalty. However, the Dutch legislature has abolished this competence, as Dutch administrative law allows for a preventive imposition of the regular periodic penalty.[277] Article 5:7 Awb, which contains the conditions for imposing this sanction, provides that an order may be imposed in the event that the risk of an offence is evident. According to settled case-law, this entails that preventive action on the basis of this provision is only permitted if it is clear that the offence will take place with a probability verging on certainty. As was outlined in section 4.3 of this chapter, Article 11 of the ECN+ Directive 2019 requires that an NCA must have at least the competence to adopt an interim measure where there is urgency due to the risk of serious and irreparable harm to competition and a prima facie (on first sight) infringement can be established. It is highly doubtful whether the rather strict test of Article 5:7 Awb meets the more flexible standard of Article 11 of the Directive.[278] In our view, for that reason, the power to adopt interim measures must be reintroduced in Dutch competition law. It is, therefore, to be welcomed that the draft Act implementing the ECN+ Directive 2019 contains a provision again granting the ACM the competence to impose a provisional order, subject to periodic penalty payments, in urgent cases.[279]

---

[276] Case 155/79 *AM&S*, ECLI:EU:C:1982:157.

[277] Kamerstukken II 2012/13, 33 622, nr. 3, p. 69.

[278] Dzino, Van de Gronden and Rusu 2019, p. 541.

[279] It is apparent from the draft Wijziging van de Mededingingswet en de Instellingswet ACM in verband met de implementatie van Richtlijn 2019/1 (Amendment of the Competition Act and Establishment Act of the Authority

Article 12h Instellingswet grants the ACM the power to adopt commitment decisions. Commitments proposed by the companies concerned are made binding by the ACM, as this authority is of the opinion that such an action is more efficient than imposing a fine or a periodic penalty. This efficiency-based condition differs from the competence of the Commission to make commitments binding as this power applies if the commitments made meet the concerns of the Commission.[280] Furthermore, Article 12 of the ECN+ Directive 2019 also requires that the condition based on the concerns of a competition authority is attached to the power to adopt commitment decisions. To date, however, the Dutch legislature does not seem to plan to change the current condition of Article 12h Instellingswet. In this respect, it must be borne in mind that some overlap exists between the Dutch and EU condition for making commitments binding: it may be assumed that, if the ACM considers that a commitment is more effective than imposing a sanction, it also holds the view that the competition concerns identified are addressed.[281]

Noteworthy is a proposal launched by the ACM in order to introduce an *ex ante* intervention mechanism to prevent anti-competitive behaviour by dominant undertakings fulfilling the role of gatekeepers on digital markets. The reason for this is that these markets are highly dynamic and driven by innovation, which entails that the current *ex post* enforcement tools fall short, as making use of these tools takes up too much time. The ACM proposes to add the new *ex ante* tool to Regulation 1/2003, which would enable the Commission and the NCAs to take swift action on digital markets.[282] In our view, for the position of the NCAs it would make more sense to add this tool to the ECN+ Directive 2019, as this piece of EU legislation deals with public enforcement on the national level. The ACM proposal suggests that the extra tool will amount to a new power, as it differs from competences such as finding an infringement, adopting an interim measure and making commitments binding.[283] This seems to be a valid point, but in our view, this extra tool will have a lot in common with the power to adopt interim measures, as both competences are geared towards taking swift action in matters of urgency. Consequently, it may make sense to regulate the *ex ante* intervention mechanism in the context of the provisions dealing with the interim measure competence. In any event, the new extra tool should be non-punitive in nature, which means that the enterprises concerned will not face any fines or damages claims, which may facilitate the adoption of commitments at an early stage.[284]

Whereas the German legislature has proposed to extend the national toolkit in order to meet the challenges of the digital markets by issuing the draft GWB-Digitalisierungsgesetz,

---

for Consumers and Markets in relation to the implementation of Directive 2019/1) that this competence would be laid down in Article 58b Mw.

[280] Regulation 1/2003, Article 9.

[281] Van de Gronden 2017, p. 258.

[282] ACM Memorandum, 'Extension of Enforcement Toolkit to Increase Effectiveness in Dealing with Competition Problems in the Digital Economy', (2019) available at <https://www.acm.nl/sites/default/files/documents/2019-08/ex-ante-tool.pdf> accessed 22 June 2020.

[283] ACM Memorandum 2019, p. 2.

[284] Ibid.

the Dutch competition authority has decided to foster that EU-wide measures will be taken in order to address these challenges. The proposal of the ACM was also endorsed by the Joint Memorandum of the Benelux competition authorities.[285] Interestingly, after the ACM had issued its proposal, the Commission has put forward that it will further explore *ex ante* rules to ensure that digital markets remain fair and contestable for innovators, businesses and new market entrants.[286] It has launched a consultation process with regard to a possible introduction of *ex ante* regulation of digital platforms.[287] The reason for this is that large online platforms are able to control increasingly important platform ecosystems in the digital economy, and businesses, as well as consumers, are heavily dependent on these platforms.[288] On top of that, the Commission has put forward that it considers introducing an instrument for addressing structural competition problems.[289] When writing this book, the outcome of the public consultation process was not yet known.

4.4.2.4 Sanctions in Dutch competition law

The Mw and also the Instellingswet confer powers upon the ACM to impose sanctions. It should be noted that these powers concern both infringements of the substantive competition rules and the provisions of a procedural nature. It is apparent from Article 89 Mw that these sanctions may also be imposed in the event that Articles 101 and 102 TFEU are violated. Apart from the Mw and the Instellingswet, the enforcement of the competition rules is governed by the Awb in the Netherlands, as this Act contains the general norms applicable to all areas of Dutch administrative law.

Enforcement of competition law is a matter of administrative law in the Netherlands and criminal law does not apply to competition offences. In the past, the Act preceding the Mw (Wet Economische Mededinging – WEM – Act on Economic Competition) was enforced by both criminal and administrative law, but with the entry into force of the Mw, this enforcement system was replaced by a system based solely on administrative law, in which great value is assigned to administrative fines. The reason for this was that criminal law enforcement had proved to be very unsuccessful, as in practice virtually no priority was given to the detection of violations of the Dutch competition rules.[290] Later, at the initiative of the Dutch parliament it was examined whether criminal law could play some additional role in competition law enforcement,[291] but eventually it was concluded by the government that criminal law enforcement should not be reintroduced into competition law, given the

---

[285] Joint Memorandum 2019, pp. 5–7.

[286] Shaping Europe's Digital Future Communication 2020.

[287] See <https://ec.europa.eu/commission/presscorner/detail/en/ip_20_977> accessed 11 June 2020.

[288] Inception Impact Assessment of 2 June 2020, (2020) <https://ec.europa.eu/info/law/better-regulation/have-your-say/initiatives/12418-Digital-Services-Act-package-ex-ante-regulatory-instrument-of-very-large-online-platforms-acting-as-gatekeepers> accessed 24 June 2020.

[289] See <https://ec.europa.eu/info/law/better-regulation/have-your-say/initiatives/12416-New-competition-tool> accessed 24 June 2020.

[290] Mok 2004, pp. 19–54.

[291] Handelingen (Discussions of the Parliament) TK 91, 15 June 2006, pp. 5562–86.

expertise needed in this area of law, and the sufficiently deterrent nature of the current administrative sanctions in place in Dutch competition law.[292]

The ACM enjoys some discretion in deciding to take up a competition law case. It has developed an approach to set priorities, highly mirroring the EU experience with this matter.[293] The Dutch judiciary has accepted that the ACM sets priorities in enforcement matters,[294] but also requires that a decision not to follow up on enforcement requests is based on sound and transparent reasoning.[295] This reasoning must, inter alia, explain why on the basis of the available findings further action is not justified, which comes down to giving a preliminary assessment of the facts in the light of the relevant competition rules. As in EU competition law, an ACM decision not to take enforcement action may be challenged in court. Under Dutch administrative law a complaint lodged, alleging that the competition rules are infringed, is regarded as a request directed to the ACM to exercise its enforcement powers; in other words, the ACM is requested to take a decision and decisions of public bodies are, of course, subject to judicial review.[296]

Fines

According to Article 56 Mw, the ACM has the authority to impose a fine in the event that the substantive competition rules are violated. Also, the fines that may be imposed upon firms not having complied with the relevant merger control rules are laid down in the Mw.[297] Violations of the rules of a procedural nature are governed by the Instellingswet. For example, a fine is due if the duty to cooperate with the ACM in investigations is not observed. Before a fine will be imposed, the ACM is obliged to issue a report setting out which rules are violated by the undertakings under investigation and revealing its intent to impose a sanction.[298] This report has a lot in common with the statement of objections that the Commission draws up in EU competition law enforcement cases.[299] The report informs the parties involved about the allegations made against them and gives them the opportunity to defend themselves. They have the opportunity to give their views on what is set out in the report, which, as a rule, will be done in a hearing organised by the ACM.

As for the level of the fine imposed due to breaches of the substantive competition rules, Article 5:46 Awb provides that the gravity of the offence, the level of culpability and the circumstances under which it has been committed must be taken into account. Furthermore, a fine may not be imposed in the absence of any fault on the part of the

---

[292] Parliamentary Documents 33 622, 2012–2013, nr. 3, explanatory memorandum, pp. 17–18.

[293] Proritering van handhavingsverzoeken door de Autoriteit Consument en Markt, Stcrt. 2016, 14564.

[294] E.g., case *CZ group*, (2004) ECLI:NL:RBROT:2004:AS3852, Rechtbank Rotterdam, 3 December 2004.

[295] E.g. case *Vereniging van Reizigers*, (2010) ECLI:NL:CBB:2010:BN4700, College Beroep voor het Bedrijfsleven, 20 August 2010, par. 7.2.5.1.

[296] Ibid, par. 7.2.1.

[297] Mw, Articles 71–75.

[298] According to Awb, Article 5:53 a report must be drafted if the fine to be imposed exceeds EUR 340. It is clear from the outset that this threshold will be exceeded in virtually every competition law case.

[299] Section 3.5.1 of this chapter.

company or person concerned, pursuant to Article 5:41 Awb. Also, it is set out in Article 5:43 Awb that double jeopardy is not permitted, which means that the principle of *ne bis in idem* must be observed.

The maximum level of the fines that may be imposed for violations of the substantive competition rules is governed by Article 57 Mw. According to Article 57(1) Mw, the maximum level is 900 000 EUR or, if this is more, 10 per cent of the turnover of the undertaking concerned or, in the event of a breach of an association of undertakings, 10 per cent of the turnover of all undertaking being a member of that association. However, it must be noted that the maximum level for breaches of the cartel prohibition is subject to a refined set of conditions, since Article 57(2) Mw sets out the following: the maximum level of such fine should be determined by multiplying the amount calculated on the basis of Article 57(1) Mw, by the number of years of the duration of the offence. As for the calculation to be made, the minimum number of years of the duration is one and the maximum is four. So, if an undertaking participated in a cartel for three years and its turnover is 1 million EUR, the maximum level of the fine is 100 000 * 3, which is 300 000 EUR. It should also be noted that the Dutch rules dealing with the maximum fining levels accommodate the issue of repeat offences. If within five years, the same or a similar violation of the cartel prohibition or of the ban on abuse of dominance occurs, the maximum fining level will be doubled on the basis of Article 57(4) Mw. The term for raising the maximum level will start to run at the moment that the decision by which the fine is imposed for the first time has become final. If a report for the same or a similar infringement has been drawn up within five years, the maximum level will be doubled. So, what matters is the period between the date of the final decision of the first (or previous) offence and the date of the report of the second (or subsequent) offence. So, in some circumstances the maximum level of the fines exceeds the threshold of 10 per cent of the turnover of the undertaking concerned, which differs from the fining competence of the Commission. In section 3.5.3 of this chapter it was put forward that in the EU case-law the threshold of 10 per cent is regarded as a general safeguard ensuring that the principle of proportionality is met. This safeguard seems to be absent in Dutch competition law in the event of cartel offences and repeat offences. For that reason, Veenbrink has argued that the Dutch judiciary should subject fines imposed in those events to a more intense proportionality review than in the case of other offences.[300]

It was outlined in section 4.3 of this chapter that Article 15 of the ECN+ Directive 2019 lays down a minimum requirement for the maximum level of the fine due. This must be 10 per cent of the worldwide turnover of the preceding business year. It is apparent from the discussion above that the Dutch fining rules are in tune with this requirement: the breaches of the cartel prohibition and repeat offences even give rise to maximum fining levels higher than the minimum requirement set out in the Directive. However, it must be pointed out that neither in the current Dutch competition rules, nor in the draft Act implementing the ECN+ Directive 2019 is it specifically provided that the *worldwide* turnover must be the benchmark for calculating the fines to be imposed. The reference is limited solely to the concept of

---

[300] Veenbrink 2020, p. 273.

turnover; in order to guarantee the correct implementation of the Directive into Dutch law, the term 'worldwide' should be added to this concept.[301]

As already stated above, the Minister of Economic Affairs has the authority to direct instructions dealing with policy matters at the ACM. An important example of such an intervention is the adoption of the Boetebeleidsregel ACM 2014 (the Policy rule on ACM fines).[302] This document specifies, in more detail than the relevant Dutch laws do, how the ACM must determine the level of the fines due. In the past, the Dutch competition authority issued its own Guidelines on fines but these were replaced by the instructions of the Minister. According to the Boetebeleidsregel ACM 2014, the point of departure for determining the fine is constituted by the turnover involved in the infringement concerned. The basis of the fines must be a proportion of this turnover, a proportion which ranges between 0 and 50 per cent. Then, the ACM examines which aggravating and mitigating factors must be taken into account. A noteworthy aggravating factor are repeat offences. In that event, the basis fine has to be raised by 100 per cent, unless this is not reasonable given the circumstances. Since the legal maximum level of the fine is doubled for repeat offenders, pursuant to Article 57(4) Mw (as stated above), it is likely that in most cases doubling the basic fine in accordance with the Boetebeleidsregel ACM 2014 will not lead to exceeding the maximum level fixed in this provision of the Mw. An interesting mitigating factor is the circumstance that the undertaking concerned has voluntarily offered compensation to parties having suffered harm. Consequently, the way such an undertaking has operated in private law disputes has its bearing on the level of fine imposed in the public law context.[303]

In contrast with EU competition law, the ACM has the power to impose fines upon managers and other individuals in charge of companies. In Dutch administrative law, this competence is granted by Article 5:1(3) Awb to administrative authorities, among which is the ACM. In this provision, a reference is made to Article 51(2) and (3) of the Dutch Criminal Code (Wetboek van Strafrecht). Accordingly, offences committed by a corporation can be imputed to its 'opdrachtgevers' (instructors) and 'feitelijk leidinggevenden' (de facto managers/actual managers). An instructor could be fined if he has given a specific instruction to infringe a provision of law.[304] A de facto manager/actual manager could be confronted with a fine, if: (1) he/she has not taken any precautionary actions against the infringement concerned, although he was competent to take such actions and had the duty to do so, and (2) he/she has willingly accepted the chance that this infringement will be committed and, therefore, he/she has furthered this illegal practice knowingly.[305]

The Instellingswet lays down the maximum fines for instructors and de facto managers/ actual managers. According to the first paragraph of Article 12n of this Act, the maximum level is 900 000 EUR. The maximum fine of 900 000 EUR is doubled for repeat offenders.[306]

---

[301] Dzino, Van de Gronden and Rusu 2019, p. 544.

[302] Boetebeleidsregel ACM 2014.

[303] Van de Gronden 2017, p. 384.

[304] Ibid, p. 386.

[305] Case *Slavenburg*, (1985) ECLI:NL:PHR:1985:AC9097, Hoge Raad, 19 November 1985.

[306] Intstellingswet ACM, Article 12n(2).

The Boetebeleidsregel ACM 2014 also specifies the conditions to be taken into account by the ACM when fining instructors and *de facto* managers/actual managers.[307] For instance, aggravating and mitigating factors must play a role in the calculation of the fine.

Leniency

In Dutch competition law, a policy on leniency is also in place, as in EU and German competition law. Like the Boetebeleidsregel ACM 2014, the leniency policy is enshrined in instructions given by the Minister to the ACM: the Beleidsregel clementie 2014 (Policy rule on leniency).[308] This document applies only to breaches of the cartel prohibition (contained in Article 6 Mw and Article 101 TFEU). According to Article 4 of Beleidsregel clementie 2014, the ACM grants immunity if the applicant is the first party to a cartel stepping forward in order to provide information enabling the ACM to carry out a specific inspection. Reduction of the fine due (ranging between 30 and 50 per cent) will be granted on the basis of Article 5 of the Beleidsregel clementie 2014, if the applicant is not the first party having stepped forward but nevertheless provides information of significantly additional value. As in EU and German competition law, the Beleidsregel clementie 2014 has introduced a marker system, on the basis of which the applicant is able to complete its request at a later stage. It is reported that leniency applications triggered many enforcement actions: between 2005 and 2009, leniency paved the way for 40 per cent of the cartel offence cases, while with regard to the cases taken up after 2009, the chairman of the board of the ACM has put forward that even more applications were made (although no exact figures were given).[309] As was pointed out in section 4.3.4 of this chapter, the ECN+ Directive 2019 obliges the Member States to lay down the leniency rules in provisions of binding law. The draft Act implementing this Directive proposes to add a new provision to the Mw (Article 58c), giving the government the authority to adopt a decree (delegated legislation) on leniency. So, if this amendment is adopted, the Dutch leniency rules will be contained in binding provisions of law laid down in delegated legislation.

When writing this book, a significant legal debate was being conducted in Dutch competition law as to how the ACM should deal with fining decisions in leniency cases. The College van Beroep voor het bedrijfsleven (Trade and Industry Appeals Tribunal, highest Dutch court in competition law) has held that the ACM is not competent to set the fine at zero in its decision, although immunity was granted to the firm concerned.[310] The case was referred back to the Rechtbank Rotterdam (District Court of Rotterdam, court of first instance in competition law cases), which ruled that the ACM decision should state that no fine was imposed on this undertaking.[311] The question, however, arises whether this is in line with the view of the College van Beroep voor het bedrijfsleven, as this court seems to have ruled that in the event no fine is due, the ACM should refrain from taking any decision finding an infringement

---

[307] Article 2.7 of this Policy rule.

[308] Beleidsregel clementie 2014.

[309] Braat 2018, pp. 70–71.

[310] Case *Clementieverzoek*, (2019) ECLI:NL:CBB:2019:329, College van Beroep voor het Bedrijfsleven, 30 July 2019.

[311] Case *Clementieverzoek*, (2019) ECLI:NL:RBROT:2019:9692, Rechtbank Rotterdam, 12 December 2019.

directed at the undertaking having successfully applied for leniency.[312] If this is true, the question arises whether the current Dutch rules dealing with leniency are compatible with the ECN+ Directive 2019, which requires that Member States have in place rules granting immunity.[313] It should be noted that in the event no official decision is adopted, the undertaking concerned does not have the official guarantee that no fine will be imposed, which would run counter to the rationale of the leniency policy and would, moreover, jeopardise the functioning of this policy due to its lack of predictability. Further case-law on this matter is much needed, but it also seems appropriate that the Dutch government, when issuing a decree on leniency, repairs the deficit resulting from the current debate on the status of the Dutch leniency rules. It should lay down provisions that are crystal clear on the competence of the ACM to take a decision finding an infringement in combination with the non-imposition of a fine on the firm enjoying immunity.

Settlements and informal enforcement

As in EU and German competition law, settlements play a role in competition law cases in the Netherlands.[314] The ACM has adopted the Richtsnoeren vereenvoudiging afdoening van boetezaken (the ACM's Guidelines for Simplified Resolution of Cases Involving a Fine),[315] dealing with a system that has a lot in common with the EU experience with settlements. In these Guidelines, the conditions are set out for applying this mechanism: the parties are, inter alia, obliged to acknowledge the facts and the legal assessment of these facts made by the ACM, they have to accept the method of calculating the fine, as well as the level of the actual fine. In return, the undertakings involved are entitled to a reduction of 10 per cent of the fine calculated. Moreover, it is outlined that the ACM will take the initiative to contact the firms concerned if the case under review seems to be fit for a simplified resolution in its view.

In addition to the official enforcement approaches outlined above, it must be noted that in some cases the ACM deals with the infringement in an informal fashion. For example, the ACM contacted two universities that were colluding on tuition fees (not fixed in the Dutch laws on higher education). After this anti-competitive practice was terminated by these institutions, the ACM decided not to take any formal enforcement decision.[316] On the one hand, informal action may be very efficient and may lead to swift resolution of the dispute

---

[312] Outhuijse 2020, p. 227.

[313] Ibid.

[314] On this matter, see Lachnit 2016, pp. 140–43.

[315] Available at <https://www.acm.nl/sites/default/files/documents/richtsnoeren-vereenvoudigde-afdoening-van-boetezaken-acm-380605.pdf> accessed 24 June 2020. The English translation is available at <https://www.acm.nl/sites/default/files/documents/2019-01/acms-guidelines-for-simplified-resolution-of-cases-involving-a-fine.pdf> accessed 24 November 2020.

[316] See Press Release of 13 July 2012, NMa accepteert maatregelen van de Uva en VU; at that time the name of the Dutch competition authority was Nederlandse Mededingingsautoriteit/NMa, Netherlands competition authority, available at <https://www.acm.nl/nl/publicaties/publicatie/10780/NMa-accepteert-maatregelen-van-UvA-en-VU> accessed 24 June 2020.

at issue, but on the other hand, such an action cannot be challenged in court and does not establish a reliable precedent.[317]

Periodic penalties

Article 56 Mw grants to the ACM the power to impose not only fines, but also periodic penalties. In the past, prior to the imposition of a penalty the drafting of a report was required in Dutch competition law. This obligation was, however, lifted[318] as such a requirement prevented the ACM from taking swift enforcement action in the view of the national legislature.[319] Article 58a Mw provides that a periodic penalty may include a structural measure, provided that this measure is proportionate and necessary for terminating the infringement concerned. Moreover, structural measures are only permitted if behavioural remedies are less effective or more intrusive for the parties concerned. In the view of the Dutch legislature, adopting a structural measure is a last resort remedy.[320] As was outlined in section 4.3 of this chapter, Article 10 of the ECN+ Directive 2019 requires, inter alia, that an NCA has the power to adopt structural measures. This is already regulated in Dutch competition law. It should be noted that unlike in EU and German competition law, this power is part of the competence to impose periodic penalties.

Appeals

The sanctions imposed by the ACM can be challenged, as is apparent from the foregoing, before the Rechtbank Rotterdam (District Court of Rotterdam) in first instance, and before College van Beroep voor het bedrijfsleven (Trade and Industry Appeals Tribunal) in last instance. Although it is apparent from Article 56 Mw, the ACM enjoys wide discretion when, inter alia, setting fines, these courts will subject these sanctions to a full review, since fines qualify as punitive sanctions for the purposes of Article 6 ECHR and Article 47 of the Charter of Fundamental Rights of the EU.[321] This level of review is also required by Article 3:4 Awb, which deals with the duty to balance interests.[322] The full review deployed by the Dutch competition law courts largely mirrors the full review the EU courts carry out on the basis of case-law such as *Chalkor*, *KME* and *Menarini*.[323] In this regard, it is noteworthy that the full review carried out by the judiciary and the expertise of the courts handling ACM cases is seen, together with some other factors, as important reasons explaining the high success rates

---

[317] Cf. also Lachnit 2016, pp. 306–8.

[318] Stroomlijningswet ACM (Act streamlining the ACM powers and proceedings), Stb. 2014, 247 and Stb. 2014, 265.

[319] Kamerstukken II 2012–2013, nr. 3, p. 19.

[320] Kamerstukken II 30 071, nr. 3, p. 11.

[321] E.g. cases *Shrimps*, (2011) ECLI:NL:CBB:2011:BP8077, College Beroep voor het bedrijfsleven, 17 March 2011; *Bicycle cartel*, (2011) ECLI:NL:CBB:BT, College Beroep voor het bedrijfsleven, 4 October 2011; *Aesculaap*, (2006) ECLI:NL:RBROT:2006:AX8428, Rechtbank Rotterdam, 13 June 2006.

[322] Slot, Swaak and Mulder 2012, pp. 191–2.

[323] Section 3.5.3 of this chapter.

of litigation in Dutch competition law: many ACM decisions are partly or entirely annulled in appeal proceedings.[324]

5 CONCLUSIONS

Over time, the powers to enforce competition law have increased considerably. The toolkit of the Commission has been extended and, next to the formal enforcement powers, an informal approach based on consensual resolution with undertakings has also been developed. It is also clear that the modernisation process of Regulation 1/2003 leading to decentralisation of the enforcement of EU competition law has led to significant changes. The NCAs are now important players, when it comes to taking action on the basis of the EU competition rules. As a result, not only the toolkit of the Commission but also the toolkits of the NCAs have been extended. Remarkably, this is the result of measures taken by both the EU and national legislatures. It is clear from the outset that the ECN+ Directive 2019 ensures that NCAs will have a minimum set of enforcement powers in competition law. On top of that, national initiatives, such as the draft GWB-Digitalisierungsgesetz, show that also national laws giving more competences to NCAs are adopted. In this regard, it should be noted that the EU competition rules and the EU norms facilitating the enforcement of these rules function in the arena of national law. The reception of these EU provisions by the national legal order may give rise to legal debates, as is, for example, testified by the recent Dutch case-law on leniency. The interplay between EU and national enforcement rules may put national legal traditions under some pressure. In our view, striking a balance between the need to ensure the uniform application of the EU competition rules and the respect for the various national legal orders is a delicate matter. Close cooperation between the Commission and the NCAs in a setting of multi-layered governance may greatly contribute to striking this balance. The need for this cooperation, in combination with the call for taking swift action, which could be a harsh issue in the time-consuming competition law proceedings, is also demonstrated by the emerging digital markets.[325] On the one hand, these (rapidly evolving) markets do not stop at the border of a particular Member State, and on the other hand, these markets do not wait for the Commission and the NCAs to complete their lengthy proceedings. In other words, the enforcement of the competition rules will lead to many challenges to meet in the future. It goes without saying that these challenges have become more urgent due to the Corona crisis of 2020. In this crisis, many businesses and consumers have become increasingly dependent on big digital networks, which shows that prompt action is needed if the operation of these networks has become subject to anti-competitive practices.

---

[324] Outhuijse 2019, pp. 208–9.

[325] Steenbergen 2020, p. 11.

9

Private enforcement of the EU antitrust rules

1 INTRODUCTION

Chapter 7 dealt with the main themes regarding enforcement of the EU antitrust rules, namely Articles 101 and 102 TFEU. We have shown that the EU antitrust prohibitions have been traditionally enforced via public enforcement mechanisms by the Commission, and since the entry into force of Regulation 1/2003, also by the NCAs and domestic courts.[1] The public enforcement system was extensively discussed in Chapter 8. It is now time to direct the attention to the private enforcement mechanisms of the EU antitrust rules, since the consumers, customers or competitors of the undertakings that infringed these rules are entitled to claim reparation in front of the national courts for the injury incurred. Therefore, these subjects may also enforce Articles 101 and 102 TFEU through the private law instruments available in the Member States.

The chapter at hand will first deal with the prerequisites of private enforcement. It distinguishes between the different legal avenues available to the antitrust infringement victims, it explains the roles different entities play in private enforcement actions, and it dwells upon the conditions that need to be fulfilled for successful damages claims. Next, the EU case-law and soft-law landmarks that shaped the EU private enforcement developments are analysed. Further, the provisions of the Private Damages Directive 2014 are discussed at length, highlighting the harmonisation effect of the various domestic private law provisions it has brought about. The discussion surrounding this Directive's provisions is grouped around the key questions that define the exercise of the right to claim damages: who can claim damages, when and how can they do so, who should pay the damages and what exactly should be paid? Importantly, in the context of such questions, this chapter also sheds light on the balance between important public enforcement tools (such as leniency programmes) and private enforcement mechanisms. Since the latest developments in the field cover primarily actions for damages, and given that such actions are the ones most often encountered in practice, the main focus of this chapter will be placed on damages claims, while other mechanisms of private enforcement, such as injunctions and collective redress tools are touched upon primarily for the sake of completeness.

---

[1] Rusu 2017 (a), p. 796.

The core of this chapter is built around the framework established by the Private Damages Directive 2014. This is so, because in our opinion, this instrument will be at the heart of the development of private enforcement in the EU in the years to come. Indeed, one of the objectives of the Directive is to foster actions for damages in the EU Member States. The Directive aims to achieve this goal by first codifying domestic rules and principles already existing in some national jurisdictions, and second by inserting new rules relating to various aspects of actions for damages. While the above endeavours are meant to ensure a level playing enforcement field when it comes to such private law actions, the Directive is likely to have a different impact in the diverse European jurisdictions.[2] This is why, in the chapter at hand, our focus on the approaches adopted in the domestic jurisdictions will differ from the previous chapters: the attention will be primarily directed at the manner in which the provisions of the Private Damages Directive 2014 were implemented in some of the domestic legal orders.

2 THE BASICS OF PRIVATE ENFORCEMENT

2.1 Actors in private enforcement

As previewed above, when the TFEU and national competition law provisions are infringed, it may very well be the case that certain subjects incur some sort of injury. Such injury may occur in practice in the form of (financial or economic) loss, due to, for example, over-charges resulting from price fixing cartels. In such settings, the customers of the cartelists pay more for the cartelised products, than they would have paid in absence of an infringement. Should these customers, or in other words direct purchasers, resell the cartelised product on a downstream market, the end-consumers (i.e. indirect purchasers in this example) are the ones incurring losses, if the direct purchasers incorporate the cartel overcharge in the price charged on the downstream market. The same rationale is also valid for abuses of dominant positions, particularly when we are talking about exploitative excessive prices. However, when it comes to Article 102 TFEU, it may also be the case that business interests of undertakings may suffer due to competition law infringements, as is the case if a dominant undertaking eliminates its competitors from the market.[3] The victims of all these kinds of infringements, namely the customers, consumers and competitors of the infringers may have an interest in using competition law to disrupt such practices and to claim compensation for the loss suffered.

However, the incentives to do so vary depending on the type of infringement and the position of the entity that suffers the injury. In the price fixing cartel example above, the customers of the infringers (i.e. those undertakings that buy inputs from the infringers) have less incentive to take action than competitors. This is so because, first, while having a better understanding of the market functioning than end-consumers, they are in a position where

---

[2] Parcu, Monti and Botta 2018, pp. 9–10.

[3] E.g. the exclusionary abuses that are the focus of the Enforcement Priorities Guidelines 2009.

they can pass on the cartel overcharge in the downstream market, and second, they may wish not to jeopardise the business relationship with their (potentially long-term) suppliers.[4] Competitors, on the other hand, may at first sight be more inclined to use competition law to bring an end to illegal practices or to compensate their losses. Similar to customers, they too are undertakings operating on a market, the functioning of which they assumedly understand. Their incentives to take action differ though, depending on the consequences of the infringement. Should they be excluded from the market due to a predatory pricing abuse of dominance for example, the competitors have all the right reasons to sue. If they operate on the same market as the price fixing cartelists however, they may think twice before bringing the infringers to court: this is so, as we will detail below when focusing on the 'umbrella pricing' phenomenon, since they may increase their prices to the cartelised market pricing level, and thus boost their revenues accordingly. Last but not least, the end-consumers in all these scenarios are the ones in the weakest position. From the outset, it is most often that the end-consumer will incur the financial overcharge of a competition law infringement, due to direct exploitative behaviour of monopolists, or due to the passing-on of (cartel) overcharges on the downstream markets. Yet, the end-consumer, despite having incentives to take action for compensating its loss, encounters the greatest obstacles to do so: it has very little information about the market functioning, it has limited resources in battling most often much stronger suppliers, and in most cases it experiences difficulties in engaging in collective actions together with other victims of the same infringement.[5] On top of this, more often than not, when looked at individually, the claims of end-consumers can be regarded as rather small.

Nevertheless, the main purpose of the private enforcement mechanisms is to allow and stimulate the victims of antitrust infringements, be they customers, consumers or competitors, to capitalise on these incentives, thus achieving the goal of corrective justice.[6]

2.2　Direct effect of the EU antitrust provisions and the role of domestic ambits

Victims of antitrust infringements may take enforcement action based on Articles 101 and 102 TFEU since these provisions have direct effect. The provisions of these articles are clear, unconditional and do not require implementing measures.[7] In *BRT v SABAM*,[8] the CJEU made clear that, as the antitrust prohibitions tend by their very nature to produce direct effects in relations between individuals, these articles create direct rights in respect of the individuals concerned, which the national courts must safeguard. Thus, the prohibitions embedded in Articles 101 and 102 TFEU have horizontal direct effect. Furthermore, this means that the victims of the infringement, as plaintiffs, may take the infringers, who are the

---

[4] Graham 2010, p. 280.

[5] On this matter, see Monti 2007, pp. 431–5.

[6] Jones, Sufrin and Dunne 2019, p. 1023.

[7] Case 26/62 *Van Gend en Loos*, ECLI:EU:C:1963:1.

[8] Case C-127/73 *BRT v SABAM*, ECLI:EU:C:1974:25, par. 15, 16.

addressees of the EU antitrust rules, to court as defendants, in order to obtain compensation for the loss incurred, or to bring an end to the illicit practice.

Despite the fact that the antitrust prohibitions discussed so far are anchored in EU law, and as we will detail in the coming paragraphs, the right itself to claim damages being also grounded in the TFEU provisions, the Commission and the EU courts do not have the competence to award damages.[9] Given the direct effect of the TFEU antitrust provisions, the victims of antitrust law infringements exercise their rights before the domestic private law courts, using domestic procedures and remedies, by virtue of the Member States' national procedural autonomy principle. This means that where EU law does not establish concrete procedural rules on the matter, the Member States' legal systems designate the courts having jurisdiction and determine the procedural conditions governing actions at law intended to ensure the protection of rights which citizens have from the direct effect of EU law. This procedural autonomy is not unlimited though, because the Member States, while observing their duty of sincere cooperation[10] and their obligation to guarantee effective judicial protection of the EU rights,[11] must make sure that the EU effectiveness and equivalence principles are observed: national rules may not make the exercise of the EU rights that domestic courts must protect virtually impossible or excessively difficult, and national procedures for EU rights enforcement must be equivalent to domestic rights enforcement procedures.[12]

As we will detail below, the principles of effectiveness and equivalence played an important role in shaping the manner in which damages actions based on EU law are conceived in the domestic ambits. These principles serve as a safe-net of protection afforded to the victims of antitrust infringements. Furthermore, the principles of effectiveness and equivalence continue to play a role in this respect, even after the latest legislative developments in the field brought about by the harmonising effect of the Private Damages Directive 2014.[13]

2.3 Types of private enforcement mechanisms

When using private enforcement mechanisms, the victims of antitrust enforcement have various avenues readily available to enforce their rights. Different categorisations of the private law actions which may be embarked on have been established. First, victims of antitrust infringements may choose to claim their rights in individual actions, or in class or collective actions. With regard to the latter, such actions are useful when economic harm is caused to a large number of natural and/or legal persons that choose to overcome the risk and costs of bringing individual actions, by bundling such single claims into a single court proceeding.[14] Collective redress actions may thus counterbalance the lack of resources normally faced by individual claimants (most often end-consumers or indirect purchasers) and may ensure a

---

[9] Whish and Bailey 2012, p. 297.

[10] Article 4(3) TEU.

[11] Article 19(1) TEU.

[12] Cases 33/76 *Rewe*, ECLI:EU:C:1976:188, par. 5; 45/76 *Comet*, ECLI:EU:C:1976:191, par. 13.

[13] Private Damages Directive 2014, Article 4.

[14] For more on this matter, see Whish and Bailey 2018, p. 323.

better access to justice to those who would normally be deterred from bringing individual actions. While class actions are more common in the US, in the EU, the availability of collective redress mechanisms is still a matter that ranges from Member State to Member State. We will return to this discussion in section 4.5 of this chapter.

A different categorisation pertaining primarily to individual actions (but to a certain extent also to collective actions)[15] distinguishes between compensatory actions and actions for injunctive relief. Injunctions are often used when the victim of an infringement needs to take immediate court action to halt an alleged anti-competitive behaviour. An example in this respect relates to businesses threatened with expulsion from the market due to alleged exclusionary behaviour of dominant undertakings. Making use of court injunction proceedings offers a faster route than public enforcement proceedings of NCAs, based on complaints, even if only for a temporary cessation of the alleged anti-competitive behaviour.[16] Compensatory actions, or actions for damages, on the other hand, pertain to some sort of loss incurred due to the anti-competitive behaviour, be it financial loss due to anti-competitive overcharges (potentially passed on to indirect purchasers), loss of profit and/or investment caused to a competitor, and so on. Such actions are geared towards compensating the loss incurred by the antitrust infringement victims.

Closely connected to the categorisation above is the distinction between the so-called 'sword' and 'shield' actions. The former entails the claimant relying on competition law when bringing a case against the alleged infringers, in order to stop the practice and/or obtain compensation for the loss. The latter refers to defendants using competition law as a defence against claims made by the infringer.[17] For example, defendants may use 'shield' actions in connection with alleged abuses of dominant positions where royalty payments are requested for IP licensing agreements. Other examples may also be nullity actions, where the defendant shields itself from a potential breach of contract, or claims of payments being owed, by arguing that the contract at hand infringes competition law and is thus (absolutely) null and void. This is particularly relevant in the context of using Article 101(2) TFEU as a so-called 'Euro-defence' against the contractual clauses which infringe Article 101(1) TFEU.[18]

Moving on, particularly (yet not exclusively) when it comes to actions for damages, private enforcement actions may be categorised as 'follow-on' or 'stand-alone' actions. The former entails a public enforcement decision/judgment finding an EU antitrust infringement, which the victim 'follows-on', by proving all the remaining elements for a successful claim, such as the loss suffered, the causal relationship between the infringement and the loss, and any other conditions required by the applicable domestic laws. In practice, it turns out that most

---

[15] E.g. Recommendation on Collective Redress 2013, Recital 9.

[16] Rodger and MacCulloch 2015, Chapter 3.

[17] Graham 2010, pp. 280–81.

[18] Rodger and MacCulloch 2015, Chapter 3. Despite the wording of Article 101 TFEU, the CJEU held in case 56/65 *Société Technique Minière*, ECLI:EU:C:1966:38, that the nullity provided in Article 101(2) TFEU only affects the individual clauses infringing Article 101(1) TFEU. Thus, the agreement as a whole is void only when those clauses are not severable from the rest of the agreement. See also Jones, Sufrin and Dunne 2019, p. 1031.

actions take the form of follow-on proceedings,[19] given primarily the limited resources individual claimants have in proving the existence of an antitrust infringement. The latter (i.e. stand-alone actions) are independent of enforcement actions of public authorities, and arise because NCAs or the Commission will not deal with a complaint, because the victim starts injunction actions, as discussed above, or because the victims aim to obtain compensation for the loss suffered. In this scenario, the injured party must prove the presence of all constitutive elements of the claim in order to obtain redress, including the existence of the infringement (which in follow-on actions is proven by a competition authority or a court).[20] For the sake of completeness, at times, follow-on actions may include a stand-alone claim, where the claimant is of the opinion that the unlawful behaviour was more extensive than established in the competition authority's decision.[21]

The last point of this discussion, at least for now, relates to the general conditions that must be fulfilled for damages claims based on EU antitrust infringements to be successful. As indicated above, classic private law theory prescribes a three-prong formula in this respect: (1) infringement of the law, (2) loss, and (3) causality between the two. Most EU Member States did not have in place specific regulations dealing with damages stemming from competition law infringements, at least not until the Private Damages Directive 2014 was implemented in their respective legal orders. Instead, general rules of damages applicable in tort (for breach of statutory duty) are used by the domestic courts for these purposes. It is thus not surprising that certain domestic civil law systems add extra elements to the three-prong recipe mentioned above: the majority of the national private law systems require establishing the infringer's fault, one way or the other: fault in relation to the infringement, in relation of the effects of the infringement, fault that may be rebutted, fault that is automatically presumed when an infringement of competition law occurs, and so on.[22] For example, Article 6:162 of the Dutch Civil Code refers to unlawful acts that can be *attributed* to the person who committed them. Also, Article 131(1) of the Slovenian Obligations code points to the liability of those who caused damages to compensate those damages, if they cannot prove that the damage has occurred without their *fault*. Article 62 of the Slovenian Competition Act further refers to damages arising from the *deliberate or negligent* violation of the competition law provisions. Also, some domestic systems, as in the UK for example, may additionally require that the statute's intention is to protect the victim against the damage.[23] From an institutional perspective, the choices made in the Member States regarding the courts competent to rule on private damages actions differ too. For example, in Romania, after the Private Damages Directive 2014 was implemented, the competent court to hear actions for damages stemming from competition law infringements is the Bucharest Tribunal, with two consecutive appeals possible, before the Bucharest Court of Appeal and

---

[19] Private Damages Directive 2014, Recital 26. See also Monti 2007, pp. 434–6.

[20] Rusu 2017 (a), p. 798.

[21] Whish and Bailey 2018, p. 307.

[22] Ashurst Report 2004.

[23] For further details on this matter, see e.g. Davidson 1985; Matthews 1984; Rodger 2003; Rusu 2017 (a).

the High Court of Cassation and Justice.[24] In the UK, a claimant seeking a remedy for an infringement of EU or UK competition law can bring an action either in the High Court (based on the Civil Procedure Rules) or in the Competition Appeal Tribunal (based on the Competition Act 1998 and the Competition Appeal Tribunal Rules 2015), the former being also able to transfer cases to the latter, based on Section 16 of the Enterprise Act 2002.[25] Choosing one of these two options comes with advantages and disadvantages. For example, before the High Court competition claims may be combined with other claims, such as a breach of contract or patent infringement. The Competition Appeal Tribunal, on the other hand, is a specialised competition forum, that has flexible procedures that may offer a faster and less expensive resolution in some cases.[26]

3 THE EU RIGHT TO CLAIM DAMAGES: CASE-LAW DEVELOPMENTS

So far, several mentions have been made of antitrust infringement victims being able to bring actions in front of the domestic courts. Also, indications were provided above that this right relates also to infringements of the EU antitrust rules. The question that follows naturally is how was this right developed in EU law?

The TFEU is silent on the matter of individual liability for damages relating to antitrust infringements. This statement also stands for Member State liability for damages for loss resulting from EU law infringements, for that matter. In this last respect, a reading of Article 19(1) TEU would indicate that such claims for damages should unfold before the domestic courts, since it is the Member States – and therefore not the EU – that must provide remedies sufficient to ensure effective legal protection in the fields covered by EU law.[27] Two aspects need to be briefly mentioned in this context: first, the failure of a Member State to fulfil its EU Treaties obligations (thus infringing EU law) is enforced by the Commission under Article 258 TFEU. However, this is a matter of public enforcement, which does not address the issue of damages resulting from the Member State's behaviour. Therefore, second, the issue of compensating the victims of such infringements for the loss incurred must be tackled. In several cases,[28] the CJEU clarified that the defaulting Member State must compensate the victims, if the EU law rule infringed is intended to confer rights on individuals, the breach is sufficiently serious, and a causal link between the breach and the loss incurred by the victims exists. This is the principle of state liability for damages, which establishes the right to compensation, flowing directly from EU law. The compensation is to

---

[24] Government Ordinance 39/2017, OJ 422/2017, Article 4.

[25] E.g. case *Sainsbury's v Mastercard*, (2015) EWHC 3472 (Ch), (2016) CAT 11.

[26] Whish and Bailey 2018, pp. 326–8.

[27] Wilman 2016, pp. 890–91.

[28] Joined cases C-6 and C-9/90 *Francovich and Bonifaci*, ECLI:EU:C:1991:428; joined cases C-46 and C-48/93 *Brasserie du Pêcheur*, ECLI:EU:C:1996:79; joined cases C-178, C-179, C-188, C-189 and C-190/94 *Dillenkofer*, ECLI:EU:C:1996:375.

be made good via national procedures unfolding before domestic courts, since as mentioned above, EU law does not set out procedural rules generally applicable to remedies relating to EU law. This discussion[29] is important since the principle of state liability for damages essentially forms the basis for establishing the EU right to damages stemming from EU antitrust infringements, acknowledged for the first time in the *Courage and Crehan* case.[30] The CJEU's rationale in this case, and the breadth of the EU right to claim damages in the context of antitrust infringements, were later on developed in rulings such as *Manfredi*, *Otis*, and *Kone*, among others.[31] It is therefore important to delve into these cases, in order to correctly understand the role the CJEU has played throughout time in laying the groundwork for the development of private enforcement of the EU antitrust rules, especially in the absence of a concrete EU procedural framework fostering damages claims stemming from the infringement of those rules.[32]

3.1 *Courage and Crehan*

The importance of this ruling cannot be overstated. As will become evident below in this chapter, the 2001 *Courage and Crehan* landmark judgment shaped to a great extent the later developments of private enforcement of the EU antitrust rules.[33] Briefly, the facts of this case are as follows: Crehan leased a pub in the UK and committed to sell Courage beer only. When Crehan found himself in a situation of not being able to pay for the beer he purchased, Courage sued for the recovery of the amounts owed. Crehan claimed that the beer supply agreement breached Article 101 TFEU and was consequently null and void according to Article 101(2) TFEU. Furthermore, Crehan argued that his business went bankrupt due to the 'beer tie' and therefore asked for damages caused by the infringement of Article 101(1) TFEU. The case reached the CJEU through a preliminary ruling reference from the English Court of Appeal, based on Article 267 TFEU.

The CJEU essentially had to clarify whether a party to a (vertical supply) contract liable to restrict competition can rely (in a shield-type action) on an Article 101 TFEU breach, to obtain relief from the other contracting party. Next, the Court had to elucidate on whether EU law precludes national rules that deny the right to rely on one's own illegal actions to

---

[29] For more on this matter, see Rusu 2017 (a), p. 799.

[30] Case C-453/99 *Courage and Crehan*, ECLI:EU:C:2001:465. Prior to the *Courage and Crehan* ruling of the CJEU, the issue of liability for European competition law infringements arose in case C-128/92 *Banks & Co Ltd v British Coal Corporation*, ECLI:EU:C:1994:130. The Court, however, did not deal with the matter of bringing actions for damages in front of the domestic court, since Articles 65 and 66 of the ECSC Treaty, which were allegedly infringed, were not directly applicable. See Braat 2018, p. 94.

[31] Joined cases C-295 to C-298/04 *Manfredi*, ECLI:EU:C:2006:461; cases C-199/11 *Otis*, ECLI:EU:C:2012:684; C-557/12 *Kone*, ECLI:EU:C:2014:1317.

[32] Some of these cases unfolded after the entry into force of the Private Damages Directive 2014, although the facts may have taken place before this time frame. We will therefore discuss various aspects of some of these cases in different sections of this chapter.

[33] Whish and Bailey 2018, p. 509; Rodger and MacCulloch 2015, Chapter 3; Graham 2010, p. 295 *et seq.*

obtain damages.[34] In this light, some authors[35] argue that the core problem in *Courage and Crehan* was not the existence in EU law of a right to bring antitrust damages actions per se, but to establish whether a party to a contract which infringes EU antitrust law can be excluded from such actions related to that contract; the CJEU was thus summoned to draw the limits to be imposed to the application of national procedural rules. The Court, while citing classic case-law that emphasises the unique nature of the EU legal order,[36] commenced by highlighting in paragraph 19 of the ruling that EU law imposes burdens on, but also gives rights to individuals, rights which arise not only when expressly granted by the Treaty, but also by virtue of obligations clearly imposed by the Treaty on individuals, Member States and EU institutions. Then, in paragraph 20 it reminds us that Article 101 TFEU is a fundamental provision, essential for accomplishing the EU tasks, specifically the functioning of the Internal Market. Further, as already pointed out above, the Court reiterated that the nullity of anti-competitive agreements embedded in Article 101(2) TFEU is absolute. In paragraph 22 it is argued that this rationale can be relied on by anyone, since anti-competitive agreements produce no effects between the contracting parties and cannot be enforced against third parties. In paragraphs 23 and 25 of the judgment the Court recalls that the EU antitrust provisions have horizontal direct effect, and therefore the domestic courts must safeguard the rights they create for individuals. Consequently, the Court rules in paragraph 24 that any individual is able to rely on breaches of these provisions, even as parties to contracts liable to restrict competition. The Court then proceeds to support its rationale by pointing out in paragraphs 26 and 27 that such a right strengthens the full effectiveness and functionality of EU antitrust law. Lastly, the domestic legal ambits, via their national procedural autonomy, and while observing the effectiveness and equivalence principles (paragraph 29), must ensure that unjust enrichment is avoided (paragraph 30), and that litigants bearing significant responsibility for the infringement do not benefit from their unlawful conduct (paragraphs 31 to 33).[37]

All in all, by establishing the EU right to claim damages, stemming directly from Articles 101 and 102 TFEU, the CJEU fostered a more meaningful private law enforcement of these rules.[38] Yet, many questions remained unanswered, since in the absence of EU harmonising rules on the matter, many procedural issues relating to the actual recovery of damages continued to depend on domestic law.[39] It comes hardly as a surprise that, after the CJEU's ruling in *Courage and Crehan*, many years of litigation followed in the domestic UK courts, before a final resolution of the original dispute was reached: the Court of Appeal awarded Mr

---

[34] Rusu 2017 (a), pp. 799–800.

[35] Braat 2018, p. 95, referring to Cisotta 2014.

[36] Case 26/62 *Van Gend en Loos*, ECLI:EU:C:1963:1; joined cases C-6 and C-9/90 *Francovich and Bonifaci*, ECLI:EU:C:1991:428; case 6/64 *Costa v E.N.E.L.*, ECLI:EU:C:1964:66.

[37] Rusu 2017 (a), pp. 799–800.

[38] Leczykiewikz 2013; Bucan 2013; Drake 2006; Temple Lang 2006.

[39] See, in this respect, the criticism put forward by Braat 2018, p. 98 and Monti 2007, p. 427 *et seq.*, especially when it comes to establishing the significance of the responsibility borne by the parties to a contract infringing the antitrust rules.

Crehan little over £130 000 in damages. This award was later on overturned by the House of Lords.[40] This court held that the UK courts must not defer to the findings of the Commission decision[41] relied upon by Mr Crehan, a decision that found a similar agreement as the 'beer tie' at issue in Mr Crehan's case to be infringing the EU cartel prohibition.[42]

3.2 *Manfredi*

The opportunity to build upon the domestic procedural leftovers of the *Courage and Crehan* ruling, and thus to further shape the domestic laws' role in the private enforcement of EU competition law context,[43] occurred in the 2006 *Manfredi* preliminary ruling case. Once again, we first need to get acquainted with the facts of this case: several insurance companies engaged in various exchanges of information between themselves, the effect of which was the increase of the premiums to be paid for compulsory civil liability insurance relating to accidents caused by various types of vehicles. The Italian competition authority and the domestic competent court decided that the information exchanges breached the (Italian and EU) cartel prohibition provisions. Manfredi (and other customers of the insurance companies involved in the cartel) sued for repayment of the overcharge resulting from the increased insurance premiums. The CJEU was called upon to answer several questions relating to the compatibility of the Italian domestic (procedural) rules with EU law, in the context of actions for damages connected with infringements of the EU antitrust provisions.

In the parts of the ruling which are relevant for the discussion at hand, the Court started by repeating almost word by word the *Courage and Crehan* rationale. In paragraph 56 to 60 it is first recalled that any individual can rely in front of the domestic courts on the invalidity of an agreement prohibited under the directly effective Article 101 TFEU and that this right strengthens the full effectiveness of the cartel prohibition. Then, in paragraphs 61 and 63 the Court rules that such victims of antitrust infringements may claim compensation where causality exists between the infringement and the harm suffered. However, the Court continues in paragraphs 62 and 64, in the absence of EU law on the matter, deference is afforded to the domestic procedural ambits in which damages claims unfold, when discussing the application of the causality concept. This is also the case when it comes to the limitation periods for starting actions in the domestic courts: it is for the domestic legal system of each Member State to prescribe the limitation period for seeking compensation for harm caused by an agreement or practice (paragraph 81). Thus, for both the causation issue and the limitation periods matter, the Court emphasised that these are points pertaining to the domestic procedural autonomy of the Member States, however, very importantly, under the obligation to observe the equivalence and effectiveness principles (paragraphs 64 and 81). Actually, in paragraphs 78, 79 and 82 the CJEU specifically detailed how short or non-suspensory domestic limitation periods infringe the effectiveness principle. Lastly,

---

[40] Case *Inntrepreneur Pub Company (CPC) and Others v Crehan*, (2006) UKHL 38.

[41] Case IV/35.079/F3 *Whitbread*, (1999) OJ L 88/26.

[42] Marco Colino 2011, p. 130.

[43] Van de Gronden 2017, p. 267.

the Court used the same rationale relating to the absence of EU law on the matter and the importance of respecting the effectiveness and equivalence principles, when discussing the award of punitive damages (i.e. damages greater than the advantage obtained by the infringers, awarded to ensure deterrence from engaging in anti-competitive practices). Starting with paragraph 89, it is made clear once again that the EU right to claim damages improves the EU antitrust rules' full effectiveness and functionality; however, when EU law does not provide rules on establishing the extent of the damages to be awarded, designing the criteria in this respect pertains to the domestic legal ambits, which must observe the effectiveness and equivalence criteria (paragraph 92). So, as is evident from paragraph 99 of the ruling, awarding punitive damages is not prohibited per se. But, the domestic laws must also ensure that unjust enrichment is avoided (paragraphs 94 and 99) and that the heads of damages, which the compensation should cover, include the actual loss – *damnum emergens*, the loss of profit – *lucrum cessans*, plus interest (paragraphs 95 and 100). While compensation for actual loss seems to be logical, in paragraphs 96 and 97 the CJEU felt the need to briefly explain the (economically and commercially driven) rationale for also considering the loss of profit and the interest as essential components of the compensation matter.[44]

The *Manfredi* ruling developed the discussion surrounding the EU right to claim damages. It clarified how the Member States' legal regimes should design important (procedural) elements of damages actions based on EU antitrust infringements. It has also highlighted the extremely important role that the effectiveness and equivalence principles play in the context of national procedural autonomy, although, especially in relation to the effectiveness principle, interpretation problems continued to linger.[45] Furthermore, despite the Court's enthusiasm for damages actions, concrete problems still remained also in relation to the Member States' substantive rules of recovery in tort, delict, restitutionary and other actions.[46] Nevertheless, the *Manfredi* ruling has drawn a more concrete dimension of the EU law/ national law interaction in the private enforcement of EU antitrust infringements.[47]

3.3 *Otis*

The 2012 *Otis*, 2014 *Kone* and 2019 *Otis II* CJEU preliminary rulings, related to the infamous elevators and escalators bid rigging cartel, further qualified the EU right to claim damages for loss resulting from EU antitrust infringements. This cartel involved Otis, Kone, Schindler and ThyssenKrupp, undertakings which allocated tenders and other contracts between themselves, in order to share markets and fix prices. The *Otis* case concerned the following jurisdictions: Belgium, Germany, Luxembourg and the Netherlands. The *Kone* case concerned the

---

[44] Rusu 2017 (a), p. 800.

[45] Jones, Sufrin and Dunne 2019, pp. 1039–42, referring primarily to Nebbia 2008 and Nazzini 2011, thoroughly debate the interpretation of the principle of effectiveness, in relation to whether its core purpose is the attainment of corrective justice, or it is to be regarded as a simple tool to increase enforcement and deter violations. See also Monti 2007, p. 429.

[46] Whish and Bailey, 2018, p. 310.

[47] Van de Gronden 2017; Afferni 2007; Rusu 2017 (a); Nebbia 2007.

same cartel, however it unfolded in the Austrian jurisdiction, on which the Commission did not focus in the *Otis* case.[48]

In *Otis*, the Court dealt with issues surrounding the principle of effective judicial protection[49] and also the private enforcement of the EU antitrust rules. To be more specific, the Court had to answer preliminary questions relating to the interpretation of the law in a situation where the Commission acted as both public enforcer having adopted an Article 101 TFEU infringement decision, and as a representative of the EU institutions which were victims of the said cartel, in a follow-on civil action for damages before the Belgian competent court. With regard to the private enforcement elements of the ruling, the Court unsurprisingly commenced by pointing to the main findings of the *Courage and Crehan* and *Manfredi* rulings: in paragraph 40 the right of any individual to rely on antitrust breaches and consequently on the invalidity of the prohibited practices is recalled; then, in paragraphs 41 and 42, the full effectiveness and practical effect of the cartel prohibition are brought in as substantiating arguments in respect of the importance of the right to claim damages, a right which strengthens the working of the EU antitrust rules and deters practices liable to restrict competition; thus, in paragraph 43, the Court repeats the *Manfredi* assertion that any person can claim compensation for the harm suffered where a causal link between the infringement and the loss exists. For the sake of clarity, the Court dedicates one brief paragraph of the ruling (paragraph 44) to stating that the EU (represented in this case by the Commission) also enjoys the right to claim damages. In paragraph 77 the Court builds up on this assertion and concludes by stating that the Commission is thus not precluded from starting domestic proceedings to fulfil the EU's right to compensation, without the defendants' (i.e. the cartelists) right to effective judicial protection being infringed. This takes us to the second set of issues dealt with in this ruling, namely the Court's interpretation of the principle of effective judicial protection. Starting with paragraph 50, the Court points to the fact that, according to the *Masterfoods* ruling[50] and Article 16 of Regulation 1/2003, national courts ruling on agreements under Article 101 TFEU, which are already the subject of a Commission decision, are obliged not to take decisions contrary to the Commission decision. This rule is also relevant for domestic actions for damages (paragraph 51). In paragraphs 52 to 54, while pointing to the obligation of sincere cooperation between the national courts, on the one hand, and the Commission and the EU courts, on the other hand, the CJEU reiterates the separation of functions between the domestic and the EU courts: the latter have the task of reviewing the legality of acts of EU institutions, a power which does not rest with the former. Nevertheless, this does not deny the defendant's right of access to a tribunal (paragraph 55), since the EU system of judicial review of Commission decisions (i.e. Article 263 TFEU and the Court's unlimited review jurisdiction regarding the public law penalty's lawfulness) offers sufficient safeguards to the defendants (paragraphs 56 to 63). In paragraph 57 the Court actually notes that the defendant brought an action in front of the EU courts for the annulment of the Commission's public enforcement decision. Neither

---

[48] Rusu 2017 (a), p. 800.

[49] Charter of Fundamental Rights of the EU, Article 47.

[50] Case C-344/98 *Masterfoods*, ECLI:EU:C:2000:689.

does the outcome discussed above breach the equality of arms principle, since Article 28(1) of Regulation 1/2003 prohibits the Commission from using information gathered during investigations for other purposes (paragraphs 71 to 74).[51] Lastly, and interestingly, the CJEU emphasised once again what has been already stated in *Manfredi*, with regard to the basic constitutive elements of civil damages actions: such actions require establishing the existence of: (1) a harmful event (i.e. an infringement of the EU antitrust rules), (2) loss, and (3) the direct link between the two. In *Otis*, it is the Commission that established the first element of this formula, namely the infringement of Article 101 TFEU, a finding which, based on the *Masterfoods* and Regulation 1/2003 rationale discussed above, the national court is obliged to accept. Yet, in follow-on actions such as the one at issue in this scenario, although the national court is required to accept that a prohibited agreement or practice exists, the existence of loss and of a direct causal link between the loss and the agreement or practice in question remains, by contrast, a matter to be assessed by the national court (paragraph 65). Even when the Commission has in its decision determined the precise effects of the infringement, it still falls on the national court to determine individually the loss caused to each of the persons who have brought an action for damages. What is striking in this respect is that when the case returned to the Belgian competent court, the Commission adduced insufficient evidence as to the causal link between the anti-competitive behaviour and the loss, and failed to prove the existence of an overcharge; therefore, no damages were granted.[52] All in all, in paragraph 66 and 67, the Court concludes that the setting discussed above regarding the Commission's role is not contrary to Article 16 of Regulation 1/2003 and therefore the Commission cannot be regarded as judge and party in its own cause in the context of such a dispute.

The *Otis* judgment has thus expanded the scope of the right to claim damages. Better phrased, it may be argued that it has enlarged the pool of potential claimants for damages in domestic follow-on proceedings, to include also administrative authorities that have established the actual EU antitrust infringement. It is true though that, in this case, the Commission represented the EU in the domestic civil action, the EU institutions here being no more and no less than customers of the cartelists, or consumers of the cartelised product. Still, the fact that an administrative institution, such as the Commission, appears to play distinct, yet (according to some) connected, roles in legal proceedings which flow from one another does not sit very comfortably with some commentators.[53] It was to this end argued that the Commission's 'double' role is unfortunate, and in order to avoid indistinctness, confusion and distrust, it would make sense to entrust another EU institution with the tasks pertaining to private enforcement.[54] All in all, the *Otis* ruling generated hot debates among competition law and fundamental rights scholars.[55]

---

[51] Rusu 2017 (a), p. 801.

[52] Case *EU v Otis and others*, (2014) A.R. A/08/06816.

[53] E.g. Beumer 2013; Hauger and Palzer 2013.

[54] Braat 2018, p. 104.

[55] Hauger and Palzer 2013; Wils 2014; Botta 2013; Braat 2018, pp. 103–4.

3.4 *Kone*

Damages claims are not necessarily restricted to claimants in a vertical chain with the defendant (i.e. direct or indirect purchasers of the cartelists), so long as it can be established that the loss caused to the claimant resulted as a consequence of the infringing conduct.[56] This scenario evidently points to the causal link element of the three-prong damages claims formula; this element was already mentioned in the *Manfredi* and *Otis* rulings discussed above. In the *Kone* case, which dealt with the same elevators and escalators cartel, the CJEU developed the discussions surrounding the causation requirement, as embedded in the relevant provisions of Austrian law, while ruling on the so-called 'umbrella pricing' phenomenon. A simple practical example may be useful here to elucidate what is meant by umbrella pricing: imagine that companies A, B, C and D are active in a given relevant market. A, B and C are members of a cartel, which has the effect of raising the price of the products they sell. This price increase creates an 'umbrella', under which D, as a non-cartelist, may also increase the price of its product to the level of the price charged by the cartelists.

In paragraph 19 of the ruling, the Court summarises what it was summoned to clarify: essentially, is domestic legislation consistent with Article 101 TFEU if it categorically excludes, for legal reasons, any civil liability of cartelists towards customers of non-cartelists, for loss caused by the non-cartelists who, having regard to the practices of the cartel, set prices higher than would otherwise have been expected in the absence of the cartel? In other words, are cartelists liable towards the non-cartelists' customers? Connected to the causation requirement, the Court noted in paragraph 31 that Austrian law categorically excluded compensation in umbrella pricing situations, because the causality between the victim's loss and the cartel was missing, due to the inexistence of direct (i.e. contractual) link between cartelist and victim, and also due to the non-cartelists' autonomous decision of applying umbrella pricing.

The Court proceeded by referring once more to the key elements of *Courage and Crehan* and *Manfredi*:[57] Articles 101 and 102 TFEU have direct effect (paragraph 20); this strengthens the EU antitrust law's full effectiveness (paragraphs 21 and 23); consequently, any person is entitled to claim compensation where causality exists between the harm suffered and the prohibited practice (paragraph 22). Further on, in absence of EU law on the matter, the domestic laws must design the exercise of the right to claim damages, including the issue of a causal relationship between the infringement and the loss incurred. Procedural autonomy is therefore important, of course, provided that the effectiveness and equivalence principles are observed (paragraphs 24 and 25). So far, the *Kone* judgment reiterates the main points of the *Courage and Crehan* and *Manfredi* rulings. In paragraph 26, the Court adds to the domestic autonomy discussion, while referring to some of its more recent case-law, including *VEBIC*,[58] that domestic law must, however, not jeopardise the EU antitrust rules' effective application. This is an important remark, reiterated in paragraph 32, in the context of clarifying that

---

[56] Jones, Sufrin and Dunne, 2019, p. 1037.

[57] Rusu 2017 (a), p. 801.

[58] Case C-439/08 *VEBIC*, ECLI:EU:C:2010:739.

causation is an element of domestic law, and as such domestic rules pertaining to causation too must ensure that EU competition law is fully effective. Such rules must specifically take into account the objective pursued by Article 101 TFEU, which aims to guarantee effective and undistorted competition in the Internal Market, and, accordingly, prices set on the basis of free competition. In this context, in paragraphs 28 to 30, the Court assesses the umbrella pricing phenomenon, as a potential cartel consequence, and concludes that compensation may be claimed from the cartelists, even in the absence of a contractual link between the victim and the cartelists, if two conditions are met (paragraph 34): (1) the cartel was (given the circumstances of the case and the relevant market's specific aspects) liable to result in umbrella pricing being applied by independent third parties, and (2) the cartelists could not ignore such circumstances. In our opinion, the second condition laid down by the CJEU is almost always fulfilled when at stake is a large cartel, with members whose aggregate market shares cover the largest part of the relevant market.[59]

The *Kone* ruling touches upon an important element of domestic damages claims based on the EU right to damages, which although mentioned in previous case-law, was left mainly untouched: the causal relationship between the infringement and the loss incurred. Although still a matter of domestic law, causation cannot be conceived in such a way as to categorically exclude liability, and consequently frustrate the EU antitrust rules' effective application. A consequence of this, particularly in umbrella pricing scenarios, is that the right to claim damages is expanded. So is the pool of potential claimants of damages, and for that matter, the cartelist's liability for damages: they are now liable to their direct and indirect customers, with whom a direct or indirect contractual relationship exists, and also to the non-cartelists' customers, due to the effects of umbrella pricing. Such expansions of the right to claim damages and of the liability of cartelists reframes the dynamics of the cartelist–competitors–customers/consumers relationship. Section 5 of this chapter will further detail specific aspects of this discussion, in particular in the context of the leniency–private enforcement relationship, which is key to maintaining a workable balance between the effective public enforcement of the cartel prohibition, on one hand, and the fulfilment of the right to claim damages, on the other hand. Essentially, the incentives to act for all parties involved in a *Kone*-like scenario have been shifted by this ruling: the 'prisoner's dilemma' recipe, mentioned in Chapter 3, and the cartelists' willingness to apply for leniency are now rethought by cartelists (as also pointed out by the defendants in *Kone*, paragraph 36), since such a move would transform them into 'sitting ducks' for private law damages claims initiated by all (cartelists' and non-cartelists') customers. Thus, they must think of a larger group of victims that would potentially need to be compensated. This risk of paying larger amounts of money in damages would arguably make cartelists think twice before applying for leniency. In a different scenario, absent a successful leniency application, if detected infringing the cartel prohibition, the cartelists must also factor in their calculations the public law fines which they may incur. Meanwhile, the non-cartelists' incentives to complain about their competitors' misconduct have also shifted, yet in a different direction, since they are more

---

[59] Veenbrink and Rusu 2014; Dunne 2014 (a).

likely now not to signal the existing anti-competitiveness, but instead to shelter under the 'umbrella effect', in order to boost their own profits.[60]

3.5 Preliminary findings

So far, we have become acquainted with the following arrangements, as far as the EU anti-trust private enforcement mechanisms are concerned: on one hand, we are dealing with EU substantive rules that prohibit agreements and practices that distort competition (Articles 101 and 102 TFEU). Next, should these provisions be infringed, there is a right to claim damages for the loss incurred, which flows directly from these EU law provisions. Yet, on the other hand, the effectuation of this right is dependent on domestic procedural rules and arrangements. This setting paints a fragmented enforcement picture in the EU Internal Market, where various conditions for bringing actions, diverse liability regimes, and at times inadequate institutional arrangements[61] existed. This is also probably why actions for damages based on EU law have been scarce in the EU Member States, and what is more, rarely successful. It is thus no surprise that the private enforcement phenomenon has been considerably underdeveloped at EU level for decades.[62] Of course, the CJEU has played its part to the fullest when it comes to furthering the right to claim damages, while aiming to maintain the coherency and effectiveness of EU law. It has done so by relying heavily on domestic procedures, which it shaped to the best of its ability in order to ensure the likely fulfilment of the right to claim damages. But, there is so much that the judiciary can do, particularly while making extensive use of the effectiveness and equivalence principles. In our opinion, these principles, crucial as they may be, should nevertheless be viewed as a (last resort) safe-net in ensuring that damages stemming from EU antitrust law infringements are not easily dispensed with in the domestic ambits. The 'absence of EU law on the matter' argument often put forward by the CJEU in its rulings, while pointing to the Member States' national procedural autonomy, seems to our mind the Court's way of signalling the existence of a legislative *lacuna*, in the area of procedural arrangements surrounding damages actions. At the same time, this is a more or less evident invitation to the EU legislator to take action and further develop such (key matters of) EU antitrust private enforcement.[63] Consequently, in the next paragraphs of this chapter, we will turn the attention to the soft-law and legislative developments brought about at EU level in the private enforcement field.

Before we do so, a last brief mention at this point relates to the ongoing role the CJEU plays. Section 3 of this chapter highlights the important contribution the Court has brought to laying the groundwork for private enforcement in the EU. This section builds on the case-law which pre-dates the adoption of the Private Damages Directive 2014. Yet, even after such legislative action has been undertaken at EU level, the Court continues to play an important role in furthering the possibilities of victims of antitrust infringements to successfully engage

---

[60] Rusu 2017 (a), pp. 801–2.

[61] Jones, Sufrin and Dunne 2019, pp. 1041–2.

[62] Rusu 2017 (b), pp. 38–9.

[63] Rusu 2017 (a), p. 802.

in actions for damages. As we will detail in the following sections of this chapter, after the 2014 moment, the Court has continued to hand down rulings which not only clarify key aspects of private enforcement, but also draw important links between private law actions for damages and other (sub-)areas of EU competition law: for example, in *Degussa*,[64] the Court clarified the boundaries of disclosing *leniency* information; in *Otis II*,[65] the link between antitrust liability and *state aid* measures was brought to light; in *Skanska*,[66] the Court turned to the notion of *undertaking* when determining the entities liable to pay civil law damages, thus bringing public law and private law liability under the same overarching regime. All in all, the Court's case-law continues to undertake a key role shaping and developing private enforcement in the EU.

4 UNDERSTANDING AND FURTHER SHAPING EU PRIVATE ENFORCEMENT THROUGH SOFT-LAW

The EU institutions took the CJEU's invitation to further work out the mechanisms of private enforcement to heart. Yet, shortly after the *Courage and Crehan* ruling, and later on, following the *Manfredi* judgment, the time was still not ripe for legislative intervention. The next best thing was thus to make recourse to soft-law documents, the general purpose of which was to provide a deeper understanding of private enforcement in the EU domestic jurisdictions, and to shape the subsequent direction of travel, when it came to the actions that needed to be undertaken, in order to make genuine private enforcement a reality in the EU. In the following paragraphs we will briefly delve into such soft-law/policy documents,[67] in a chronological order, going, for the sake of completeness, also over the more recent recommendations and actions which accompany and nuance the legislative developments embedded in the Private Damages Directive 2014.

4.1 The Ashurst Report 2004

In 2004, a report was commissioned in order to identify and analyse the obstacles to successful damages actions in the Member States based on infringements of competition law.[68] The Report[69] sought to map the *status quo* of private enforcement claims and to find ways to improve the effectiveness of domestic and EU private enforcement. Its findings were based on a comparative analysis of the national legislation and jurisprudence regarding the enforcement of the EU (and where necessary) domestic competition rules. The Report found

---

[64] Case C-162/15 P *Evonik Degussa*, ECLI:EU:C:2017:205.

[65] Case C-435/18 *Otis II*, ECLI:EU:C:2019:1069.

[66] Case C-724/17 *Skanska*, ECLI:EU:C:2019:204.

[67] Braat 2018, pp. 107–20 extensively dwells upon the content, objectives and recommendations of some of these soft-law documents.

[68] Whish and Bailey 2018, p. 310.

[69] Ashurst Report 2004.

that there was a wide-ranging diversity in the approaches taken by the Member States, when it comes to both EU and purely domestic actions. It identified diverse national and procedural obstacles to the more efficient development of the system of private competition litigation,[70] specifically with regard to the standing requirements of victims, the rules on evidence, discovery, causation, limitation periods, and so on. Last but not least, as already indicated in the paragraph above, the Report revealed low levels of private enforcement through damages claims: in between 1962 and 2004, approximately 60 instances were reported where actions were brought in front of the domestic courts based on both EU and national competition law; in 23 cases damages were awarded, out of which only 12 were based on EU competition law infringements.

4.2 The Green Paper 2005

As a follow-up to the findings of the Ashurst Report 2004, the Commission published the Green Paper 2005 on damages actions.[71] This discussion document was intended to stimulate debate and launch a consultation process at the European level regarding private enforcement, for the purpose of setting out different options for further reflection and possible action to improve the functioning of both follow-on and stand-alone actions.[72] It specifically discussed the conditions for starting damages actions and, similar to the Ashurst Report, it identified the obstacles thereto, especially with respect to matters concerning access to evidence, fault requirements, the passing-on defence, litigation costs, jurisdictional conflicts, and more. The Green Paper 2005 also dwelt upon the balance between the roles public and private enforcement mechanisms fulfil, and the (deterrence and/or compensation) goals they respectively aim to achieve. It argued that these two enforcement systems should be coordinated in an optimal way, especially when talking about matters surrounding the leniency policies. In this last respect, the Green Paper proposed to exclude the discoverability of leniency applications in damages actions, to instate a rebate on damages for the leniency applicant, and to eliminate its joint and several liability.[73] In many respects, the Green Paper's points were influenced by the experience in the US, most evidently when it comes to the introduction of double damages for cartel infringements and the exclusion of the passing-on defence.[74] For the period when these proposals were put forward, and given the actual level of development of private enforcement in the Member States at that time, one may remark that the action points envisioned by the Commission were quite daring. It comes as no surprise that the Member States' reactions to the Commission's views were not always the most favourable.

---

[70] Bucan 2013, p. 76.

[71] Accompanied by Staff Working Paper 2005.

[72] Braat 2018, pp. 108–9.

[73] On the Member States' reaction to these proposals, see Braat 2018, pp. 111–16.

[74] Wils 2017, p. 21.

4.3 The White Paper 2008

While picking up those positive findings of the Green Paper 2005, and encouraged by the European Parliament to continue its work in the field of private enforcement, the Commission issued the follow-up White Paper 2008.[75] The Paper detailed the proposals meant to overcome the obstacles to effective damages actions. The proposals aimed to improve the legal conditions for victims to exercise their right to reparation of all damage suffered as a result of a breach of the EC antitrust rules. In this respect, the White Paper was focused on the compensation function of private enforcement. Further, it also contained clear references regarding the preservation of the strong public enforcement of the TFEU antitrust provisions by the Commission and the NCAs, while at the same time ensuring that the design of the private enforcement system complements, but does not replace or jeopardise, public enforcement. The White Paper dropped some of the daring proposals present in its predecessor, the Green Paper 2005,[76] and adapted some of the points relating to the protection to be conferred to leniency applicants. The Commission argued that adequately protecting from disclosure the corporate statements submitted by leniency applicants is key to prevent disadvantaging the applicant when compared to its co-infringers. In this respect, it was proposed to bar disclosure of all corporate statements, regardless whether the leniency applications are accepted or not, and even if they do not lead to any public enforcement decision finding an infringement. The liability for damages was also to be reduced for the immunity recipient, to cover only the damages of its direct and indirect purchasers, thus offering predictability to the immune undertaking as far as the scope of the damages go. As with the Green Paper 2005, the stakeholders' reactions to the White Paper 2008 were quite mixed,[77] and therefore no legislative action has been taken yet on the private enforcement front.

Nevertheless, the Commission's efforts to develop private enforcement in the EU did not cease. 2013 was a fruitful year, in which three developments occurred: the Commission issued a legislative Proposal for a Directive on Damages Actions,[78] a Communication on Quantifying Harm in such actions[79] and a Recommendation on Collective Redress.[80] The first document constitutes an important step, since it signalled clearly that binding EU law was well on its way. However, since the next section of this chapter will examine the actual Private Damages Directive 2014 at length, we will focus in the next few paragraphs only on the 2013 Communication on Quantifying Harm and on the Recommendation on Collective Redress.

---

[75] Accompanied by Staff Working Paper 2008 and Impact Assessment 2008.

[76] Wils 2017, p. 21.

[77] The contributions submitted in response to the Green and White Papers may be found at the following links, respectively: <http://ec.europa.eu/competition/antitrust/actionsdamages/green_paper_comments.html> and <http://ec.europa.eu/competition/antitrust/actionsdamages/white_paper_comments.html> accessed 5 June 2020.

[78] Proposal for the Private Damages Directive 2013.

[79] Communication on Quantifying Harm 2013.

[80] Recommendation on Collective Redress 2013.

4.4 The Communication on Quantifying Harm 2013

Although issued before the Private Damages Directive 2014 was signed into law, the Communication on Quantifying Harm 2013 is meant to complement the provisions of the Directive. The Communication is accompanied by a Practical Guide,[81] aiming to help national courts and parties to antitrust damages actions in the often complex task of quantifying damages. The Practical Guide 2013 provides an overview of the main economic methods, techniques and empirical insights available to quantify damages in practice.[82] The Communication is rather brief and mainly tackles the interaction between the national rules and the rules and principles of EU law. As far as the guidance offered to the domestic courts and other stakeholders, reference is made to the Practical Guide, in which we find detailed explanations on matters such as: working with counterfactual scenarios, using simulation models and cost-based and finance-based analysis, quantification tools for exploitative and exclusionary practices, respectively, and so on. The Practical Guide 2013 is complex and requires economic and legal skills to decipher its contents. Nevertheless, it undoubtedly adds flesh and blood to the skeleton provisions on quantifying harm embedded in Article 17 of the Private Damages Directive 2014.

4.5 The Recommendation on Collective Redress 2013

Another soft-law document complementing the Private Damages Directive 2014 is the Recommendation on Collective Redress 2013. Since the Directive applies to any damages actions in the antitrust field, it also applies to collective damages actions in those Member States where they are – or will be – available.[83] Indeed, Article 2(4) of the Directive defines the concept of 'action for damages' as an action under national law by which a claim for damages is brought before a national court by an alleged injured party, or by someone acting on behalf of one or *more* alleged injured parties, thus not excluding collective actions per se from its scope. However, the Directive itself does not require Member States to introduce collective redress mechanisms for the enforcement of Articles 101 and 102 TFEU.[84] Consequently, such actions remain within the legal competence of the Member States, while the Recommendation on Collective Redress 2013 simply invited them to introduce collective redress mechanisms in their domestic private enforcement systems, by 26 July 2015.

In some jurisdictions (also outside the EU) collective redress mechanisms are very useful tools not only in competition law matters, but also in other consumer-related fields.[85] When connected to the antitrust matter, especially when looking at the experience the US jurisdiction has built around the so-called 'class-actions',[86] collective mechanisms serve both

---

[81] Practical Guide 2013.

[82] See <http://ec.europa.eu/competition/antitrust/actionsdamages/index.html> accessed 6 June 2020.

[83] Ibid.

[84] Private Damages Directive 2014, Recital 13.

[85] Whish and Bailey 2018, p. 323.

[86] Jones, Sufrin and Dunne 2019, p. 1023 *et seq.*

compensating the antitrust infringements victims' losses, and the deterrence of future anti-competitive behaviour. Yet, such US mechanisms are characterised by a combination of features that are very specific to the US, including jury trial, one-way shifting of costs, wide pre-trial discovery, contingent fee agreements and an 'opt-out' mechanism.[87]

Given the wide array of issues that surround collective actions in private enforcement, it seems reasonable to spend a bit more time on discussing their merit. After all, such mechanisms are a hotly debated topic not only in business circles, but also in the academic environment. In the paragraphs above we already previewed some of the benefits of collective damages actions: such actions are useful when more victims incurred harm, and they choose to overcome the risk and costs of bringing individual actions. Collective actions thus counterbalance the lack of resources normally faced by individual claimants and limit deterrence from bringing individual actions.[88]

Such concerns were tentatively addressed at EU level, as early as the Green Paper 2005, which in answering the question of whether special procedures should be made available for bringing collective actions and protecting consumer interests, pointed out two potential options: (1) action for consumer associations without depriving individual consumers of bringing an individual claim, and (2) action by groups of purchasers other than final consumers. Especially with regard to the first option, issues such as standing, the distribution and quantification of damages, were identified as points of further reflection. The White Paper 2008 further strengthened the feel that there is a clear need of collective redress mechanisms. It built upon the items discussed in the Green Paper 2005 and proposed a combination of two complementary mechanisms of collective redress, to address effectively the antitrust-related concerns mentioned above: (1) representative actions on behalf of identified or identifiable victims brought by qualified entities (e.g. consumer associations, state bodies, trade associations), designated in advance or certified on an ad hoc basis by a Member State, and (2) 'opt-in' collective actions, in which victims expressly decide to combine in one single action their individual claims for the harm suffered. In close relation to this latter proposal, victims were thought of as not deprived from bringing individual actions for damages, provided that safeguards for avoiding double compensation exist. Indeed, the key choice in determining an appropriate collective redress model is between the opt-in and opt-out forms of action. The former entails that claimants take action to be included in the collective claim proceedings, while in the case of the latter model, claimants with the same interest are included in the proceedings by default, unless they expressly exclude themselves. While the opt-out model reduces costs for the defendants and the courts, the opt-in model can be criticised for being under-inclusive and ineffective.[89] Following the US class-action model, some of the EU Member States (e.g. Denmark, Portugal) have chosen for tailor-made versions of the opt-out model in their domestic collective mechanisms.[90]

Getting back to the contents of the Recommendation on Collective Redress 2013, we can

---

[87] Bucan 2013, p. 78.

[88] Rodger and MacCulloch 2015, Chapter 3.

[89] Ibid.

[90] Bucan 2013, p. 89.

observe though that the Commission has not changed its mind on this choice. It recommends the Member States to introduce opt-in collective redress mechanisms in their legal orders, while also suggesting observance of the following principles: providing for both injunctive and compensatory relief; designing fair, equitable, timely and not prohibitively expensive procedures; preventing abuse of collective redress litigation, for instance by prohibiting contingency fees; affording a central role to the judge, and suchlike.[91] It may be thus observed that the Recommendation is not driven or guided by the US system of class actions. Furthermore, the Recommendation is not limited to damages actions for infringements of Articles 101 and 102 TFEU. It covers both injunctive and compensatory collective redress, and concerns violations of all rights granted under EU law, including in particular consumer rights. This signals that the Commission views collective redress as a more general topic on the European agenda for consumers.[92]

To this end, the next step in the process of furthering collective redress in the EU was taken in 2018, when the Commission announced its New Deal for Consumers,[93] which although focused on consumer law issues, and again, not necessarily on antitrust matters, proposes inter alia that consumer bodies should be able to seek redress on behalf of a group of consumers.[94]

In the expectation of collective redress mechanisms making their way into binding EU law, the situation in the domestic jurisdictions of the EU Member States differs extensively. While in certain jurisdictions, such as Slovakia, collective redress mechanisms do not exist, other jurisdictions have more or less comprehensive provisions on collective action, enacted either before the 2013 Commission Recommendation, or based specifically on its provisions. For example, in Hungary, until 2018 it was only the competition authority that could initiate class actions based on Article 92 of the Competition Act; however, only if the competition infringement concerns a large group of individuals, and after the competition authority has initiated public enforcement proceedings, and only within the limitation period of three years from the date when the infringement occurred. As of 2018, the Act on Civil Court Procedures provides that class actions can also be initiated by private parties for the purpose of enforcing a claim arising from a consumer contract, in labour lawsuits, or in relation to damage to health directly caused by unforeseen environmental factors. In Poland, the 2009/2010 Act on Class Actions allows for group actions in relation to anti-competitive behaviour, based on Article 72 of the Polish Civil Code, for groups of ten persons or more, who have claims of similar type, and whose claims are based on one and the same set of facts. At the other end of the spectrum, countries like the Netherlands and the UK have more comprehensive experience with collective redress mechanisms. In the Netherlands, several possibilities for collective action exist: collective settlement claims, collective action, and action on the basis of transfer of claims. These types of actions are based on diverse provisions of the Dutch Civil Code, Code of Civil Procedure and the Act on Collective Settlements. Recent developments

---

[91] Whish and Bailey 2018, p. 323.

[92] Wils 2017, p. 23; Oude Elferink and Braat 2014, p. 218.

[93] Press Release IP/18/3041.

[94] Whish and Bailey 2018, p. 324.

were incorporated in the 2019 Bill on the Settlement of Damages in Collective Actions, which deals with standing requirements for claims vehicles, and allows such entities to claim damages in collective actions based on the opt-out principle. It also provides that collective actions must have a sufficiently close connection to the Dutch jurisdiction, which is the case, for example, if the majority of claimants are Dutch residents or if the events based on which the claim is built took place in the Netherlands.[95] In the UK, actions for damages before the High Court may take different shapes: a group litigation order, representative actions, or a single trial of multiple claims, based on the English civil procedural rules. Collective actions may be brought also before the Competition Appeal Tribunal, based on Sections 47 *et seq.* of the Competition Act 1998. Since 2015 not only opt-in class actions are allowed, but also actions based on the opt-out principle, due to the changes brought about by the Consumer Rights Act 2015. The Competition Appeal Tribunal controls collective actions by issuing collective proceedings orders, when claims raise the same, similar or related issues of fact or law and are suitable to be brought in collective proceedings. This order appoints a class representative for the collective action. The damages that the Tribunal may award may be paid to the class representative or to other persons the Tribunal deems fit. Based on Section 49 of the Competition Act 1998, the Competition Appeal Tribunal may also approve the collective settlement of claims in collective proceedings.[96]

4.6 Some recent soft-law developments

In order to further complement the Directive's provisions, one of the latest developments the Commission is engaged in relates to providing guidance to the national courts on the matter of quantifying the passing-on of overcharges. This is a difficult exercise that the domestic courts, legal practitioners and the parties to damages actions have to engage in. Therefore, guidance in this respect is crucial, a fact acknowledged specifically in Article 16 of the Private Damages Directive 2014. As an initial step, a study[97] was commissioned in 2016 on the matter of passing-on of overcharges. Drawing on relevant economic theory and quantitative methods, as well as relevant legal practice and rules, the Study provides a practical framework for assessing and quantifying passing-on effects.[98] The Study focuses on key passing-on issues such as the relevant cost effects, the impact of buyer power, the relationship between passing-on and volume effects, disclosure of documents, use of economic experts and parallel proceedings, and suchlike.

Based on the findings of this study, the Commission issued a set of draft Guidelines on estimating passing-on of overcharges, as part of a public consultation.[99] The Guidelines on passed-on overcharges was then adopted in 2019.[100] Essentially, this document aims to pro-

---

[95] For more on collective actions in the Netherlands, see Van de Gronden 2017; Zippro 2009.

[96] Whish and Bailey 2018, p. 330 *et seq.*

[97] Study on Passing-on of Overcharges 2016.

[98] See <http://ec.europa.eu/competition/antitrust/actionsdamages/index.html> accessed 5 June 2020.

[99] Draft Guidelines on Passed-on Overcharges 2018.

[100] Guidelines on Passed-on Overcharges 2019.

vide legal and economic guidance to national courts and the other stakeholders involved. It describes the procedural instruments available to national courts when assessing the existence of overcharges passed on to indirect customers, the national courts' power to estimate the amount of the overcharge that was passed on, and by way of handy examples, an overview of the most common economic methods and techniques to quantify passed-on overcharges. The Guidelines are intended to complement the Communication on Quantification of Harm 2013 and the Practical Guide 2013.[101]

4.7 Findings so far

By now, we can conclude that the Commission puts great value on soft-law documents as far as the private enforcement field is concerned. There are several reasons for this, or better yet, various roles that soft-law fulfils. First, soon after the acknowledgement of the existence of an EU right to claim damages, the Commission used soft-law mechanisms to collect data on the various domestic approaches to private enforcement, to stir debate about the next steps to be undertaken at EU level, and to test-drive potential options for furthering damages claims and other mechanisms based on EU law. Thus, such actions are to be viewed as necessary precursors of the legislative means adopted later on (i.e. the Private Damages Directive 2014), meant to shape the stakeholders' views and increase public transparency in the field of private enforcement. The second category of soft-law documents are the ones complementing the Directive. Two types of such documents may be identified in this category: first, those pertaining to areas of the law for which no specific legislative provisions exist at EU level, such as collective redress. Essentially, here we are talking about areas of the law that are probably still too sensitive for the Member States to agree on common binding European standards. Where such topics did not make it into the Directive, and are consequently left within the Member States' competence, the next best thing is adopting non-binding recommendations, which may still shape domestic practice. Speaking of the Member States, the second type of documents complementing the Directive are those that should help the domestic authorities work with the Directive's provisions. In other words, such soft-law documents further the Directive's provisions, while providing clarity and certainty exactly to those who work with them on a daily basis.

All in all, soft-law action is a tool the Commission finds useful in competition law, across all its sub-fields. There is no reason to treat private enforcement any different. Therefore, it is to be expected that further private enforcement guidelines and recommendations will be issued at EU level in the years to come.

5 THE PRIVATE DAMAGES DIRECTIVE 2014

Having discussed the case-law and soft-law initiatives meant to further private enforcement of the EU antitrust rules, it is now time to focus on the legislative developments embodied in

---

[101] See <http://europa.eu/rapid/press-release_IP-18-4369_en.htm> accessed 5 June 2020.

the Private Damages Directive 2014. First, we will dwell upon some general aspects regarding the Directive, in order to place its adoption in the correct context, and also to correctly understand its provisions and their relationship with the CJEU's case-law and with the national relevant private law provisions. In close connection to this setup, we will then analyse its core provisions in a systematic manner, focusing on specific questions surrounding the main issue of how damages are awarded once the EU antitrust rules have been infringed.

5.1 The basics

First, the legal bases on which the Directive has been adopted: Articles 103 and 114 TFEU. This discussion is important for understanding the need for adopting the Directive and also the goals that it is supposed to foster. On one hand, Article 103 TFEU allows adopting directives and regulations to give effect to the EU antitrust principles, measures which should be designed to ensure compliance with the cartel and dominance abuse TFEU prohibitions. Article 114 TFEU, on the other hand, is known as the 'Internal Market legal basis', since it allows approximating domestic rules which have as their object the establishment and functioning of the Internal Market. Recital 8 of the Private Damages Directive 2014 provides that there are differences in the Member States' applicable liability regimes. This creates an uneven playing field, which affects the antitrust infringers, but has consequences also for the exercise of the fundamental freedoms (particularly the freedom of establishment, the free movement of goods and services). This setting may negatively affect both competition and the Internal Market's proper functioning. Therefore, constructing the Directive on these dual legal bases is appropriate. Indeed, Article 1(1) states that the Directive intends to foster undistorted competition in the Internal Market and remove obstacles to its proper functioning, by ensuring equivalent protection throughout the EU for anyone who suffered harm resulting from antitrust infringements.[102]

Second, Article 1(2) continues by pointing out that the Directive's aim is to coordinate the antitrust enforcement performed by NCAs and the enforcement of the antitrust rules in damages actions before national courts. The Directive thus brings about the harmonisation of the respective domestic rules. Here we are talking about non-exhaustive harmonisation, since the Directive does not deal with the entire spectrum of private enforcement: it does not deal with fault requirements, legal costs, causation, among others;[103] it is concerned with damages actions as defined in Article 2(4), a definition which is essentially built around the subjects who may start proceedings in front of the domestic courts. The non-harmonised items remain within the Member States' national procedural autonomy, in the 'absence of EU law on the matter'. Recital 11 of the Private Damages Directive 2014 exemplifies this discussion with reference to inter alia causality, imputability, adequacy or culpability. The Member States may maintain such conditions for compensation in their legal regimes, if the

---

[102] Rusu 2017 (a), pp. 802–3.

[103] 'Editorial Comments: "One Bird in the Hand . . ." The Directive on Damages Actions for Breach of the Competition Rules' (2014) 51 Common Market Law Review 5, p. 1338; Parcu, Monti and Botta 2018, p. 42 *et seq.* See also Private Damages Directive 2014, Recitals 10, 11, 13.

CJEU's case-law on the effectiveness and equivalence principles, which continue to shape *all* national rules and procedures for the exercise of damages claims, is respected.[104] This last assertion is crucial for correctly understanding the relationship between the Directive's provisions, the national law provisions, and the CJEU's case-law. Indeed, Article 4 of the Directive codifies the principles of effectiveness and equivalence, as general principles of the Directive. This means that these principles, as they stem from the case-law of the Court, are relevant not only for the private enforcement areas of the law which are outside the scope of the Directive. They are relevant also for *all* those domestic rules relating to private damages, which due to the Directive's (where is the case, minimum) harmonisation technique, go beyond the standard of protection put forward by this EU legislative instrument. For example, if Member States choose to enact limitation periods longer than the ones the Directive prescribes in Article 10(3), such provisions should apply equally to both actions based on domestic law and on EU law.

Third, while speaking of the relationship between the Directive's provisions and the case-law of the CJEU, the Directive's codification exercise does not stop at the principles of effectiveness and equivalence. It also incorporates in its text the EU right to claim damages, put forward in *Courage and Crehan* (Articles 1(1) and 3(1)), and the heads of damage (i.e. actual loss, loss of profit, and interest, as acknowledged in *Manfredi*), which are confirmed in the context of the general principle prescribing a right to full compensation, as embedded in Article 3: essentially, compensation should place the antitrust infringement victim in the position in which it would have been had the infringement not been committed. However, the Directive deviates from the *Manfredi* rationale when it comes to punitive damages, since according to Article 3(3) any overcompensation should be avoided. Consequently, the effectiveness and equivalence assessment of punitive damages in *Manfredi* was no longer tenable once the Directive entered into force, since such damages are prohibited altogether. The punitive damages now fall outside the 'absence of EU law rules on the matter' discussion.

Fourth, since one of the aims of the Directive is to coordinate public and private enforcement mechanisms, a brief note on the relationship between NCAs' decisions and damages claims is in order at this point. Article 9 provides that a final public enforcement infringement decision irrefutably establishes the existence of the breach (i.e. the infringement's nature, its material, personal, temporal and territorial scope)[105] for the purpose of damages actions before the national courts of that Member State. If this decision stems from another Member State, it should have at least the value of prima facie evidence that an antitrust breach occurred, to be appraised as appropriate, along with any other evidence adduced by the parties, according to national law. This approach is consistent with Article 16 of Regulation 1/2003 and the *Masterfoods* ruling,[106] and it should aid the victims by providing them with a more concrete and even basis regarding the proof of antitrust infringements having occurred. This is so, especially if read in conjunction with Article 17(2) of the Directive, which puts forward a rebuttable presumption that cartel infringements cause

---

[104] Private Damages Directive 2014, Article 4. See also Rusu 2017 (a), p. 803.

[105] Private Damages Directive 2014, Recital 34.

[106] Wils 2017, p. 30.

harm.[107] In other words, Article 9 of the Private Damages Directive 2014 adds considerable value for domestic follow-on actions, especially those unfolding in front of the courts of the Member States struggling with their public–private law mechanisms coordination, or of the Member States experiencing problems in handling NCA decisions issued in another Member State. Even more so, Article 9 adds considerable value in jurisdictions where no framework relating to the binding nature of NCA decisions was previously in place, such as France and Italy.[108] In France, Article L.481-2 was added to the French Code of Commerce, according to which, where the existence of an anti-competitive practice and its attribution to a person have been established by a decision pronounced by the competition authority or by the appeal court, which can no longer be the subject of an ordinary appeal for the part relating to this finding, a non-rebuttable presumption is established. Such a decision adopted by a competition authority or court of another Member State constitutes a means of proof of the commission of the anti-competitive practice. Other Member States, such as the Netherlands, remarkably, chose not to implement the provisions of paragraph 2 of Article 9. According to the Dutch legislator, this provision does not require implementation because, pursuant to Article 152(1) of the Dutch Code of Civil Procedure, evidence can, unless the law determines otherwise, be furnished by any means. This means that a decision of a foreign competition authority or review court can be used as evidence before a Dutch court. The admissibility of evidence is nevertheless left to the discretion of the domestic court, unless the law determines otherwise. One may argue that the Dutch approach does not amount to correct implementation of the Private Damages Directive 2014, in this respect, since it arguably may diminish the value of Article 9(2). In Germany, on the other hand, the implementation of Article 9 of the Directive in Section 33b of the GWB goes beyond the requirements of the Directive, since a final decision of a competition authority or court, regarding the infringement of Articles 101 and 102 TFEU, always binds the German courts handling actions for damages, regardless in which Member State the competition authority or court that took that decision is established. This approach can be arguably expected to boost follow-on litigation in Germany.

Fifth, speaking of implementation matters, Article 21(1) requires the Member States to bring into force the laws, regulations and administrative provisions necessary to comply with the Directive. The Member States opted for one of the following three alternatives when complying with this requirement: first, amending the Civil Codes, the Codes of Civil Procedure, the Commercial Codes, and so on, as was the case for the Netherlands and France, for example; second, new rules were incorporated in the domestic competition acts, or the domestic competition acts were amended to transpose the provisions of the Directive, as was the case, for example, with the ninth amendment of the German GWB; third, new legislation/government ordinances were introduced specifically to implement the Directive, as is the case, for example, in Romania.[109]

Sixth, and lastly for now, while implementing the Directive's provisions, some Member States chose to extend the scope of the Directive's provisions beyond EU competition law,

---

[107] Rusu 2017 (a), p. 803.

[108] Parcu, Monti and Botta 2018, pp. 10–11.

[109] Government Ordinance 39/2017, OJ 422/2017.

covering actions for damages resulting from breaches of domestic competition law.[110] In France, the implementation expanded the scope of the Directive's provisions even further than that, to damages claims concerning abuses of economic dependency, an aspect which is not provided for in EU law.[111] In other Member States, such as the Netherlands, for example, the Implementation Act only concerns infringements of EU competition law and infringements of Dutch competition law as far as such an infringement has an effect on trade between the Member States (the parallel application of EU and Dutch competition law). The Implementation Act does not apply to infringements of Dutch competition law itself, the Dutch legislator having chosen to deal with such matters in a separate legislative proposal.[112]

Having placed the Directive in context, it is now time to focus on its specific provisions which should help us answer the following questions: who can claim damages, when should reparation be asked for, what means and tools should be used to this end, who should pay the damages, and lastly, what should be paid?

5.2 Who can claim damages?

The answer to this question may be summarised in a very straightforward manner, while pointing to the EU right to claim damages, as put forward in the *Courage and Crehan* ruling, and as embedded in Article 3(1) of the Directive: any natural or legal person who suffered harm caused by an antitrust infringement may claim and obtain full compensation. Several categories of parties may fall under this generous formulation. First, the direct purchasers of the cartelised product/service, or of the product/service which is the object of the antitrust infringement, be they consumers, undertakings or public authorities, may claim damages in front of the domestic courts. This is confirmed in Recitals 13 and 44 and in Article 12(1) of the Directive, as a corollary to the full effectiveness of the right to full compensation. Second, if one pays close attention to the definition of actions for damages in Article 2(4) of the Directive, as we have pointed out above, such actions may also be initiated by a third party on behalf of one or more alleged injured parties. In the same vein, a natural or legal person that succeeded in the right of the alleged injured party, including the person that acquired the claim, may also start damages proceedings. Third, if we are to recall the situation which occurred in the *Courage and Crehan* ruling, infringers also enjoy the right to claim damages, provided that no benefit is drawn from their own unlawful conduct, if they bear significant responsibility for the competition distortion.[113] To be more precise, in this practical situation, the purchaser in a vertical agreement which infringes the antitrust rules may also claim damages caused by such an infringement. Fourth, as indicated by Articles 12 to 15 and Recitals 13, 41 and 44 of the Directive, in economic reality, it may often be the case that the products which are the object of the antitrust infringement are purchased and then resold on the

---

[110] In Romania, for example, see Government Ordinance 39/2017, OJ 422/2017, Articles 2(l) and 3(1).

[111] Article L 420-2(2) of the French Code de Commerce. See also S. Solidoro, 'Private Antitrust Enforcement in France' in Parcu, Monti and Botta 2018, p. 173.

[112] Rusu and Looijestijn-Clearie 2017 (b), p. 376.

[113] Rusu 2017 (a), p. 805.

markets downstream. This means that the overcharge which results from the infringement may be passed on to natural or legal persons who do not have a direct contractual link with the antitrust infringers. These so-called indirect purchasers too have a right to claim damages if they have incurred a loss due to the passing-on of overcharges on the downstream markets where they have purchased the product. Fifth, if one is to recall the *Kone* umbrella pricing scenario, the direct and indirect purchasers of the non-cartelists (yet, competitors of the cartelists on the same relevant market) who have engaged in such pricing behaviour also have the right to claim damages, if they suffered harm, and irrespective of the fact that no direct contractual relationship with the antitrust infringers exists. This stems from the liability provisions embedded in Article 11(6) of the Directive, which will be also mentioned below. Sixth, and lastly for now, the broad formulation of Article 11(6) of the Directive (i.e. 'injured parties other than the direct or indirect purchasers or providers of the infringers') also includes third parties, who are not active as suppliers or customers on the market affected by a cartel, but who have incurred losses as a result of that cartel. The CJEU made this clear in the *Otis II* 2019 preliminary ruling, which occurred in the context of the same elevators and escalators cartel which was at hand in *Otis* and *Kone*. It is important to first note that, since the facts of the *Otis II* case unfolded before the entry into force of the Private Damages Directive 2014, there is no reference in the Court's judgment to this legislative instrument. In *Otis II*, the Province of Upper Austria granted subsidies to clients of the cartel. These loans entailed higher amounts than they would have otherwise, in the absence of the cartel. The CJEU held that if the domestic court determines that this entails a loss, in that the Province of Upper Austria had the possibility of making more profitable investments, and if this injured party establishes a causal connection between that loss and the cartel, it may seek damages from the cartelists for the losses suffered.[114] Importantly, the Court, following the Advocate General's Opinion, argued that the guarantee of the full effectiveness of Article 101 TFEU and effective protection against the adverse effects of an infringement of competition law would be seriously undermined if the possibility of requesting compensation for loss caused by a cartel were limited to suppliers and customers of the market affected by the cartel. That would from the outset systematically deprive potential victims of the possibility of requesting compensation. Consequently, it is not necessary that the loss suffered by such an injured third party presents, in addition, a specific connection with the 'objective of protection' pursued by Article 101 TFEU.[115]

Let us now focus on the fourth category of claimants identified above, namely the indirect purchasers, since it is with respect to such actors that practical challenges are more prone to occur. As pointed out above, the lack of a direct contractual link between the purchasers in the downstream markets and the antitrust infringers in the upstream market does not exclude the indirect purchasers from the possibility to rely on the EU right to claim damages. This is because, as pointed out in Recital 39 of the Private Damages Directive 2014, the overcharge in the upstream market may have been entirely or partially passed on downstream by the (intermediary) direct purchasers, who incorporated the cartel overcharge in the price

---

[114] Case C-435/18 *Otis II*, ECLI:EU:C:2019:1069, par. 32–34.
[115] Ibid, par. 27, 31.

they charge their consumers or customers. This matter relates greatly to the question of who should pay the damages and what proportion of the damage should be covered by the infringers, a question which will be tackled in the paragraphs below; for the purpose of the discussion at hand, the relevant question is what course of action should the victims go for, and what defences are available to the infringers in case a (partial) passing-on of overcharges occurred. The so-called 'passing-on defence' relates to the cartelists being able to defend against the direct purchasers who pass on the overcharge to the consumers downstream and then claim damages from the cartelists upstream. The US federal private enforcement system does not accept such a defence invoked by the infringers. Furthermore, the US federal anti-trust enforcement system does not confer standing to the indirect purchasers downstream (most often, end-consumers) either, when they would want to sue the infringers upstream directly, in order to obtain reparation for the overcharge that was passed on to them by the direct purchasers.[116] Nevertheless, in the US, under state law, the indirect purchasers are afforded the possibility to seek damages.[117] In the European context, passing-on may be read between the lines as early as *Courage and Crehan* and *Manfredi*: both rulings speak of *any* individual who has suffered harm (meaning, indirect purchasers too), and of prevent-ing the occurrence of unjust enrichment (e.g. by allowing infringers to use the passing-on defence against direct purchasers, who could otherwise become unjustly enriched). Yet, as we pointed out above, the Green Paper 2005 adopted a similar approach to the US, overlooking the passing-on defence. However, the White Paper 2008 reversed this stance, by suggesting that infringers may rely on the passing-on defence, and indirect purchasers should enjoy a rebuttable presumption that the overcharge was passed on to them.[118] The Private Damages Directive 2014 builds on this latter approach, by acknowledging both the passing-on defence and the standing of indirect purchasers in actions for damages. This makes sense, given the right to full compensation embedded in Article 3 of the Directive, which we will discuss below in section 5.7 of this chapter.

So far, it becomes apparent that the passing-on matter may be used as a defence by the antitrust infringers, against the direct purchasers who, according to the infringers' views, have incorporated the overcharge in the prices charged downstream. This stems from the provisions of Article 13 of the Private Damages Directive 2014. According to Article 14 of the same Directive, the passing-on argument may also be used as an offensive action by the indirect purchasers, in a direct action against the infringers, when claiming that the harm caused by the overcharge reached them all the way in the downstream market. Regardless of which setting is at hand (i.e. offensive or defensive action), Article 12(1) of the Directive provides that compensation of harm exceeding that caused by the infringement of antitrust law to the claimant, as well as the absence of liability of the infringer, should be avoided. In this respect, the Member States are obliged to lay down procedural rules ensuring that compensation for the actual loss incurred does not exceed the overcharge harm which occurred at each particular level of the supply chain. Also, the right to claim and obtain

---

[116] Cases *Hanover Shoe v United Shoe Machinery*, (1968) 392 US 481 and *Illinois Brick v Illinois*, (1977) 431 US 720.

[117] On the reasoning behind this approach, see OECD 2006.

[118] Rusu 2017 (a), p. 806.

compensation for the loss of profit due to a full or partial passing-on of the overcharge should be safeguarded.[119]

When using the passing-on argument as a defence, Article 13 of the Directive is relevant. The actors in such actions are the antitrust infringers, as defendants, and the direct purchasers, as plaintiffs claiming damages. The defendants have the burden of proving that the overcharge was fully or partially passed on, since they are the ones trying to defend themselves from paying multiple and sometimes overlapping amounts to both direct and indirect purchasers. In order to substantiate such proof, the defendants may reasonably require disclosure of evidence from the direct purchaser or from third parties. In practice, due to the overcharge being passed on, the direct purchasers who have absorbed the overcharge in their prices charged downstream do not incur injuries, or incur injuries only with regard to the part of the overcharge which was not passed on. This is where the risk of unjust enrichment becomes visible, if the direct purchaser passes on the overcharge and is also able to claim damages for that overcharge. The situation becomes complicated if the indirect purchaser too claims damages for the overcharge passed on to it. In order to avoid situations of multiple liabilities or absence of liability, for that matter, Recital 44 and Article 15 of the Directive provide rules meant to avoid such liability complications arising from actions for damages by claimants from different levels in the supply chain.[120] In this respect, national courts, particularly where they find that passing-on has been proven, should be able to take due account, by procedural or substantive means available under EU and national law, of the following issues: (1) any damages action related to the same infringement, brought by claimants from other levels in the supply chain, (2) the resulting judgments referring to point (1), and (3) relevant information in the public domain resulting from the public enforcement of competition law.

When the passing-on argument is used as an offensive action, Article 14 of the Directive is relevant. Here we are talking about the indirect purchasers claiming that the overcharge resulting from the antitrust infringement was absorbed by the direct purchasers and it has reached them in the downstream market, through higher prices that were paid to the direct purchasers. In this setting, the indirect purchasers in the downstream market initiate actions for damages against the antitrust infringers in the upstream market. Where the existence of a claim for damages or the amount of compensation to be awarded depends on whether, or to what degree, an overcharge was passed on to the claimant, the burden of proving the existence and scope of such a passing-on rests with the claimant, who again may reasonably require disclosure of evidence from the infringers or from third parties. While reading Recitals 39 and 41 of the Directive, it seems reasonable to have the indirect purchasers bear the burden of proof, since it is them who claim they suffered harm, and not the direct purchasers, who incorporated (part of) the overcharge in their prices downstream. The situation is a bit more complex though, than in cases where the passing-on matter is used as a defence. This is so because the causation between the harm and the infringement is more remote in cases involving indirect purchasers. As a reminder, causality is an item not harmonised by the Directive's provisions, thus still depending on legal and factual circumstances

---

[119] Private Damages Directive 2014, Article 12(2) and (3).

[120] Strand 2014.

governed by domestic laws, which must abide by the effectiveness and equivalence principles. Nevertheless, the Directive comes to the help of indirect purchasers, by providing in Article 14(2) that they shall be deemed to have proven that a passing-on occurred when they show that: (1) the defendant committed an infringement, (2) the infringement resulted in an overcharge for the direct purchaser, and (3) the indirect purchaser purchased the goods/services that were the object of the infringement, or has purchased goods/services derived from or containing them. As helpful as this may be, this is nevertheless a rebuttable presumption that passing-on has occurred, since the infringers may demonstrate credibly that the overcharge was not, or was not entirely, passed on to the indirect purchaser. Also, the Article 14(2) presumption relates only to the *existence* of passing-on, and not to the *rate* of passing-on (i.e. the extent to which the overcharge was passed on). This latter aspect remains within the domestic autonomy ambit, governed by the national rules and procedures, under the effectiveness and equivalence principles.[121]

Speaking of domestic jurisdictions, it is important to mention that the passing-on doctrine was already recognised in some of the EU Member States, even before the Private Damages Directive 2014 came into force, primarily through the jurisprudence of the domestic courts.[122] Yet, Botta[123] argues that this 'passing-on jurisprudence' seems to be built on different premises than the EU case-law on private enforcement: while the latter often points to the need to preserve the effective enforcement of EU competition law, the former seems to be based more on the compensatory nature of civil damages actions. Furthermore, the domestic approaches to passing-on in the Italian, French and German jurisdictions seem to be showing important differences when it comes to how the passing-on doctrine is practically applied. The former two jurisdictions, prior to the implementation of the Private Damages Directive 2014, did not acknowledge a reversal of the burden of proof in relation to the passing-on defence. In other words, in Italy and France, it was up to the claimant (i.e. the direct customer) to prove that it has not passed the price overcharge downstream. In Germany, furthermore, the use of legal presumptions facilitating the legal standing of indirect purchasers was often regarded with scepticism.[124] The benefit of the Private Damages Directive 2014, when it comes to passing-on, is that such diverging approaches in national case-law are ironed out. This may very well mean that the domestic case-law referred to above will go through important revisions. For the purposes of implementation, most Member States copied (almost) verbatim in their legislation the text of Articles 12–14 of the Private Damages Directive 2014, dealing with indirect purchasers and the passing-on doctrine.[125] Some states, however, chose not to implement certain provisions of the Directive dealing with this topic. For example, in the

---

[121] Ibid, p. 376; Rusu 2017 (a), pp. 806–7.

[122] E.g. cases *ORWI*, Bundesgerichtshof 28 June 2011, KZR 75/10, in Germany; *Le Gouessant*, Cour de Cassation 15 May 2012, 11-18495, in France; *Indaba*, Corte di Appello di Torino, 6 July 2000, in Italy.

[123] Botta 2017.

[124] Ibid, p. 881 *et seq.*

[125] In Romania, for example, see Government Ordinance 39/2017, OJ 422/2017, Articles 12–14. In Ireland, see Part 4 of Statutory Instrument No. 43/2017 – European Union (Actions for Damages for Infringements of Competition Law). In Spain, see Articles 78–80 of the Competition Law.

Netherlands, Article 193p of the Civil Code implements only the first sentence of Article 13 of the Private Damages Directive 2014. The Dutch legislator deemed it unnecessary to implement the second sentence which states that the defendant bears the burden of proof that the overcharge was passed on. According to the Dutch legislator the sentence is already catered for in Article 150 of the Code of Civil Procedure, which deals with allocation of the burden of proof, and in Article 843a, which already allows the defendant the possibility to reasonably require disclosure of evidence from the claimant or third parties.[126] The German legislator opted for an interesting approach too, when implementing the second sentence of Article 13. Section 33c of the GWB provides that in case of purchases at excessive price, the harm incurred by the purchaser shall be *deemed* to be remedied to the extent that the purchaser has passed on the overcharge resulting from an infringement to its customers. The injured party's right to claim compensation for lost profits under Section 252 of the German Civil Code shall remain unaffected, to the extent that such loss of profit is the result of the passing-on of the overcharge.

5.3 Limitation periods and their suspension: when should damages actions be initiated?

By now, it is clear that the EU right to claim damages may be relied on by any person who has suffered harm due to infringements of the antitrust rules. However, this right may not be exercised indefinitely. Actions before domestic courts may be initiated only within a given time frame. This matter relates to the limitation periods imposed by the domestic laws for starting damages actions. The Private Damages Directive 2014 harmonises the domestic rules which provide for such limitation periods. In this respect, Article 10(1) of the Directive refers to the domestic rules which determine when the limitation period begins to run, the duration thereof, and the circumstances under which it is interrupted or suspended, while Recital 36 makes it clear that such rules should not unduly hamper the bringing of actions for damages. This is particularly important in follow-on actions which build upon an infringement established by a competition authority or a review court, and therefore it is key to allow for damages actions to be started after the conclusion of the public enforcement proceedings. To this end, Article 10(4) of the Directive provides that the suspension or interruption of the limitation period (as the case may be in domestic law) shall be ensured if an NCA takes public enforcement investigative or decision-making action connected to practices to which the action for damages relates. The suspension shall end at the earliest of one year after the infringement decision has become final or after the proceedings are otherwise terminated. For the sake of completeness, it has to be mentioned that limitation periods can also interfere with the parties' intentions to engage in consensual dispute resolution. Recital 49 and Article 18(1) of the Directive come to the rescue in this respect: in order to provide the infringers and the victims with a genuine opportunity to come to an agreement on the compensation to be paid, before bringing proceedings before national courts, the limitation periods should be suspended for the duration of any consensual dispute resolution process. However, this

---

[126] Rusu and Looijestijn-Clearie 2017 (b), p. 377.

suspension benefits only those parties that are or that were involved or represented in the consensual dispute resolution.

Regarding the moment when limitation periods begin to run, Article 10(2) of the Directive makes it crystal clear that this cannot take place before the antitrust infringement has ceased, and the claimant knows, or can reasonably be expected to know: (1) of the behaviour and the fact that it constitutes an infringement, (2) of the fact that the infringement caused it harm, and (3) the identity of the infringer. These provisions rightfully tackle the potentially problematic scenarios envisioned by the Court in the *Manfredi* ruling, particularly in connection with short limitation periods which begin to run from the day on which the alleged anticompetitive practice was adopted, or when the infringements are continuous or repeated, in which case there would be a real possibility that the limitation period expires even before the infringements were ended.[127] Another example of problematic limitation periods can be found in the more recent *Cogeco* case.[128] This judgment was handed down after the adoption of the Private Damages Directive 2014. However, the facts of the case did not fall under the temporal application of the Directive. The limitation period aspect dealt with in this case was therefore handled in light of the principle of effectiveness. The CJEU ruled that this principle precludes a national limitation period of three years, which, first, starts to run from the date on which the injured party was aware of its right to compensation, even if the infringer is not known and, secondly, may not be suspended or interrupted in the course of proceedings before the national competition authority. The Court therefore held that such a provision of national law renders the exercise of the right to full compensation practically impossible or excessively difficult. After the Directive is fully and correctly implemented in a national law system such scenarios are arguably less likely to occur and potential enforcement gaps of the kind discussed above should thus be closed.

Moving on, Article 10(3) of the Directive demands that limitation periods for bringing damages actions should be of at least five years. This is quite a generous deadline, which if combined with the possibility of suspension or interruption, and considering when the limitation period begins to run (according to Article 10(2) of the Directive), may result in proceedings commencing in practice many years after the infringement has ended.[129] What is more, the language used in Article 10 (i.e. *at least* five years, suspension shall end *at the earliest* one year after . . ., and so on) suggests that the harmonisation technique employed by the Directive when it comes to limitation periods is that of minimum harmonisation. This means that the Member States are allowed to regulate above the EU law minimum standard, by providing, for example, for longer limitation periods, as long as the principles of effectiveness and equivalence are observed. On this note, indeed, Recital 36 of the Directive allows Member States the possibility to maintain or introduce absolute limitation periods that are of general application, provided that the duration of such absolute limitation periods does not render practically impossible or excessively difficult the exercise of the right to full compensation.

---

[127] Joined cases C-295 to C-298/04 *Manfredi*, ECLI:EU:C:2006:461, par. 78, 79.

[128] Case C-637/17 *Cogeco*, ECLI:EU:C:2019:263.

[129] Jones, Sufrin and Dunne 2019, p. 1051.

There are no surprises as far as the implementation of the limitation period provisions of the Private Damages Directive 2014 in the Member States' legal orders. Most Member States have chosen the five-year period required by the Directive. This period has nevertheless produced important consequences in certain Member States, more than in others. For example, in Spain the five-year period now embedded in Article 74 of the Competition Law replaces the (rather short) one-year limitation period previously used based on Article 1968 of the Civil Code. In other Member States, like Germany, the GWB provides different deadlines, prescribed based on different circumstances relating to the degree of knowledge of the infringement. Section 33h of the Act provides limitation periods as short as five years and as long as 30 years.

5.4 Disclosure of evidence

By now, it should be clear who is entitled to claim damages and when such proceedings should be initiated. It is now time to dwell upon the question of how should such claims be substantiated in front of the domestic courts, or better yet, how can victims have access to the necessary evidence to prove that they have suffered harm, and also the extent of that harm. With regard to the first matter, we have already provided above that Article 17(2) of the Directive puts forward a rebuttable presumption that cartels cause harm. As we will detail below, when speaking of infringements performed jointly by multiple undertakings, this presumption is quite useful for the victims. On the same note, as already pointed out in section 5.1 above, particularly in follow-on actions, Article 9 of the Directive provides extra help for the victims when it comes to proving that an infringement has occurred. With regard to the second matter, namely the extent of the harm suffered, the matter of disclosure of evidence becomes relevant. Articles 5 to 8 of the Directive are relevant in this respect.

Recitals 14 and 15 of the Directive provide that actions for damages typically require a complex factual and economic analysis. The evidence necessary to prove a claim for damages is often held exclusively by the opposing party or by third parties, and is not sufficiently known by, or accessible to, the claimant. Since such information asymmetry may be detrimental to the effective exercise of the right to full compensation, a clear system regulating the disclosure of evidence relevant to the claim is necessary, for more vigorous private enforcement.[130] Such a system must nevertheless also protect the defendants in actions for damages. This is why, in certain circumstances, such as when the passing-on argument is put forward (Articles 13 and 14 of the Directive), not only the claimants, but also the defendants may reasonably require the disclosure of relevant evidence. Furthermore, the national courts should be able to order that evidence be disclosed by third parties, including public authorities, too. In this last respect though, the principles of legal and administrative cooperation under EU or national law must apply. All in all, the matters surrounding the disclosure of evidence must be treated with care, since, more often than not, they essentially entail a balancing of opposing interests, some of which may be favoured and others which may be jeopardised, if disclosure is ordered or not, respectively. This is probably why the

---

[130] Wagner-von Papp 2016, p. 1.

disclosure provisions were not designed to reach as far as they potentially could: essentially, the Directive enables national courts to order disclosure, but does not mandate disclosure.[131] Whether this approach will suffice to ensure more meaningful private enforcement in the EU remains to be seen.

Article 5 of the Directive provides the main rules on disclosure of evidence.[132] These rules are meant to provide the bare bones of the disclosure exercise, since the Member States may always adopt rules providing for wider disclosure, according to the last paragraph of this Article, however, without prejudice to important items connected to the disclosure process: protecting confidential information (Article 5(4)), observing the legal professional privilege principle (Article 5(6)) and affording the party summoned with the disclosure of evidence the right to be heard (Article 5(7)). Essentially, the domestic courts must be able to order the disclosure of evidence which lies in the control of the defendant, the claimant or a third party. Nevertheless, this disclosure must not be absolute. When speaking of claimants requesting the disclosure of evidence, Article 5(1) of the Directive sets certain important criteria to be met: first, the claimant must put forward a reasoned justification containing reasonably available facts and evidence sufficient to support the plausibility of the claim for damages. This means that the claimant must make a plausible assertion that it has suffered harm, caused by the defendant. It may do so by pointing to, among other issues, an infringement decision of a competition authority and to the presumption embedded in Article 17(2) of the Directive. Second, the claimant may not request all sorts of evidence which may or may not be useful for its claim. According to Article 5(2), the disclosure must pertain only to specified items of evidence or relevant categories of evidence circumscribed as precisely and as narrowly as possible, on the basis of the reasonably available facts in the reasoned justification. Recital 16 clarifies that where a request for disclosure aims to obtain a category of evidence, that category should be identified by reference to common features of its constitutive elements such as the nature, object or content of the documents the disclosure of which is requested, the time during which they were drawn up or other criteria, provided that the evidence falling within the category is relevant within the meaning of this Directive. Third, and in very close connection to the previous two requirements mentioned, according to Article 5(3), the disclosure of evidence should be proportionate. As mentioned above, since the domestic courts deal with opposing interests, they should take into account the legitimate interests of all parties concerned, although the interest of undertakings to avoid actions for damages shall naturally not constitute an interest that warrants protection.[133] When performing the proportionality check, the domestic courts should pay close attention in particular to the following items: how is the claim, or the defence, supported by the available facts and evidence put forward in the disclosure request; the scope and cost of disclosure; the prevention of non-specific searches for information of questionable relevance; the potentially confidential nature of the information sought, which may nevertheless be disclosed if effective protection

---

[131] Ibid.

[132] Braat 2018, pp. 128–9.

[133] Private Damages Directive 2014, Article 5(5).

mechanisms are in place.[134] Recital 18 of the Directive provides examples of such protection mechanisms, which should in any case not impede the exercise of the right to compensation: redacting sensitive passages in documents, conducting hearings *in camera*, restricting the persons allowed to see the evidence, and instructing experts to produce summaries of the information in an aggregated or otherwise non-confidential form.

As provided above, relevant evidence may be in the possession of competition authorities. The domestic courts should be able to request these authorities to disclose relevant evidence. Nevertheless, the disclosure of such information should not unduly detract from the effectiveness of the antitrust enforcement performed by the Commission and the NCAs. This is why, according to Recital 21, the effectiveness and consistency of the application of the EU antitrust rules by these authorities require a common EU approach on the disclosure of evidence that is included in the file of a competition authority. This approach is essentially provided in Article 6 of the Directive, which complements the basics embedded in Article 5, discussed above, with stricter rules and requirements. The starting point here is that the disclosure of items in the file of a competition authority should be a 'last resort' instrument in the hands of the parties: Article 6(10) allows for such disclosure only when no other (third) party is able to provide that evidence.[135] Also, the disclosure should not pertain to every document relating to proceedings under Article 101 or 102 TFEU. Indeed, according to Article 6(3), the Directive does not cover the disclosure of internal documents of, or correspondence between, competition authorities. Also, it is highly unlikely that the action for damages will need to be based on *all* the evidence in the file relating to those proceedings. Such wide, generic disclosure would actually be disproportionate, and at the end of the day, incompatible with the requesting party's duty to specify the items of evidence or the categories of evidence as precisely and narrowly as possible. According to Recital 23, proportionality is important when disclosing evidence from a competition authority's file, since the disclosure of evidence may risk unravelling the investigation strategy of the authority by revealing which documents are part of the file, or it may risk having a negative effect on the way in which undertakings cooperate with the authorities. Once again, one must recall that one of the objectives of the Directive is achieving a better coordination between private and public enforcement mechanisms. In this respect, Article 6 supplements the proportionality requirements of the disclosure of evidence exercise, embedded in Article 5(3), by requiring the national courts to allow the NCA to submit its proportionality-related observations, if there are any (Article 6(11)), and also pay attention to the following items (Article 6(4)): whether the disclosure request has been formulated specifically with regard to the nature, subject matter or contents of documents submitted to a competition authority or held in the file thereof, rather than by a non-specific application concerning documents submitted to a competition authority; whether the party requesting disclosure is doing so in relation to an action for damages before a national court; the need to safeguard the effectiveness of the public enforcement of competition law.

Particularly in this last respect, Article 6 brings clarity as to which evidence may or may

---

[134] Ibid, Article 5(4).

[135] Wils 2017, p. 31.

not be disclosed, by creating a three-prong categorisation of the documents which are in a competition authority's file. First, the so-called 'grey list' documents relate to evidence or categories of evidence which, according to Article 6(5), may be disclosed only after a competition authority, by adopting a decision or otherwise, has closed its proceedings, with the exception of decisions on interim measures. To reflect this stance, the Commission has amended its rules regarding the conduct of proceedings, so that the Directive's provisions on disclosure are consistently observed.[136] Getting back to Article 6(5) of the Directive, its provisions relate to information that was prepared by a natural or legal person specifically for the authority's proceedings (e.g. witness statements, replies to requests for information), information that the authority has drawn up and sent to the parties in the course of its proceedings (e.g. statements of objection), and withdrawn settlement submissions. The practical effect of temporarily protecting such documents from disclosure is to discourage 'stand-alone' actions running in parallel with public enforcement proceedings, and to encourage instead follow-on actions. Given the suspension of domestic proceedings during public enforcement action, provided in Article 10 of the Directive, this should not necessarily be a problem for claimants.[137]

Second, the so-called 'black-listed' documents may, according to Article 6(6), never be disclosed for the purpose of actions for damages. These documents include leniency statements and settlement submissions, as defined in Article 2(16) and (18) of the Directive. Recital 26 of the Directive makes it clear that the black list should be limited to *voluntary* and *self-incriminating* leniency statements and settlement submissions (and verbatim quotations from them included in other documents), in order to ensure that the injured parties' right to compensation is not unduly interfered with. All other documents accompanying such statements and submissions remain disclosable.[138] The same recital further explains the rationale for protecting the voluntary and self-incriminating leniency statements and settlement submissions from disclosure: leniency programmes and settlement procedures are important public enforcement tools, allowing, more often than not, the detection, efficient prosecution and sanctioning of cartels. The public enforcement decisions taken to this end benefit greatly effective follow-on actions for damages. If self-incriminating documents produced solely for the purpose of cooperating with the authorities in the public enforcement process (i.e. leniency and settlements) were to be disclosed, the incentives for such cooperation would be seriously undermined.[139] Furthermore, such disclosure would yield more severe civil or even criminal liability[140] than in the case of those co-infringers not cooperating with the competition authorities. Therefore, in order to preserve the 'whistle-blowing' incentives, the Directive argues that protection needs to be granted to leniency statements and settlement submissions, when it comes to the application of the disclosure of evidence rules. Of course, this stance raises fundamental questions as to the relationship between private and public

---

[136] Conduct of Proceedings Regulations 2004 and 2015.

[137] Wils 2017, p. 36.

[138] Chirita 2018.

[139] Veenbrink and Rusu 2014, p. 113; Wils 2017, p. 33.

[140] E.g. Contreras 2017.

enforcement means of the antitrust rules.[141] As we will see below, this relationship extends also to the liability that immunity recipients bear towards the infringement victims, when reported to the liability incurred by the co-infringers. The leniency and private enforcement balance that emerges in this respect will be discussed at length in section 5.6 of this chapter.

For now, it is time to move to the third category of evidence discussed in Article 6 of the Directive. Paragraph 9 of this Article contains the so-called 'residual' category of documents that may be subject to disclosure, namely evidence in the file of a competition authority that does not fall into any of the categories listed in Article 6 (i.e. grey list or black list documents). The disclosure of such documents, including evidence that exists independently of the proceedings of a competition authority (the so-called 'pre-existing information')[142] may be ordered by the domestic courts at any time in actions for damages.

This approach to the first and third categories of evidence ensures that injured parties retain sufficient alternative means by which to obtain access to the relevant evidence that they need in order to prepare their actions for damages. In the same respect, according to Recital 27 and Article 6(7), national courts should themselves be furthermore able, upon a reasoned request by a claimant, to access the black-listed documents in order to verify whether the contents thereof fall outside the definitions of leniency statements and settlement submissions laid down in the Directive. Any content falling outside those definitions should be disclosable under the relevant conditions: the authors of the evidence in question may also have the possibility to be heard; national courts may request assistance only from the competent competition authority; other parties or third parties are not permitted access to that evidence. Lastly, if such black-listed documents are located in the file of the Commission, and the domestic court deems it important to have access to them in order to ensure the effectiveness of the victims' right to obtain compensation, recourse may be made to the national court's prerogative to request the Commission to transmit the file, based on Article 15(1) of Regulation 1/2003. Should the Commission refuse this, after weighing up the relevant interests in the case, the domestic court could test the validity of the Commission's negative decision by formulating a preliminary ruling question under Article 267 TFEU, or the claimant could make an application for annulment based on Article 263 TFEU.[143]

A further note over here needs to be made in relation to the limits placed on the use of evidence obtained from the file of a competition authority, and the penalties relating to evidence handling. First, regarding the discussion on limits, Article 7 provides that the evidence legally obtained based on the provisions of Article 6 can only be used in an action for damages by the person who obtained it, or by a natural or legal person that succeeded to that person's rights, including a person that acquired that person's claim. This applies also to situations where the evidence was obtained by a legal person forming part of a corporate group constituting a single undertaking: other legal persons belonging to the same undertaking should also be

---

[141] Rusu 2017 (b), pp. 16–17.

[142] Private Damages Directive 2014, Recital 28. See also the definition of 'pre-existing information' provided in the Private Damages Directive 2014, Article 2(17).

[143] Wils 2017, p. 35.

able to use that evidence.[144] Article 7(2) and (3) provide that black-listed evidence, and the grey-listed documents before the competition authority has closed its proceedings, should be either deemed inadmissible in actions for damages, or should otherwise be protected under the applicable national rules. Moreover, such evidence should not become an object of trade.[145] The rationale here is rather straightforward, namely to ensure the full effect of the limits on the disclosure of evidence set out in Article 6. Second, with regard to the penalties relating to evidence handling, Article 8 of the Directive is relevant. The rules provided in this respect are meant to curb the temptation to destroy or hide evidence that would be useful in substantiating an injured party's claim for damages, once such an action has been initiated. To this end, the domestic courts should be able to impose effective, proportionate and dissuasive penalties when orders for disclosure of evidence or obligations to protect confidential information are not complied with, when relevant evidence is destroyed, and when the limits of use of evidence imposed by Article 7 are breached. Article 8(2) and Recital 33 provide that penalties shall include the possibility to draw adverse inferences, such as presuming the relevant issue to be proven or dismissing claims and defences in whole or in part, and the possibility to order the payment of costs. Such penalties may be particularly effective in preventing undue delays and potentially abusive behaviour.

The domestic implementation of the disclosure of evidence provisions of the Private Damages Directive 2014 is also quite diverse and complex. In the Netherlands, a new section, entitled 'Access to documents in cases concerning the infringement of competition law' was inserted into the Code of Civil Procedure (Articles 844–850). Article 843a of the Code of Civil Procedure governs the discovery of documents in Dutch civil procedural law and grants wider access to documents than Article 5 of the Private Damages Directive 2014. The new section in the Code of Civil Procedure was necessary, especially when the Directive's provisions deviate from the provisions of Article 843a. For example, according to Article 845, by derogation from Article 843a(4), the person who has at his/her disposal or in his/her custody documents concerning an action for damages due to an infringement of competition law is not required to grant access to copies or extracts of such documents if there are serious grounds for not doing so. Otherwise, Article 846, which implements Article 6(6) of the Private Damages Directive 2014, states in no uncertain terms that copies or extracts of leniency statements and settlement submission available only from the file of a competition authority shall not be disclosed, as they do not constitute evidence in actions for damages due to an infringement of competition law.[146] At the other end of the spectrum, in Spain, the Directive added significant value as far as evidence disclosure is concerned, to the point where the initial drafts of the implementation Act aimed to extend the application of these rules to all civil litigation. As things stand though, the disclosure rules, which were fully implemented in Spanish legislation (Article 283bis(a)–(k) of the Procedural Civil Code),

---

[144] Private Damages Directive 2014, Article 7(1), Recital 31.

[145] Ibid, Recital 32.

[146] For a full account of the evidence disclosure provisions added to the Dutch legislation due to the implementation of the Directive, see Rusu and Looijestijn-Clearie 2017 (b), p. 377 *et seq.*

apply now only to antitrust damages actions. Maillo[147] argues that the changes brought about by the Directive greatly improve access to evidence since, prior to the implementation, this matter was one of the significant bottlenecks in starting damages actions in Spain, both prior and during the trial. Articles 256.1.2a and 297 of the Procedural Civil Code regulated preliminary proceedings and measures of assurance of evidence respectively, however, both provisions having limited scope. Once the trial started, Articles 328 *et seq.* of the Procedural Civil Code provided for certain disclosure possibilities, however, again modest in their reach. In France Title VIII (particularly Articles L.483-1 *et seq.*) of the Code de Commerce, introduced by Ordinance 2017-303 of the French Government, implements the access to evidence provisions of the Directive. Prior to the implementation, the general rules governing civil procedure were applicable (Articles 10–11 and 132–142 of the Civil Procedural Code), and still are, as long as they do not conflict with the implementation of the Private Damages Directive 2014. The implementation brought about some peculiar changes to the French system. For example, while implementing Article 5 of the Directive, Article L.483-1 of the Code de Commerce permits claimants to request the disclosure of *categories* of evidence, whereas before the implementation, only *well-defined items* could be requested for disclosure. Nevertheless, Article R.483-1 prescribes that such categories of evidence must be identified as precisely and narrowly as possible, by reference to common and relevant characteristics of its constituent elements, such as the nature, the object, the time of the establishment or content of the documents for which communication or production is requested. Further, Solidoro[148] remarkably argues that the balancing exercise the national judges need to engage in while assessing the conflicting interests regarding evidence disclosure, as prescribed by Article 5(3) of the Directive, is a novelty for French procedural law. The same author argues that the black-list/grey-list dichotomy contained in Article 6(5) and (6) of the Directive impacted the discretion the French Competition Authority previously enjoyed, as far as disclosing its files in court proceedings, a system which was arguably designed to strengthen the cooperation between this NCA and the national courts. After the Directive's implementation, however, Article L.483-5 of the Code de Commerce prohibits national courts to order the French Competition Authority from disclosing leniency statements and settlement submissions. Lastly for now, Article 8 of the Private Damages Directive 2014 requests the Member States to enact provisions enabling the courts to impose effective, proportionate and dissuasive penalties when orders for disclosure of evidence or obligations to protect confidential information are not complied with. A striking diversity may be observed as far as what Member States considered effective and dissuasive penalties in this respect. For example, in Slovakia fines of up to 500 EUR for a single refusal to produce documents, and up to 2000 EUR for repeat offenders in this respect. In Romania, fines range from between little over (national currency equivalent of) 100 EUR to 1000 EUR for natural persons, to 0.1 to 1 per cent of the undertaking's turnover in the previous financial year, for legal persons.[149] In Hungary, based on Article 88/Q(2) of the Competition Act the maximum amount of fine that may be

---

[147] J. Maillo, 'Antitrust Damages Claims in Spain' in Parcu, Monti and Botta 2018, pp. 168–9.

[148] S. Solidoro, 'Private Antitrust Enforcement in France' in Parcu, Monti and Botta 2018, p. 187.

[149] Government Ordinance 39/2017, OJ 422/2017, Article 8.

imposed is around (national currency equivalent of) 160 000 EUR. In Poland, Articles 27 and 28 of the Act on Claims for Damages put forward an interesting setup: fines up to (national currency equivalent of) 5000 EUR may be imposed if a disclosure of evidence is requested in bad faith, or if evidence is used for other purposes than the pending proceedings. However, there is no fine set for non-compliance with a disclosure order. Instead, very much in line with Article 8(2) of the Private Damages Directive 2014, courts may consider as established the facts which were supposed to be established by the requested evidence, unless the entity not complying with the disclosure order proves otherwise (i.e. rebuttable presumption).

5.5 Liability of infringers: who must pay the damages?

Once we have seen who can claim damages and what are the tools available to this end, it is now time to turn our attention to the question of, who is liable to pay damages? The answer here is those who have infringed the antitrust rules, since it is these undertakings that did not observe the responsibility of not infringing the cartel and abuse of dominance prohibitions. This was so even before the enactment of the Private Damages Directive 2014, as signalled by the case-law of the CJEU discussed above, which embodied the infringers' liability for damages in the essence of the concept of the EU right to claim compensation (e.g. claiming damages for loss caused by a contract or by conduct liable to restrict or distort competition). Furthermore, the private law liability of the infringers to compensate the harm caused must be acknowledged regardless of the fines and sanctions imposed through Commission or NCAs' public enforcement decisions, and irrespective of whether leniency immunity or fine reductions have been obtained. This makes sense having in mind the separate nature of the public and private enforcement systems and the respective goals they serve. Nevertheless, we must make it clear on this note that, as already pointed out several times above, the functions of leniency tools and of private damages claims interact in practice, and the consequences of the interplay between the two can raise fundamental enforcement questions. We will deal with such matters in the following section 5.6 of this chapter.

At this point, the discussion needs to be nuanced with regard to the identity of those who are liable to pay damages. If the infringement of the antitrust rules has been performed by a single undertaking, this entity should be the one covering the full compensation to which all the victims of the infringement are entitled. This is the case, for example, of abusive practices performed by a dominant undertaking, which infringes Article 102 TFEU.

On a side note to this discussion, the matter of the parental/(economic) successor liability for the subsidiary's/previously existing company's antitrust infringements has to be dealt with. The question here is whether civil liability of a parent or successor company for infringements performed by other companies may be established. This discussion is relevant given that in public enforcement proceedings, when it comes to the fines that must be paid by the undertakings infringing the antitrust rules, the concept of the single economic unit comes into play. We have discussed the doctrine of the single economic unit in Chapter 2. It is settled case-law of the CJEU[150] that the anti-competitive behaviour of a wholly owned subsidiary

---

[150] Cases C-97/08 P *Akzo Nobel*, ECLI:EU:C:2009:536; C-516/15 P *Akzo Nobel*, ECLI:EU:C:2017:314.

may be imputed to the parent company, when both form part of the same economic unit. In such a setting, the parent company is actually presumed to exercise decisive influence over its wholly owned subsidiary, unless it adduces sufficient evidence to show that the subsidiary acts independently on the market, and therefore it will be regarded as jointly and severally liable for the payment of any fine imposed on the subsidiary. In later case-law,[151] the Court pointed out that an entity that is not responsible for the infringement can nevertheless be penalised for that infringement, if the entity that has committed the infringement has ceased to exist, either in law or economically. This happens when the assets of the infringer are transferred to independent undertakings. Therefore, the restructuring (via whatever means) of the infringing companies' structure does not necessarily create a new undertaking that is free of liability for the conduct of its predecessor, where, from an economic point of view, the two entities are identical. This is essentially an embodiment of the principle of economic continuity. Thus, in public enforcement, parental liability and liability of economic and legal successors exists and it is strongly embedded in EU law. In other words, liability follows those assets, as confirmed also by Article 13(5) of the ECN+ Directive 2019, which states that for the purpose of imposing fines on parent companies and legal and economic successors of undertakings, the notion of undertaking applies.[152]

Can (and must) this approach be transposed to civil law liability in private damages claims too? This issue is not dealt with in the Private Damages Directive 2014, and thus, one might have thought that in the absence of EU law, its regulation is left to the competence of the Member States, who must observe the principles of effectiveness and equivalence when dealing with it. So, according to some authors, an analogous application of the public enforcement line of reasoning, in order to establish the civil liability of a parent company or successor for other companies' actions, is not required in EU law.[153] Nevertheless, there are other authors who argued, based on a textual interpretation of the Private Damages Directive 2014, as well as based on the widely recognised goal of ensuring a consistent interpretation of EU law, that it is likely that parent company liability will become the general rule in EU competition law, thus covering also private damages proceedings.[154] The Court had the opportunity to settle this matter in the *Skanska* preliminary ruling. The key question that the Court had to answer was whether the determination of the entities liable to pay damages should be done on the basis of national provisions and the EU principle of effectiveness, or whether this determination pertains to EU law, being directly embedded in the interpretation of Article 101 TFEU? Following the Opinion of Advocate General Wahl,[155] the Court reached the reasonable conclusion that the concept of undertaking, and for that matter, the concepts of single economic unit and economic continuity, play the same role when establishing liability in actions for damages, as they play when determining the entities liable in cases concerning fines (i.e. public enforcement). Consequently, establishing which entities should be

---

[151] Cases C-280/06 *ETI*, ECLI:EU:C:2007:775; T-531/15 *Coveris*, ECLI:EU:T:2018:885.

[152] Rusu 2019.

[153] Van Leuken 2016.

[154] Koenig 2017; Koenig 2018.

[155] Case C-724/17 *Skanska*, Opinion of Advocate General Wahl, ECLI:EU:C:2019:100.

held liable to pay damages is a constitutive condition of liability governed by EU law, namely Article 101 TFEU: it is, in the words of the Advocate General, the other side of the coin of the right to claim compensation for harm caused by a breach of EU antitrust law. Therefore, establishing the liability of (economic) successors and, logically for that matter, the liability of parent companies, too, are not matters pertaining to the procedural autonomy of the Member States. They flow directly from EU law. This means, according to the Court's ruling in *Skanska*, that an individual may seek compensation from a company that has continued the economic activity of an EU antitrust law infringer.

Returning to the infringer's liability discussion, the matter becomes slightly more complicated when the infringement is performed jointly by several undertakings.[156] Recital 37 of the Private Damages Directive 2014 provides that where this is the case (e.g. a cartel), it is appropriate to hold those co-infringers jointly and severally liable for the entire harm caused. What this means in practice for the victims of the infringement is spelled out in Article 11(1): each cartelist is bound to compensate the harm in full, and the victims have the right to require full compensation from any cartelist, until fully compensated. Continuing this line of reasoning, according to Article 11(5) and Recital 37, the co-infringer who covered the amounts due in this respect may subsequently recover from the other cartelists whatever payment exceeded its share.[157] However, this contribution of the co-infringers is only marginally touched upon in the Directive. Essentially, the Member States shall ensure that an infringer may recover a contribution from any other infringer, the amount of which shall be determined in the light of their relative responsibility for the harm caused by the infringement. The determination of that share as the relative responsibility of a given infringer, and the relevant criteria such as turnover, market share or role in the cartel, is a matter for the applicable national law, while respecting the principles of effectiveness and equivalence.

To our mind, the cartelists' joint and several liability is probably the most likely scenario to achieve full compensation for the victims. At the same time, this setup pressures the infringers to cover upfront large amounts in damages. The Directive, however, creates certain exceptions to this rule, thus placing limits on the liability of certain categories of antitrust infringers.[158]

First, SMEs, as defined in the Commission SME Recommendation 2003, are, according to the provisions of Article 11(2) of the Directive, only liable towards their direct and indirect purchasers. The joint and several liability of SMEs is thus removed when it comes to fully compensating *all* victims of the cartel. However, this is so only if the SME at hand has a market share under 5 per cent at any time during the infringement, and the application of the normal rules of joint and several liability would irretrievably jeopardise its economic viability and cause its assets to lose all their value. Should these cumulative conditions not be met, the benefit of the exception is removed. Similarly, according to Article 11(3) of the Directive, no exception from the joint and several liability may be granted to those SMEs which have

---

[156] For the sake of completeness, the parental/successor liability discussion above applies equally to situations of single infringer and multiple infringers.

[157] Rusu 2017 (a), p. 804.

[158] Ibid.

been proven to be 'ring-leaders' (i.e. undertakings that have led the infringement or have coerced other undertakings to participate therein) or are repeat offenders. The Directive's recitals do not explain why the SME exception was created. However, one may support this approach by pointing to the Commission's ongoing general policy of supporting such undertakings, which make up for more than 99 per cent of Europe's businesses.[159] Also, the SME exception may have been introduced in order to mitigate the side effects of the immunity recipient exception, which will be discussed next. As we will see below, the undertaking that receives immunity under a leniency programme may also escape the joint and several liability rule, on top of avoiding the public enforcement fine. The remaining co-infringers, possibly SMEs, may have to pay large fines (through public enforcement decisions) and also compensate jointly all damages incurred by the infringement victims. If these SMEs cannot cope with their payment obligations and eventually exit the market, the immunity recipient may become the largest market player, or even a monopolist.[160]

The second exception to the joint and several liability rule relates to the so-called consensual dispute resolution mechanisms, as embedded in Chapter VI of the Private Damages Directive 2014. Such mechanisms, and the settlement resulting from these processes, are defined in Article 2(21) and (22) of the Directive, as any mechanism enabling parties to reach the out-of-court resolution of a dispute concerning a claim for damages, such as arbitration, mediation or conciliation. Consensual dispute resolution mechanisms are important in the private enforcement of the EU antitrust rules, and they should consequently be encouraged, since, according to Recital 48, they reduce uncertainty for infringers and injured parties and mitigate the drawbacks of extensive litigation. In this respect, Article 18 of the Directive provides rules for the suspension of litigation proceedings, when parties decide to engage in consensual dispute resolution after an action for damages for the same claim has been brought before a national court. Furthermore, according to Recitals 51 and 52 and Article 19 of the Directive, an infringer that pays damages through consensual dispute resolution should not be placed in a worse position vis-à-vis its co-infringers, than it would otherwise be without the consensual settlement. Therefore, in principle, it should thus not pay a total amount of compensation exceeding its relative responsibility for the harm caused by the infringement. Indeed, according to Article 19(1), following a consensual settlement, the claim of the settling injured party is reduced by the settling co-infringer's share of the harm that the infringement inflicted upon the injured party. Further, according to Article 19(2) and (3), the infringers that consensually settled with the victims cannot be held by the non-settling co-infringers to contribute to the remaining claim, except where the non-settling co-infringers cannot pay the damages that correspond to the remaining claim of the settling injured party. The latter possibility may, however, be expressly excluded under the terms of the consensual settlement.[161]

As briefly previewed above, the third exception to the joint and several liability rule, in case

---

[159] Press Release IP/10/1390. See also Action Plan for SMEs 2011.

[160] Case C-289/04 P *Showa Denko v Commission*, Opinion of Advocate General Geelhoed, ECLI:EU:C:2006:52. See also Wils 2017, pp. 28–9.

[161] Wils 2017, p. 30.

of infringements committed jointly by multiple undertakings, relates to those undertakings that were granted immunity from public enforcement fines under a leniency programme, the so-called 'immunity recipients'.[162] We must recall at this point that, according to Article 1(2), one of the goals of the Private Damages Directive 2014 is to better coordinate the public and private enforcement mechanisms of the antitrust rules. According to the provisions embedded in Article 11(4), immunity recipients are exempted from the joint and several liability rule, since they are liable only to their direct and indirect purchasers or providers, unless full compensation cannot be obtained from the co-infringers. Thus, when it comes to covering the damages of purchasers and providers other than those that the immunity recipient has a direct or indirect relationship with, the immunity recipient sits at the end of the co-infringers list from whom the victims may claim damages. Therefore, the immunity recipient will be held liable to purchasers or providers other than its own, only when the other co-infringers can no longer compensate those damages. As previewed above, according to Article 11(5) of the Directive, a consequence of this is that if a co-infringer (i.e. infringer that has not received immunity from fines) has actually covered the full compensation for all the cartel victims, this co-infringer could only recoup from the immunity recipient the amount pertaining to the harm this immunity recipient caused to its own direct or indirect purchasers or providers.[163] Furthermore, this also means that if the infringement caused harm to injured parties other than the infringers' direct or indirect purchasers or providers, the immunity recipient's contribution to compensating such damages is determined in light of its relative responsibility for that harm. In this last respect, this provision embedded in Article 11(6) of the Directive essentially reflects the Court's umbrella pricing case-law, as shaped in the *Kone* ruling discussed above, and also the *Otis II* scenario regarding the right of third parties, not active as suppliers or (direct or indirect) purchasers of the infringers on the same relevant market, to also claim damages for injury caused by the infringement.

The question that may be raised here is what is the Directive's rationale regarding the immunity recipient exception? The answer is very much similar to the one provided above, when talking about the rationale behind protecting leniency statements from disclosure, under Article 6(6) of the Directive, yet the arguments go beyond the idea of *protection* only. Recital 38 of the Directive indeed highlights the value attached to the information provided by immunity recipients when uncovering secret cartels and justifies the *rewards* that should be awarded in private enforcement proceedings to such cooperating undertakings. In this respect, the Directive first *protects* the immunity recipient from potential excessive litigation: this is because the immunity recipient's cooperation mitigates the harm which could have been caused, had the infringement continued; it is therefore appropriate to protect them from undue exposure to damages claims, bearing in mind that the decision of the competition authority finding the infringement may become final for the immunity recipient before it becomes final for other undertakings which have not received immunity, thus potentially making the immunity recipient the preferential target of litigation: a so-called 'sitting duck'.

---

[162] For the definition of the concepts of 'leniency programme', 'immunity recipient' and also other relevant concepts in this context, see Private Damages Directive 2014, Article 2(15) to (19).

[163] Rusu 2017 (a), p. 805.

In other words, the victims would be inclined to seek damages in follow-on actions from the first infringer for which an infringement of the antitrust rules has been proven, namely the immunity recipient. Second, the Directive *rewards* the immunity recipient by limiting, in principle, its private damages liability: such undertakings are relieved from joint and several liability for the entire harm caused, as any contribution they must make vis-à-vis co-infringers does not exceed the amount of harm caused to its own direct or indirect purchasers/providers, provided that the co-infringers are able to cover the rest of the damages. That share of the contribution should be determined in accordance with the same rules used to determine the contributions between infringers.

The *protection* and *rewards* afforded to the immunity recipients in private enforcement proceedings, and also black-listing the leniency statement when it comes to evidence disclosure, as discussed in section 5.4. above, obviously pertain to the delicate balance between the public and private enforcement means of the (EU) antitrust rules. This is so, having in mind the goals that these two enforcement systems aim for, the incentives provided to the market players to cooperate with the public enforcement authorities, and the infringement victims' right and ability to obtain full compensation for the harm incurred. Since this discussion has developed in an interesting manner in recent years, through the case-law of the CJEU and via the Private Damages Directive 2014, and since it raises fundamental challenges to our understanding of the equilibrium between public and private enforcement mechanisms, specifically when talking about leniency and private damages claims, we will dwell upon its intricacies in the following section of this chapter.

The implementation of the liability provisions of the Private Damages Directive 2014 in the Member States differs from jurisdiction to jurisdiction. In some Member States, such as Romania, Article 11 was implemented in its entirety by incorporating the Directive's text verbatim in the domestic legislation.[164] In other Member States, such as the Netherlands, the legislator chose to implement this provision only in part. For example, Article 11(6) dealing with umbrella pricing scenarios is not implemented into a separate provision of Dutch law since this provision is already catered for on the basis of Article 6:102 read in conjunction with Articles 6:101 and 6.10 of the Dutch Civil Code, dealing with joint fault and the internal contribution in the performed joint obligation and of the liable persons towards each other, respectively.[165] The same stands for the provisions of Article 12 of the Directive, which was not implemented since the Dutch legislator argues that existing Dutch law is already in line with this Directive provision. In Spain, prior to the Private Damages Directive's implementation, Article 1,137 of the Civil Code put forward as a general rule for cases dealing with non-contractual liability the so-called 'pooled' liability. In practice, courts have established the so-called 'improper solidarity' for those cases where several persons are liable for the same facts, without being able to identify individual shares of liability. This improper solidarity is only valid where the court establishes it and only with regard to the infringers sued by the victim. The implementation of Article 11 of the Private Damages Directive 2014 in Article 73 of the Spanish Competition Law creates a special rule

---

[164] Government Ordinance 39/2017, OJ 422/2017, Article 11.

[165] Rusu and Looijestijn-Clearie 2017 (b), p. 376.

for antitrust damages actions, which deviates from other non-contractual liability cases. For antitrust damages cases all co-infringers are now jointly and severally liable, regardless which one was sued.[166] In the UK, Peyer[167] argues that the Directive's provisions on joint and several liability will particularly impact on claimants who settle their claims, on claimants who seek damages from immunity recipients and on defendants who seek contribution from their co-defendants, particularly because the exceptions embedded in Articles 11 and 19 had no predecessors in English law, prior to the Directive's implementation. The Civil Liability Act 1978 simply provided in its first two sections that any person liable in respect of any damage suffered by another person may recover contribution from any other person liable in respect of the same damage (whether jointly with him or otherwise) and that the amount of the contribution recoverable from any person shall be such as may be found by the court to be just and equitable having regard to the extent of that person's responsibility for the damage in question. The implementation of the Private Damages Directive 2014 moves away from this discretion that the domestic judge exercised in this respect.

5.6 The relationship between leniency and private enforcement of the antitrust rules

Chapter 7 dealt with, among other issues, the general aspects that characterise the relationship between the public and private enforcement mechanisms of the EU antitrust rules. There, we concluded that these two enforcement systems are closely linked to each other: there are complementary goals that are aimed for, and tools that are employed in order to ensure the effectiveness of the prohibition provided in Articles 101 and 102 TFEU. There are also overlaps between the goals and mechanisms pertaining to the public and private enforcement systems. Chapter 3, dealing with the economics of competition law, also pointed in this direction when talking about the rationale behind certain public enforcement policies and the incentives of the market players to work together with the competition enforcement authorities. Lastly, in several instances, the chapter at hand also made remarks about the inter-relationship between the leniency programmes (as important tools or public enforcement of the antitrust rules) and actions for damages. It is now time to delve into this discussion, in order to clarify its development over time.

In Chapter 8 we discussed that it is very difficult for competition authorities to detect covert anti-competitive practices, and in order to tackle this problem, competition authorities have developed leniency programmes, meant to stimulate undertakings to break secret cartels. Such programmes are valuable public enforcement tools which help competition authorities to establish infringements of Article 101 TFEU or of the domestic cartel prohibitions. This stance is acknowledged also in the Private Damages Directive 2014, as pointed out in the sections above. Yet, establishing such infringements yields problems for the antitrust infringers on the private enforcement front. This is so, regardless of the immunity from public fines, or

---

[166] J. Maillo, 'Antitrust Damages Claims in Spain' in Parcu, Monti and Botta 2018, p. 158 *et seq.*

[167] S. Peyer, 'Private Antitrust Enforcement in England and Wales after the EU Damages Directive' in Parcu, Monti and Botta 2018, pp. 107–11.

reductions of those fines, as the case may be, that the cartelists may benefit from under the leniency rules. When speaking of private enforcement actions which, more often than not, take the form of follow-on actions subsequent to the finding of an antitrust infringement by the competition authorities, the infringers are confronted with two interconnected concerns: liability for damages, on one hand, and disclosure of evidence necessary for plaintiffs when seeking compensation, on the other hand. In other words, tensions have arisen between the need to ensure the effectiveness of the victims' right to claim compensation, and the effectiveness of the leniency programmes of competition authorities.[168]

This was so, even before the enactment of the Private Damages Directive 2014. With regard to the former aspect, namely liability for damages, this was clear as early as the *Courage and Crehan* ruling of the CJEU which, once again, established an EU right to claim damages caused by antitrust infringements, a right that may be enforced by any person who has suffered harm. This breadth of the category of persons entitled to claim damages has been shaped in time through the rulings of the Court, to include direct (and indirect) purchasers (with regard to the latter, if the passing-on doctrine is accepted), parties to an anti-competitive agreement (if they do not bear significant responsibility for the infringement), public institutions establishing the actual infringement (as was the case in *Otis*), direct and indirect purchasers that are victims of the so-called umbrella pricing practices (as was the case in *Kone*) and third parties not active as purchasers or suppliers on the relevant market, who have nevertheless suffered damages (as was the case in *Otis II*). We can already see that if an infringement of the cartel prohibition is established, the liability of the infringers to pay damages was quite extensive, even before the Private Damages Directive 2014 came into force. As briefly explained in Chapter 3, this setting puts pressure on cartelists, and impacts on their incentives to apply for leniency. At the end of the day, what is the benefit of confessing to the antitrust infringement, and avoiding or limiting the subsequent public law fines, if later on the risk of paying large amounts in damages is present? The calculation of whether it is worth breaking the cartel or not is put into a different perspective.

Yet, such a threat for the cartelists was not really tangible if, for the purpose of actually obtaining compensation for the harm incurred, the victims still needed to prove the extent of the harm. As portrayed above, such proof relies heavily on the evidence that the victims need to present in front of the civil law courts, evidence which is not easy to gather. It is in this respect that victims were tempted to ask the competent courts to order the infringers or the NCAs to disclose relevant pieces of evidence, which could help them substantiate their claims for damages.[169] The scope of such disclosure, as far as the antitrust infringement victims are concerned, obviously included leniency documents. This was the case in the *Pfleiderer* ruling,[170] where the CJEU was called upon to clarify whether the disclosure of leniency materials in private damages actions may or may not be precluded. Despite the position of the Commission, of some NCAs and of Advocate General Mazak, who argued that the disclosure of such self-incriminating statements voluntarily provided by leniency applicants

---

[168] Van de Gronden 2017, p. 344 *et seq.*; Bucan 2013, pp. 69–70.

[169] Jones, Sufrin and Dunne 2019, p. 1042.

[170] Case C-360/09 *Pfleiderer*, ECLI:EU:C:2011:389. See also Völcker 2012.

would reduce the attractiveness of leniency applications, and thus of the effectiveness of the cartel prohibition (paragraphs 25 to 27),[171] the CJEU, in a preliminary ruling, opted for a different, more balanced approach to be taken by the national courts, when it comes to access to leniency documents under national disclosure rules. The Court first recalled the lack of EU law rules on leniency and disclosure of evidence (paragraph 20), and thus the Member States through their procedural autonomy must handle such disclosure claims (paragraphs 23 and 24). Next, the *Courage and Crehan* rationale regarding the importance of private enforcement, especially in light of the need to ensure the effectiveness of the EU antitrust provisions, is emphasised (paragraphs 28 and 29). Then, when it comes to the victims' applications for disclosure of leniency documents, the Court points to the need of national rules to respect the principles of effectiveness and equivalence, and makes it clear that the national courts, when deciding whether to grant or refuse such access, must weigh the respective interests in favour of disclosure of the information and in favour of the protection of that information provided voluntarily by the leniency applicant, on a case-by-case basis, according to national law, and taking into account all the relevant factors in the case (paragraphs 30 to 32). In later case-law, the disclosure of leniency documents discussion was further nuanced. In the *Donau Chemie* preliminary ruling,[172] the Court dealt with national (Austrian) rules prohibiting disclosure to third parties of court files relating to the public enforcement of the competition law rules, including leniency documents, unless all parties to these proceedings agreed on such disclosure. In this case, access to the file was requested in order to gather evidence enabling an assessment of the nature and amount of the potential loss suffered by the petitioner, and to determine whether it was appropriate to bring an action for damages against the antitrust infringers. The Court proceeded by referring to its earlier rulings (*Francovich, Courage and Crehan, Manfredi*) highlighting the EU right to claim damages, the importance of this right for strengthening the effectiveness of the EU antitrust rules and for the protection of the victims against adverse effects of the antitrust infringements, the lack of EU law procedural rules on the matter, and the need for the exercise of the national procedural autonomy to observe the equivalence and effectiveness principles (paragraphs 20 to 27). Then, while referring extensively to the *Pfleiderer* rationale,[173] especially when it comes to the weighing exercise the national courts must engage in on a case-by-case basis, the Court pointed out that, in competition law in particular, any rule that is rigid, by providing for absolute refusal of disclosure, is liable to undermine the effective application of Article 101 TFEU and the rights that provision confers on individuals (paragraph 31). Such rules naturally infringe the principle of effectiveness, especially when the victims have no other way of obtaining that evidence (paragraph 32).[174] Yet, the Court argues in paragraph 33, generalised access to all evidence in the file may lead to infringement of other rights conferred by EU law (e.g. protection of professional and business secrecy, protection of personal data). That is why weighing

---

[171] Jones, Sufrin and Dunne 2019, p. 1042.

[172] Case C-536/11 *Donau Chemie*, ECLI:EU:C:2013:366.

[173] Hirst 2013.

[174] In case C-365/12 P *EnBW*, ECLI:EU:C:2014:112, the Court clarified that access should be required when relevant evidence was not available through alternative mechanisms.

all interests at stake, taking into account all the relevant factors in the case, is important. Giving the parties to the court proceedings the possibility to object to the disclosure, without giving reasons, but obviously in an effort to protect their own interests, makes the weighing process impossible, especially when it comes to the protection of overriding public interests or the legitimate overriding interests of other parties, who may not have alternative recourse to fulfil their compensation rights (paragraphs 37 to 39). Speaking of overriding public interests, the importance of leniency programmes for the effectiveness of the cartel prohibition is recalled (paragraph 40 *et seq.*): rules on access to file must not be applied in such a manner as to undermine public interests such as the effectiveness of national leniency programmes. Nevertheless, systematic refusals of disclosure without taking into account all the relevant factors in the case is not to be accepted. Given the importance of actions for damages in ensuring the maintenance of effective competition in the EU, the argument that there is a risk that access to evidence contained in a file in competition proceedings which is necessary as a basis for those actions may undermine the effectiveness of a leniency programme in which those documents were disclosed to the competent competition authority cannot justify a refusal to grant access to that evidence (paragraph 46). By contrast, if disclosure would be refused, the infringers would not only benefit from leniency, but they would also circumvent their compensation obligations. Therefore, the refusal may only be based on overriding reasons relating to the protection of the interest relied on and applicable to *each document* to which access is refused (paragraph 47). If a given document may actually undermine the public interest relating to the effectiveness of the national leniency programme (*as a whole*, to our minds) that non-disclosure of that document may be justified (paragraph 47).[175]

Whereas the *Courage and Crehan*, *Manfredi*, *Otis* and *Kone* cases established extensive liability for damages on behalf of the antitrust infringers, the *Pfleiderer* and *Donau Chemie* rulings opened the gates for victims to ask for disclosure of relevant leniency documents in order to substantiate their private damages claims. The Court seemed to obviously favour private damages actions over leniency programmes, despite the potential chilling effect on leniency applications.[176] Once again, the cartelists' incentives to apply for leniency are significantly decreased, when faced with a wide pool of victims potentially able to claim damages, and with a victim-friendly approach to evidence disclosure. The balance between public and private mechanisms of antitrust enforcement thus seems severely unbalanced. What is extremely relevant to mention in this context is that all these cases unfolded, as the Court rightfully repeatedly emphasised, in the absence of EU rules prescribing procedural systems for damages claims to materialise. This setting was prone to make litigation in the domestic ambits, and particularly disputes on disclosure in follow-on claims, more complex and burdensome for the parties.[177] This is the context in which we must place the Private Damages Directive 2014 provisions dealing with the equilibrium between leniency and private damages claims. In fact, as we pointed out above, the Court's remarks about the absence of EU law on the matter may be perceived as an invitation to the EU legislator to regulate this field.

---

[175] For more discussions on the *Pfleiderer*, *Donau Chemie*, and *EnBW* rulings of the Court, see Braat 2018, pp. 41–5.

[176] Rusu 2017 (b), p. 38; Veenbrink and Rusu 2014; Hirst 2013.

[177] Hirst 2013.

Indeed, when talking about this equilibrium, the Directive's procedural harmonisation[178] exercise actually tackles exactly the points built up by the Court in its rulings: liability of infringers and disclosure of evidence, in the context of the importance of leniency programmes and of fulfilling the right to claim damages. It may be (rightfully, some say) argued that the Directive has 'rebalanced the uneven balance' between such public and private enforcement mechanisms, by reducing the immunity recipient's joint and several liability for the harm caused, and by black-listing self-incriminating voluntary leniency statements from disclosure.[179] On this note, once the Directive came into force and was properly implemented in the Member States, one may thus argue that the relevance of the *Pfleiderer* and *Donau Chemie* rulings remains residual. Nevertheless, the newly established equilibrium is a fragile one and it should not be taken for granted. This is so especially in light of arguments that may be put forward as to the generous regime created for immunity recipients. Some may argue that the Private Damages Directive 2014 has over-tipped the balance too far in the opposite direction, when compared to the case-law of the CJEU, especially when it comes to the liability discussion: the immunity recipient now avoids the public law fine and also the obligation to compensate victims other than its own direct and indirect purchasers, unless the co-infringers can compensate such damages. This means that the co-infringers might be severely financially affected by public law fines they may have to pay and the extensive damages they will have to cover. This setting may leave the immunity recipient in a stronger market position when compared to the pre-infringement period. Whether such arguments will be truly verified in the future remains to be seen. But for now, we may observe a clear inclination on behalf of the Commission to protect the incentives to be the first one to apply for leniency.

Surprisingly or not, the CJEU has embarked on this approach too, while attempting to further shape and clarify the private/public enforcement balance after the entry into force of the Private Damages Directive 2014. This time, the Court's contribution relates to the disclosure of leniency evidence discussion. In *Degussa*,[180] the Court clarified the boundaries which the Commission needs to adhere to when disclosing leniency information. The Court's approach is very much in tune with the Directive's approach: first, it makes a distinction between leniency statements (the so-called 'corporate statements'), as defined in Article 2(16) of the Directive, and 'pre-existing information', as defined in Article 2(17), a distinction previously not made in *Pfleiderer* and *Donau Chemie*,[181] rulings which refer merely to leniency documents. Second, in paragraph 87 of the ruling, the Court points out that

---

[178] Sauter 2016, p. 135.

[179] See also Van de Gronden 2017, pp. 347–8, who also points to the changes brought to the Leniency Notice 2006, in order to take good account of the Court's case-law on the matter and of the provisions of the Private Damages Directive 2014. See paragraph 35(a) of the amended Leniency Notice 2006, which now states that the Commission will not at any time transmit leniency corporate statements to national courts for use in actions for damages for breaches of the EU antitrust provisions, this being without prejudice to the situation referred to in Article 6(7) of the Private Damages Directive 2014.

[180] Case C-162/15 P *Evonik Degussa*, ECLI:EU:C:2017:205.

[181] Hirst 2013.

the publication, in the form of verbatim quotations, of information from the documents provided by an undertaking to the Commission in support of a statement made in order to obtain leniency differs from the publication of verbatim quotations from that statement itself. Whereas the first type of publication should be authorised, subject to compliance with the protection owed, in particular to business secrets, professional secrecy and other confidential information, the second type of publication is not permitted in any circumstances. Indeed, this is in line with Recital 26 (and Article 6(6), for that matter) of the Directive which bars the disclosure of leniency statements and verbatim quotations from them included in other documents (e.g. in a Commission infringement decision), and in line with Article 6(9) of the Directive, which allows the disclosure at any time in actions for damages of documents that exist independently of the proceedings of a competition authority (including 'pre-existing information'). In practice, more often than not, leniency/corporate statements are especially important for immunity recipients, whereas leniency applicants generally rely on 'pre-existing documentation'. This is because the leniency statements of non-immunity receiving leniency applicants (the second, third, and so on undertaking in line) need further corroboration with documentation, when contested, if they are to be considered of 'significant added value' by the Commission.[182] In other words, immunity recipients rely on leniency statements, whereas leniency applicants rely more on 'pre-existing documentation'. Whereas the former are always barred from disclosure, the latter may be disclosed in an easier manner. The result of this judgment is thus an increased protection for immunity recipients, whereas applicants for reduction of a fine come off badly. Consequently, the incentives to be the first to apply for leniency are indeed further strengthened.[183]

5.7 Extent of damages: qualification and quantification of harm

We have shown above that classic private law theory requires the claimant to prove the existence of at least the following elements, for a successful claim for damages: (1) infringement of the law, (2) loss, and (3) causality between the two. The expectation would therefore be that the claimant must prove the harm incurred. Nevertheless, the Directive shifts the weight onto the infringers' shoulders, by instating in Article 17(2) a rebuttable presumption that cartels cause harm. This presumption undoubtedly helps the victims of the antitrust infringements in their endeavour to obtain compensation, especially given the known hurdles they need to overcome to this end. Speaking of the compensation that the victims are entitled to, this necessarily needs to be connected with the harm incurred. This discussion entails the matters of *qualification* and *quantification* of harm.[184]

The question of qualification of harm essentially relates to what the victims can hold the infringers liable for. In other words, what can the victims ask for through an action for damages, or better yet, what are the heads of damages? The starting point is the right to full compensation embedded in Article 3 of the Directive. Compensation must place the person

---

[182] Leniency Notice 2006, par. 25.

[183] Veenbrink 2017.

[184] Wilman 2016, p. 898 *et seq.*

who has suffered harm due to an antitrust infringement in the position in which it would have been had the infringement not been committed. As pointed out several times before, this covers the actual loss, the loss of profit and the payment of interest, fully in line with the *Manfredi* ruling of the CJEU.[185] What the right to full compensation should not cover, though, is punitive, multiple or other types of damages, contrary to what the Court stated in the same ruling, when it accepted that punitive damages may be awarded in domestic law if the effectiveness and equivalence principles are observed. First, by excluding such damages from the ambit of the right to full compensation, the Directive seeks to avoid overcompensation of the victims. What this approach essentially amounts to is that everyone who has suffered harm due to antitrust law infringements may obtain exactly what they are entitled to: no more, and hopefully no less. Second, the exclusion of punitive (and other types of such) damages is consistent with the approach to the issue of passing-on of overcharges, embedded in Article 12 of the Directive. Third, taking punitive damages outside the ambit of the heads of damages that may be claimed is also in line with the general aims of antitrust enforcement: indeed, actions for damages aim (among other goals) for compensating the victims of the infringements, as we have shown in Chapter 7. It is true that private enforcement mechanisms also possess a deterrent element, thus *contributing* to the effective enforcement of the antitrust rules. However, in our opinion, this is so not necessarily in relation to the actual types of damages to be awarded. To our mind, it is the mere threat of multiple damages claims from various categories of victims that may function as a deterrence from engaging in anti-competitive practices. Consequently, we view the deterrence objective of the enforcement of the antitrust rules to be primarily served by the public enforcement mechanisms, which are at the disposal of competition authorities.[186] Fourth, and in close connection to the point made just above, prohibiting the award of punitive damages is also consistent with the EU fundamental principle of *ne bis in idem* (and with Article 16 of Regulation 1/2003 and the *Masterfoods* judgment, for that matter), especially when thinking of follow-on actions, based on a Commission or NCA decision fining the infringers.[187] In such cases indeed, imposing a fine and punitive damages on the wrongdoer would lead to a violation of the principle of *ne bis in idem*.

When speaking of the quantification of the harm incurred, the question that needs to be answered is how should the compensation be calculated? The starting point here is that the injured party who has proven that it has suffered harm, luckily by making use also of the Article 17(2) presumption that cartels cause harm, still needs to prove the extent of the harm in order to obtain damages.[188] In practice, this exercise also turns out to be one of the bottlenecks for successful damages litigation, since as emphasised by Recital 45 of the Directive, the quantification of harm is a costly and fact-intensive process, requiring complex

---

[185] Joined cases C-295 to C-298/04 *Manfredi*, ECLI:EU:C:2006:461, par. 95–97, 100.

[186] On the (protective) role of private enforcement mechanisms, see Monti 2007, p. 425 *et seq*. On the inherent superiority of public enforcement for deterrence and punishment, see Wils 2017, pp. 17–21.

[187] Wils 2017, pp. 25–26; Wils 2009, pp. 21–2.

[188] Private Damages Directive 2014, Recital 45.

economic modelling.[189] On top of this, the information asymmetries between the parties and the application of the counterfactual principle (i.e. estimating how the market would have evolved had there been no infringement) further complicate the achievement of completely accurate quantification results.[190] Article 17 of the Directive is relevant when it comes to the quantification of harm. On a quick glance though, one may observe that Article 17(1) of the Directive sets a low threshold,[191] since it only requires the Member States to ensure that the burden and standard of proof that the claimants must meet regarding the quantification of harm should be consistent with the effectiveness principle. Consequently, in absence of clear EU law rules on the matter of quantifying harm, the safe-net principles of effectiveness and equivalence are important. This stems clearly from Recital 46 of the Directive, which also provides that these principles continue to shape the national courts' determination of the requirements that the claimant must meet when proving the amount of the harm suffered, of the methods used in quantifying the amount, and of the consequences of not fully meeting those requirements. The bottom line here is that the EU legislator, while relying heavily on the work done by the domestic courts when it comes to quantification of harm, opted for flexibility, while using rebuttable presumptions and estimates, rather than rigid concepts such as fixed rates for setting the damages. Such flexibility may indeed be appropriate, because by not being bound to bright-line compensation thresholds and formulas, the national courts will be less likely to award overcompensation.[192]

It may be true that the domestic judges are equipped to apply the domestic rules on quantification of harm. Nevertheless, when it comes to antitrust infringements, the matter may be somewhat more complex, due to the reasons briefly explained above (the need to use economic models, applying the counterfactual principle, and suchlike). This is where the Directive provides the domestic courts with extra tools for the purpose of smoothly quantifying the harm relating to private damages claims: first, Article 17(1) gives the courts the power to estimate the amount of the harm (again, according to national procedures), when it is proven that harm was incurred, but it is practically impossible or excessively difficult to precisely quantify the harm suffered on the basis of the evidence available. Second, when the domestic courts still encounter problems in this respect, they may make recourse to the expertise of the NCAs, which may provide guidance and assistance to the domestic courts on the determination of the quantum of damages.[193] Third, and lastly, Recital 46 of the Directive speaks also of providing general guidance at EU level, which is meant to ensure coherence and predictability when domestic courts quantify harm in actions for damages. This is where the Communication on Quantifying Harm 2013 and the Practical Guide 2013 may be referred to as useful tools for the domestic judges.[194]

---

[189] Wilman 2016, p. 899.

[190] Private Damages Directive 2014, Recital 46. See also Rusu 2017 (a), p. 807.

[191] Wilman 2016, p. 900.

[192] Wilman 2016, p. 900; Rusu 2017 (a), p. 808.

[193] Private Damages Directive 2014, Article 17(3), Recital 46.

[194] Strand 2014, pp. 383–5.

6 CONCLUSIONS

The private enforcement of the EU antitrust rules witnessed a different process of development than the public enforcement mechanisms described in the previous chapter of this book. The lack of EU law rules on the matter of private enforcement allowed the Member States to develop quite diverse private enforcement mechanisms, based on the specificity of their domestic private law rules. This setting led to a noticeable fragmentation of the antitrust private enforcement regimes in the EU, raising considerable problems not only for the injured parties requiring reparation, but also for those liable to cover the damages.[195] The underdevelopment of the antitrust private enforcement system at EU level was supplemented and furthered by the Court's intervention, which created important principles and laid down useful rules meant to aid the antitrust victims in fulfilling their right to full compensation for the harm incurred. However, the case-law of the CJEU cannot do it all.

This is where the EU legislator continued the work of the Court, by adopting the Private Damages Directive 2014. This instrument further paves the way to more meaningful private enforcement of the EU antitrust rules in the EU Member States. It provides more instruments and more certainty to the parties concerned, it aims to level the playing field for damages actions in different EU jurisdictions, and it stimulates victims to engage in such actions, thus contributing to a more effective and balanced enforcement of the EU antitrust rules. Importantly, the Directive also resets the balance between the value attached to public enforcement mechanisms (i.e. leniency) and private enforcement tools (i.e. actions for damages). However, all these important steps forward are contingent on the Directive's implementation in the national legal orders. When writing this book, all Member States have implemented the Directive, although some of them while encountering some delays.[196] Litigants rely on the provisions of national law after the implementation of the Private Damages Directive 2014. This means that for the Directive's success, a lot depends on the correct implementation of its provisions by the Member States. Should implementation be faulty, it must be borne in mind that it is settled case-law of the CJEU[197] that directive provisions are not capable of having horizontal direct effect. This means that if incorrectly implemented, the Directive's provisions will not be applicable, thus potentially questioning the effectiveness of the private enforcement system of EU antitrust law. The domestic judge would then be bound to apply the domestic legal provisions, eventually interpreted in consistence with the Directive's provisions.

While the implementation process is thus key, the domestic examples we provided in this chapter highlight that the Directive was more impactful in certain domestic legal orders than in others. This makes sense, given that some domestic private enforcement systems have already exhibited solid features even before the enactment of the Directive. It is in this respect, probably, that some of such Member States did not hesitate in retaining their

---

[195] Rusu 2017 (a), p. 808.

[196] See <https://eur-lex.europa.eu/legal-content/EN/NIM/?uri=uriserv:OJ.L_.2014.349.01.0001.01.ENG> accessed 7 June 2020.

[197] Case C-91/92 *Dori*, ECLI:EU:C:1994:292.

domestic mark, or better yet national flavours, in the manner in which actions for damages unfold in practice. The enactment and implementation of the Private Damages Directive 2014 is, however, not the end of the road as far as private enforcement of antitrust law is concerned, since the Directive deals primarily with private damages actions. It is to be expected that EU action will follow in other matters pertaining to the private enforcement of the said rules, such as collective redress. Until then, for such non-harmonised matters, reliance on the domestic laws of the Member States and on the principles of equivalence and effectiveness continue to be important, while the case-law of the Court remains of high relevance.

PART IV
CONCENTRATION CONTROL

10
Concentration control

1 INTRODUCTION

This chapter deals with the manner in which the Commission and the NCAs examine concentration transactions. This activity is commonly referred to as merger control. As will become apparent in this chapter, the scrutiny of concentrations performed by competition authorities has many similarities with, but also differences from the approach employed in antitrust law. These differences relate to, for example, the legal basis for controlling concentrations, the timing of assessing their effects, the jurisdictional division between competition authorities, the substantive appraisal test, and so on. At least some of these differences in approach are often linked to the specificity of various types of concentrations, in that such transactions create structural changes in the market which may be permanent, or in any case, long lasting.[1] Mergers, acquisitions, takeovers, joint ventures, and the like are common occurrences in day-to-day economic life, and often occur in so-called 'waves', normally triggered by technological shocks, regulatory changes and availability of financing.[2] Such transactions may be performed due to a multitude of reasons, and may trigger diverse effects, impacting various areas of the law: competition law, corporate law, financial and tax law, among others. As far as competition law is concerned, the purpose of examining concentrations is to ensure that reorganisations of undertakings do not cause lasting damage on competition, thus maintaining the process of competition in the market, and consequently maximising consumer welfare. Unlike company law, which views mergers and acquisitions from the shareholders' standpoint, the competition law scrutiny of concentrations is carried out in the public interest.[3] Thus, concentration control has become a key pillar in almost all modern competition systems throughout the world.[4]

The chapter at hand will discuss the concentration control phenomenon in the EU. It will focus first on a few generic issues (i.e. motives of merger activity, forms of concentrations, the rationale behind creating the EU concentration control system). Then the discussion

---

[1] Jones, Sufrin and Dunne 2019, p. 1059.

[2] On the emergence and development of mergers and acquisitions (M&A) as a global economic phenomenon, see Lianos, Korah and Siciliani 2019, pp. 1482 *et seq.*, 1487.

[3] Kokkoris and Shelanski 2014, p. 10; Whish and Bailey 2018, p. 836.

[4] Whish and Bailey 2018, p. 832.

will move to the architecture of the EU concentration control rules, pursuant to the Merger Control Regulation 2004: jurisdictional aspects, the procedure for assessing concentrations and the substantive appraisal test. Last but not least, certain international aspects and the concentration control experience in some domestic jurisdictions will be visited, to highlight the specificity of national merger control regimes in the EU.

2 PREREQUISITES OF CONCENTRATION CONTROL

2.1 Motivations and drivers

There are various reasons why undertakings would want to grow externally through mergers, acquisitions and other types of concentrations. Such reasons may be categorised in multiple ways: economic and non-economic drivers, pro-competitive and anti-competitive motives, or depending on the interested party and the strategies it may pursue (i.e. drivers relating to shareholders, managers, competitors, and the like).[5]

From a shareholders' perspective, M&A deals are pursued with a view to increasing shareholder value, the expectation being that the transaction creates synergies unachievable should the deal not take place. This is also connected to the undertakings' perceived operational efficiency and success, triggered by the desire to achieve optimal scale to perform their business. Such synergies are expected to either increase revenues or reduce costs, or both: for example, this can be achieved by replacing underperforming management with better skilled staff, thus disciplining existing management; by combining R&D activities of multiple firms, aiming to create a more successful product; by achieving economies of scale or scope through eliminating fixed costs, or costs common to the merging parties, or through the possibility of commercialising complementary products, thus also penetrating new sectors of the economy, and so forth. These aspects point to an increase in efficiency for the merged entity, and at the same time, also to a larger scale achieved through concentration. This larger scale is attractive for businesses, since a larger firm may have greater bargaining power in the market, it may acquire more stable access to supplies, and it may gain access to more and cheaper financing sources. Also, firms may find it attractive to acquire businesses active in various sectors of the economy, since this diversified portfolio will allow them to spread the risk of their operations. Furthermore, undertakings may, through various sorts of acquisitions, target key assets of other businesses, such as patented technologies and know-how, efficient large-scale production plants, or existing distribution networks. Especially with regard to the latter, forward acquisitions (i.e. producers acquiring wholesalers or retailers) may open access to distribution networks in an easier and probably cheaper fashion, than creating such a network from scratch. In a similar fashion (cross-border) acquisitions may allow firms to enter new markets.

As far as other players in the market are concerned, concentration deals may provide

---

[5] On the various drivers for M&As, see Lianos, Korah and Siciliani 2019, p. 1485 *et seq.*; Whish and Bailey 2018, p. 833 *et seq.*; Jones, Sufrin and Dunne 2019, pp. 1060–61; Schenk 2006.

opportunities to exit a particular industry. Especially these days, when technological progress seems to have burst beyond expectations, it is not uncommon for entrepreneurs to invest in setting up businesses that create innovative products and services, solely for the purpose of selling the business at a profit. Mergers may also provide a 'market exit' for those entities that would otherwise face inevitable liquidation. Thus, production plants could be kept in place, employees may not lose their jobs, creditors would avoid the risk of not getting paid, and generally speaking, the stability of the industry sector would not be jeopardised. At the opposite side of the spectrum, as discussed above, instead of exiting an industry, mergers and acquisitions may accommodate penetrating a particular sector of the economy, or the consolidation of firms' position in a given industry. A particular facet of this discussion is the creation of so-called national champions, that is, firms large enough to compete on an international scale. Governments may find this an attractive route, for reasons relating to industrial policy, or to incentivise technical and economic progress and international trade. Yet, the flipside of such an approach relates to running the risk of unduly altering the structure of markets, thus undermining competition domestically. Furthermore, a national champion, favoured by such policies and thus freed from the disciplining effect of national competitive pressure, may actually end up lacking the skills necessary to compete internationally. That is why such growth of firms should be achieved while competing on the merits and in an environment affording a level playing field to the market players. Speaking of growth, above we mentioned the desire of undertakings to grow to their perceived optimal scale for performing their business. There is often a thin line between growth as such, and growth triggered by the desire to increase or leverage one's market power. The latter, if allowed, may result in elimination of efficient competitive pressure, the suspension of rivalry between competitors, or vertical foreclosure effects, as the case may be.

Last but not least, mergers and acquisitions may also be triggered by non-economically rational motives. The managers' desire to keep their jobs, or their overconfidence in their ability to achieve cost or revenue-related synergies, but also their greed, the 'rush' some may experience when 'making a deal', the fear of not missing out in the process of industry consolidation, and consequently the imitation/herding behaviour when seeing competitors engage in M&A transactions, have all been identified in legal and economic literature as potential triggers for concentrations. In this context, many studies[6] evaluate the profitability of concentration transactions, in various sectors of the economy, and based on diverse benchmarks and hypotheses. Some authors[7] argue that merger control is not the appropriate tool to deal with the problems that non-economically driven mergers may create, be they profitable or not. Other authors[8] plead for restructuring current merger control policies, in an attempt for society to escape the burden of uneconomic mergers.

---

[6] On such studies, see Kokkoris and Shelanski 2014, pp. 6–9; Schenk 2006.

[7] Whish and Bailey 2018, p. 835.

[8] Schenk 2006.

2.2 Categorisations

So far, various terms have been used in reference to concentration transactions: mergers, acquisitions, takeovers, joint ventures, and the like. We will clarify these terms' meaning in section 3.1.1, while discussing jurisdictional matters in EU merger control. For now, it is important to distinguish between broad categories of concentrations, having in mind the pre-transaction relationship between the parties.[9] This is important in order to elucidate the effects such transactions may create and the theories of harm that may be employed by competition authorities when scrutinising these effects.

Horizontal transactions involve parties which are active or potentially active in the same (product and geographic) market, at the same level of the supply chain. For example, the producer of soft-drink A merges with its competitor, producer of soft-drink B. *Vertical* transactions occur between players that operate at different, but complementary, levels of the production and distribution chain, for the same final product. For example, the car manufacturer X acquires the showroom facilities of car salesman Y, active on the downstream retail market. *Conglomerate* transactions take place between parties which are neither actual nor potential competitors (as is the case for horizontal deals), and which do not produce goods which could be used by the others (as is the case for vertical deals), meaning that they are not functionally related.

This categorisation already points to (some of) the types of effects that concentrations can lead to: horizontal, vertical and conglomerate effects. Such effects, which will be extensively discussed in section 3.3.4 below, may occur individually in a given case, but specific scenarios may also entail one and the same concentration exhibiting several types of such effects. For now it suffices to state that the practice of competition authorities shows that horizontal transactions are most likely to raise anti-competitive issues, while vertical and conglomerate transactions may have ambivalent effects: on one hand they may create efficiencies, while on the other hand, they may also create competitive harm.[10] Regardless of the type of transaction, when anti-competitive effects are possible, competition authorities are prone to intervene. For the sake of transparency and legal certainty about the types of effects that warrant intervention, competition authorities often use soft-law instruments, which describe the approach to concentrations that entail such effects.[11]

2.3 Rationale for (EU) merger control

Merger control is meant to scrutinise those transactions that are prone to create lasting damage on competition, thus aiming to maintain the process of competition in the market, and consequently to maximise the welfare of consumers. In this respect, the rationale behind developing merger control systems is very much congruent with the objectives of antitrust

---

[9] Whish and Bailey 2018, pp. 830–31; Lindsay and Berridge 2017, p. 28 *et seq.*

[10] E.g. Non-Horizontal Merger Guidelines 2008, par. 11–15.

[11] E.g. the Commission's Horizontal Merger Guidelines 2004 and Non-Horizontal Merger Guidelines 2008; in the UK, the CMA's Merger Assessment Guidelines 2010; in France, Lignes Directrices 2013.

law. Yet, when it comes to mergers, this rationale may often be viewed as multi-sided, in that concentrations resonate with other areas of the law too, and with diverse interests of various stakeholders. This is why, especially when viewed within national boundaries contexts, merger control tools may be used by governments to prevent foreign takeovers of strategic domestic firms, to avoid massive unemployment situations, or to further domestic industrial policy aims. In other words, national governments may use merger control policies in order to further objectives which are peculiar to their respective jurisdictions.

At EU level, the matter has to be viewed from a historical perspective: while antitrust rules at European level have been embedded in the EEC and ECSC Treaties, merger control was only present in Article 66 of the ECSC Treaty. This is because, given the post-Second World War circumstances, the signatory states of the ECSC Treaty deemed it important to control the coal and steel industries, in order to ensure that a third World War was not going to erupt. Unlike the ECSC Treaty, the EEC Treaty covered a wider range of sectors and aimed for a more complex set of goals. The achievement of such objectives, particularly the market integration goal, required the adoption of further regulatory measures. Merger control was thus not embedded in the EEC Treaty, given the reluctance of the signatory states to cede the power to control transactions taking place in a wider spectrum of the economy towards supranational entities. Further, given the post-Second World War political realities, the concentration of economic power could also have been viewed as a vehicle to assist European industry to regain its international competitiveness.[12]

M&A activity prompted thus consequences not only regarding the companies involved, but also regarding the structure of the European markets. It is in this respect that the Commission felt that the growth of important market players and the functioning of the markets required supervision. Yet, European primary law conferred no *specific* tools for this task. In Memorandum 1966, the Commission signalled that Article 102 TFEU could be used to tackle those transactions that would lead to the strengthening of a dominant position. This actually happened in the *Continental Can* case,[13] when the CJEU validated the approach that Article 102 TFEU could be used to tackle structural abuses of market power, that is, a dominant undertaking abusing its position by acquiring a competitor and thereby strengthening its dominance.[14] It goes without saying that a pre-existing dominant position must have been in the cards, though. The question whether this Treaty provision could be used to tackle a concentration which creates a dominant position was not considered by the Court. This stance fuelled the subsequent actions of the Commission, which pushed towards the adoption of a specific instrument at EU level for controlling concentrations, by putting forward a draft Regulation in 1973.[15] This and several other proposals, which were put forward during the 1980s, failed in receiving support from the Member States. This was due to strategic differences in opinion regarding jurisdictional aspects (i.e. for which kind of transactions should national sovereignty be relinquished?) and substantive appraisal criteria (i.e. should non-competition

---

[12] Rusu 2010, p. 65 *et seq.*; Kokkoris and Shelanski 2014, p. 15 *et seq.*

[13] Case 6/72 *Continental Can*, ECLI:EU:C:1973:22.

[14] Jones, Sufrin and Dunne 2019, p. 1067; Sauter 2016, p. 198.

[15] (1973) OJ C 92/1.

– social and industrial policy – concerns play a role in appraising concentrations?). On top of this, the CJEU acknowledged in the *Philip Morris* judgment[16] that an acquisition of shares in a competing company, which is the subject matter of agreements entered into by companies which remain independent after the entry into force of the agreements, must be examined from the point of view of Article 101 TFEU. This is so because such an acquisition may serve as an instrument for influencing the commercial conduct of the companies in question, particularly when the investing company obtains legal or *de facto* control of the commercial conduct of the other company. Consequently, not only Article 102 TFEU (after *Continental Can*), but also Article 101 TFEU (after *Philip Morris*) could be used to address competition issues arising from M&As, despite the fact that these Treaty provisions were never designed to control such transactions, and exhibit visible shortcomings in their application to concentrations (e.g. there must be a dominant position to apply Article 102 TFEU, there must be some sort of coordination to apply Article 101 TFEU, and suchlike).

These circumstances, coupled with a general feeling of unease in the business community regarding the *ex post* application of Articles 101 and 102 TFEU to concentrations, and with the pressing need of having a European framework for controlling structural reorganisations in the market, in order to ensure the completion of the Internal Market integration project, triggered the adoption of the Merger Control Regulation 1989, the first Merger Control Regulation at EU level.[17] The legal bases for this Regulation were the current Articles 103 and 352 TFEU, meaning that the Regulation was meant to give effect to the principles embedded in Articles 101 and 102 TFEU. In our opinion, this should be read as the Merger Control Regulation 1989 filling the gaps that Articles 101 and 102 TFEU exhibited when being applied to concentration transactions. To this end, the Regulation put forward jurisdictional, substantive and procedural rules allowing the Commission to appraise concentrations that can have an impact on the EU market. The Regulation was supported by many soft-law documents, some of which are still valid today (in an updated form). It was later amended by Regulation 1310/97, particularly in relation to jurisdictional thresholds. Further, in an effort to optimise the functioning of the control system, the Commission issued the Green Paper 2001, signalling a comprehensive review of the Regulation.[18] This resulted in the adoption of the Merger Control Regulation 2004, the EU Merger Control Regulation currently in force, accompanied by Implementing Regulation 2004.

May Articles 101 and 102 TFEU still be applied to concentrations, even after 1989? Jones, Sufrin and Dunne[19] aptly and systematically explain why this risk is minimal and unlikely to materialise. Essentially, as discussed below, concentrations with an EU dimension should fall under the Merger Control Regulation, whereas those concentrations that do not have an EU dimension should fall under national laws of the Member States. The Merger Control Regulation cannot disapply Articles 101 and 102 TFEU, which constitute primary EU law. However, it disapplies the EU Regulations implementing these articles, including Regulation

---

[16] Joined cases 142 and 156/84 *BAT and Reynolds*, ECLI:EU:C:1987:490.

[17] Rusu 2010, p. 92 *et seq.*; Kokkoris and Shelanski 2014, p. 25.

[18] Jones, Sufrin and Dunne 2019, p. 1068.

[19] Ibid, pp. 1097–8.

1/2003.[20] So, the Commission, although it could in theory use the EU antitrust provisions to deal with concentrations, would not be able to enforce these provisions in practice. The only possibility envisioned by the authors to witness the application of Articles 101 or 102 TFEU to concentrations is by virtue of their direct effect. In such a setting, a private party could, at least in theory, challenge the compatibility of a concentration with Article 101 or Article 102 TFEU before a national court.

Moving on, Recitals 2–5 of the Merger Control Regulation 2004 spell out the aims of this EU instrument: the Regulation was adopted as an essential driver for the further development of the Internal Market, and more specifically as part of a system ensuring that competition in the Internal Market is not distorted, for the ultimate purpose of achieving the aims of the Treaty. The Regulation comes in the context of the enlargement of the EU and of the lowering of international barriers to trade and investment, which will continue to result in major corporate reorganisations, which are desirable if they are in line with the requirements of dynamic competition and when they are capable of increasing the competitiveness of European industry. Nevertheless, this process of corporate reorganisation should not result in lasting damage to effective competition. While the adoption of the Merger Control Regulations is to be viewed in the context of the Internal Market project and of the goals of the EU Treaties,[21] thus also aiming for fostering societal welfare,[22] the Commission has clearly adopted the consumer welfare standard for the purpose of assessing mergers. This stems evidently not only from the Commission's Horizontal Merger Guidelines 2004,[23] but also from numerous speeches of various Competition Commissioners throughout time.[24] While the Commission expressed a clear preference for this standard of appraisal, it must be noted that the consumer welfare standard is not the only conceivable benchmark for merger control. Concentration control may also be geared towards fostering other interests, such as those of producers or competitors, or (non-competition-related) public interests relating to industrial or social policy; therefore, appraisal standards alternative to the consumer welfare standard have been developed by competition authorities around the world (e.g. the Canadian competition authority uses the weighted surplus standard).[25]

3 THE EU MERGER CONTROL SYSTEM

The merger control system currently applicable at EU level is built on the Merger Control Regulation 2004. This EU instrument is supported by several soft-law documents.[26] Also,

---

[20] Merger Control Regulation 2004, Article 21(1).

[21] Sauter 2016, p. 197.

[22] Rusu 2010.

[23] Horizontal Mergers Guidelines 2004, par. 8, 79.

[24] E.g. Monti 2001; Kroes 2005; Almunia 2010.

[25] On the various objectives of merger control, including a comprehensive literature review in this respect, see Kokkoris and Shelanski 2014, pp. 32–43; Lindsay and Berridge 2017, pp. 36–40.

[26] E.g. Consolidated Jurisdictional Notice 2008; Simplified Procedure Notice 2013; Case Referral Notice 2005;

the case-law of the EU courts has proven to be instrumental in shaping the development of EU merger control over time, especially at the time the transition was made from the Merger Control Regulation 1989 to its 2004 successor.[27] The Merger Control Regulation 2004 contains jurisdictional, procedural and substantive rules, which will be discussed in the following (sub)sections.

3.1 Jurisdiction

Recitals 8 and 9 of the Merger Control Regulation 2004 signal that the Regulation applies to significant structural changes, the market impact of which goes beyond the national borders of any one Member State. Such concentrations should, as a general rule, be reviewed exclusively at EU level. Concentrations not covered by the Regulation come, in principle, within the jurisdiction of the Member States. Thus, the scope of application of the Merger Control Regulation should be defined according to the geographical area of activity of the undertakings involved in the concentration and be limited by quantitative thresholds in order to cover those concentrations which have an EU dimension. In this light, Articles 1 and 3 of the Merger Control Regulation 2004 provide the two cumulative jurisdictional criteria for its application: (1) there should be a *concentration* which (2) has an *EU dimension*.

3.1.1 The concept of concentration

Article 3 of the Merger Control Regulation 2004 and paragraphs 7–123 of the Consolidated Jurisdictional Notice 2008 provide the qualitative criteria a concentration must meet. Should this not be the case, and consequently should the Merger Control Regulation not apply, the transaction may fall under the national merger control rules (if the respective domestic qualitative thresholds are met), or under the EU and/or national antitrust rules, particularly Article 101 TFEU, or its domestic equivalent. It may also be the case that such a transaction may be reviewed by the Commission under Article 101 TFEU, whereas domestic authorities treat the transaction as a concentration and review it under the domestic merger control rules.[28] Article 3 and Recital 20 of the Merger Control Regulation 2004 and paragraph 7 of the Consolidated Jurisdictional Notice 2008 define the concept of concentration as covering operations bringing about a lasting change in the control of the undertakings concerned and

---

Remedies Notice 2008; Ancillary Restraints Notice 2005; Horizontal Merger Guidelines 2004; Non-Horizontal Merger Guidelines 2008; Notice on Access to Commission File 2005. For a complete list of the merger control soft-law documents, see <https://ec.europa.eu/competition/mergers/legislation/legislation.html> accessed 11 March 2020.

[27] In cases T-310/01 *Schneider*, ECLI:EU:T:2002:254; T-5/02 *Tetra Laval*, ECLI:EU:T:2002:264; T-342/99 *Airtours*, ECLI:EU:T:2002:146, three prohibition decisions adopted by the Commission were annulled by the GC (Court of First Instance, at the time). Many commentators argue that this turn of events was an important contributing factor to the decision to revamp the Merger Control Regulation 1989. See e.g. Kokkoris and Shelanski 2014, p. 30; Rusu 2010, p. 148 *et seq.*; Lianos, Korah and Siciliani 2019, p. 1506; Sauter 2016, p. 201.

[28] See Kokkoris and Shelanski 2014, p. 121, referring to case COMP/38.064/F2 *Covisint*, (2001) OJ C 49/04. See Press Release IP/01/1155.

therefore in the structure of the market. The lasting kind that the change of control must exhibit need not be permanent, yet the period of the underlying concentration agreement must be sufficiently long (e.g. ten years or more).[29]

According to Article 3(1) and (4) of the Merger Control Regulation 2004, such a change of control may occur via: mergers (Article 3(1)(a)), acquisitions (Article 3(1)(b)) or full-function joint ventures (Article 3(4)). The Consolidated Jurisdictional Notice 2008 provides extensive guidance as to each type of concentration.

3.1.1.1 Mergers

Mergers[30] occur where two or more independent undertakings amalgamate into a new undertaking and cease to exist as separate legal entities (i.e. fusion). A merger may also occur when an undertaking is absorbed by another, the latter retaining its legal identity while the former ceases to exist as a legal entity (i.e. absorption). Essentially, mergers entail transactions which result in the creation of a single economic unit/entity.[31] The distinctive feature of mergers is that at least one entity ceases to exist. There may, however, be situations where two or more undertakings, while retaining their individual legal personalities, establish contractually a common economic management, leading to a *de facto* amalgamation of the undertakings concerned into a single economic unit. Such situations are to be treated as mergers, under Article 3(1)(a) of the Merger Control Regulation 2004.[32]

3.1.1.2 Acquisitions

Since mergers entail at least one entity ceasing to exist, in practice, mergers occur less often than acquisitions, as described in Article 3(1)(b) of the Merger Control Regulation 2004. Such acquisitions of control, by undertakings or by persons already controlling at least another undertaking, do not entail entities ceasing to exist. Instead, the parties to the transactions remain active, yet what makes such transactions concentrations is the fact that there is a change of control of at least one undertaking's (i.e. the target) behaviour. It is nevertheless important to clearly distinguish between mergers and acquisitions, for the purpose of establishing who must notify the transaction to the relevant authorities.[33]

Depending on the manner in which acquisitions are completed in practice, we may deal with acquisitions of assets (such as important production plants or equipment, patents or other IP rights, client base of specific businesses, and more), or acquisitions of shares/securities/interests. Depending on how many entities acquire control over the target, we may

---

[29] Case COMP/M. 2903 *Daimler Chrysler/Deutsche Telekom*, (2003) OJ L 300/73.

[30] For the sake of clarity, the term 'merger' may be perceived as having a broad and narrow meaning. In the broad sense, mergers are synonymous with concentrations (e.g. when referring to the Merger Control Regulation). In the narrow sense of the term, mergers are to be perceived as the form of concentration referred to in Article 3(1)(a) of the Merger Control Regulation 2004 (i.e. legal mergers performed through fusions or absorptions).

[31] For further discussions on this matter, see Kokkoris and Shelanski 2014, p. 122.

[32] Consolidated Jurisdictional Notice 2008, par. 9, 10 and the case examples cited therein. See also Whish and Bailey 2018, pp. 853, 854.

[33] Jones, Sufrin and Dunne 2019, p. 1072. See also section 3.2.1 of this chapter.

deal with acquisitions of sole or joint control. Similarly, depending on the features of the target acquired, we may deal with acquisitions of the whole or parts of undertakings. Lastly, contingent on whether the parties to a transaction willingly consent to the transaction, the deal may or may not amount to a so-called hostile takeover. Either way, whether an operation gives rise to an acquisition of control depends on a number of legal and/or factual elements.[34]

The concept of control,[35] which is the gateway to establishing the existence of a concentration, is broadly defined in Article 3(2) of the Merger Control Regulation 2004:

> control shall be constituted by rights, contracts or any other means which, either separately or in combination and having regard to the considerations of fact or law involved, confer the possibility of exercising decisive influence on an undertaking, in particular by: a) ownership or the right to use all or part of the assets of an undertaking; b) rights or contracts which confer decisive influence on the composition, voting or decisions of the organs of an undertaking.

The key in understanding the essence of the notion of control is therefore the *decisive influence* concept, which is not defined per se in the Regulation. Attention should be paid to the fact that the Regulation requires merely the *possibility to* exercise such influence over the target undertaking. It must not be demonstrated that this influence will be or has been exercised. Nevertheless, the possibility of exercising that influence must be effective.[36] Decisive influence does not necessarily entail obtaining absolute control over an undertaking. What the Commission will be interested in is the decisive influence, which has a certain weight.[37] The boundaries of this concept have been tested in practice: while acquisitions of majority voting rights likely (but not always) result in the exercise of decisive influence, it may also be the case that acquisitions of smaller shareholding packages (i.e. considerably below the 50 per cent mark) could amount to control, provided that the remaining shares are widely dispersed, or the holder of the remaining shares must not be consulted for strategic decisions.[38] Thus, the question of whether decisive influence, and therefore control, exists is to be determined pragmatically, the essential ingredient being that of an influence over the business strategy of the undertaking(s) concerned. This fact should be determined in light of all relevant circumstances of the given case.[39]

Although above we mentioned that the concept of decisive influence does not necessarily entail absolute control, it can be viewed as somewhat demanding, especially when compared to standards in force in certain domestic jurisdictions. In the UK, for example, the concept of control is broadly conceived, so as to cover the ability to 'materially influence' an enterprise's policy. In practice, the existence of an ability to exercise 'material influence' is presumed for

---

[34] Consolidated Jurisdictional Notice 2008, par. 17.

[35] For more discussions on this matter, see Broberg 2004; Rusu 2014 (a).

[36] Consolidated Jurisdictional Notice 2008, par. 16.

[37] Broberg 2004, p. 742.

[38] E.g. case IV/M.258 *CCIE/GTE*, (1992) OJ C 225/14.

[39] Marco Colino 2019, pp. 432–3.

shareholdings of 25 per cent and above; exceptionally, even a shareholding of less than 15 per cent in a direct competitor might attract scrutiny, where other factors indicating the exercise of such influence are present.[40]

Returning to EU law aspects, control is normally acquired by persons or undertakings which are the holders of the rights or are entitled to use the rights conferring control under the contracts concerned. However, there may be situations in which an entity uses another entity to acquire control, as a vehicle for the acquisition. In such scenarios, control is acquired by the entity which in reality is behind the operation and in fact enjoys the power to control the target undertaking.[41] When control is acquired by one entity only, that is, the acquirer alone can exercise decisive influence over the target, we are dealing with *sole control* scenarios.[42] According to paragraphs 54 and following of the Consolidated Jurisdictional Notice 2008, sole control may be exercised positively (i.e. determining the target's strategic commercial decisions, through the acquisition of a majority of voting rights) or negatively (i.e. when only one shareholder is able to veto strategic decisions in an undertaking, but this shareholder does not have the power, on his own, to impose such decisions). Further, sole control may be acquired on a *de jure* or a *de facto* basis. The former scenario occurs in cases of acquisitions of majority shareholdings, or through minority shareholdings if specific rights (e.g. preferential shares allowing the minority shareholder to determine the target's strategic behaviour, or to appoint more than half of the members of its supervisory or administrative boards) are attached to such participations. The latter scenario occurs, for example, when a minority shareholder is highly likely to achieve a majority at the shareholders' meetings, given the level of its shareholding and the evidence resulting from the presence of share-holders in the shareholders' meetings in previous years.[43] In such settings, diverse criteria (such as the position of other shareholders, dispersion of remaining shares, structural or economic links between shareholders, and the like) are evaluated on a case-by-case basis to verify this likelihood. When control is acquired by two or more entities that have the possi-bility to exercise decisive influence over the target, we are dealing with *joint control* scenarios. Unlike sole control, which confers upon a specific shareholder the power to determine the strategic decisions in an undertaking, joint control is characterised by the possibility of a deadlock situation resulting from the power of two or more parent companies, by virtue of a common understanding, to veto proposed strategic decisions (essentially, negative control). Joint control can be achieved on a *de jure* (e.g. formal agreement between the companies) or a *de facto* basis (where a strong common interest exists between the minority shareholders to the effect that they would not act against each other in exercising their rights in relation to the joint venture).[44] Given the many forms in which joint control may materialise and the

---

[40] E.g. case *BSkyB/ITV*, (2008) CAT 25, Court of Appeal (2010) EWCA Civ 2. See Rusu 2014 (b), pp. 497–8 and the literature cited therein.

[41] Merger Control Regulation 2004, Article 3(3)(a) and (b); Consolidated Jurisdictional Notice 2008, par. 13; case T-282/02 *Cementbouw*, ECLI:EU:T:2006:64.

[42] E.g. case COMP/M.754 *Anglo American Corporation/Lonrho*, (1998) OJ L 149/21.

[43] Cases COMP/M.3330 *RTL/M6*, (2004) OJ C 95/35; IV/M.1519 *Renault/Nissan*, (1999) OJ C 178/14.

[44] Consolidated Jurisdictional Notice 2008, par. 62, 63; case COMP/JV.55 *Hutchison/RCPM/ECT*, (2003) OJ L 223/1;

ensuing intricacies that such transactions often entail, the Consolidated Jurisdictional Notice 2008 dedicates paragraphs 62 to 82 to shedding light on such matters.

Lastly, it is not only acquisitions of control that trigger the application of the Merger Control Regulation 2004, but also changes in the quality of control, for example from sole to joint control or vice versa, or changes in the number or identity of joint controlling entities. However, the internal restructuring of an undertaking, for example through changes from negative to positive control or changes in the level of shareholdings of the same controlling shareholders, without changes of the powers they hold in the company and of the composition of the control structure of the company, does not amount to a concentration.[45]

3.1.1.3 Full-function joint ventures

Article 3(4) of the Merger Control Regulation 2004 provides that the creation of a joint venture performing on a lasting basis all the functions of an autonomous economic entity is also to be regarded as a concentration. Joint ventures are generally defined as business arrangements between parties who undertake a specific economic activity *together*, activity the performance of which is beyond their individual capacity (e.g. R&D, production, distribution).[46] Thus, joint ventures are created by the so-called parent undertakings, which jointly control such newly created entities. The Merger Control Regulation 2004 applies to so-called *full-function* joint ventures. It is important to delineate full-function from non-full-function joint ventures, since it is only the former that fall under the provisions of the Regulation, while the latter may qualify for scrutiny under the EU (and/or domestic) antitrust provisions dealing with agreements between undertakings. Paragraphs 91–105 of the Consolidated Jurisdictional Notice 2008 discuss the concept of full-functionality in depth.

The starting point in understanding the concept of full-functionality is Article 3(4) of the Merger Control Regulation 2004: the performance on a lasting basis of all the functions of an autonomous economic entity. For a joint venture to qualify as full-function, it must exhibit certain features.[47] It must be economically autonomous (i.e. autonomous from an operational perspective), which does not necessarily entail autonomy as regards the adoption of its strategic decisions. Such strategic decisions remain at the disposal of the parent undertakings.[48] It must operate on a market, just like any other undertaking. It must have a management dedicated to its day-to-day operations, and access to sufficient resources including finance, staff (not necessarily employed by the joint venture itself)[49] and assets (tangible and intangible).[50] The joint venture must not perform activities which are simply auxiliary to the parents' business activities, for example, when the joint venture is limited to

---

Lianos, Korah and Siciliani 2019, p. 1536.

[45] Consolidated Jurisdictional Notice 2008, par. 83–90. See e.g. cases COMP/M.3440 *ENI/EDP/GdP*, (2005) OJ L 302/69; IV/M.023 *ICI/Tioxide*, (1990) OJ C 304/27.

[46] Kokkoris and Shelanski 2014, p. 141.

[47] Rusu 2010, pp. 18–19.

[48] Consolidated Jurisdictional Notice 2008, par. 93.

[49] Case COMP/M.2992 *Brenntag/Biesterfeld/JV*, (2003) OJ C 84/5.

[50] Consolidated Jurisdictional Notice 2008, par. 94.

R&D, or distribution of the parents' products. Neither must it be fully dependent on sales to or purchases from its parents, which are active on upstream or downstream markets, respectively. It must thus have independent access to the market, a matter which will be assessed on a case-by-case basis.[51] Last but not least, the joint venture must be intended to operate on a lasting basis (e.g. the agreement through which it is created is concluded for an indefinite period of time). It is only if this is the case that structural changes of the undertakings concerned (may) occur.[52]

Under the first Merger Control Regulation 1989, a distinction was made in Article 3(2) between 'cooperative' and 'concentrative' joint ventures. This distinction essentially relates to the behaviour of the parent companies. Cooperative joint ventures have as an object or effect the coordination of the competitive behaviour of the parent undertakings, which remain independent. For example, the parents would remain active on the market (or a neighbouring market), and use the joint venture as a vehicle of coordination. Such a joint venture would not fall under the Merger Control Regulation and it was meant to be assessed under the EU antitrust provisions. Concentrative joint ventures do not entail coordination between the parents, or between the parents and the joint venture, but entail the existence of an entity that has all the attributes of an independent economic actor. An example in this respect is where the parents completely withdraw from the market and 'concentrate' their respective activities in the joint venture, which actively replaces their presence on the market. From 1989 until 1998, the Commission made a sharp, formal cartel/concentration distinction when it came to joint ventures.[53] This boundary was redrawn by Regulation 1310/97, which focused on the full-functionality criteria, discussed above. After 1998, and under the current Merger Control Regulation 2004, the creation of a full-function joint venture, irrespective of the fact that it exhibits cooperative or concentrative features, is regarded as a concentration, and therefore falls under the procedural rules of the said Regulation. This change enhances legal certainty for the parties, as joint ventures, be they with cooperative or concentrative features, must be notified to the Commission, as long as the full-functionality criteria is met. The difference between the two types of effects is nevertheless maintained when it comes to the substantive analysis of such concentration transactions: cooperative aspects are appraised in light of Article 101 TFEU, whereas the concentrative features of a full-function joint venture are scrutinised based on the same substantive test as full-blown mergers and acquisitions.[54] We will return to this discussion in section 3.3.7.2 below.

3.1.1.4 Situations which do not amount to concentrations

Article 3(5) of the Merger Control Regulation 2004 specifies certain types of operations which, although seeming similar to the transactions discussed above, in that they may entail

---

[51] Consolidated Jurisdictional Notice 2008, par. 97–102. See e.g. cases IV/M.556 *Zeneca/Vanderhave*, (1996) OJ C 188/10; IV/M.751 *Bayer/Hüls*, (1996) OJ C 271/16. See also Lorenz 2013, p. 249; Whish and Bailey 2018, p. 858.

[52] E.g. case COMP/M. 2903 *Daimler Chrysler/Deutsche Telekom*, (2003) OJ L 300/73; Consolidated Jurisdictional Notice 2008, par. 103–105.

[53] Kokkoris and Shelanski 2014, pp. 142–3.

[54] On this matter, see Rusu 2010, p. 16 *et seq.*

acquisitions of controlling interests (but not of assets), do not constitute concentrations.[55] In this category of exceptions will fall the acquisition of securities by credit or other financial institutions, on an investment basis, provided that the voting rights are not exercised other than to protect the investment, the acquisition of control according to the law of a Member State relating to liquidation, winding up, insolvency, cessation of payments, compositions or analogous proceedings, and acquisition by financial holding companies in relation to such matters. In an era where institutional investors play an increasingly important role in the global economy, the frequency of such transactions tends to intensify. One can imagine that competition issues could occur, especially in situations of interlocking shareholdings in competitors active in concentrated sectors.[56] A prospective revision of the Merger Control Regulation could take such concerns into account.

3.1.1.5 The minority shareholdings discussion

A similar statement may be made in connection with non-controlling minority shareholding acquisitions. At the beginning of the 2010s, the Commission seriously contemplated amending the Merger Control Regulation's thresholds to bring within its scope such transactions which, although currently falling short of conferring control over target undertakings, may create competition issues in the market place. The discussions surrounding non-controlling minority shareholdings in the EU were triggered by the Commission's inability to appropriately deal with Ryanair's minority shareholding acquisition in its competitor Aer Lingus.[57] Extensive research[58] suggests that some acquisitions of non-controlling minority shareholdings, be they in the form of corporate rights or financial interests, may secure the acquirer's presence in the target's structure, its involvement in the target's internal matters, and generally speaking, influence the direction of the business, on one hand, or may alter the incentives the acquirer has to behave in a certain way or to compete less vigorously, on the other hand. Somewhat similar to fully fledged concentrations, minority shareholdings may thus create horizontal, vertical or market entry effects, which may be problematic from a competition point of view.[59] Such concerns caused certain domestic jurisdictions (e.g. the UK, Germany) to regulate minority shareholding transactions in their national merger control laws. The Commission, after a series of public consultations, multiple studies and staff working documents,[60] issued the White Paper 2014, which puts forward a system allowing it to tackle minority shareholdings as low as 5 per cent, which create 'competitively significant links' between the undertakings concerned. The White Paper 2014 even designed

---

[55] Consolidated Jurisdictional Notice 2008, par. 110–116; see e.g. case COMP/M.2978 *Lagardère/Natexis/VUP*, (2004) OJ L 125/54.

[56] Whish and Bailey 2018, p. 859; Lianos, Korah and Siciliani 2019, pp. 1541–2.

[57] Case M.4439 *Ryanair/Aer Lingus*, (2006) OJ C 274/10; T-342/07 *Ryanair*, ECLI:EU:T:2010:280; T-411/07 *Aer Lingus*, ECLI:EU:T:2010:281.

[58] E.g. Salop and O'Brien 2000; Reynolds and Snapp 1986; Gilo, Moshe and Spiegel 2006.

[59] For a more extensive overview of such effects, see Rusu 2017 (c), p. 228 *et seq.*

[60] For a list of such documents, see <https://ec.europa.eu/competition/mergers/publications_en.html> accessed 20 March 2020.

a procedural roadmap for assessing such transactions, entailing a 'targeted transparency control', which was advertised as presenting lighter burdens on the business community than the full-blown merger control review applicable to concentrations.[61] Despite these efforts, the minority shareholdings discussion in the EU seems to have been parked, after Commissioner Vestager stated in a 2015 speech that the balance between the concerns that minority shareholdings raise and the procedural burdens of the targeted transparency control system of competitively significant links may not be the right one and that the issues need to be examined further.[62]

3.1.2 The concept of EU dimension

Once a transaction meets the requirements to be labelled as a concentration, for the Merger Control Regulation 2004 to apply, the concentration needs to have an EU dimension. Article 1 of the Merger Control Regulation 2004 and paragraphs 124–128 of the Consolidated Jurisdictional Notice 2008 shed light on the criteria to establish the EU dimension. Essentially, the transaction needs to exceed a certain 'size' to qualify for review under the Regulation, since it is these large transactions that may have an impact that goes beyond the national borders of any one Member State. Should the transaction amount to a concentration, yet not have an EU dimension, the national concentration regimes of the Member States may be applicable. Deciding whether a concentration meets the EU dimension characterisation is done by reference to the turnover of the parties involved in the transaction. Thus, Article 1 of the Merger Control Regulation 2004 introduces a quantitative dimension to the jurisdictional test, additional to the qualitative test embedded in Article 3. Article 1 thus provides a bright-line test, allocating the EU and national jurisdictions, respectively, a test which can be applied relatively simply, objectively and easily.[63] Article 1 of the Merger Control Regulation 2004 contains two alternative thresholds by which a concentration may be labelled as having an EU dimension.

Article 1(2) provides that a concentration has an EU dimension where:

(a) the combined aggregate worldwide turnover of all the undertakings concerned is more than EUR 5000 million; and (b) the aggregate EU-wide turnover of each of at least two of the undertakings concerned is more than EUR 250 million, unless each of the undertakings concerned achieves more than two-thirds of its aggregate EU-wide turnover within one and the same Member State.

Article 1(3) provides that a concentration that does not meet the thresholds laid down in paragraph 2 has an EU dimension where:

(a) the combined aggregate worldwide turnover of all the undertakings concerned is more than EUR 2500 million; (b) in each of at least three Member States, the combined

---

[61] See Rusu 2015 (a) and (b), for more extensive analysis of the White Paper 2014 proposals.

[62] Vestager 2015.

[63] Jones, Sufrin and Dunne 2019, p. 1078.

aggregate turnover of all the undertakings concerned is more than EUR 100 million; (c) in each of at least three Member States included for the purpose of point (b), the aggregate turnover of each of at least two of the undertakings concerned is more than EUR 25 million; and (d) the aggregate EU-wide turnover of each of at least two of the undertakings concerned is more than EUR 100 million, unless each of the undertakings concerned achieves more than two-thirds of its aggregate EU-wide turnover within one and the same Member State.

There is no mention in either of these paragraphs of a requirement that the undertakings concerned be domiciled in the EU territory, nor that the transaction should take place in the EU. This highlights the extraterritorial dimension that jurisdictional matters in EU merger control assume.[64] However, these thresholds do shed light on the size of the undertakings involved and on their presence in the EU. The lower thresholds embedded in Article 1(3) were introduced by Regulation 1310/97, and are designed to catch those smaller concentrations, which nevertheless may have an impact on at least three Member States, and which would otherwise be subject to control in these domestic jurisdictions. To date, a limited number of cases have fallen within this threshold.[65] Further, both paragraphs contain the so-called 'two-thirds rule', according to which, even when the turnover thresholds are met, when each of the undertakings concerned achieves more than two-thirds of its aggregate EU-wide turnover within one and the same Member State, the concentration is labelled as not having an EU dimension. This means that the control of such a transaction is left to the respective Member State.[66] This makes sense, given that the effects of such a transaction will probably be felt primarily in that domestic jurisdiction.

The two-thirds rule puts forward an element of flexibility, in order to ensure the proper allocation of cases between the Commission and the NCAs. It is important to note that the Commission is constantly looking to improve the functioning of the EU dimension thresholds. In its Report on the Functioning of the Merger Control Regulation 2009, it indicated that the two-thirds rule may allow mergers with EU relevance to escape its scrutiny, and pleaded for the revision of this rule. For example, the merger between E.ON and Ruhrgas escaped the Commission's assessment and it was assessed under German law by the domestic authorities: the BKA (i.e. the German competition authority) prohibited the merger; then, the German Government decided to conditionally approve the transaction, despite the fears expressed about the impact of the merger on competition throughout the EU; subsequently,

---

[64] E.g. case IV/M.887 *Boeing/McDonnell Douglas*, (1997) OJ L 336/16; case COMP/M.2220 *General Electric/Honeywell*, (2001) OJ L 48/1, Commission prohibition decision confirmed by the GC in case T-209/01 *Honeywell International*, ECLI:EU:T:2005:455. See Whish and Bailey 2018, p. 859; Marco Colino 2019, p. 436; Kokkoris and Shelanski 2014, p. 157.

[65] E.g. case COMP/M.2867 *UPM-Kymmene/Morgan Adhesives*, (2002) OJ C 284/4; case M.4439 *Ryanair/Aer Lingus*, (2006) OJ C 274/10, Commission prohibition decision confirmed by the GC in case T-342/07 *Ryanair*, ECLI: EU:T:2010:280.

[66] Marco Colino 2019, p. 435. See, e.g. case *Lloyds TSB Group/Abbey National*, (2001) Cm 5208, investigated by the UK authorities.

the Higher Regional Court of Düsseldorf reversed the Economics Minister's decision, based on procedural errors, thus blocking the transaction.[67] Therefore, the flexibility of the two-thirds rule, as it currently stands, also has a dangerous flipside, since it may allow national governments the possibility to create so-called national champions in key sectors of the economy.

In 2016–17 the Commission launched a consultation on procedural and jurisdictional aspects of EU merger control[68] which, going beyond the two-thirds rule, was meant to test the effectiveness of purely turnover-based jurisdictional thresholds. This is because particularly in certain sectors, such as the digital and pharmaceutical industries, the acquired company, while having generated little turnover, may play a competitive role, hold commercially valuable data, or have a considerable market potential for other reasons. Such deals (some of which may also take the form of so-called 'killer acquisitions') often do not meet the EU dimension criteria. Nevertheless, such transactions may have an impact on the EU market and should therefore be evaluated by the Commission. For example, the *Facebook/WhatsApp*[69] transaction did not have an EU dimension, due to the low turnover of one of the parties (WhatsApp). The deal was nevertheless cleared by the Commission, after the parties successfully argued based on Article 4(5) of the Merger Control Regulation 2004[70] that the transaction should be handled by the Commission, rather than an NCA. All in all, the Commission is currently looking into the possibility to introduce extra criteria (e.g. related to the value of the transaction, as recently introduced in Germany and Austria), in order to bring such concentrations within the scope of the EU merger control regime,[71] yet to date, no specific measures have been taken in this respect.

The thresholds embedded in Article 1 of the Merger Control Regulation 2004 are framed with a view to the *turnover* of the *undertakings concerned*. These notions are explained in Article 5 and paragraph 129 and following of the Consolidated Jurisdictional Notice 2008. The first step is to identify which are the undertakings concerned in a given concentration transaction. Then, their turnover is calculated to see if the concentration has an EU dimension.

3.1.2.1 Undertakings concerned

Identifying the undertakings concerned depends on the type of transaction at hand. In a merger, the undertakings concerned are each of the merging entities.[72] In case of acquisitions of sole control, the undertakings concerned are the acquiring undertaking (even if it is simply a subsidiary of a group of companies, unless the subsidiary is merely an acquisition vehicle)

---

[67] See Jones and Davies 2015, pp. 98–9; OECD 2004, p. 143.

[68] See <https://ec.europa.eu/competition/consultations/2016_merger_control/index_en.html> accessed 17 March 2020.

[69] Case COMP/M.7217 *Facebook/WhatsApp*, (2014) C/2014/7239 final.

[70] See section 3.1.4.1 of this chapter.

[71] Crémer, de Montjoye and Schweitzer 2019, p. 10 and Chapter 6; Vestager 2016; Vestager 2019 (a); Lianos, Korah and Siciliani 2019, p. 1559; Joint Memorandum 2019.

[72] Consolidated Jurisdictional Notice 2008, par. 132.

and the target undertaking.[73] If the acquisition entails a change from joint to sole control, one shareholder normally acquires the stake previously held by the other shareholder(s). The undertakings concerned are then the acquiring shareholder and the joint venture.[74] In the case of acquisition of joint control of a newly created undertaking, the undertakings concerned are each of the companies acquiring control of the newly set-up joint venture. If the target is a pre-existing undertaking, the undertakings concerned are each of the undertakings acquiring joint control on the one hand, and the pre-existing acquired undertaking on the other.[75] If one or more shareholders acquire control, either by entry or by substitution of one or more shareholders, when joint control exists both before and after the operation, the undertakings concerned are the shareholders (both existing and new) who exercise joint control and the joint venture itself.[76] If a joint venture acquires control of another company, the undertakings concerned are the target and the joint venture (unless the joint venture is set up as a 'shell' company, in which case the parent companies will individually be considered as the undertakings concerned).[77] If natural persons that carry out economic activities acquire a company, or if they already control another company, the undertakings concerned are the target undertaking and the individual acquirer.[78]

3.1.2.2 Turnover

Next, the concept of *turnover* relates to revenues from the sale of products and the provision of services in the EU. Paragraphs 157–60 and 197–202 of the Consolidated Jurisdictional Notice 2008 discuss the calculation and geographic allocation of turnover, for products and services, respectively. Particularly for services, due to their diversity, many different situations may arise and the underlying legal and economic relations have to be carefully analysed. Article 5(1) of the Merger Control Regulation 2004 refers to the turnover obtained from the ordinary activities of the undertakings concerned, that is, the normal course of their business, meaning that extraordinary income derived from, for example, the sale of businesses or of fixed assets, is excluded from the calculation, whereas, for example, aid granted to undertakings by public bodies is included in the calculation, if it is directly linked to the sale of products and the provision of services by the undertaking.[79] Also, the turnover calculation does not include the so-called internal turnover, which results from internal transfers between undertakings belonging to the same group, as described in Article 5(4) of the Merger Control Regulation 2004, that is, those undertakings in which the undertaking concerned, directly or indirectly, owns more than half the capital or business assets, or has the power to exercise more than half the voting rights, or has the power to appoint more

---

[73] Ibid, par. 134, 135.

[74] Ibid, par. 138. See case IV/M.023 *ICI/Tioxide*, (1990) OJ C 304/27.

[75] Consolidated Jurisdictional Notice 2008, par. 139, 140.

[76] Ibid, par. 143. See case IV/M.376 *Synthomer/Yule Catto*, (1993) OJ C 303/5.

[77] Consolidated Jurisdictional Notice 2008, par. 145.

[78] Ibid, par. 151. See case IV/M.082 *Asko/Jacobs/Adia*, (1991) OJ C 132/13.

[79] Consolidated Jurisdictional Notice 2008, par. 161, 162. See case IV/M.156 *Cereol/Continentale Italiana*, (1992) OJ C 7/7.

than half the members of the supervisory board, the administrative board or bodies legally representing the undertakings[80] or has the right to manage the undertakings' affairs.[81] The rationale in this respect is to exclude the proceeds of business dealings within a group, so as to take account of the real economic weight of each entity in the form of market turnover. In other words, the turnover calculation is meant to capture the total volume of the economic resources that are being combined through the operation,[82] irrespective of whether the economic activities are carried out directly by the undertaking concerned, or whether they are undertaken indirectly via undertakings with which the undertaking concerned possesses such links. Thus, the amounts taken into account by the Merger Control Regulation 2004 reflect only the transactions which take place between the group of undertakings, on the one hand, and third parties, on the other. This means that when calculating the turnover of the undertaking concerned for the purpose of establishing the (in)existence of an EU dimension, this turnover shall be calculated by adding together the respective turnovers of the undertakings belonging to the same group, while avoiding double counting.[83] Paragraph 175 and following of the Consolidated Jurisdictional Notice 2008 contain very detailed information on how to identify the undertakings whose turnover should be taken into account, essentially detailing the criteria of Article 5(4) of the Merger Control Regulation 2004. Importantly, these criteria, including the 'right to manage the undertakings' affairs', are not coextensive with the notion of 'control' under Article 3(2). According to paragraph 184 of the Consolidated Jurisdictional Notice 2008, there are significant differences between Articles 3 and 5 of the Merger Control Regulation 2004 (particularly when talking about *de facto* control), as those provisions fulfil different roles.[84] Moving on, according to Article 5(2) of the Merger Control Regulation 2004, where the concentration consists of the acquisition of parts of one or more undertakings, only the turnover relating to the parts which are the subject of the concentration are taken into account with regard to the seller. Two or more transactions in this respect, the so-called 'staggered operations', which take place within a two-year period, between the same entities are treated as one and the same concentration. According to Article 5(1) of the Merger Control Regulation 2004, the turnover calculation is made with reference to the net turnover of the previous financial year, that is, after deduction of sales rebates and of value added tax and other taxes directly related to turnover. Turnover calculation should thus reflect the real economic strength of the undertakings.[85] Lastly, Article 5(3) of the Merger Control Regulation 2004 and paragraphs 206–220 of the Consolidated Jurisdictional Notice

---

[80] E.g. cases IV/M.187 *Ifint/Exor*, (1992) OJ C 88/13; IV/M.062 *Eridania/ISI*, (1991) OJ C 204/12.

[81] E.g. cases COMP/M.1741 *MCI Worldcom/Sprint*, (2003) OJ L 300/1; IV/M.1046 *Ameritech/Tele Danmark*, (1998) OJ C 25/18.

[82] Lianos, Korah and Siciliani 2019, p. 1556.

[83] Merger Control Regulation 2004, Article 5(4) and (5); Consolidated Jurisdictional Notice 2008, par. 167, 168, 175. See also par. 178 for an illustrative graphic example of how calculation of turnover in relation to group of undertakings is to be performed.

[84] Kokkoris and Shelanski 2014, p. 159; Lianos, Korah and Siciliani 2019, p. 1557; Whish and Bailey 2018, p. 855.

[85] Consolidated Jurisdictional Notice 2008, par. 164.

2008 provide specific rules for the calculation of turnover of credit and other financial institutions, as well as insurance undertakings.

3.1.3 The one-stop-shop principle

The Merger Control Regulation is premised on the idea that structural reorganisations which affect the Internal Market should be assessed on a unitary European framework, rather than be subject to multiple appraisals in the jurisdictions of the Member States where a transaction may create effects. This EU-wide framework is known as the one-stop-shop principle, embedded in Article 21 of the Merger Control Regulation 2004. Its essence entails that, subject to review by the EU courts, the Commission alone may take decisions, based on the Merger Control Regulation 2004, in respect of concentrations having an EU dimension, and no Member State may apply its national (competition) rules, unless one of the case referral scenarios (discussed below) occurs, or unless the Member States intend to protect certain legitimate interests recognised under EU law (such as, but not limited to, public security, plurality of the media and prudential rules).[86] In this latter case, the Member States retain their powers to apply domestic rules to concentrations taking place in such sectors. Their action must be appropriate and proportionate for achieving the relevant interest. All in all, the one-stop-shop principle is meant to eliminate double review, administrative inefficiency, delays, unnecessary expenses and uncertainty, while the possibility of conflicting decisions is avoided.[87]

The introduction of the one-stop-shop system in EU merger control yielded consequences for a diverse range of stakeholders. The business community demanded such a system, given the conflicting environment businesses were finding themselves in: on one hand, the Internal Market project was presenting them with increased cross-border opportunities, while on the other hand, they were facing multiple and at times diverging national merger review procedures and criteria, a situation which was obviously burdensome. The national governments' motivation to support the EU framework was more diverse, but nevertheless congruent in supporting the creation of a one-stop-shop EU merger control system: France, for example, saw this as an opportunity to translate the 'national champion' policy into a 'European champion' type of vision. France also felt that German merger control, already in a robust shape in the 1980s, limited the expansion of French businesses. Germany, on the other hand, supported the European framework since it feared that laxer merger laws in other Member States may be to the detriment of German businesses.[88]

Summing up, the one-stop-shop principle ensures a clear division of competences between the EU and the domestic concentration control systems: the Commission applies the Merger Control Regulation 2004, whereas domestic merger control is governed solely by national laws. The one-stop-shop principle thus entails a centralisation of cases at the Commission level, opposite to the antitrust enforcement decentralisation that Regulation 1/2003 brought

---

[86] Merger Control Regulation 2004, Article 21(4) and Recitals 17–19. On the functioning of the 'legitimate interest clause', including relevant practical examples, see Whish and Bailey 2018, pp. 872–5.

[87] Whish and Bailey 2018, p. 865.

[88] On these matters, see Monti 2007, pp. 247–8.

about.[89] Yet, this division of competences is not rigid: the system of case referrals between the NCAs and the Commission ensures the proper allocation and appraisal of all concentrations in the appropriate forum, in accordance with the principle of subsidiarity.

3.1.4 Case referrals

A key prerequisite for the one-stop-shop principle to achieve its aims is that concentrations are notified to the Commission. (Most) domestic merger control systems in the Member States also require the notification of concentrations before their practical implementation. The notification step[90] is important when discussing the case referral mechanisms, since the (re-)allocation of a case may take place either before or after the transaction is notified to the relevant authority: that is, pre-notification and post-notification referrals. A different way of categorising case referrals in EU merger control is from the standpoint of the entity trigger-ing the (re-)allocation of the case: that is, referrals initiated by the parties to the transaction and referrals initiated by competition authorities. For the sake of clarity, the case referral mechanism is a bi-directional one: a case may be reallocated from the Commission to the NCA(s), or vice versa, from the NCA(s) to the Commission. The Case Referral Notice 2005 extensively deals with all these scenarios.

The rationale behind the case referral system is spelled out in the introductory paragraphs of the Case Referral Notice 2005: the turnover criteria confer legal certainty for the merging parties, yet taken by themselves only, they accommodate only a limited degree of flexibil-ity. Furthermore, the Merger Control Regulation 1989 envisaged reallocation of cases only in exceptional circumstances. The Merger Control Regulation 2004 revised this stance, by accommodating broader possibilities to derogate from the turnover jurisdictional criteria, while continuing to abide by the guiding principles: (1) of having transactions investigated by the most appropriate authority, having regard to the specific characteristics of the case, as well as the tools and expertise available to the authority; (2) the one-stop-shop principle, and the avoidance (as much as possible) of fragmentation of cases (i.e. partial referrals); and (3) legal certainty, from the perspective of all parties involved.[91]

3.1.4.1 Pre-notification referrals

Paragraph 6 of the Case Referral Notice 2005 provides that a case referral may be triggered before a formal filing in any (Member State or EU) jurisdiction, thereby affording merging companies the possibility of ascertaining, at an early stage, in which jurisdiction their trans-action will be scrutinised. Such pre-notification referrals have the advantage of alleviating additional costs and delays associated with post-filing referrals. Pre-notification referrals may be initiated only by the parties to a concentration transaction.

---

[89] Sauter 2016, p. 196.

[90] See section 3.2.1 of this chapter.

[91] Case Referral Notice 2005, par. 2–14.

Article 4(4) of the Merger Control Regulation 2004
This provision did not exist in the Merger Control Regulation 1989. As it now stands, this mechanism provides the parties to a concentration with the possibility to inform the Commission, by means of a reasoned submission (Form RS – contained in Annex III of the Implementing Regulation 2004), that the concentration may significantly affect competition in a market within a Member State which presents all the characteristics of a distinct market. Therefore, according to the parties' view, the concentration should be examined, in whole or in part, by the NCA in that Member State. This does not mean that the concentration necessarily produces detrimental effects on competition.[92] Article 4(4) thus deals with concentrations that have an EU dimension, which may nevertheless be appraised by the NCAs of the Member States where competition effects may occur. Sections 2–5 of Article 4(4) and paragraph 49 of the Case Referral Notice 2005 outline the procedural steps for successfully reallocating the case from the Commission to the domestic authorities. Both the Commission and the concerned NCAs must agree to the case referral. A lack of response on behalf of these authorities within the deadlines specified by Article 4(4) equals consent. When the case is reallocated to the national authorities, these authorities will apply their national laws to the (parts of) the concentration referred. Statistics[93] show that until February 2020, 173 requests were submitted to the Commission under Article 4(4), while refusals to refer the case to the NCA(s) are yet to occur.

Article 4(5) of the Merger Control Regulation 2004
This Article provides for a similar process as Article 4(4), yet this time, the concentration does not have an EU dimension, but it is capable of being reviewed under the national competition laws of at least three Member States. The parties may, before any notification to the competent NCAs, inform the Commission, via Form RS, that the concentration should be examined by the Commission. Sections 2–5 of Article 4(5) and paragraph 49 of the Case Referral Notice 2005 outline the procedural steps for successfully referring the case to the Commission. It is important that no Member State from those concerned by the transaction disagrees with the referral. If at least one Member State disagrees with the referral, it cannot be performed. If no disagreements occur, the case is deemed to acquire an EU dimension and is thus referred to the Commission which has exclusive jurisdiction over it. The parties must then notify the Commission, using the customary method (discussed below in section 3.2.1). The referral process under Article 4(5) embodies perfectly the benefits of the one-stop-shop control system: parties do not have to engage in multiple filings, they avoid unnecessary costs, and the deal is assessed by the best placed authority. Until February 2020, more than 350 referral requests have been made under Article 4(5); only seven refusals to refer have been registered so far.[94]

---

[92] Merger Control Regulation 2004, Recital 16; Case Referral Notice 2005, par. 61.

[93] See <https://ec.europa.eu/competition/mergers/statistics.pdf> accessed 31 March 2020.

[94] Ibid.

3.1.4.2 Post-notification referrals

The post-notification referrals mirror the general setup of the pre-notification referrals, in that they entail a reallocation of cases. However, there are at least two main differences with the referrals based on Article 4 of the Merger Control Regulation 2004: first, the referrals in question occur after a concentration is notified to the authority competent to scrutinise it, based on the jurisdictional criteria in force; second, post-notification referrals are always initiated by the competition authorities (the NCA(s), either on own motion, or based on an invitation from the Commission). Further, as detailed just below, the rationale of introducing post-notification referrals in the text of the EU Merger Control Regulations is somewhat special.

Article 9 of the Merger Control Regulation 2004

This provision is also known as the 'German clause', since it was inserted in the Merger Control Regulation 1989 at the request of Germany, which was keen at that time to retain the power to appraise large concentrations that may have an impact on its territory.[95] Article 9 of the Merger Control Regulation 2004 allows the Commission to refer a (part of a) concentration that has been notified to it, to an NCA, at its own initiative, or at the request of that particular Member State.[96] Thus, a concentration that has an EU dimension may be referred for investigation under the domestic law of the Member State concerned. Pursuant to Article 9(2) of the Merger Control Regulation 2004 this may be done only if:

a) the concentration threatens to affect significantly competition in a market within that Member State, which presents all the characteristics of a distinct market, or b) the concentration affects competition in a market within that Member State, which presents all the characteristics of a distinct market and which does not constitute a substantial part of the Internal Market.

In the former situation (Article 9(2)(a)), the Commission must first verify whether those legal criteria (i.e. the existence of such a distinct market and threat) are met. It may then decide to refer the case, or a part thereof, exercising its administrative discretion. In the latter scenario (Article 9(2)(b)), the Commission must (i.e. has no discretion) make the referral if the legal criteria are met (i.e. the affected market does not constitute a substantial part of the Internal Market, in light of, for example, the economic importance of the services and territories concerned, the volume of cross-border trade, and suchlike).[97] Article 9 prescribes detailed procedural rules regarding referrals to the NCAs, addressed both to the Commission and the NCAs, including strict deadlines. Once a referral is made, that (part of the) case should be assessed based on the domestic law of the Member State concerned. Statistics[98] show that,

---

[95] Rusu 2010, p. 102; Jones, Sufrin and Dunne 2019, p. 1087.

[96] E.g. case COMP/M.5881 *ProSiebenSat.1 Media/RTL Interactive/JV*, (2010) OJ C 219/19.

[97] Case Referral Notice 2005, par. 50. See also Lianos, Korah and Siciliani 2019, p. 1561.

[98] See <https://ec.europa.eu/competition/mergers/statistics.pdf> accessed 31 March 2020.

until February 2020, out of the 121 referral requests under Article 9, the large majority (about 85 per cent) were (at least partially) granted by the Commission.[99]

Article 22 of the Merger Control Regulation 2004

This provision mirrors the 'German clause', as it entails a concentration without an EU dimension, which is notified to one or more NCAs, and which affects trade between the Member States and threatens to significantly affect competition within the territory of that/ those Member State(s). The NCAs concerned may request the Commission to investigate the transaction based on the provisions of the Merger Control Regulation 2004. Article 22 is known as the 'Dutch clause', since it was inserted in the text of the Regulation at the request of the Netherlands, which, at that time, did not have merger control rules in its domestic legislation. Article 22 and paragraph 50 of the Case Referral Notice 2005 provide the procedural steps that a successful referral requires. After such a referral request is lodged by one or more NCAs, more Member States may join the request. The Commission is not obliged to accept jurisdiction. It may accept the referral for the whole or parts of a case.[100] When it takes on the case, national proceedings in the referring Member State(s) are terminated and the Commission examines the case pursuant to rules embedded in the Merger Control Regulation 2004, on behalf of the requesting state(s). In such a scenario, it is nevertheless not excluded that there are Member States which choose not to request the involvement of the Commission. Such non-requesting states may continue to apply their respective national laws to the concentration in question. Statistics show that requests arising from one Member State only are scarce (only four registered until February 2020, out of a total of 41 requests made so far),[101] while most referrals entail joint requests of several Member States, in cases where, essentially, the Commission would be the best placed authority to deal with the cross-border effects of the case.[102] Rejections of referrals are equally rare (only four registered so far).[103] Given the proliferation of merger control systems in almost all jurisdictions of the EU (except Luxembourg, which to date has no merger control system in place), one could imagine that the Dutch clause would lose its value throughout time. Nevertheless, referral requests based on Article 22 continue to occur, though seldom (approximately one request/ year).[104] In any case, just as with referrals based on Article 4(5) of the Merger Control Regulation 2004, the 'Dutch clause' has its advantages: saving private and public resources connected with multiple investigations, addressing the lack of particular remedies in certain domestic jurisdictions, and so on.[105]

---

[99] E.g. case M.7612 *Hutchison 3G UK/Telefónica UK*, (2016) OJ C 357/15.

[100] E.g. case M.4980 *ABF/GBI Business*, (2008) available at <https://ec.europa.eu/competition/elojade/isef/case_details.cfm?proc_code=2_M_4980> accessed 31 March 2020.

[101] See <https://ec.europa.eu/competition/mergers/statistics.pdf> accessed 31 March 2020.

[102] Jones, Sufrin and Dunne 2019, p. 1096.

[103] E.g. case M.4124 *Coca Cola Hellenic Bottling Company/Lanitis Bros*, (2006) Commission Decision of 24 February 2006.

[104] E.g. case M.8788 *Apple/Shazam*, (2018) OJ C 106/16.

[105] Kokkoris and Shelanski 2014, p. 167.

3.1.4.3 Potential revision of the case referral system

The White Paper 2014 noted that the case referral system could be enhanced,[106] particularly regarding pre- and post-notification referrals from Member States to the Commission. The White Paper 2014 proposed to abolish the two-step procedure of Article 4(5) of the Merger Control Regulation 2004, consisting of the submission of a Form RS and then of the formal notification; it also proposed to assign jurisdiction for the entire European Economic Area (EEA) to the Commission, if it accepts a referral pursuant to Article 22 of the Merger Control Regulation 2004. The White Paper 2014 also tackled some of the perceived shortcomings of Article 4(4) referrals, specifically dealing with the substantive thresholds for such referrals: the parties were no longer to be required to claim that the transaction may 'significantly affect competition in a market' to qualify for a referral. Showing that the transaction is likely to have its main impact in a distinct market in the Member State would suffice. Removing this 'element of self-incrimination' was perceived to potentially lead to an increase in the number of Article 4(4) requests. Despite the support that such proposals received,[107] no reform of the case referrals system has been operated so far.

3.2 Procedure

Once the Commission's jurisdiction is established in respect of a given concentration, the procedural rules of the Merger Control Regulation 2004 (and the supporting hard-law and soft-law documents) apply. We will discuss the procedural steps of the Commission's appraisal of the concentration, in the following sections. Before that, two preliminary points must be mentioned.

First, the Simplified Procedure Notice 2013 sets out the conditions under which the Commission usually adopts a short-form decision declaring a concentration compatible with the Internal Market, pursuant to a simplified procedure, in cases where the concentration does not raise competition concerns. In practice, this is the case more often than not, with years when more than half of the cases notified to the Commission are handled under this procedure. According to paragraphs 5 and 6 of this Notice, certain categories of concentrations can benefit from this procedure, such as: joint ventures with no, or negligible, actual or foreseen activities within the EEA territory, certain conglomerate concentrations, certain concentrations involving low market shares (below 20 per cent for horizontal and below 30 per cent for vertical transactions), and so forth. The simplified procedure will apply unless the safeguards or exclusions set forth in paragraphs 8–19 of the Notice are applicable (e.g. when the parties' market shares may not be precisely established, where coordination issues between the parties may occur, and so on), in which case, the Commission may launch an investigation and/or adopt a full decision under the Merger Control Regulation 2004. The 2013 'Simplification Package',[108] widened the scope of the simplified procedure even further

---

[106] White Paper 2014, par. 59–75.

[107] See   <https://ec.europa.eu/competition/consultations/2016_merger_control/summary_of_replies_en.pdf> accessed 31 March 2020.

[108] MEMO/13/1098.

for concentrations that are unlikely to raise competition problems. The 2016–17 consultation on procedural and jurisdictional aspects of EU merger control[109] identified additional options for procedural simplification: exempting certain categories of cases from the notification and standstill obligations; setting up a self-assessment system with the possibility of a voluntary notification for selected categories of cases, and suchlike. No legal developments have been registered in this respect yet.

Second, in practice it is common for contact to exist between representatives of the parties and the Commission prior to the formal notification of the concentration. Any contacts of this nature are entirely voluntary.[110] The Commission's Best Practices Guidelines 2004 provide important guidance in this respect, which may alleviate from the outset incomplete notifications, and may allow the Commission to identify sufficiently early the information it needs to run an efficient investigation.

3.2.1 Mandatory prior notification

Article 4(1) of the Merger Control Regulation 2004 provides that a concentration with an EU dimension shall be notified to the Commission prior to its implementation and following the conclusion of the agreement, the announcement of the public bid or the acquisition of a controlling interest. Notification may also take place where the undertakings concerned demonstrate to the Commission a good faith intention to conclude an agreement or, in the case of a public bid, where they have publicly announced an intention to make such a bid, provided that the intended agreement or bid would result in a concentration with an EU dimension. From the outset, it has to be noted that submitting the notification is mandatory. Large fines, of 10 per cent maximum of the aggregate turnover of the undertakings concerned, may be imposed on the parties when they intentionally or negligently fail to notify a concentration.[111]

As shown above,[112] the prior notification requirement is essential for the one-stop-shop control system and for the case referral mechanisms to function. Also, mandatory prior notification is a defining feature of the EU merger control system, which is thus conceived as an *ex ante* exercise, as opposed to the enforcement of the EU antitrust rules, which functions in an *ex post* manner. In other words, the competition impact of concentrations with an EU dimension is assessed before the transaction is implemented, and thus, before it may produce its effects. The *ex ante* control method is argued as necessary to ensure effective control of structural changes in the market. Such effective control was in turn viewed as necessary to ensure a system of undistorted competition in the Internal Market, in furtherance of a policy conducted in accordance with the principle of an open market economy with free competition.[113] Further, the *ex ante* control choice may be viewed from the perspective of

---

[109] See <https://ec.europa.eu/competition/consultations/2016_merger_control/index_en.html> accessed 31 March 2020.

[110] Marco Colino 2019, p. 445.

[111] Merger Control Regulation 2004, Article 14(2)(a).

[112] Sections 3.1.3 and 3.1.4.

[113] Ibid, Recitals 24, 34.

the business community. As discussed in section 2.3 above, market players signalled from early on that *ex post* (antitrust) methods of control are ill-suited for concentrations, which are business operations that require speedy assessment and legal certainty. *Ex ante* control obviously fulfils such needs more satisfactorily than *ex post* control.[114] From the moment the Merger Control Regulation 1989 entered into force, until February 2020, the Commission received 7674 notifications of concentrations.[115]

Notifications are done by submitting the so-called Form CO, or Short Form CO, in case the simplified procedure applies (contained in Annexes I and II of the Implementing Regulation 2004). Filling in Form CO is costly and time-consuming. It requires the parties to provide comprehensive information about the transaction, about themselves, about the ownership and control of the entities involved in the deal, about the markets involved, the parties' market shares, the position of competitors, the rationale for the concentration, and so forth. The Form CO itself and the provisions of the Implementing Regulation 2004 provide valuable information as to how the form should be filled in and what supporting documentation needs to be provided. Submitting a complete Form CO to the Commission is a key moment in the EU merger control procedure: the complete Form CO makes the notification effective, and it thus triggers the start of the strict timetable for the appraisal process (discussed in section 3.2.3 below).[116]

It is important for the parties to a transaction to understand who exactly needs to perform the notification of the concentration. The obligation to notify rests on different entities, depending on the type of transaction at hand. Article 4(2) of the Merger Control Regulation 2004 and Article 2 of the Implementing Regulation 2004 shed light on this matter. In case of a merger, it is the merging parties that should notify the deal. In case of acquisition of joint control, it is the parties who jointly acquire control that must notify the Commission. When dealing with a full-function joint venture, it is the 'parents' of the joint venture that must comply with the notification requirement. The only situation in which the notification must be done by a single entity is when the acquirer must notify its acquisition of sole control over a target.

The parties obliged to notify the concentration are responsible for the accuracy of the information provided. There are important consequences when supplying incorrect or misleading information in the (Short) Form CO notification. First, Article 5(4) of the Implementing Regulation 2004 clarifies that such information shall be considered to be incomplete information, which consequently cannot amount to an effective notification, thus delaying the process.[117] Second, based on Article 14(1)(a) of the Merger Control Regulation

---

[114] On the *ex ante/ex post* enforcement choice in EU merger control, see Rusu 2010, p. 111 *et seq.*

[115] See <https://ec.europa.eu/competition/mergers/statistics.pdf> accessed 31 March 2020.

[116] Implementing Regulation 2004, Articles 5 and 7–10. Based on Article 4(3) of the Merger Control Regulation 2004, the Commission shall publish the fact that it received the notification, indicating inter alia the date when the notification was received. When the notification is complete, it is the date when the Commission received the notification that triggers the timetable. When the notification is incomplete, the time limits start running when the complete information is received by the Commission.

[117] Merger Control Regulation 2004, Article 10(1).

2004, these entities may also be subject to a fine of 1 per cent maximum of the aggregate turnover of the undertaking or association of undertakings concerned, when they intentionally or negligently supply incorrect or misleading information in a submission, certification, notification or supplement thereto.[118] Such fines apply also to submissions performed via Form RS, in cases of referral procedures. Also, pursuant to Articles 6(3)(a) and 8(6)(a) of the Merger Control Regulation 2004, the Commission may revoke its decision clearing a notified concentration (and it has done so on one occasion in the past), where it is based on incorrect information for which one of the undertakings is responsible.

3.2.2 Suspension of concentrations

The essence of the *ex ante* control system requires that concentrations are not implemented by the parties before they are notified to and cleared by the appropriate authority. Otherwise, the whole purpose of effectively controlling structural market changes before they take place would be emptied of substance.

Article 7 of the Merger Control Regulation 2004 therefore places a standstill obligation on the parties, also known as the prohibition of 'gun-jumping': a concentration with an EU dimension, or without an EU dimension but referred to the Commission based on Article 4(5), may not be (fully or partly)[119] implemented until the Commission approves it. The parties should thus not perform actions which may result in change of control,[120] neither should they share information in contravention to the EU competition law rules. Failure to abide by such requirements, which happens rarely, may result in the imposition of hefty fines, of 10 per cent maximum of the aggregate turnover of the undertakings concerned, when the parties intentionally or negligently implement the concentration in breach of the standstill obligation (Article 14(2)(b)).[121] Even when such fines are imposed, this does not mean that the concentration necessarily falls apart. Article 7(4) of the Merger Control Regulation 2004 makes it clear that the validity of the transaction performed in breach of the notification requirement or of the gun-jumping prohibition depends on the subsequent clearance or prohibition decision of the Commission. Before such a decision is adopted, the Commission may impose interim measures which are appropriate to restore or maintain conditions of effective competition.[122] In case the already implemented transaction is declared incompatible with the Internal Market, and thus prohibited, the Commission may adopt such interim measures, but based on Article 8(4), it may go further and require the undertakings concerned to dissolve the merger, or dispose of all shares or assets acquired, so as to restore

---

[118] See e.g. the 110 million EUR fine imposed on Facebook, for providing misleading information regarding the acquisition of WhatsApp. Press Release IP/17/1369.

[119] An example of partial implementation may be found in case IV/M.993 *Bertelsmann/Kirch/Premiere*, (1999) OJ L 53/01.

[120] E.g. case C-633/16 *Ernst & Young*, ECLI:EU:C:2018:371.

[121] See e.g. the 125 million EUR fine imposed on Altice for controlling PT Portugal before the Commission's clearance. Press Release IP/18/3522. See also case C-10/18 P *Marine Harvest ASA* (succeeded by *Mowi ASA*), ECLI:EU:C:2020:14.

[122] Merger Control Regulation 2004, Article 8(5).

the prior-implementation situation, or it may take any other measure appropriate to achieve such restoration as far as possible.[123]

There are two exceptions to the standstill rule. First, Article 7(2) provides the so-called 'automatic' derogation for public bids: the standstill obligation does not apply in case of a public bid, or of a series of transactions in securities admitted to trading on a market, by which control is acquired from various sellers. Two conditions need to be fulfilled in this respect: the concentration must be notified without delay, and the acquirer does not exercise the voting rights attached to the securities in question or does so only to maintain the full value of its investments, based on a derogation granted by the Commission under the second possible exception to the standstill obligation, provided in Article 7(3). This second exception entails the Commission granting, on request from the parties, an 'express' derogation from this obligation. It may do so while taking into account the effects the suspension may have on one or more undertakings concerned or on a third party and the threat to competition posed by the concentration. Such derogations, totalling 126 until February 2020,[124] may be, however, made subject to conditions and obligations in order to ensure conditions of effective competition. Failure to observe such conditions may result in the imposition of fines of 10 per cent maximum of the aggregate turnover of the undertaking concerned, based on Article 14(2)(d) of the Merger Control Regulation 2004.

3.2.3 Appraisal phases, time limits and Commission decisions

Merger control entails strict time limits imposed on the Commission to perform the concentration assessment. The applicable deadlines are provided in Article 10 of the Merger Control Regulation 2004. The EU merger control system is designed in two separate phases. Phase I is a streamlined procedure leading to a first decision regarding the notified concentration. This phase enables the Commission to speedily deal with matters less likely to create competition issues. Phase II of the procedure contains a more substantial review of the concentration, when the Phase I review deems this necessary.[125] In the most extreme of situations, a concentration appraisal procedure (Phase I and Phase II) must be completed within a maximum of 160 working days, from the moment the notification was received. The Commission publishes details about the notification in the *Official Journal*, to make it clear when 'the clock starts ticking'. This publication also gives third parties the opportunity to react to the concentration, by providing documents and statements, which may prove useful during the appraisal process. The Implementing Regulation 2004 details the procedural steps and requirements contained in the Merger Control Regulation 2004, as far as deadlines, decisions on substance, enforcement procedures, and the like.

---

[123] This is not always an easy task. In case T-411/07 *Aer Lingus*, ECLI:EU:T:2010:281, the divestment of a minority shareholding could not be executed based on the provisions of Article 8(4). See Rusu 2014 (a) and (b), Rusu 2015 (b).

[124] See <https://ec.europa.eu/competition/mergers/statistics.pdf> accessed 31 March 2020.

[125] Marco Colino 2019, pp. 447–8; Kokkoris and Shelanski 2014, p. 174.

3.2.3.1 Phase I

Article 6(1) of the Merger Control Regulation 2004 states that the Commission shall examine the notification as soon as it is received. According to Article 10(1), Phase I should be completed within 25 working days, starting from the day following the day when the complete notification was received. Phase I may be extended to 35 working days, in cases where the Commission receives a 'German clause' request from a Member State, or where the undertakings concerned offer commitments pursuant to Article 6(2) with a view to rendering the concentration compatible with the Internal Market, no later than 20 working days after the notification was submitted.[126] These periods may be suspended if the parties fail to meet a deadline imposed for submitting requested information to the Commission.[127]

During Phase I, the Commission makes an initial determination on the merits, regarding the compatibility of the notified concentration with the Internal Market.[128] To this end, it may request information from the parties and perform other enforcement activities (discussed in section 3.2.4).

Commitments

In Phase I, the Commission may accept commitments put forward by the parties who aim to have their transaction approved. For example, divestments by the parties of specific assets or packages of shares, or granting access to infrastructure or technologies, may remove the Commission's doubts as to the concentration's compatibility with the Internal Market. The Remedies Notice 2008 details the types of commitments that may be suitable in a given case (i.e. primarily structural and only exceptionally behavioural),[129] and the conditions and procedural requirements to follow in this respect. This soft-law document is extremely useful for the parties, since identifying and applying the right remedy is often a complicated matter. For example, in case of divestitures,[130] which are the most common kind of remedies applied in EU merger control, the divested business needs to be viable and appropriately preserved during the divestment process, the buyer needs to be suitable, in that it should be able to effectively compete with the merged entity, and the divestiture should be set up in a fitting time frame. The parties must also prove that the commitments are proportionate to the competition problem identified, and that they eliminate the problem entirely. To this end, the commitments must be comprehensive and effective, and capable of timely implementation.[131] According to paragraph 81 of the Remedies Notice 2008, commitments in Phase I can only be accepted where the competition problem is straightforward, readily identifiable and can easily be remedied through clear-cut measures that render entering into an in-depth investigation unnecessary. The Commission may make such commitments binding, as a condition for clearing the concentration. Should the undertakings fail to observe such binding

---

[126] Implementing Regulation 2004, Article 19(1).

[127] Merger Control Regulation 2004, Article 10(4).

[128] Kokkoris and Shelanski 2014, p. 174.

[129] Remedies Notice 2008, par. 17.

[130] Ibid, par. 97 *et seq.*

[131] Merger Control Regulation 2004, Recital 30; Remedies Notice 2008, par. 9. See also Lorenz 2013, p. 300.

obligations, they may incur a fine of 10 per cent maximum of their aggregate turnover, based on Article 14(2)(d), or a periodic penalty payment, not exceeding 5 per cent of their average daily aggregate turnover for each working day of non-compliance, based on Article 15(1)(c). They may also have their clearance decision revoked by the Commission, based on Article 6(3)(b). This entails that the Commission may resume Phase I or II proceedings, without being bound by the time limits in Article 10(1).[132] At the other end of the spectrum, in isolated and exceptional circumstances, it may also be possible for the Commission to waive commitments which were already made binding as a condition to clear a concentration. Such a waiver may be granted based on the parties' request, and if the Commission's investigation reveals that permanent, significant and unforeseeable developments took place since the conditional clearance (e.g. during the divestiture process), affecting the evolution of the competitive landscape, and thus rendering the commitments no longer necessary for the transaction's compatibility with the Internal Market.[133]

At the end of the Phase I timeline, the Commission must adopt a decision. Failure to do so within the specified deadlines results in the concentration being declared compatible with the Internal Market, and thus 'tacitly' approved.[134] Phase I decisions are based on Article 6 of the Merger Control Regulation 2004, and they may embody the following outcomes:[135]

- Article 6(1)(a): the concentration does not fall within the scope of the Regulation (less than 1 per cent of the cases), because it is not a concentration, or it does not have an EU dimension;
- Article 6(1)(b): the concentration with an EU dimension does not raise serious doubts as to its compatibility with the Internal Market and is therefore approved without any modifications. This finding extends also to the so-called 'ancillary restraints', which are restrictions directly related and necessary to the concentration. This means that any terms of the transaction which might fall within either Article 101 TFEU, or national competition law, are cleared at the same time as long as they bear a sufficiently close relation to the concentration itself.[136] Further, short-form clearances adopted through the simplified procedure are also based on Article 6(1)(b). Almost 90 per cent of the concentrations notified to the Commission are handled under Article 6(1)(b);
- Article 6(2), in conjunction with Article 6(1)(b): approximately 5 per cent of the notified concentrations with an EU dimension raise serious doubts as to their compatibility with the Internal Market, yet the commitments put forward by the parties remove those doubts. The transaction is then (conditionally) cleared, subject to the parties abiding by the obligations imposed through the Commission's decision;

---

[132] Merger Control Regulation 2004, Article 6(4). A similar approach to waiving the time limit obligations is also present in Article 8(7).

[133] E.g. Press Release IP/20/967.

[134] Merger Control Regulation 2004, Article 10(6).

[135] For the relevant statistics, see <https://ec.europa.eu/competition/mergers/statistics.pdf> accessed 31 March 2020.

[136] Marco Colino 2019, p. 448.

- Article 6(1)(c): when the concentration with an EU dimension raises serious doubts as to its compatibility with the Internal Market, which cannot be addressed via commitments, the Commission adopts a decision to initiate proceedings.[137] This decision marks the commencement of Phase II in-depth analysis of the concentration. Such decisions are adopted in approximately 5 per cent of the cases. An Article 6(1)(c) decision brings about certain consequences: first, the conclusion of the procedure must be based on a decision adopted based on Article 8(1)–(4) of the Merger Control Regulation 2004, unless the undertakings concerned abandon the concentration; second, the decision to initiate Phase II is an intermediary act, meant to allow the Commission to adopt a final decision as to the concentration's compatibility with the Internal Market. Therefore, although framed as a *decision* (i.e. a judicially reviewable act based on Article 263 TFEU), the Article 6(1)(c) decision cannot be appealed against, in front of the EU courts. The parties must instead wait for the completion of Phase II proceedings, and lodge an appeal against the final decision adopted based on Article 8.[138] However, Phase I decisions which *close the proceedings* are susceptible to be appealed against, for example as detailed in section 3.2.5 below, by third parties unhappy with the result of the Commission's conclusions.

3.2.3.2 Phase II

This phase of the appraisal process is dedicated only to those cases that cannot be solved in Phase I, due to the complexity of the issues they raise. Phase II thus entails an in-depth investigation of the relevant aspects of the concentration. Given the daunting tasks that the Commission must accomplish in this phase of the appraisal process, the timetable is more generous than in Phase I: Article 10(3) provides that Phase II should be completed within 90 working days from the adoption of the Article 6(1)(c) decision. This deadline may be extended to 105 working days, if the parties put forward commitments meant to render the concentration compatible with the Internal Market, within the first 55 working days.[139] Further extensions are possible, up to a grand total of 125 working days for Phase II, either requested unilaterally by the parties, or agreed upon with the Commission. Article 10(4) regarding the suspension of these deadlines applies similarly to the manner in which 'stopping the clock' works in Phase I. Failure to conclude the Phase II proceedings within the specified deadlines will render the concentration compatible with the Internal Market, again similarly to the Phase I outcome, when deadlines are not met.[140]

Phase II is a substantively and procedurally 'charged' process. Regarding substance, most of what takes place during Phase II relates to the application of the substantive appraisal test of Article 2 of the Merger Control Regulation 2004, in order to assess the concentration's compatibility with the Internal Market. For example, market investigations are performed,

---

[137] Remedies Notice 2008, par. 86.

[138] Cases C-188/06 P *Schneider*, ECLI:EU:C:2007:158; T-902/16 *HeidelbergCement*, ECLI:EU:T:2017:846.

[139] Merger Control Regulation 2004, Article 10(3). According to Implementing Regulation 2004, Article 19(2), such commitments may only be put forward during the first 65 working days since the initiation of Phase II.

[140] Merger Control Regulation 2004, Article 10(6).

economic evidence is evaluated, the effects of the concentrations on the market are scrutinised, countervailing and efficiency concerns are examined. Such matters are discussed in
section 3.3 below. Procedurally, in Phase II, the parties may be interviewed, inspections may
be performed, the Advisory Committee on Concentrations (composed of representatives of
the NCAs)[141] and other Directorates-General may be consulted, a statement of objections
may be issued, commitments may be negotiated, and so forth.

The statement of objections is a key step in the process, when the Commission intends
to prohibit the concentration, approve it subject to conditions, or when it intends to apply
fines to the undertakings concerned.[142] Communicating the Commission's objections in
writing to the parties gives them the opportunity to communicate their views and provide
information that addresses the Commission's concerns. The statement of objections is normally issued when the Commission's doubts about the concentration are not removed, and
it must contain all elements of law and fact on which the objections are based. This statement
is, however, only a preparatory act, that cannot be appealed against in front of the EU
courts. Also, the Commission's final decision adopted based on Article 8 must not be fully
identical in rationale with the statement of objections. Nevertheless, radical changes in the
Commission's thinking must be justified when the final decision is appealed against by the
parties, and if the Court is not satisfied with such justifications, the Commission's decision
may be annulled.[143]

Regarding commitments in Phase II, much of what was stated above, with regard to Phase
I commitments, is applicable, including, for example, the value of the Remedies Notice 2008
and the sanctions and periodic penalty payments which may be imposed based on Articles
14 and 15 of the Merger Control Regulation 2004. Nevertheless, commitments in Phase I and
in Phase II of the procedure must be viewed from different standpoints, as the Commission
applies different tests to such remedies: the former are meant to remove the Commission's
serious doubts as to whether the concentration will result in a significant impediment to
effective competition, whereas the latter should be sufficient to eliminate such significant
impediments to effective competition in the market.[144] Effective remedies in merger control
are a complex issue and have been the subject of continuous concern for the Commission.
In 2005, it has issued a comprehensive study on the design, implementation and likely
effectiveness of remedies, in an effort to improve future action in this field.[145] Lastly about
commitments and remedies, (Phase I or II) conditional clearances may be cumbersome. The
implementation of the commitments may take a long time and, depending on the type of
remedies chosen, they may require complex monitoring.[146]

---

[141] Ibid, Article 19(3)–(7).

[142] Implementing Regulation 2004, Articles 13(2)–(4), 16.

[143] Kokkoris and Shelanski 2014, pp. 178–9; Jones, Sufrin and Dunne 2019, p. 1106. See e.g. case T-310/01 *Schneider*,
ECLI:EU:T:2002:254.

[144] Case T-119/02 Royal Philips Electronics, ECLI:EU:T:2003:101. See Lindsay and Berridge 2017, pp. 593–4.

[145] Press Release IP/05/1327.

[146] Whish and Bailey 2018, pp. 882, 907–15; Monti 2007, pp. 283–91; Kokkoris and Shelanski 2014, Chapter 14;
Lindsay and Berridge 2017, Chapter 20.

At the end of Phase II, the Commission must reach one of the following outcomes:[147]

- Article 8(1): about a quarter of the Phase II cases result in the concentration being deemed compatible with the Internal Market and thus cleared by the Commission. This means that the serious doubts that triggered the initiation of Phase II did not turn out to be true. A decision based on Article 8(1) also covers the potential ancillary restraints;
- Article 8(2): more than half of the Phase II cases conclude with the concentration being cleared by the Commission, after the parties modify their transaction to meet the Commission's concerns, and thus render the concentration compatible with the Internal Market. The parties' commitments may result in obligations being attached to the Commission's decision;
- Article 8(3): in 30 cases only, until February 2020, concentrations have been declared incompatible with the Internal Market and thus blocked by the Commission. A prohibition decision may only be adopted after a Phase II in-depth analysis of the concentration, and definitely not in Phase I proceedings. Prohibition decisions are rare, yet interesting to study, because such decisions shed more light on what a significant impediment to effective competition means.[148] Also, more often than not, prohibition decisions call into question essential elements of the merger control phenomenon, be they of a conceptual, substantive or fundamental nature. For example, in *Airtours*, and *Tetra Laval*,[149] matters relating to the standard of proof in Commission decisions were at stake; in *Ryanair/Aer Lingus*[150] the concept of concentration was put to the test; in *GE/Honeywell*[151] and *Deutsche Börse/NYSE Euronext*[152] questions were raised regarding the coherency of international cooperation in merger control procedures, as the EU and US authorities were contemplating, and in *GE/Honeywell* actually reached, diverging appraisal outcomes; lastly, in the *Siemens/Alstom* decision[153] the 'European champion' discussion and arguments relating to public interest considerations in merger control assessment were revived, when the Commission refused to allow the creation of an EU dominant player in the markets for very high-speed trains and various types of railway and metro signalling systems, a player which the merging parties argued to be better suited to compete internationally with Chinese and US competitors.[154]

---

[147] For the relevant statistics, see <https://ec.europa.eu/competition/mergers/statistics.pdf> accessed 31 March 2020.

[148] See section 3.3 of this chapter.

[149] Cases T-342/99 *Airtours*, ECLI:EU:T:2002:146; T-5/02 *Tetra Laval*, ECLI:EU:T:2002:264.

[150] Case M.4439 *Ryanair/Aer Lingus*, (2006) OJ C 274/10; T-342/07 *Ryanair*, ECLI:EU:T:2010:280.

[151] Case COMP/M.2220 *General Electric/Honeywell*, (2001) OJ L 48/1; T-209/01 *Honeywell International*, ECLI:EU:T:2005:455.

[152] Case M.6166 *Deutsche Börse/NYSE Euronext*, (2014) OJ C 254/8; T-175/12 *Deutsche Börse*, ECLI:EU:T:2015:148.

[153] Case M.8677 *Siemens/Alstom*, (2019) OJ C 300/14.

[154] Siemens CEO, essentially pleading for the creation of a European market force, argued that 'it is naive to think individual European states can compete with China and America'. See J. Revill, 'Siemens Makes Last Ditch Appeal for EU to Approve Rail Merger', available at <https://www.euronews.com/2019/01/30/siemens-misses-first-quarter-profit-forecast-as-power-problems-persist > accessed 7 April 2020. Commissioner Vestager, on the other hand,

Article 8(4)–(7) of the Merger Control Regulation 2004 provides the Commission with powerful and complex instruments, to be used in case the parties have already implemented a transaction declared incompatible with the Internal Market, when they breached the conditions attached to a clearance, or when they use deceit or submit incorrect information during the proceedings. The Commission may adopt interim measures, appropriate to restore or maintain conditions of effective competition; it may revoke the clearance, without being bound by the Article 10(3) time limits; lastly, it may also dissolve the concentration in order to restore the situation prevailing prior to the implementation of the concentration. To secure the practical implementation of interim measures or the dissolution of a concentration, the Commission may impose on the parties fines of 10 per cent maximum of their aggregate turnover and periodic penalty payments not exceeding 5 per cent of their average daily aggregate turnover for each working day of non-compliance with the obligations imposed by the Commission.[155]

3.2.4 Investigation and enforcement measures

In order to enable the Commission to reach Phase I or Phase II decisions, the Merger Control Regulation 2004 provides it with investigation and sanctioning powers.

3.2.4.1 Sanctions

As mentioned above, the Commission may impose fines (of up to 1 or 10 per cent of the aggregate turnover of the undertakings concerned, depending on the type of breach) or fix periodic penalty payments (of up to 5 per cent of the aggregate turnover of the undertakings concerned), where the merging parties, for example, do not notify a concentration with an EU dimension, breach the standstill obligation, provide misleading or incorrect information in a notification, do not comply with obligations contained in conditional clearance decisions, do not dissolve a concentration when ordered to do so, and so on. These sanctions do not have a criminal law nature.[156] Article 14(3) provides that fines should take due account of the nature, gravity and duration of the infringement. Also, as with other competition law fines imposed by the Commission, Article 16 of the Merger Control Regulation 2004 makes it clear that the CJEU has unlimited jurisdiction within the meaning of Article 261 TFEU to review (i.e. cancel, reduce or increase) fine or periodic penalty payment Commission decisions.

3.2.4.2 Investigation powers

Similar to antitrust enforcement, the sanctions discussed above may be imposed also for breaching the investigation measures deployed by the Commission during the procedure.

---

stated that 'Siemens and Alstom are both champions in the rail industry. Without sufficient remedies, their merger would have resulted in higher prices. . . . The Commission prohibited the merger because the companies were not willing to address [the Commission's] serious competition concerns'. See Press Release IP/19/881. As a reaction to the prohibition, the French and German Ministers of Economy reacted by issuing the Franco-German Manifesto 2019, suggesting radical EU merger control policy shifts.

[155] Merger Control Regulation 2004, Articles 14(2)(c) and 15(1)(d).

[156] Ibid, Article 14(4).

The *procedural powers* and *safeguards* contained in the Merger Control Regulation 2004 resemble significantly, and are substantially in line[157] with, those contained in Regulation 1/2003 and the ECN+ Directive 2019, discussed in Chapter 8. It will therefore suffice to say that the Commission may *request information* (including interviews) and *perform inspections* (which may also be performed by the NCAs, in accordance with their national laws, according to Article 12 of the Merger Control Regulation 2004).

Requests for information

In both Phases I and II, based on Article 11, the Commission routinely requests information from various stakeholders, such as the undertakings concerned, their customers and competitors, and also governments and other competent authorities of the Member States, in order to carry out its appraisal tasks. Information requests may be performed via simple requests (Article 11(2)), in which case the parties must not comply, but if they choose to do so, they must submit correct and complete information, under the sanction of a fine (Article 14(1) (b)). When information requests are performed via formal decisions, which are judicially reviewable by the EU courts (Article 11(3)), the parties must not only respond within the specified deadline, but they must also provide correct and complete information, under the sanction of a fine (Article 14(1)(c)) or a periodic penalty payment (Article 15(1)(a)). The instruments described in this paragraph resemble closely those powers of the Commission in Articles 18, 19, 23 and 24 of Regulation 1/2003.

Inspections

The same assertion may be made with regard to the Commission's powers of inspection in concentration control cases, based on Article 13 of the Merger Control Regulation 2004. This power, and also the powers conferred to the officials authorised to perform the inspection, are in line with the powers embedded in Article 20 of Regulation 1/2003. It is striking that the power to inspect other premises (embedded in Article 21 of Regulation 1/2003) is missing from the text of the Merger Control Regulation 2004. At the time of the adoption of the Merger Control Regulation 2004, it was believed that such powers are important for uncovering cartels and less so for merger investigations.[158] Nevertheless, when it comes to inspecting business premises, the Commission officials have the powers to enter any premises of the undertakings, examine books, make copies, seal records or premises, and ask clarification questions. They may do so, on the basis of a written authorisation (Article 13(3)), in which case the undertakings are not obliged to cooperate, but if they do so, they must provide correct and complete information and answers, under the sanction of fines imposed based on Article 14(1)(d) and (e). When the Commission orders the inspection via an Article 13(4) decision (again, judicially reviewable by the EU courts), the undertakings must submit to the inspection, under the sanction of a fine (Article 14(1)(d) and (e)). Should they oppose such inspections, the Commission officials may make use of national authorities' assistance (including the police), and may have to apply for a (precautionary) judicial authorisation

---

[157] Marco Colino 2019, p. 454.

[158] Monti 2002 (a).

in the national courts.[159] Similar to inspections ordered based on Article 20 of Regulation 1/2003, the national court, in its decision on whether to grant such an authorisation or not, may check the authenticity and proportionality of the Commission's envisioned inspection, but not the necessity for the actual inspection. All in all, these powers of inspection, as far-reaching as they may seem, have not proven to be very significant in practice so far, since the Commission is most often able to collect all the information it needs via the powers conferred by Article 11 of the Merger Control Regulation 2004.[160]

3.2.4.3 Safeguards

The Commission's procedural powers are counterbalanced by the safeguards conferred onto the notifying parties, during concentration control procedures: for example, the statement of objections and the parties' rights of defence (especially in cases when the Commission intends to adopt decisions of initiating Phase II, conditional derogations from the standstill obligation, conditional clearances adopted in Phase II, prohibitions, fines and periodic penalties).[161] In such cases the parties have the right of access to file and the right to be heard, enshrined in Article 41 of the EU Charter of Fundamental Rights. Article 18 of the Merger Control Regulation 2004 and Chapters IV and V of the Implementing Regulation 2004 discuss these safeguards. The effectuation of the procedural rights of the parties is supervised by the Hearing Officer, who is a Commission official outside the case team that investigates the transaction, generally tasked with ensuring the objectivity of the process.[162]

3.2.5 Appeals against Commission decisions

Once the Commission adopts a decision, (conditionally) clearing or prohibiting a concentration, or imposing a fine or a periodic penalty payment, such decision is binding on the entities to whom it is addressed, according to Article 288 TFEU. According to Article 263(4) TFEU, in conjunction with paragraphs (2) and (6), any natural or legal person may lodge appeal proceedings in front of the GC (and then further appeal on points of law only in front of the CJEU) against such decisions, within two months of publication, if such persons are the addressees of the decision, or they are directly and individually concerned by such decision, on grounds of lack of competence, infringement of an essential procedural requirement, of the Treaties, or of any rule of law relating to their application, or misuse of powers. Appeals are thus possible on both procedural and substantive matters, in both situations the EU courts testing the legality of the Commission decisions.

For an appeal to be admissible, the party lodging the appeal must first have standing to do so. The parties to a concentration have automatic standing, since they are the addressees of the Commission decision, be it a decision on substance or a sanctioning decision on procedural grounds. This obviously includes decisions prohibiting a concentration, as happened

---

[159] Merger Control Regulation 2004, Article 13(6)–(8).

[160] Lorenz 2013, p. 302.

[161] Merger Control Regulation 2004, Article 18(1).

[162] On the role of the Hearing Officer, see Kokkoris and Shelanski 2014, p. 182. On access to file, see the Notice on Access to Commission File 2005 and Public Access Regulation 2001.

in, for example, *Schneider*, *Airtours*, and *Tetra Laval*,[163] and in exceptional circumstances, conditional clearances, as was the case in *Cementbouw*.[164] Further, Article 18(4) of the Merger Control Regulation 2004 grants third parties (e.g. customers or competitors) the right to be heard. They too have the right to appeal a Commission decision, most often a clearance decision (whether conditional or not),[165] if they prove that the Commission decision is of 'direct and individual concern' to them, based on the well-known *Plaumann* criteria,[166] that is, the decision prejudices their competitive position and their legal position is affected in a way that is particular to them, or differentiates them from all other persons.[167] For example, in the *KPN* case,[168] KPN successfully challenged the Commission's decision clearing Liberty Global's acquisition of control over Ziggo: the GC annulled the Commission's decision, on the ground that it did not fully state the reasons of its conclusion that the merger would not lead to vertical anti-competitive effects on the potential market for premium pay TV sports channels in the Netherlands. Moving on, employees, as third parties to a concentration transaction, are normally not granted *locus standi*,[169] yet works councils or labour unions appeal if their right to be heard under Article 18(4) of the Merger Control Regulation 2004 has been infringed.[170]

Next, the act which is appealed against must produce binding legal effects. In this context we refer to Commission decisions, adopted both with regard to procedural matters or on the substance of the case. Nevertheless, some acts adopted by the Commission are not susceptible to judicial review: decisions to initiate Phase II proceedings based on Article 6(1)(c) of the Merger Control Regulation 2004, or statements of objections cannot be appealed against, since these are intermediary/preparatory acts, meant to facilitate the adoption of a final decision.

Moving on, one needs to be aware of the role the review courts play in merger control appeals. Regarding sanctions, Article 16 of the Merger Control Regulation 2004 provides that the CJEU has unlimited jurisdiction to cancel, reduce or increase fines or periodic penalties. When it comes to the merits of the case, the Merger Control Regulation 2004 is silent as to the courts' role. In the courts' case-law, however, it became apparent that the EU courts do not have full jurisdiction when reviewing the merits of the Commission decision. They must not reassess the facts underlying a Commission decision, and they may only annul a decision if an error of fact, law or assessment has been committed. The courts should abstain from entering into the merits of the Commission's complex economic assessment or to substitute

---

[163] Cases T-310/01 *Schneider*, ECLI:EU:T:2002:254; T-342/99 *Airtours*, ECLI:EU:T:2002:146; T-5/02 *Tetra Laval*, ECLI:EU:T:2002:264.

[164] Case T-282/02 *Cementbouw*, ECLI:EU:T:2006:64; C-202/06 P *Cementbouw*, ECLI:EU:C:2007:814.

[165] For a rare successful challenge by a third party to an unconditional clearance, see case T-464/04 *Impala*, ECLI:EU:T:2006:216.

[166] Case 25/62 *Plaumann*, ECLI:EU:C:1963:17.

[167] Kokkoris and Shelanski 2014, p. 562.

[168] Case T-394/15 *KPN*, ECLI:EU:T:2017:756.

[169] E.g. cases T-96/92 *Nestlé*, ECLI:EU:1995:77; T-12/93 *Vittel*, ECLI:EU:1995:78.

[170] Kokkoris and Shelanski 2014, p. 565.

their own economic assessment for that of the Commission. In other words, the Commission enjoys a margin of discretion/appreciation when it comes to complex economic matters. That does not mean that the EU courts must refrain from reviewing the Commission's interpretation of information of an economic nature. Not only must the EU courts establish, inter alia, if the evidence relied on is factually accurate, reliable and consistent, but also whether that evidence contains all the information which must be taken into account in order to assess a complex situation, and whether it is capable of substantiating the conclusions drawn from it. Such review is all the more necessary in case of a prospective (i.e. *ex ante*) analysis required when examining planned concentrations.[171] Botteman[172] summarises clearly what the EU courts expect from the Commission when it appraises concentrations: conducting a thorough and painstaking investigation, complying with the relevant procedural rules, adequately stating the reasons for its decision, correctly relating the facts on which the decision is based and not committing any manifest error of appraisal or misuse of powers.[173]

Appeals may take years, a period during which the operation of the challenged Commission decision is not suspended.[174] Since 2001, the GC may grant the parties the possibility to follow a fast-track process, if the urgency of the issues raised and the complexity of the case call for such a course of the procedure. The normal oral and written, reply and rejoinder phases of the court proceedings follow slightly different paths, and the case is normally given priority on the Court's docket. This may result in a GC judgment being rendered as early as 7 months from the application to the Court.[175] In exceptional circumstances, the GC may also grant interim relief via a reasoned order, to the parties or to third parties affected by the transaction, without prejudging the outcome of the case.[176]

Lastly, should an appeal be successful, in that the GC annuls the whole or part of a Commission decision, certain consequences result from such a judgment. The annulment is legally effective only as regards the parties who successfully challenged the decision, that is, complainants and third parties that intervened in the procedure.[177] Next, according to Article 10(5) of the Merger Control Regulation 2004, the concentration must be re-examined by the Commission, however, in light of the current market conditions, with a view to adopting a decision pursuant to Article 6(1). This entails that the parties must submit a new notification or supplement the original notification. In the *KPN* case, the acquisition of Ziggo by Liberty Global was reappraised by the Commission, after the GC annulled the initial Commission decision in October 2017, and conditionally cleared in May 2018.[178] Moving on, when the Commission decision is annulled, the claimants may start damages proceedings against

---

[171] Cases C-12/03 P *Commission v Tetra Laval*, ECLI:EU:C:2005:87, par. 39; C-413/06 *Impala*, ECLI:EU:C:2008:392, par. 145.

[172] Botteman 2006, p. 80

[173] Rusu 2010, pp. 146–62.

[174] Jones, Sufrin and Dunne 2019, p. 1181; Kokkoris and Shelanski 2014, p. 571.

[175] E.g. case T-87/05 *EDP*, ECLI:EU:T:2005:333.

[176] E.g. case T-88/94 R *Kali und Salz* (1994) ECR II-263.

[177] Kokkoris and Shelanski 2014, p. 572.

[178] Press Release IP/18/3984.

the Commission, based on Article 340(2) TFEU, with regard to the loss suffered due to the wrongful prohibition of the concentration. Such actions are infrequent,[179] and rarely successful, primarily due to the high threshold generally required for establishing the non-contractual liability of EU institutions. In merger control especially, given the complexity of the cases and the Commission's margin of discretion regarding economic assessment, the EU courts are rather unlikely to find that a sufficiently serious error, or breach, has been established on behalf of the Commission.

3.3 Substantive analysis

According to Article 2(1) of the Merger Control Regulation 2004, the substantive appraisal of a notified concentration essentially entails an assessment, in accordance with the objectives of the Regulation, of whether the transaction is or is not compatible with the Internal Market. The CJEU made it clear in *Impala*[180] that the Regulation does not put forward a presumption of compatibility or incompatibility with the Internal Market. The Commission must thus assess the economic outcome attributable to the concentration which is most likely to ensue, based on a range of factors, in order to assert this (in)compatibility with the Internal Market. The prospective nature of the Commission's assessment is a natural consequence of the *ex ante* control system choice made in the Merger Control Regulations (1989 and 2004). In practice, the Commission developed a framework of analysis, meant to evaluate the market developments and the effects which are prone to result from a given concentration. The following sections are dedicated to discussing the elements of this assessment framework.

The core of the substantive analysis is contained in Article 2 of the Merger Control Regulation 2004. The benchmark against which a transaction will be labelled as compatible or incompatible with the Internal Market is embedded in paragraphs 2 and 3, which essentially provide that the key to this matter is whether the transaction would or would not significantly impede effective competition (SIEC) in the Internal Market or in a substantial part of it, in particular as a result of the creation or strengthening of a dominant position. This has come to be known as the SIEC substantive test in EU merger control.[181] Article 2(1) of the Merger Control Regulation 2004 indicates the range of factors the Commission should take into account while scrutinising a concentration: the need to maintain and develop effective competition in view of, among other things, the structure of all the markets concerned and the actual or potential competition from undertakings located either within or outside the EU, the market position of the undertakings concerned and their economic and financial power,

---

[179] E.g. cases T-212/03 *MyTravel*, ECLI:EU:T:2008:315; T-351/03 *Schneider*, ECLI:EU:T:2007:212. When writing this book, case T-834/17 *UPS* was pending, after the Commission decision prohibiting the *UPS/TNT Express* transaction was annulled. See case COMP/M.6570 *UPS/TNT Express*, (2014) OJ C 137/8; GC judgment in case T-194/13 *UPS*, ECLI:EU:T:2017:144, confirmed on appeal by the Court of Justice in case C-265/17 P *Commission v UPS*, ECLI:EU:C:2019/23.

[180] Case C-413/06 *Impala*, ECLI:EU:C:2008:392, par. 48, 52.

[181] Merger Control Regulation 2004, Article 2(4) puts forward a different substantive test applicable to cooperative full-function joint ventures. See section 3.3.7.2 of this chapter.

the alternatives available to suppliers and users, their access to supplies or markets, any legal or other barriers to entry, supply and demand trends for the relevant goods and services, the interests of the intermediate and ultimate consumers, and the development of technical and economic progress provided that it is to consumers' advantage and does not form an obstacle to competition. The Horizontal Merger Guidelines 2004 and Non-Horizontal Merger Guidelines 2008 offer detailed explanations as to the Commission's interpretation of these factors.

3.3.1 From dominance to SIEC

The SIEC test is the result of fierce debates surrounding the merits of the fundamental question of what substantive features call for the prohibition of a concentration. The Merger Control Regulation 1989 used slightly different language when it comes to the substantive test. In Article 2 it provided that the substantive criteria should be whether the concentration creates or strengthens a dominant position, as a result of which effective competition would be significantly impeded in the Internal Market or in a substantial part of it. This was known as the 'dominance test', since a dominant position constituted an indispensable condition to be taken into account.

The origins of the dominance test may be traced back to the ECSC Treaty and one could safely assume that the choice to rely on this notion as the main appraisal criterion in the Merger Control Regulation 1989 can be linked to the degree of familiarity with, and large body of case-law and decisional practice on the dominance concept under Article 102 TFEU.[182] While the notion of dominance had the same meaning under both Article 102 TFEU and the Merger Control Regulation 1989, namely a position of economic strength enabling the undertaking at hand to behave to an appreciable extent independently of competitors, customers and consumers, the practical applicability of the concept differed in these areas of law. For example, while dominance in antitrust law requires a static analysis of the market structure, to enable the conclusion of existence of market power, in merger control a more dynamic and forward-looking approach is attached to evaluating dominance. Connected to this, in merger control cases, a causal link must exist between the creation or strengthening of dominance through a concentration and the adverse impact on competition.[183] In antitrust analysis, on the other hand, such a link must not necessarily be established between dominance and abuse, for Article 102 TFEU to apply. Last but not least, in antitrust law, the dominance concept is applied *ex post*, while in merger control *ex ante*.[184]

The dominance test embedded in the Merger Control Regulation 1989 was constructed on two limbs: first, the creation or strengthening of a dominant position and second, the resulting impediment to effective competition.[185] The test was meant to be applied in a teleological/result-oriented manner so as to give effect to the Merger Control Regulation's purpose. Despite this approach, certain gaps were identified between the policy aims of

---

[182] Rusu 2010, p. 36.

[183] Joined cases C-68/94 and C-30/95 *Kali und Salz*, ECLI:EU:C:1998:148, par. 115.

[184] Rusu 2010, pp. 36–7; Kokkoris and Shelanski 2014, pp. 46–7.

[185] E.g. Selvam 2004; Fountoukakos and Ryan 2005.

catching all anti-competitive concentrations and the ability to detect them through the use of the dominance test, leaving certain enforcement 'blind spots', especially when it comes to oligopolistic markets.[186] Specifically, in the *Airtours* case,[187] it became apparent that a merger between undertakings active on an oligopolistic market may damage competition even if a single dominant position is not created. The Commission blocked the merger between Airtours and First Choice, on the ground that the merger would create a collective dominant position between the three largest short-haul package holiday companies in the UK. Kokkoris and Shelanski[188] argue that the Commission's decision was controversial and ambiguous, since it could also be interpreted as a case of non-coordinated effects in an oligopolistic market. Controversies stem also from the fact that the Commission, in its decision, seems to have expanded the notion of collective dominance that the EU courts worked with in previous case-law, like *Kali und Salz*, *CMB* and *Gencor*.[189] In *Airtours* specifically, the post-merger market shares of the major players in the relevant market would have settled around the following values: Airtours/First Choice approximately 32 per cent, Thomson approximately 27 per cent, Thomas Cook approximately 20 per cent. This scenario, according to the Commission's rationale, would have created incentives for these players to cease competing with one another. The Commission took the view that the ability of firms to engage in tacit collusion was not essential in this case, as it was sufficient that the concentration made it rational for the firms at hand to reduce competition among themselves. The deal was thus blocked, even though the market in which it was meant to take place did not display the typical characteristics favouring collusion: the product was not homogeneous, the market was dynamic and barriers to entry were low.[190] On appeal, the GC concluded that the Commission's decision to block the transaction, far from basing its prospective analysis on cogent evidence, was vitiated by errors of assessment. The Commission thus failed to prove to the requisite legal standard that the concentration would give rise to a collective dominant position, of such a kind as significantly to impede effective competition in the relevant market. In paragraph 62 of its judgment, the GC formulated strict criteria for establishing a collective dominant position:

1. There must be sufficient market transparency for all members of the dominant oligopoly to be aware, sufficiently precisely and quickly, of the way in which the other members' market conduct is evolving.
2. The situation of tacit coordination between the members of the dominant oligopoly must be sustainable over time, that is, there must be an incentive not to depart from the

---

[186] Baxter and Dethmers 2005; Völcker 2004; Rusu 2010, pp. 36–9. On the possible practical scenarios which would fall outside the scope of the dominance test, see Lindsay and Berridge 2017, pp. 41–4.

[187] Case T-342/99 *Airtours*, ECLI:EU:T:2002:146.

[188] Kokkoris and Shelanski 2014, p. 245.

[189] Joined cases C-68/94 and C-30/95 *Kali und Salz*, ECLI:EU:C:1998:148; joined cases C-395 and 396/96 P *CMB*, ECLI:EU:C:2000:132; case T-102/96 *Gencor*, ECLI:EU:T:1999:65. See also section 3.3.4.2 below.

[190] Lianos, Korah and Siciliani 2019, p. 1502; Rusu 2010, p. 149.

common policy on the market. This also entails the existence of adequate deterrents to ensure that the undertakings are not departing from the common policy.

3.   The foreseeable reaction of current and future competitors, as well as of consumers, would not jeopardise the results expected from the common policy.[191]

Such transactions, even if they are not to lead to the coordination of the behaviour of the market players active on such oligopolistic markets (i.e. so-called non-collusive oligopolies), may be prone to increase concentration in the market and to remove important competitive constraints. This may result in so-called unilateral effects, since the parties may increase prices, due to the reduced or inexistent rivalry post-merger. In absence of establishing the creation or strengthening of a dominant position, such unilateral effects could not be tackled under the Merger Control Regulation 1989 substantive test. This enforcement gap was acknowledged by the Commission in its Green Paper 2001, although it viewed it as more hypothetical than real. The Commission engaged in a debate about the merits of shifting to an 'SLC-type substantive test', used in jurisdictions such as the UK, Ireland, Canada, and the US. This SLC criterion essentially tests whether a concentration would lead to a substantial lessening of competition (SLC) in the market, without necessarily requiring a finding of dominance. Thus, concentrations in oligopolistic markets such as discussed just above may be better addressed by an SLC-type test, since such a test is argued to be better focused on inter-firm dynamics, empirical evidence, economic analysis and allows for clearer identification of remedies.[192] Both procedural and substantive arguments were put forward in favour of switching the EU substantive test in this direction, ranging from international coherency between appraisals performed in different jurisdictions, to the ability of focusing on more merger-related concerns than just structural ones, thus better accounting for the transaction's effects on the conditions of competition, for the synergies and for the efficiencies resulting from concentrations. Nevertheless, the dominance test continued to have its supporters: Mario Monti, Competition Commissioner in the early 2000s, put forward a proposal to elucidate the EU test so as to make it clear that the dominance test also covers situations of non-collusive oligopolies. The proposal was meant to clarify that 'one or more undertakings shall be deemed to be in a dominant position if, with or without coordinating, they hold the economic power to influence appreciably and sustainably the parameters of competition, in particular, prices, production, quality of output, distribution or innovation, or appreciably to foreclose competition'.[193]

The Merger Control Regulation 2004 addressed the concerns connected to the dominance test in an intelligent manner. The SIEC test contains almost identical wording as the

---

[191] In case C-413/06 *Impala*, ECLI:EU:C:2008:392, par. 120–126, the CJEU approached these criteria from a slightly different angle, yet with similar language, which is not inconsistent with the approach taken by the GC in *Airtours*. According to Jones, Sufrin and Dunne 2019, pp. 1134–5, the EU courts' approaches accord with the economists' views of the conditions required for coordinated effects.

[192] Kokkoris and Shelanski 2014, p. 67.

[193] See Rusu 2010, pp. 40–46, for a more extensive account of the pro- and con-arguments regarding the dominance/SLC debate. See also Kokkoris and Shelanski 2014, pp. 62–72.

dominance test, yet the two limbs of the old test are reversed, bringing the impediment to effective competition to the heart of the substantive test, and transforming the dominance criterion into a mere example of such restrictions of competition, albeit the most important one. This approach preserved the language with which the Commission, the courts and the companies were familiar, and also the continued relevance of the case-law and practice under the dominance test.[194] Furthermore, the new EU substantive test was brought somehow closer to the spirit of the SLC test,[195] without necessarily linking the EU's approach to concepts and interpretations foreign to this jurisdiction.[196] The SIEC test also represents a clear move towards a more effects-based approach in EU competition law, which relates to focusing on the impact of a given concentration on the market and on competition (rather than on formalistic criteria relating to the degree of market power). Lastly for now, the adoption of the SIEC test entails the closing of the enforcement gap signalled with regard to unilateral effects on oligopolistic markets. Recital 25 of the Merger Control Regulation 2004 clarifies that the new substantive test may be used to efficiently tackle non-collusive oligopolies: the notion of 'significant impediment to effective competition' in Article 2(2) and (3) should be interpreted as extending, beyond the concept of dominance, only to the anti-competitive effects of a concentration resulting from the non-coordinated behaviour of undertakings which would not have a dominant position on the market concerned. Thus, one could argue that the adoption of the SIEC criterion broadened the Commission's jurisdiction to prohibit mergers.[197]

This means that after the Merger Control Regulation 2004 entered into force, the Commission could, at least theoretically, tackle concentrations that create: (1) unilateral effects due to single firm dominance (scenarios for which the Commission's practice was unlikely to change due to retaining the dominance requirement as an example of significant impediment to effective competition); (2) coordinated effects that are generally due to joint or collective dominance (based on the *Airtours* and *Impala* criteria); (3) unilateral effects, even without a single dominant position being created or strengthened (and even if the merger would not involve the market leader, but the second and third strongest players in the market).[198] This latter scenario especially signals that the enforcement gap on oligopolistic markets can now be regarded as effectively closed. In order to appease those concerned with the Commission's appetite for broader intervention in such concentrated markets, even on deals involving smaller firms, Recital 32 of the Merger Control Regulation 2004 states that where the parties' market share does not exceed 25 per cent, the Commission's interest is limited based on the Regulation.

Speaking of closing the unilateral effects enforcement gap, there have been few cases after the adoption of the SIEC test which could not have been effectively tackled under the old

---

[194] Merger Control Regulation 2004, Recital 26.

[195] See also the comparison drawn by Lindsay and Berridge 2017, p. 50.

[196] Rusu 2010, pp. 45–6; Selvam 2004, p. 67.

[197] Lindsay and Berridge 2017, p. 45.

[198] Sauter 2016, pp. 202–3; Lindsay and Berridge 2017, p. 41; Filippelli 2013.

dominance test. One example is the *T-Mobile Austria/Tele.ring* case.[199] In this case, neither single firm dominance, nor tacit collusion could be established. The Commission found that post-merger a market structure with two major and two smaller operators would have been created. The transaction would have eliminated a maverick, and increase the symmetry between the two leading market players. This could have resulted in price increases. Therefore, even though T-Mobile would not have had the largest market share in the market post-merger, the removal of important competitive constraints previously exerted on the market leaders would have resulted in a significant impediment to effective competition. The transaction was nevertheless conditionally cleared after T-Mobile submitted commitments.[200]

3.3.2 Market definition

Defining the relevant product and geographic market is a necessary precondition for assessing a concentration's compatibility with the Internal Market. Much of the discussion in this context overlaps with the market definition exercise in antitrust cases. This seems reasonable, having in mind that paragraph 1 of the Notice on Relevant Market 1997 states that the Notice applies to both antitrust and merger control cases.

Market definition is not an end in itself, but rather a tool to identify and define the boundaries of competition between firms. It serves to establish the framework within which the Commission's policy is applied, its main purpose being to identify in a systematic way the competitive constraints that the undertakings involved in a given case face.[201] Thus, a great deal of energy is dispensed in identifying the wide range of product/service and geographic markets which can be affected in a concentration case. This is true primarily in complex cases, in which the Commission may actually identify different market definition scenarios, against which it will test the theories of harm appropriate for the given case (i.e. a 'better safe than sorry' approach). In the large majority of cases, the Commission leaves the market undefined, because even in the most restrictively defined market, the concentration would not result in competition concerns.[202]

Much like in antitrust cases, in concentration control too the battle between the Commission and the undertakings concerned will relate to how narrow or how broad the markets are defined. The parties will normally argue for wider definitions of the (product and/or geographic) markets, since this will ensure a lower market share count on their behalf. Especially in concentration control cases, the wider the market, the more attracted would the parties be by the national/European champion status, an argument which, as we discussed above in this chapter, should be treated with utter care by the Commission. Overall, one can say that certain sectors are more prone than others to accommodate wider market definitions, going as far as global from a geographic standpoint, especially when talking about low transport costs, low or inexistent barriers to entry, highly technical products, products

---

[199] Case COMP/M.3916 *T-Mobile Austria/Tele.ring*, (2007) OJ L 88/44.

[200] Lianos, Korah and Siciliani 2019, pp. 1512–13; Lorenz 2013, p. 275.

[201] Notice on Relevant Market 1997, par. 2.

[202] See Sauter 2016, p. 200, who argues this percentage to be 70 per cent of the cases handled by the Commission. See e.g. cases M.232 *PepsiCo/General Mills*, (1992) OJ C 228/6; M.833 *Coca-Cola/Carlsberg*, (1998) OJ L 145/41.

generally traded globally or, more recently, products and services pertaining to the digital economy.[203]

From a product/service perspective, the relevant market definition in concentration control cases uses the familiar tools, such as the SSNIP test, the physical characteristics and intended use of the products/services, and their price, as indicated in the relevant provisions of the Notice on Relevant Market 1997.[204] Again, much like in antitrust cases, the Commission investigates the demand-side and the supply-side substitutability of products/services.[205]

However, in concentration control cases one must be aware of the *ex ante* nature of intervention, as opposed to *ex post* control in antitrust cases. This means that the Commission takes a forward-looking approach not only to identify *existing* overlaps which may lead to a significant impediment to effective competition, but also when it comes to predicting how markets will evolve post-merger.[206] To this end, they will often employ various types of quantitative and empirical techniques and statistical tests in the market definition exercise.[207] In the same vein, sections 6 to 8 of Form CO require the notifying parties to provide the Commission, at an early stage of the process, with comprehensive information in relation to the markets that may be affected by the concentration: that is, in the case of horizontal relationships, markets where two or more parties to a concentration have a combined market share of 20 per cent or more and, in the case of vertical relationships, where their individual or combined market share is more than 30 per cent at one or more levels of the market.[208]

3.3.3 Market shares and concentration levels

Once the relevant markets affected by the concentration are defined, the Commission will proceed to assessing the market shares and thus the structure of the markets, and in doing so, it will essentially calculate the concentration level in the market. These tools may be regarded as useful first indications about the competitive importance of the parties involved in the concentration,[209] with regard to the extent to which they may control supplies or purchases. They will also provide an indication of the possibilities to profitably raise prices post-merger at a level higher than the pre-merger scenario. Further, evaluating market shares and concentration levels may paint a picture of the position of competitors in the respective markets.[210] Nevertheless, as reliable an indicator as market shares may be, one needs to have realistically understood the specificities of each sector and the particularities of each

---

[203] Jones, Sufrin and Dunne 2019, p. 1115.

[204] While writing this book, the process for reviewing the Notice on Relevant Market 1997 was launched. See <https://ec.europa.eu/info/law/better-regulation/have-your-say/initiatives/12325-Evaluation-of-the-Commission-Notice-on-market-definition-in-EU-competition-law> accessed 25 May 2020. See also Vestager 2019 (b).

[205] Lorenz 2013, pp. 264–74.

[206] See also Rusu 2010, p. 181 *et seq.*

[207] Kokkoris and Shelanski 2014, pp. 209–19; Lindsay and Berridge 2017, Chapter 3.

[208] Whish and Bailey 2018, p. 888.

[209] Horizontal Merger Guidelines 2004, par. 14; Non-Horizontal Merger Guidelines 2008, par. 24.

[210] Lindsay and Berridge 2017, p. 197 *et seq.*

market,[211] in order to perform a thorough competition assessment. For example, in novel, innovation-driven markets, in dynamic industries, such as computer gaming[212] or electronic communications,[213] the trustworthiness of market share data may be less reliable. Either way, an accurate picture of the market shares held by the parties is helpful in merger control cases: in *Cementbouw*,[214] the GC clarified that the existence of very large market shares and the relationship between the merging parties' market shares and their competitors, especially those of the next largest, is relevant evidence of the existence of a dominant position.

A finding of dominance is, however, not always a 'must'; the SIEC test may be successfully applied even in the absence of dominance. While there is no formal market share threshold in EU merger control which will trigger the Commission's 'radar', certain so-called filtering mechanisms are used in practice: for example, Recital 32 of the Merger Control Regulation 2004 provides that where the market share of the undertakings concerned does not exceed 25 per cent the transaction is not liable to create a significant impediment to effective competition. Some authors[215] regard this threshold as a safe harbour, establishing a rebuttable presumption that such concentrations are compatible with the Internal Market. Of course, market shares must be perceived from different standpoints, depending on the type of transaction at hand. The Horizontal Merger Guidelines 2004 (paragraphs 17–18) and the Non-Horizontal Merger Guidelines 2008 (paragraph 25) indicate the market share thresholds which the Commission regards as the baseline for employing the various theories of harm in its assessment, thresholds which, however, do not give rise to legal presumptions per se.[216] For vertical and conglomerate transactions, the Commission is unlikely to find (coordinated or unilateral) concerns where the merged entity's market share post-merger, in each of the markets concerned, is below 30 per cent. For horizontal transactions, several thresholds may be taken into account: (1) very large market shares, that is, 50 per cent or more, may in themselves be evidence of the existence of a dominant market position.[217] However, smaller competitors may act as a sufficient constraining influence if, for example, they have the ability and incentive to increase their supplies. (2) Post-merger market shares below 50 per cent, but over 40 per cent:[218] such a scenario may raise competition concerns in view of other factors, such as the strength and number of competitors, the presence of capacity constraints, or the extent to which the products of the merging parties are close substitutes. (3) On somewhat rare occasions, post-merger market shares below 40 per cent may also trigger competition concerns, in light of the factors mentioned under (2).[219]

The interpretation of the market shares held by the market players must take into account

---

[211] Horizontal Merger Guidelines 2004, par. 15.

[212] E.g. case COMP/M.5008 *Vivendi/Activision*, (2008) OJ C 137/6.

[213] Case COMP/M.7217 *Facebook/WhatsApp*, (2014) C/2014/7239 final.

[214] Case T-282/02 *Cementbouw*, ECLI:EU:T:2006:64, par. 201.

[215] Lorenz 2013, p. 277.

[216] E.g. Horizontal Merger Guidelines 2004, par. 21; Non-Horizontal Merger Guidelines 2008, par. 27.

[217] E.g. cases T-102/96 *Gencor*, ECLI:EU:T:1999:65; T-221/95 *Endemol*, ECLI:EU:T:1999:85.

[218] Case COMP/M.2337 *Nestlé/Ralston Purina*, (2001) OJ C 239/8.

[219] Case IV/M.1221 *Rewe/Meinl*, (1999) OJ L 274/1.

their dynamics, that is, their volatility, on one hand, and, since concentration control is essentially an *ex ante* exercise, the prediction of future market developments, on the other hand. According to paragraph 15 of the Horizontal Merger Guidelines 2004, the Commission normally uses *current* market shares in its competitive analysis, which may be adjusted to reflect reasonably certain future changes, for instance in the light of exit, entry or expansion. Post-merger market shares are calculated on the rebuttable assumption that the post-merger combined market share of the merging parties is the sum of their pre-merger market shares. However, evidence of likely so-called market share shrinkage post-merger may be accepted, when customers may switch suppliers to maintain leverage over the merged entity, and competitors may change pricing and output decisions, to account for the merger. Such reactions show that high market shares may erode fast.[220] Moving on, historical data may be used if market shares have been volatile. Changes in historic market shares may provide useful information about the competitive process and the likely future importance of various competitors, for example, by indicating whether firms have been gaining or losing market shares.

Besides asserting the division of market shares between the market players, the Commission also investigates the market's concentration level, in order to assert to what extent supply or purchase activities are concentrated in the hands of a few market players. Both the Horizontal Merger Guidelines 2004 and the Non-Horizontal Merger Guidelines 2008 use the Herfindahl-Hirschman Index (HHI) to measure market concentration, although this is not the only instrument that may be used for this purpose.[221] The HHI is calculated by summing the squares of the individual market shares of all the firms in the market.[222] The HHI value will depend on the features of the market, that is, the number of players and their market power. It may range from almost 0 points, in markets with a very large number of players, to 10 000 points, in markets which are fully monopolised. Thus, the absolute level of the HHI can give an initial indication of the competitive pressure in the market. If after the merger, the level of concentration in the market is less than 1000 points for horizontal mergers, competition concerns are unlikely to occur.[223] If for horizontal mergers the post-merger HHI value is between 1000 and 2000 points, competition issues may arise, yet the establishment of such concerns requires investigation of particular factors. Certain benchmarks are taken into account in this respect. For example, the change in the HHI (known as the 'delta') between the pre-merger and the post-merger status in the market is a useful proxy for the change in concentration directly brought about by the merger. The Horizontal Merger Guidelines 2004 provide handy indications: when the post-merger HHI value is between 1000 and 2000 points and the delta is below 250, or when the post-merger HHI value is above 2000 points and the delta is below 150, problems are unlikely to occur. The incremental increase of market concentration is indeed very small. Competition problems may occur if the delta exceeds

---

[220] Lindsay and Berridge 2017, pp. 230–31. See e.g. cases COMP/M.1672 *Volvo/Scania*, (2001) OJ L 143/74; COMP/M.1882 *Pirelli/BICC*, (2003) OJ L 70/35; IV/M.42 *Alcatel/Telettra*, (1999) OJ L 122/48.

[221] E.g. Concentration Ratios and the Lerner Index.

[222] Horizontal Merger Guidelines 2004, par. 16 and footnotes 18, 19.

[223] Ibid, par. 19.

these values, or even if this is not the case, one or more of the following factors are present: a merger involves a potential entrant or a recent entrant with a small market share; one or more merging parties are important innovators in ways not reflected in market shares; there are significant cross-shareholdings among the market participants; one of the merging firms is a maverick firm with a high likelihood of disrupting coordinated conduct; indications of past or ongoing coordination, or facilitating practices, are present; one of the merging parties has a pre-merger market share of 50 per cent or more.[224] While the Commission argues in paragraph 21 of the Horizontal Merger Guidelines 2004 that the HHI levels and the deltas do not create presumptions regarding the existence of absence of competition concerns per se, in *Sun Chemical*,[225] the GC argued that the greater the margin by which the HHI and delta thresholds are exceeded, the more the HHI values will be indicative of competition concerns.

The Non-Horizontal Merger Guidelines 2008 approach this matter somewhat differently, in that they are silent as far as deltas are concerned. These Guidelines simply state that when the post-merger HHI is below 2000 points, competition problems are unlikely, and it will thus not investigate such transactions, unless special circumstances may be present: for example, mergers involving a company likely to expand significantly in the near future, due to recent innovation; the existence of significant cross-shareholdings or cross-directorships among the market participants; one of the merging firms is a firm with a high likelihood of disrupting coordinated conduct; the presence of indications of past or ongoing coordination, or facilitating practices.[226]

3.3.4 The counterfactual and theories of harm

The *ex ante* concentration control method requires a prediction exercise of how the effects of the merger will unfold. The Commission makes it clear in both the Horizontal Merger Guidelines 2004 (paragraph 9) and the Non-Horizontal Merger Guidelines 2008 (paragraph 20) that in assessing the competitive effects of a merger, it compares the competitive conditions that would result from the notified merger with the conditions that would have prevailed without the merger. In most cases the competitive conditions existing at the time of the merger constitute the relevant comparison for evaluating the effects of a merger. In certain circumstances, the Commission may take into account future changes to the market that can reasonably be predicted.[227] It may, in particular, take account of the likely entry or exit of firms if the merger did not take place, when considering what constitutes the relevant comparison. It will also look into the manner in which parallel and overlapping mergers (i.e. mergers in contemplation or executed at the same time, in the same market) must be factored in the substantive appraisal of given concentrations.[228]

---

[224] Ibid, par. 20.

[225] Case T-282/06 *Sun Chemical*, ECLI:EU:2007:203, par. 138.

[226] Non-Horizontal Merger Guidelines 2008, par. 25–26.

[227] E.g. cases IV/M.1846 *Glaxo Wellcome/SmithKline Beecham*, (2000) OJ C 170/6; COMP/M.2547 *Bayer/Aventis Crop Science*, (2004) OJ L 107/1.

[228] On parallel and overlapping mergers, see Rusu 2010, p. 175 *et seq.*

These considerations form part of the so-called counterfactual principle.[229] Essentially, a concentration would only be prohibited if it will result in a significant impediment of effective competition. Should there be no significant change in the level of competition, the transaction should be allowed to go through.[230] If the conditions of competition are bound to change, an evaluation of the counterfactual proves even more important. Many examples may be provided in this respect, some of which may be somewhat counterintuitive: a merger resulting in price drops may be prohibited if it is proven that prices would have fallen further;[231] if a transaction results in a decline of conditions of competition, it may not be prohibited if it is proven that the conditions of competition would have worsened to a more serious degree;[232] a merger may also not be prohibited, if it does not increase the degree of cooperation between the parties[233] or if it does not aggravate an existing competition issue,[234] and suchlike. The counterfactual is thus important for establishing whether there is a causal link between the transaction and the effects of a given concentration. Ascertaining this causation requires a good understanding of: (1) the pre-merger status on the market; (2) whether and, if so, how the pre-merger market status is likely to change in absence of the transaction; (3) the post-merger market status; (4) the differences between points (2) and (3) above. While point (2) essentially relates to the counterfactual, point (4) reveals the effects of the appraised concentration.

To uncover these effects, the Commission evaluates the elements (non-exhaustively) listed in Article 2(1) of the Merger Control Regulation 2004, however, without treating the list contained therein as a mechanical checklist to be completed in each and every case appraisal. The Commission is in control of the theory or theories of harm it intends to employ in a given case and it enjoys a certain degree of discretion as far as taking or not taking into account certain factors.[235] The competitive analysis in a particular case is thus based on an *overall assessment* of the foreseeable impact of the concentration in the light of the *relevant* factors and conditions. This involves an evaluation of both the pro- and anti-competitive factors pertaining to the concentration.

The manner in which the effects of a concentration manifest themselves in practice, and the weight attached to their appraisal is dependent on the type of transaction at hand: horizontal and non-horizontal (i.e. vertical or conglomerate) concentrations. For both types of transactions, when it comes to investigating whether a significant impediment to effective competition may occur, the Commission will apply theories of harm in its appraisal process

---

[229] On the counterfactual principle see Lindsay and Berridge 2017, Chapter 5.

[230] Case T-342/99 *Airtours*, ECLI:EU:T:2002:146, par. 82.

[231] Horizontal Merger Guidelines 2004, footnote 7.

[232] E.g. case COMP/M.2810 *Deloitte & Touche/Andersen*, (2002) OJ C 200/9.

[233] E.g. case COMP/M.5181 *Delta Airlines/Northwest Airlines*, (2008) OJ C 281/3.

[234] E.g. case COMP/M.6381 *Google/Motorola Mobility*, (2012) OJ C 75/1.

[235] Horizontal Merger Guidelines 2004, par. 12–13; Non-Horizontal Merger Guidelines 2008, par. 21; case T-282/06 *Sun Chemical*, ECLI:EU:2007:203, par. 57.

which relate to non-coordinated (unilateral) and/or coordinated effects.[236] Such effects may occur in transactions between actual or potential competitors.[237]

Regarding potential competitors, coordinated or non-coordinated effects may occur if the potential competitor significantly constrains the behaviour of the firms active in the market (e.g. it may enter the market without incurring significant sunk costs). For a merger with a potential competitor to have significant anti-competitive effects, two basic conditions must be fulfilled: the potential competitor must already exert a significant constraining influence or there must be a significant likelihood that it would grow into an effective competitive force, and there must not be a sufficient number of other potential competitors, which could maintain sufficient competitive pressure after the merger.[238] From the above we can gather that this discussion relates to the elimination of (actual or perceived) potential competition. Such an outcome may result in consumer harm particularly in concentrated markets with high barriers to entry. In such cases, the Commission normally assesses the incentives and abilities of each candidate entrant and the likely development of competition in that market.[239]

In the paragraphs below we will dwell upon unilateral and coordinated effects in effects in more detail, in relation to horizontal and non-horizontal transactions, respectively.

3.3.4.1 Horizontal unilateral effects

Such effects entail the removal of important competitive constraints and the reduction of competitive pressure on the remaining competitors in the market. This may have several consequences: the merging parties may acquire enhanced market power, which may in turn lead to higher prices and/or lower output or quality; the remaining competitors in the market may resort to similar behaviour, when faced with price increases by the merged entity, especially since they are no longer pressured by the same competitive constraints which existed pre-merger. The typical example of horizontal unilateral effects which significantly impede effective competition is the creation of a single dominant position, especially when there is a significant gap between the degree of market power of the merged entity and its closest competitor. Unilateral effects may also occur due to concentrations performed in oligopolistic markets, without necessarily resulting in single dominance.[240]

The Horizontal Merger Guidelines 2004 dwell upon (exemplificative) factors to be evaluated, in order to decide whether significant unilateral effects result from a concentration, factors which are very much in tune with those (non-exhaustively) listed in Article 2(1) of the Merger Control Regulation 2004. Once again, the *overall* evaluation performed by the Commission is what counts, since such factors perceived in isolation may not necessarily be

---

[236] Horizontal Merger Guidelines 2004, par. 22; Non-Horizontal Merger Guidelines 2008, par. 17–19.

[237] Horizontal Merger Guidelines 2004, par. 58–60; Non-Horizontal Merger Guidelines 2008, par. 7.

[238] E.g. cases COMP/M.1630 *Air Liquide/BOC*, (2004) OJ L92/1; IV/M.1439 *Telia/Telenor*, (2001) OJ L 40/1; COMP/M.1853 *EDF/EnBW*, (2002) OJ L 59/1.

[239] Lindsay and Berridge 2017, pp. 380–81.

[240] Merger Control Regulation 2004, Recital 25; Horizontal Merger Guidelines 2004, par. 24–25.

decisive. The essence of these factors boils down to the parties' degree of market power or their relationship with competitors:

- If the merged entity has *large market shares*, it is very likely it has market power. The larger the addition of market share post-merger, the more likely it is that a significant impediment to effective competition will occur. Although this is only a first indication of (increases in) market power, market shares are normally important factors in the assessment.[241] For example, in *Olympic/Aegean*[242] a prohibition decision was adopted since the merged entity would have had very high combined market share post-merger (about 80 per cent of the flights and 90 per cent of the capacity on the Greek market).

- If the parties are *close competitors*, the higher the degree of substitutability between the merging parties' products/services, the more likely it is that the merging firms will raise prices significantly.[243] The market definition, and especially understanding the issue of product substitutability and differentiation (based on brand image, technical specifications, quality, level of service, geographic considerations, and the like) is key in this respect. Transactions between companies whose products are regarded as close substitutes by consumers may thus be problematic, since the concentration would remove important competitive pressure. The rivalry between the parties, which is an important source of competition on the market, may thus be a central factor in the Commission's analysis. For example, in *Unilever/Sara Lee Body Care*,[244] the Commission found that post-merger Unilever could have the incentive to raise prices for its Dove and Rexona deodorants, since Sara Lee's Sanex brand was no longer exerting any competitive pressure on Unilever's brands. The divestiture of Sanex was needed in order to approve this transaction.

- Moving further, the *rivalry between the merging firms*, on one hand, *and the rival producers active in the market post-merger*, on the other hand, is also important: such rivals, which produce close substitutes to the merging parties' products may constrain the merged entity's incentive to raise prices, especially if customers are able to switch in a timely manner to such alternative sources of supply.[245] Post-merger rivals may also reposition or expand their product lines, although this may entail sunk costs. All in all, it is less likely that a concentration will significantly impede effective competition, when there is a high degree of substitutability between the products of the merging parties and those supplied by rival producers. For example, in *Volvo/Renault VI*,[246] the analysis showed that customers regarded Scania and DAF as particularly good substitutes for

---

[241] Horizontal Merger Guidelines 2004, par. 27.

[242] Case COMP/M.5830 *Olympic/Aegean*, (2012) OJ C 195/10.

[243] Horizontal Merger Guidelines 2004, par. 28–30.

[244] Case COMP/M.5658 *Unilever/Sara Lee Body Care*, (2010) OJ C 147/04.

[245] Horizontal Merger Guidelines 2004, par. 31: customers may be vulnerable to price increases if they cannot switch suppliers easily, or they face substantial switching costs. A merger may affect such customers' ability to protect themselves, and may thus raise competition issues.

[246] Case IV/M.1980 *Volvo/Renault VI*, (2000) OJ C 301/23.

Volvo in the French heavy truck market, and thus the transaction between Volvo and Renault VI raised no competition concerns.

- In close connection to the rationale above, it may, however, be the case that the merging parties' *rivals are unlikely to increase their supply* substantially, if prices increase. This will be the case, for example, if the expansion of capacity is costly. This scenario, which is prone to take place when goods are relatively homogeneous, may result in the merged entity being incentivised to reduce output and increase prices, which in turn may be labelled as a significant impediment to effective competition.[247]

- Paragraph 36 of the Horizontal Merger Guidelines 2004 also foresees potential competition problems when the merged entity is left in a position where it would have the ability and incentive to *make the expansion of smaller firms and potential competitors more difficult* or otherwise restrict the ability of rival firms to compete.[248] A good part of this discussion thus relates to the concept of barriers to entry (discussed below in section 3.3.5.2), but also to the discussion just above about the strength of competitors to constrain the merged entity not to take action detrimental to competition.

- In close connection to the second bullet point of this enumeration, *important competitive pressure may be removed* via a concentration, even when the parties are not *close* competitors.[249] If one of the parties is a so-called maverick firm, its market share is not a realistic representation of its actual influence in the competitive process in the market. In other words, mavericks may be tougher competitors than they may initially seem. In *Boeing/McDonnell Douglas*,[250] the Commission acknowledged that although the market share of McDonnell Douglas has been continuously declining, its impact on the conditions of competition in the market for large commercial aircraft was higher than reflected by its market share in the year previous to the transaction. The Commission conditionally approved this deal after Phase II proceedings.

- Last but not least, paragraph 38 of the Horizontal Merger Guidelines 2004 sheds light on an interesting scenario, dealing with *innovation*. In markets where innovation is an important competitive force, a merger may increase the firms' ability and incentive to bring new innovations to the market and, thereby, the competitive pressure on rivals to innovate in that market. Nevertheless, effective competition may be significantly impeded by a merger between two important innovators, for instance between two companies with 'pipeline' products related to a specific product market. Such considerations were extensively assessed by the Commission in the *Dow/DuPont* deal, which impacted on several segments of the agrochemical sector.[251] The Commission acknowledged that innovation, both to improve existing products and to develop new active ingredients, is a key element of competition between companies in the pesticides

---

[247] Horizontal Merger Guidelines 2004, par. 32–35.

[248] Cases COMP/M.1741 *MCI Worldcom/Sprint*, (2003) OJ L 300/1; COMP/M.1795 *Vodafone Airtouch/Mannesmann*, (2003) OJ C 300/10.

[249] Horizontal Merger Guidelines 2004, par. 37–38.

[250] Case IV/M.887 *Boeing/McDonnell Douglas*, (1997) OJ L 336/16.

[251] Case M.7932 *Dow/DuPont*, (2017) OJ C 353/05.

industry, where only five players were globally active throughout the entire R&D process. It identified concerns which could have led to a significant impediment to effective competition: first, the parties were competing head-to-head in a number of important herbicide, insecticide and fungicide innovation areas. There was thus a likelihood that post-merger, they would have had an incentive to discontinue such development efforts. Second, the Commission was of the opinion that the merged entity would have lower incentives and a lower ability to innovate than Dow and DuPont separately. The merged entity would have allegedly cut back on the amount they spent on developing innovative products. The concentration was eventually conditionally cleared as the parties agreed to divest the relevant DuPont pesticide businesses and its global R&D organisation, as well as relevant assets in Dow's petrochemical business.[252]

The Horizontal Merger Guidelines 2004 do not put forward a specific theory of harm dedicated to horizontal unilateral effects in oligopolistic markets, in which no market leader may be identified. The Commission's assessment of such mergers will address the same factors as discussed above, in order to evaluate whether in the post-merger market the oligopolistic interdependence is altered and the incumbent firms may thus adopt pricing and production structures which may adversely impact competition: they could increase prices, given the price increase that the merged entity would engage in, and also given the potential output reduction of the merged entity, which might induce consumers to switch to the non-merging market rivals.[253] Concentrations relating to such non-collusive oligopolies are exactly the types of deals that the adoption of the SIEC test in the Merger Control Regulation 2004 was meant to address. In recent years, the Commission has dealt with such scenarios. For example, in *UPS/TNT Express*,[254] the merger would have *created* a non-collusive oligopoly, with very few competitors in most EU markets for express delivery of small packages. Absent any countervailing factors, the Commission concluded that price increases post-merger would have been incentivised. Consequently, it prohibited the transaction. The GC annulled this prohibition since the rights of defence of UPS were not respected. The action for damages started by UPS in this respect is currently pending.[255] In *Hutchison UK/Telefónica UK*,[256] the Commission prohibited this transaction since it was prone to remove an important competitor and leave only two mobile network operators to challenge the merged entity. The Commission feared that this would lead to less choice and higher prices for the end-consumers, as well as hampered development of the UK mobile network infrastructure and reduced ability of mobile virtual operators to compete.[257] The GC annulled this decision too, since the Commission's application of the assessment criteria of the unilateral effects was argued to be vitiated by several errors of law and of assessment.

---

[252] Press Release IP/17/772; Lianos, Korah and Siciliani 2019, pp. 1518–23.

[253] Kokkoris and Shelanski 2014, p. 243 *et seq.*

[254] Case COMP/M.6570 *UPS/TNT Express*, (2014) OJ C 137/8.

[255] Case T-834/17 *UPS*.

[256] Case M.7612 *Hutchison 3G UK/Telefónica UK*, (2016) OJ C 357/15.

[257] Press Release IP/16/1704.

In particular, the GC pointed out that the mere effect of reducing competitive pressure on the remaining competitors is not, in principle, sufficient in itself to demonstrate an SIEC in the context of a theory of harm based on non-coordinated effects. The GC emphasised that Article 2(3) of the Merger Control Regulation 2004 must be interpreted in the light of Recital 25 thereof, which lays down two cumulative conditions in order that non-co-ordinated effects arising from a concentration may, under certain circumstances, result in an SIEC: the concentration must involve (1) the elimination of important competitive constraints that the merging parties had exerted upon each other and (2) a reduction of competitive pressure on the remaining competitors.[258]

3.3.4.2 Horizontal coordinated effects

Paragraphs 39–57 of the Horizontal Merger Guidelines 2004 deal with concentrations that lead to coordinated effects, or in other words the creation or strengthening of a collective dominant position. This is a complex discussion, which, as the language used suggests, links also with the EU antitrust provisions.[259] Indeed, as early as the *ICI*[260] and *Hoffmann-La Roche*[261] cases, the EU courts have clarified that parallel behaviour does not in itself amount to a concerted practice, unless concertation is a plausible explanation of such behaviour, and that a dominant position must be distinguished from parallel conduct typically observed in oligopolistic markets. In such markets, characterised by the presence of a small number of players who acknowledge their interdependence and ineffectiveness of forceful competition between themselves, some sort of interaction between the players exists, while a dominant firm determines its conduct unilaterally.[262] Jones, Sufrin and Dunne[263] rightfully argue that Article 101 TFEU prohibits explicit, but not tacit collusion. Nevertheless, explicit collusion is hard to detect. Article 102 TFEU provides a less than ideal tool for controlling tacit collusion. Thus, it is critical that the merger control system is able to prevent concentrations that might lead to collusion (whether explicit or tacit) on a market.

The Horizontal Merger Guidelines 2004[264] provide that some market structures may be such that firms would consider it possible, economically rational, and hence preferable, to adopt on a sustainable basis a course of action aimed at selling at increased prices. A merger in a concentrated market may significantly impede effective competition, through the creation or the strengthening of a collective dominant position, because it increases the likelihood that firms are able to coordinate their behaviour and raise prices, reduce output or capacity, divide markets, allocate customers or contracts, and so on, even without resorting to agreements or concerted practices within the meaning of Article 101 TFEU. A merger may also make coordination easier, more stable or more effective for firms that were

---

[258] Case T-399/16 *CK Telecoms UK Investments*, ECLI:EU:T:2020:217, par. 96–97.

[259] On collective dominance, see Filippelli 2013.

[260] Case 48/69 *ICI*, ECLI:EU:C:1972:70.

[261] Case 85/76 *Hoffmann-La Roche*, ECLI:EU:C:1979:36.

[262] Kokkoris and Shelanski 2014, p. 262.

[263] Jones, Sufrin and Dunne 2019, p. 1131.

[264] Par. 39–40.

already coordinating before the merger, either by making the coordination more robust or by permitting firms to coordinate on even higher prices. The Horizontal Merger Guidelines 2004 build on the criteria for establishing a collective dominant position, put forward by the GC in *Airtours*, while spelling out four elements which must be identified to conclude that a concentration may lead to coordinated effects:[265] (1) it is relatively simple to reach a common understanding on the terms of coordination; (2) firms must be able to monitor to a sufficient degree whether the terms of coordination are being adhered to; (3) there is some form of credible deterrent mechanism that can be activated if deviation is detected; (4) the reactions of current and future competitors not participating in the coordination, as well as customers, should not be able to jeopardise the results expected from the coordination.

In the *Impala* ruling[266] the CJEU clarified that the *Airtours* conditions, and thus the conditions listed just above, should not be applied in isolation and in a mechanical manner. Instead, the overall economic mechanism of a hypothetical tacit coordination should be taken into account. The *Impala* ruling[267] also nicely recalls the experience the Commission and the EU courts had with the concept of collective dominance prior to 2004: in *Kali und Salz*[268] it was made clear that the concept of collective dominant position is included in that of dominant position within the meaning of Article 2 of the Merger Control Regulation 1989. In *CMB*[269] the existence of an agreement or of other legal links between the undertakings concerned is not essential to a finding of a collective dominant position. Such a finding may be based on other connecting factors and would depend on an economic assessment and, in particular, on an assessment of the structure of the market in question. Thus, as confirmed in *Gencor*,[270] a collective dominant position could be held by the members of a tight oligopoly. In paragraph 122 of the *Impala* ruling, the Court concludes: a collective dominant position significantly impeding effective competition may arise as the result of a concentration where, in view of the actual characteristics of the relevant market and of the alteration to those characteristics that the concentration would entail, the latter would make each member of the oligopoly, as it becomes aware of common interests, consider it possible, economically rational, and hence preferable, to adopt on a lasting basis a common policy on the market with the aim of selling at above competitive prices, without having to enter practices falling under Article 101 TFEU and without any actual or potential competitors, let alone customers or consumers, being able to react effectively.

The language used in *Impala* is definitely reminiscent of the Horizontal Merger Guidelines 2004. The Guidelines elaborate on the four factors mentioned above and spell out further supporting assessment aspects that facilitate their realisation:

---

[265] Horizontal Merger Guidelines 2004, par. 41, 44 *et seq.*

[266] Case C-413/06 *Impala*, ECLI:EU:C:2008:392, par. 125–126.

[267] Ibid, par. 119–121.

[268] Joined cases C-68/94 and C-30/95 *Kali und Salz*, ECLI:EU:C:1998:148.

[269] Joined cases C-395 and 396/96 P *CMB*, ECLI:EU:C:2000:132.

[270] Case T-102/96 *Gencor*, ECLI:EU:T:1999:65.

- Reaching the terms of coordination:[271] if firms can easily arrive at a common perception of how coordination should work, coordination is more likely. Several aspects may facilitate this: a less complex and stable economic environment; a limited number of symmetric players in the market, in terms of cost structures, market shares, capacity, vertical integration, and so forth; few products, which are homogeneous; relatively stable conditions of supply and demand; little internal growth of undertakings; limited role of innovation; limited market entry; and so on. Even if such conditions are not fully met, or if the economic environment is complex, this does not mean that coordination may not be achieved. Firms may establish simple pricing rules that reduce the complexity of coordinating on a large number of prices; they may exchange information through trade associations, or use information received through cross-shareholdings or participation in joint ventures.

- Monitoring deviations:[272] firms need to be able to monitor each other's behaviour, to make sure that deviation from coordination does not occur, through, for example, lowering prices, increasing output or improving quality. Firms may be tempted to do this at times, in order to increase their market shares and win new customers. For monitoring to be effective, markets need to be transparent. This is more likely to be the case when there are fewer players active in the market and transactions take place in the public space, rather than behind closed doors. Generally speaking, what counts is what the players can infer from the signals they receive from the market: for example, are lost sales due to an overall low level of demand or due to a competitor deviating? Even in the absence of significant market transparency, firms may nevertheless engage in practices which have the indirect effect of easing the monitoring task: cross-directorships in joint ventures, most-favoured-customer clauses, voluntary publication of information, exchange of information through trade associations, and the like may increase transparency or help competitors interpret the choices made.

- Deterrent mechanism:[273] a credible threat of timely and sufficient retaliation by the players involved in the coordination keeps firms from deviating. Coordination is only sustainable if the consequences of deviations are sufficiently severe. Timing and the certainty of activation of a deterrent mechanism are important in this respect. Much will depend on the features of the market: for retaliation to be timely, the market needs to be transparent. If orders in the market are infrequent and large in volume, severe retaliation may be difficult to implement, since the gain from deviating at the right time may be large, certain and immediate, whereas the losses from being punished may be small and uncertain and only materialise after some time. The credibility of the retaliatory mechanism depends on the incentives of the coordinating firms, and on the willingness of some of them to incur some losses (e.g. price wars, increasing of capacity) for the sake of punishing deviations. Also, retaliation may also take place in other markets than the one where the concentration takes place (through, for example,

---

[271] Horizontal Merger Guidelines 2004, par. 44–48.

[272] Ibid, par. 49–51.

[273] Ibid, par. 52–55.

breaking up joint ventures or selling shares in jointly owned companies), if the firms at hand have commercial interactions in such other markets.

- Reactions of outsiders:[274] coordination can only be successful if the actions of non-coordinating firms and potential competitors, as well as customers, cannot jeopardise the outcome expected from coordination. For example, if the coordinating firms reduce capacity, this market gap should not be able to be filled in by the non-coordinating players increasing their output capacity. Market entry barriers and countervailing customer power are important in assessing the weight of the reactions of outsiders. Sections 3.3.5.1 and 3.3.5.2 below will elaborate on these concepts.

Cases involving coordinated effects of horizontal concentrations do not occur very often. This is partly due to the strict features that markets in which concentrations might occur need to exhibit. Recently, the Commission used this theory of harm, for example in *AB InBev/SABMiller*,[275] a transaction between the world's largest two brewers. The Commission expressed concerns of tacit coordination between the merged entity and other brewers, in what proved to be a tightly oligopolistic market. It, however, cleared the merger based on the commitment to divest the SABMiller EU beer business. In *Holcim/Cemex West* and *Cemex/ Holcim Assets*,[276] the Commission identified the cement sector as one being susceptible to coordination, but cleared both mergers unconditionally, since they were unlikely to make possible coordination easier, more stable or more effective.[277]

3.3.4.3 Non-horizontal unilateral and coordinated effects

Paragraphs 12–14 of the Non-Horizontal Merger Guidelines 2008 highlight that vertical and conglomerate deals are often less problematic than horizontal concentrations, since they do not entail loss of direct competition and may provide substantial scope for efficiencies. Nevertheless, such transactions may lead to significant impediments to effective competition. Just like horizontal transactions, vertical and conglomerate ones may create unilateral and coordinated effects. It is thus no surprise that the Non-Horizontal Merger Guidelines 2008 often rely on the rationale and mechanisms of the Horizontal Merger Guidelines 2004. The Non-Horizontal Merger Guidelines 2008 frame the discussion for both types of non-horizontal mergers in terms of changes to the ability and incentive of the merging parties, or their competitors, as the case may be, to compete in ways that cause harm to consumers.[278]

---

[274] Ibid, par. 56–57.

[275] Case M.7881 *AB InBev/SABMiller*, (2017) OJ C 198/1.

[276] Cases M.7009 *Holcim/Cemex West*, (2014) available at <https://ec.europa.eu/competition/mergers/cases/deci sions/m7009_20140605_20682_3836837_EN.pdf>; M.7054 *Cemex/Holcim Assets*, (2014) available at <https:// ec.europa.eu/competition/mergers/cases/decisions/m7054_20140909_20682_4001455_EN.pdf>. Both links were accessed on 14 May 2020.

[277] Whish and Bailey 2018, p. 895.

[278] Non-Horizontal Merger Guidelines 2008, par. 15.

Unilateral effects

Non-coordinated/unilateral effects relate primarily to foreclosure, although vertical integration may also lead to other types of competition issues: for example, gaining access to commercially sensitive information regarding the upstream or downstream activities of rivals, which allows adjusting the pricing strategies downstream, to the detriment of consumers.[279] When it comes to vertical transactions, the Guidelines make a distinction between *input foreclosure*, that is, the concentration is likely to raise the costs of downstream rivals by restricting their access to an important input, and *customer foreclosure*, that is, the transaction is likely to foreclose upstream rivals by restricting their access to a sufficient customer base.[280]

Input foreclosure must not result in competitors downstream exiting the market per se. The benchmark for establishing consumer harm is whether the increased input costs would lead to higher prices for consumers. An overall assessment of the post-merger ability and incentive to substantially foreclose access, as well as whether the foreclosure strategy would have a significant detrimental effect on competition downstream, is performed by the Commission.[281] Input foreclosure may embody many shapes: refusal to deal with competitors downstream, restricting supplies, increasing prices, degrading the quality of the input supplied, or technologically altering it so that rivals' products are no longer compatible.[282] For input foreclosure to yield results, the input must be important for the downstream production process,[283] and the vertically integrated firm resulting from the concentration must have a significant degree of market power in the upstream market. Alternatively, if the input market is oligopolistic in nature, restrictions of access to inputs by the merged entity may reduce the competitive pressure exercised on remaining input suppliers, which could thus raise prices for the non-vertically integrated downstream players.[284] Furthermore, for input foreclosure to produce results, the foreclosure must be profitable, taking into account how the merged entity's supplies of inputs to competitors downstream will affect not only the profits of its upstream division, but also of its downstream division. The merged entity must thus factor in the likelihood of capturing diverted downstream demand from foreclosed rivals, and how this may profit the downstream division of the merged entity.[285] At the end of the day, input foreclosure may lead to significant impediments to effective competition through price increases in the downstream markets and raising barriers to entry to potential

---

[279] Ibid, par. 78.

[280] Ibid, par. 30.

[281] Ibid, par. 31–32.

[282] E.g. cases COMP/M.2861 *Siemens/Drägerwerk/JV*, (2003), OJ L 291/1; COMP/M.3998 *Axalto/Gemplus*, (2006) OJ C 196/8; COMP/M.4314 *Johnson & Johnson/Pfizer Consumer Healthcare*, (2007) OJ C 39/6.

[283] E.g. cases COMP/M.4561 *GE/Smiths Aerospace*, (2007) OJ C 31/1; COMP/M.4094 *Ineos/BP Dormagen*, (2006) available at <https://ec.europa.eu/competition/mergers/cases/decisions/m4094_20060810_20682_en.pdf> accessed 12 May 2020.

[284] Non-Horizontal Merger Guidelines 2008, par. 33–38.

[285] Ibid, par. 40–43. See e.g. cases COMP/M.3943 *Saint-Gobain/BPB*, (2005) available at <https://ec.europa.eu/com petition/mergers/cases/decisions/m3943_20051109_20310_en.pdf> accessed 12 May 2020; COMP/M.4314 *Johnson & Johnson/Pfizer Consumer Healthcare*, (2007) OJ C 39/6.

competitors. When assessing the overall impact on effective competition, the Commission will look into the strength of the likely foreclosed rivals, the presence of buyer power, likely efficiencies, or the likelihood of entry in the upstream market.[286]

Customer foreclosure occurs where a supplier integrates with an important customer in a downstream market. Thus, potential rivals in the upstream market may no longer have access to a sufficient customer base downstream. The same factors relied upon when discussing input foreclosure are relevant for assessing customer foreclosure,[287] yet their perception has to be taken from the perspective of access to downstream customers, rather than upstream supplies: ability to foreclose access to downstream markets, incentives to do so, and overall likely impact on effective competition. The rationale is thus very much similar as discussed above:[288] no upstream market exit is actually necessary; customer foreclosure may take various shapes in practice, which creates detriments to the upstream rivals; the customer must have a significant degree of market power in the downstream market; the likely foreclosure must be profitable; and so forth. All in all, foreclosing a sufficiently large part of rivals upstream, or creating barriers to enter the upstream market, may have an adverse impact downstream, and harm consumers: the merger may reduce the upstream rivals' ability to compete and thus the downstream rivals may be put at a competitive disadvantage due to raised input costs. Further, the merged entity may profitably raise prices or reduce the overall output on the downstream market.[289]

Foreclosure is also a concern for conglomerate transactions. The Commission's approach is based again on the same three factors:[290] ability to foreclose rivals, incentives to do so, and overall likely impact on prices and choice. Given that conglomerate concentrations involve parties not directly related in a horizontal or vertical manner, the Commission will typically focus on those cases where the parties are nevertheless active in closely related markets (e.g. mergers involving suppliers of complementary products or products that belong to the same product range, or a range of products that is generally purchased by the same set of customers for the same end use).[291] Competition may be hampered by such concentrations when the combination of products in related markets may confer on the merged entity the ability and incentive to leverage a strong market position from one market to another by means of tying or bundling or other exclusionary practices. Such actions may reduce actual or potential rivals' ability to compete, and thus decrease the competitive pressure on the merged entity, which becomes free to increase its prices. In order to be able to foreclose competitors, the merged entity must have a significant degree of market power, which does not necessarily amount to dominance, in one of the markets concerned. It must be the case that there is a large common pool of customers for the individual products concerned. The more customers

---

[286] Non-Horizontal Merger Guidelines 2008, par. 47–57.

[287] Whish and Bailey 2018, pp. 900–901.

[288] Non-Horizontal Merger Guidelines 2008, par. 58, 60, 61, 68. See e.g. cases COMP/M.2822 *EnBW/ENI/GVS*, (2003) OJ L 248/51; COMP/M.1879 *Boeing/Hughes*, (2004) OJ L 63/53.

[289] Non-Horizontal Merger Guidelines 2008, par. 72, 74, 75.

[290] Ibid, par. 95–104, 105–110, and 111–118, respectively.

[291] Ibid, par. 5, 91.

tend to buy both products (instead of only one of the products), the more demand for the individual products may be affected through bundling or tying.[292]

While Commission decisions in conglomerate cases are rare,[293] some of the most controversial cases it handled relate to such mergers. For example, both the *GE/Honeywell*[294] and *Tetra Laval/Sidel*[295] cases resulted in prohibitions which, although ending up in being heavily criticised by the EU courts on appeal, confirmed the Commission's right to intervene in conglomerate mergers. It has to be acknowledged in this respect that both these transactions were handled before the entry into force of the Merger Control Regulation 2004. The Commission investigated the conglomerate effects of these mergers and concluded that the deals would have created incentives for the merged entities to leverage market power between related markets. In *GE/Honeywell*, the Commission feared that the merger would strengthen GE's existing dominant position in the markets for jet engines for large commercial aircraft and regional aircraft and create a dominant position in avionics, non-avionics and corporate jet engines, markets in which Honeywell was the leading supplier of such products. According to the Commission, and contrary to the views of the US authorities, which had already cleared the deal, this would have allowed prospective strategies to be employed, which would have resulted in short-run price cuts, followed by market exit of competitors, and consequently price increases in the longer run. In *Tetra Laval/Sidel*, Tetra was the world's market leader in liquid food carton packaging, while Sidel produced packaging equipment, being an important player in the production of SBM machines, that produce PET bottles. The Commission considered that the merger would strengthen Tetra Laval's dominant position in the market for aseptic carton packaging machines and cartons and create a dominant position in the market for PET packaging equipment. It held that the merged entity would be able to exploit its dominant position on the carton markets by leveraging into the market for PET packaging equipment. By foreclosing competitors in the SBM machines market, Sidel could have ended up dominating it. The EU courts annulled the Commission's decision, stressing that the likelihood of such leveraging must be based on sufficiently convincing, plausible and cogent evidence.[296] Nevertheless, the Non-Horizontal Merger Guidelines 2008, which are still used today, can be considered a reflection of the Commission's attempt to acknowledge the criticism put forward by the EU courts in these two cases.[297]

Coordinated effects

Such effects may occur in the context of vertical and conglomerate deals too. The Non-Horizontal Merger Guidelines 2008 do not spend much time on this aspect, as the framework set out for coordinated effects in the Horizontal Merger Guidelines 2004 also applies to

---

[292] Ibid, par. 93–94, 99–100

[293] E.g. case M.8124 *Microsoft/LinkedIn*, (2016) C/2016/8404 final.

[294] Case COMP/M.2220 *General Electric/Honeywell*, (2001) OJ L 48/1; T-209/01 *Honeywell International*, ECLI:EU:T:2005:455.

[295] Case M.2416 *Tetra Laval/Sidel*, (2004) L 43/13.

[296] Standard of proof in merger control is discussed in section 3.3.6 below.

[297] Jones, Sufrin and Dunne 2019, pp. 1160–65.

coordinated effects resulting from non-horizontal concentrations.[298] Essentially, vertical and conglomerate concentrations may facilitate anti-competitive coordination, even in the absence of practices prohibited by Article 101 TFEU. Such transactions too may change the nature of competition in such a way that players previously not coordinating their behaviour are post-merger significantly more likely to coordinate. The same four proxies[299] are used to evaluate this possibility, as in the case of horizontal concentrations:

- Reaching the terms of coordination: a vertical concentration may increase the symmetry and degree of transparency between the market players. In turn, this may facilitate reaching a common understanding on the terms of coordination. This is important because, when foreclosure occurs, the number of effective competitors in the market reduces, thus making coordination easier.
- Monitoring deviations: market transparency makes it easier to monitor prices too. When foreclosure occurs, a reduced number of market players facilitates monitoring each other's action in the market.
- Deterrent mechanism: a vertically integrated company may be in a position to more effectively punish rival companies when they choose to deviate from the terms of coordination, because it is either a crucial customer or supplier to them.
- Reactions of outsiders: vertical concentrations may reduce the scope for outsiders to destabilise the coordination by increasing the barriers to enter the market.

3.3.5 Countervailing factors and efficiencies

A finding that a concentration may lead to an anti-competitive outcome may nevertheless be counterbalanced by so-called countervailing factors. In other words, there may be practical circumstances or market effects which, in the *overall* assessment that the Commission performs, may render the existence of a SIEC unlikely, on one hand, or mitigate the magnitude of the SIEC by outweighing the concentration's anti-competitive effects, on the other hand. Such scenarios may result in clearing concentrations which would have otherwise been blocked, or considerably amended. In the following subsections we will briefly discuss the following factors: buyer power, market entry, the failing firm defence and efficiencies.[300]

3.3.5.1 Buyer power

Customers/buyers may exercise constraints on the behaviour of the merged entity, thus preventing it from engaging in behaviour which may impede effective competition, or neutralising its market power. Buyer power may be relevant both in horizontal and non-horizontal mergers. Yet, it is only the Horizontal Merger Guidelines 2004 (paragraphs 64–67) that

---

[298] Non-Horizontal Merger Guidelines 2008, par. 79 and 119.

[299] Ibid, par. 82–90.

[300] See also Lindsay and Berridge 2017, Chapters 14–19; Kokkoris and Shelanski 2014, Chapters 10–13; Gore, Lewis, Lofaro and Dethmers 2013, p. 288 *et seq.*

contain information on how this factor should be construed in practice.[301] Buyer power relates to the bargaining strength that the buyer has vis-à-vis the seller in commercial negotiations due to its size, its commercial significance to the seller and its ability to switch to alternative suppliers.

Cases in which factors relating to buyer power tipped the balance in favour of a concentration are rare, since fairly exceptional market conditions need to be present.[302] For example, a customer must be able to credibly threaten to resort, within a reasonable time frame, to viable alternative sources of supply, should the supplier decide to increase prices, or alter the supply conditions. The buyer could do so by immediately switching to other suppliers, by credibly threatening to vertically integrate into the upstream market or to sponsor upstream expansion or entry, by delaying purchases, and so on. The buyer thus needs to be large and sophisticated, rather than small and active in fragmented industries. Furthermore, offsetting the anti-competitive effects of a concentration will depend on the buyer's actual incentive to utilise its power, and the breadth of the customers' segments affected by the post-merger deteriorated conditions of competition. It goes without saying that buyer power needs to be present and effective post-merger, since although pre-merger buyer power is important, it may nevertheless be reduced by the merger.[303]

3.3.5.2 Market entry/potential competitors

Market entry of new competitors may similarly be relevant for both horizontal and non-horizontal concentrations, and yet it is only the Horizontal Merger Guidelines 2004 that provide insights in this matter.[304] From the Commission's standpoint, if such market entry is sufficiently easy, a concentration in that market is unlikely to pose any significant anti-competitive risk.[305] In *Nestlé/Perrier*,[306] the Commission made it clear that entry must be competitively meaningful and effective, in order to constrain the merged entity's behaviour. In *Olympic/Aegean*,[307] it pointed out that the threat of entry must be immediate and actual.

For market entry to pose sufficient constraints on the merged entity, and thus deter or defeat any anti-competitive effects of the concentration, it must meet certain requirements. Entry must first be *likely*. This means that it must be sufficiently profitable, taking into account the price effects of injecting additional output into the market and the potential

---

[301] Par. 51, 76 and 114 of the Non-Horizontal Merger Guidelines 2008 point to Section V on countervailing buyer power in the Horizontal Merger Guidelines 2004.

[302] Jones, Sufrin and Dunne 2019, p. 1139, referring to A. Ezrachi and M. Ioannidou, 'Buyer Power in European Union Merger Control' (2014) European Competition Journal 69. See e.g. cases IV/M.42 *Alcatel/Telettra*, (1999) OJ L 122/48; COMP/M.1882 *Pirelli/BICC*, (2003) OJ L 70/35; M.1225 *Enso/Stora*, (1999) OJ L 254/9; M.833 *Coca-Cola/Carlsberg*, (1998) OJ L 145/41.

[303] Horizontal Merger Guidelines 2008, par. 66–67.

[304] Par. 51, 76 and 114 of the Non-Horizontal Merger Guidelines 2008 point to Section VI on entry in the Horizontal Merger Guidelines 2004.

[305] Horizontal Merger Guidelines 2004, par. 68.

[306] Case IV/M.190 *Nestlé/Perrier*, (1992) OJ L 356/1.

[307] Case COMP/M.5830 *Olympic/Aegean*, (2012) OJ C 195/10.

responses of the incumbents. Second, entry must be *timely*, that is, sufficiently swift and sustained. A two-year period is regarded as meeting this requirement in general, but the Commission acknowledges that the characteristics and dynamics of the market, as well as the specific capabilities of potential entrants call for a case-by-case approach. Third, entry must be of *sufficient scope and magnitude*, meaning that small-scale entry into some market 'niche', may not be considered sufficient.[308]

If these three criteria are met, the presumption that high market shares entail the existence of market power may be overridden, even in extreme cases leading to or bordering monopoly power. For example, in *Western Power Distribution/Hyder*[309] and *HP/Compaq*,[310] the Commission cleared such mergers, as barriers to entry were low and there were many potential credible competitors ready to enter, or already planning to enter the market. Both transactions were actually cleared in Phase I, even though in the latter deal the merged entity was supposed to hold 85–95 per cent of the market share.

The ease of accessing new markets is inevitably connected to the concept of barriers to entry: the lower they are, the more likely and timely entry of new competitors would be; vice versa, when entry barriers are high, price increases or reductions of output or quality by the merging firms would not be significantly constrained by entry. Much of what was discussed in this context in section 2.2.2.2 of Chapter 6 is relevant here too. In line with economic theory, the Commission interprets barriers to entry as specific features of a given market, which give incumbent firms advantages over potential competitors.[311] These may be legal, technical or strategic advantages.[312] Legal advantages relate to regulatory (tariff-related or not) barriers, which essentially limit the number of market participants, for example, by restricting the number of licences, or requiring to obtain a licence.[313] Technical and strategic advantages are essentially circumstances which make it difficult for any firm to compete successfully with the incumbent: for example, preferential access to essential facilities or natural resources, innovation and R&D, access to data and IP rights, sunk costs, economies of scale and scope, the existence of distribution and sales networks, and suchlike.[314] Factors such as consumer loyalty, advertising or switching costs on behalf of customers may also inhibit entry, particularly in digital and technology-driven markets.

Lastly for now, barriers to *exit* may also be telling when it comes to the likelihood of market entry, since if exit proves to be costly, the risks associated with entering a market are higher. When, however, barriers to exit and entry are inexistent, and so are sunk costs, such markets may be labelled as contestable. If there are potential entrants, which have similar

---

[308] Horizontal Merger Guidelines 2004, par. 69, 72–75.

[309] Case COMP/M.1949 *Western Power Distribution/Hyder*, (2000) available at <https://ec.europa.eu/competition/mergers/cases/decisions/m1949_en.pdf> accessed 5 May 2020.

[310] Case COMP/M.2609 *HP/Compaq*, (2002) OJ C39/23.

[311] Horizontal Merger Guidelines 2004, par. 70.

[312] Ibid, par. 71.

[313] Case COMP/M.1795 *Vodafone Airtouch/Mannesmann*, (2003) OJ C 300/10.

[314] E.g. cases M.833 *Coca-Cola/Carlsberg*, (1998) OJ L 145/41; M.68 *Tetra Pak/Alfa Laval*, (1991) OJ L 290/35; M.4854 *TomTom/Tele Atlas*, (2008) OJ C 237/12.

costs as the incumbent merged entity, the latter will take into account such circumstances when establishing its market tactics. The incumbent merged entity will thus be unlikely to increase prices and reduce output, even in a situation of monopoly, out of fear of so-called 'hit and run' market entry by such potential entrants.[315]

3.3.5.3 Failing firm defence

The failing firm defence was first recognised in the EU in the so-called *Kali und Salz* case.[316] The rationale of the Commission decision in this case, which stood the EU courts' test, is now reflected in the Horizontal Merger Guidelines 2004. The Guidelines acknowledge that, in exceptional circumstances,[317] an otherwise problematic concentration is nevertheless compatible with the Internal Market if one of the merging parties is a failing firm. In other words, a SIEC would occur regardless of whether the merger would take place, since the firm in question would exit the market in any case. Thus, the competitive structure of the market would deteriorate to at least the same extent in absence of the merger. The burden of proving this counterfactual scenario rests with the merging parties.[318] This is not an easy bar to clear. Three cumulative conditions, belonging to two different stages of analysis, must be met. The first stage relates to establishing the correct counterfactual, entailing conditions 1 and 2: the allegedly failing firm would, in the near future, be forced out of the market because of financial difficulties, if not taken over by another undertaking; there is no less anti-competitive alternative purchase than the notified concentration. The second stage of analysis relates to comparing the counterfactual to the post-merger scenario: the third condition is thus ascertaining whether, in the absence of a merger, the assets of the failing firm would inevitably exit the market.[319]

(Successful) failing firm cases, also known as rescue merger cases, are rare.[320] For example, in the first *Olympic/Aegean* case,[321] the Commission prohibited the concentration, since (among other reasons) none of the three conditions of the failing firm defence were met. Olympic, a newly privatised Greek airline company, could not be regarded as failing. Nevertheless, in the second *Olympic/Aegean* case,[322] Olympic was in a far worse state than before: it registered massive losses since its privatisation, and it was essentially surviving only due to the loans it was receiving. The Commission observed that no other serious buyer could be identified, the failing firm would have left the market in any case, and its existing market share would have been, in any event, captured by the competing acquirer, Aegean Airlines. Therefore, the Commission cleared this transaction.

---

[315] Lindsay and Berridge 2017, p. 536.

[316] Joined cases C-68/94 and C-30/95 *Kali und Salz*, ECLI:EU:C:1998:148.

[317] Horizontal Merger Guidelines 2004, par. 12, 89–91.

[318] Lianos, Korah and Siciliani 2019, p. 1614.

[319] Lindsay and Berridge 2017, p. 538.

[320] E.g. cases COMP/M.2876 *Newscorp/Telepiù*, (2004) OJ L 110/73; COMP/M.2314 *BASF/Pantochim/Eurodiol*, (2002) OJ L 132/45.

[321] Case COMP/M.5830 *Olympic/Aegean*, (2012) OJ C 195/10.

[322] Case COMP/M.6796 *Olympic/Aegean*, (2015) OJ C 25/05.

The very demanding criteria for successfully using the failing firm defence have triggered pleas for relaxing the failing firm test.[323] This could prove important, particularly in times of, or during the aftermath of economic recession, or in relation to the COVID-19 crisis, for that matter. The Commission has, however, not shown signals of amending its policy in this respect yet.

3.3.5.4 Efficiencies

The discussion surrounding efficiencies in EU merger control has caught traction in connection with the adoption of the Merger Control Regulation 2004, and is very much connected to the shift from the dominance to the SIEC appraisal test. Even before this shift, there were supporters of the possibility to apply an efficiency defence in the context of the dominance test.[324] Nowadays, Recital 29 of the Merger Control Regulation 2004 states in no uncertain terms: to determine the impact of a concentration on competition, it is appropriate to take account of any substantiated and likely efficiencies put forward by the undertakings concerned. It is possible that the efficiencies brought about by the concentration counteract the effects on competition, and in particular the potential harm to consumers that it might otherwise have, and that, as a consequence, the concentration would not significantly impede effective competition. Paragraphs 76–88 of the Horizontal Merger Guidelines 2004 provide guidance as to how the Commission perceives efficiencies in practice. In a nutshell, taking efficiencies into account must be done in the context of the *overall* competitive appraisal of the transaction, in light of the factors mentioned in Article 2(1) of the Merger Control Regulation 2004, in order to evaluate whether the concentration will lead to a significant impediment to effective competition. If the efficiency gains meet the criteria specified in the Guidelines, such an overall assessment may lead to the conclusion that there are no grounds for declaring the transaction incompatible with the Internal Market, pursuant to Article 2(3) of the same Regulation.[325]

The Non-Horizontal Merger Guidelines 2008 point, on several instances, to the provisions of Section VII of the Horizontal Merger Guidelines 2004, suggesting that the latter's methods and techniques are valid for, and applicable to, non-horizontal mergers too. Indeed, vertical and conglomerate concentrations may provide substantial scope for efficiencies, which are likely to enhance the ability and incentive of the merged entity to act pro-competitively for the benefit of consumers, thereby counteracting the adverse effects on competition which the transaction might otherwise have. Actually, invoking efficiency considerations in non-horizontal concentrations may even be less burdensome, given that the parties' activities may be complementary to each other, and the integration of such activities in a single firm may significantly cut costs.[326]

Efficiencies may arise from various sources connected to a given concentration (horizontal or non-horizontal): economies of scale or scope, production rationalisation, removal of

---

[323] Lindsay and Berridge 2017, pp. 551–2.

[324] Monti 2002 (b). See case COMP/M.2876 *Newscorp/Telepiù*, (2004) OJ L 110/73.

[325] Horizontal Merger Guidelines 2004, par. 76–77.

[326] Non-Horizontal Merger Guidelines 2008, par. 12–14, 21, 22, 28, 52–57, 77.

so-called double marginalisation and transaction costs, direct or indirect network effects, and the like.[327] They may also take diverse forms in practice (e.g. cost savings, intensified R&D activities, improved quality of products and services, and more) and they may be categorised according to diverse criteria (i.e. allocative, productive, transactional, dynamic, and so on).[328] Yet, to be taken into account in the Commission's appraisal, efficiency claims put forward by the parties must meet the cumulative conditions discussed below. The pattern of approaching the efficiency conditions in merger control resembles to a certain extent the approach taken in antitrust law, namely Article 101(3) TFEU and the CJEU's case-law and the Commission's decisional practice on Article 102 TFEU.

Efficiencies must first *benefit consumers*.[329] Consumers must not be worse off as a result of the concentration. Efficiencies must thus be substantial, timely and likely to be realised in those markets where it is otherwise expected that competition concerns would occur. They may be embodied in lower prices, or improved quality of services or products. Lower prices often result from marginal and variable (but less likely fixed) costs savings, which are passed on to the consumers. The merged entity must be incentivised to pass on such savings, and the competitive pressure from actual or potential competitors is important to this end. That is why mergers to monopoly are unlikely to cohabitate well with efficiency considerations. Second, efficiencies must be *merger-specific*.[330] They must be a direct consequence of the notified transaction and cannot be achieved to a similar extent by less anti-competitive, realistic and attainable alternatives, of a non-concentrative or concentrative nature. A proportionality assessment is thus part of the efficiencies' evaluation. Third, the proposed efficiencies must be *verifiable*.[331] They must be likely to materialise and must be substantial enough to counteract a concentration's potential harm to consumers. The more precise and convincing the efficiency claims are, the better the Commission can evaluate the claims. This means that parties must provide all relevant information (e.g. internal documents, studies, historical market data, and suchlike) to allow the quantification of efficiencies or the foreseeability of a clearly identifiable positive and non-marginal impact on consumers.

Merging parties, who have the burden of proof regarding these conditions, are very rarely successful in convincing the Commission. This does, however, not stop them in putting forward complex efficiency claims, especially in recent cases. For example, in the *UPS/TNT Express* prohibition decision,[332] the projected (mostly fixed) cost savings were acknowledged, but they were deemed unlikely to be passed on to consumers and thus unfit to outweigh the likely price increases. In the *FedEx/TNT Express* Phase II clearance decision,[333] efficiencies were again acknowledged, although they were deemed as less relevant in the overall

---

[327] Ibid, par. 54–57. See also Lianos, Korah and Siciliani 2019, pp. 1612–13.

[328] For more on such matters, see e.g. Ilzkovitz and Meiklejohn 2006; Camesasca 2000; Van den Bergh, Camesasca and Giannaccari 2017.

[329] Horizontal Merger Guidelines 2004, par. 79–84.

[330] Ibid, par. 85.

[331] Ibid, par. 86–88.

[332] Case COMP/M.6570 *UPS/TNT Express*, (2014) OJ C 137/8.

[333] Case M.7630 *FedEx/TNT Express*, (2016) OJ C 450/09.

assessment, primarily given that the parties were not close competitors. Further, the *Ryanair/ Aer Lingus* prohibition decision[334] is a perfect exemplification of why concentrations to (near-)monopoly power are unlikely to be saved by efficiencies. The efficiencies put forward in this case were deemed not merger-specific, since similar cost savings to those proposed could have been achieved in the absence of the transaction. Similar arguments as in all these cases were present in *Deutsche Börse/NYSE Euronext*,[335] again a transaction in which efficiencies were deemed insufficiently substantial and non-specific. Actually, the Commission went so far as to argue that the merged entity would capture a good part of the claimed cost savings, thus reducing the benefits consumers were supposed to receive.

3.3.6 Standard of proof

In section 3.2.5 above, while dealing with the review of the Commission's concentration control decisions, we mentioned what is expected from the Commission when it comes to ensuring that such a decision passes the EU courts' test. This discussion pertains to the standard of proof that Commission decisions must meet in concentration control cases. This matter, although eminently touching upon procedural aspects of the appraisal process, is also very important as far as the substantive analysis is concerned, and it ties in with the counterfactual discussion touched upon in section 3.3.4 above. The question here is: how far must the Commission go in proving a (prospective) significant impediment to effective competition, in order to prohibit a concentration? This discussion is even more important given the *ex ante* nature of concentration control, which assumedly requires meeting a high evidentiary threshold. Indeed, in *Tetra Laval*[336] for example, the CJEU stated that the prospective analysis must be carried out with great care since it does not entail the examination of past events (for which often many items of evidence are available, which make it possible to understand the causes) or of current events, but rather a prediction of events which are more or less likely to occur in the future, if a prohibition decision is not adopted. Such an analysis requires several steps: first, an evaluation of the future conduct which the Commission contends will be engaged in by the merged entity and the other operators following the merger, by means of the assessment of the economic outcome attributable to the concentration which is most likely to ensue. For a prohibition decision to be adopted, the SIEC must be the direct and immediate effect of the concentration, stemming from future decisions by the merged entity. This is the case when such decisions are made possible by and are economically rational because of the alteration of the characteristics and the structure of the market caused by the concentration. Second, an assessment is performed by means of a prospective analysis of the reference market, of whether that future conduct will probably lead to a situation in which effective competition in the relevant market is significantly impeded.[337]

The standard of proof in EU merger control is not embedded in the Merger Control Regulation 2004. Yet, the case-law of the EU courts sheds light on the degree of likelihood the

---

[334] Case M.4439 *Ryanair/Aer Lingus*, (2006) OJ C 274/10.

[335] Case M.6166 *Deutsche Börse/NYSE Euronext*, (2014) OJ C 254/8.

[336] Case C-12/03 P *Commission v Tetra Laval*, ECLI:EU:C:2005:87, par. 42.

[337] Case T-399/16 *CK Telecoms UK Investments*, ECLI:EU:T:2020:217, par. 112–118.

Commission must establish regarding the competition harm resulting from a transaction.[338] Since the Commission's analysis is the result of an assessment based on hypotheses, it cannot be required that proof be adduced that the scenarios and theories of harm underpinning that assessment will *inevitably* occur. This means that, when ruling on a concentration's compatibility with the Internal Market, the Commission must not prove 'beyond any reasonable doubt' that anti-competitive effects will occur with absolute certainty. Instead, given the prospective analysis that needs to be carried out, the Commission must adopt a decision based on a 'balance of probabilities'. This means that there is no general presumption in favour of or against that compatibility. Thus, the Commission must establish with a *sufficient degree of probability* that a concentration will create a SIEC before it prohibits it. The EU courts have used concepts such as '(most) likely', 'probably', 'in all likelihood', 'sufficiently realistic' and the like, to describe the standard of proof in concentration control cases. To meet this standard, the Commission must discharge a body of evidence which is 'cogent', 'coherent', 'consistent', 'specific', 'reliable' and 'convincing'. In *Tetra Laval*, but not only,[339] it became apparent that this essentially entails a heavy burden on the Commission to prove how a SIEC will take place in the future. This analysis consists of an examination of how a concentration might alter the factors determining the state of competition on a given market. This makes it necessary to envisage various chains of cause and effect with a view to ascertaining which of them are the most likely.

The standard of proof is not necessarily altered by the (choice of) theory of harm put forward by the Commission. Its body of evidence will still need to meet the thresholds mentioned just above, regardless of which theory of harm is employed. Similarly, the principle of symmetry requires the Commission to meet the same standard when it comes to prohibiting a concentration, as when clearing it. Nevertheless, the complexity of a case, and consequently of the theory of harm employed, are taken into account when assessing the plausibility of the various consequences the concentration may have. For example, the more prospective the analysis is and the chains of cause and effect dimly discernible, uncertain and difficult to establish, the more the quality of the evidence produced by the Commission in order to establish that it is necessary to adopt a prohibition decision is important. In other words, the more a theory of harm advanced in support of a SIEC is complex or uncertain, the more demanding the EU courts must be as regards the specific examination of the evidence submitted by the Commission.[340] In the same vein, particularly demanding standards seem to exist also in cases involving the so-called failing firm defence, where one must assert that a particular asset would 'inevitably' leave the market.

---

[338] Joined cases C-68/94 and C-30/95 *Kali und Salz*, ECLI:EU:C:1998:148; cases T-342/99 *Airtours*, ECLI:EU:T:2002:146; C-12/03 P *Commission v Tetra Laval*, ECLI:EU:C:2005:87; T-464/04 *Impala*, ECLI:EU:T:2006:216; C-413/06 *Impala*, ECLI:EU:C:2008:392; T-399/16 *CK Telecoms UK Investments*, ECLI:EU:T:2020:217. On standard of proof, see Rusu 2010, pp. 146–60; Kokkoris and Shelanski 2014, pp. 195–8.

[339] Cases C-12/03 P *Commission v Tetra Laval*, ECLI:EU:C:2005:87, par. 43; C-413/06 *Impala*, ECLI:EU:C:2008:392, par. 47; T-399/16 *CK Telecoms UK Investments*, ECLI:EU:T:2020:217, par. 108.

[340] Cases C-413/06 *Impala*, ECLI:EU:C:2008:392, par. 41; T-399/16 *CK Telecoms UK Investments*, ECLI:EU:T:2020:217, par. 110–111.

The heavy burden carried by the Commission seems to become even heavier when, in one and the same case, the analysis is based on *several theories of harm*. In such a case, the Commission is required to produce sufficient evidence to demonstrate with a *strong probability* the existence of significant impediments following the concentration. Thus, the standard of proof applicable in such cases may be regarded as stricter than that under which a SIEC is 'more likely than not', on the basis of a 'balance of probabilities'. Nevertheless, even in such cases entailing the application of several theories of harm, the standard of proof will not reach the 'beyond any reasonable doubt' threshold.[341]

When the standard of proof is not met, the Commission decision will be annulled by the GC. The successive annulments in *Schneider, Airtours,* and *Tetra Laval*[342] triggered the Commission to strengthen its decision-making processes, to improve the quality and quantity of evidence and economic analysis set out in its merger decisions.[343] Since then, Commission decisions, especially in complex cases, can cover hundreds of pages, containing diverse categories of evidence and intricate economic analyses, meant to thoroughly clear the (SIEC-related) standard demanded by the courts. To our minds, this is to be appreciated, especially given the challenges current and future economic developments are bound to bring forward in concentration cases, for example, in digital markets.

3.3.7 Substantive analysis and Article 101 TFEU
In a couple of instances, the relationship between the substantive analysis in concentration control and the use of Article 101 TFEU needs to be elucidated.

3.3.7.1 Ancillary restraints
Articles 6 and 8 of the Merger Control Regulation 2004 provide that clearance decisions are deemed to also cover the so-called ancillary restraints, that is, the restrictions directly related and necessary to the implementation of the concentration. Thus, any terms of the transaction which might fall within Article 101 TFEU are cleared at the same time, if they bear a sufficiently close relation to the concentration itself.[344] Such terms agreed by the concentrating parties escape Article 101 TFEU scrutiny.

Undertakings often conclude agreements attached to the concentration transaction which are vital to the functioning of the concentration, or without which, the concentration would not be concluded: for example, non-competition clauses, licence agreements, purchase and/ or supply obligations, and the like. Such agreements must meet a set of objective criteria: they must be closely linked to the concentration itself and they must be necessary to the implementation of the concentration.[345] It is important to correctly establish if a restriction

---

[341] Case T-399/16 *CK Telecoms UK Investments*, ECLI:EU:T:2020:217, par. 117–118.

[342] Cases T-310/01 *Schneider*, ECLI:EU:T:2002:254; T-342/99 *Airtours*, ECLI:EU:T:2002:146; T-5/02 *Tetra Laval*, ECLI:EU:T:2002:264.

[343] Jones, Sufrin and Dunne 2019, p. 1111, referring to A. Witt, 'From Airtours to Ryanair: Is the More Economic Approach to EU Merger Law Really about More Economics?' (2012) 49 Common Market Law Review 217.

[344] Marco Colino 2019, p. 448

[345] E.g. case T-112/99 *Métropole Télévision*, ECLI:EU:T:2001:215, par. 106.

is ancillary or not, because in the latter case, the application of EU and domestic antitrust law comes back in the picture.[346] Recital 21 of the Merger Control Regulation 2004 provides that ancillary restraints are automatically covered by the Commission decision, without the Commission having to assess such restrictions in individual cases. This means that it is for the undertakings concerned to self-assess which restrictions are ancillary, as they normally do under antitrust analysis. The Commission will not state in a clearance decision which restraints are ancillary: it will provide guidance only in the case of specific novel or unresolved issues giving rise to genuine uncertainty, other disputes having to be resolved before national courts.[347] In order to provide appropriate guidance to the concerned parties, the Commission issued the Ancillary Restraints Notice 2005 (replacing its 2001 predecessor), which sets out the principles for assessing to what extent the most common types of agreements are deemed ancillary.[348]

3.3.7.2 Cooperative dimension of full-function joint ventures

In section 3.1.1.3 above, we indicated that certain aspects of full-function joint ventures require a particular type of substantive appraisal. Specifically, while all full-function joint ventures are deemed as concentrations and are thus procedurally bound to the Merger Control Regulation 2004, it is only their concentrative aspects that are substantively assessed under the SIEC test. Article 2(4) of this Regulation provides that when the creation of a full-function joint venture has as its object or effect the coordination of the competitive behaviour of undertakings that remain independent (i.e. the joint venture's parents), such coordination shall be appraised in accordance with the criteria of Article 101(1) and (3) TFEU, with a view to establishing whether or not the operation is compatible with the Internal Market. In other words, the cooperative aspects of full-function joint ventures are appraised in light of these Treaty provisions. This analysis takes place 'within' the concentration control procedure and it entails two steps:[349] first, the Commission analyses whether the parents retain, to a significant extent, activities in the same, upstream, downstream, neighbouring or closely related market as the joint venture; second, it assesses whether the coordination which is the direct consequence of the creation of the joint venture affords the parents the possibility of eliminating competition in respect of a substantial part of the products/services in question.[350]

When it comes to coordination and joint ventures, tensions may arise because Article 101 TFEU analysis is less benign than a SIEC analysis under the Merger Control Regulation 2004.[351] Nevertheless, in practice, the Commission does not draw a significant distinction between classic coordinated effects analysis (embedded in the SIEC test) and an assessment of coordination under Article 2(4) and (5). It normally first identifies the markets for analysis. If the parents are not active or potential competitors in the same, upstream, downstream,

---

[346] E.g. case COMP/39.736 *Siemens/Areva*, (2012) OJ C 280/8.

[347] Whish and Bailey 2018, p. 905.

[348] Ancillary Restraints Notice 2005, par. 4.

[349] E.g. case COMP/M.3099 *Areva/Urenco/ETC*, (2006) OJ L 61/11.

[350] Merger Control Regulation 2004, Article 2(5).

[351] Lindsay and Berridge 2017, p. 473 *et seq.*

neighbouring or closely related market as the joint venture, coordination may be ruled out.[352] Second, it identifies the mechanism for coordination: for example, price, output, market sharing, exchange of information, and so forth. Third, the Commission assesses the parties' incentive and ability to coordinate, to evaluate the likelihood of coordination taking place. Coordination may be more likely if the joint venture's business is important when compared to the parents' retained activities, and vice versa.[353] Fourth, the Commission looks into whether the coordination is likely to deliver an appreciable effect on competition, in light of the parents' market share, the viability of actual or potential competitors and buyer power,[354] aspects which essentially relate to the parents' actual ability to coordinate. Fifth, the Commission determines whether there is a causal link between the creation of the joint venture and the likelihood of coordination. Lastly, when the Commission concludes that this may be the case, it will engage the Article 101(3) TFEU analysis. This has, however, not happened to date, since such coordination concerns are normally handled through commitments.

3.3.8 Substantive appraisal of concentrations in the digital economy

One of the most interesting challenges relating to competition law enforcement nowadays is posed by the emergence of digital markets. Concentration control is no different. The substantive assessment of concentrations in digital markets must take into account certain specific features of the technology M&A phenomenon. Technology giants like Facebook, Google, Amazon, Apple, Microsoft and the like have engaged in many transactions in the recent past. Most of these transactions are pure acquisitions of young companies, more often than not of small(er) size. Such deals rarely entail horizontal effects, most being of conglomerate nature, the targets' products or services being often complementary to those offered by the acquirer.[355] Deals in the technology environment may often be pro-competitive, bringing about synergies resulting from the combination of innovative ideas, on one hand, with skills, assets and resources, on the other hand. Yet, scenarios resulting in concentration of control over valuable and non-replicable data or resources may also occur. This can lead to better data access for the merging parties than for their competitors, thus reinforcing the already very strong positions large technology companies may already possess, or in other words, strengthening their degree of market power. Other scenarios may entail creating the possibility to leverage market power, to foreclose actual competition, or to prevent market entry of potential rivals.

The technology-related concentrations that the European Commission has dealt with

---

[352] E.g. case COMP/JV.19 *KLM/Alitalia*, (1999) available at <https://ec.europa.eu/competition/mergers/cases/deci sions/jv19_en.pdf> accessed 4 May 2020.

[353] E.g. case COMP/M.3178 *Bertelsmann/Springer*, (2005) available at <https://ec.europa.eu/competition/mergers/ cases/decisions/m3178_20050503_20682_en.pdf> accessed 4 May 2020.

[354] E.g. cases IV/JV.1 *Telia/Telenor/Schibsted*, (1998) available at <https://ec.europa.eu/competition/mergers/cases/ decisions/jv1_en.pdf>; COMP/M.1413 *Thomson-CSF/Racal Electronics*, (1999) available at <https://ec.europa.eu/ competition/mergers/cases/decisions/m1413_en.pdf>. Both links were accessed on 4 May 2020.

[355] Joint Memorandum 2019, pp. 1–3.

so far were handled more or less expediently. For example, the *Apple/Shazam* deal was cleared without commitments, although it entailed a longer (Phase II) in-depth evaluation. The *Microsoft/LinkedIn*[356] transaction was cleared in Phase I, however, with commitments relating primarily to maintaining interoperability of competing professional social networks with Microsoft's products, and ensuring that PC manufacturers and distributors would be free not to install LinkedIn on Windows-equipped computers. Such outcomes may point out that the SIEC test, in general, and the 'strengthening of dominance' criterion, in particular, remain a sound basis for assessing the concentrations in the digital sector.[357] The theories of harm, on the other hand, as sound as they may be, may require some updating, according to the Commission's 2019 Report on Competition Policy for the Digital Era.

For example, where a dominant platform with strong positive network effects and data access, which constitute significant barriers to entry, acquires a low turnover target which nevertheless has a large and/or fast-growing user base and a high future market potential, such an acquisition may result in early elimination of potential competitive threats. This scenario goes beyond traditional conglomerate theories of harm relating to the foreclosure of rivals' access to inputs, since it can serve the acquirer the possibility to strengthen its dominance by increasing retention of users and user loyalty. The current EU control system could be better equipped according to this 2019 Report in order to better protect the ability of competitors to enter markets, especially when competition in the market is typically reduced and competitive threats typically come from the fringe. Beyond this, the control system should also accommodate horizontal elements into the conglomerate theories of harm. Such elements would help identify if the target is really a potential or actual competitor of the acquirer, a question which is key when it comes to applying the counterfactual principle in merger control cases. Often times, it is very difficult to determine if the target will grow to become a significant competitive force in a timespan which is not too long.[358] Horizontal-related questions may be also useful to identify whether the acquirer can benefit from barriers to entry linked to network effects or use of data, or whether the acquisition increases market power, particularly via barriers to entry. Other proposals to improve the concentration control exercise in digital markets relate to the standard and burden of proof that the Commission and competition authorities should adhere to.[359] For instance, questions have been raised whether a 'balance of harms' approach should be adopted in digital markets-related cases, whereby competition authorities, instead of considering only the *likelihood* of harm caused by a specific concentration, would also take into account the *scale* of potential competition harm of the transaction. That is, merger control would be stricter in cases where dominant platforms that enjoy significant network effects and barriers to entry acquire (potential) competitors. Next, where an acquisition would plausibly be part of such a strategy, a proposal relates to altering the burden of proof rules, yet without necessarily creating a presumption against the legality of such transactions: instead of requiring the Commission

---

[356] Case M.8124 *Microsoft/LinkedIn*, (2016) C/2016/8404 final.

[357] Crémer, de Montjoye and Schweitzer 2019, p. 116.

[358] Joint Memorandum 2019, p. 3; Crémer, de Montjoye and Schweitzer 2019, p. 116.

[359] Joint Memorandum 2019, p. 2; Crémer, de Montjoye and Schweitzer 2019, p. 11.

(or competition authorities) to show that the concentration would have a negative impact on the market before blocking it or imposing remedies, the burden could be placed on the parties (or better yet, the acquirer), when it comes to showing the lack of competitive harm, or that the adverse effects on competition are offset by merger-specific efficiencies. Lastly for now, proposals for scrutinising technology mergers more intensely have gone so far as to suggest exploring *ex post* control possibilities for transactions that may have an impact on the digital ecosystem.[360] To our minds, this avenue is worth exploring, especially given the rapid pace with which digital markets evolve. This may make it difficult for the Commission (or competition authorities) to predict the future market dynamics and the expected effects of a given deal, in a pure *ex ante* approach.

All in all, the digitalisation phenomenon brings about challenges as far as substantive appraisals of certain types of concentrations are concerned. While no EU merger control legislative amendments have been adopted yet, the debate surrounding the topic of making EU merger control 'future and technology-proof' is certainly rich.[361] Forthcoming decisional practice of the Commission, with potential inspiration drawn from the domestic ambits, may shed more light on the actual need to upgrade the EU merger control substantive appraisal mechanisms.

4 BEYOND THE EU MERGER CONTROL SYSTEM: INTERNATIONAL ASPECTS AND DOMESTIC EXPERIENCE

More often than not, concentrations have impact on multiple markets and jurisdictions. The EU merger control system must thus be placed in the broader context. First, this context relates to the relationship with the Member States. Second, the interaction with third countries must be kept in mind. Third, despite the fact that the enforcement of the EU concentration control rules is not decentralised, as is the case with the enforcement of Articles 101 and 102 TFEU, the practice of the NCAs and domestic courts of the Member States with enforcing national merger control laws is valuable, when it comes to grasping the full breadth of the M&A phenomenon in the EU. Thus, while markets and business strategies are constantly evolving, so are (and should) the concentration control mechanisms used by competition authorities. Studying and sharing domestic experience and best practices provide invaluable benefits to this end.

4.1 Relationship with the Member States' authorities

Concentration control, as part of competition policy, must observe the principle of sincere cooperation embedded in Article 4(3) TEU. This entails the existence of strong ties between

---

[360] Joint Proposal 2019.

[361] E.g. Furman Report 2019; OECD 2016; OECD 2018; Netherlands' Ministry of Economic Affairs and Climate Policy 2019.

the Commission and the NCAs, and between EU law and domestic law for that matter. Many examples may be provided in this respect, ranging from the functioning of the case referral mechanisms, to the active assistance of Commission inspections by NCAs,[362] to the joint adoption (by the Commission and the NCAs) of best practices for handling cross-border concentrations falling outside the EU one-stop-shop system.[363] For the sake of completeness, it is important to mention that Article 19 of the Merger Control Regulation 2004 focuses on the liaison between the Commission and the NCAs, particularly when it comes to the role of the Advisory Committee on Concentrations. This committee is composed of representatives of the NCAs. It issues opinions when the Commission intends to adopt Phase II and sanctioning decisions. Despite their non-binding character, the Commission is expected to take the utmost account of the opinions delivered by the Committee.

4.2 Relationship with third countries

Once a concentration has an EU dimension, the Merger Control Regulation 2004 applies, regardless where the parties to the transaction are established, where most of their business is performed, where the transaction is completed, whether competition effects are limited in the EU, or if the deal was already cleared in another jurisdiction. This is because the Commission's jurisdiction is not triggered by the (potential) existence of an effect on trade between the Member States, but by the size of the undertakings concerned. Jones, Sufrin and Dunne refer in this respect to the 'long arm' of the Merger Control Regulation. The authors argue that the Commission's scrutiny of some transactions has been extremely politically sensitive in nature.[364] We have already mentioned the *GE/Honeywell* deal,[365] prohibited in the EU and cleared in the US. Another, out of many, example is the *Gencor/Lonrho* transaction,[366] found to be non-problematic by the South African authorities, yet prohibited by the Commission, despite the fact that the parties were claiming that their joint venture had no activities within the EU, was not implemented within the EU, and did not have an immediate, direct and substantial effect within the EU.[367] Such outcomes are a direct consequence not only of differing substantive and procedural standards in different jurisdictions, but also of deferring institutional strength and/or political views about given transactions. They also paint a tough picture for companies operating, or aiming to operate, at a global or internationally oriented scale, who must engage in multiple filings, while hoping for genuine

---

[362] Merger Control Regulation 2004, Article 11.

[363] See EU Merger Working Group, 'Best Practices on Cooperation between EU National Competition Authorities in Merger Review', available at <https://ec.europa.eu/competition/ecn/nca_best_practices_merger_review_en.pdf> accessed 17 April 2020.

[364] Jones, Sufrin and Dunne 2019, pp. 1182–3.

[365] Case COMP/M.2220 *General Electric/Honeywell*, (2001) OJ L 48/1; T-209/01 *Honeywell International*, ECLI:EU:T:2005:455.

[366] Case M.619 *Gencor/Lonrho*, (1997) OJ L 11/30; T-102/96 *Gencor*, ECLI:EU:T:1999:65.

[367] Jones, Sufrin and Dunne 2019, pp. 1184–5; Lianos, Korah and Siciliani 2019, p. 1497 *et seq.*; Fox and Gerard 2017, p. 257 *et seq.*

inter-institutional cooperation between competition authorities, and eventually consistent appraisals in the various jurisdictions concerned. And yet, despite the benefits the EU one-stop-shop system brings about, this is not always the case. As we will see in section 4.3. below, the magnitude of such issues may be further exacerbated by Brexit.

In any event, such problems are acknowledged by the competition authorities throughout the world and steps have been taken, mostly in the context of the work performed within the ICN. The best practices recommendations issued by this network are, however, non-binding and their implementation is left to the discretion of its members, acting through unilateral, bilateral or multilateral arrangements. Thus, in the absence of a true approximation of the merger control standards worldwide, the Merger Control Regulation 2004 foresees the basics of the reciprocity that should be expected in the treatment afforded by third countries to EU companies involved in concentrations overseas. Article 24 provides that whenever the Commission learns of difficulties encountered by EU companies involved in such transactions, or that a third country does not grant these EU undertakings treatment comparable to that granted by the EU to undertakings from that country, the Commission may request a Council mandate for negotiating comparable treatment for the EU undertakings in third countries, while respecting the obligations assumed by the EU under international bilateral or multilateral agreements.

4.3 A brief note on Brexit

The UK's withdrawal from the EU will render it as a third country. This, of course, is bound to have consequences on how the EU concentration control rules are applied to UK companies, but also for the relationship between the Commission and the respective NCA. In late 2018 to early 2019, the UK CMA and the Commission have respectively issued guidance notices on the main implications for stakeholders in case of a so-called 'no-deal' Brexit.[368] In the meantime, the CMA's guidance was withdrawn in March 2020. Many opinions nevertheless arose as to the implications of the UK's leaving the EU, for undertakings being engaged in, or contemplating concentrations somehow connected to the UK.[369]

From the Commission's standpoint, the Brexit Notice 2019 restates in no uncertain terms the exclusive jurisdiction of the Commission in the EU, over concentrations with an EU dimension, based on the one-stop-shop principle. This setup applies, regardless of the nationality or country of incorporation or where the headquarters of a company are located. Brexit thus does not have an impact on the applicability of the Merger Control Regulation 2004 to UK companies when the jurisdictional criteria as set out in this Regulation are fulfilled. But on top of this, post-Brexit, concentrations involving UK companies may actually be subject to dual review, by the Commission under the Merger Control Regulation 2004 and by the CMA, under the domestic UK rules, similar to how the *GE/Honeywell* and *Gencor/Lonrho* deals described above were evaluated in multiple jurisdictions. The Notice also gives

---

[368] Brexit Guidance 2018; Brexit Notice 2019.

[369] Too many to mention, but a Google search 'Brexit merger control' would reveal a myriad blogposts and opinion pieces, written primarily by practitioners.

indications on certain procedural rules relating to the application of the Merger Control Regulation 2004, for example, relating to the relevant date for establishing jurisdiction, the calculation of EU-wide turnover to exclude amounts realised in the UK, and the impossibility of performing inspections pursuant to Article 13 of the Regulation on UK territory. Specific information is provided with regard to pre- and post-notification case referrals from the UK to the Commission, based on Articles 4(5) and 22 of the Merger Control Regulation 2004: importantly, after its withdrawal from the EU, the UK is no longer empowered to refer cases to the Commission or to join referral requests by other Member States under Article 22. As far as substance is concerned, post-Brexit, the Commission is no longer competent to find that a planned concentration would (or would not) significantly impede effective competition in UK national or sub-national markets. Should new (tariff or non-tariff) EU–UK trade barriers arise, the Commission will assess their consequences on a case-by-case basis, while acknowledging that this may have an impact on the competitive assessment including the suitability and viability of remedies. Lastly for now, all Commission decisions already adopted under the Merger Control Regulation 2004 (including decisions imposing conditions and obligations) remain valid after Brexit. As far as already imposed remedies are concerned, some leniency is shown, as parties may request the Commission to waive, modify or substitute commitments which address competition issues in UK markets only, or markets including only the UK and a third country.

4.4 Experience in domestic jurisdictions

In most EU countries the assessment of concentrations follows a roughly similar pattern to the one described in the sections above, with reference to the Commission's approach to M&As. Despite the lack of decentralisation in EU merger control, many jurisdictions have modelled their merger control laws and enforcement techniques after the EU merger control system.[370] Nevertheless, important domestic specificities still exist. We will turn our attention to this discussion in the following paragraphs.

4.4.1 The Netherlands

The control of concentrations in the Netherlands is based on Chapter 5 of the Competition Law (Mw) which came into force in 1998. Certain procedural aspects regarding the enforcement of the said law in relation to concentrations are embedded in the General Act on Administrative Law (Algemene wet bestuursrecht) and a great deal of guidance is contained in the Dutch NCA's soft-law documents, such as the Best Practices on Merger Control Cases (Spelregels bij concentratiezaken) and the Remedies Guidelines (Richtsnoeren Remedies). A high degree of similarity exists between the Dutch and the EU concentration control systems, to the point where one could argue that a comparable effect to the decentralisation of antitrust enforcement is reached in practice.[371] The ACM is tasked to control those transactions that qualify as concentrations (i.e. mergers, acquisitions of control and full-function

---

[370] Van de Gronden 2017, p. 214.

[371] Ibid, pp. 214–15.

concentrative or cooperative joint ventures, according to Article 27 Mw), as long as the turnover thresholds embedded in Article 29 of the same law are met: the aggregate worldwide turnover of the undertakings concerned in the previous calendar year exceeds 150 million EUR and the individual turnover in the Netherlands of each of at least two of the undertakings concerned was at least 30 million EUR in the previous calendar year. Concentrations in specific economic sectors may be held to abide by different thresholds, as is the case in the healthcare sector, or different calculations of the turnover (which normally follows the rules embedded in Book 2 of the Dutch Civil Code), as is the case for financial and credit institutions. In isolated instances, based on Article 29(3) the thresholds may be lowered for certain categories of undertakings, for a period of five years, a period which can be extended: for example, in the healthcare sector the turnover thresholds mentioned above are lowered to 55 million and 10 million EUR respectively, provided that at least two of the undertakings concerned have achieved a turnover of 5.5 million EUR from the provision of healthcare in the preceding calendar year. This rule applies from 1 January 2018 until 1 January 2023.[372]

For transactions that meet these criteria a prior notification to the ACM is required, based on Article 34 Mw. Failure to notify may result in the imposition of fines, alongside the transaction being rendered null and void, based on Article 3:40(2) of Book 3 of the Dutch Civil Code. The mandatory prior notification requirement also entails the prohibition of gun-jumping, which if not observed, may again lead to fines being imposed.[373] However, exemptions from the standstill obligation may be provided by the ACM, especially in cases where the target is in financial distress. Article 34(2) provides a different route for concentrations which involve a healthcare provider that employs 50 or more persons. Such deals need to be first notified to the Dutch Healthcare Authority (NZa), which checks whether the parties have taken due account of the interests of stakeholders. This procedure also entails a standstill obligation. Once the transaction is cleared by the NZa, it then needs to be filed with the ACM, which will perform its investigation in the customary manner. It is expected that upcoming legislative changes in the Netherlands will transfer the procedural check tasks mentioned above, from the NZa to the ACM.[374]

The ACM's appraisal procedure is divided into two phases. In Phase I, based on Article 37(1), the ACM must decide within one month whether the concentration can create competition problems. Of course, the clock may be stopped if further clarifications are needed from the notifying parties. Article 37(2) provides that if the ACM has reason to believe that the concentration could significantly impede effective competition on the Dutch market or part thereof, in particular as a result of the creation or strengthening of a dominant position, it may determine that an authorisation ('vergunning') is required for the transaction to be carried through. Should no authorisation be required, the concentration may be approved,

---

[372] 'Besluit tijdelijke verruiming toepassingsbereik concentratietoezicht op ondernemingen die zorg verlenen', available at <https://wetten.overheid.nl/BWBR0023022/2018-01-01> accessed 25 May 2020.

[373] Fines may, based on Article 74(1) Mw, amount to 900 000 EUR or 10 per cent of the company's annual turnover, whichever is higher.

[374] See <https://gettingthedealthrough.com/area/20/jurisdiction/17/merger-control-netherlands/> accessed 21 April 2020.

possibly with commitments. Phase II of the investigation can thus only be started if competition problems are identified in Phase I. A striking difference with the EU control system is that Phase II is initiated by the parties, who submit a request for an authorisation based on Article 41(1), and not by the ACM. Article 41 also provides that operating without such a licence is prohibited, meaning that the concentration cannot be implemented in its absence. It goes without saying that the refusal by the ACM to grant the authorisation amounts to the concentration being prohibited. If the authorisation is granted, possibly with conditions (most often of a structural nature), the concentration may be implemented. Phase II investigations, which according to Article 44 cannot last longer than 13 weeks, are rare in the Netherlands, and so are prohibition decisions, by refusing to grant the concentration authorisation.[375] Despite the fact that no fast-track procedure exists in Dutch merger control, most cases which do not raise competition concerns are dealt with within three to four weeks, and are cleared via a so-called short-form decision. As far as the sectors in which M&A activity is the most visible in the Netherlands, in recent years, the healthcare sector stood out evidently. The 2019 ACM's Annual Report indicated that the focus in the coming years will also be extended to (among other key sectors) the digital economy.[376] As can be seen in the recent conditional clearance of August 2019 in the *Sanoma Learning/Iddink Group* acquisition, the ACM is indeed following on its promise. In this decision, the ACM made binding remedies dealing with data access and equal access to digital platforms, meant to support innovation in the markets for digital educational materials.[377]

Two striking features of the Dutch merger control system relate to prohibition decisions. First, Article 41(3) Mw contains a specific rule relating to undertakings tasked with the performance of an SGEI. When such an undertaking is engaged in a concentration investigated by the ACM, the authority can refuse to grant the authorisation mentioned in the previous paragraph, only when such a refusal does not impact on the performance of the tasks entrusted to the undertaking in question. Such a ground for the approval of a concentration is not present in the EU Merger Control Regulation 2004, despite the EU legal system's extensive degree of familiarity with the SGEI concept. Second, based on Article 47 Mw, when an authorisation is refused by the ACM, the Minister of Economic Affairs may nevertheless, at the request of the parties (within four weeks from ACM's refusal), issue such an authorisation permitting the concentration, for reasons relating to (economic or non-economic) public interest which outweigh the foreseeable competition restrictions resulting

---

[375] E.g. case 14.0982.24 *Albert Schweitzer Ziekenhuis/Stichting Rivas Zorggroep*, ACM decision of 15 July 2015; Rechtbank Rotterdam, 29 September 2016, ECLI:NL:RBROT:2016:7373.

[376] E.g. ACM's 2018 Phase II clearance decision in the *Bergman Clinics and NL Healthcare Clinics* case, <https://www.acm.nl/en/publications/acm-clears-merger-between-bergman-clinics-and-nl-healthcare-clinics>; ACM's 2018 'failing firm defence' clearance decision in the *ZorgSaam Zorggroep Zeeuws-Vlaanderen and Warmande* case, <https://www.acm.nl/nl/publicaties/groen-licht-overname-warmande-door-zorgsaam-waarborgt-continuiteit-oud erenzorg-zeeuws-vlaanderen>. See also the ACM's recent Annual Reports, available at <https://www.acm.nl/en/about-acm/our-organization/annual-reports>. All links were accessed on 21 April 2020.

[377] See <https://www.acm.nl/en/publications/acm-conditionally-clears-acquisition-iddink-group-sanoma-learni ng> accessed 21 April 2020.

from the concentration. This is a discretionary power of the Minister (and not a right to give instructions to the ACM in specific cases), which obviously comes carrying a high degree of political sensitivity, and therefore should seldom be made use of.[378] Recently, such an authorisation permitting a concentration under strict conditions was issued in relation to PostNL's acquisition of Sandd, which was initially prohibited by the ACM.[379]

Speaking of prohibitions of concentrations, the ACM may adopt such decisions only if the substantive criteria for assessing concentrations are met. Between 1998 until 2007, when legislative changes were operated to the Mw, the Dutch concentration control system used the so-called dominance test. As of 2007, in line with the 2004 amendments to the EU Merger Control Regulation, the Dutch NCA too adopted the SIEC test, which is aimed at identifying significant impediments to effective competition on the Dutch market or a part thereof, the most common example of which being still the creation or strengthening of a dominant position.[380] The ACM investigates horizontal, vertical and conglomerate concentrations, while drawing inspiration as far as the specificities of the SIEC test is concerned from the Commission's Horizontal Merger Guidelines 2004 and Non-Horizontal Merger Guidelines 2008. For example, for horizontal deals the focus of ACM's appraisal is on the actual economic effects of the concentration, including also issues raised by unilateral effects or the potential resulting efficiency gains.[381] Again, similar to the approach adopted under the Merger Control Regulation 2004, the appraisal of the cooperative aspects of full-function joint ventures is not performed with a view to the SIEC test, but with reference to the cartel prohibition requirements embedded in Article 6(1) and (3) Mw.[382]

The decisions adopted by the ACM in relation to concentration transactions which fall under the provisions of the Mw are subject to judicial review, in first instance in front of the District Court Rotterdam (Rechtbank Rotterdam), and in further appeal in front of the Trade and Industry Appeal Tribunal (College van Beroep voor het bedrijfsleven). Both the merging parties and third parties (if they qualify as interested parties under Dutch law) may start appeal proceedings. The intensity of the review performed by the Dutch judiciary is highly reminiscent of the review performed by the EU courts on the Commission decisions adopted based on the Merger Control Regulation 2004. It is thus not surprising that the case-law of the Dutch courts[383] points, for example, to the ACM's discretion regarding the interpretation

---

[378] See Van de Gronden 2017, p. 223; see also <https://gettingthedealthrough.com/area/20/jurisdiction/17/merger-control-netherlands/> accessed 21 April 2020.

[379] E.g. <https://www.rijksoverheid.nl/actueel/nieuws/2019/09/27/onder-strenge-voorwaarden-vergunning-voor-overname-sandd-door-postnl> accessed 25 May 2020.

[380] Mw, Articles 37(2) and 41(2). See also Van de Gronden 2017, p. 218.

[381] Only one example of an 'efficiency case' exists in the ACM's practice: case 6424/427 *Ziekenhuis Walcheren/ Oosterscheldeziekenhuizen*, (2009) available at <https://www.acm.nl/nl/publicaties/publicatie/2359/Ziekenhuis-Walcheren-en-Oosterscheldeziekenhuizen-mogen-onder-voorwaarden-fuseren-concentratiebesluit> accessed 21 April 2020.

[382] Mw, Article 37(3).

[383] E.g. case *Nuon en Essent*, (2006) ECLI:NL:CBB:2006:AZ3274, College van Beroep voor het bedrijfsleven, 28 November 2006.

of complex economic matters, but also to the judges' role in checking whether the evidence provided is materially correct, reliable and consistent, and can support the conclusions of the ACM's appraisal. For example, in 2016 the Trade and Industry Appeal Tribunal annulled the ACM's decision prohibiting the concentration between biscuit producers AA ter Beek and Continental Bakeries,[384] for improper definition of the relevant markets, while the District Court Rotterdam upheld (on appeal by a competitor of the merging parties) the ACM's decision clearing unconditionally the change from joint to sole control of KPN in Reggefiber, since sector-specific regulation applicable to these companies was regarded as adequate to alleviate competition concerns.[385] These courts may annul not only ACM merger decisions, but also ministerial authorisations permitting a concentration, as was recently the case of the District Court Rotterdam annulling the authorisation issued by the Ministry of Economic Affairs in the *PostNL/Sandd* deal, mentioned just above. The District Court argued that the authorisation was tainted by errors, since the Minister had not addressed the competition risks identified by the ACM, while the line of reasoning put forward was rather thin. When writing this book, the Ministry is examining appeal possibilities.[386]

4.4.2 Germany

The control of concentration transactions in Germany is based on Chapter VII of the GWB 1958 (as amended) and is performed by the BKA (Federal Cartel Office), an independent federal authority assigned to the German Federal Ministry of Economic Affairs and Energy. The Monopolkommission, composed of five specialists, issues every two years an expert opinion assessing the level and the foreseeable development of business concentration in Germany. It also issues reports on particular subjects, at the request of the government or on its own initiative.[387] Much like the BKA, the Monopolkommission acts in an independent manner, yet unlike the BKA, it is not regarded as a competition authority, in the meaning of German competition law, since it does not have enforcement powers or the power to adopt binding decisions.[388] The BKA is recognised at EU level as one of the pioneers of competition law enforcement in the EU. This assertion is very much true as far as merger control is concerned as well, the BKA's prolific work in this field regularly covering more than 1000 notified concentrations/year.

The German concentration control system is conceived as an (hybrid) *ex ante* mechanism, prior notification of the transaction to the BKA being necessary,[389] when the jurisdictional tests are met; concentrations that are subject to control and have been examined according to the merger control procedure must again be notified to the BKA after they have been put

---

[384] Case *AA ter Beek and Continental Bakeries v ACM*, College van Beroep voor het bedrijfsleven, 11 February 2016, ECLI:NL:CBB:2016:23.

[385] Case *Vodafone v ACM*, Rechtbank Rotterdam, 12 May 2016, ECLI:NL:RBROT:2016:3476; Appeal, College van Beroep voor het bedrijfsleven, 14 February 2018, ECLI:NL:CBB:2018:16.

[386] See <https://uitspraken.rechtspraak.nl/inziendocument?id=ECLI:NL:RBROT:2020:5122> accessed 11 June 2020.

[387] GWB, Chapter 8.

[388] On the role of the BKA and the Monopolkommission, see Van de Gronden and De Vries 2006.

[389] GWB, Section 39.

into effect.[390] While this may be regarded as a mere formality, sanctions may nevertheless be imposed for failure to notify the effectuation of a merger, based on Section 81 of the GWB. Concentrations in specific sectors must abide by additional rules. For example, in the media sector, separate authorities[391] may intervene in order to ensure the existence of sufficient diversity of opinion. In any case, for non-regulated sectors, the jurisdictional steps are spelled out in in Sections 35 and 37 of the GWB.

First, two alternative thresholds are provided in the former Section: first, the combined turnover of the participating undertakings in the last financial year must exceed 500 million EUR worldwide, and the German turnover of two undertakings concerned must exceed 25 million EUR and 5 million EUR, respectively. The second alternative highlights our previous assertion regarding the BKA being a pioneer in competition law enforcement at EU level, since it was the first European authority to introduce transaction value thresholds, meant to catch those deals falling under the threshold mentioned above, and specifically those occurring in digital markets. This threshold entails: a combined aggregate worldwide turnover of all undertakings concerned exceeding 500 million EUR; an undertaking concerned having a turnover over 25 million EUR in Germany; neither the target nor any other undertaking concerned having a turnover in Germany over 5 million EUR; the consideration for the acquisition exceeding 400 million EUR; and the target having substantial operations in Germany (also known as the *local nexus* clause). Further differences from the EU concentration control performed by the Commission relate to the presence in the GWB of a so-called *de minimis* clause (Section 35(2)) and a *minor market* clause (Section 36(2)(2)), both of which entail concentrations not subject to control and therefore not needing a prior notification.[392] Furthermore, a pragmatic approach is adopted in respect of the so-called *domestic effects* clause in Section 185 of the GWB, which essentially provides that for a concentration to be subject to control and the notification requirement, it must have sufficient effects within Germany. While this provision, and the inherent ambiguity that the notion of *sufficient* effects entails, may leave open important jurisdictional questions, the BKA has issued guidelines meant to assist the stakeholders in asserting whether the notification thresholds are indeed met in a given case.[393]

Second, the notion of concentration has a broader meaning than in EU merger control. According to Section 37 of the GWB, this notion covers not only the acquisition of all or a substantial part of the assets of another company and the acquisition of direct or indirect control over (parts of) another company. The notion of concentration also covers acquisitions of shares resulting in 25 per cent or more or 50 per cent or more shareholding in the target's capital or voting rights and any other combination of undertakings enabling the sole

---

[390] GWB, Section 39(6). See also Bundeskartellamt Information Leaflet 2005 (currently under review).

[391] Kommission zur Ermittlung der Konzentration im Medienbereich – KEK (Commission on Concentration in the Media).

[392] Bundeskartellamt Information Leaflet 2005 (currently under review), pp. 4–5.

[393] Bundeskartellamt, 'Guidance on Domestic Effects in Merger Control', (2014) available at <https://www.bundeskartellamt.de/SharedDocs/Publikation/EN/Merkblaetter/Leaflet%20-%20Guidance%20document%20domestic%20effects%202014.pdf?__blob=publicationFile&v=2> accessed 28 April 2020.

or joint, direct or indirect exercise of a material competitive influence on another undertaking. These last points concerning the notion of concentration in the GWB entail that the BKA is competent to scrutinise non-controlling minority shareholdings, when the 'competitively significant influence test' is met. This may be so independent of the acquired shareholding's level (which at times may be lower than 25 per cent).[394] Cases such as *Axel Springer/Stilke*[395] and *Mainova/Aschaffenburger Versorgungs AG*[396] reveal that the BKA construes this threshold broadly: such influence is normally found where the minority shareholder's interests need to be taken into account by the target's other shareholders and management. The influence must factually impact the target's behaviour, without necessarily being decisive. Several factors, evaluated on a case-by-case basis, may lead to this conclusion: the ability to appoint the members of the board of directors, significant veto rights, personal interlocks, and so on.[397]

Similar to the EU merger control mechanism, the BKA uses the SIEC appraisal test when scrutinising concentrations, however, only since 2013, when the shift from the dominance test to SIEC was made in German merger control. The concept of dominance, however, continues to be relevant today, as evidenced by the fact that the 2012 Guidance on Substantive Merger Control,[398] which explains how the single firm and collective dominance scenarios are to be interpreted in horizontal, vertical and conglomerate mergers, continues to play a role in the BKA's work. The GWB (Section 18) interprets dominance as situations where an undertaking has no competitors, is not exposed to substantial competition, or has a paramount market position in relation to its competitors. This is presumed to be the case where an undertaking has a market share of at least 40 per cent, or three or fewer undertakings have a combined market share of at least 50 per cent (i.e. collective dominance). Keeping up with the digitalisation trends, the GWB also sheds light on the factors which should be taken into account when discussing dominance in the context of multi-sided markets and networks, and acknowledges that markets may exist for the purpose of competition investigations, irrespective of whether goods or services are provided free of charge.[399] Moving on, the BKA interprets the concept of SIEC as situations where, through the merger, the companies involved gain a scope of action that is no longer sufficiently controlled by competition. This would enable a company to raise its prices, lower product quality, cut back on innovation investments or worsen its offer in any other way without incurring the risk of losing its customers. From this point on, there are no major surprises, since the German control analytical framework is quite consistent with the EU merger control approach, as far as theories of harm are concerned. Certain somewhat peculiar aspects are nevertheless worth mentioning:

---

[394] E.g. case *A-TEC Industries/Norddeutsche Affinerie*, (2008) OLG Düsseldorf, Kart 5/08 (V), WuW/E DE-R 2462.

[395] Case *Axel Springer/Stilke*, (1997) WuW/E DE-R 607.

[396] Case *Mainova/Aschaffenburger Versorgungs AG*, (2004) VI-2 Kart 14/04 (V), WuW/E DE-R 1639.

[397] Knable Gotts 2012; Rusu 2014 (b); Schmidt 2013; Riis-Madsen, Stephanou and Kehoe 2012.

[398] See <https://www.bundeskartellamt.de/SharedDocs/Publikation/EN/Leitlinien/Guidance%20-%20Substantive%20Merger%20Control.pdf?__blob=publicationFile&v=6> accessed 28 April 2020.

[399] GWB, Section 18(2a) and (3a).

Section 36 of the GWB specifically acknowledges as countervailing factors the efficiency defence and the failing firm defence in newspapers or magazine publishing markets, and it also provides for the *minor market* clause mentioned above; all these items prevent the prohibition of a transaction that would otherwise significantly impact effective competition, in particular through the creation or strengthening of a dominant position. Joint ventures follow a different assessment regime than under the EU merger control system: they must be assessed against the SIEC test and, in addition, all cooperative aspects of the joint venture must be reviewed under the restrictive practices provisions of the GWB (thus not as part of the merger control process). This assessment may be performed either in parallel or after the merger procedure (e.g. after a merger control clearance). Similarly, the so-called ancillary restraints between the merging parties are not automatically cleared together with the concentration itself. Instead, they may be reviewed under the restrictive practices provisions of the GWB, yet they are often exempted if they are necessary and indispensable to the successful implementation of the concentration and the EU law and practice are taken into account.[400]

The procedural blueprint again follows the EU merger control system, with two investigation phases:[401] Phase I (lasting for a maximum of one month) in which the BKA may (conditionally or unconditionally) clear the transaction, or decide to start in-depth investigations. Phase II proceedings (lasting for four months) may be closed by way of formal decision, (conditionally or unconditionally) clearing the concentration, or in the event the substantive test requirements are met, and no exception may be raised, based on Section 36(1) and (2), the BKA may prohibit the deal. In the event remedies are imposed in order to clear a merger, these may not amount to continued control of the behaviour of the undertakings involved.[402] Prohibitions are rare,[403] much like in EU merger control, yet a distinctive feature of German merger control is that BKA prohibition decisions may be overruled by the Federal Minister for Economic Affairs and Energy. While the BKA is adamant about its task to control concentrations solely from a competition law perspective, if a transaction's competition restraints are outweighed by advantages to the economy as a whole or if the transaction is justified by overriding public interests, the Minister has nevertheless the discretion to clear it. Section 42 of the GWB provides the conditions under which such a ministerial authorisation may be adopted. Interestingly, the competitiveness of the undertakings concerned in markets outside Germany shall be taken into account, which points to a national champion type of a policy. However, this is toned down by making it clear that ministerial authorisations may only be granted if the scope of the competition restraint does not jeopardise the market economy system. Ministerial authorisations are also rare[404] and, just like all Phase

---

[400] See <https://gettingthedealthrough.com/area/20/jurisdiction/11/merger-control-germany/> accessed 28 April 2020.

[401] GWB, Section 40.

[402] GWB, Section 40(3). See also Bundeskartellamt Remedies Guidance 2017.

[403] E.g. case *CTS Eventim/Four Artists*, B6-35/17, Bundeskartellamt, 23 November 2017.

[404] E.g. the conditional authorisation given for the merger between E.ON and Ruhrgas discussed in section 3.1.2 above and the conditional authorisation in the transaction between EDEKA and Kaiser's Tengelmann, 17 March 2016;

II decisions of the BKA, are subject to review by the Higher Regional Court of Düsseldorf, and further review by the Federal Court of Justice only on points of law. Third parties too may appeal such decisions, but only if they were granted admission as interveners during the BKA proceedings, and if they manage to prove that their competitive interests are materially affected by the transaction.

Lastly for now, the BKA has always been at the forefront of the debate relating to digitalisation and merger control.[405] A good part of the proposals discussed in section 3.3.8 above find their roots in documents and initiatives in which the BKA has had a leading role.[406] It is thus no surprise that the recent draft Act on Digitalisation of German Competition Law (GWB-Digitalisierungsgesetz)[407] contains concepts which should allow more effective enforcement in digital markets. This 2019 draft Act also aims to better focus the merger control exercise in Germany, for example by increasing certain elements of the jurisdictional and *de minimis* thresholds and by abolishing the post-merger completion notification to the BKA. For allowing better assessment of complex cases the Phase II timetable may be increased from four to five months, while the rules on ministerial approvals may also be streamlined.

4.4.3 Austria

In Austria, Part I, Chapter III of the Cartel Act 2005 (Kartellgesetz) contains rules applicable to concentrations (including the so-called media mergers). The Competition Act (Wetbewerbsgesetz), as amended in 2017, contains procedural and enforcement rules applicable in Austrian merger control.

Section 7 of the Kartellgesetz defines the transactions falling under the Act. These include not only classic M&A deals and full-function joint ventures, but also non-controlling minority shareholdings: that is, the direct or indirect acquisition of shares in a target if post-acquisition the shareholding is or exceeds 25 per cent, transactions resulting in at least half of the management or members of the supervisory boards of two or more undertakings being identical, or any other connection of undertakings which allows one undertaking to have a

---

see <https://www.bundeskartellamt.de/SharedDocs/Meldung/EN/Meldungen%20News%20Karussell/2017/25_08_2017_OLG_EDEKA_KT.html> accessed 19 June 2020.

[405] Developments relating to digitalisation and merger control are on the agenda of NCAs in other Member States too. In section 4 of Chapter 6 we discussed the 2020 Position Paper of the French NCA (L'Autorité de la concurrence 2020). The role of the so-called structuring platforms in the digital economy has implications for the merger control system, too, according to this NCA. As far as mergers falling below the notification thresholds are concerned, it is therefore proposed, for example, to have the Commission and the NCAs informed of mergers implemented by structuring platforms, or to permit voluntary notifications by the concerned undertakings, thus allowing platforms to remove doubts about future possible intervention by competition authorities. See also 'French Competition Authority Proposes Competition Reforms for Digital Platforms', available at <https://www.osborneclarke.com/insights/french-competition-authority-proposes-competition-reforms-digital-platforms/> accessed 19 June 2020.

[406] E.g. Competition Law and Data 2016; Joint Proposal 2019; Market Power of Platforms and Networks 2016.

[407] See   <https://www.d-kart.de/wp-content/uploads/2019/10/GWB-Digitalisierungsgesetz-Fassung-Ressortabst-immung.pdf> accessed 28 April 2020.

direct or indirect dominant influence over another undertaking.[408] The turnover thresholds contained in Section 9 point to the combined worldwide turnover of all the undertakings concerned exceeding 300 million EUR; the combined Austrian turnover of all the undertakings concerned exceeding 30 million EUR; and the individual worldwide turnover of at least two of the undertakings concerned each exceeding 5 million EUR. A recent amendment of the Kartellgesetz introduced a new threshold, linked to the value of the transaction, meant to catch acquisitions of low turnover, yet 'pricy' targets. These are transactions which, on top of specific worldwide and domestic turnover requirements, must exceed 200 million EUR value of consideration, and the target is active to a large extent on the Austrian market.[409] Media mergers, on the other hand, report to different (i.e. considerably higher) turnover thresholds.

Section 9 also provides that transactions meeting the above stated thresholds must be notified to the Austrian Federal Competition Authority (Bundeswettbewerbsbehörde) before their implementation. This authority, together with the Federal Cartel Prosecutor (Bundeskartellanwalt), as statutory/official parties,[410] share jurisdiction in Phase I merger control investigations (lasting for four weeks, according to Section 10 of the Kartellgesetz). The Federal Competition Authority is also 'advised' by the Competition Commission (Wettbewerbskommission) as far as requesting the initiation of in-depth investigations. Both the Federal Competition Authority and the Federal Cartel Prosecutor have the competence to initiate Phase II merger control proceedings (lasting for five months, according to Section 14 of the Kartellgesetz), in front of the Cartel Court (Kartellgericht), which is part of the Higher Regional Court of Vienna. It is the Cartel Court that adopts merger control decisions (conditionally or unconditionally) clearing or prohibiting the transaction. In other words, the Federal Competition Authority and the Federal Cartel Prosecutor do not clear per se concentrations in Phase I. They may simply choose not to request the initiation of Phase II proceedings, at times because they are convinced by the remedies proposed by the notifying parties in Phase I. The institutional and procedural framework in Austrian merger control is thus quite complex, and differs significantly from the EU setup.

The same assertion stands as far as the substantive assessment of concentrations is concerned: Section 12 of the Kartellgesetz requires the Cartel Court to appraise mergers on the basis of the dominance test: that is, whether the transaction creates or strengthens a dominant position. This test nevertheless is capable to accommodate various theories of harm, such as vertical and conglomerate effects, and collective dominance. Uncertainty still exists as far as the possibility to tackle unilateral effects in oligopolistic markets, under this test.[411] The

---

[408] E.g. cases BWB/Z-2121 *Saubermacher Dienstleistungs-AG/Kärntner Restmüllverwertungs GmbH,* (2013) available at <https://www.bwb.gv.at/zusammenschluesse/zusammenschluss/id/2108/>; BWB/Z-2660 *Funke Mediengruppe GmbH & Co. KGaA/Axel Springer Media Impact GmbH & Co. KG,* (2015) available at <https://www.bwb.gv.at/news/news_2015/detail/news/z_2660_funke_mediengruppe_gmbh_co_kg_und_axel_springer_se/>. Both Links were accessed on 23 April 2020.

[409] Kartellgesetz, Section 9(4).

[410] Ibid, Sections 11, 40.

[411] See <https://gettingthedealthrough.com/area/20/jurisdiction/25/merger-control-austria/> accessed 23 April 2020.

concept of dominance is again differently conceived, when compared to its EU law meaning. According to Section 4, dominance is presumed where an undertaking's market share is greater than 30 per cent, or greater than 5 per cent, and it is facing competition from no more than two other undertakings; or greater than 5 per cent and it is one of the four largest undertakings on the relevant market that together hold at least 80 per cent of the relevant market. Collective dominance is also presumed where a group of three or fewer undertakings has a market share of at least 50 per cent or a group of five or fewer undertakings has a share of at least two-thirds of the relevant market. These presumptions entail that it is the notifying parties that must prove that their transaction will not lead to such market dominance. Furthermore, unlike the Merger Control Regulation 2004, the Kartellgesetz does not put forward a specific substantive test for assessing the cooperative aspects of full-function joint ventures. Also, media mergers (even those that would be caught under the Merger Control Regulation 2004) will be investigated by the Austrian authorities under a specific test, which checks their impact on media diversity.[412] On a connected note, the Cartel Court may, notwithstanding the competition analysis discussed above, clear a concentration which is necessary and economically justified to maintain or improve international competitiveness of the undertakings concerned. Furthermore, the efficiency defence is actually embedded in the Kartellgesetz (Section 2.1). The failing firm defence is, however, not mentioned in the Cartel Act 2005. Nevertheless, the Supreme Court (which acts as appellate body when it comes to the Cartel Court's merger control decisions), has accepted this defence in practice when it comes to restructuring concentrations which strengthen a dominant position.[413] Speaking of judicial review, the Cartel Court's decisions may only be appealed against by the merging parties and the statutory/official parties. Third parties do not enjoy this right, regardless of their interest or their previous involvement in the Cartel Court's proceedings.

Overall, more than 400 merger control cases are handled by the Austrian authorities every year. Very few (less than ten cases/year), however, enter Phase II investigations, while prohibitions are extremely rare.

5 CONCLUSIONS

Concentration control in the EU has come of age. While the Commission's concentration control work, based on the Merger Control Regulation(s), differs in certain important respects from the approach adopted in EU antitrust law, the end goals of these two branches of competition law remain congruent. So are the theories of harm used, the key concepts and principles employed, the investigation methods used, and the cooperation relationship between the Commission and the NCAs. A stark difference between antitrust and merger control enforcement, though, relates to the lack of decentralisation of the enforcement of the EU merger control rules. Nevertheless, most EU Member States have steadily aligned

---

[412] Kartellgesetz, Section 13.

[413] See <https://gettingthedealthrough.com/area/20/jurisdiction/25/merger-control-austria/> accessed 23 April 2020.

their domestic concentration control systems to the EU model, thus creating a (more or less) coherent M&A oversight mechanism in the EU. This does not, however, mean that domestic institutional, substantive and procedural specificities ceased to exist. To the contrary, some of the national law examples we discussed above prove that some Member States retained strong views about how concentrations should be handled on their own territories.

While in both substance and enforcement, the Commission and the domestic authorities have developed modern tools for controlling concentration transactions in the past three decades, the concentration control system must be perceived as constantly evolving. Economic developments continuously pose challenges to the manner in which merger control law(s) should be conceived and applied. One of the latest of such challenges stems from the novelties brought about by the digital era. Both the Commission and the NCAs have showed openness to engage with concentrations occurring in digital markets. The coming years will bring about interesting developments in this respect.

PART V

COMPETITION RULES ADDRESSED TO THE MEMBER STATES

11

The state and competition

1 INTRODUCTION

One of the aims of competition law is to stimulate competition between undertakings and, accordingly, most rules of this area of law are addressed at undertakings. However, the competition process could also be hindered by actions of the state. For that reason, special rules dealing with these actions are developed in EU competition law. The relationship between the state and competition has given rise to complicated questions. It should be noted that EU Internal Market law and, more in particular, the Treaty provisions on free movement, deal with the policies of the Member States and the effect of these policies on competition in the Internal Market. It is therefore of great importance to explore to which state actions the EU competition law and Internal Market law rules apply. Many national laws and policies are capable of influencing competition. From that perspective, it may seem fit to review a wide range of state measures under the competition law rules. However, the CJEU has decided to walk down another avenue: measures of Member States fall within the ambit of EU competition law, if these measures are directly related to the operation of undertakings.[1] If this is not the case, only EU Internal Market law may provide the relevant framework for review. In the event that state actions are directly related to the operation of undertakings, both the Treaty provisions on competition and the EU Internal Market rules may apply. In other words, only specific links with undertakings justify applying the competition rules to undertakings.

It is apparent from the setup of the EU competition law rules and the case-law of the EU courts that in three categories of measures specific links occur between the state and undertakings. The first category concerns state measures that jeopardise the useful effect of the Treaty provisions on competition. In the case-law of the CJEU an approach is developed in order to preclude Member States from taking such measures.[2] This approach is referred to as the useful effect doctrine. At the centre of the second category of measures is Article 106 TFEU. This provision governs public undertakings and undertakings having exclusive and special rights. The third category focuses on state aid given to undertakings and is regulated

---

[1] Cf. cases C-2/91 *Meng*, ECLI:EU:C:1993:885; C-245/91 *Ohra*, ECLI:EU:C:1993:887.

[2] E.g. cases C-13/77 *INNO/ATAB*, ECLI:EU:C:1977:185; C-198/01 *CIF*, ECLI:EU:C:2003:430.

by Articles 107–109 TFEU. As the last category is of great importance in legal practice, the next chapter of this book is entirely devoted to the subject of state aid.

In this chapter the useful effect doctrine as well as Article 106 TFEU will be discussed. The evolution of the second limb of Article 106 TFEU has given rise to the emergence of the concept of Services of General Economic Interest (SGEI). This concept is closely related to public services. As SGEIs enable Member States to strike a balance between competition and goals of public (and social) interest and, accordingly, are of great importance for the national welfare states, special attention will be paid to these services. The issues surrounding the state and competition have prompted national legislatures to adopt laws governing these issues. A few examples will be discussed in this chapter. At the end of this chapter a set of conclusions will be drawn.

2 THE USEFUL EFFECT DOCTRINE

According to Article 4(3) TEU, the Member States are obliged to take any measure in order to fulfil their obligations under EU law. This principle is referred to as Union loyalty or sincere cooperation. Before the entering into force of the Treaty of Lisbon, this principle was enshrined in Article 5 of the TEC. From this Treaty provision the CJEU has derived the obligation for the Member States not to adopt any measure that is capable of jeopardising the useful effect of Article 101 TFEU or Article 102 TFEU.[3] In the past, reference was also made to Article 3(f) (later sub (g)),[4] which sets out that the Union was based on a system of undistorted competition. This reference was left out in later case-law[5] and the text underlining the importance of undistorted competition was moved from the Treaty to Protocol 27 annexed to the Treaty of Lisbon.[6]

2.1 Union loyalty and the Treaty provisions on competition

All in all, Article 4(3) TEU in combination with Article 101 TFEU or Article 102 TFEU precludes Member States from taking measures that run counter to the ban on anti-competitive agreements or on the abuse of dominance, respectively.[7] It should be noted that the majority of the case-law on the useful effect doctrine is concerned with Article 101 TFEU. Only a few cases are related to Article 102 TFEU. In our view, this difference can be explained by pointing to Article 106 TFEU, which is about undertakings having special rights and their position being reinforced by the government. This Treaty provision focuses on undertakings having a strong position on the market, which is exactly what Article 102 TFEU aims to regulate. For

---

[3] Case C-13/77 *INNO/ATAB*, ECLI:EU:C:1977:185.

[4] Ibid, par. 29.

[5] E.g. case C-35/96 *Commission v Italy*, ECLI:EU:C:1998:303.

[6] Internal Market and Competition Protocol 2008.

[7] E.g. joined cases C-184 to 187, C-194, C-195 and C-208/13 *API*, ECLI:EU:C:2014:2147; joined cases C-532 and C-538/15 *Eurosaneamientos*, ECLI:EU:C:2016:932.

that reason, in many cases it is not necessary to carry out a review under Article 4(3) TEU in conjunction with Article 102 TFEU, as Article 106(1) TFEU in combination with Article 102 TFEU provide an adequate framework to that effect.

Article 4(3) TEU in conjunction with Article 101 TFEU may be infringed by two means. First, a violation is found if a Member State requires or encourages the adoption of practices (such as an agreement) contrary to Article 101 TFEU or reinforces the effects of these practices.[8] Accordingly, in such circumstances a clear link exists between action taken by a state body and an anti-competitive practice of undertakings. The state action can be composed of: requiring a certain conduct, encouraging a certain conduct, or reinforcing the effects of a certain conduct. If, for example, a piece of national law obliges undertakings to be engaged in price fixing cartels, the state requires undertakings to set up anti-competitive practices. Another example is that a state stimulates undertakings to agree on price fixing by promising particular benefits, if such an agreement is concluded. Lastly, there could be reinforcement of the effects of practices contrary to Article 101 TFEU if a price cartel is declared generally binding by the government.

Second, a violation is found if the state divests its own rules of the character of legislation by delegating to undertakings the responsibility for intervening on the market.[9] In that event, there is improper delegation of powers from the state to economic operators. If, for instance, a state body delegates the power to allocate production quotas for the relevant market players to undertakings or an association of undertakings, Article 4(3) TEU in conjunction with Article 101 TFEU are infringed.[10]

As already stated, only limited case-law is available as regards Article 102 TFEU in relation to Article 4(3) TEU. According to the judgments that do deal with these two provisions, Member States are precluded from placing an undertaking in a position of economic strength in order to enable this undertaking to prevent competition, leading to behaviour independent of its competitors and of its customers and consumers.[11]

The question has arisen as to whether a state measure depriving the EU competition rules from their useful effect could be justifiable. Can a Member State rely on an exception in cases involving the useful effect doctrine? The CJEU has already hinted at this possibility in *Pavlov*.[12] At issue in this case was the question whether a Dutch collective pension scheme, which was declared generally binding by the government for self-employed medical specialists, was compatible with the useful effect doctrine. The CJEU ruled that the scheme under review was compatible with EU law, as it was designed to realise objectives in the social domain.[13] The question was left open whether the state measure concerned did not constitute an infringement or whether it was restrictive, but justifiable on the basis of an exception.

---

[8] E.g. joined cases C-184 to 187, C-194, C-195 and C-208/13 *API*, ECLI:EU:C:2014:2147, par. 29; joined cases C-532 and C-538/15 *Eurosaneamientos*, ECLI:EU:C:2016:932, par. 35.

[9] Ibid.

[10] Case C-198/01 *CIF*, ECLI:EU:C:2003:430.

[11] Cases 85/76 *Hoffmann-La Roche*, ECLI:EU:C:1979:36, par. 38; C-38/97 *Librandi*, ECLI:EU:C:1998:454, par. 27.

[12] Joined cases C-180 and C-184/98 *Pavlov*, ECLI:EU:C:2000:428.

[13] Ibid, par. 98.

In *API*,[14] which concerned the transport sector in Italy, the CJEU shed more light on the matter of justification. At issue was the level of the minimum operating costs, which was determined by a body representing the transport companies. The CJEU found that the useful effect of Article 101 TFEU was jeopardised, as pursuant to the applicable rules of Italian law, the decisions taken by this body were mandatory for operators in the transport sector. The CJEU, however, moved on to examine whether these decisions were justifiable given the objectives pursued. It specifically referred to the approach developed in *Wouters*.[15] As was outlined in section 2.2.3 of Chapter 5, in this case the CJEU held that anti-competitive practices may be permitted if the restrictive effects caused are inherent to the objectives to be achieved. This exception is referred to as the 'EU-style Rule of Reason'. The aim of the Italian rules at stake was to protect road safety. The CJEU found, however, that fixing the minimum operating costs was not appropriate to achieve this goal and that, therefore, these rules went beyond what was necessary to achieve the said goal. Further case-law must be awaited, but it is clear that in *API* the CJEU took an enormous leap in the process of accepting that an exception is available in cases involving the useful effect doctrine.

2.2 The decentralised application of the useful effect doctrine

As with Articles 101 and 102 TFEU, the norms derived from Article 4(3) TEU in conjunction with Article 101 TFEU or Article 102 TFEU have direct effect. This entails that domestic courts must review national legislation and other national measures under Article 4(3) TEU in conjunction with Article 101 TFEU or Article 102 TFEU, if the compatibility with the useful effect doctrine is at stake.

On top of that, the CJEU has decided in *CIF* that an NCA must also set aside rules of national law that are incompatible with this doctrine. The CJEU pointed out that the duty to disapply national legislation contravening EU law does not only apply to national courts but to all organs of the state too, including administrative authorities.[16] In this regard, the CJEU referred to its judgment in *Fratelli Costanzo*,[17] where it held that all organs of the administration, including decentralised authorities such as municipalities, are obliged to apply directive provisions having direct effect. In this case, the CJEU concluded that the municipality concerned had to refrain from giving effect to provisions of national law which conflicted with the directive provision having such effect.

It is apparent from *CIF* that an NCA not only has the power, but even the duty to apply the useful effect doctrine in cases where national legislation is found to deprive Article 101 TFEU or Article 102 TFEU of their useful effect. Moreover, it seems that every national authority having been entrusted with the task to apply Articles 101 and 102 TFEU is also competent to review national legislation under the useful effect doctrine. It could be argued that, to a certain extent, the CJEU has created a new competence for NCAs to scrutinise

---

[14] Joined cases C-184 to 187, C-194, C-195 and C-208/13 *API*, ECLI:EU:C:2014:2147.

[15] Case C-309/99 *Wouters*, ECLIEU:C:2002:98.

[16] Case C-198/01 *CIF*, ECLI:EU:C:2003:430, par. 49.

[17] Case 103/88 *Fratelli Costanzo*, ECLI:EU:C:1989:256.

whether a piece of national legislation gives rise to competition concerns.[18] This could lead to an incidental review by an NCA of a certain national law in a particular enforcement case undertaken against firms restricting competition by aligning their commercial policies with these laws.[19] If the outcome of this review points to the incompatibility with the useful effect doctrine, the NCA must act as if this national law does not exist and, as a result, must reach the conclusion that the undertakings concerned have violated EU competition law.[20] For instance, if a national law requires the conclusion of a price cartel, the NCA must decide that it is not permitted for the undertakings involved to comply with this law and that, by doing so, they have violated Article 101 TFEU.

This raises the question how this approach sits with the principle of legal certainty. Companies may usually assume that laws adopted by the state must be observed, rather than ignored. In order to solve this problem of legal certainty, the CJEU has held in *CIF* that, as long as national legislation does not leave any room for manoeuvre and the NCA decision finding the incompatibility has not become final, the undertakings concerned cannot be penalised.[21] However, if they continue to act in accordance with this legislation once the NCA decision has become final, sanctions may be imposed.[22] In other words, future anti-competitive conduct may and must even be subject to enforcement actions by the NCA. It should be noted that in the event that legislation contrary to the useful effect doctrine allows for autonomous actions on the part of the undertakings, it is, in the CJEU's view, appropriate not only to penalise future, but also past conduct. The reason for this is that under such legislation, undertakings remain subject to Articles 101 and 102 TFEU.[23] In this respect, it should be noted that according to settled case-law, only in the event that national legislation eliminates any possibility of competitive activity, the restrictive effects cannot be attributed to the undertakings concerned and, accordingly, solely in those circumstances they cannot be held liable.[24] If the national laws only confine themselves to encouraging or making possible anti-competitive behaviour, undertakings remain liable for violating Article 101 TFEU or Article 102 TFEU. However, to this finding the CJEU also added that national laws encouraging or making possible anti-competitive conduct may be regarded as a mitigating factor for the calculation of the level of the penalties imposed.[25]

In *CIF*, the CJEU only dealt with the liability of the undertakings complying with anti-competitive national laws. The other side of the coin is, of course, the liability of the Member State that has enacted such laws. It should be noted that in EU law an approach is developed addressing this matter, which entails that Member States may be held liable for damages caused by national laws infringing the useful effect doctrine. It is settled case-law

---

[18] Steyger 2003; Mortelmans 2003.

[19] Verschuur 2010, p. 60.

[20] Ibid.

[21] See case C-198/01 *CIF*, ECLI:EU:C:2003:430, par. 53–55.

[22] Ibid, par. 55.

[23] Ibid, par. 56.

[24] Joined cases C-359 and C-379/95 *Ladbroke*, ECLI:EU:C:1997:531, par. 33.

[25] Case C-198/01 *CIF*, ECLI:EU:C:2003:430, par. 57.

that measures adopted by Member States in violation of EU law may give rise to state liability, if: (1) these measures amount to a sufficiently serious breach, (2) the provisions of EU law at issue confer rights upon individuals, and (3) a causal link exists between the breach of the obligation resting on the state and the damages suffered.[26] It goes without saying that this case-law also applies to national measures being incompatible with the useful effect doctrine. If the conditions set out in the case-law are satisfied, the Member State concerned is obliged to grant compensation. However, it has to be pointed out that the condition of sufficiently serious breach amounts to a hurdle that is hard to overcome, as in many cases an in-depth analysis is required as to whether the national measure under review is incompatible with the useful effect doctrine. Furthermore, the quantification of the harm suffered may also give rise to a heated legal debate.

3 ARTICLE 106 TFEU

The TFEU contains one specific set of rules dealing with a special group of undertakings, which are laid down in Article 106 TFEU. Public undertakings or undertakings having exclusive or special rights are governed by this Treaty provision. At first, the prohibition addressed to the Member States, which is enshrined in Article 106(1) TFEU and which has given rise to complicated case-law, will be discussed. Subsequently, attention will be paid to the exception, which is laid down in paragraph 2 of this Treaty provision, and is centred around the concept of SGEIs. Then, Article 106(3) TFEU, which confers certain powers upon the Commission, will be briefly dealt with.

3.1 Article 106(1) TFEU: the special undertakings and the state

When the Treaty of Rome, establishing the EEC, was drafted, it was acknowledged that the competition process could not only be distorted by private firms, but also by state actions. Therefore, a provision, which is now Article 106(1) TFEU, was inserted in the Treaty, imposing specific obligations on the Member States. With regard to public undertakings and undertakings granted exclusive or special rights, Member States are precluded from adopting measures that run contrary to the Treaty provisions, in particular Article 18 TFEU (the ban on discrimination on grounds of nationality) and Articles 101–107 TFEU. It is apparent from the references made, that the competition rules play an important role in applying Article 106(1) TFEU. The case-law of the CJEU dealing with this Treaty provision is mainly concerned with Article 102 TFEU (dominance) rather than with the other rules contained in the Treaty. In our view, this is for obvious reasons, as at the heart of Article 106(1) TFEU are undertakings that have obtained market power due to measures taken by the state.

In fact, two conditions must be distinguished for establishing an infringement of Article 106(1) TFEU. First, the measures taken by the state apply to a special group of undertakings.

---

[26] E.g. joined cases C-46 and C-48/93 *Brasserie du Pêcheur*, ECLI:EU:C:1996:79; joined cases C-6 and C-9/90 *Francovich and Bonifaci*, ECLI:EU:C:1991:428.

Second, these measures give rise to competition issues. As the majority of the judgments delivered under Article 106(1) TFEU are related to Article 102 TFEU, the discussion will only focus on the dominance problems resulting from the state measures taken.

Below, these two conditions will be explored. In this regard, it must be noted that, for Article 106(1) TFEU to be applicable, the trade between the Member States must also be influenced. This condition is inherent to almost all provisions of EU competition law, including Articles 101 and 102 TFEU. As in cases on cartels and abuse of dominance, a potential effect suffices for finding an intra-Union effect in a case involving Article 106(1) TFEU.[27]

3.1.1 First condition: the special undertakings

It is striking that the TFEU does not define what is meant by 'public undertakings', 'exclusive rights' and 'special rights'. However, such definitions can be found in the Transparency Directive 2006, which imposes obligations of an institutional nature upon a Member State, when creating and regulating undertakings falling within the scope of Article 106(1) TFEU.

According to Article 2(b) of this Directive, a public undertaking is any undertaking over which the public authorities of a Member State may exercise directly or indirectly a dominant influence. This influence could result from ownership, financial participation, or the rules governing the undertaking concerned. In practice, most of the case-law on Article 106(1) TFEU concerns undertakings having exclusive or special rights. Accordingly, it is of great importance to give a definition of these two types of rights.

Article 1(f) of the Directive provides that the term exclusive rights means rights that are granted by a Member State to one undertaking through any kind of instrument reserving it the right to provide a particular service or to be engaged in a certain activity within a given geographical area. In other words, the undertaking having such rights is the sole entity entitled to provide this service or to be engaged in this activity. As a rule, exclusive rights create monopoly power for the enterprises being granted these rights.

There is a special right pursuant to Article 1(g) of the Directive, if a limited number of undertakings are granted the right to provide a particular service or to be engaged in a certain activity. From the drafting of this provision it is clear that the term special rights means that two or more enterprises operate on a market within a given geographical area.

Exclusive and special rights have in common that the number of companies which are given access to a certain market is limited. It goes without saying that such actions have their bearing on the competition process. The essential difference between the two types of rights is that an exclusive right only allows for one player on the market, whereas special rights permit more players to operate on the market.

3.1.2 Second condition: competition issues

In deciding whether the creation of public undertakings or creating exclusive or special rights amounts to an infringement, the CJEU could, theoretically, opt for four approaches.[28] In the *absolute sovereignty approach* a Member State has the absolute competence in relation to

---

[27] E.g. case C-475/99 *Ambulanz Glöckner*, ECLI:EU:C:2001:577, par. 48.

[28] Edward and Hoskins 1995, p. 159; Schweitzer 2011, pp. 16–17.

legal monopolies and similar matters, which means that no violation of Article 106(1) TFEU can be found. According to the *absolute competition approach*, the granting of exclusive or special rights results in a per se violation of Article 106(1) TFEU. It is not a surprise that these two approaches were too drastic to be seriously considered. A choice had to be made between the following two possibilities: the *limited sovereignty approach*, according to which the creation of legal monopolies and similar positions were permitted as long as this would not contravene the EU competition law rules, and the *limited competition approach*, entailing that creating monopolies and similar positions is only permitted where this is justified by a public interest goal.

In some old cases, the CJEU had suggested that it adhered to the *limited competition approach*, by deciding that the mere creation of, for example, an exclusive right amounts to a violation under Article 106(1) TFEU and that, accordingly, this action was only acceptable if a justification ground could be relied upon. In *Corbeau*,[29] it held that a statutory monopoly for mail delivery was only permitted if an exception could be relied upon and, by putting forward this point of view, it hinted that this statutory monopoly in itself implied an infringement. In later case-law, however, the CJEU took another route by stressing that the sole granting of exclusive or special rights or the creation of a public undertaking does not automatically lead to the conclusion that Article 106(1) TFEU is violated. Although this inevitably impacts the competition process, the CJEU required in this case-law that the state measure concerned somehow leads to a violation of Article 102 TFEU. It should be recalled that the applicability of Article 106(1) TFEU is combined with that of another Treaty provision, which is in most of the cases Article 102 TFEU. In dominance cases, the CJEU has made it clear that the mere existence of a dominant position does not automatically lead to a violation of Article 102 TFEU. In the same vein, it was held that Article 106(1) TFEU in combination with Article 102 TFEU were only violated if the state measure under review (the granting of exclusive or special rights, or the creation of a public undertaking) leads to an abuse of dominance within the meaning of Article 102 TFEU. The test to be carried out is whether the undertaking concerned is led by the exclusive or special rights granted to abuse its dominant position, or whether those rights are liable to create a situation in which that undertaking is led to be engaged in abusive behaviour.[30] In other words, the state measure at stake forces or makes an enterprise to abuse its dominant position. It is clear that, finally, the CJEU has adopted the *limited sovereignty approach* in relation to Article 106(1) TFEU[31] and, by doing so, has given considerable leeway to the Member States for granting exclusive and special rights, as well as creating public undertakings.

It is apparent from the test developed in this approach that somehow a link must be established between the state measure under review and the abusive behaviour concerned. To a certain extent, this abuse has to be imputed to the public authority having given a strong position to an undertaking. This entails that in order to find an infringement, at first, it should

---

[29] Case C-320/90 *Corbeau*, ECLI:EU:C:1993:198.

[30] E.g. joined cases C-115, C-116 and C-117/97 *Brentjens*, ECLI:EU:C:1999:434, par. 93; case C-475/99 *Ambulanz Glöckner*, ECLI:EU:C:2001:577, par. 39.

[31] Schweitzer 2011, pp. 17–18.

be established whether the state measure has created an undertaking falling within the scope of Article 106(1) TFEU, then it must be explored whether the practices of this undertaking satisfy the conditions that are set out by Article 102 TFEU, and finally, a link between these practices and the state measure under review must be demonstrated. As a result, not only an analysis based on Article 106(1) TFEU must be conducted, but also all (very extensive) steps required under an Article 102 TFEU assessment have to be taken. It is, therefore, inevitably necessary to define the relevant market, to establish dominance, and to examine whether the practices of the undertaking involved amount to abuse.

Illustrative in this respect is the judgment in *Ambulanz Glöckner*.[32] At issue was the transport of ill people in emergency and non-emergency circumstances in a region of Germany. To start with, it was found that Article 106(1) TFEU constituted the relevant legal framework, as a public authority has granted to a particular group of medical aid organisations the special right to provide ambulance transport services. Then, the relevant market was analysed and two markets were defined: emergency transport services and (regular) patient transport. Subsequently, the assessment showed that the medical aid organisations concerned occupied a dominant position on both markets. The next step concerned whether there was abusive behaviour. If a newcomer wishes to enter the market for non-emergency transport, the competent German authorities consulted the medical aid organisations and only if those organisations did not raise any objections, the new operators were allowed to enter the market. The point was, however, that allowing new competitors would put under pressure the continuous provision of emergency patient transport and for that reason, the medical aid organisations were not willing to give their consent. In practice, the medical aid organisations had, therefore, a monopoly position on both ambulance markets. As a result, the economic power of the medical aid organisations on the emergency market was leveraged to the non-emergency market, which led to limiting the provision of services to the detriment of consumers, contrary to Article 102(b) TFEU. This abuse was inherent in the system set up by the German authorities and, therefore, it could be imputed to these authorities. As a link between the regional public system for ambulance services and the abusive behaviour could be established, Article 106(1) TFEU in conjunction of Article 102 TFEU were violated.

It is clear from the outset that the review to be carried out is very complicated. A thorough analysis is required, which is even more complex than the assessment carried out on the basis of Article 102 TFEU alone. In our view, this is striking, as it can hardly be denied that state interventions amounting to the creation of exclusive or special rights have a considerable bearing on the competition process.

Given the complexity of the test explained above, it is not a surprise that Article 106(1) TFEU cases have hardly reached the CJEU recently. In our view, this is also due to another reason. As exclusive and special rights are prone to render access to the market difficult or even impossible, the argument can also be made that the free movement of services or the freedom of establishment may have been restricted.[33] Over the years, the CJEU has

---

[32] Case C-475/99 *Ambulanz Glöckner*, ECLI:EU:C:2001:577.

[33] In its case-law on the Treaty provisions on free movement, the CJEU deploys a test based on market access. National measures liable to render the access to a national market less attractive are deemed to restrict free movement. See in

found that statutory monopolies for providing gambling services,[34] but also for supplying ambulance services[35] and social insurance services,[36] are restrictive measures for the purpose of EU free movement law. For plaintiffs, this is a less burdensome course of action for challenging exclusive and special rights, than basing their claims on the somewhat ambiguous Article 106(1) TFEU. Under free movement law, each exclusive or special right is likely to be found to be restrictive. This means that it all comes down to examining whether this right is justifiable in the light of the Treaty exceptions for free movement or the overriding requirements of general interest (Rule of Reason). Moreover, it must be outlined that the Services Directive 2006, which covers a wide range of activities and is, as the free movement rules, part of EU Internal Market law, provides that national requirements that reserve access to a service activity to a particular provider by virtue of the specific nature of this activity are only permitted, in so far as they pursue a public interest objective in a proportionate and non-discriminatory way.[37] As a result, it should be argued that in EU Internal Market law the CJEU has decided to apply the *limited competition approach* to national measures granting exclusive or special rights to enterprises.[38] Above, it is argued that the room for manoeuvre for Member States is considerable under the *limited sovereignty approach* deployed in Article 106 TFEU cases. This room for manoeuvre is, however, limited by the CJEU through the back door, as it has based the interpretation of the prohibitions contained in EU free movement law on the *limited competition approach*. Accordingly, the Member States must base their policies leading to the granting of exclusive and special rights on sound arguments related to the need to achieve public interest goals. From this perspective, the added value of Article 106(1) TFEU seems to be limited.

3.2 Article 106(2) TFEU: Services of General Economic Interest and their role as exception

It follows from Article 106(2) TFEU that the concept of SGEI can be invoked as an exception. It is apparent from the case-law of the CJEU that the scope of the exception of Article 106(2) TFEU is broader than the scope of the prohibition contained in Article 106(1) TFEU. Not only public authorities wishing to justify their state measures,[39] but also undertakings being entrusted with an SGEI mission may rely on Article 106(2) TFEU.[40] Consequently, practices contrary to Article 101 TFEU or Article 102 TFEU may be permitted, if the conditions of

---

this respect, inter alia, cases C-19/92 *Säger*, ECLI:EU:C:1993:125; C-442/02 *CaixaBank France*, ECLI:EU:C:2004:586. See on this matter, Barnard 2019, pp. 220–24.

[34] E.g. case C-203/08 *Betfair*, ECLI:EU:C:2010:307.

[35] Cf. case C-113/13 *Azienda sanitaria*, ECLI:EU:C:2014:2440.

[36] E.g. cases C-355/00 *Freskot*, ECLI:EU:C:2003:298; C-350/07 *Kattner Stahlbau*, ECLI:EU:C:2009:127.

[37] Services Directive 2006, Article 15(2)(d) and (3). See, in this regard, case C-171/17 *Commission v Hungary*, ECLI:EU:C:2018:881.

[38] Schweitzer 2011, pp. 19–20.

[39] E.g. case C-203/96 *Chemische Afvalstoffen Dusseldorp*, ECLI:EU:C:1998:316, par. 65.

[40] E.g. case C-393/92 *Almelo*, ECLI:EU:C:1994:171, par. 46–50.

Article 106(2) TFEU are satisfied. It should be noted that not only competition distortions, but also restrictions of free movement could be justified. In other words, the concept of SGEI constitutes also an exception in EU free movement law. It was put forward that the prohibition contained in Article 106(1) TFEU does not have much added value. The same conclusion cannot be drawn for the exception of Article 106(2) TFEU given its scope, which is broader than the prohibition of the first paragraph of this Treaty provision.

SGEIs concern tasks that play an important role in the society of the Member States. Classical examples of these tasks are delivery of mail, public transport and the supply of electricity. At the heart of these activities is the operation of networks that are needed to provide essential services to citizens. Another significant category of activities is related to the social welfare state of the Member States. These cases revolve around matters, such as pension schemes, healthcare and social housing. Accordingly, the way EU law deals with SGEIs has its bearing on the organisation of the national welfare states in the EU. The concept of SGEI is a means to strike a balance between market integration and public interest goals (social policy, health, continuous supply of energy, and suchlike) in EU law.[41]

Two conditions must be satisfied in order to rely on Article 106(2) TFEU successfully. In the first place, a task to provide SGEI must be entrusted to an operator. In the second place, the performance of the task assigned would be obstructed if competition may not be restricted. In our view, this comes down to requiring that the restriction of competition does not go beyond what is necessary.

According to the first condition, the undertaking concerned must be entrusted to provide an SGEI by the state. In many cases, this entrustment is based on a legislative act or decision taken by a public authority.[42] However, over the years, the CJEU has accepted that an SGEI mission could be derived from (a system of) plans, legal provisions and contracts.[43] The CJEU has even construed such a mission on the basis of a set of provisions of national law stipulating that everyone must have access to a certain service (universal access).[44] The CJEU is rather flexible in assuming that an SGEI is entrusted to an operator and, by doing so, has given Member States considerable leeway in organising their social welfare states and other public interest matters. Moreover, in settled case-law it is stressed that it is up to the Member States to designate a particular activity as an SGEI mission, the entrustment of which can only be called into question in the event of a manifest error.[45] The Member States enjoy a wide margin of discretion in this respect.[46] The Union courts will carry out a marginal review as to whether the boundaries of the discretion are exceeded. In *BRT v SABAM*,[47]

---

[41] Vast literature is available on the role of SGEI. See, inter alia, Cremona 2011; Krajewski, Neergaard and Van de Gronden 2009.

[42] Case C-127/73 *BRT v SABAM*, ECLI:EU:C:1974:25.

[43] E.g. cases C-393/92 *Almelo*, ECLI:EU:C:1994:171; C-203/96 *Chemische Afvalstoffen Dusseldorp*, ECLI:EU:C: 1998:316.

[44] Cases C-437/09 *AG2R*, ECLI:EU:C:2011:112; T-289/03 *BUPA*, ECLI:EU:T:2008:29.

[45] E.g. case C-171/17 *Commission v Hungary*, ECLI:EU:C:2018:881, par. 49.

[46] Buendía Sierra 1999, p. 281.

[47] Case C-127/73 *BRT v SABAM*, ECLI:EU:C:1974:25.

for example, the CJEU found that the management of copyrights did not amount to an SGEI. The Commission seems to have adopted a stricter view by putting forward that SGEI missions may only be created if a particular service cannot be provided on the market under acceptable circumstances.[48] In our view, it is questionable whether this view is entirely in line with the settled case-law, which underlines the autonomy of the Member States regarding the designation of SGEIs.

The second condition of Article 106(2) TFEU requires that competition is solely restricted in so far as this is needed with a view to the task entrusted. It is clear from the outset that this means that the proportionality principle must be complied with. However, it is apparent from the case-law of the CJEU that this principle is dealt with in a way that differs from the settled case-law on, for example, free movement law. In the latter area of law, the CJEU deploys the test of the less restrictive means, which comes down to examining whether the objectives set can be achieved by instruments restricting free movement in less intrusive ways than the measures under review.[49] In *Corbeau*, however, the CJEU did not start from this test in interpreting the proportionality principle of Article 106(2) TFEU. Rather, it held that competition distortions resulting from the implementation of an SGEI mission are permitted, if these distortions are necessary in order to perform the task assigned under economically acceptable circumstances.[50] At issue was the delivery of (small) mail on a continuous and stable basis, as the aim of the national monopoly under review was to satisfy specific needs of the population. The point was that commercially oriented enterprises would concentrate on the most profitable activities, leaving the other activities to the undertaking entrusted with the task to guarantee the universal provision of the service. This would put under pressure the economic viability of this task. In other words, the company having the SGEI mission should have the possibility to offset the less profitable sectors against the profitable sector.[51] This mission must satisfy specific needs of economic operators, and services not related to these needs must be dissociated from it.[52] So, the CJEU put forward that some additional postal services (not being part of the traditional mail delivery), such as collection from the senders' address, were dissociable from the SGEI mission and, therefore, the monopoly should not be extended to these services.

In fact, by deciding that an SGEI has to be supplied under economically acceptable circumstances, the CJEU has accommodated the market failure of 'cherry-picking' in its test.[53] The main concern of the economically acceptable circumstances lies in the problem that commercially oriented enterprises will only offer the most profitable services, which are the 'cherries' on the market. Thus, in the *Albany* case,[54] the CJEU accepted that a Dutch provider

---

[48] E.g. SGEI Communication 2012, par. 48.

[49] E.g. cases 120/78 *Cassis de Dijon*, ECLI:EU:C:1979:42, par. 8–13; C-368/95 *Familiapress*, ECLI:EU:C:1997:325, par. 19. On this matter, see Barnard 2019, pp. 176–8.

[50] Case C-320/90 *Corbeau*, ECLI:EU:C:1993:198, par. 16.

[51] Ibid, par. 17–18.

[52] Ibid, par 19.

[53] See Van de Gronden 2013 (a), p. 252; Zhu 2020, p. 100.

[54] Case C-67/96 *Albany*, ECLI:EU:C:1999:430; joined cases C-115, C-116 and C-117/97 *Brentjens*, ECLI:EU:C:1999:434;

was granted the legal monopoly of managing a supplementary pension fund in order to prevent that other providers would only offer services to customers having low-risk profiles. Above, the case of *Ambulanz Glöckner* was discussed. The preservation by the state of the non-emergency transport of patients to medical aid organisations already having a monopoly position on the market for emergency transport of patients was found to be anti-competitive. However, this was justifiable on the basis of the concept of SGEI in the view of the CJEU, as it had to be prevented that commercial ambulance companies would concentrate on patient transport at daytime in urban areas, which would make the emergency transport of patients in remote areas too cost-intensive. In other words, the restrictive practices were needed in order to guarantee the provision of the ambulance services under economically acceptable circumstances. In *AG2R*,[55] the task to provide cover for particular health risks was assigned to one specific insurance company. The exclusion of other providers was justified in the eyes of the CJEU, as the task given amounts to an SGEI mission and competition from other market players could put under pressure the fulfilment of this mission. Also, in this case, the test of the economically acceptable circumstances was applied.

The cases discussed above show that it is settled case-law that the principle of proportionality must be interpreted as to accommodate the test of the economically acceptable circumstances. It has been argued that this is a 'Member State friendly' test, as it is more flexible than the test of the less restrictive means.[56] However, there is an important downside to the current case-law. It is important to note that the requirement of dissociation is part of the proportionality test. The task assigned must not cover services, the provision of which is not necessary for attaining an economic equilibrium. As a matter of fact, this requires that an SGEI mission is defined with great precision. It must be clear which task must be assigned and which activities must be included in this task, in order to guarantee performance under economically acceptable circumstances. However, it has been already pointed out that for finding an entrustment of an SGEI mission, the CJEU has not only accepted a legislative act or an explicit act assigning this task, but also a set of general rules, obligations of a general nature, and contracts suggesting that such a mission is created. As a result, it may be difficult to delineate what an SGEI mission entails and to establish its boundaries. The problem with this is that dissociating services from the task entrusted, which is an essential part of the proportionality principle, will be a complex matter.[57] In some cases, strikingly, the CJEU did not even pay attention to the issue of dissociation. In *AG2R*, for example, the CJEU held that it was permitted to assign the task to provide cover for particular health risks to only one insurer, in order to prevent adverse selection on the basis of risk profiles, without verifying whether some of the insurance service activities were dissociable. Consequently, it cannot be ruled out that the CJEU approved a mission that was too broad from the perspective of the proportionality principle.

All in all, it is clear from the outset that the case-law of the CJEU has evolved in a direction

case C-219/97 *Drijvende Bokken*, ECLI:EU:C:1999:437.

[55] Case C-437/09 *AG2R*, ECLI:EU:C:2011:112.

[56] Prosser 2010, p. 327.

[57] Van de Gronden 2013 (a), p. 257.

based on a genuine respect for the competences of the Member States. The provision of many services is shielded from the impact of competition law, as they qualify as SGEIs and the national systems governing these tasks are found to be compatible with the proportionality principle.

In the previous section, it was outlined that exclusive and special rights are deemed to restrict free movement in EU Internal Market law and that, accordingly, the validity of these rights depends on the assessment carried out under the relevant exceptions. It is remarkable that, as a rule, these cases are not dealt with under Article 106(2) TFEU, according to which the need to supply an SGEI is not only capable of justifying competition distortions but also restrictions of free movement, under the 'classical' free movement exceptions (Rule of Reason and Article 52 TFEU). However, in its interpretation of these justifications, the CJEU has accommodated arguments that are typical for Article 106(2) TFEU.[58] For example, in cases concerning social security and free movement, the CJEU has accepted that the aim to preserve the financial balance of a social security scheme constitutes a Rule of Reason justification, which justifies the granting of an exclusive right to one particular provider.[59] One of the core elements of preserving the financial balance is to prevent that commercially oriented companies would offer insurance cover to wealthy or healthy persons, leaving persons who are less fortunate to the operator being entrusted with a special task. This is exactly the problem of 'cherry-picking', which plays an important role also under assessments based on Article 106(2) TFEU. In cases dealing with the Services Directive 2006, the exceptions are also interpreted in line with the case-law of the CJEU on Article 106(2) TFEU. In a Hungarian case on mobile payment services,[60] the CJEU accepted that the provision of these services constituted an SGEI, as Hungary had entrusted the supply thereof to an enterprise in order to guarantee that every citizen had access to these services. However, Hungary had not stated any reason explaining why the creation of the exclusive right under review was necessary in order to perform the task concerned in a cost-effective manner. The benchmark of cost-effective performance is closely related to the matter of financial balance in our view.

From this analysis it is apparent that, formally, SGEI missions are not referred to frequently in EU Internal Market law, but that, in substance, these missions play a key role in justifying cases concerning, inter alia, social security. As a result, the concept of SGEI plays an important role both in competition law and in Internal Market law. As this concept takes as a point of departure values such as universal access, the recipient of the services concerned is not only regarded as a consumer, but also as a citizen.[61] In other words, to a certain extent, the developments related to SGEIs also contribute to the evolution of European citizenship,[62] as these services could be qualified as socio-economic rights for EU citizens.[63] It should be stimulated that every citizen residing in the EU has access to services that play a key role in

---

[58] E.g. cases C-355/00 *Freskot*, ECLI:EU:C:2003:298; C-372/04 *Watts*, ECLI:EU:C:2006:325.

[59] E.g. case C-350/07 *Kattner Stahlbau*, ECLI:EU:C:2009:127, par. 85–91.

[60] Case C-171/17 *Commission v Hungary*, ECLI:EU:C:2018:881.

[61] Cf the White Paper on SGI 2004, p. 4; SGEI Communication 2012, point 45.

[62] E.g. SGI Communication 2001, point 64. See also Ross 2007, p. 1065; Van Eijken 2014, pp. 134–8.

[63] Van Eijken 2014, p. 138.

modern society. Against the backdrop of this role, more attention will be paid to SGEIs and other related concepts in section 4 of this chapter.

3.3 Article 106(3) TFEU: legislative and supervisory powers of the European Commission

Article 106(3) TFEU assigns to the Commission the task to ensure compliance with the obligations set out in that Article. To that effect, two powers are conferred upon the Commission. The first power enables this Union institution to carry out supervision, by taking decisions regarding individual cases. The second category concerns the power to enact legislation containing binding rules of general application.

In the past, the Commission frequently took decisions in order to establish an infringement of Article 106 TFEU.[64] However, since 2000 this supervisory competence has hardly been used anymore.[65] Companies being confronted with distortions of competition resulting from exclusive or special rights could request the Commission to take an enforcement decision on the basis of Article 106(3) TFEU. However, in this respect, the Commission enjoys a wide margin of discretion and may, therefore, decide not to initiate a proceeding based on this Treaty provision.[66] The Commission is not obliged to take action upon a complaint lodged by an individual.

As for the legislative powers of the Commission, it must be stressed that according to settled case-law this competence is limited to the measures outlined in Article 106 TFEU.[67] These measures concern matters such as exclusive and special right, as well as SGEIs. In other words, it is not permitted for the Commission to adopt general harmonisation measures.[68] In the past, Article 106(3) TFEU has been used for adopting directives liberalising network markets, such as the telecommunications sector.[69] Nowadays, EU laws requiring that network markets are opened up are based on Article 114 TFEU, which contains the general legal basis for measures establishing and promoting the EU Internal Market. This development is not surprising, as basing measures on Article 106(3) TFEU is, to a certain extent, controversial from the perspective of democratic legitimacy. The reason for this is that the European Parliament and the Council are not involved in the decision-making process.[70] Nevertheless, it should be stressed that the Commission, when exercising its powers, must observe the general principles of EU law.[71]

The increased use of other legal bases enshrined in the TFEU does not mean that Article 106(3) TFEU has become obsolete, as some specific measures are still adopted on the basis

---

[64] E.g. case *AENA and others*, (2000) OJ L 208/36.

[65] Buendía Sierra 2016, p. 281.

[66] Case C-141/02 *max.mobil Telekommunikation Service*, ECLI:EU:C:2005:98, par. 68–73.

[67] Case C-202/88 *France v Commission*, ECLI:EU:C:1991:120, par. 23–25.

[68] Kapteyn and VerLoren van Themaat 2003, p. 694.

[69] Ibid, pp. 694–5.

[70] Jones, Sufrin and Dunne 2019, p. 638.

[71] Whish and Bailey 2018, p. 248.

of this Treaty provision. An important example is the (already mentioned) Transparency Directive 2006, which introduces a set of rules dealing with separate accounting and similar matters for undertakings falling within the scope of Article 106 TFEU.

It is apparent from the drafting of Article 106(3) TFEU that the competence of the Commission is limited to adopting directives and decisions, as a reference to regulations is left out in this Treaty provision. However, the Commission has adopted decisions imposing obligations of general nature on the addressees. For example, in the next chapter, the Commission SGEI Decision 2011 will be discussed. This Decision exempts national measures financing the supply of particular social services from the scope of the EU state aid rules. From this example, it is apparent that the disadvantages of not having the power to adopt regulations can (largely) be circumvented by adopting a decision.

4 SOME REFLECTIONS ON SERVICES OF GENERAL ECONOMIC INTEREST

From the discussion above it is apparent that Article 106(1) and Article 106(3) TFEU have become less important over the years, whereas the concept of SGEI of Article 106(2) TFEU has expanded. In that regard, it is important to note that SGEIs are part of an overarching category, namely Service(s) of General Interest (SGI). In our view SGIs concern the entrustment of the performance of a task in the public interest.[72] These services are classified by the Member States as being of general interest and, therefore, subject to specific public service obligations.[73] These obligations must guarantee that citizens get access to the services concerned. Although the Treaty does not make any reference to this concept, it is referred to in other sources of EU law, such as the Services Directive 2006[74] and Commission soft-law documents.[75] SGIs encompass both economic and non-economic activities.[76] The non-economic SGIs are services that are supplied in the public interest without falling within the scope of EU competition law and Internal Market law.[77] Consequently, the entities supplying these services are not engaged in economic activities and do not, accordingly, qualify as undertakings. It is clear from the outset that the term used for an economic SGI is SGEI, which entails that the operators entrusted with the task concerned are undertakings for the purpose of EU competition law, and that their services are normally provided for remuneration in the sense of Article 57 TFEU, which contains the definition of the concept of service used in free movement law.[78]

Another term encountered is Social Service of General Interest (SSGI). According to the

---

[72] Neergaard 2009, p. 21; Van de Gronden 2009, pp. 234–5.

[73] Quality Framework for SGI Communication 2011, p. 3.

[74] Services Directive 2006, Recital 17.

[75] E.g. White Paper on SGI 2004; Quality Framework for SGI Communication 2011, p. 3.

[76] E.g. Quality Framework for SGI Communication 2011, p. 3.

[77] Van de Gronden 2009, p. 235.

[78] Neergaard 2009, pp. 23 and 24.

Commission, these are services responding to the needs of vulnerable citizens and are based on the principles of solidarity and equal access.[79] In its soft-law documents, the Commission distinguishes two categories of SSGIs: (1) statutory and complementary social security schemes covering the main risks of life, and (2) services provided directly to the person, such as social assistance services and social housing.[80] It is important to note that SSGIs can be both of economic and non-economic nature.[81] In our view, this entails that the concept of SSGIs is mainly a policy term, the aim of which is to explain to what extent particular social activities are covered by EU competition law and Internal Market law. As a legal concept, its 'raison d'être' may be questioned: either an SSGI is of economic nature, which means that it is also an SGEI, or it is non-economic, which entails it is a non-economic SGI. In other words, in order to establish which rules of EU law apply, it is not necessary to determine whether an activity qualifies as an SSGI. For that reason, in what follows no attention will be paid to SSGI,[82] as the setup of the current chapter is to discuss the main lines of the rules dealing with the state, competition and SG(E)I.

During the last 20 years, the concept of SGEI has seen major changes. For example, the Commission has issued a wide variety of communications and other soft-law documents.[83] An important moment was the entering into force of the Treaty of Lisbon in 2009. Apart from Article 106(2) TFEU, since then, three sets of rules are in place dealing with SG(E)I. Article 14 TFEU lays down general rules for SGEI, which means that non-economic SGIs are not covered by this Treaty provision. Article 36 of the Charter of Fundamental Rights of the EU specifically deals with SGEIs, which again means that non-economic SGIs are excluded. A Protocol is annexed to the Treaty of Lisbon that focuses on SGIs in general, including non-economic SGIs.[84]

Article 14 TFEU provides that both the EU and its Member States are obliged to ensure the proper functioning of SGEIs. This is a very general obligation but it can serve as source of inspiration for interpreting more specific rules in the area of, for example, competition and Internal Market law. Article 14 TFEU also confers upon the Union legislature the power to adopt regulations setting out the principles and conditions for the provision, commissioning and funding of SGEIs. It is striking that under Article 106(3) TFEU, which enables the Commission to enact legal acts on, inter alia, SGEIs, only directives and decisions may be adopted, while under Article 14 TFEU, the regulation is the sole instrument to be used by the Union legislature for setting general conditions for SGEIs. Are these differences the result of errors or are special purposes served? In any event, it is hard to understand the rationale

---

[79] See <https://ec.europa.eu/info/topics/single-market/services-general-interest_en> accessed 23 June 2020.

[80] E.g. Biennial Report 2013, p. 2.

[81] E.g. SGI/SSGI Communication 2007, p. 5; SSGI Lisbon Programme Communication 2006, p. 4; Quality Framework for SGI Communication 2011, pp. 3–4.

[82] On the confusion caused by the term SSGI, see Szyszczak, Neergaard and Van de Gronden 2013, pp. 601–4.

[83] These documents are available, inter alia, at <https://ec.europa.eu/info/topics/single-market/services-general-interest_en#documents> and <https://ec.europa.eu/competition/state_aid/overview/public_services_en.html> both accessed 23 June 2020.

[84] SGI Protocol 2008.

underpinning the differences in the instruments to be used. It should be noted that to date no regulations are based on Article 14 TFEU[85] and, accordingly, a discussion on the role of regulations in Article 14 TFEU is solely of an academic nature. In terms of democratic legitimacy, it is striking that Article 106(3) TFEU is still used and the legal basis of Article 14 TFEU has remained untouched, as the last provision requires the involvement of the European Parliament and the Council.[86] Consequently, the added value of Article 14 TFEU only lies in the policy linking clause, which obliges the EU and the Member States to take the position of SGEI seriously when taking action in the various policy fields. It does, therefore, not come as a surprise that, in some cases, the CJEU has made references to Article 14 TFEU in order to support its statement that Member States enjoy a wide margin of discretion, when it comes to the organisation of SGEIs.[87] In a case, the GC even held that, given this wide margin of appreciation, the Commission had rightly drawn the conclusion that an EU measure guaranteeing adequate social protection and access to sustainable long-term care could not be based on Article 14 TFEU.[88]

Article 36 of the Charter of Fundamental Rights of the EU has given access to SGEIs the status of a fundamental right. The drafting of this provision is, however, striking. It states that the Union must recognise and respect access to SGEIs as provided for in the national laws of the Member States. The aim of this is to promote the social and territorial cohesion of the Union. It takes some imagination to find out to what extent the respect for national competences for organising SGEIs amounts to a fundamental right. Furthermore, such respect for national action is more likely to contribute to territorial cohesion of the Union (meaning the territorial cohesion of the respective Member States) than to social cohesion. If national implementation of social policy falls short, respect for this national action does not 'promote' social cohesion. However, it may be assumed that, as with Article 14 TFEU, the added value of Article 36 of the Charter is that this provision could function as a policy linking clause. It is therefore not surprising that provisions of EU law are interpreted in the light of this Charter provision.[89] The inclusion of Article 36 in the Charter may have as a result that the SGEIs are not only regarded as exceptions to the market rules, but also as a concept reflecting the important role of solidarity.[90]

The Protocol on SGI emphasises that it belongs to the Member States to provide, to

---

[85] Although Article 14 TFEU has not served as a legal basis yet, in EU legislation based on, e.g., Article 114 TFEU, references are made to Article 14 TFEU in order to highlight the significance of Article 14 TFEU. See e.g. Cross-Border Parcel Delivery Regulation 2018, Recital 2.

[86] Cf. Schweitzer 2011, p. 54.

[87] E.g. cases T-151/11 *Telefónica de España*, ECLI:EU:T:2014:631, par. 156–159; T-462/13 *Comunidad Autónoma del País Vasco*, ECLI:EU:T:2015:902, par. 50; joined cases C-66 to C-69/16 *Comunidad Autónoma del País Vasco*, ECLI:EU:C:2017:999, par. 83; cases C-293/14 *Hiebler*, ECLI:EU:C:2015:843, par. 42; T-295/12 *Germany v Commission*, ECLI:EU:T:2014:675, par. 45; T-309/12 *Zweckverbandkörperbeseitigung*, ECLI:EU:T:2014:676, par. 105.

[88] Case T-44/14 *Bruno Constantini*, ECLI:EU:T:2016:223, par. 19–35.

[89] Case C-121/15 *Association nationale des opérateurs détaillants en énergie*, ECLI:EU:C:2016:637, par. 40.

[90] Pedreschi 2020, p. 76

commission and to organise non-economic SGIs. It also states that the Union and its Member States share values in respect of SGEIs. A particular value mentioned is that national, regional and local authorities enjoy a wide discretion in organising, commissioning and providing SGEIs close to the users. On top of that, it is pointed out that the diversity of the SGEIs is also a common value, as the needs and preferences of users may differ given differences of geographical, social and cultural situations. From this perspective, the Protocol approaches SGIs, including SGEIs, from the angle of the national competences.[91] In the case-law, the emphasis on these national competences is used in order to underline the wide discretion of the Member States in designating SGEI missions.[92] However, in the Protocol the emphasis on the national competences is 'blended' with setting out values entailing that SGEIs must comply with particular requirements. It is specifically stipulated that the services provided must be of a high level of quality, safe and affordable. Moreover, the operation of SGEIs must be in accordance with the principles of equal treatment and the promotion of universal access and of the rights of the users. From this, it is apparent in our view that the Protocol sets an EU benchmark for SGEIs and it is, for that reason, not free of obligations for the Member States.[93] Against this backdrop, it is not a surprise that the Commission has referred to the Protocol as the Framework for the policy dealing with SG(E)I.[94] The values requiring SGEIs' specific standards may serve as a stepping stone for further Europeanisation of these services. To date, it is unclear whether the Protocol is capable of increasing this Europeanisation, but it does serve as a tool for interpreting concrete provisions of EU law.[95]

It should be noted that an important element of SGEIs is that the access to essential services is guaranteed to all. This aim is put under pressure by the Corona crisis of 2020.[96] In our view, it is apparent from the foregoing discussion that SGEIs may experience a renaissance. So far, the developments resulting from the Lisbon Treaty have been of a general nature: amending Article 14 TFEU (which was Article 16 TEC), introducing a Protocol on SGIs, and reinforcing the status of the Charter, including Article 36. The EU may consider making use of its competences laid down in Article 14 TFEU to enact a regulation in order to set out how access for all to SGEIs must be achieved. In other words, concrete SGEI policies may be developed at the EU level.[97]

---

[91] Cases C-171/17 *Commission v Hungary*, ECLI:EU:C:2018:881, par. 48–49; T-533/10 *DTS Distribuidora de Televisión Digital*, ECLI:EU:T:2014:629, par. 124–126; T-461/13 *Commission v Spain*, ECLI:EU:T:2015:891, par. 61.

[92] Case C-121/15 *Association nationale des opérateurs détaillants en énergie*, ECLI:EU:C:2016:637, par. 40–44.

[93] Van de Gronden and Rusu 2012, p. 426.

[94] SGI/SSGI Communication 2007, pp. 9–11, 14.

[95] E.g. case T-462/13 *Comunidad Autónoma del País Vasco*, ECLI:EU:T:2015:902, par. 50; joined cases C-66 to C-69/16 *Comunidad Autónoma del País Vasco*, ECLI:EU:C:2017:999, par. 83; case C-293/14 *Hiebler*, ECLI:EU:C:2015:843, par. 42.

[96] This problem is pointed out by the Commission in its Temporary Framework 2020.

[97] In this regard it must be pointed out that EU measures governing specific regulatory matters are already in place and that these measures pay due consideration to the role of SGEI. See Zhu 2020, p. 137 *et seq.*

5 NATIONAL RULES ON THE STATE AND COMPETITION: A FEW EXAMPLES

In various Member States, special laws dealing with the state and competition are also in place. Below, several of those laws will be discussed. Special attention will be paid to concepts similar to SGEIs, such as public services, as these concepts play an important role in debates on the relationship between the state and the market. Below, at first, attention will be paid to some of the laws in place in some EU Member States. Then, a comparative approach will be adopted, by touching upon the US 'State action doctrine'.

5.1 EU Member States

5.1.1 France

According to French law, public authorities are also bound by the competition rules. Article L410-1 of the French Code de Commerce (Commercial Code) provides that these rules apply to all production, distribution and service activities, including those carried out by public entities. Against the backdrop of the French tradition of state intervention, it is not surprising that the application of the competition law rules to public bodies has given rise to heated debates.[98] Eventually, it was accepted that these bodies were not immune from competition law.[99] Article L410-1 of the Commercial Code pays some attention to the so-called 'service public' (public service). It is stressed that the competition rules apply in particular in the context of public service agreements.

In France, the notion of *service public* has a very long-standing tradition. In the first half of the twentieth century it was developed in French law, more in particular by Léon Duguit.[100] The EU concept of SGEI is closely related to the French notion of *service public*.

The purpose of the notion of *service public* was the obligation of the state to promote the development of society.[101] The concept of *service public* contains both limits to, and legitimation of state action.[102] Thus, limiting the use of state power is an important element of this French concept. Strikingly, the function of the EU rules on SGEI is, to a certain extent, to limit market forces, as these rules justify restrictions of competition if this is necessary with a view to the proper functioning of these services.

Traditionally, the *service public* were provided by the state or local authorities.[103] Over the years, it has been accepted that also private entities were entrusted with the task to provide *service public*, especially in network sectors, such as water, gas, electricity and railways.[104] In the classic model, the notion of *service public* was related to direct public man-

---

[98] Vogel 2015, p. 194.

[99] On this matter, see Vogel 2015, pp. 194–5.

[100] Schweitzer 2011, p. 13.

[101] Dreyfus 2009, p. 270.

[102] Ibid.

[103] Bauby and Simile 2010, p. 203.

[104] Ibid, pp. 203–4.

agement by authorities, such as the police, justice and educational bodies, as well as to large national enterprises in the field of postal services, telecommunications, energy, transport and railways.[105]

In France, *service public* can be created by the legislature and by public authorities.[106] An example is the establishment of a *service public* of dissemination of public data, generated by the entity concerned; also, the exploitation of a cafeteria in a town centre could be designated as such a public service.[107]

In legal doctrine, the question has arisen how to identify *service public* supplied especially by private entities. According to the Conseil d'Etat,[108] first the will of the legislator has to be examined. Is its aim to assign a *service public* mission to the enterprise concerned?[109] If this is not specifically set out in the laws, the following three elements must be considered in order to find out whether such a mission is given: the award of special powers to the private entity, the existence of a general interest requirement and control of the administration.[110] As for the first condition, the Conseil d'Etat argued that in the event a private entity is not granted state authority powers, the *service public* nature can be derived from a set of criteria (*faisceau d'indices*): to be taken into account are aspects related to the character of the general interest, the conditions of creation, organisation and functioning, the obligations imposed on the entity, and the controls established to verify compliance with the established objectives.[111]

It is not required that the service concerned is not supplied through private initiative; it suffices that the creation of a *service public* mission serves the cause of a particular public interest.[112] As *service public* can be supplied by private entities, they may be of economic nature. Such a service is referred to as '*service public industriel et commercial*'.[113] Moreover, it is considered that designing an activity as a *service public* is at the free discretion of the state; if a public interest dimension is given to an activity by the state, it becomes a *service public*.[114] However, it is required that principles of competition, more in particular of equal treatment, are observed.[115] As was already stated, Article L410-1 of the Commercial Code specifically articulates the duty to comply with competition law in the context of public service agreements.

The functioning of the *service public* must be in line with principles set out in the French

---

[105] Ibid, p. 211.

[106] See Tifine 2019, Partie 5, Chapter 2, Section II.

[107] Ibid.

[108] CE, Sect. 22 February 2007, Association du personnel relevant des établissements pour inadaptés (APREI), req. No 264541.

[109] See Dreyfus 2009, p. 273.

[110] Ibid.

[111] Ibid.

[112] See Tifine 2019, Partie 5, Chapter 2, Section II.

[113] Ibid, Partie 5, Chapter 2, Section I.

[114] Schweitzer 2011, p. 14.

[115] See Tifine 2019, Partie 5, Chapter 2, Section II.

laws, particularly in the laws of Roland (Lois de Roland).[116] These principles, which are partly echoed in the EU Protocol on SGI, concern the continuous provision of the *service public* at issue, the responsiveness to evolving social needs and interests, and equal treatment.[117]

5.1.2 Germany

In Germany, the concept of '*Daseinvorsorge*' has been developed. Forsthoff had introduced this concept in the 1930s, as the modern individual was incapable of producing the goods and services he needed (due to developments such as industrialisation) and, therefore, the state had to ensure that all individuals were provided with the essential goods and services.[118] As a result, the state had the right to intervene on the market to provide public services.[119] In the 1990s, the concept of *Daseinvorsorge* witnessed a renaissance triggered, inter alia, by EU law, but nevertheless the exact contours of this concept remained unclear.[120] It is apparent from the German case-law that this concept was primarily developed in the context of the social welfare state.[121] So, it was considered that the population was entitled to have access to drinking water but also to services such as gas, electricity, district heating, as well as postal and telecommunication services.[122] Furthermore, it is not surprising that *Daseinvorsorge* includes infrastructural works, such as the construction of roads, too.[123] *Daseinvorsorge* can be derived from pieces of national legislation, from the need to ensure access for all to particular goods or services, and from the purpose of the delivery of the goods and services concerned, that is, the general interest of the population concerned.[124] It is permitted that the public services concerned are supplied not only by public bodies, but also by private entities.[125] Under current German law, it is not required that all the essential services are provided by the state, but the state and its organs are responsible for ensuring that somehow these services are provided (the task of which may be entrusted to private entities) and that the social needs of the population are satisfied.[126]

Apart from the discussions surrounding *Daseinvorsorge* it should be noted that in German competition law it is accepted that the competition law rules are applied to undertakings owned or managed by public authorities. Article 185(1) GWB stipulates that the provisions dealing with restrictive agreements and dominant positions apply to these enterprises. In other words, publicly owned and managed companies are not immune from German competition law. However, it is set out specifically that fees and contributions of public law do

---

[116] Ibid, Partie 5, Chapter 2, Section III.

[117] Ibid.

[118] Schweitzer 2011, p. 15.

[119] Ibid.

[120] See Krajewski 2011, pp. 29–32.

[121] Ibid, p. 32.

[122] Ibid, pp. 32–3.

[123] Ibid, p. 34.

[124] Ibid, p. 36.

[125] Ibid.

[126] Bull 2008, pp. 9–10.

not fall within the scope of the German provisions on the abuse of dominance. The question arose whether it was appropriate to review the tariffs and contributions determined by public water management companies and municipalities under these provisions, as such matters are usually governed by tax law.[127] However, this carve-out does not exclude that the TFEU provisions on competition law may apply, if the activities under review amount to economic activities for the purposes of EU law.[128] In that event, Article 106(2) TFEU could be relied upon in order to justify restrictive practices. In this regard, it must further be noted that pursuant to Article 185(1) GWB the German national bank (Bundesbank), as well as the Credit Bank for Reconstruction (Kreditanstalt für Wiederaufbau) are not governed by German competition law. The reason for this is that these public institutions, entrusted with the task to intervene on financial and capital markets in the public interest, must comply with strict requirements of impartiality fixed in national law.[129]

5.1.3 The Netherlands

In Dutch law, no specific doctrine is developed for public services, as is the case in French law (*service public*) and German law (*Daseinvorsorge*). However, provisions mirroring Article 106(2) TFEU (which governs SGEIs) are enshrined in the Mw. Article 11 Mw provides that restrictive agreements in violation of the Dutch cartel prohibition may be justifiable if one of the parties to these agreements is entrusted with an SGEI mission. As with Article 106(2) TFEU, this provision of Dutch competition law is directly applicable, which means that, in proceedings, parties can rely upon it when confronted with a claim that the cartel prohibition is infringed. Article 25 Mw contains an exception for SGEIs in the event that abuse is made of a dominant position contrary to Article 24 Mw. Strikingly, unlike both Article 106(2) TFEU and Article 11 Mw, an undertaking must apply for prior authorisation from the ACM in order to rely on Article 25 Mw. In other words, a dominant firm having an SGEI mission, and supposing that it may be engaged in anti-competitive behaviour under Article 24 Mw, can only justify this behaviour if it asks for permission to do so from the ACM in advance. As making a request for such a permission would come down to confessing that competition issues have arisen, it may be expected that companies are not willing to make such application under Article 25 Mw.[130] The Dutch rules on merger control also pay due consideration to the need to provide SGEIs. Pursuant to Article 41(3) Mw, the ACM is not allowed to refuse clearance of a merger, if one of the parties involved is entrusted with the task to provide SGEIs and such a refusal obstructs the performance of this task.

Furthermore, it must be noted that provisions specifically dealing with the state and the market (*Markt en Overheid*) are laid down in the Dutch Act on Competition 2011. According to these rules of conduct, the enforcement of which is entrusted to the ACM, any public authority is obliged to refrain from being engaged in particular anti-competitive practices. For example, every public body carrying out economic activities has the duty to charge at

---

[127] See Bechtold and Bosch 2018, p. 781.

[128] Ibid, p. 782.

[129] Ibid.

[130] Van de Gronden 2017, p. 445.

least full-cost prices (prices below the costs incurred by this body are not permitted). Another example is the ban on favouring a public company at the expense of other companies. It should be noted that there are exceptions that may be invoked by the public authorities in order to justify their practices contrary to the provisions on the state and the market. Strikingly, pursuant to one of these exceptions, these provisions do not apply if an action undertaken by a particular public body serves the general interest. On first sight, this may lead to a lenient carve-out enabling public authorities to circumvent the rules of conduct. However, it is apparent from the case-law that this exception can only be invoked if the public body concerned bases its finding on a sound line of reasoning and if it is made clear that economic operators are not able to serve the general interest at issue by supplying services or products under their conditions.[131] Furthermore, the public body is obliged to limit the disadvantages of the companies involved as much as possible, which could entail that financial compensation has to be given.[132]

5.2 State action doctrine in the US

Accommodating the role of state interventions in assessments carried out under the competition rules does not only take place in the EU and its Member States, but also in US antitrust law. To that effect, the state action doctrine is developed in US antitrust law. The point of departure of this doctrine is the delineation of the powers of the federal government and of the States of the US. In essence, the doctrine is a principle of federalism, as it resolves tensions arising from US federal antitrust law and state regulation.[133]

In the case *Parker v Brown*,[134] the Supreme Court recognised the state action doctrine for the first time, by ruling that US antitrust law does not apply, if a State of the US adopts a measure that creates a regulatory regime leading to displacing competition.[135] At issue in *Parker v Brown* were price and supply restrictions adopted by private firms on the market for raisins, which was approved by a state committee. Other examples relate to the laws enacted by some States of the US in order to authorise physicians to engage in collective bargaining with health insurers.[136]

From later case-law it is apparent that two conditions must be satisfied for the state action doctrine to be applicable.[137] First, the restraint at issue has to be a practice that is clearly articulated and affirmatively expressed as state policy. Second, the policy under review must be actively supervised by the State itself. The first condition means that: (1) the State permits

---

[131] Cases *Q-park Operations Netherlands*, ECLI:NL:2018:660, College van Beroep voor het Bedrijfsleven, 18 December 2018; *Jachthaven Wolderwijd (Wolderwijd marina)*, ECLI:NL:CBB:2018:661, College van Beroep voor het Bedrijfsleven, 18 December 2018.

[132] Cases *Q-park Operations* and *Jachthaven Wolderwijd, supra.*

[133] Inman and Rubinfeld 1996–97, p. 1205.

[134] Case *Parker v Brown*, (1943) 317 U.S. 341, 63 S.Ct. 307.

[135] Areeda and Hovenkamp 2006, pp. 42–50.

[136] Blair and Coffin 2004–05, p. 1732.

[137] Case *California Retail Liquor Dealers Ass'n v Midcal Aluminum Co.*, (1980) 445 U.S. 97, 100 S. Ct. 937.

the activity, and (2) the State has the clear intention of displacing federal antitrust scrutiny.[138] In other words, it must be clear from the outset that the measure taken by the State would have adverse effects on competition. The second condition implies that it is for the State to decide to what extent competition is substituted by regulation, as long as adequate public control is in place wherever this regulation has substantially weakened competition.[139] As a result, rubber-stamping by a public authority of a State will not suffice for triggering the state action doctrine.[140] In the context of state regulation, private parties must be precluded from acting in their own interest rather than the public interest, which means that state policies should not be captured by the industry being subject by the regulation concerned.[141]

From the foregoing, it is apparent that the institutional framework of the state regulation concerned is of great importance for finding that federal antitrust laws are not violated. The review should not be primarily geared towards balancing the objectives pursued and the restraints resulting from the state regulation. The reason for this is that the underlying principle of the state action doctrine is the protection of state legislative sovereignty in a federal system.[142] Consequently, this doctrine has a very eminent constitutional dimension. However, there is also an element related to the goals to be achieved. It has to be examined whether the state regulation leading to anti-competitive restraints somehow furthers the public authority's conception of the public interest.[143] All in all, in US law the general feeling is that the judiciary should not be given the mandate to ensure that state regulation only produces competitive results.[144] In this view, the balancing of the need to stimulate competition and the protection of public interest goals should take place in the political process.

The US state action doctrine is difficult to interpret and to apply. However, it is clear that its main goal is of a constitutional nature, as it safeguards the powers of the States vis-à-vis the federal government. Consequently, this doctrine differs greatly from the approach developed on the basis of Article 106(2) TFEU in EU law.[145] At the heart of the latter concept is the scrutiny of the necessity of the restraints of competition in order to guarantee the provision of the essential services under review. This requires an appraisal of the trade-offs between the public policy objectives at play and the competition process on the Internal Market. As a result, in EU law it has been accepted that the judiciary scrutinises whether national laws pay sufficient respect to the competition process. It should be borne in mind that the EU is an international organisation aiming at removing obstacles to free trade. In our view, inherent to the process of removing these obstacles is the judicial review of national measures that may distort competition in the Internal Market.

---

[138] Areeda and Hovenkamp 2006, p. 75.

[139] Ibid, p. 63.

[140] Ibid, p. 65.

[141] Inman and Rubinfeld 1996–97, p. 1262.

[142] Ibid, p. 125.

[143] Semeraro 2000–01, p. 212.

[144] Hovenkamp 2008, p. 234.

[145] Van de Gronden 2013 (b), p. 126.

6 CONCLUSIONS

In its case-law, the CJEU has struggled with striking a balance between the EU system of undistorted competition and the competences of the Member States to intervene on the market. The point of departure is that competition law only applies in so far as a link exists between state action and the undertakings operating on a given market. This has resulted in tests which are difficult to apply and that have given rise to complicated legal debates. The steps to be taken for establishing an infringement of Article 106(1) TFEU are so complex that hardly any litigation has occurred under this provision for the last ten years. Also, the US experience with the state action doctrine shows that applying the antitrust rules to measures adopted by public authorities is capable of giving rise to a lot of uncertainty and complex assessments. On top of that, this experience discloses that the relationship between state measures and a common market has a constitutional dimension. Then again, the creation of the useful effect doctrine in EU law, as well as the French, German and Dutch rules on competition and public authorities demonstrate that there is a case for control of the actions undertaken by state organs on the market. From the case-law on the EU Internal Market rules it can also be derived that such a control may have great merit.

In our view, EU law faces the challenge to develop a coherent set of rules, based on a well-designed test, that does justice to both the proper functioning of the Internal Market and the special role of the state (seeking to represent the public interest). Moreover, the respect for the national competences to intervene on markets for a good cause should also be accommodated in such rules. In other words, the provisions on the state and the market should have a 'horizontal element' and a 'vertical element'. The horizontal element is concerned with reconciling the tensions resulting from the clash between the competition process and the public interest. The vertical element is geared towards coordinating between the EU and national competences.

In our view, the design of these rules should allow for making trade-offs between competition distortions and public interest objectives. Concepts such as SG(E)I, *service public*, and *Daseinvorsorge*, constitute nice stepping stones for making such trade-offs. It is of great importance that in the various jurisdictions these concepts are elaborated on and will be related to both EU competition law and Internal Market law. Now, SGEIs function mainly as an exception in competition law, *service public* delineates the competences of the state and *Daseinvorsorge* stimulates the state to provide services and goods needed by its citizens. Somehow, the core elements of these concepts must be brought together, supplemented by elements from valuable experiences with similar matters in other EU Member States, in order to build a robust concept of SGIs/public services, and to develop a sustainable vision on the relationship between the EU Internal Market, the national social welfare states and modern society.[146]

---

[146] Zhu 2020, pp. 38–40, 270–71.

12
State aid law

1 INTRODUCTION

When it comes to state and competition, the Treaty provisions on state aid, enshrined in Articles 107–109 TFEU, are of great importance. In legal practice, this area of law plays a very significant role. It appears that many Member States grant financial support to undertakings. It goes without saying that such support is capable of seriously distorting competition. Therefore, according to Article 107(1) TFEU the point of departure is that giving state aid to undertakings is not permitted. Under specific circumstances, however, state aid could be allowed.

The general framework of Articles 107–109 TFEU is that Member States must refrain from granting state aid to undertakings, if this aid is capable of distorting competition in the Internal Market and influencing the trade between the Member States. However, particular reasons may justify that such aid is given by the Member States in order to achieve certain objectives of public interest, as, for example, envisaged by Article 107(2) and (3) TFEU. It is of great interest to note that it is only for the Commission to decide whether national state aid measures are justifiable under these Treaty provisions. The official terminology used for finding a measure justified is concluding that this measure is compatible with the Internal Market. The Commission must adopt a decision stating that the national aid is compatible with the Internal Market. Therefore, Article 108(3) TFEU provides that national state aid measures must be notified to the Commission and may not be put into effect as long as no approval is given by this EU institution. This procedural rule is known as the standstill provision. If a Member State grants state aid without respecting the standstill provision, that is, without prior approval given by the Commission, this aid must be paid back, if the Commission detects it and, moreover, finds it incompatible with the Internal Market.[1] In other words, the sanction for failing to notify financial support given to undertakings is very serious and far-reaching: it will affect the validity of the national state aid measure.

In this chapter, the prohibition on state aid will be discussed. Then, it will be explored under which conditions state aid is justifiable. Subsequently, attention will be paid to procedural matters: how are the TFEU provisions on state aid enforced both in European and national law?

---

[1] E.g. case C-39/94 *SFEI v La Poste*, ECLI:EU:C:1996:285, par. 43.

2 ARTICLE 107(1) TFEU: THE BAN ON STATE AID

Article 107(1) TFEU contains the ban on state aid. According to this provision, Member States are precluded from granting any aid to undertakings, which distorts competition in the Internal Market. In essence, the prohibition of Article 107(1) TFEU is violated, if state aid is given to undertakings, by which competition in the Internal Market is restricted and the trade between the Member States is impacted. This comes down to satisfying the following conditions for Article 107(1) TFEU to be applicable: (1) the national measure under review constitutes state aid, (2) the aid concerned is given by the state or through state resources, (3) competition in the Internal Market is distorted, and (4) the trade between the Member States is influenced.[2] In this respect, it must be noted that the Commission has adopted the Notion of State Aid Notice 2016, which codifies the case-law of the EU courts on this matter. This Notice is of great help for interpreting Article 107(1) TFEU.

In *Pearle*,[3] the CJEU decided that all conditions laid down in Article 107(1) TFEU must be fulfilled for the ban on state aid to be applicable. Accordingly, an economic benefit granted to a specific undertaking by the state is not in violation of this ban, if competition in the Internal Market is not distorted or the trade between the Member States is not influenced. As a result, the Member State concerned is not obliged to notify this aid measure to the Commission for the simple reason that Article 107(1) TFEU does not apply, and that, accordingly, it is not required to comply with the standstill provision. In other words, the scope of the standstill provision is limited to national measures that satisfy all the conditions spelled out in Article 107(1) TFEU.

2.1 The concept of state aid

The concept of state aid, which is the first condition mentioned, must be interpreted in an expansive way. As with the concept of undertaking, the term 'state aid' is based on a functional interpretation. The case-law of the CJEU takes the effects of national measures as the point of departure, rather than their legal form or qualification according to national law. The term state aid encompasses all positive benefits, such as subsidies and interventions mitigating the charges that are normally included in the budget of the undertakings.[4] There is state aid if the costs that should have been borne by an enterprise or enterprises are covered by public bodies. Accordingly, subsidies but also tax reductions could fall within the ambit of Article 107(1) TFEU.[5] Furthermore, a loan given at favourable rates to companies could amount to state aid for the purposes of Article 107(1) TFEU.[6] The selling of real estate by the government to a corporation for a considerably low price could also be regarded as state aid.[7]

---

[2] E.g. case C-345/02 *Pearle*, ECLI:EU:C:2004:448, par. 33.

[3] Ibid.

[4] See case C-39/94 *SFEI v La Poste*, ECLI:EU:C:1996:285, par. 58.

[5] E.g. joined cases C-197 and C-203/11 *Libert*, ECLI:EU:C:2013:288, par. 79, 80.

[6] E.g. case T-16/96 *Cityflyer*, ECLI:EU:T:1998:78, par. 50–57.

[7] E.g. case C-239/09 *Seydaland Vereinigte Agrarbetriebe*, ECLI:EU:C:2010:778, par. 31.

It is clear from the broad definition given by the CJEU that not only subsidies but also other interventions of public bodies may give rise to state aid issues.

The question has arisen how to establish that a particular transaction of the state constitutes state aid. Some transactions are permitted, whereas other transactions could be very problematic. The test to be carried out is whether a private investor would have been engaged in a transaction similar to the state's transaction under review. In the Notion of State Aid Notice 2016 this analysis is referred to as the 'market economic investor test'.[8] It should be examined whether the transaction concerned is carried out under normal market conditions. In this respect, it is not important whether the transaction carried out by the state serves a specific purpose or aims to achieve a particular (social or environmental) objective.[9] Furthermore, it should not be examined what the maximum profitability of an investment would have been, but rather the benchmark is whether a private investor would have made the same investment as the public authority did.[10]

When the market economic investor test is deployed, it is of great importance that the findings are based on an overall assessment, which entails that all relevant evidence is taken into account in order to verify whether a private investor would not have been prepared to grant financial facilities comparable to those given by the state body concerned.[11] Furthermore, the financial situation of the beneficiary must be explored with great care.[12]

Another important element of the concept of state aid relates to the matter of selectivity. It is settled case-law that the benefits given to all market operators do not constitute state aid. If, for example, the national legislature lowers the general taxation on corporations, it may be assumed that every company profits. No harm to competition can be identified, which does not justify the applicability of Article 107(1) TFEU. A key element of the term state aid is, accordingly, selectivity.[13] A certain degree of selectivity is required for assuming that particular undertakings are favoured. A state intervention granting benefits to all relevant market operators does not favour specific companies.

Especially, in cases where national tax laws are reviewed under Article 107(3) TFEU, the matter of selectivity is of great importance. Tax benefits given to one or a limited group of undertakings are likely to be considered as state aid, whereas this is not the case in the event that every company is entitled to those benefits. Accordingly, in the cases on tax rulings, where the national authorities establish in advance the application of the national tax rules to a particular case, one of the most prominent issues is whether a wide range of companies would be eligible to receive the favoured treatment a particular large enterprise was given.[14] If so, the tax benefits are not selective. In contrast, if only a limited number of companies

---

[8] Notion of State Aid Notice 2016, par. 75.

[9] E.g. case C-487/06 *British Aggregates Association*, ECLI:EU:C:2008:757.

[10] Case T-791/16 *Real Madrid Club de Fútbol*, ECLI:EU:T:2019:346, par. 86.

[11] Case T-732/16 *Valencia Club de Fútbol*, ECLI:EU:T:2020:98, par. 134.

[12] Case T-901/16 *Elche Club de Fútbol*, ECLI:EU:T:2020:97, par. 94–95.

[13] E.g. case C-143/99 *Adria-Wien Pipeline*, ECLI:EU:C:2001:598, par. 34.

[14] E.g. cases SA.38944 *Luxembourg Alleged Aid to Amazon*, (2014/C) OJ C 44/13, par. 48–57; SA.38373 *Ireland/Apple*, (2014/C) OJ L 187/1, par. 225–226; SA.38374 *The Netherlands/Starbucks*, (2014/C) OJ C 460/03, par. 229–230.

are eligible while other enterprises are not entitled to the favourable treatment concerned in similar circumstances, the tax benefits under review are selective and fall within the ambit of Article 107(1) TFEU.[15] In two important cases on tax rulings the GC has held that the existence of an advantage is determined by reference to normal taxation rules: the tax benefits granted must be compared with the tax burden that the undertaking in question would otherwise have had to bear in accordance with the normal rules of taxation.[16] In this respect, the GC accepted that the Commission used the arm's length principle as a benchmark for establishing whether the company concerned had received an advantage.[17] According to this principle, the conditions of transactions of affiliated companies of one conglomerate enterprise are compared with the conditions of the transactions of independent companies; the question is whether the transaction of the companies of the conglomerate enterprise is based on a remuneration reflecting the functions performed (such as the transfer of IP rights), which also requires that the assets involved and the risks at play are taken into account.[18]

2.2 State resources

The second criterion is related to the resources of the state. For Article 107(1) TFEU to be applicable, the aid under review must be financed out of the public purse. The economic benefits given must be imputed to state bodies.[19] Giving state aid involves a financial sacrifice being made by a public body. It is clear from the outset that a subsidy given by a public body, such as a minister or a board of a municipality, to an undertaking amounts to aid imputable to the state. In this regard, it must be noted that the notion of state is a broad concept: it does not only encompass public authorities operating at the national level, but also regional and local authorities. The imputability must be inferred from a set of indicators arising from the circumstances of the case and the context in which the measure was taken.[20] In specific circumstances, even aid given by a public undertaking can be imputed to the state.[21] If, for instance, the decision to be taken by a public company on a request for aid must be made in accordance with the requirements set out by public authorities, or if this decision must be based on instructions given by public authorities, the conclusion could be drawn that the economic benefits at play are financed out of the public purse.[22] Also aid which is given through a third party used as an intermediary may be imputable to the state. For example, in

---

[15] Notion of State Aid Notice 2016, par. 170.

[16] Joined cases T-755 and T-759/15 *Luxembourg and Fiat*, ECLI:EU:T:2019:670, par. 318; joined cases T-760/15 and T-636/16 *The Netherlands and Starbucks*, ELCI:EU:T:2019:669, par. 153; cases T-696/17 *Havenbedrijf Antwerpen*, ECLI:EU:T:2019:652, par. 129; T-865/16 *Fútbol Club Barcelona*, ECLI:EU:T:2019:113, par. 54–68; C-374/17 *A-Brauerei*, ECLI:EU:C:2018:1024, par. 21–22.

[17] Joined cases T-760/15 and T-636/16 *The Netherlands and Starbucks*, ELCI:EU:T:2019:669, par. 151–170.

[18] Ibid, par. 9.

[19] E.g. joined cases C-72 and C-73/91 *Sloman Neptun*, ECLI:EU:C:1993:97.

[20] Joined cases T-98, T-196 and T-198/16 *Banca Tercas*, ECLI:EU:T:2019:167, par. 84.

[21] Notion of State Aid Notice 2016, par. 40–42.

[22] Case C-482/99 *France v Commission*, ECLI:EU:C:2002:294, par. 55.

the cases *Germanwings*, *Volotea* and *easyJet Airline*, the GC held that funds were transferred by a regional authority to airport operators, which, on their turn, transferred these funds to particular airlines.[23] Of importance in this regard was the degree of control exerted by this regional authority.[24] However, in the event that a private entity gives financial support, the Commission may not confine itself to simply putting forward that, given the circumstances, it is unlikely that the state did not exert control over this private entity when the latter granted aid to certain undertakings.[25] A profound analysis specifying the relevant facts and details is required in such cases and ill-founded assumptions must be avoided. For example, regular prudential control exercised by a central bank of a Member State over private banks does not automatically entail that a measure must be imputed to this Member State.[26]

2.3 Distortion of competition in the Internal Market

The third condition focuses on the anti-competitive effects of state aid. Financial support given by the state to undertakings falls within the scope of Article 107(1) TFEU, in so far as competition in the Internal Market is distorted. Examining the effects on competition under Article 101 TFEU or Article 102 TFEU entails a deep and profound analysis of the economic and legal circumstances. In contrast, the assessment to be carried out under Article 107(1) TFEU is less substantial. It suffices to compare the position of the beneficiary undertaking with the position of its competitors operating in intra-Union trade.[27] It is not required to establish that the national aid measure at hand actually distorts competition, but rather it should be examined whether that aid is liable to do so.[28] In other words, it is not very difficult to find anti-competitive effects if a public authority favours an undertaking or a specific group of undertakings by granting economic support. Such measures decrease the costs of the beneficiaries, which their competitors, operating in similar circumstances, still have to bear themselves. Moreover, in principle, aid intended to release a company from costs it would normally have to bear in its normal activities distorts competition.[29] In its Notion of State Aid Notice 2016, the Commission even contends that granting a financial advantage to an enterprise operating in a liberalised sector generally leads to distortions of competition.[30] In our view, however, the simple finding that in a specific sector the markets are opened up and the beneficiary concerned operates in this sector does not justify the conclusion that

---

[23] Cases T-716/17 *Germanwings*, ELCI:EU:T:2020:181, par. 71–106; T-607/17 *Volotea*, ELCI:EU:T:2020:180, par. 83–98; T-8/18, *easyJet Airline*, ECLI:EU:T:2020:182, par. 117–140.

[24] See cases T-716/17 *Germanwings*, ELCI:EU:T:2020:181, par. 91; T-607/17 *Volotea*, ELCI:EU:T:2020:180, par. 94–96; T-8/18, *easyJet Airline*, ECLI:EU:T:2020:182, par. 129–131.

[25] Joined cases T-98, T-196 and T-198/16 *Banca Tercas*, ECLI:EU:T:2019:167, par. 89.

[26] Ibid, par. 115–124.

[27] E.g. cases 730/79 *Philip Morris*, ECLI:EU:C:1980:209, par. 11; C-148/04 *Unicredito Italiano*, ECLI:EU:C:2005:774, par. 56

[28] Case C-372/97 *Italy v Commission*, ECLI:EU:C:2004:234, par. 44.

[29] Case C-659/17 *INPS*, ECLI:EU:T:2019:633, par. 32.

[30] Notion of State Aid Notice 2016, par. 187.

competition is restricted. Although the test to be carried out is lenient, it must be made clear how the competition process, at least potentially, could be affected by the public support given. It should be explained how the benefits given impact the competition conditions on the market or are likely to impact these conditions. In short, some form of economic analysis has to be carried out, although it is not required that this analysis is very detailed.

2.4 Trade between the Member States

The fourth condition underlines the Union dimension of the TFEU provisions on state aid: the trade between the Member States must be influenced for Article 107(1) TFEU to be applicable. It is apparent from case-law that the conditions regarding the distortion of competition and the effect on intra-Union trade are inextricably linked.[31] As with the condition of distorting competition, the position of the company having received state aid must be compared with the companies competing in intra-Union trade, in order to find an effect on the trade between the Member States. Accordingly, the position of the beneficiary must be reviewed against the backdrop of the undertakings providing goods or services in other Member States. It is not a surprise that, as with the condition of competition distortion, it suffices to find a hypothetical effect on the trade between the Member States. Consequently, the analysis carried out for verifying whether (potential) effects on competition in the Internal Market occur may be recycled when examining the impact on the trade between the Member States. Public support can even be considered of being capable of influencing intra-Union trade, if the beneficiary undertaking is not engaged in cross-border activity.[32] The strengthening of a domestic player on the market by public support could prevent competitors from other Member States from entering the market. Therefore, also financial advantages that are relatively small could have an effect on intra-Union trade. If it cannot be excluded that foreign companies may be interested in supplying goods or services on the domestic market concerned, a small amount of aid can change the competition conditions on the market considerably, by reducing the costs of a certain company. If the profit margins are relatively small, mitigating the costs of a particular company may place this company in a better position compared to other undertakings.

Irrespective of the potential effects of relatively small aid, the Commission has adopted the so-called State Aid *De Minimis* Regulation 2013. This Regulation deals with small aid amounts by coming up with a special approach for these aids. Aid not exceeding 200 000 EUR over any period of three years is deemed to be compatible with the Internal Market. The threshold set relates to aids given to one particular undertaking by all public authorities in a given EU Member State. Thus, the entire amount of aid granted must not exceed the ceiling of 200 000 EUR. Accumulation of all public support received is an important issue to be taken into account. The relevant period for establishing whether the cumulated aid exceeds the threshold of the *De Minimis* Regulation 2013 is three years.

---

[31] Joined cases T-298, T-312, T-313, T-315, T-600 to 607/97, T-1, T-3 to T-6 and T-23/98 *Alzetta*, ECLI:EU:T:2000:151, par. 81.

[32] Notion of State Aid Notice 2016, par. 191.

It should be noted that the *De Minimis* Regulation 2013 is ambiguous with regard to the reason for carving out aid not exceeding 200 000 EUR over any period of three years. Pursuant to Article 3(1) of this Regulation, aid not in excess of this amount is 'deemed not to meet all the criteria in Article 107(1) of the Treaty . . .' In our view, this suggests that small aid amounts do not fall within the ambit of the prohibition enshrined in this Treaty provision. Strikingly, it is not specified which condition is not met, although it may be assumed that the remark on non-fulfilment is connected with the trade between the Member States, probably in close relation to the distortion of competition in the Internal Market. In any event, non-fulfilment entails that the obligation to notify and, accordingly, the standstill provision do not apply. However, Article 3(1) of the *De Minimis* Regulation 2013 specifically stipulates that the small aid amounts are 'exempt from the notification requirement in Article 108(3) of the Treaty . . .'. It is not clear why a state aid measure that is deemed not to satisfy all the conditions of Article 107(1) TFEU should be exempted from this obligation. Exempting such measures suggests that Article 107(1) TFEU does apply, but that these measures are considered to be compatible with the Internal Market. This difference between non-fulfilment of the conditions and exempting national measures is an important difference, as the final say on interpreting the conditions of Article 107(1) TFEU rests with the CJEU, whereas the Commission has the sole power to exempt national measures under Article 107(2) and (3) TFEU, decisions which are, of course, subject to review by the Union courts. Hopefully, in the future it will be clarified on which assumption Article 3(1) of the *De Minimis* Regulation 2013 is based. That said, our view is also that the *de minimis* rule is very useful for legal practice, as it makes it clear that certain small aid amounts are permitted under EU law without prior notification. The *De Minimis* Regulation 2013 expires on 31 December 2020 and, for that reason, the Commission launched a public consultation process in 2019.[33] When writing this book, the outcome of this consultation was not yet known.

2.5 The concept of state aid and Services of General Economic Interest

Member States finance the supply of many essential services, such as hospital services, social services and transport. If these services are provided by undertakings for the purposes of EU competition law, state aid issues can arise. Such issues are capable of jeopardising the proper functioning of services that play a key role in the national welfare states. It should be noted that the standstill provision applies to national measures financing undertakings, even if these undertakings are entrusted with special tasks, such as hospitals, social housing companies and transport enterprises. If state aid is granted without prior permission of the Commission, this aid should be recovered. It goes without saying that this would put under pressure the access for all to services that are significant in the national welfare states.

In order to address the problems arising from the standstill provision, the CJEU has developed a special approach for services the access to which must be guaranteed. It has drawn on Article 106(2) TFEU when designing this approach. Pursuant to this provision

---

[33] See <https://ec.europa.eu/competition/consultations/2019_de_minimis/index_en.html> accessed 22 June 2020.

the application of the Treaty provisions on, for example, competition and state aid may not obstruct the provision of SGEIs. According to settled case-law, services the supply of which are entrusted by a state body to a particular enterprise or group of enterprises qualify as SGEIs.[34] Article 106(2) TFEU shows that SGEIs deserve special treatment in EU law.

The CJEU has pointed out that the provision of these services often incurs additional costs for the company entrusted with an SGEI mission. It, therefore, held in *Altmark*[35] that as long as the financial support given by the state is aimed at compensating these costs, Article 107(1) TFEU is not violated.[36] The national measure at hand is not considered as state aid within the meaning of this Treaty provision. The economic benefits given do not constitute an advantage, as it is compensation given for the costs incurred with the supply of the special services concerned. Due to the compensatory character of these benefits, the company entrusted with a special task does not enjoy a real financial advantage and, accordingly, the aid granted does not have the effect of putting this company in a more favourable competition position than other companies.[37] In the CJEU's view the compensation given does not satisfy all the conditions for the concept of state aid.

The CJEU has adopted a compensatory approach when it comes to financing SGEI. It could also have opted for walking down another road, which would have stressed the need to protect the competition process in the Internal Market. In fact, Advocate General Léger, who was requested to hand down two Opinions by the CJEU, was in favour of the state aid approach. In his view, the purposes that a national measure financing SGEI seeks to serve is not of interest for the qualification of that measure under Article 107(1) TFEU.[38] Only the effects should be taken into account and that would have implied that the national measure under review in *Altmark* amounted to state aid and was caught by Article 107 TFEU. The public interest goals to be achieved could have been taken into account in the context of the exceptions, in the view of the Advocate General. It is clear from the outset that such an approach sits well with the overall setup of the state aid rules: the interpretation of the state aid ban is geared towards the effects of the public support given, while the adverse effects of this ban are moderated by exceptions. But the Opinion of the Advocate General did not address the problems arising from the standstill provision.

Eventually, the CJEU decided not to follow its Advocate General, but to give the Member States some leeway for financing SGEI. The great advantage of this decision is that the problems surrounding non-compliance with the standstill obligation are solved. The downside of this is, however, that effects do play a role in the interpretation on the ban on state aid, which makes this interpretation less comprehensive and coherent.

In any event, it should be stressed that the CJEU tried to strike a balance between respect for the competences of the Member States and the need to protect the competition process on the market. The CJEU formulated four conditions that must be met in order to benefit

---

[34] E.g. case C-127/73 *BRT v SABAM*, ECLI:EU:C:1974:25.

[35] Case C-280/00 *Altmark*, ECLI:EU:C:2003:415.

[36] Case C-53/00 *Ferring*, ECLI:EU:C:2001:627.

[37] Case C-280/00 *Altmark*, ECLI:EU:C:2003:415, par. 87.

[38] E.g. case C-280/00 *Altmark*, Opinion of Advocate General Léger, ECLI:EU:C:2002:188, par. 80.

from the compensatory approach. These conditions are cumulative, which entails that Article 107(1) TFEU is violated if one of them is not satisfied. According to the first condition the enterprise concerned must be entrusted with the discharge of a public service obligation (PSO). It is striking that the term used is not SGEI. However, it is apparent from later case-law that SGEI and PSO are identical terms.[39] The second condition is that the parameters for the compensation given are established in advance in an objective and transparent manner. The third condition requires that the compensation given does not go beyond what is necessary. Fourth, if the task to discharge PSO is not awarded through a public procurement procedure, the level of the compensation must be calculated on the basis of the costs of a well-run company.

In subsequent case-law, the CJEU has clarified these conditions and given more guidance.[40] Also, the Commission has intervened by issuing binding rules and publishing guidelines.[41] For a great part, this case-law of the CJEU and the interventions of the Commission are concerned with the interpretation of exceptions. The concept of SGEI does not only play a role in applying the ban on state aid but is also a constituent element of a few exceptions. In the section below dealing with the exceptions, attention will be paid to the SGEI communications and rules adopted by the Commission.

3 EXCEPTIONS IN EU STATE AID LAW

Article 107(2) and (3) TFEU contain exceptions to the prohibition to grant state aid. Particular interests could justify national state aid measures, which means that these measures are found compatible with the Internal Market. It is apparent from the procedural rules laid down in Article 108 TFEU that the Commission has the sole power to decide that a national state aid measure is compatible with the Internal Market. For that reason, Member States must notify their state aid measures in order to benefit from the exceptions of Article 107(2) and (3) TFEU. Furthermore, the Commission has adopted Block Exemptions. According to these exemptions the obligation to notify is lifted for certain aid measures that satisfy the particular conditions. Such aid is deemed to be compatible with the Internal Market. Unlike Article 107(2) and (3) TFEU, it is not required for Member States to notify the Commission in order to rely on Block Exemptions. As a result, the last category of exceptions gives more leeway to the Member States than the first category does. In this respect, it must also be noted that Block Exemptions reduce the workload of the Commission, as the national measures covered by these exemptions do not need to be examined.

In this section, the exceptions laid down in Article 107(2) and (3) TFEU will be discussed.

---

[39] Case T-289/03 *BUPA*, ECLI:EU:T:2008:29, par. 96.

[40] E.g. case C-706/17 *Achmea AB*, ECLI:EU:C:2019:407; joined cases C-66 to C-69/16 *Comunidad Autónoma del País Vasco*, ECLI:EU:C:2017:999; cases C-649/15 *TV2/Danmark*, ECLI:EU:C:2017:835; C-660/15 *Viasat Broadcasting UK*, ECLI:EU:C:2017:178; C-185/14 *EasyPay*, ECLI:EU:C:2015:716.

[41] See for this package <http://ec.europa.eu/competition/state_aid/legislation/sgei.html> accessed 10 June 2020.

Then, the Block Exemptions will be addressed; the discussion of these exemptions will be limited to the two most important ones.

3.1 The Treaty exceptions

Both Article 107(2) TFEU and Article 107(3) TFEU provide that certain public interest goals are capable of justifying state aid measures. As significant differences exist between these two provisions, they will be discussed separately.

3.1.1 What is the added value of Article 107(2) TFEU?

Article 107(2) TFEU is a striking provision for various reasons. To start with, this provision does not leave any discretionary power to the Commission. It simply states that aid shall be compatible with the Internal Market if the measure concerned aims at achieving one of the objectives outlined. Although notification is required in order to benefit from Article 107(2) TFEU,[42] the Commission must approve the aid under review, as soon as one of the interests mentioned in this Treaty provision is at issue. Then again, it cannot be excluded that discussion could arise as to whether the conditions outlined in this Treaty provision are satisfied. Does the Commission enjoy some discretion in interpreting these conditions? Furthermore, it may be doubted whether all aid specified in Article 107(2) TFEU is connected with an economic activity. The aid measures set out in Article 107(2)(a) TFEU constitute financial support of a social character given to individual consumers. Only in very limited circumstances are such consumers also engaged in economic activities and, accordingly, are undertakings for the purposes of competition law. Article 107(2)(c) TFEU refers to aid that must be given to address the economic problems resulting from the division of Germany in the aftermath of the Second World War. More than 25 years ago Germany was unified again and, in its case-law, the CJEU has held that the financing of the costs incurred with this reunification are not covered by this Treaty provision.[43] As a result, the exception laid down therein is no longer of use. What is left is Article 107(2)(b) TFEU, which justifies aid to make good damages caused by natural disasters or exceptional occurrences. It is clear from the outset that in legal practice the exceptions of Article 107(2) TFEU are of limited importance.

3.1.2 The exception of Article 107(3) TFEU: great relevance

Article 107(3) TFEU provides that aid granted in order to pursue specific objectives could be considered to be compatible with the Internal Market. It is clear from the drafting of this provision that the Commission has discretion in deciding whether a national aid measure is permitted. Unlike Article 107(2) TFEU, national aid must not be approved for the sole reason that it is concerned with one of the interests listed.

---

[42] Hancher, Ottervanger and Slot 2016, p. 127.

[43] Case C-277/00 *Germany v Commission*, ECLI:EU:C:2004:238.

3.1.2.1 Overview

Pursuant to Article 107(3)(a) TFEU, aid given in areas where the standard of living is abnormally low or where serious unemployment exists may be permitted. What is meant by 'abnormally low' and 'serious unemployment' must be assessed from the perspective of the entire European Union.[44] In order for Article 107(3)(a) TFEU to be applicable, a particular area must be in a state of underdevelopment in comparison with the economic situation of all EU Member States' areas.

Article 107(3)(b) TFEU provides that aid promoting the implementation of an important project of common European interest or remedying a serious disturbance in the economy of a Member State could be approved by the Commission. The general concepts used in this provision allow for a wide variety of interests to be covered. The Commission has, for example, relied on Article 107(3) TFEU in the financial crisis of 2008. Many national decisions adopted in order to rescue banks in difficulty were approved by the Commission on the ground that a serious disturbance of the economy needed to be remedied.[45] The point is, however, that in Article 107(3) TFEU reference is made to the economy of a Member State and no attention is paid to an economic problem that is of a European or global nature. However, given the serious and urgent nature of the financial problems at play at that time, the Commission had no other choice than to make use of the possibilities of Article 107(3)(b) TFEU.

At the heart of Article 107(3)(c) TFEU is aid granted to facilitate the development of certain economic activities or of certain economic areas. This provision is, inter alia, concerned with regional aid like Section (a) of this provision. The significant difference is, nevertheless, that under Section (c) the benchmark is the economic situation in one particular Member State, whereas under Section (a), as already outlined, the entire European Union is the point of reference.[46] In prosperous countries, some regions can still lag behind in economic development, which may justify relying on the Treaty exception under Section (c), while invoking the exception under Section (a) is not an option. The CJEU has specifically held that the exemption contained in Section (c) is wider in scope than the one contained in Section (a).[47] It should be noted that regional aid will only be eligible for approval under Section (c) if trading conditions are not adversely affected to an extent contrary to the common interest of the EU.

Article 107(3)(d) TFEU governs aid granted in order to promote culture and heritage conservation. It is remarkable that this specific interest is singled out in EU state aid law and is given special attention. The majority of the Commission Decisions approving national measures on the basis of Section (d) relate to cinema and TV production.[48] This does not come as a surprise, as in this industry much money is spent on large projects.

To conclude, it must be pointed out that Article 107(3)(e) TFEU gives the power to the

---

[44] Case C-113/00 *Spain v Commission*, ECLI:EU:C:2002:507, par. 65.

[45] Hancher, Ottervanger and Slot 2016, pp. 143–4.

[46] Case C-113/00 *Spain v Commission*, ECLI:EU:C:2002:507, par. 65.

[47] Case C-248/84 *Germany v Commission*, ECLI:EU:C:1987:437, par. 19.

[48] Faull and Nikpay 2014, p. 1974.

Council to specify which other categories of aid may be approved by the Commission. The extended list of national aid measures eligible for approval must be laid down in an EU regulation.

The Commission enjoys a wide margin of appreciation when reviewing national aid measures under Article 107(3) TFEU. As was already stated, the chapeau of this Treaty provision says that the national measures under review may be compatible with the Internal Market, which suggests that a margin of appreciation is assigned to the Commission. Furthermore, the drafting of the interests that may justify national aid, such as an important project of common European interest and the need to remedy a serious disturbance of the economy, leaves considerable room for manoeuvre. In order to give guidance, the Commission has issued Communications and Guidelines that explain how it will make use of the powers under Article 107(3) TFEU.[49] For example, the Commission has adopted the Environmental Protection and Energy Guidelines 2014. In these Guidelines, reference is made to Article 107(3)(c) TFEU. This suggests that the Commission is of the opinion that environmental aid facilitates the development of certain economic activities. An important criterion that the Commission will apply is whether the national aid at issue is to increase the level of environmental protection compared to the level that would have been achieved in the absence of this aid.[50] Furthermore, the need for intervening by giving state aid must be shown, which entails that it is explained which market failures have to be addressed.[51] Moreover, the appropriateness of the aid concerned must be demonstrated. This means, inter alia, that it should be shown that no less restrictive means are available.[52] It does not come as a surprise that the aid must also be proportionate.[53] On top of that, the aid must amount to incentive effects prompting a change in behaviour.[54] The date of expiry of the Environmental Protection and Energy Guidelines 2014 is 31 December 2020 and, as a result, the Commission launched a consultation process in 2019.[55] In this regard, it must be noted that, when writing this book, the Commission was in the midst of developing policies for addressing the problems of global warming and related environmental problems, policies which are known as the Green Deal. The Competition Commissioner, Margrethe Vestager, has put forward that the state aid rules will be used in order to achieve the goals of the Green Deal.[56]

[49] These documents are available at <http://ec.europa.eu/competition/state_aid/legislation/legislation.html> accessed 10 June 2020.

[50] Environmental Protection and Energy Guidelines 2014, par. 30.

[51] Ibid, par. 34–37.

[52] Ibid, par. 40–48.

[53] Ibid, par. 69–80.

[54] Ibid, par. 49–68.

[55] See <https://ec.europa.eu/competition/consultations/2019_eeag/index_en.html> accessed 10 June 2020.

[56] Vestager 2020 (a) and (b).

3.1.2.2 Modernisation

Over the years, the Commission has modernised its approach to its assessment of national state aid measures under Article 107(3) TFEU. In 2005, it published its State Aid Action Plan,[57] which was a consultation document. In 2012, the Commission adopted its Communication EU State Aid Modernisation (SAM 2012). In this Communication, the Commission made clear that its intention is to approve state aid aimed at targeting market failures.[58] In addition, in the Commission's view state aid will be effective in achieving the public interest goals set when it has an incentive effect: companies must be encouraged to undertake activities that would not have been carried out in the absence of the aid concerned.[59] It goes without saying that serious disruptive effects for the proper functioning of the competition process in the Internal Market must be avoided. A systematic assessment of the potential negative effects of the aid notified will be made.[60] The parameters to be taken into account are distortions of allocative and dynamic efficiency, subsidy races and market power. The positive and negative effects of a particular aid measure have to be balanced, although this may prove difficult in practice.[61] All in all, the Commission has adopted a more economic approach to the national state aid measures it reviews under Article 107(3) TFEU. In 2019, the measures taken in the context of the SAM 2012 were subject to public consultation.[62]

3.1.2.3 The Corona crisis

In 2020, the Commission made use of its powers under Article 107(3) TFEU in order to respond to the Corona crisis. It published the Temporary Framework for State Aid 2020. In this Framework, it is set out which state aid measures adopted by the Member States in order to address the economic problems caused by the pandemic of 2020 are to be approved. As was stated above, pursuant to Article 107(3)(b) TFEU, the Commission has the authority to declare compatible with the Internal Market aid remedying serious disturbance of the economy. On the basis of this provision, national schemes giving temporary limited amounts of aid to undertakings facing sudden shortage of liquidity may be approved according to the Framework.[63] Another means of addressing liquidity problems is giving aid in the form of guarantees on loans. The financial support consisting of limited amounts of aid and aid in the form of guarantees on loans may also be granted through financial intermediaries, such as credit institutions.[64] Subject to conditions set out in the Temporary Framework for State Aid 2020, the Commission will also consider such measures compatible with the Internal

---

[57] State Aid Action Plan 2005.

[58] SAM 2012, par. 12.

[59] Ibid.

[60] Ibid, par. 18.

[61] Faull and Nikpay 2014, p. 1965.

[62] See <https://ec.europa.eu/competition/consultations/2019_gber_deminimis/index_en.html> accessed 10 June 2020.

[63] Temporary Framework for State Aid 2020, par. 21–23.

[64] Ibid, par. 28–31.

Market.[65] Moreover, subsidies given in order to finance interest rates for loans of companies having liquidity problems may be accepted by the Commission if certain conditions are met.[66] Furthermore, it must be pointed out that other national aid measures may also be approved by the Commission, for example, measures financing COVID-19 relevant research[67] and financing investments made in order to support infrastructures required for mass production of COVID-19 relevant products.[68] In sum, the Temporary Framework for State Aid 2020 has enabled the Commission to approve a wide array of national state aid measures,[69] which is unprecedented in our view, even in comparison with the financial crisis. It must be borne in mind that financial support given to many sectors of the economy is accepted under the EU state aid rules in order to prevent a very serious and dramatic economic downturn.

The possibilities of financing undertakings facing serious problems are not limited to approvals based on Article 107(3)(b) TFEU, as the Commission has also put forward that the Member States' state aid measures may also benefit from EU rules already in place[70] before the Corona crisis, such as the Block Exemptions.[71] Furthermore, in May 2020 it was announced that the Commission would propose a Solvency Support Instrument, the purpose of which is to enable equity support to businesses all over Europe.[72] The European Investment Bank is supposed to play an important role in giving this financial support.[73]

The leeway given by the Commission to the Member States to deal with the Corona crisis should be welcome. However, it is also worrying that the financial capacity differs from Member State to Member State and that, accordingly, finding a balance is very difficult.[74] Nevertheless, striking this balance is of great significance in order to prevent competition distortions in the EU Internal Market. On top of that, some businesses, not having been granted any financial support, may feel harmed, since their competitors have received large sums of public money. Against this backdrop, it is not surprising that Ryanair has announced to take legal action against the public bailouts of other airlines.[75]

3.1.3 Article 106(2) TFEU: Services of General Economic Interest

As was already stated, national measures financing SGEIs may be regarded as compensatory measures that do not fall within the scope of Article 107(1) TFEU. However, in *Altmark*, the

---

[65] Ibid, par. 24–25.

[66] Ibid, par. 26–27bis.

[67] Ibid, par. 34–35.

[68] Ibid, par. 36–37.

[69] For an overview of the measures approved by the Commission, see <https://ec.europa.eu/competition/state_aid/what_is_new/covid_19.html> accessed 10 June 2020.

[70] Temporary Framework for State Aid 2020, par. 11 *et seq.*

[71] Looijestijn-Clearie 2020.

[72] See Vestager 2020 (d).

[73] Ibid.

[74] Buendía and Dovalo 2020, p. 7.

[75] See S. Saeed, 'Ryanair Goes to War against Coronavirus Bailouts', available at <https://www.politico.eu/article/ryanair-goes-to-war-against-coronavirus-bailouts/> accessed 14 June 2020.

CJEU made it clear that four conditions must be met for concluding that these measures do not constitute state aid. As a result, much financial support given with a view to SGEIs is state aid, that is, when one or more of these conditions are not satisfied. However, it is not excluded that this support may be compatible with the Internal Market. Article 106(2) TFEU provides that enterprises entrusted with the operation of an SGEI are only subject to the rules contained in the Treaty, in so far as the application of these rules does not prevent them from performing the tasks assigned to them. Particular reference is made to the competition rules, which include EU state aid law. Consequently, the need to carry out an SGEI mission could justify that state aid is granted. The Commission has the authority to approve such aid on the basis of Article 106(2) TFEU. Pursuant to the procedural rules laid down in Article 108 TFEU, it is up to the Commission to decide on the compatibility of national aid with the Internal Market and, accordingly, Member States can only rely on Article 106(2) TFEU if they have notified the measures financing SGEI to the Commission. In other words, next to Article 107(2) and (3) TFEU it should be concluded that Article 106(2) TFEU also contains an exception, on which the Commission may base its finding that national aid is compatible with the Internal Market.

The Commission enjoys a wide margin of appreciation when deciding on the justifiability of national aid in the light of Article 106(2) TFEU. As with Article 107(2) and (3) TFEU the Commission has published guidance as to how it will make use of its powers to approve SGEI state aid. In this regard, the most important document is the European Union State Aid Framework for State Aid in the Form of Public Service Obligation.[76] As already stated, the concepts of PSO and SGEI are identical. In this Framework it is outlined that the SGEI mission at hand must be based on a national entrustment act specifying this mission and the methods of calculating compensation. The content and duration of this mission must be clearly articulated. Furthermore, the amount of compensation given must not go beyond what is necessary to cover the net costs of providing the SGEI concerned, including a reasonable profit. It is even required that the Member State financing a certain SGEI introduces incentives for the efficient provision of SGEI of high standard.[77] This obligation does not apply if complying with it is not feasible or appropriate. Furthermore, a system of separate accounting must be in place, if the enterprise entrusted with the task to provide SGEI does not only supply these services, but is also engaged in other economic activities (which probably are of a more commercial nature).[78] The State Aid Framework 2012 specifically states that overcompensation must be avoided. Aid that is in excess of the costs incurred with the performance of the task assigned and a reasonable profit is regarded as overcompensation.

The Commission has approved various national measures aimed at financing the supply of SGEI. For example, it was called upon to shed light on the organisation of the Dutch social housing sector.[79] The Dutch authorities granted economic benefits to social hous-

---

[76] State Aid Framework 2012.

[77] Ibid, par. 39.

[78] Ibid, par. 44.

[79] Case E 2/2005 and N 642/2009 *The Netherlands existing and special project aid to housing corporations*, (2009) C/2009/9963 final, Commission Decision of 15 December 2009.

ing companies providing housing services to low-income groups. As these companies were engaged in economic activities (letting dwellings in exchange for payment), the financial support they receive from the government amounted to state aid. The Commission was of the opinion that the task of Dutch social housing companies to rent out dwellings below market price to citizens not having a high income qualified as an SGEI mission.[80] However, at first, this mission was not clearly defined, as it was left open how to distinguish low-income groups from high-income groups. The Dutch authorities solved this matter by defining the target group for social housing through an income ceiling (which was, of course, subject to inflation correction). At the time of the Decision taken by the Commission in the Dutch social housing case this ceiling was set at 33 000 EUR per year, which included the lowest-earning 43 per cent of the population.[81] In this regard it should be noted that one of the policy aims of the Dutch government was to stimulate that various income groups live together in one neighbourhood, which could have positive effects on underdeveloped neighbourhoods. This policy of social mixity and social cohesion was accepted by the Commission, as it was based on clear and transparent rules. The social housing companies were permitted to rent out 10 per cent maximum of the dwellings to higher-income groups, which entailed that at least 90 per cent of the remaining dwellings were reserved exclusively to lower-income groups.[82] The Commission decided to approve the aid given to the Dutch social housing companies on the basis of Article 106(2) TFEU, as the tasks of these companies were based on well-defined SGEI missions. This Decision has given rise to much litigation,[83] which shows that financing SGEIs may lead to complicated legal issues. Eventually, the GC upheld the Decision taken by the Commission with regard to the Dutch financing of social housing.[84]

3.2 Block Exemptions

The obligation to notify enables the Commission to oversee the national aid measures that the Member States wish to take. The downside of this is, however, that examining and approving these measures is time-consuming and leads to considerable administrative burdens, both on the part of the Commission and the Member States. The Commission had to handle a relatively high number of applications entailing aid measures with only limited impact. This prevented the Commission from taking action against serious infringements of the state aid rules, more particularly against violations resulting from non-notified measures.

In order to strike a better balance between the need of oversight activities and the wish to reduce the administrative burden connected with the notification procedure, the Commission

---

[80] Ibid, par. 51–55.

[81] Ibid, par. 57.

[82] Ibid, par. 58.

[83] Cases T-202/10 *Stichting Woonlinie*, ECLI:EU:T:2011:765; T-203/10 *Stichting Woonpunt*, ECLI:EU:T:2011:766; C-132/12 *Stichting Woonpunt*, ECLI:EU:C:2014:100; C-133/12 *Stichting Woonlinie*, ECLI:EU:C:2014:105; T-202/10 *RENV, Stichting Woonlinie*, ECLI:EU:T:2015:287; T-203/10 *RENV, Stichting Woonpunt*, ECLI:EU:T:2015:285; C-414/15 *Stichting Woonlinie*, ECLI:EU:C:2017:215; C-415/15 *Stichting Woonpunt*, ECLI:EU:C:2017:216.

[84] Joined cases T-202 *RENV II* and T-203/10 *RENV II, Stichting Woonlinie and Woonpunt*, ECLI:EU:T:2018:795.

adopted the so-called Block Exemptions. The most significant difference between these instruments and the exceptions laid down in Article 107(2) TFEU, Article 107(3) TFEU and Article 106(2) TFEU is that the former category lifts the obligation to notify, whereas the latter category requires prior notification. To put it differently, the Block Exemptions leads to self-assessments carried out by the Member States wishing to grant state aid. It should be pointed out that in *Bayerische Motoren Werke*,[85] the CJEU has held that the Commission has the sole power to declare state aid measures compatible with the Internal Market and that, accordingly, the applicability of a Block Exemption only leads to the lifting of the obligation to notify.[86] Accordingly, the legal effect generated is of a formal nature. Compliance with the conditions of a Block Exemption does not justify the finding that the state aid measure is compatible with the Internal Market. It is for the Commission to decide this. In other words, compliance with these conditions amounts at most to a presumption that the measure at hand is compatible with the Internal Market.[87] In fact, in *Bayerische Motoren Werke*, the CJEU has made a distinction between the presumed compatibility of national aid with the Block Exemptions and the actual compatibility of national aid after the Commission has adopted an official Decision on the basis of, for example, Article 107(3) TFEU.[88] This subtle distinction gives rise to various kinds of questions related to legal certainty which the CJEU has to address in future cases.

As for the reason to introduce Block Exemptions in EU state aid law, a striking parallel exists with EU antitrust law.[89] As was pointed out in Chapters 5, 7 and 8, the enforcement of Articles 101 and 102 TFEU was decentralised with the entering into force of Regulation 1/2003 on 1 May 2004. Pursuant to Article 3 of this Regulation, it is up to the undertakings party to a restrictive agreement to assess whether this agreement satisfies conditions laid down in Article 101(3) TFEU. As a result of this, the Commission had the opportunity to free-up staff and to focus on detecting serious infringements of the EU antitrust rules. In the same vein, the General Block Exemption Regulation 2014, which entered into force on 1 July 2014, alleviates the administrative burden of the Commission and, accordingly, paves the way for boosting the enforcement of the state aid rules and prioritising cases involving serious violations of those rules. According to the Commission's estimation based on data obtained in 2012, 75 per cent of the state aid measures adding up to approximately two-thirds of aid amounts would be exempted by the General Block Exemption Regulation 2014.[90] In this regard, the outcome of the *Bayerische Motoren Werke* case may be a little worrying, as Member States may feel tempted to notify (some) aid measures fulfilling the conditions of a Block Exemption, as compliance with these conditions only amounts to a presumption of compatibility.[91]

---

[85] Case C-654/17 *Bayerische Motoren Werke*, ECLI:EU:C:2019:634.

[86] Ibid, par. 155.

[87] Nicolaides 2019, p. 343.

[88] Ibid, p. 344.

[89] Sauter 2016, p. 430.

[90] Press Release IP/14/587.

[91] Nicolaides 2019, p. 345.

3.2.1 The General Block Exemption

The Council has enacted the Enabling Regulation 2015, which gives power to the Commission to adopt Block Exemptions in EU state aid law. According to Article 1, the Commission may, by means of regulations, declare that particular categories of aid are compatible with the Internal Market and are, therefore, exempted from the obligation to notify. This Article specifies the various categories of aid which are subject to the Commission competence concerned. As already stated, the Commission has made use of this power by adopting the General Block Exemption.

In Article 1 of the Commission's General Block Exemption Regulation 2014 the categories of aid benefiting from this exemption have been listed. It is clear from the outset that this list must not contain more and other categories than those mentioned in the Enabling Regulation 2015 of the Council. The power of the Commission is limited to what is set out in this Council Regulation. Article 2 of the General Block Exemption Regulation 2014 defines some important concepts and, inter alia, clarifies what is meant by the various categories of aid listed in Article 1. For example, Article 1(c) of the General Block Exemption Regulation 2014 provides that aid for environmental protection falls within the scope of this exemption. Article 2(101) of this Regulation states that any action designed to remedy or prevent damage to physical surroundings or natural resources, to reduce the risk of such damage, or to lead to a more efficient use of natural resources (like energy-saving measures) is regarded as environmental protection. Given the large number of definitions to be given, Article 2 is very long, which is, however, needed in order to guarantee legal certainty. The aim of the General Block Exemption Regulation 2014 is lifting the obligation to notify, the violation of which will lead to the recovery of the aid given. As a result, it should be crystal clear whether a certain aid measure falls within the scope of the Block Exemption, which shows the need for a comprehensive and long list of definitions.

The fact that a particular state aid category is mentioned in Article 1 of the General Block Exemption Regulation 2014 does not automatically lead to the applicability of this exemption. The national measure at hand must satisfy the conditions set out in this exemption. Two sets of conditions are in place. The first set applies to all categories of aid, whereas the second set of conditions specifically governs a particular category.

As regards the general conditions, Article 5 of the General Block Exemption Regulation 2014 is of great relevance. According to this provision the aid given must be transparent, which means that it is possible to calculate precisely the gross equivalent of this aid in advance. In general, subsidies will be transparent, as these instruments normally come down to giving a certain amount of money to undertakings. Other economic benefits, such as loans or the selling of real estate below the market price, could give rise to issues in this regard.

Article 4 of the General Block Exemption Regulation 2014 reveals the rationale of the obligation of the transparency of aid. The obligation to notify is lifted in so far as the thresholds set out in this provision are not exceeded. For each category of aid, a threshold is set. For instance, investment aid for environmental protection must not, as a rule, be in excess of 15 million EUR per undertaking, per investment project.[92] It is clear from the

---

[92] General Block Exemption Regulation 2014, Article 4(1)(s).

outset that this threshold can only be applied if the gross equivalent of the aid concerned is calculated.

Another important general condition to be met is related to the incentives of the national aid measures. Pursuant to Article 6 of the General Block Exemption Regulation 2014 it is required that the national state aid measure has an incentive effect. The beneficiary has to be stimulated to undertake a specific project or carry out particular activities. Article 6 specifies in great detail how to establish whether a national aid measure has an incentive effect. Generally, the undertaking concerned must be obliged to submit a written application for the aid to the competent authorities of the Member States before work on the project or activity starts. This application must contain details, such as the description of the project, location of the project and the list of the project costs.[93] The reason for requiring an incentive effect is that aid not having such effect is not capable of addressing market failures.[94]

It goes without saying that specific conditions vary from aid category to aid category. Articles 13–56c of the General Block Exemption Regulation 2014 lay down the various conditions for aid falling within the scope thereof. Article 36, for example, concerns investment aid enabling undertakings to go beyond the standards laid down in EU environmental laws, or to increase the level of environmental protection in absence of such Union laws. Section 5 of this provision specifies how to determine the extra investment costs needed. Section 6 stipulates that the aid intensity ought not to exceed 40 per cent of the eligible cots. However, this level is increased by 10 per cent for medium-sized enterprises and by 20 per cent for small undertakings.[95]

If both the general and specific conditions are met, the obligation to notify is lifted for the national aid measure at hand. These measures are presumed to be compatible with the Internal Market according to Article 3 of the General Block Exemption Regulation 2014. If one of the conditions is not met, this obligation is not lifted, which entails that the measure concerned, in its entirety, must be notified to the Commission.[96] When a public authority finds that it has granted state aid not in accordance with the conditions of the General Block Exemption Regulation 2014, it must take action on its own initiative and order the recovery of this aid.[97]

It should be noted that the Block Exemption will expire on 31 December 2020. Given the need for the Commission to reduce its workload there is a strong chance that a new block exemption will be adopted or the duration of the present one will be extended (probably subject to some amendments). In any event, when writing this book, the Commission launched a public consultation with regard to a new or renewal of the General Block Exemption.[98]

---

[93] Ibid, Article 6(2).

[94] Hancher, Ottervanger and Slot 2016, p. 214.

[95] General Block Exemption Regulation 2014, Section 7, Article 36. Section 8 further increases the level of aid intensity for investments located in underdeveloped regions.

[96] Case C-654/17 *Bayerische Motoren Werke*, ECLI:EU:C:2019:634, par. 158–159.

[97] Case C-349/17 *Eesti Pagar*, ECLI:EU:C:2019:172, par. 95.

[98] See <https://ec.europa.eu/competition/consultations/2020_gber/index_en.html> accessed 22 June 2020.

3.2.2 SGEI as Block Exemption

Since the *Altmark* ruling, it is clear that the relationship between the EU state aid rules and SGEI requires special attention. The aftermath of this ruling has led to new case-law but also to the adoption of a package of measures by the Commission. The result of these actions is that in every stage of the assessment of a national state aid measure, SGEI could play a role. In *Altmark* itself, the need to finance SGEI could constitute a reason for finding that the ban on state aid is not violated. As already stated, measures that do not meet all the *Altmark* conditions still qualify as state aid but may be approved by the Commission on the basis of Article 106(2) TFEU. In order to give the Member States more leeway in financing certain SGEIs, the Commission has adopted a Decision that lifts the obligation to notify with regard to these SGEI. In fact, this Decision works in the same way as the General Block Exemption Regulation 2014, as national aid measures are deemed to be compatible with the Internal Market without prior notification.

The official name of this EU measure is the Commission Decision of 20 December 2011 on the Application of Article 106(2) of the Treaty to State Aid in the Form of Public Service Compensation Granted to Certain Undertakings Entrusted with the Operation of SGEI.[99] As already pointed out, SGEI and PSO are identical concepts. The legal basis for this instrument is Article 106(3) TFEU, which gives, quite strikingly, the Commission the power to adopt directives or decisions. It may be assumed that the absence of reference to regulations in this Treaty provision made the Commission adopt a decision. In any event, the 2011 Commission Decision contains generally binding rules, which exempts particular forms of national aid measures from the notification obligation.

3.2.2.1 The conditions of the SGEI Block Exemption

Article 2 of this Decision lists the national measures that fall within its scope. This provision refers to SGEI compensation not exceeding 15 million EUR (also known as compensation given to SMEs providing SGEI), SGEI compensation given to hospitals providing medical care, SGEI compensation given to providers of certain social services[100] and SGEI compensation given to enterprises providing transport services to remote areas. As with the General Block Exemption Regulation 2014, these national measures do not need to be notified provided that certain conditions are met. Two sets of conditions are in place. The first group of conditions concerns the act of entrustment, while the second group relates to the method of calculating the compensation to be given.

Article 4 of the SGEI Decision 2011 requires that the operation of the SGEI mission is entrusted to the enterprises concerned, by way of one or more acts, the form of which may be determined by the Member States. The design of this act must comply with the conditions outlined in this provision. For example, the content and duration of the mission assigned must be specified, the compensation mechanisms and the parameters for calculating, controlling

---

[99] SGEI Decision 2011.

[100] SGEI Decision 2011, Article 2 mentions the following social services: health and long-term care, childcare, access to and reintegration into the labour market, social housing as well as the care and social inclusion of vulnerable groups.

and reviewing must be described, and the arrangements for avoiding and recovery of any overcompensation must be pointed out.[101]

At the heart of the second group of conditions is the method of calculating the level of the compensation that will be granted. Article 5 of the SGEI Decision 2011 provides that the amount of compensation may not exceed what is necessary to cover the net costs incurred with the operation of the SGEI mission including a reasonable profit. Furthermore, the costs must be calculated in accordance with commonly accepted accounting rules. Moreover, the competent authorities of the Member States are obliged to carry out regular checks in order to prevent overcompensation.[102] It should be borne in mind that the SGEI Decision 2011 applies, inter alia, to hospital and social services. By emphasising the importance of the method of the calculation of the compensation, the Commission, in fact, requires that these services should be supplied in an efficient way.[103] If sound mechanisms for cost calculation are not in place, the national measures of financing the hospital and social services are not exempted from the obligation to notify.

3.2.2.2 The 'bigger picture' of EU state aid law and SGEI

It must be recalled that the SGEI Decision 2011 is part of an encompassing package dealing with financing SGEI. At the end of 2011 and in the course of 2012, the following measures were adopted by the Commission: the SGEI Communication 2012, the State Aid Framework 2012, the SGEI Decision 2011, and the SGEI *De Minimis* Regulation 2012. The latter contains a *de minimis* approach that is specifically targeted towards national measures financing SGEIs, and may be regarded as *lex specialis* in relation to the general state aid approach towards *de minimis* aid. According to the SGEI *De Minimis* Regulation 2012, the threshold for not notifying minor aids is raised to 500 000 EUR (over any period of three years).

The measures of the 'Altmark Package' deal with the various aspects of the assessment of national SGEI measures under the Treaty provisions on state aid. They also do justice to the emerging importance of SGEI, which is also apparent from Article 14 TFEU, according to which the proper functioning of SGEI must be guaranteed, Article 1 of the SGI Protocol 2007, which underlines the essential role of SGEI, and Article 36 of the Charter of Fundamental Rights of the EU, which focuses on the access for all to SGEI. Given the variety of the legal instruments of the *Altmark* package it may be difficult to see the bigger picture. The following scheme, which specifies which steps should be taken for reviewing SGEI measures under the EU state aid rules, could be helpful:[104]

1. Does the SGEI *De Minimis* Regulation 2012 apply?
2. If not, are all the conditions of the *Altmark* judgment fulfilled?
3. If not, does the SGEI Decision 2011 apply?

---

[101] SGEI Decision 2011, Article 4(a), (d) and (e).

[102] Ibid, Article 6.

[103] Van de Gronden and Rusu 2013, p. 214.

[104] Buendía Sierra and Panero Rivas 2013, p. 132.

4.   If not, can the national state aid measure be justified on the basis of Article 106(2) TFEU after notification to the Commission?

The State Aid Framework 2012 serves as guidelines as to how the Commission will exercise its competences under Article 106(2) TFEU. In section 3.1.3 of this chapter, some attention was already paid to this Framework. In its SGEI Communication 2012, the Commission gives guidance on all the steps that must be taken in order to examine whether national aid measures financing SGEI are in line with EU state aid law. Issues such as the concept of undertaking, the SGEI *De Minimis* Regulation 2012 and the SGEI Decision 2011 are addressed in this Communication. Strikingly, the Commission contends in this Communication that it is not appropriate to designate the supply of certain services or goods as SGEI, if these goods or services are satisfactorily provided on the market.[105] Although the assessment of whether no market failures occur is limited to verifying whether the Member State concerned has made a manifest error,[106] the point of view taken by the Commission does not sit well with the settled case-law of the CJEU. According to this case-law, it is within the competences of the Member States to designate SGEI.[107] A Commission finding in a particular case that the service or good concerned is already supplied adequately on the market, a point of view which is likely to be highly contestable, could interfere with this national competence. It should be awaited to see to what extent such a finding can withstand the test of critical appraisal by the CJEU.

When writing this book, the Commission was in the midst of an evaluation process verifying whether the SGEI rules dealing with health and social services meet the objectives of the *Altmark* Package.[108] In our view, the concept of SGEI is capable of playing an important role in the future, as, for example, the Corona crisis of 2020 has shown that the continuous provision of essential products and services (such as medicines, food and medical devices) may give rise to serious issues.[109] Member States may endeavour to secure this provision by giving financial support to enterprises playing a key role in this respect. For instance, a Member State could try to guarantee that a particular product, being of great interest to the national healthcare system, is produced on its territory by giving large amounts of money to the companies being able to manufacture these products in order to stimulate these companies to move their production facilities to the Member State concerned. Consequently, the Commission may consider shaping the SGEI rules in order to strike a balance between the

---

[105] SGEI Communication 2012, par. 48.

[106] Ibid.

[107] E.g. case C-67/96 *Albany*, ECLI:EU:C:1999:430, par. 103, 105. See also Buendía Sierra and Panero Rivas 2013, p. 136.

[108] See <http://ec.europa.eu/competition/state_aid/legislation/sgei.html> and <https://ec.europa.eu/info/law/better-regulation/have-your-say/initiatives/11835-Evaluation-of-State-aid-rules-for-health-and-social-services-of-general-economic-interest-and-SGEI-De-Minimis> both accessed 22 June 2020.

[109] For example, in its Temporary Framework 2020, par. 6–16, the Commission has shed light on the antitrust assessment of business cooperation projects dealing the shortage of essential products and services during the Corona crisis.

goal of undistorted competition and the need to secure that essential products and services are supplied not only in a particular Member State but throughout the entire EU.

4 THE ENFORCEMENT OF EU STATE AID LAW

From the foregoing it is apparent that national measures constituting state aid and not benefiting from Block Exemptions must be notified to the Commission. It is also required to notify a state aid measure that was approved in the past but will be amended, even if the group of undertakings eligible for the aid concerned will be restricted.[110] Article 108(3) TFEU clearly stipulates that notified aid that is not (yet) approved by the Commission may not be put into practice. This rule is known as the standstill obligation, as already noted. The CJEU has held that this obligation entails that in the absence of notification to the Commission, it is also not permitted to implement the national aid measure concerned.[111] Diligent undertakings must be aware that state aid is subject to prior notification to the Commission and for that reason, in principle, they cannot entertain legitimate expectations in absence of such a notification.[112] Relying on the principle of legitimate expectations by firms having received unnotified financial support is not successful in virtually all state aid cases. Legitimate expectation can even not arise if a national authority has granted state aid based on an incorrect interpretation of the conditions of a Block Exemption; misapplying these conditions by a Member State does not entail that the beneficiary is exonerated from paying back the aid received.[113]

It is clear from the outset that the Commission plays an important role in enforcing the EU state aid rules, as it plays a key role in the notification process. However, the CJEU made clear that a national actor also occupies an important place in this respect. In its case-law it decided that the standstill obligation has direct effect. As a result, domestic courts have the power to apply the last sentence of Article 108(3) TFEU and, accordingly, non-compliance with the standstill provision can be made subject to national litigation. Thus, it is possible to enforce this provision by national law. Theoretically, only the standstill provision has direct effect and the other Treaty provisions on state aid, such as Article 107(1) TFEU,[114] do not have such effect, as it is up to the Commission to review the national state aid measures in the light of the Internal Market. In practice, however, applying the standstill provision by a national court entails that this court examines whether the measure under review is caught by Article 107(1) TFEU. This implies that all the elements of this ban, including the complicated matters surrounding the *Altmark* ruling in SGEI cases, must be scrutinised by the national court called upon to apply the standstill provision.

All in all, both the Commission and the national courts are entrusted with important

---

[110] Case C-585/17 *Dilly's Wellnesshotel*, ECLI:EU:C:2019:969, par. 49–63.

[111] Case C-39/94 *SFEI v La Poste*, ECLI:EU:C:1996:285, par. 39.

[112] Case C-148/04 *Unicredito Italiano*, ECLI:EU:C:2005:774, par. 104.

[113] Case C-349/17 *Eesti Pagar*, ECLI:EU:C:2019:172, par. 101–106.

[114] E.g. cases 78/76 *Steinike*, ECLI:EU:C:1977:52, par. 8–9; C-301/87 *Boussac*, ECLI:EU:C:1990:67, par. 15.

enforcement tasks in EU state aid law. At first, the position of the Commission will be explored. Subsequently, the role that domestic courts are supposed to play will be pointed out.

4.1 Enforcement by the Commission

The main procedural principles of the notification procedure are contained in Article 108 TFEU. These principles are elaborated on in Regulation 2015/1589. In this Regulation a distinction is made between authorised aid and unlawful aid. Authorised aid means that the national measure concerned is notified in accordance with the EU rules, and approved by the Commission,[115] whereas in the event of unlawful aid, notification is not given and nevertheless implementation has taken place in contravention of Article 108(3) TFEU.[116] More precisely, authorised aid is part of the more encompassing term 'existing aid', which, apart from aid approved by the Commission is composed of aid that already existed before the TFEU entered into force in the Member State concerned.[117]

Chapter II of Regulation 2015/1589 deals with the notification procedure. Pursuant to Article 4, the Commission examines a national aid measure, as soon as it is notified. This is the first stage of the state aid investigation. After completion of the first stage of the procedure the Commission can take three decisions. In the first place it can find that the notified measure does not amount to state aid. The Commission is required to record that finding by way of a decision.[118] As a consequence, a third party has the right to challenge the finding of the non-applicability of Article 107(1) TFEU, as a decision is subject to appeal before the GC and higher appeal in front of the CJEU. In the second place, the Commission can take a decision stating that the measure under review falls within the scope of Article 107(1) TFEU, but is compatible with the Internal Market, for example, on grounds related to one of the interests mentioned in Article 107(3) TFEU. This is known as the decision not to raise objections,[119] which is also subject to judicial review by the Union courts. In the third place, the Commission may be of the opinion that the notified measure gives rise to serious issues under EU state aid law or, at least, it may entertain some doubts as to whether the measure concerned should be permitted. In that event, it decides to move to the second stage of the investigation procedure, by taking the decision to initiate the formal investigation procedure.[120] Even this decision may be appealed against, but normally the Member States and undertakings concerned will wait for the outcome of the formal investigation procedure.[121]

---

[115] Regulation 2015/1589, Article 1(b)(11).

[116] Ibid, Article 1(f).

[117] Ibid, Article 1(b)(i).

[118] Ibid, Article 4(2).

[119] Ibid, Article 4(3).

[120] Ibid, Article 4(4).

[121] A rare example is the appeal of the municipality of Eindhoven (the Netherlands) against a decision of the Commission to start the formal investigation procedure. This decision concerned a transaction concluded between this municipality and the football club PSV (the best football club of the Netherlands). Before the General Court was

When deciding on the notifications made by the Member States in the first stage of the investigation procedure, the Commission is bound by stringent deadlines. Pursuant to Article 4(5) of Regulation 2015/1589, the decision must be taken within two months, a period which can be extended with the consent of both the Commission and the Member State concerned. If the Commission fails to meet this timeframe, the aid under review is deemed to have been authorised by the Commission according to Article 4(6) of Regulation 2015/1589. It is clear that the sanction for not respecting the applicable deadline is very serious.

At the end of the second stage of the investigation procedure (the formal investigation procedure), the Commission can take three decisions. In the first place, the Commission can find (by means of a decision subject to judicial review) that on a closer inspection, the notified measure did not fall within the scope of Article 107(1) TFEU after all.[122] In the second place, the Commission can take a decision stating (probably following modifications made by the Member State concerned) that the doubts expressed earlier are removed and the aid concerned is compatible with the Internal Market.[123] In that event, the Commission has adopted a positive decision. The Commission is entitled to attach conditions to a positive decision, subject to which aid may be considered to be compatible with the Internal Market. Such a decision is known as a conditional decision.[124] It goes without saying that these decisions may be appealed against before the Union courts. In the third place, the Commission can decide that the notified aid is not compatible with the Internal Market and will not be authorised. This is known as a negative decision,[125] which is, unsurprisingly, often challenged before the GC and the CJEU.

The time limits that are in place in the formal investigation procedure are less strict than the limits applicable in the first stage of the investigation procedure. According to Article 9(6) of Regulation 2015/1589, the point of departure is that the Commission takes a decision within 18 months from the opening of the procedure. This time limit can be extended by common agreement between the Commission and the Member State concerned. In sharp contrast with the first stage of the investigation procedure, the sanction for failing to meet this deadline is not very serious. In the event that the Commission does not meet the time limit of the formal investigation stage, the aid under review is not deemed to be approved. What a Member State could do is to request the Commission to take a decision on the basis of the available information within 2 months. It is doubtful whether such a request would be in the interest of this Member State if no sufficient information is available. Article 9(7) of Regulation 2015/1589 specifically provides that, in the absence of information supporting the

---

able to hand down its judgment, the Commission adopted a decision ending the formal investigation procedure. According to this decision, the transaction at hand did not constitute state aid and, consequently, the procedure before the GC no longer had relevance and was, therefore, closed. See Order of the President of the GC in case T-370/13 *Eindhoven*, ECLI:EU:T:2016:516.

[122] Regulation 2015/1589, Article 9(2).

[123] Ibid, Article 9(3).

[124] Ibid, Article 9(4).

[125] Ibid, Article 9(5).

claim that the notified aid is compatible with the Internal Market, the Commission is entitled to take a negative decision.

It is clear from the outset that, after the Commission took a negative decision, recovery is not an issue if the Member State concerned observed the standstill provision of Article 108(3) TFEU; in that case, no public financial support is given to any company. Conversely, a Member State that did not live up to this rule and did grant state aid must take action upon a negative decision of the Commission. Such state aid is regarded as unlawful aid.[126] Article 16(1) of Regulation 2015/1589 provides that the Commission has to order recovery of unlawful state aid, if it has found this aid incompatible with the Internal Market. The money to be paid back by the beneficiary undertaking must include interest at an appropriate rate, fixed by the Commission pursuant to Article 16(2) of Regulation 2015/1589.

The Commission has the authority to start investigations concerning unlawful aid on its own initiative.[127] In this regard, it must be pointed out that the failure to comply with the standstill provision does not automatically entail that the aid concerned is incompatible with the Internal Market.[128] Consequently, the Commission is obliged to examine whether such aid may be justifiable on the grounds set out in Article 107(2) and (3) TFEU and Article 106(2) TFEU.

Then again, the proper functioning of supervisory mechanisms, envisaged by Article 108 TFEU, must not be jeopardised. Therefore, the Commission has the power to take interim measures in order to remedy the adverse effects resulting from the obligation to give prior notification of state aid.[129] In our view, the possibility to take interim measures strikes a balance between, on the one hand, the duty of the Commission to review an aid measure in the light of the Internal Market even in the absence of notification, and, on the other hand, the obligation of the Member States to respect the standstill provision. It should be borne in mind that the obligation to notify is one of the key pillars on which the entire system of the enforcement of the EU state aid rules rests. The matter of interim measures is dealt with in Article 13 of Regulation 2015/1589. According to this provision the Commission has the authority to order a Member State to suspend the implementation of an unlawful state aid measure (suspension injunction). It is even possible for the Commission to require the provisional recovery of the aid granted (recovery injunction), provided that the following conditions are met: (1) there are no doubts about the aid character of the measure concerned, (2) there is urgency to act, and (3) a serious risk of substantial and irreparable damage to a competitor exists. Suspension measures may be taken both after the initiation of the formal investigation stage and at the moment the Commission officially decides to open the formal investigation stage, having evidence that the Member State concerned is not willing to cooperate (sufficiently).[130] Moreover, it goes without saying that these measures must

---

[126] Ibid, Article 1(f).

[127] Ibid, Article 12.

[128] See case C-301/87 *Boussac*, ECLI:EU:C:1990:67, par. 11.

[129] Ibid, par. 16–20.

[130] Case C-456/18 *Hungary v Commission*, ECLI:EU:C:2020:241, par. 43.

be in accordance with the principle of proportionality.[131] If a suspension measure does not contain the reasons for the swift interventions made, this measure will be annulled for having breached the obligation, laid down in Article 296 TFEU, to state reasons.[132]

As regards the procedural rules for reviewing unlawful aid, Regulation 2015/1589 refers to the provisions dealing with lawful aid.[133] To a large extent these rules are similar. There is, however, an important difference between these two procedures. In the proceedings regarding possible unlawful aid, the Commission is not bound by time limits.[134] Consequently, the Commission may spend a lot of time on investigating unlawful aid.

4.2 Enforcement by the domestic courts

As already pointed out, the standstill provision enshrined in Article 108(3) TFEU has direct effect according to settled case-law of the CJEU.[135] As a result, the domestic courts are obliged to apply this provision. Thus, the domestic courts play a significant role in enforcing the EU state aid rules.

4.2.1 General observations

A company faced with (unlawful) aid given to a competitor may start litigation at the national level. Before a domestic court, it could argue that the public authority concerned has violated the standstill provision by giving financial support to another undertaking. Once a national court has found non-compliance with the standstill provision, it is obliged to order the public authority concerned to recover the aid granted.

As already stated, it is the sole power of the Commission to decide whether national aid is compatible with the Internal Market and, accordingly, the domestic courts must confine themselves to applying the standstill provision, without giving any judgment on the compatibility with the Internal Market. However, as also already pointed out, it is inevitable for a national court to verify whether all the conditions of the state aid ban of Article 107(1) TFEU are satisfied, when applying the standstill provision. The simple reason for this is that the standstill provision applies as far as a national measure falls within the scope of this ban. This implies that a domestic court must examine whether a particular measure constitutes state aid, distorts competition on the market and has an effect on intra-Union trade. As is apparent from the *Altmark* ruling, compensation given by a state body is not deemed to amount to state aid, if the (rather complicated) conditions set out in this ruling are met. Accordingly, when applying the standstill provision and examining whether the measure under review is caught by the ban on state aid, the domestic court concerned must also verify whether these conditions are fulfilled. This court is, therefore, forced to go into the details of national measures financing SGEIs. As indicated above, the Commission has adopted Block Exemptions in

---

[131] Ibid, par. 41.

[132] Ibid, par. 78.

[133] Regulation 2015/1589, Article 15 (1).

[134] Ibid, Article 15 (2).

[135] E.g. case C-39/94 *SFEI v La Poste*, ECLI:EU:C:1996:285, par. 39.

order to lift the obligation to notify for specific aid measures. This entails that national courts must also examine whether a state aid measure, which is subject to their review, falls within the scope of the Block Exemptions. Accordingly, they must scrutinise whether the conditions set out in these exemptions are satisfied. All in all, it is clear that the task of the national courts is not concerned with a simple procedural matter, but rather comes down to dealing with a wide range of EU state aid law issues. This task encompasses the interpretation of the concept of aid, the conditions of the *Altmark* ruling, and so on. The only matters that are not subject to the review of the domestic courts are related to Article 107(2) and (3) TFEU, as well as Article 106(2) TFEU.

The point of departure is that domestic courts order the recovery of the entire amount of unlawful state aid given to an undertaking. In *CELF*,[136] the CJEU has ruled that this includes the interest in respect of the period of unlawfulness. The rationale of this approach is that during this period the beneficiary company was not obliged to take a loan from the bank or other private investors. By recovering the interest, the competition distortions are remedied. The competition conditions on the market are restored. Regulation 2015/1589 contains, as already pointed out, a provision for calculating interest, by the Commission, in the event that this EU institution orders recovery of unlawful aid. This Regulation does not specify how national courts must determine the rate of the interest to be paid. Therefore, domestic courts must deal with this issue in accordance with national law. In its Notice on the Enforcement of State Aid Law by National Courts,[137] the Commission has given some guidance as to how to calculate the interest rates. It is important to take the nominal aid amount as the starting point.[138] Furthermore, the Commission is of the opinion that the method used by a national court for calculating the interest must not be less strict than the method foreseen in Regulation 2015/1589. The point is, however, that this Regulation limits itself to stating that rates must be appropriate and must be payable from the date from which the unlawful aid was at the disposal of the beneficiary, until the date of recovery. This leaves much room for manoeuvre. In fact, EU state aid law hardly contains any requirements for calculating the interest rates. All in all, the domestic courts have a wide margin of discretion, when it comes to calculating the interest rates and it may be expected that in many cases this gives rise to heated debates in the courtroom.

4.2.2 Procedural issues

It is up to national law to lay down the rules governing procedures in which state aid issues are raised. To date, these matters are not subject to EU harmonisation. Accordingly, both in private and public law procedures, a national court could be called upon to apply the standstill procedure. If, for example, a piece of land is sold below the market price by a municipality, it is likely that a private law court has to deal with the state aid issues resulting from this transaction. Conversely, a decision, by which a public authority grants a subsidy

---

[136] Case C-199/06 *CELF*, ECLI:EU:C:2008:79.

[137] Notice on Enforcement by National Courts 2009.

[138] Ibid, par. 41(a).

to an undertaking, can be challenged before an administrative court in many EU Member States. Such proceedings will be governed by national administrative law.

Although no EU harmonisation measures are in place, some requirements of EU law must be complied with. It should be noted that, according to settled case-law of the CJEU, the national procedural rules must be in line with the principles of equivalence and effectiveness,[139] including the right to an effective remedy and to a fair trial laid down in Article 47 of the Charter of Fundamental Rights of the EU.

Domestic courts must ensure that aid that is granted in contravention with the standstill obligation will be recovered. Two situations must be distinguished: either the domestic court is called upon to follow up on a decision of the Commission obliging the beneficiaries to pay back aid, or it has to decide on a domestic dispute involving a litigant claiming that the standstill provision is violated. In the first situation, national law must allow for immediate and effective execution of the recovery decision.[140] In the event national procedural rules prevent this, national courts are obliged to leave these rules unapplied.[141] In the second situation, in the same vein, the court must guarantee immediate and effective recovery in our view, if it finds a violation of the standstill provision in a case between various national parties. National procedural rules preventing the recovery of unlawful aid in national disputes also infringe the principle of effectiveness.

This principle has also some ramifications for the national rules on standing. In *Streekgewest Westelijk Noord-Brabant*,[142] at issue was the question whether particular individuals must have standing in order to challenge a state aid measure. In this case, the aid given was funded by levies imposed on certain companies. In the CJEU's view, every individual who has an interest in relying on the standstill provision must have standing and must be able to bring a case to a national court.[143] It does not matter whether the individual concerned has been affected by distortions of competition due to the state aid measure at issue. The only fact that must be taken into account is that the tax concerned is an integral part of the national measure that is implemented in contravention of the standstill provision. As a result, the companies that have paid the levies at stake must have the right to challenge these levies before a national court. It is apparent from *Streekgewest Westelijk Noord-Brabant* that the direct effect of the standstill provision has an impact on the national procedural rules for admissibility.

In *Residex*,[144] the CJEU was called upon to shed light on the relationship between national private law and the standstill provision. In this case, a national public authority provided a guarantee in order to cover a loan granted by a finance company to an undertaking. It was apparent from the facts that this undertaking would have not been able to obtain such a loan under normal market circumstances. Consequently, the guarantee granted by the

---

[139] Cases 33/76 *Rewe*, ECLI:EU:C:1976:188; 45/76 *Comet*, ECLI:EU:C:1976:191.

[140] Notice on Enforcement by National Courts 2009, par. 64.

[141] Case C-232/05 *Commission v France*, ECLI:EUC:2006:651, par. 49–53.

[142] Case C-174/02 *Streekgewest Westelijk Noord-Brabant*, ECLI:EU:C:2005:10.

[143] Ibid, par. 19.

[144] Case C-275/10 *Residex*, ECLI:EU:C:2011:814.

public authority amounted to state aid and the standstill provision was not respected, as no notification was made to the Commission. However, the question arose which consequences had to be drawn from the non-compliance with the standstill obligation. Was the domestic court obliged to declare that the guarantee granted was void? In *Residex*, the CJEU stressed that it is for the national courts to draw all the necessary conclusions of the infringement of this obligation in accordance with national law. It is required that unlawful aid will be repaid in order to eliminate the distortions of competition. The decision taken by the national court must lead to restoring the competition situation existing prior to the state aid measure concerned. If this result can only be achieved by cancelling the guarantee granted, the domestic court must decide that this act is void. However, if the result of restoring the competition situation can also be achieved by other means, it is not compulsory for the national court to apply the sanction of nullity. It is apparent from the *Residex* case that the standstill provision may have ramifications for national private law. Also, in *Arriva Italia*, the CJEU stressed that a national private law court should draw all necessary inferences from a violation of the standstill provision; this concerns both the validity of the act under review and the recovery of the financial support not notified to the Commission.[145] The result of the court ruling must be that the situation prior to the payment of the unlawful aid is restored.[146]

Both national courts and the Commission enforce the EU state aid rules and, accordingly, parallel proceedings may be pending at both the national and EU level, as could be the case in antitrust law too. These parallel proceedings may lead to complicated procedural issues. In *Lufthansa*,[147] the CJEU shed light on these matters. It held that, as soon as the Commission initiated a formal investigation procedure, the domestic courts dealing with the same state aid measure (that has not been notified) must stay their procedures. This approach is in line with the outcome of the *Masterfoods* ruling,[148] which is about parallel proceedings in antitrust cases. However, staying a national proceeding is sufficient in cases concerning Article 101 TFEU or Article 102 TFEU, whereas in EU state aid law this is not. The point is that aid that has already been granted will continue to distort competition, as long as it is being implemented. Therefore, the national courts may decide to suspend the implementation of the state aid measure at stake, or order other provisional measures. As regards the last measures, it may be assumed that it could be ordered to provisionally pay back the non-notified aid. In any event, it is required that the national court adopts all measures necessary to address the problems arising from the infringement of the standstill provision. The obligation to take these measures is derived by the CJEU from the obligation of sincere cooperation of Article 4(3) TEU.

As is apparent from *CST Azienda della Mobilità*[149] and *Buonotourist*,[150] previous rulings of national courts dealing with state aid measures are not binding upon the Commission.

---

[145] Case C-385/18 *Arriva Italia*, ECLI:EU:C:2019:1121, par. 84.

[146] Ibid, par. 85.

[147] Case C-284/12 *Lufthansa*, ECLI:EU:C:2013:755.

[148] Case C-344/98 *Masterfoods*, ECLI:EU:C:2000:689.

[149] Case C-587/18 *CST Azienda della Mobilità*, ECLI:EU:C:2020:150.

[150] Case C-586/18 *Buonotourist*, ECLI:EU:C:2020:152.

In these cases, certain state aid measures had been subject to judgments handed down by the Italian Council of State. Subsequently, the Commission took action, as it was of the opinion that the EU state rules were violated. The national procedural rules on *res judicata* (the authority of a final decision) did not preclude the Commission from doing so, as this Union institution has the exclusive competence to assess the compatibility of national state aid measures with the Internal Market.[151] If national rulings do not call into question the state aid given, it is still possible that the Commission may intervene and order recovery. This does not mean, however, that the Commission is free to intervene whenever it seems fit to do so. On the contrary, Article 17(1) of Regulation 2015/1589 provides that the Commission must order recovery of state aid within 10 years from the day the unlawful aid was awarded. This limitation term may be interrupted if action with regard to this measure is taken.[152] In the event that national authorities recover the unlawful aid, the national rules on limitation periods apply, subject, however, to the EU conditions of effectiveness and equivalence.[153] These conditions have ramifications for the national procedural rules. It is not permitted that the national limitation period expires before the Commission has adopted its recovery decision, or that the expiration of this national limitation period is caused by delayed action on the part of the competent national authorities.[154]

The principle of sincere cooperation between the Commission and national courts is elaborated on in Article 29 of Regulation 2015/1589. The first section of this provision provides that a national court may ask the Commission to give information in its possession, or its opinion on questions concerning the application of the EU state aid rules. When responding to such requests, the Commission acts in its capacity as *amicus curiae*. Article 29(2) of Regulation 2015/1589 stipulates that the Commission may intervene in national proceedings in which issues of EU state aid law are at stake. The Commission has the right to submit written observations and may even, with the permission of the court in question, make oral observations.

It is clear from the outset that Article 29 of Regulation 2015/1589 highly mirrors what is stipulated in Article 15 of Regulation 1/2003. The last provision deals with the cooperation between the Commission and the national courts in antitrust cases, and is discussed in Chapter 8. The aim of the provisions on cooperation between national courts and the Commission is to guarantee the uniform application of the EU state aid and antitrust rules. There is one striking difference between Article 29 of Regulation 2015/1589 and Article 15 of Regulation 1/2003. The first provision requires that the Commission informs the Member State concerned of its intention to submit observations in advance, whereas such an obligation is absent in Article 15 of Regulation 1/2003. From this difference it may be derived that state aid cases are more sensitive for Member States, than cases concerning Article 101 TFEU or Article 102 TFEU.

---

[151] Cases C-587/18 *CST Azienda della Mobilità*, ECLI:EU:C:2020:150, par. 92–97; C-586/18 *Buonotourist*, ECLI:EU:C:2020:152, par. 92–97.

[152] Regulation 2015/1589, Article 17(2).

[153] Case C-627/18 *Nelson Antunes da Cunha*, ECLI:EU:C:2020:321, par. 41.

[154] Ibid, par. 49–61.

5 CONCLUSIONS

The EU state aid rules are interpreted by the EU courts in an expansive way. All national measures leading to the transfer of public means to undertakings could fall within the scope of these rules. The basic setup of the Treaty provisions on state aid is crystal clear: aid distorting competition and impacting intra-Union trade is not permitted, save for prior approval by the Commission. Over time, this structure has become highly complicated, because a special approach for financing SGEIs has been developed and the obligation to notify has been lifted for specific national aid measures. In our view, these developments were triggered by the wish to smoothen the sharp edges of the standstill provision. More leeway is given to the Member States to finance various kinds of activities or projects, while the workload of the Commission is reduced. The downside of this is that EU state aid law is increasingly hard to interpret and to apply.

Both the Commission and the national courts are responsible for enforcing the Treaty provisions on state aid. During the last years, the Commission has concentrated on the serious infringements of the state aid rules, leaving the other cases to the national enforcement level. It may be expected that national courts will increasingly be confronted with complicated cases, given the tendency to decentralise the application of the state aid rules. So, the measures taken to guarantee the uniform application, such as the *amicus curiae* mechanism, are of great importance. The same is true for the guidance given by the Commission on various state aid issues.

In the years to come EU state aid law will be confronted with great challenges. For example, action should be taken in order to deal with the problems resulting from global warming (e.g. the Green Deal) and the Corona crisis of 2020. When writing this book, the Commission has launched several public consultations dealing with these challenges. Accordingly, it may be expected that the direction of travel of EU state aid law will change (probably considerably). In this respect, an important aim will be striking a balance between the goal of undistorted competition in the EU Internal Market and the significant public interest issues at play in these turbulent times.

PART VI

CONCLUSIONS

13

Conclusions: the evolving role of European competition law

A turning point in the development of EU competition law was the adoption of Regulation 1/2003. This piece of EU law has given a tremendous boost to the application of the EU competition rules at the national level and has led to the emancipation of the NCAs. The latter development was also spurred by the enactment or modernisation of the national competition law systems in many EU Member States. This development was perfectly in tune with the political views on the role of markets of that time. As it becomes clear from the analysis carried out in this book, the substantive national rules are for a great part modelled after the European equivalent provisions of competition law. The substantive rules were subject to a process of spontaneous harmonisation and, accordingly, compulsory harmonisation was not needed. The national rules dealing with procedures, organisational issues and enforcement, on the other hand, varied from Member State to Member State. It is, therefore, not surprising that the EU has adopted the ECN+ Directive 2019, the aim of which is to harmonise these matters. Strikingly, the harmonisation measures taken in the field of competition law do not concern the substantive rules, but matters of an institutional nature. On top of this, it should be noted that the Private Damages Directive 2014 has streamlined the national rules for the private enforcement of competition law.[1]

From the perspective of the decentralisation process it may be argued that EU competition law has been a success story. The EU has succeeded in involving a wide array of national authorities in the application and enforcement of the competition rules in order to ensure that the markets are competitive across Europe. However, changing political views on the role of markets, new developments, such as the emergence of digital markets, crises, and even the changing global circumstances show that EU competition law is subject to a heated debate. These developments will shape the application and enforcement of the competition rules. Although, the drafting of Articles 101 and 102 TFEU is still in accordance with the competition rules of the first European Treaties, the concepts, prohibitions and exceptions embodied in these Treaty provisions are very flexible and able to respond to new developments. Furthermore, the adaptions of the secondary law measures and the soft-law documents are also a possible avenue in this regard.

---

[1] These matters are discussed in Chapters 7–9.

1 THE EUROPEAN AND NATIONAL DIMENSIONS OF COMPETITION LAW

The decentralisation process has led to the creation of the ECN, in which the Commission works together with the NCAs of the Member States. This is an excellent example of a multi-layered governance system, tied together with the Treaty provisions on competition, EU secondary legislation, numerous Commission soft-law documents, national provisions of competition law and non-binding national rules. In other words, in the EU, the system of competition law has been turned into an impressive structure of complex rules aimed at making markets competitive. As competitiveness is at the heart of this system, economic theories have played and continue to play an important role in interpreting the various sets of competition rules. As is demonstrated in some chapters of this book, an important theme is the effect-based analysis, which requires that the decisions and rulings adopted are based on a sound economic appreciation of the impact of the (anti-competitive) practices, contractual arrangements, and other transactions under review. Applying the competition rules means that a profound understanding of the market is gained, based, for example, on an adequate theory of harm.

The Commission has given much guidance based on economic insights, as to how the various prohibitions and exceptions must be interpreted. Since the national substantive competition rules are modelled after the equivalent Treaty provisions, the former rules must also be interpreted in accordance with this guidance. In other words, national competition law is further Europeanised and, in relation to this, it must be stressed that soft-law documents of the Commission set out in great detail how to deal with specific issues. Accordingly, the influence of the Commission on the daily work of the NCAs and the national courts is considerable. National competition law has, undeniably, a European dimension for a great part.

However, it should be also pointed out that EU competition law has gained a national dimension too. The NCAs give effect to the EU competition rules by making use of the national frameworks of their jurisdictions. As a result, the EU norms interact with the national norms, and this process results in the addition of a national layer to the EU competition rules. The NCAs and the national courts reviewing their decisions are called upon to apply the EU competition rules to new cases and, accordingly, these national bodies are compelled to fine-tune these rules in order to respond to the new challenges. For example, the emergence of digital markets has inspired various NCAs to consider how the competition rules (including the Treaty provisions on competition) should be made fit for these markets. Such actions may even lead to proposals for amendments to be implemented at the national level. Furthermore, various Member States have in place competition rules that do not mirror the European equivalent competition provisions, but rather complement these provisions. For example, in France a provision laid down in the Commercial Code specifically prohibits abusively low pricing without requiring that the firm concerned is dominant. The German GWB contains a provision setting out how to establish dominance in digital markets. All in all, it is clear that the decentralisation process of EU competition law does not result in national systems which confine themselves to copying what is set out at the EU level. It is inevitable that principles, concepts and approaches developed at the EU level are elaborated on and made fit for the national arena in domestic competition law. This does not necessarily entail that this national course of action is incompatible with EU law; rather this course leads to the reception of the European norms of competition law in accordance with the national circumstances and, eventually, to a national layer further building upon the European layer. The supremacy of EU (competition) law does not need to be framed as a one-size-fits-all approach, but rather it could be also seen as a doctrine allowing for national refinement.

The decentralisation process does not only concern the competition rules directed at undertakings but also the law governing state action in relation to competition. Revealing in this respect is the *CIF* judgment of the CJEU (mentioned in section 2.2 of Chapter 11),[2] according to which, NCAs are competent, and even obliged, to apply the 'useful effect' norm. This norm precludes Member States from jeopardising the useful effect of the Treaty provisions on competition and, accordingly, the result of the *CIF* judgment is that NCAs must review national legislation in the light of this norm. More importantly, the settled case-law of the CJEU on the standstill provision in EU state aid law stimulates as well as obliges the national courts to subject national state aid measures to EU scrutiny. Unnotified aid not being detected by the Commission may still be confronted with recovery claims, namely before domestic courts.

2 ENFORCEMENT OF THE COMPETITION RULES

The enforcement of the EU competition law rules has evolved considerably during the last 15 years. It could be argued that the law dealing with this enforcement has come of age. An impressive enforcement toolkit for public enforcement is now available, containing classic tools, such as (high) fines and penalties, and specific tools, such as the leniency policy, the settlement procedure and commitment decisions. It is apparent from Chapter 8 that not only the former but also the latter tools have contributed to the efficient enforcement of the competition rules significantly. Regulation 1/2003 and ECN+ Directive 2019 set the scene for the Commission and the NCAs. Moreover, the enforcement actions of these authorities have been assessed in the light of fundamental rights, in the case-law of the courts. The litigation initiated by the stakeholders has enabled the European courts to build an extensive body of law dealing with significant enforcement matters. It goes without saying that efficient enforcement is an important value adhered to in EU competition law, since uniform application of EU law is of utmost importance in the European integration process. Nonetheless, a wide range of safeguards has been developed in EU competition law, such as the legal privilege and the *nemo tenetur* principle. As in EU competition law the (financial) stakes are high and more often than not large enterprises are involved in proceedings conducted by the Commission, many significant issues concerning safeguards have been debated at great length before the Union courts, which, in their turn, had to settle these disputes by deciding on the fundamental questions at play. Litigation in competition law has been a good breeding ground for the development of safeguards. It goes without saying that this process

---

[2] Case C-198/01 *CIF*, ECLI:EU:C:2003:430.

will not stop, and that competition law cases will continue to give rise to the development of important enforcement principles.

A very important building block of the enforcement structure in place is constituted by the ECN. As enforcement is now in the hands of a great number of NCAs, mechanisms are needed in order to ensure the uniform application of the EU competition rules. Coordination and cooperation within the ECN greatly contribute to this aim. On top of that, mechanisms are also in place in order to stimulate that the Commission and the NCAs work together with the national judiciary. Although EU law takes precedence over national law, these mechanisms are sensitive and, to a certain extent, even controversial, since judicial bodies are supposed to review the actions of administrative authorities, rather than cooperating with them. However, to date the CJEU seems to have accepted these cooperation mechanisms by holding that interventions of the Commission made in national proceedings before domestic courts, with a view to the efficient working of the EU competition rules, must be accepted by these domestic courts.[3] Guidance given by the Commission and the NCAs to domestic courts contributes significantly to the efficient enforcement of competition law, but given the independent position of the judiciary, the public bodies involved should proceed with great care.

Moreover, it should be noted that due to the Private Damages Directive 2014, the private enforcement of the competition rules has been stimulated. As a result, private law courts also play a role in this enforcement. It has to be waited and seen whether enforcement of the competition rules by private law means will take off in the EU Member States in the years to come. In any event, the endeavour of the EU is to involve private law courts in the enforcement of competition law substantially. The interaction between national private law and the competition rules may lead to interesting developments and the enrichment of both the EU and the domestic legal orders.

A very important means for fostering the uniform application of EU competition law are the notices, communications and guidelines issued by the Commission. Although these soft-law documents are not binding, great authority is assigned to them. As a result, these documents are not only used by the Commission and the Union courts when handling cases, but also by NCAs and domestic courts in matters concerning EU competition law. The notices, communications and guidelines contribute greatly to the enforcement of EU competition law, but it should be borne in mind that the final say in interpretation issues rests with the CJEU.

The enactment of the ECN+ Directive 2019 shows that the toolkit of the NCAs should be evaluated frequently. The aim of this Directive is to ensure that the NCAs dispose of a minimum set of enforcement tools. Also, at the national level, action is taken in order to extend this toolkit. A nice example is the GWB-Digitalisierungsgesetz (GWB Digitalisation Act),[4] according to which the German competition authority should be granted new enforcement powers in order to address, inter alia, digital market-specific issues. Another interesting

---

[3] Case C-429/07 *Inspecteur van de Belastingdienst/X BV*, ECLI:EU:C:2009:359. See discussion in Chapter 8, section 4.2.2.

[4] This draft bill is available at <https://www.bmwi.de/Redaktion/DE/Downloads/G/gwb-digitalisierungsgesetz-referentenentwurf.pdf?__blob=publicationFile&v=10 > accessed 23 June 2020.

example is the proposal made by the Dutch competition authority for introducing *ex ante* regulation of internet platforms,[5] which was followed up by a proposal made by the European Commission.[6]

3 THE EMERGENCE OF DIGITAL MARKETS

It is not a coincidence that the proposals for new enforcement powers are related to the digital markets. During the last years, competition authorities have been confronted with problems that are typical to these markets. Big Data play a key role in the online services provided by high-tech companies operating, for example, internet platforms, to their customers. On first sight, these services seem to be supplied free of charge. A closer look, however, reveals that the collected data are used for commercial purposes: targeted advertisements, for instance, are based on these data. The platforms are two- or even multi-sided: the collection of data from one side of the platform leads to the sale of commercial products or services on the other side(s) of the platform. Traditionally, price has played a central role in many competition law matters. As many digital services 'run on' Big Data, the authorities entrusted with the task to interpret and apply competition law are confronted with the question whether the role of price needs to be re-evaluated. This is a major and daunting undertaking, as price is deemed to be a decisive factor in many classical questions of competition law (hardcore restrictions, the definition of the relevant market, predatory pricing, and the like). In our view, it should be borne in mind that the collection of data is supposed to result in the supply of products and services for remuneration, as well as in profitable activities, at the end of the day. In other words, at least on one side of the platform prices do matter and money is paid. The novelty of the internet platforms lies in the interplay between the collection of data and its subsequent use.

It is clear that the emergence of the digital markets has led to a process of transformation of the modes of supply of various products and services. As a result, various principles, approaches and concepts of competition law need rethinking. As was clear from section 2.2.2.4 of Chapter 6, the occurrence of network effects is an important feature to pay due consideration to: large enterprises operate internet platforms and similar services. It may be assumed that especially the competition rules dealing with dominance are of great importance in order to respond to these effects. This means, as is clear from Chapter 6, that well-established concepts related to abusive behaviour must be re-evaluated. It is, therefore, not surprising that one of the NCAs has called for a reconceptualisation of the essential facilities doctrine.[7] The outcome of the cases brought against players such as Google may also shed more light on the relationship between the ban on the abuse of dominance and digital markets. In this regard, it must also be pointed out that the emergence of digital markets

---

[5] ACM Memorandum 2019.

[6] See   <https://ec.europa.eu/info/law/better-regulation/have-your-say/initiatives/12416-New-competition-tool> accessed 23 June 2020.

[7] This is a proposal of the French NCA. See Chapter 6, section 4.2.

brings about privacy issues, as the data provided by consumers and processed by huge high-tech firms are of a personal nature for a great deal. The German *Facebook* case (discussed in Chapter 6) reveals the delicate interplay between these issues and competition law, and also the different appreciations of this interplay. One of the questions to be addressed is to what extent the finding that the privacy rules are not observed should have an impact on the interpretation and application of the competition rules.

A very important concern is that successfully intervening in digital markets requires swift action. Innovation is one of the driving forces of these markets and is, also, of a rapidly evolving nature. The point is that the decision process in competition law is time-consuming as well as complex, especially in cases in which new fundamental questions are raised. The next example is revealing in terms of duration of the proceeding: on 10 February 2000 the Commission announced its intention to examine the impact of Windows 2000 on competition, on 24 March 2004 it imposed a fine on Microsoft and on 17 September 2007 the GC handed down a judgment[8] upholding this decision.[9] Against this backdrop, it is, therefore, not surprising that proposals are put forward to allow for rapid interventions. Various avenues may be explored in this regard. The conditions for adopting interim measures may be relaxed,[10] but also new instruments based on *ex ante* regulation could be developed.[11] When writing this book, the Commission had launched a consultation process in order to explore the latter option.[12] All in all, it is clear from these initiatives that it is a common feeling that competences enabling competition authorities to intervene with necessary urgency on digital markets are needed.

All in all, it is clear from the outset that the emergence of digital markets has posed new challenges to competition law. It may be expected that these challenges will have a considerable impact on the direction of travel of this area of law. It is likely that the interpretation and application of the substantive rules will change. Moreover, also significant amendments regarding procedural and enforcement matters are in the pipeline.

4 CRISES AND CHANGING GLOBAL CIRCUMSTANCES

It should be noted that, normally, the Commission acts as initiator for triggering new developments, such as the decentralisation process of EU competition law as well as the enhancement and harmonisation of the enforcement powers of the NCAs (brought upon by the ECN+ Directive 2019). This is different for the developments spurred by the pressure

---

[8] Case T-201/04 *Microsoft*, ECLI:EU:T:2007:289.

[9] These data are derived from <https://ec.europa.eu/competition/elojade/isef/case_details.cfm?proc_code=1_377 92> accessed 25 June 2020.

[10] In Germany, this is proposed by the GWB-Digitalisierungsgesetz. See Chapter 8, section 4.4.1.3.

[11] See Chapter 8, section 4.4.2.3.

[12] See <https://ec.europa.eu/info/law/better-regulation/have-your-say/initiatives/12416-New-competition-tool> accessed 27 June 2020.

resulting from the changing global circumstances. In Chapter 10,[13] it was outlined that the Commission prohibited the merger between Siemens and Alstom and, accordingly, refused to approve that an EU dominant player was created on the market for very high-speed trains, as well as for various railway and signalling systems.[14] It did not accept the argument that a 'European champion' had to be created in order to match the competition of enterprises from countries such as China. This decision has triggered various stakeholders to take action and, in fact, question the current framework of EU competition law. The German and French competition authorities jointly published a manifesto in order to advocate for 'a European industrial policy fit for the 21st Century'.[15] These plans do not only encompass a common strategy for funding technology and innovation, but also call for taking into greater consideration the State control exercised by third countries and the subsidies granted by these countries; this should result in a different approach to defining relevant markets. In the view of the French and German authorities, the Commission must pay due consideration to competition at global scale; in other words, a market definition must accommodate the benefits received from, and the control exercised by, third country governments, such as the Chinese government. It is not a coincidence that in 2020 the Commission started its review of the current Notice on market definition,[16] by inviting the stakeholders and the public to give their views.[17] In this review process, the challenge for the Commission is to strike a balance between the need to address the changing circumstances of globalisation and the benefits of the well-established approach to competition issues. The Commission has to cope with political pressure, as is clear, inter alia, from a Report issued by the French Parliament, in which it is stated that although EU competition law has its merits, the application of this law must be changed in order to address the challenges posed by the emergence of China as an economic player on the global level and the increasing importance of the digital economy.[18] The example of the *Siemens/Alstom* case is specifically mentioned, in order to explain that, currently, the application of the EU competition rules turns a blind-eye to the aggressive policies of the other economic global powers.[19] Against this backdrop, the White Paper issued by the Commission on levelling the playing field as regards foreign subsidies[20] does not come as a surprise. In this White Paper, it is acknowledged that subsidies and other actions of third countries may have distortive effects on the EU Internal Market. The introduction of various instruments is proposed, such as the adoption of a 'module' enabling the Commission (or another authority) to prohibit certain investments or acquisitions in the EU. The plans proposed do not stand alone, but are closely connected with recent measures,

---

[13] Section 3.2.3.2.

[14] Case M.8677 *Siemens/Alstom*, (2019) OJ C 300/14.

[15] Franco-German Manifesto 2019.

[16] Notice on Relevant Market 1997.

[17] See <https://ec.europa.eu/info/law/better-regulation/have-your-say/initiatives/12325-Evaluation-of-the-Commission-Notice-on-market-definition-in-EU-competition-law> accessed 26 June 2020.

[18] See Assemblée nationale 2019, p. 49.

[19] Ibid, pp. 49–50.

[20] White Paper 2020.

such as the EU Foreign Direct Investment Regulation 2019. EU competition law is thus bound to encounter important developments in the future, which are likely to be triggered by 'bottom-up criticism'. In our view, it should not be forgotten that the ICN could also play an important role in this respect. This network could issue best practices in order to stimulate a global level playing field.

Another global problem that will have its bearing on competition law is climate change. The response of the EU to this serious problem is known as the Green Deal. State aid will be used in order to mobilise industry and businesses for a clean and circular economy.[21] For that reason, the state aid Guidelines including those dealing with the environment and energy will be evaluated.[22] It is clear that the Green Deal is capable of having a considerable impact on EU state aid law. However, it should be noted that also other areas of competition law may be influenced. An important question is, for example, whether a restrictive agreement may be justifiable due to the environmental objectives it pursues. In Chapter 5 it was discussed to what extent the approach developed in *Wouters*[23] and subsequent case-law, as well as Article 101(3) TFEU,[24] accommodates concerns of public interest. A fair chance exists that this discussion will be further stimulated by the Green Deal. It is likely that the Commission and the NCAs will be called upon to assess whether particular restrictive arrangements have to be approved given their significant contribution to addressing the problems of climate change. Closely related to this question is the issue whether certain practices of a dominant under-taking may be acceptable in the light of a Green Deal specific objective. A similar question may be asked with regard to merger control. The Green Deal stimulates to rethink particular principles, concepts and approaches in EU competition law.

Another challenge is posed by Brexit. When writing this book, the outcome of the nego-tiations between the EU and the UK concerning their future partnership was not yet known. However, given the close economic and business ties between the UK and the EU Member States, it is clear from the outset that cooperation in the field of competition law is inevitable. The competent competition authority of the UK, the CMA, will be responsible for handling all merger cases, which impact the UK jurisdiction, including the large transactions that satisfy the thresholds of the EU Merger Control Regulation 2004. It should be avoided that parallel concentration control proceedings in the EU and the UK will have a chilling effect on business. Also, many commercial activities and, accordingly, anti-competitive practices will cover the territory of both the EU and the UK. Thus, joint enforcement efforts are needed to tackle the resulting concurrence problems. This calls for setting up a new structure of cooperation and for revisiting the role of the ECN. Since the economies on the continent and on the island are closely intertwined as a result of the European integration process of the last 40 years, many firms must comply with both the EU and the UK competition rules. In the event that the EU and UK rules will take a different path, this may pose a considerable

---

[21] Green Deal Communication 2019, p. 9.

[22] Ibid, p. 18.

[23] Case C-309/99 *Wouters*, ECLIEU:C:2002:98, discussed in Chapter 5, section 2.2.3.

[24] This matter was discussed in Chapter 5, section 3.2, with reference to the Commission's approval of a restrictive agreement due to environmental protection considerations, case IV.F.1/36.718 *CECED*, (2000) OJ L 187/47.

administrative burden on the companies concerned. This problem may be prevented from occurring if the EU and the UK are able to set up mechanisms leading to convergence in their systems of competition law. All in all, it should be observed that Brexit will not let EU competition law remain untouched.

In 2020 the world was hit by a terrible pandemic, which had its bearing on the EU and, therefore, also on EU competition law: COVID-19 caused by the Corona virus. The response of many countries, including the EU Member States, was the introduction of a lockdown. These lockdown measures paralysed many economic and other activities and, for that reason, an unprecedented amount of state aid was given by the Member States to undertakings, in order to compensate for the losses suffered. As was pointed out in section 3.1.2 of Chapter 12, the Commission approved virtually all national state aid measures. On the one hand, state intervention was needed in order to protect the national economies and the EU Internal Market. On the other hand, the problem is that state aid may have serious disruptive effects. The financial capacity of the government varies from Member State to Member State, whereas some undertakings do benefit from the emergency schemes and others do not. For that reason, it is of utmost importance that EU state aid policy carried out during the Corona crisis will be evaluated in order to learn lessons from this crisis. It should be established what impact the Commission's 'massive approval' of the national Corona aid measures has had on the efficiency and the credibility of EU state aid law, and on the functioning of the EU Internal Market. In that regard, it must be noted that funding and financial arrangements were also created at the EU level in order to address the Corona crisis, despite the intense debates and discussions between the Member States preceding these EU actions.[25] It is important to note that these EU actions did amount to some degree of solidarity at the EU level;[26] such solidarity is capable of mitigating the potential disruptive effects of the national state aid measures. In section 2.2.3 of Chapter 5 it was outlined that the Commission, together with the NCAs, gave guidance under which circumstances cooperation projects set up by undertakings in order to ensure the supply of essential products and services, such as medicines, were permitted under EU competition law. The endeavour of this guidance was to prevent that Article 101 TFEU and the national equivalent provisions would jeopardise the necessary measures taken by undertakings in the wake of this crisis. In Chapter 6, attention was paid to the gatekeepers' role of enterprises operating internet platforms. The Corona crisis has shown that many businesses and consumers in the EU are heavily dependent on these kinds of digital facilities and other digital services. This raises the question what this means for the way Article 102 TFEU and the national equivalent provisions have to be applied to these digital facilities and services. All in all, access to essential goods and services turned out to be a serious problem during the crisis. For that reason, it cannot be excluded that the concept of Services of General (Economic) Interest,[27] which is concerned with tackling such issues, will see a revival.

As with the Green Deal developments, the Corona crisis has revealed that important

---

[25] On these EU measures, see Neergaard and De Vries 2020, pp. 24–31.

[26] Ibid, p. 31.

[27] This concept was discussed both in Chapters 11 and 12.

questions on the relationship between competition law and public interests have to be addressed. Given the immense and long-term harm caused by the Corona crisis, it may be expected that balancing these interests will remain high on the agenda in the years to come.

5 WHAT IS EUROPEAN COMPETITION LAW ABOUT?

In the first chapter of this book we put forward that EU competition law aims, at least, to foster some rivalry between undertakings. Competition on the merits is beneficial for consumer welfare, for the Internal Market and for various other goals. In our view, competition law stimulates to review business and even state measures in order to establish whether they contribute to the achievement of these objectives. At the end of the day, competition law is all about appreciating the gains of the free market and balancing these gains with other significant values and benefits.

Bibliography

G. Afferni, 'Case: ECJ – *Manfredi v Lloyd Adriatico*' (2007) 3 *European Review of Contract Law* 2

H. Andersson, *Dawn Raids under Challenge: Due Process Aspects on the European Commission's Dawn Raid Practices* (Hart Publishing 2018)

P.E. Areeda and D. Turner, 'Predatory Pricing and Related Practices under Section 2 of the Sherman Act' (1975) 88 *Harvard Law Review* 697

P.E. Areeda and H. Hovenkamp, *Antitrust Law: An Analysis of Antitrust Principles and Their Application* (vol IA, 3rd edn, Aspen Publisher 2006)

A. Bach, 'Commentary on Section 54 of the GWB' in U. Immenga and E.-J. Mestmäcker (eds), *Wettbewerbsrecht: Band 2 Kommentar zum Deutschen Kartellrecht* (6th edn, 2020), available at <https://beck-online.beck.de/?vpath=bibdata/komm/ImmengaKoWbR_5_Band2/cont/ImmengaKoWbR.htm> accessed 20 June 2020

D. Bailey, 'Presumptions in EU Competition Law' (2010) 31 *European Competition Law Review* 9

C. Barnard, *The Substantive Law of the EU: The Four Freedoms* (6th edn, Oxford University Press 2019)

S. Baxter and F. Dethmers, 'Unilateral Effects under the European Merger Regulation: How Big Is the Gap?' (2005) 26 *European Competition Law Review* 7

R. Bechtold and W. Bosch, *Gesetz gegen Wettbewerbsbeschränkungen, Kommentar* (9th edn, C.H. Beck 2018)

R. van den Bergh, P. Camesasca and A. Giannaccari, *Comparative Competition Law and Economics* (Edward Elgar Publishing 2017)

A.E. Beumer, 'Interactie tussen fundamentele rechten en mededinging: het arrest Otis' (2013) (1/2) *Nederlands Tijdschrift voor Europees Recht* 7

S. Bishop and M. Walker, *The Economics of EC Competition Law* (3rd edn, Sweet & Maxwell 2010)

R.D. Blair and K.L Coffin, 'Physician Collective Bargaining: State Legislation and the State Action Doctrine' (2004–05) 26 *Cardozo Law Review* 101

M. Botta, 'Commission Acting as Plaintiff in Cases of Private Enforcement of EU Competition Law: Otis' (2013) 50 *Common Market Law Review* 4

M. Botta, 'The Principle of Passing on in EU Competition Law in the Aftermath of the Damages Directive' (2017) 25 *European Review of Private Law* 5

M. Botta and K. Widermann, 'Exploitative Conducts in Digital Markets: Time for a Discussion after the Facebook Decision' (2019) 10 *Journal of European Competition Law & Practice* 8

Y. Botteman, 'Mergers, Standard of Proof and Expert Economic Evidence' (2006) 2 *Journal of Competition Law & Economics* 1

J. Bourgeois and D. Waelbroeck (eds), *Ten Years of Effects-Based Approach in EU Competition Law: State of Play and Perspectives* (Bruylant 2012)

B. Braat, *The Relation between Leniency and Private Enforcement: Towards an Optimum of Overall Competition Law Enforcement?* (Paris Legal Publishers 2018)

S. Brammer, *Horizontal Aspects of the Decentralisation of EU Competition Law Enforcement* (PhD Dissertation 2008) available at <https://core.ac.uk/download/pdf/34435674.pdf> accessed 24 June 2020

S.-P. Brankin, 'The Substantive Standard behind the Object/Effect Distinction Post-Cartes Bancaires' (2016) 37 *European Competition Law Review* 9

M.P. Broberg, 'The Concept of Control in the Merger Control Regulation' (2004) 29 *European Competition Law Review* 12

N. Bucan, *The Enforcement of EU Competition Rules by Civil Law* (Wolf Legal Publishers 2013)

J.L. Buendía Sierra, *Exclusive Rights and State Monopolies under EC Law: Article 86 (former Article 90) of the EC Treaty* (Oxford University Press 1999)

J.L. Buendía Sierra, 'Enforcement of Article 106 (1) TFEU by the European Commission and the EU Courts' in P. Lowe, G. Monti and M. Marquis (eds), *European Competition Law Annual 2013* (Hart Publishing 2016), p. 279

J.L. Buendía Sierra and J.M. Panero Rivas, 'The Almunia Package: State Aid and Services of General Economic Interest' in E. Szyszczak and J.W. van de Gronden (eds), *Financing Services of General Economic Interest: Reform and Modernization* (TMC Asser Press/Springer 2013), p. 125

J.L. Buendía and A. Dovalo, 'State Aid versus COVID-19: The Commission Adopts a Temporary Framework' (2020) 19 *European State Aid Law Quarterly* 1

H.P. Bull, 'Daseinsvorsorge im Wandel der Staatsformen' (2008) 47 *Der Staat* 1

P. Camesasca, *European Merger Control: Getting the Efficiencies Right* (Intersentia 2000)

A.D. Chirita, 'The Disclosure of Evidence under the Antitrust Damages Directive 2014/104/EU' in V. Tomlenovic, N. Bodiroga-Vukobrat, V. Butorac Malnar and I. Kunda (eds), *EU Competition and State Aid Rules: Public and Private Enforcement* (Springer 2018), p. 147

R. Cisotta, 'Some Considerations on the Last Developments on Antitrust Damages Actions and Collective Redress in the European Union' (2014) 10 *The Competition Law Review* 1

P. Van Cleynenbreugel, 'Associations of Undertakings and Their Decisions in the Wake of Mastercard' (2015) 36 *European Competition Law Review* 6

M. Contreras, 'Incentives to Apply for Leniency: Criminalising Cartel Offences in Spain' in A. Looijestijn-Clearie, C.S. Rusu and J.M. Veenbrink (eds), *Boosting the Enforcement of EU Competition Law at the Domestic Level* (Cambridge Scholars Publishing 2017), p. 71

M. Cremona (ed), *Market Integration and Public Services in the European Union* (Oxford University Press 2011)

K. Cseres, 'The Controversies of the Consumer Welfare Standard' (2006) 3 *Competition Law Review* 2

M.H. Dabbah, *International and Comparative Competition Law* (Cambridge University Press 2010)

S. Davidson, 'Actions for Damages in the English Courts for Breach of EEC Competition Law' (1985) 34 *International and Comparative Law Quarterly* 1

C. Decker, *Economics and the Enforcement of European Competition Law* (Edward Elgar Publishing 2009)

S. Drake, 'Scope of *Courage* and the Principle of "Individual Liability" for Damages: Further Development of the Principle of Effective

Judicial Protection by the Court of Justice' (2006) 31 *European Law Review* 6

M. Dreyfus, 'Experiences in the Member States: France' in M. Krajewski, U. Neergaard and J.W. van de Gronden (eds), *The Changing Legal Framework for Services of General Interest in Europe: Between Competition and Solidarity* (TMC Asser Press/Cambridge University Press 2009), p. 269

N. Dunne, 'It Never Rains but It Pours? Liability for "Umbrella Effects" under EU Competition Law in *Kone*' (2014 (a)) 51 *Common Market Law Review* 6

N. Dunne, 'The Role of Private Enforcement within EU Competition Law' (2014 (b)) 16 *Cambridge Yearbook of European Legal Studies* 143

N. Dunne, *Competition Law and Economic Regulation: Making and Managing Markets* (Cambridge University Press 2015)

N. Dzino, 'Independence Requirements in Directive 2019/1 and the Case of the Netherlands' in C.S. Rusu, A. Looijestijn-Clearie, J. Veenbrink and S. Tans (eds), *New Directions in Competition Law Enforcement* (Wolf Legal Publishers 2020), p. 37

N. Dzino and C.S. Rusu, 'Public Enforcement of EU Competition Law: A Circle of Trust?' (2019) 12 *Review of European Administrative Law* 1

N. Dzino, J.W. van de Gronden and C.S. Rusu, 'ECN+ Richtlijn: toegevoegde waarde en betekenis voor het publieke handhavingssysteem in Nederland' (2019) 67 *SEW: Tijdschrift voor Europees en economisch recht* 12

D. Edward and M. Hoskins, 'Article 90: Deregulation and EC Law – Reflections Arising from the XVI Fide Conference' (1995) 32 *Common Market Law Review* 1

C.-D. Ehlermann, 'Implementation of EC Competition Law by National Antitrust Authorities' (1996) 17 *European Competition Law Review* 2

H. van Eijken, *European Citizenship and the Constitutionalisation of the European Union* (Europa Law Publishing 2014)

E. Elhauge and D. Geradin, *Global Competition Law and Economics* (Hart Publishing 2011)

N. Esken, A. von Graevenitz, D. Slobodenjuk, M. Kammer, R. Jorias, T. Lemmens and A. Gronemeyer, 'Germany' in D. Sokol, D. Crane and A. Ezrachi (eds), *Global Antitrust Compliance Handbook* (Oxford University Press 2014), p. 279

J. Faull and A. Nikpay (eds), *The EU Law of Competition* (3rd edn, Oxford University Press 2014)

M. Filippelli, *Collective Dominance and Collusion: Parallelism in EU and US Competition Law* (Edward Elgar Publishing 2013)

K. Fountoukakos and S. Ryan, 'A New Substantive Test for EU Merger Control' (2005) 26 *European Competition Law Review* 277

K. Fountoukakos, M. Nuys, J. Penz and P. Rowland, 'The German FCO's Decision against Facebook: A First Step towards the Creation of Digital House Rules?' (2019) 18 *Journal of Competition Law* 1

E. Fox and D. Gerard, *EU Competition Law: Cases, Texts and Context* (Edward Elgar Publishing 2017)

C. Fratea, 'Commitment Decisions and Private Actions for Damages in EU Competition Law in Light of the Gasorba Judgment: A New Opening from the Court of Justice of the European Union?' (2018) 39 *European Competition Law Review* 12

A. Fuchs, 'Commentary on Sections 18–19 of the GWB' in U. Immenga and E.-J. Mestmäcker (eds), *Wettbewerbsrecht: Band 2 Kommentar zum Deutschen Kartellrecht* (6th edn, 2020), available at <https://beck-online.beck.de/?vpath=bibdata/komm/ImmengaKoWbR_5_Band2/cont/

ImmengaKoWbR.htm> accessed 20 June 2020

D. Geradin and N. Petit, 'Price Discrimination under EC Competition Law: The Need for a Case-by-Case Approach' (2005) College of Europe GCLC Working Paper 07/05

D. Geradin, A. Layne-Farrar and N. Petit, *EU Competition Law & Economics* (Oxford University Press 2012)

D.J. Gerber, *Global Competition: Law, Markets and Globalization* (Oxford University Press 2010)

A. Gerbrandy, 'Addressing the Legitimacy Problem for Competition Authorities Taking into Account Non-Economic Values: The Position of the Dutch Competition Authority' (2015) 5 *European Law Review* 769

A. Gerbrandy, 'Solving a Sustainability-Deficit in European Competition Law' (2017) 40 *World Competition* 4

A. Gerbrandy, 'Conceptualizing Big Tech as "Modern Bigness" and Its Implications for European Competition Law' (2018) available at <https://ec.europa.eu/competition/information/digitisation_2018/contributions/anna_gerbrandy.pdf> accessed 21 May 2020

D. Gilo, Y. Moshe and Y. Spiegel, 'Partial Cross Ownership and Tacit Collusion' (2006) 37 *RAND Journal of Economics* 1

P.P.J. van Ginneken, 'Case Comment on Case T-112/99' (2002) 2 *Markt en Mededinging* 79

D. Gore, S. Lewis, A. Lofaro and F. Dethmers, *The Economic Assessment of Mergers under European Competition Law* (Cambridge University Press 2013)

I. Graef, 'Market Definition and Market Power in Data: The Case of Online Platforms' (2015) 38 *World Competition* 4

C. Graham, *EU and UK Competition Law* (Pearson 2010)

J.W. van de Gronden, 'The Services Directive and Services of General (Economic) Interest' in M. Krajewski, U. Neergaard and J.W.

van de Gronden (eds), *The Changing Legal Framework for Services of General Interest in Europe: Between Competition and Solidarity* (TMC Asser Press/Cambridge University Press 2009), p. 233

J.W. van de Gronden, 'Services of General (Economic) Interest in EU Competition Law' in C. Heide-Jorgensen, C. Bergqvist, U. Neergaard and S. Troels Poulsen (eds), *Aims and Values in Competition Law* (DJØF Publishing 2013 (a)), p. 241

J.W. van de Gronden, 'Transnational Competition Law and Public Services' in C. Herrmann, M. Krajewski and J.P. Terhechte, *European Yearbook of International Economic Law 2013* (Springer 2013 (b)), p. 109

J.W. van de Gronden, *Mededingingsrecht in de EU en Nederland* (Uitgeverij Paris 2017)

J.W. van de Gronden, 'Services of General Interest and the Concept of Undertaking: Does EU Competition Law Apply?' (2018) 41 *World Competition* 2

J.W. van de Gronden, 'Big Data en Mededingingsrecht: Is Artikel 102 VWEU klaar voor de uitdaging?' (2019) 68 *Ars Aequi* 5

J.W. van de Gronden and S.A. de Vries, 'Independent Competition Authorities in the EU' (2006) 2 *Utrecht Law Review* 1

J.W. van de Gronden and C.S. Rusu, 'Services of General (Economic) Interest Post-Lisbon' in M. Trybus and L. Rubini, *The Treaty of Lisbon and the Future of European Law and Policy* (Edward Elgar Publishing 2012), p. 413

J.W. van de Gronden and C.S. Rusu, 'The Altmark Update and Social Services: Toward a European Approach' in E. Szyszczak and J.W. van de Gronden (eds), *Financing Services of General Economic Interest: Reform and Modernization* (TMC Asser Press/Springer 2013), p. 185

L. Hancher, T. Ottervanger and P.J. Slot (eds), *EU State Aids* (5th edn, Sweet & Maxwell 2016)

C. Harding and J. Joshua, *Regulating Cartels in Europe: A Study of Legal Control of Corporate Delinquency* (Oxford University Press 2003)

N.F.W. Hauge and C. Palzer, 'Investigator, Prosecutor, Judge . . . and Now Plaintiff? The Leviathanian Role of the European Commission in the Light of Fundamental Rights' (2013) 36 *World Competition* 4

K. Hellingman and L.J.M. Mortelmans, *Economisch Publiekrecht: Rechtswaarborgen en Rechtsinstrumenten* (Kluwer 1989)

Y. Heng Alvin Sng, 'The Distinction between "Object" and "Effect" in EU Competition Law and Concerns after Groupement des Cartes Bancaires (C-67/13P)' (2016) 37 *European Competition Law Review* 5

N. Hirst, 'Donau Chemie: National Rules Impeding Access to Antitrust Files Liable to Breach EU Law' (2013) 4 *Journal of European Competition Law & Practice* 6

T. Hoppner, 'Defining Markets for Multi-Sided Platforms: The Case of Search Engines' (2015) 38 *World Competition* 3

H. Hovenkamp, *The Antitrust Enterprise: Principle and Execution* (Harvard University Press 2008)

P. Ibáñez Colomo, 'Appreciability and *De Minimis* in Article 102 TFEU' (2016) 7 *Journal of European Competition Law and Practice* 10

P. Ibáñez Colomo, 'Finding the Appropriate Legal Test in EU Competition Law: On Presumptions and Remedies', (2018 (a)) available at <https://chillingcompetition.com/2018/11/02/finding-the-appropriate-legal-test-in-eu-competition-law-on-presumptions-and-remedies/> accessed 12 June 2020

P. Ibáñez Colomo, 'The Android Decision Is Out: The Exciting Legal Stuff beneath the Noise', (2018 (b)) available at <https://chillingcompetition.com/2018/07/18/the-android-decision-is-out-the-exciting-legal-stuff-beneath-the-noise-by-pablo/> accessed 16 June 2020

P. Ibáñez Colomo, 'Persistent Myths in Competition Law (V): There is No Such Thing as an Abuse by Object (or by Effect) under Article 102 TFEU', (2020) available at <https://chillingcompetition.com/2020/01/10/persistent-myths-in-competition-law-v-there-is-no-such-thing-as-an-abuse-by-object-or-by-effect-under-article-102-tfeu/> accessed 12 June 2020

F. Ilzkovitz and R. Meiklejohn (eds), *European Merger Control: Do We Need an Efficiency Defence?* (Edward Elgar Publishing 2006)

R.P. Inman and D.L. Rubinfeld, 'Making Sense of the Antitrust State Action Doctrine: Resolving the Tension between Political Participation and Economic Efficiency' (1996–97) 75 *Texas Law Review* 1203

M. Israel, J. MacLennan and J. Jeram, 'Vertical Restraints in an Online World: Competition Authorities Gear up Their Enforcement Approach in the Digital Economy' (2019) 18 *Journal of Competition Law* 1

J.H. Jans, S. Prechal and R.J.G.M. Widdershoven (eds), *Europeanisation of Public Law* (2nd edn, Europa Law Publishing 2015)

A. Jones and J. Davies, 'Merger Control and the Public Interest: Balancing EU and National Law in the Protectionist Debate' in B.E. Hawk (ed), *International Antitrust Law & Policy* (Juris Publishing 2015), p. 63

A. Jones, B. Sufrin and N. Dunne, *EU Competition Law: Text, Cases, and Materials* (7th edn, Oxford University Press 2019)

H.W. de Jong, 'Nederland: het kartelparadijs van Europa?' *Economische Statische Berichten* [Economic statistics messages], 14 March 1990

M. Kadar, 'European Union Competition Law in the Digital Era' (2015) 4 *Zeitschrift für Wettbewerbsrecht* 342

P. Kapteyn and P. VerLoren van Themaat, *Het*

recht van de Europese Gemeenschappen (6th edn, Kluwer 2003)

Y. Katsoulacos and F. Jenny (eds), *Excessive Pricing and Competition Law Enforcement* (Springer 2018)

W. Kerber, 'Digital Markets, Data, and Privacy: Competition Law, Consumer Law and Data Protection' (2016) 11 *Journal of Intellectual Property Law* 856

I. Klauß and D.J. dos Santos Goncalves, 'Germany: General – Price Comparison Websites' (2018) 38 *European Competition Law Review* N66

I. Knable Gotts (ed), *The Merger Control Review* (Law Business Research 2012)

C. Koenig, 'An Economic Analysis of the Single Economic Entity Doctrine in EU Competition Law' (2017) 13 *Journal of Competition Law and Economics* 2

C. Koenig, 'Comparing Parent Company Liability in EU and US Competition Law' (2018) 41 *World Competition* 1

I. Kokkoris and H. Shelanski, *EU Merger Control: A Legal and Economic Analysis* (Oxford University Press 2014)

A.P. Komninos, 'Public and Private Antitrust Enforcement in Europe: Complement? Overlap?' (2006) 3 *The Competition Law Review* 1

M. Krajewski, *Grundstrukturen des Rechts öffentlicher Dienstleistungen* (Springer 2011)

M. Krajewski, U. Neergaard and J.W. van de Gronden (eds), *The Changing Legal Framework for Services of General Interest in Europe: Between Competition and Solidarity* (TMC Asser Press/Cambridge University Press 2009)

T.G. Krattenmaker, R.H. Lande and S.C. Salop, 'Monopoly Power and Market Power in Antitrust Law' (1987) 76 *Georgetown Law Journal* 241

E. Lachnit, *Alternative Enforcement of Competition Law* (Boom Juridische Uitgevers 2016)

S. Lavrijssen, 'What Role for National Competition Authorities in Protecting Non-Competition Interests after Lisbon?' (2015) 37 *European Law Review* 5

D. Leczykiewikz, 'Enforcement or Compensation? Damages Actions in EU Law after the Draft Common Frame of Reference' in J. Devenney and M. Kenny (eds), *The Transformation of European Private Law: Harmonisation, Consolidation, Codification or Chaos?* (Cambridge University Press 2013), p. 276

R. van Leuken, 'Parental Liability for Cartel Infringements Committed by Wholly Owned Subsidiaries: Is the Approach of the European Court of Justice in Akzo Nobel also Relevant in a Private-Law Context?' (2016) 24 *European Review of Private Law* 3/4

I. Lianos, V. Korah and P. Siciliani, *Competition Law: Analysis, Cases, & Materials* (Oxford University Press 2019)

A. Lindsay and A. Berridge, *The EU Merger Regulation: Substantive Issues* (5th edn, Sweet & Maxwell 2017)

A. Looijestijn-Clearie, 'Staatsteun en Corona' [State aid and Corona] (2020) (2) *Tijdschrift voor Staatsteun* [Journal for State aid law] 97

E. Loozen, 'The Application of a More Economic Approach to Restrictions by Object: No Revolution after All (T-Mobile Netherlands, C-8/08)' (2010) 31 *European Competition Law Review* 4

M. Lorenz, *An Introduction to EU Competition Law* (Cambridge University Press 2013)

I. Maher, 'Functional and Normative Delegation to Non-Majoritarian Institutions: The Case of the European Competition Network' (2009) 7 *Comparative European Politics* 409

D. Mandrescu, 'The SSNIP Test and Zero-Pricing Strategies: Considerations for Online Platforms' (2018 (a)) 2

European Competition and Regulatory Law Review 4

D. Mandrescu, 'Applying (EU) Competition Law to Online Platforms: Reflections on the Definition of the Relevant Market(s)' (2018 (b)) 41 *World Competition* 3

D. Mandrescu, 'Ex-Ante Competition Law Enforcement and Online Platforms: A Tool with No Clear Instructions' (2019) available at <https://coreblog.lexxion.eu/ex-ante-competition-law-enforcement-and-online-platforms-a-tool-with-no-clear-instructions/> accessed 11 June 2020

A. Manganelli, A. Nicita and M.A. Rossi, 'The Institutional Design of European Competition Policy' (2010) EUI Working Papers RSCAS 2010/79

S. Marco Colino, *Competition Law of the EU and UK* (7th edn, Oxford University Press 2011)

S. Marco Colino, *Competition Law of the EU and UK* (8th edn, Oxford University Press 2019)

K. Markert, 'Commentary on Sections 20 of the GWB' in U. Immenga and E.-J. Mestmäcker (eds), *Wettbewerbsrecht: Band 2 Kommentar zum Deutschen Kartellrecht* (6th edn, 2020), available at <https://beck-online.beck.de/?vpath=bibdata/komm/ImmengaKoWbR_5_Band2/cont/ImmengaKoWbR.htm> accessed 20 June 2020

S. Martin, *Advanced Industrial Economics* (2nd edn, Wiley-Blackwell 2001)

M.H. Matthews, 'Negligence and Breach of Statutory Duty' (1984) 4 *Journal of Legal Studies* 3

M.R. Mok, *Kartelrecht I De Mededingingswet* (Kluwer 2004)

F. Montag, 'The Case for a Reform of Regulation 17/62: Problems and Possible Solutions from a Practitioner's Point of View' (1998) 22 *Fordham International Law Journal* 3

G. Monti, *EC Competition Law* (Cambridge University Press 2007)

G. Monti, 'Strengthening National Competition Authorities' (2018) 13 *The Competition Law Review* 2

B. Mooij and C.S. Rusu, 'Innovation and EU Competition Law: In Need of a Narrative for Where the Money Is Put' (2016) 43 *Legal Issues of Economic Integration* 2

K.J.M. Mortelmans, 'Noot bij het CIF-arrest' (2003) (11) *SEW: Tijdschrift voor Europees en economisch recht* 404

A. Mulder and M.R. Mok, *Kartelrecht* (Alphen aan de Rijn 1962)

A. Mundt, 'Digitalization Revolutionizes the Economy and the Work of Competition Authorities' (2017) CPI Antitrust Chronicle, available at <https://www.competitionpolicyinternational.com/wp-content/uploads/2017/02/CPI-Mundt.pdf> accessed 12 June 2020

G. Murray, 'In Search of the Obvious: Groupement des Cartes Bancaires and "by Object" Infringements under EU Competition Law' (2015) 36 *European Competition Law Review* 2

C.I. Nagy, *EU and US Competition Law: Divided in Unity? The Rule on Restrictive Agreements and Vertical Intra-brand Restraints* (Routledge 2013)

R. Nazzini, 'The Objective of Private Remedies in EU Competition Law' (2011) *Global Competition Litigation Review* 131

P. Nebbia, 'So What Happened to Mr Manfredi? The Italian Decision Following the Ruling of the European Court of Justice' (2007) 28 *European Competition Law Review* 591

P. Nebbia, 'Damages Actions for the Infringement of EC Competition Law: Compensation or Deterrence?' (2008) 33 *European Law Review* 23

U. Neergaard, 'Services of General Economic Interest: The Nature of the Beast' in M. Krajewski, U. Neergaard and J.W. van de Gronden (eds), *The Changing Legal Framework for Services of General Interest in*

Europe: Between Competition and Solidarity (TMC Asser Press/Cambridge University Press 2009), p. 17

U. Neergaard and S.A. de Vries, '"Whatever is necessary . . . will be done": Solidarity in Europe and the Covid-19 Crisis' (2020) 14 *EU Law Live 2020*, 24 April

P. Nicolaides, 'Presumed versus Actual Compatibility of State Aid with the Internal Market: Annotation on the Judgment of the Court of Justice (Fifth Chamber) of 29 July 2019 in Case C-654/17 P *Bayerische Motoren Werke AG v European Commission*' (2019) 3 *European State Aid Law Quarterly* 339

G. Niels, H. Jenkins and J. Kavanagh, *Economics for Competition Lawyers* (2nd edn, Oxford University Press 2016)

R. O'Donoghue and J. Padila, *The Law and Economics of Article 102 TFEU* (Hart Publishing 2013)

A.T. Ottow, *Market and Competition Authorities: Good Agency Principles* (Oxford University Press 2015)

E. Oude Elferink and B. Braat, 'De richtlijn betreffende schadevergoedingsacties wegens inbreuken op de mededingingsregels' (2014) 7 *Nederlands Tijdschrift voor Europees Recht* 216

A. Outhuijse, *Effective Public Enforcement of Cartels: Explaining the High Percentages of Litigation and Successful Litigation in the Netherlands* (Ridderprint 2019)

A. Outhuijse, 'Kroniek: Bestuurs- en civielrechtelijke rechtspraak mededingingsrecht 2019' (2020) 58 *SEW: Tijdschrift voor Europees en economisch recht* 168

P.L. Parcu, G. Monti and M. Botta (eds), *Private Enforcement of EU Competition Law: The Impact of the Damages Directive* (Edward Elgar Publishing 2018)

L. Parret, *Side Effects of the Modernisation of EU Competition Law: Modernisation as a Challenge to the Enforcement System of EU Competition Law and EU Law in General* (Wolf Legal Publishers 2011)

G.M. Pelecanos, N.G. Gerakinis and A.T. Themelis, 'Greece' in D. Sokol, D. Crane and A. Ezrachi (eds), *Global Antitrust Compliance Handbook* (Oxford University Press 2014), p. 297

V. Pereira, 'Algorithm-Driven Collusion: Pouring Old Wine into New Bottles or New Wine into Fresh Wineskins?' (2018) 39 *European Competition Law Review* 5

M. Petr, 'Seven Years after Toshiba: Time to Rethink Parallel Proceedings within the ECN?', in C.S. Rusu, A. Looijestijn-Clearie, J. Veenbrink and S. Tans (eds), *New Directions in Competition Law Enforcement* (Wolf Legal Publishers 2020), p. 79

J. Philippe, M. Trabucchi and A. Guyon, 'France' in D. Sokol, D. Crane and A. Ezrachi (eds), *Global Antitrust Compliance Handbook* (Oxford University Press 2014), p. 259

E. Pijnacker Hordijk, 'Netherlands' in M. Dolmans and H. Mostyn (eds), *The Dominance and Monopolies Review* (4th edn, Law Business Research 2016), p. 250

C. Pleatsikas and D. Teece, 'The Analysis of Market Definition and Market Power in the Context of Rapid Innovation' (2001) 19 *International Journal of Industrial Organization* 5

R. Podszun and F. Brauckmann, 'GWB-Digitalisierungsgesetz: Der Referentenentwurf des BMWi zur 10. GWB Novelle' (2019) 11 *Gesellschafts- und Wirtschaftsrecht* 24

R. Posner, *Antitrust Law: An Economic Perspective* (University of Chicago Press 1976)

L.F. Predreschi, *Public Services in EU Trade and Investment Agreements* (Asser Press/Springer 2020)

T. Prosser, 'EU Competition Law and Public Services' in E. Mossialos, G. Permanand, R. Baeten and T.K. Hervey (eds), *Health Systems Governance in Europe: The Role of European*

Union Law and Policy (Cambridge University Press 2010), p. 315

F. Prunet, 'France/Commentary' in Y. Hofhuis (ed), *Competition Law in Western Europe and the USA* (Kluwer Law International 1976), Supplement No. 429, May 2020

M. Pustlauk, 'BGH, Beschluss vom 26.2.2013, Az KRB 20/12 (Grauzementkartell): Zur Verfassungsmässigkeir von Kartellgeldbussen gem. § 81 Abs. 4 Satz 2 GWB 2005' (2013) *Zeitschrift des Instituts für Energie- und Wettbewerbsrecht in der Kommunalen Wirtschaft* (EWeRK) 5

E. Reille, 'France: Abuse of a Dominant Position – Pharmaceutical Sector' (2018) 39 *European Competition Law Review* 5

R.J. Reynolds and B.R. Snapp, 'The Competitive Effects of Partial Equity Interest and Joint Ventures' (1986) 4 *International Journal of Industrial Organisation* 2

C. Riis-Madsen, S. Stephanou and K. Kehoe, 'Reform of the EU Merger Regulation: Looking Out for the Minority' (2012) *CPI Antitrust Chronicle* 1

B. de Rijke, 'The Netherlands' in M. Dolmans and H. Mostyn (eds), *The Dominance and Monopolies Review* (7th edn, Law Business Research 2019), p. 316

F. Rizzuto, 'The ECN Plus Directive: The Harmonization of National Procedural Rules Governing the Parallel Enforcement of EU Competition Law in the Internal Market' (2019) 40 *European Competition Law Review* 12

V. Robertson, 'Delineating Digital Markets under EU Competition Law: Challenging or Futile?' (2017) 12 *The Competition Law Review* 2

B. Rodger, 'Private Enforcement and the Enterprise Act: An Exemplary System of Awarding Damages' (2003) 24 *European Competition Law Review* 3

B.J. Rodger, 'United Kingdom' in B.J. Rodger (ed), *Landmark Cases in Competition Law* (Wolters Kluwer Law & Business 2013), p. 319

B. Rodger and A. MacCulloch, *Competition Law and Policy in the EU and UK* (Routledge 2015)

M. Ross, 'Promoting Solidarity: From Public Services to a European Model of Competition?' (2007) 44 *Common Market Law Review* 4

C.S. Rusu, *European Merger Control: The Challenges Raised by Twenty Years of Enforcement Experience* (Wolters Kluwer Law & Business 2010)

C.S. Rusu, 'EU Merger Control and Acquisitions of (Non-Controlling) Minority Shareholdings: The State of Play' (2014 (a)) Competition Law Scholars Forum – Working Papers Series 10

C.S. Rusu, '(Non-Controlling) Minority Shareholdings as Self-Standing Transactions under EU Merger Control Analysis: Prospective Solutions' (2014 (b)) 37 *World Competition* 4

C.S. Rusu, 'Targeted Transparency Control of Competitively Significant Links: Heading towards Regulatory Overkill?' (2015 (a)) (1/2) *Romanian Competition Journal* 1/2

C.S. Rusu, 'The 2014 White Paper on EU Merger Control: Added Value for (Non-Controlling) Minority Shareholdings?' (2015 (b)) 11 *European Competition Journal* 1

C.S. Rusu, 'Workload Division after the *Si.mobil* and *easyJet* Rulings of the General Court' (2015 (c)) 11 *Competition Law Review* 1

C.S. Rusu, 'Eturas: Of Concerted Practices, Tacit Approval, and the Presumption of Innocence' (2016) 7 *Journal of European Competition Law & Practice* 6

C.S. Rusu, 'EU Antitrust Law Infringements and Private Damages Actions: How to Hold Cartelists Liable for Damages' (2017 (a)) 66 *Ars Aequi* 10

C.S. Rusu, 'The Commission Communication on Ten Years of Antitrust Enforcement under Regulation 1/2003: Prospective Priorities and Challenges' in A. Almasan and P. Whelan (eds), *The Consistent Application of EU*

Competition Law: Substantive and Procedural Challenges (Springer International Publishing 2017 (b)), p. 23

C.S. Rusu, 'Minority Shareholdings in the EU: Between Economics, Corporate Law, Antitrust and Merger Control' in H. Koster, F.J.L. Pennings and C.S. Rusu (eds), *Essays on Private and Business Law* (Eleven International Publishing/Boom Publishers 2017 (c)), p. 221

C.S. Rusu, 'The Real Challenge of Boosting the EU Competition Law Enforcement Powers of NCAs: In Need of a Reframed Formula?' (2018) 13 *The Competition Law Review* 1

C.S. Rusu, 'Case C-724/17 *Skanska*: The Journey or the Destination?' (2019) Radboud Economic Law Blog, 3, available at <https://www.ru.nl/law/research/radboud-economic-law-conference/radboud-economic-law-blog/2019/case-724-17-vantaan-kaupunki-sis-ncc-asfaltmix/> accessed 19 June 2020

C.S. Rusu and A. Looijestijn-Clearie, 'Domestic Enforcement of EU Antitrust and State Aid Rules: Status Quo and Foreseen Developments' in A. Looijestijn-Clearie, C.S. Rusu and J.M. Veenbrink (eds), *Boosting the Enforcement of EU Competition Law at the Domestic Level* (Cambridge Scholars Publishing 2017 (a)), p. 2

C.S. Rusu and A. Looijestijn-Clearie, 'The Implementation of the Private Damages Directive 2014/104/EU in the Netherlands' (2017 (b)) 67 *Wirtschaft und Wettbewerb* 7/8

C.S. Rusu, A. Looijestijn-Clearie and M. Veenbrink, 'State of the Art and Prospective Directions in the Digitalisation of Economic Law' in M. Veenbrink, A. Looijestijn-Clearie and C.S. Rusu (eds), *Digital Markets in the EU* (Wolf Legal Publishers 2018), p. 1

S. Salop and D. O'Brien, 'Competitive Effects on Partial Ownership: Financial Interest and Corporate Control' (2000) 67 *Antitrust Law Journal* 3

W. Sauter, *Coherence in EU Competition Law* (Oxford University Press 2016)

H. Schenk, 'Merger and Concentration Policy' in P. Bianchi and S. Labory, *Mergers and Concentration Policy: International Handbook of Industrial Policy* (Edward Elgar Publishing 2006), p. 153

F. Scherer and D. Ross, *Industrial Market Structure and Economic Performance* (3rd edn, Houghton Mifflin 1990)

M.P. Schinkel, L. Tóth and J. Tuinstra, 'Discretionary Authority and Prioritizing in Government Agencies' (2020) 30 *Journal of Public Administration Research and Theory* 2

J.P. Schmidt, 'Germany: Merger Control Analysis of Minority Shareholdings – A Model for the EU?' (2013) *Horizons, Concurrences: Revue des droits de la concurrence* 2

U. Schnelle and V. Soyez, 'Cartels 2020: Germany' (2020) available at <https://www.globallegalinsights.com/practice-areas/cartels-laws-and-regulations/germany> accessed 24 June 2020

U. Schwalbe, 'Market Definition in the Digital Economy: An Overview of EU and National Case Law' (2019) Concurrences, e-Competitions Market Definition in the Digital Economy, Art No 91832, available at <https://www.concurrences.com/en/bulletin/special-issues/market-definition-in-the-digital-economy-en/market-definition-in-the-digital-economy-an-overview-of-eu-and-national-case-en> accessed 19 June 2020

H. Schweitzer, 'Services of General Economic Interest' in M. Cremona (ed), *Market Integration and Public Services in the European Union* (Oxford University Press 2011), p. 11

V. Selvam, 'The EC Merger Control Impasse: Is There a Solution to This Predicament?' (2004) 25 *European Competition Law Review* 1

S. Semeraro, 'Demystifying Antitrust State Action Doctrine', (2000–01) 24 *Harvard Journal of Law & Public Policy* 1

C. Shapiro, 'Theories of Oligopoly Behaviour' in R. Schmaleense and R. Willig (eds), *Handbook of Industrial Organisation* (vol 1, North Holland 1989), p. 329

C. Shapiro, 'Antitrust in Time of Populism' (2018) 61 *International Journal of Industrial Organization* 714

K. Sidiropoulos, '*Post Danmark II*: A Clarification of the Law on Rebates under Article 102 TFEU' (2016) available at <https://europeanlawblog.eu/2015/12/11/post-danmark-ii-a-clarification-of-the-law-on-rebates-under-article-102-tfeu/> accessed 24 May 2020

A. Sinclair, 'Proposal for a Directive to Empower National Competition Authorities to Be More Effective Enforcers (ECN+)' (2017) 8 *Journal of European Competition Law & Practice* 10

P.J. Slot, C.R.A. Swaak and M.S. Mulder, *Inleiding mededingingsrecht* (6th edn, Boom Juridische Uitgevers 2012)

P. Solano Diaz, 'EU Competition Law Needs to Install a Plug-In' (2017) 40 *World Competition* 3

J. Steenbergen, 'Challenges for Enforcers' in C.S. Rusu, A. Looijestijn-Clearie, J. Veenbrink and S. Tans (eds), *New Directions in Competition Law Enforcement* (Wolf Legal Publishers 2020), p. 1

E. Steyger, 'Annotatie bij het arrest CIF' (2003) *Administratiefrechtelijke Beslissingen* (AB), 387

G. Stigler, *The Organization of Industry* (University of Chicago Press 1968)

K. Stockmann, 'Commentary on Sections 51–53 of the GWB' in U. Immenga and E.-J. Mestmäcker, *Wettbewerbsrecht: Band 2 Kommentar zum Deutschen Kartellrecht* (6th edn, 2020), available at <https://beck-online.beck.de/?vpath=bibdata/komm/ImmengaKoWbR_5_Band2/cont/ImmengaKoWbR.htm> accessed 20 June 2020

M. Strand, 'Indirect Purchasers, Passing-on and the New Directive on Competition Law Damages' (2014) 10 *European Competition Journal* 2

M.E. Stucke and A. Ezrachi, *Competition Overdose: How Free Market Mythology Transformed Us from Citizen Kings to Market Servants* (Harper Collins Publishers 2020)

M.E. Stucke and A.P. Grunes, *Big Data and Competition Policy* (Oxford University Press 2016)

E. Szyszczak, U. Neergaard and J.W. van de Gronden, 'Conclusions' in U. Neergaard, E. Szyszczak, J.W. van de Gronden and M. Krajewski (eds), *Social Services of General Interest in the EU* (Asser Press/Springer 2013), p. 595

J. Temple Lang, '*Inntrepreneur* and the Duties of National Courts under Article 10 EC' (2006) 5 *Competition Law Journal* 4

P. Tifine, *Droit administratif français* (4th edn, 2019) available at <https://www.revuegeneraledudroit.eu/blog/2013/08/10/droit-administratif-francais-cinquieme-partie-chapitre-2/> accessed 23 June 2020

C. Townley, *Article 81 EC and Public Policy* (Oxford University Press 2009)

H. Vedder, *Competition Law and Environmental Protection in Europe: Towards Sustainability?* (Europa Law Publishing 2003)

H. Vedder, 'Spontaneous Harmonisation of National (Competition) Laws in the Wake of the Modernisation of EC Competition Law' (2004) 1 *The Competition Law Review* 1

H.H.B. Vedder and J.F. Appeldoorn, *Mededingingsrecht: Beginselen van Europees en Nederlands mededingingsrecht* (3rd edn, Europa Law Publishing 2019)

J.M. Veenbrink, 'No One Wants to Be a Smoking Duck: A Commentary on Case C-162/15 P – *Evonik Degussa*' (2017) Radboud Economic Law Blog 4, available at <https://

www.ru.nl/law/research/radboud-economic-law-conference/radboud-economic-law-blog/2017/one-wants-smoking-duck-commentary-case-162-15/> accessed 19 June 2019

J.M. Veenbrink, *Criminal Law Principles and the Enforcement of EU and National Competition Law: A Silent Takeover?* (Kluwer Law International 2020)

J.M. Veenbrink and C.S. Rusu, 'Case Comment: C-557/12 *Kone*' (2014) 10 *The Competition Law Review* 1

M. Veenbrink, A. Looijestijn-Clearie and C.S. Rusu (eds), *Digital Markets in the EU* (Wolf Legal Publishers 2018)

S. Verschuur, *Overheidsmaatregelen en het toezicht van nationale mededingingsautoriteiten: De consequenties van het arrest CIF voor nationale mededingingsautoriteiten en overheden* (Boom Juridische Uitgevers 2010)

L. Vogel, *French Competition Law* (LawLex/Bruylant 2015)

S.B. Völcker, 'Mind the Gap: Unilateral Effects Analysis Arrives in EC Merger Control' (2004) 25 *European Competition Law Review* 7

S.B. Völcker, 'Case C-360/09, *Pfleiderer AG* v. *Bundeskartellamt*, Judgment of the Court of Justice (Grand Chamber) of 14 June 2011' (2012) 49 *Common Market Law Review* 2

S.A. de Vries, *Tensions with the Internal Market: The Functioning of the Internal Market and the Development of Horizontal and Flanking Policies* (Europa Law Publishing 2006)

F. Wagner-von Papp, 'Access to Evidence and Leniency Materials' (2016) available at <https://papers.ssrn.com/sol3/papers.cfm?abstract_id=2733973> accessed 25 June 2020

S. Waller, 'Towards a Constructive Public-Private Partnership to Enforce Competition Law' (2006) 29 *World Competition* 3

R.H. Weber, 'Competition Law Issues in the Online World' (2017) 20th St. Gallen International Competition Law Forum, available at <https://www.bratschi-law.ch/fileadmin/daten/dokumente/publikation/2013/04_April/SSRN-id2341978.pdf> accessed 12 June 2020

R. Wesseling, *The Modernisation of EC Antitrust Law* (Hart Publishing 2000)

P. Whelan, *The Criminalization of European Cartel Enforcement: Theoretical, Legal, and Practical Challenges* (Oxford University Press 2014)

R. Whish and D. Bailey, *Competition Law* (7th edn, Oxford University Press 2012)

R. Whish and D. Bailey, *Competition Law* (9th edn, Oxford University Press 2018)

M.P.M. Wiggers, R.A. Struijlaart and J.W. Dibbits, *Digital Competition Law in Europe: A Concise Guide* (Wolters Kluwer 2019)

F.G. Wilman, 'The End of the Absence? The Growing Body of EU Legislation on Private Enforcement and the Main Remedies It Provides For' (2016) 53 *Common Market Law Review* 4

W. Wils, 'Should Private Antitrust Enforcement be Encouraged in Europe?' (2003) 26 *World Competition* 3

W. Wils, 'Is Criminalization of EU Competition Law the Answer?' (2005) 28 *World Competition* 2

W. Wils, 'The Relationship between Public Antitrust Enforcement and Private Actions for Damages' (2009) 32 *World Competition* 3

W. Wils, 'The Compatibility with Fundamental Rights of the EU Antitrust Enforcement System in which the European Commission Acts both as Investigator and as First-Instance Decision Maker' (2014) 37 *World Competition* 1

W. Wils, 'Private Enforcement of EU Antitrust Law and Its Relationship with Public

Enforcement: Past, Present and Future' (2017) 40 *World Competition* 1

W.P.J. Wils, 'Independence of Competition Authorities: The Example of the EU and Its Member States' (2019) 42 *World Competition* 2

E.J. Zippro, *Privaatrechtelijke handhaving van mededingingsrecht* (Kluwer 2009)

L. Zhu, *Services of General Economic Interest in EU Competition Law: Striking a Balance between Non-Economic Values and Market Competition* (Asser Press/Springer 2020)

Index